SUPERMAN BATMAN

VOLUME 3

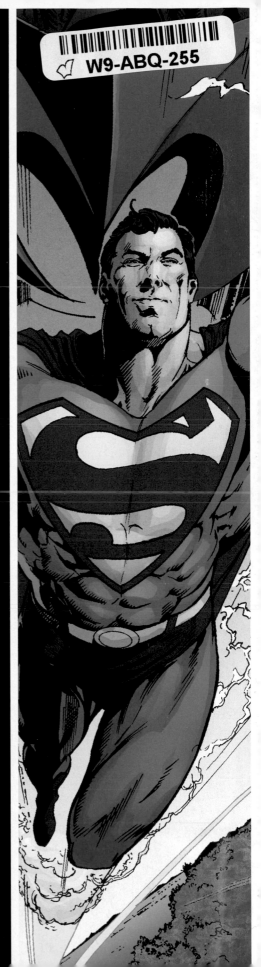

MARK VERHEIDEN
MARC GUGGENHEIM
JOE KELLY
WRITERS

ETHAN VAN SCIVER
PAT LEE
MATTHEW CLARK
RON RANDALL
JOE BENITEZ
KEVIN MAGUIRE
ED MCGUINNESS
RYAN OTTLEY
SEAN MURPHY
CARLO BARBERI
PENCILLERS

CRAIG YEUNG
ANDY LANNING
MARLO ALQUIZA
VICTOR LLAMAS
DEXTER VINES
CLIFF RATHBURN
SEAN MURPHY
DON HILLSMAN II
BOB PETRECCA
ANDY OWENS
RODNEY RAMOS
INKERS

GUY MAJOR
DANNY LUVISI
CHRIS CHUCKRY
DAVE McCAIG
COLORISTS

ROB LEIGH
COMICRAFT
LETTERERS

ETHAN VAN SCIVER
AND MOOSE BAUMANN
COLLECTION COVER ARTISTS

BATMAN CREATED BY BOB KANE WITH BILL FINGER
SUPERMAN CREATED BY JERRY SIEGEL AND JOE SHUSTER
SUPERGIRL BASED ON CHARACTERS CREATED BY
JERRY SIEGEL AND JOE SHUSTER.
BY SPECIAL ARRANGEMENT WITH THE JERRY SIEGEL FAMILY
OMAC CREATED BY JACK KIRBY.

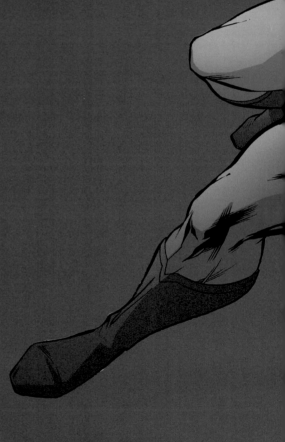

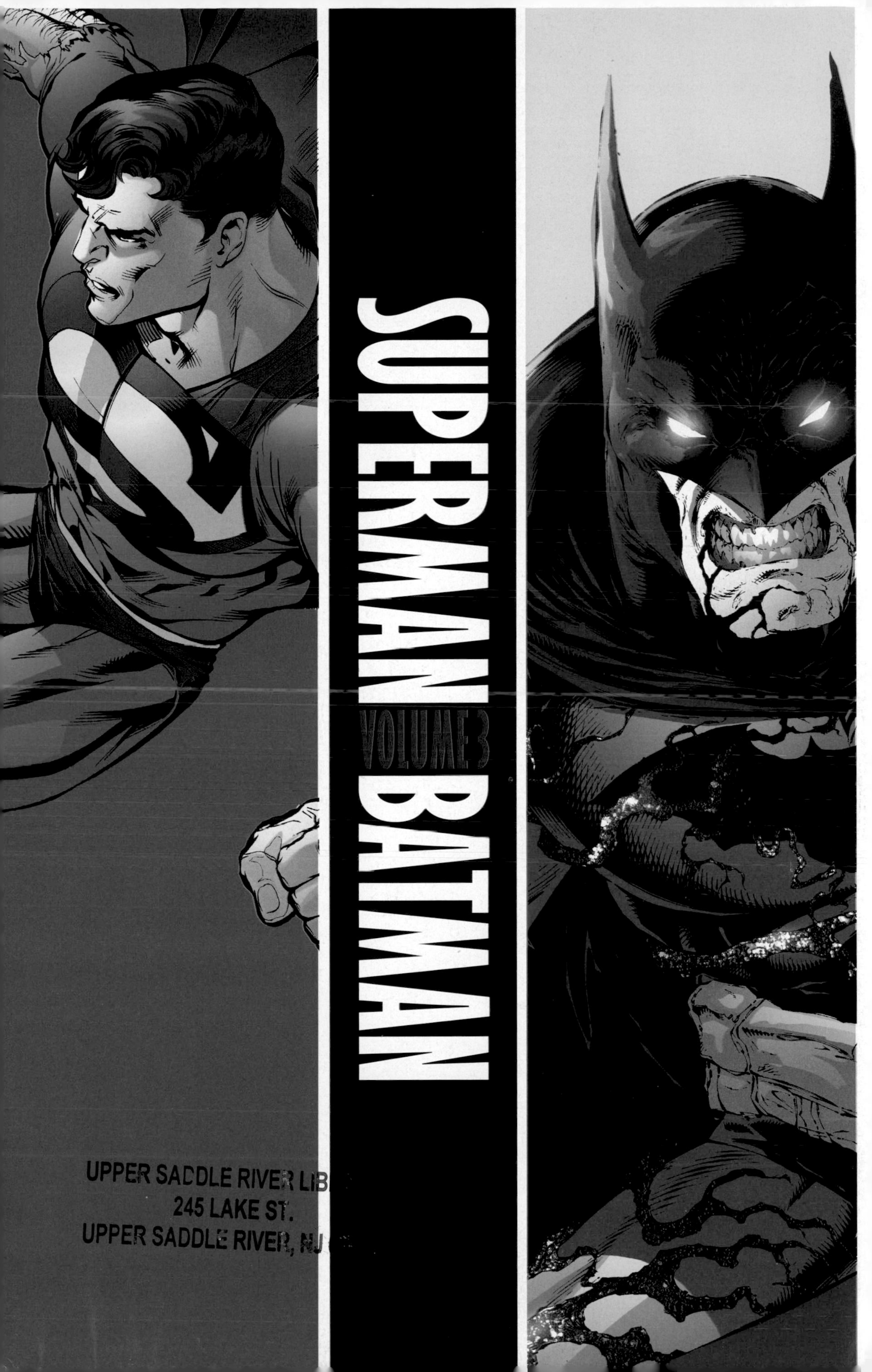
SUPERMAN
VOLUME 3
BATMAN

Eddie Berganza Editor–Original Series Jeanine Schaefer Associate Editor–Original Series Adam Schlagman Assistant Editor–Original Series
Jeb Woodard Group Editor – Collected Editions Steve Cook Design Director–Books Damian Ryland Publication Design

Bob Harras Senior VP – Editor-in-Chief, DC Comics

Diane Nelson President Dan DiDio and Jim Lee Co-Publishers Geoff Johns Chief Creative Officer
Amit Desai Senior VP – Marketing & Global Franchise Management Nairi Gardiner Senior VP – Finance
Sam Ades VP – Digital Marketing Bobbie Chase VP – Talent Development
Mark Chiarello Senior VP – Art, Design & Collected Editions John Cunningham VP – Content Strategy
Anne DePies VP – Strategy Planning & Reporting Don Falletti VP – Manufacturing Operations
Lawrence Ganem VP – Editorial Administration & Talent Relations Alison Gill Senior VP – Manufacturing & Operations
Hank Kanalz Senior VP – Editorial Strategy & Administration Jay Kogan VP – Legal Affairs
Derek Maddalena Senior VP – Sales & Business Development Jack Mahan VP – Business Affairs
Dan Miron VP – Sales Planning & Trade Development Nick Napolitano VP – Manufacturing Administration
Carol Roeder VP – Marketing Eddie Scannell VP – Mass Account & Digital Sales
Courtney Simmons Senior VP – Publicity & Communications
Jim (Ski) Sokolowski VP – Comic Book Specialty & Newsstand Sales Sandy Yi Senior VP – Global Franchise Management

SUPERMAN/BATMAN VOLUME 3

DC Comics, 2900 West Alameda Ave., Burbank, CA 91505
Printed by RR Donnelley, Salem, VA, USA. 2/26/16. First Printing.
ISBN: 978-1-4012-6480-2

Library of Congress Cataloging-in-Publication Data

Names: Verheiden, Mark, author. | Guggenheim, Marc, author. | Kelly, Joe, 1971- author. | Van Sciver, Ethan, illustrator. | Lee, Pat, 1975- illustrator. | Clark, Matthew, 1970- illustrator. | Yeung, Craig, illustrator. | Lanning, Andy, illustrator. | Alquiza, Marlo, illustrator. | Major, Guy, illustrator. | LuVisi, Dan, illustrator. | Chuckry, Chris, illustrator. | McCaig, Dave, illustrator. | Leigh, Rob, illustrator. | Van Sciver, Ethan, illustrator. | Baumann, Moose, illustrator. | Comicraft (Firm) illustrator.
Title: Superman/Batman. Volume 3 / Mark Verheiden, Marc Guggenheim, Joe Kelly, writers ; Ethan Van Sciver, Pat Lee, Matthew Clark [and seven others], pencillers ; Craig Yeung, Andy Lanning, Marlo Alquiza [and eight others], inkers ; Guy Major, Danny LuVisi, Chris Chuckry, Dave McCaig, colorists ; Rob Leigh, ComiCraft, letterers ; Ethan Van Sciver & Moose Baumann, collection cover artists.
Description: Burbank, CA : DC Comics, [2016] | "Batman created by Bob Kane with Bill Finger" | "Superman created by Jerry Siegel and Joe Shuster, by special arrangement with the Jerry Siegel family"
Identifiers: LCCN 2015044476 | ISBN 9781401264802 (paperback)
Subjects: LCSH: Graphic novels. | Superhero comic books, strips, etc. | BISAC: COMICS & GRAPHIC NOVELS / Superheroes.
Classification: LCC PN6728.S9 S8725 2016 | DDC 741.5/973–dc23
LC record available at http://lccn.loc.gov/2015044476

PEFC Certified
Printed on paper from sustainably managed forests and controlled sources
PEFC
PEFC/29-31-75
www.pefc.org

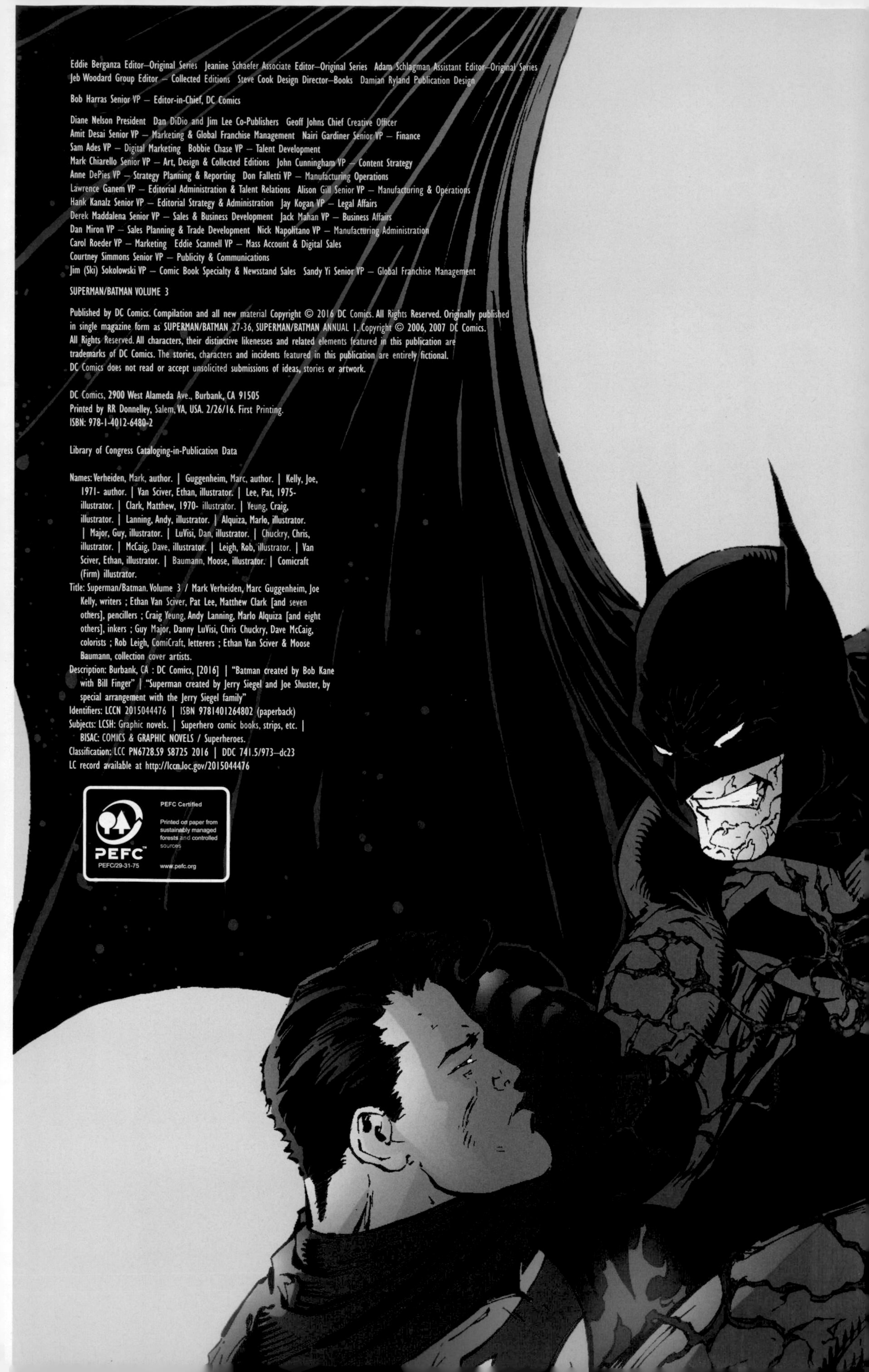

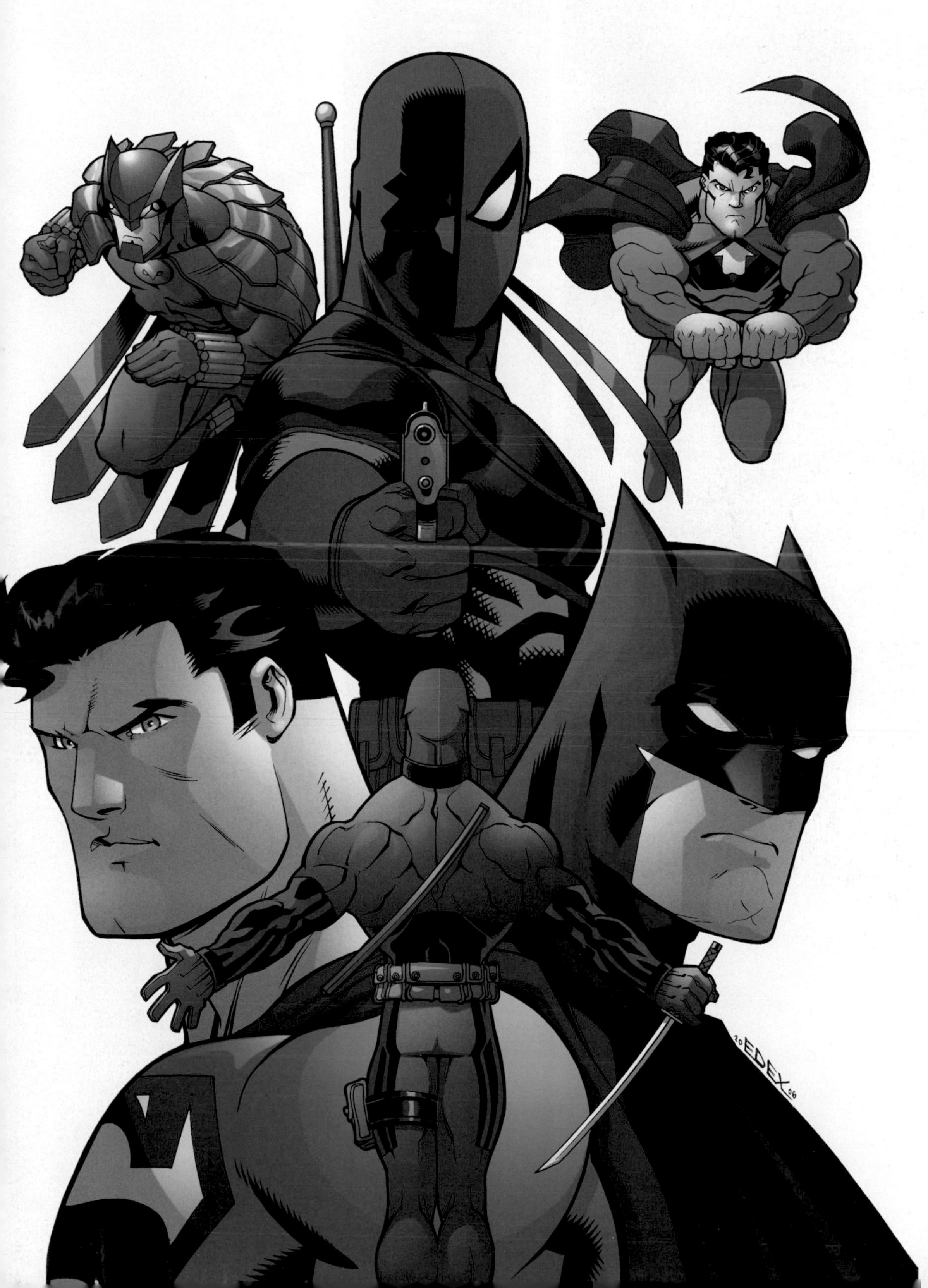
20EDEX06

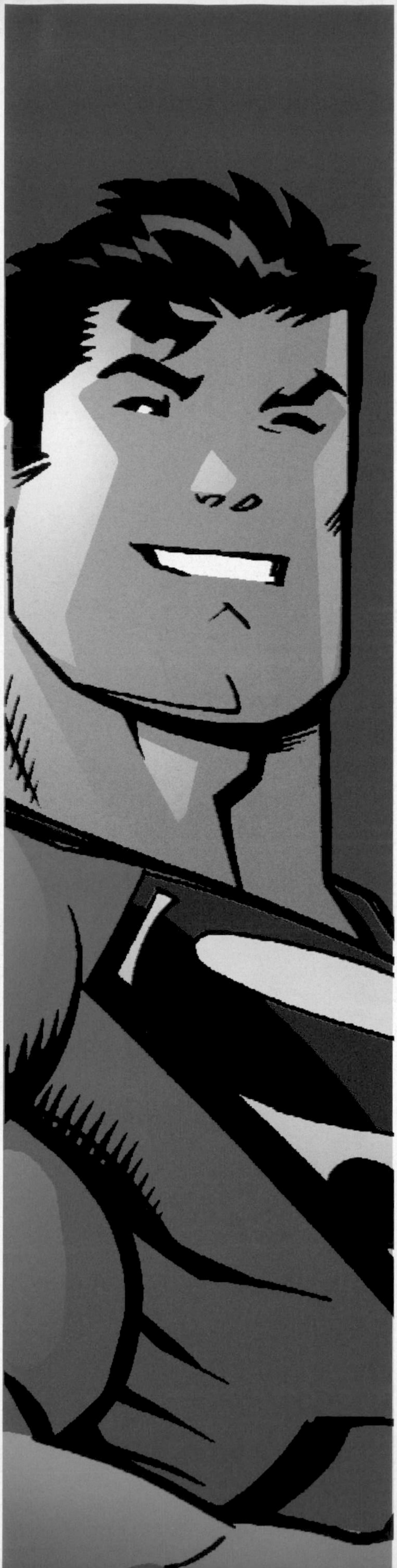

STOP ME IF YOU'VE HEARD THIS ONE . . .

JOE KELLY
WRITER

ED MCGUINNESS
RYAN OTTLEY
SEAN MURPHY
CARLO BARBERI
PENCILLERS

DEXTER VINES
CLIFF RATHBURN
SEAN MURPHY
DON HILLSMAN II
BOB PETRECCA
ANDY OWENS
RODNEY RAMOS
INKERS

GUY MAJOR
COLORIST

ROB LEIGH
LETTERER

ED MCGUINNESS
DEXTER VINES
&
GUY MAJOR
COVER

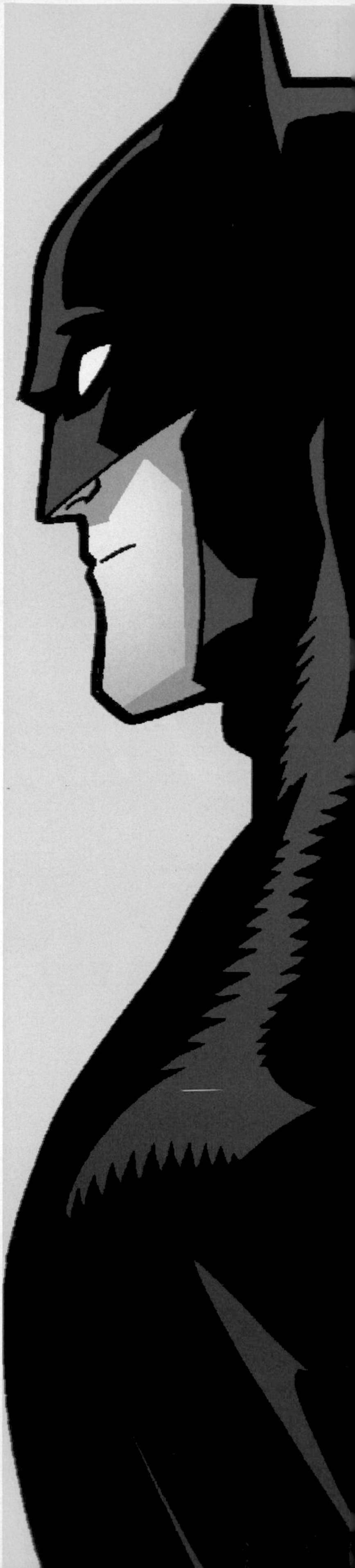

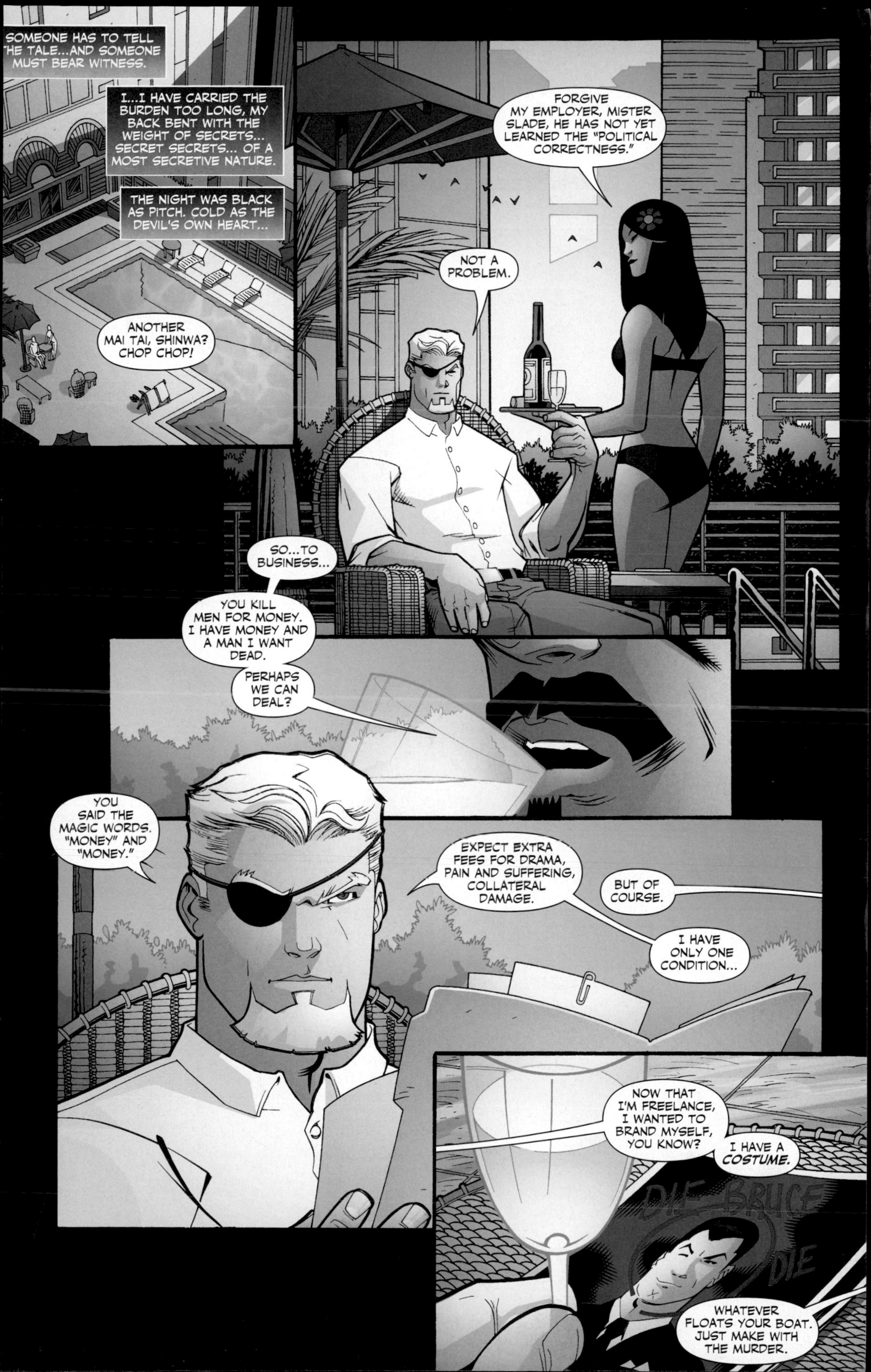
SOMEONE HAS TO TELL THE TALE...AND SOMEONE MUST BEAR WITNESS.
I...I HAVE CARRIED THE BURDEN TOO LONG, MY BACK BENT WITH THE WEIGHT OF SECRETS... SECRET SECRETS... OF A MOST SECRETIVE NATURE.
THE NIGHT WAS BLACK AS PITCH. COLD AS THE DEVIL'S OWN HEART...
ANOTHER MAI TAI, SHINWA? CHOP CHOP!
FORGIVE MY EMPLOYER, MISTER SLADE, HE HAS NOT YET LEARNED THE "POLITICAL CORRECTNESS."
NOT A PROBLEM.
SO...TO BUSINESS...
YOU KILL MEN FOR MONEY. I HAVE MONEY AND A MAN I WANT DEAD.
PERHAPS WE CAN DEAL?
YOU SAID THE MAGIC WORDS. "MONEY" AND "MONEY."
EXPECT EXTRA FEES FOR DRAMA, PAIN AND SUFFERING, COLLATERAL DAMAGE.
BUT OF COURSE.
I HAVE ONLY ONE CONDITION...
NOW THAT I'M FREELANCE, I WANTED TO BRAND MYSELF, YOU KNOW?
I HAVE A *COSTUME.*
DIE BRUCE DIE
WHATEVER FLOATS YOUR BOAT. JUST MAKE WITH THE MURDER.

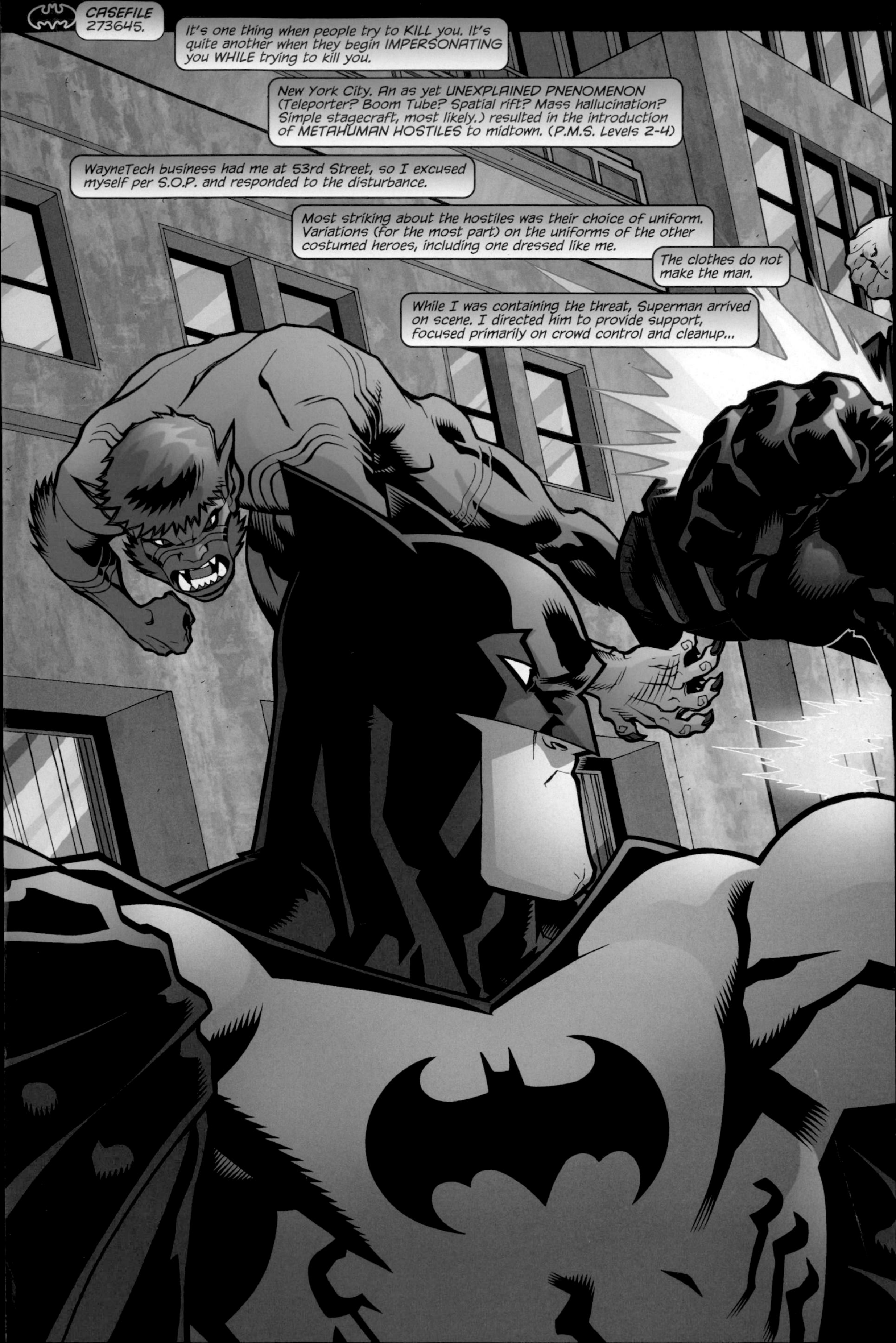
CASEFILE 273645.
It's one thing when people try to KILL you. It's quite another when they begin IMPERSONATING you WHILE trying to kill you.
New York City. An as yet UNEXPLAINED PNENOMENON (Teleporter? Boom Tube? Spatial rift? Mass hallucination? Simple stagecraft, most likely.) resulted in the introduction of METAHUMAN HOSTILES to midtown. (P.M.S. Levels 2-4)
WayneTech business had me at 53rd Street, so I excused myself per S.O.P. and responded to the disturbance.
Most striking about the hostiles was their choice of uniform. Variations (for the most part) on the uniforms of the other costumed heroes, including one dressed like me.
The clothes do not make the man.
While I was containing the threat, Superman arrived on scene. I directed him to provide support, focused primarily on crowd control and cleanup...

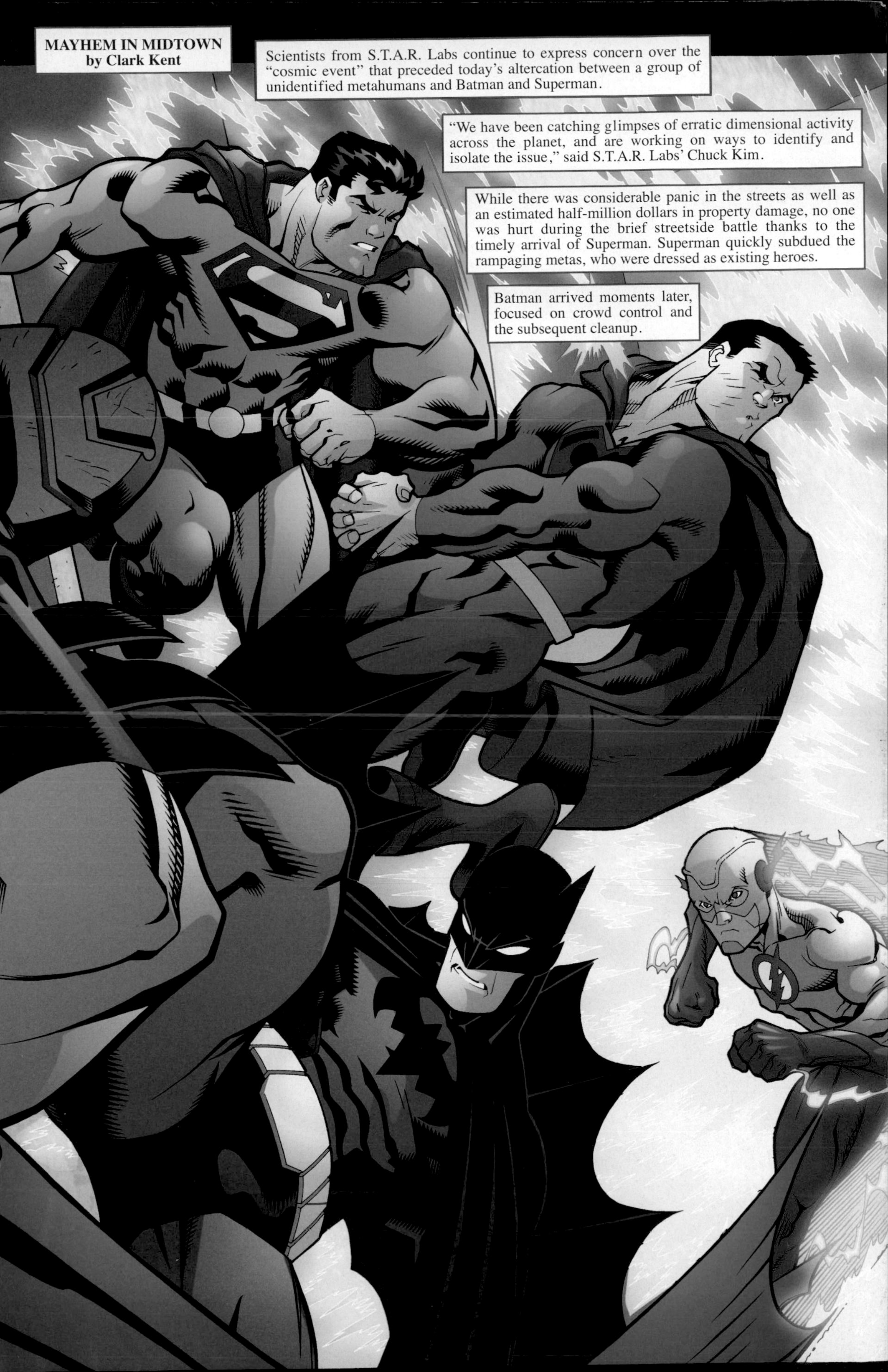
MAYHEM IN MIDTOWN
by Clark Kent
Scientists from S.T.A.R. Labs continue to express concern over the "cosmic event" that preceded today's altercation between a group of unidentified metahumans and Batman and Superman.
"We have been catching glimpses of erratic dimensional activity across the planet, and are working on ways to identify and isolate the issue," said S.T.A.R. Labs' Chuck Kim.
While there was considerable panic in the streets as well as an estimated half-million dollars in property damage, no one was hurt during the brief streetside battle thanks to the timely arrival of Superman. Superman quickly subdued the rampaging metas, who were dressed as existing heroes.
Batman arrived moments later, focused on crowd control and the subsequent cleanup.

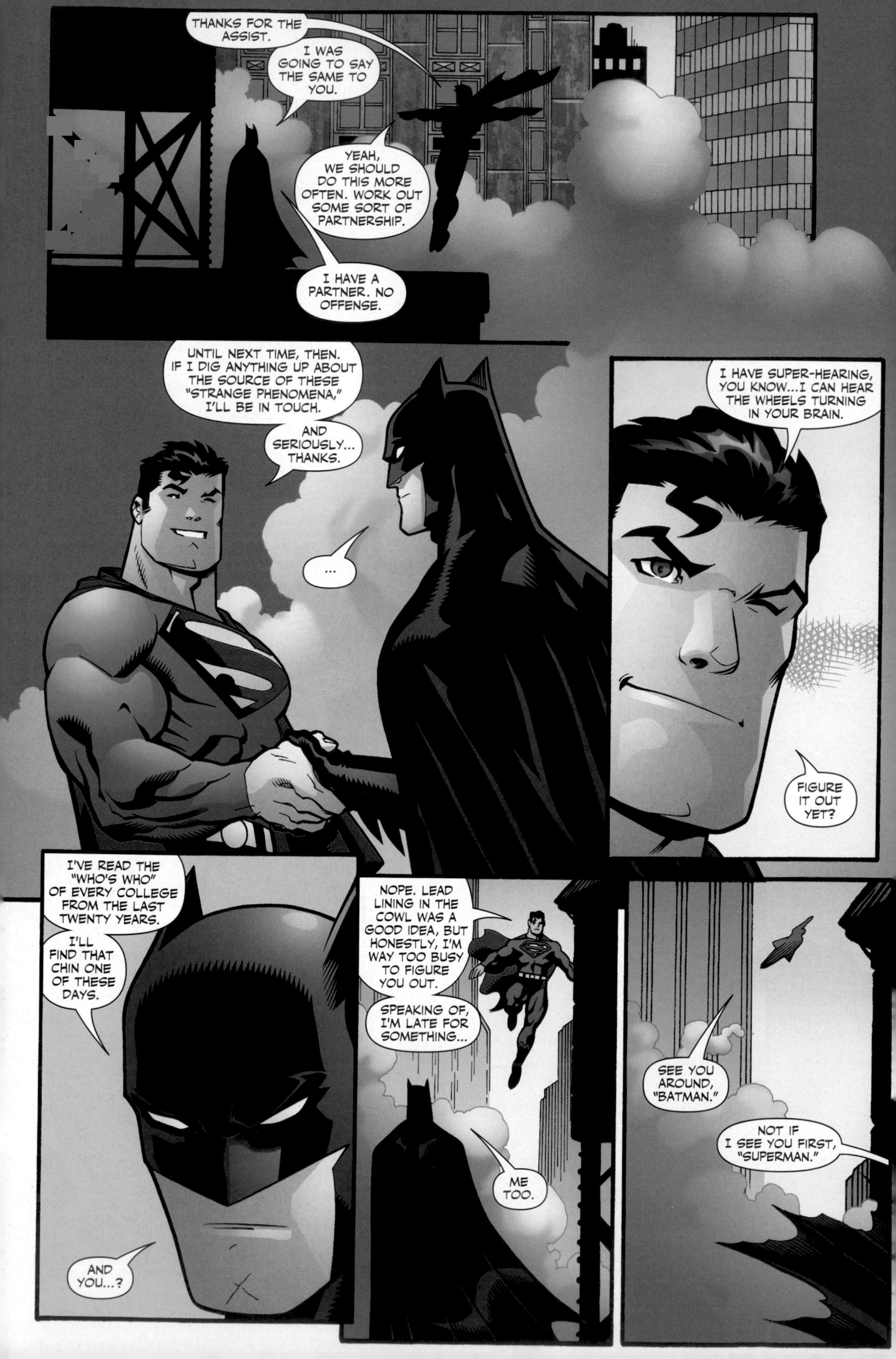
THANKS FOR THE ASSIST.
I WAS GOING TO SAY THE SAME TO YOU.
YEAH, WE SHOULD DO THIS MORE OFTEN. WORK OUT SOME SORT OF PARTNERSHIP.
I HAVE A PARTNER. NO OFFENSE.
UNTIL NEXT TIME, THEN. IF I DIG ANYTHING UP ABOUT THE SOURCE OF THESE "STRANGE PHENOMENA," I'LL BE IN TOUCH.
AND SERIOUSLY... THANKS.
...
I HAVE SUPER-HEARING, YOU KNOW...I CAN HEAR THE WHEELS TURNING IN YOUR BRAIN.
FIGURE IT OUT YET?
I'VE READ THE "WHO'S WHO" OF EVERY COLLEGE FROM THE LAST TWENTY YEARS.
I'LL FIND THAT CHIN ONE OF THESE DAYS.
AND YOU...?
NOPE. LEAD LINING IN THE COWL WAS A GOOD IDEA, BUT HONESTLY, I'M WAY TOO BUSY TO FIGURE YOU OUT.
SPEAKING OF, I'M LATE FOR SOMETHING...
ME TOO.
SEE YOU AROUND, "BATMAN."
NOT IF I SEE YOU FIRST, "SUPERMAN."

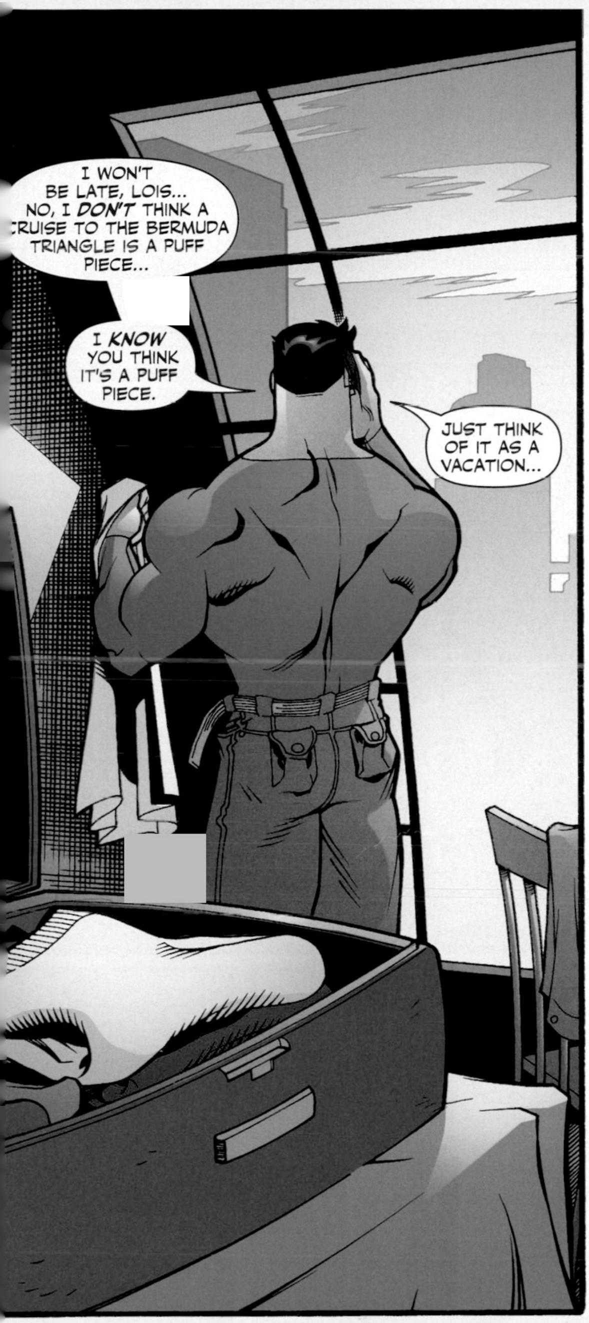
I WON'T BE LATE, LOIS... NO, I *DON'T* THINK A CRUISE TO THE BERMUDA TRIANGLE IS A PUFF PIECE...
I *KNOW* YOU THINK IT'S A PUFF PIECE.
JUST THINK OF IT AS A VACATION...

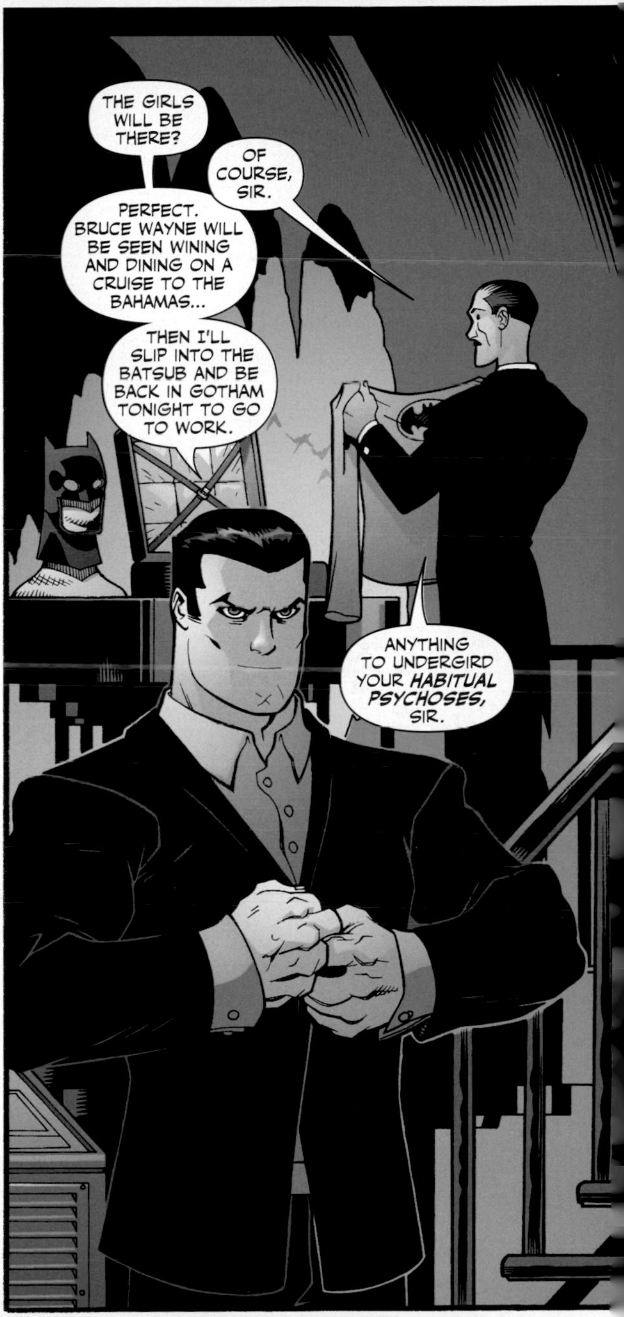
THE GIRLS WILL BE THERE?
OF COURSE, SIR.
PERFECT. BRUCE WAYNE WILL BE SEEN WINING AND DINING ON A CRUISE TO THE BAHAMAS...
THEN I'LL SLIP INTO THE BATSUB AND BE BACK IN GOTHAM TONIGHT TO GO TO WORK.
ANYTHING TO UNDERGIRD YOUR *HABITUAL PSYCHOSES,* SIR.

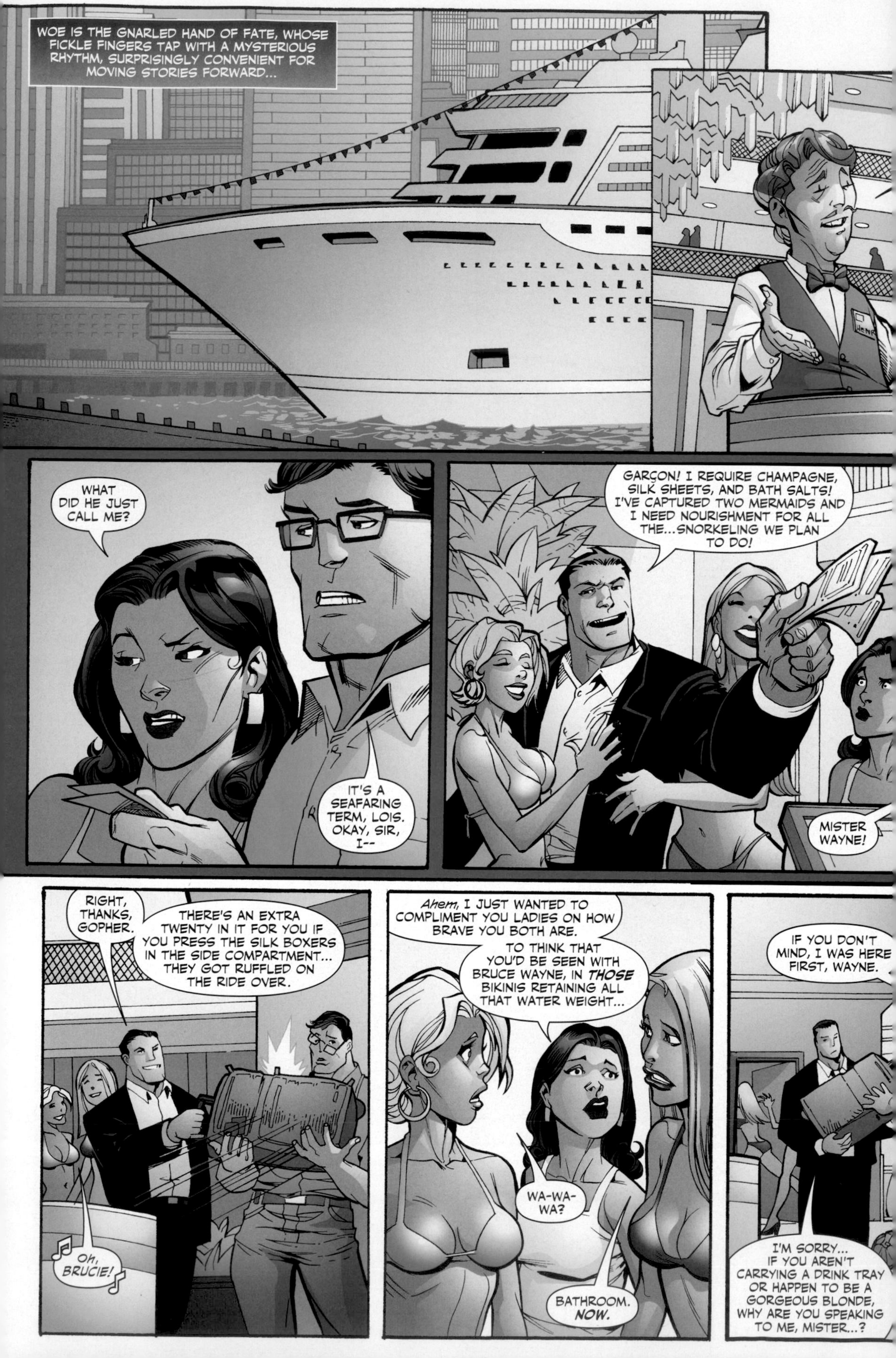
WOE IS THE GNARLED HAND OF FATE, WHOSE FICKLE FINGERS TAP WITH A MYSTERIOUS RHYTHM, SURPRISINGLY CONVENIENT FOR MOVING STORIES FORWARD...
WHAT DID HE JUST CALL ME?
IT'S A SEAFARING TERM, LOIS. OKAY, SIR, I--
GARÇON! I REQUIRE CHAMPAGNE, SILK SHEETS, AND BATH SALTS! I'VE CAPTURED TWO MERMAIDS AND I NEED NOURISHMENT FOR ALL THE...SNORKELING WE PLAN TO DO!
MISTER WAYNE!
RIGHT, THANKS, GOPHER.
THERE'S AN EXTRA TWENTY IN IT FOR YOU IF YOU PRESS THE SILK BOXERS IN THE SIDE COMPARTMENT... THEY GOT RUFFLED ON THE RIDE OVER.
Oh, BRUCIE!
Ahem, I JUST WANTED TO COMPLIMENT YOU LADIES ON HOW BRAVE YOU BOTH ARE.
TO THINK THAT YOU'D BE SEEN WITH BRUCE WAYNE, IN *THOSE* BIKINIS RETAINING ALL THAT WATER WEIGHT...
WA-WA-WA?
BATHROOM. *NOW.*
IF YOU DON'T MIND, I WAS HERE FIRST, WAYNE.
I'M SORRY... IF YOU AREN'T CARRYING A DRINK TRAY OR HAPPEN TO BE A GORGEOUS BLONDE, WHY ARE YOU SPEAKING TO ME, MISTER...?

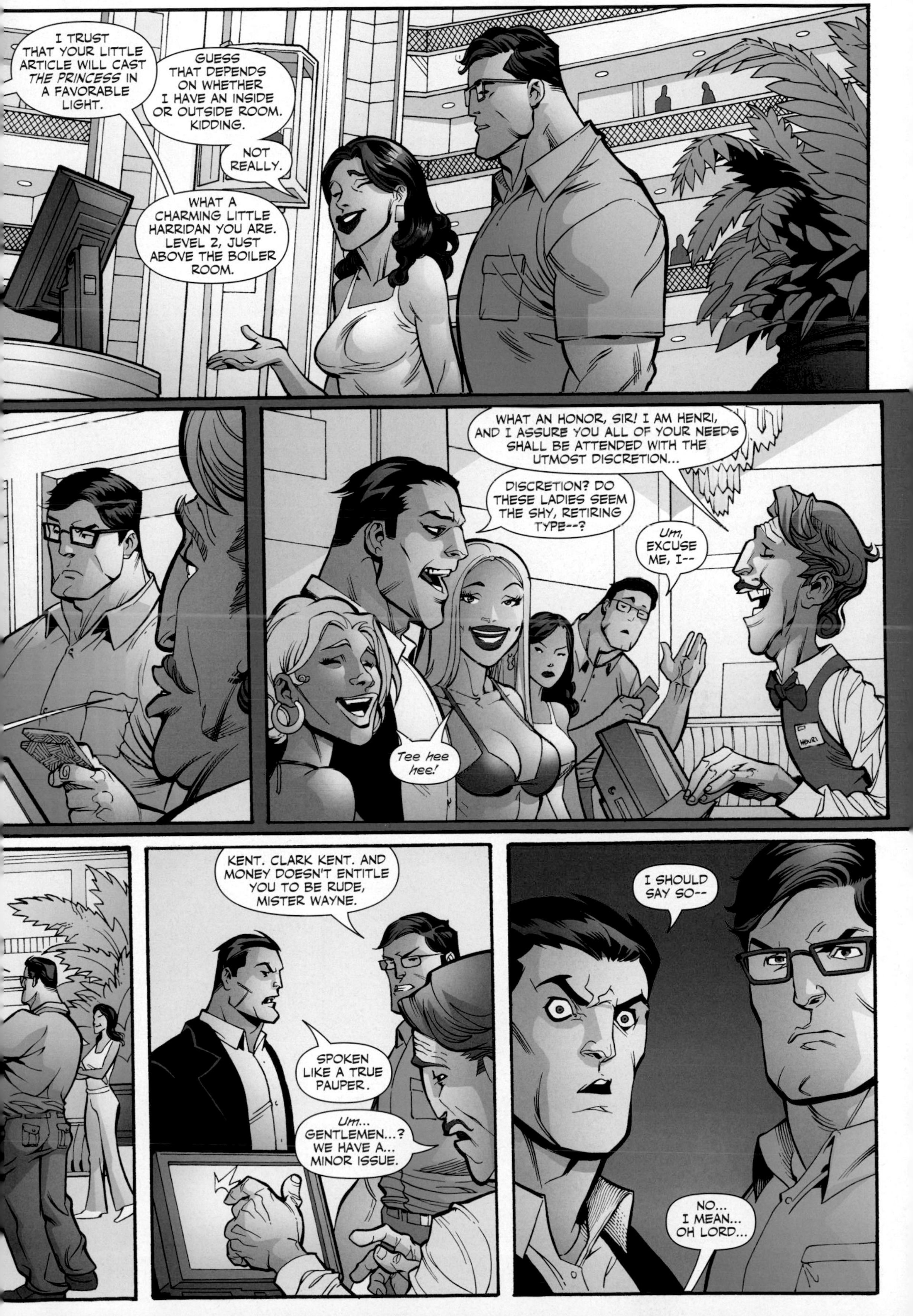
I TRUST THAT YOUR LITTLE ARTICLE WILL CAST *THE PRINCESS* IN A FAVORABLE LIGHT.
GUESS THAT DEPENDS ON WHETHER I HAVE AN INSIDE OR OUTSIDE ROOM. KIDDING.
NOT REALLY.
WHAT A CHARMING LITTLE HARRIDAN YOU ARE. LEVEL 2, JUST ABOVE THE BOILER ROOM.
WHAT AN HONOR, SIR! I AM HENRI, AND I ASSURE YOU ALL OF YOUR NEEDS SHALL BE ATTENDED WITH THE UTMOST DISCRETION...
DISCRETION? DO THESE LADIES SEEM THE SHY, RETIRING TYPE--?
Um, EXCUSE ME, I--
Tee hee hee!
HENRI
KENT. CLARK KENT. AND MONEY DOESN'T ENTITLE YOU TO BE RUDE, MISTER WAYNE.
SPOKEN LIKE A TRUE PAUPER.
Um... GENTLEMEN...? WE HAVE A... MINOR ISSUE.
I SHOULD SAY SO--
NO... I MEAN... OH LORD...

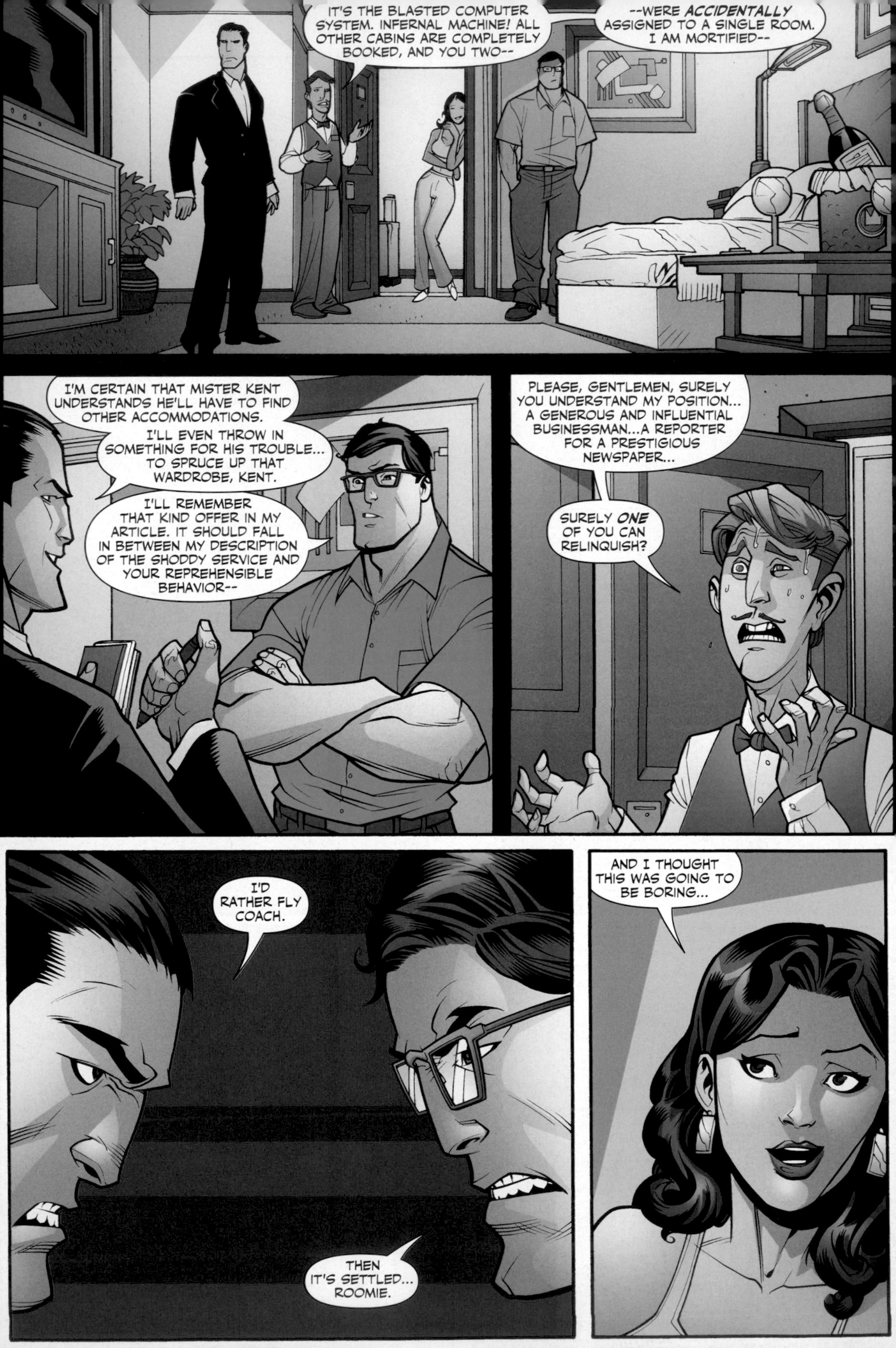

IT'S THE BLASTED COMPUTER SYSTEM. INFERNAL MACHINE! ALL OTHER CABINS ARE COMPLETELY BOOKED, AND YOU TWO--
--WERE *ACCIDENTALLY* ASSIGNED TO A SINGLE ROOM. I AM MORTIFIED--
I'M CERTAIN THAT MISTER KENT UNDERSTANDS HE'LL HAVE TO FIND OTHER ACCOMMODATIONS.
I'LL EVEN THROW IN SOMETHING FOR HIS TROUBLE... TO SPRUCE UP THAT WARDROBE, KENT.
I'LL REMEMBER THAT KIND OFFER IN MY ARTICLE. IT SHOULD FALL IN BETWEEN MY DESCRIPTION OF THE SHODDY SERVICE AND YOUR REPREHENSIBLE BEHAVIOR--
PLEASE, GENTLEMEN, SURELY YOU UNDERSTAND MY POSITION... A GENEROUS AND INFLUENTIAL BUSINESSMAN...A REPORTER FOR A PRESTIGIOUS NEWSPAPER...
SURELY *ONE* OF YOU CAN RELINQUISH?
I'D RATHER FLY COACH.
THEN IT'S SETTLED... ROOMIE.
AND I THOUGHT THIS WAS GOING TO BE BORING...

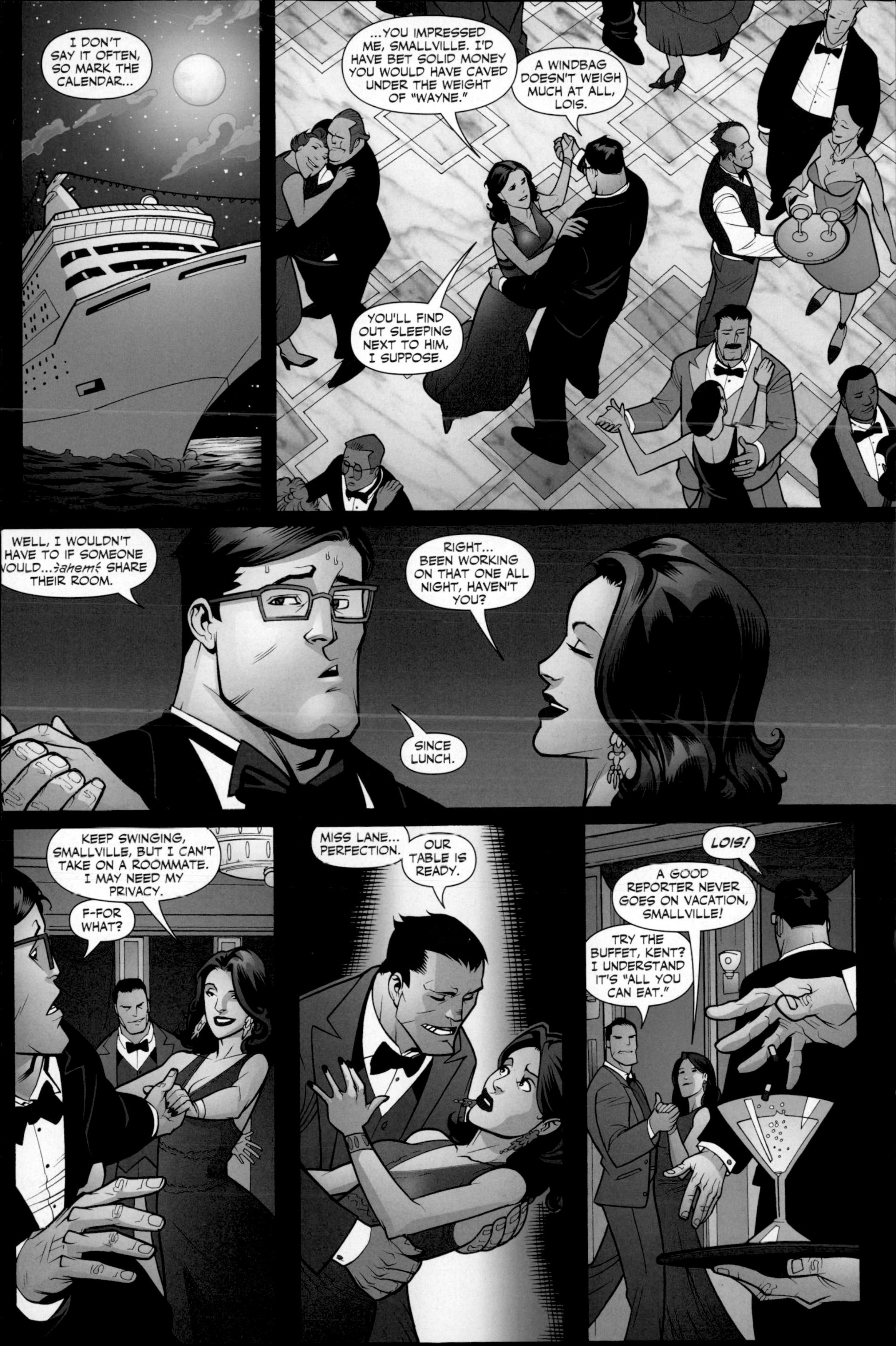
I DON'T SAY IT OFTEN, SO MARK THE CALENDAR...
...YOU IMPRESSED ME, SMALLVILLE. I'D HAVE BET SOLID MONEY YOU WOULD HAVE CAVED UNDER THE WEIGHT OF "WAYNE."
A WINDBAG DOESN'T WEIGH MUCH AT ALL, LOIS.
YOU'LL FIND OUT SLEEPING NEXT TO HIM, I SUPPOSE.
WELL, I WOULDN'T HAVE TO IF SOMEONE WOULD...*AHEM* SHARE THEIR ROOM.
RIGHT... BEEN WORKING ON THAT ONE ALL NIGHT, HAVEN'T YOU?
SINCE LUNCH.
KEEP SWINGING, SMALLVILLE, BUT I CAN'T TAKE ON A ROOMMATE. I MAY NEED MY PRIVACY.
F-FOR WHAT?
MISS LANE... PERFECTION.
OUR TABLE IS READY.
LOIS!
A GOOD REPORTER NEVER GOES ON VACATION, SMALLVILLE!
TRY THE BUFFET, KENT? I UNDERSTAND IT'S "ALL YOU CAN EAT."

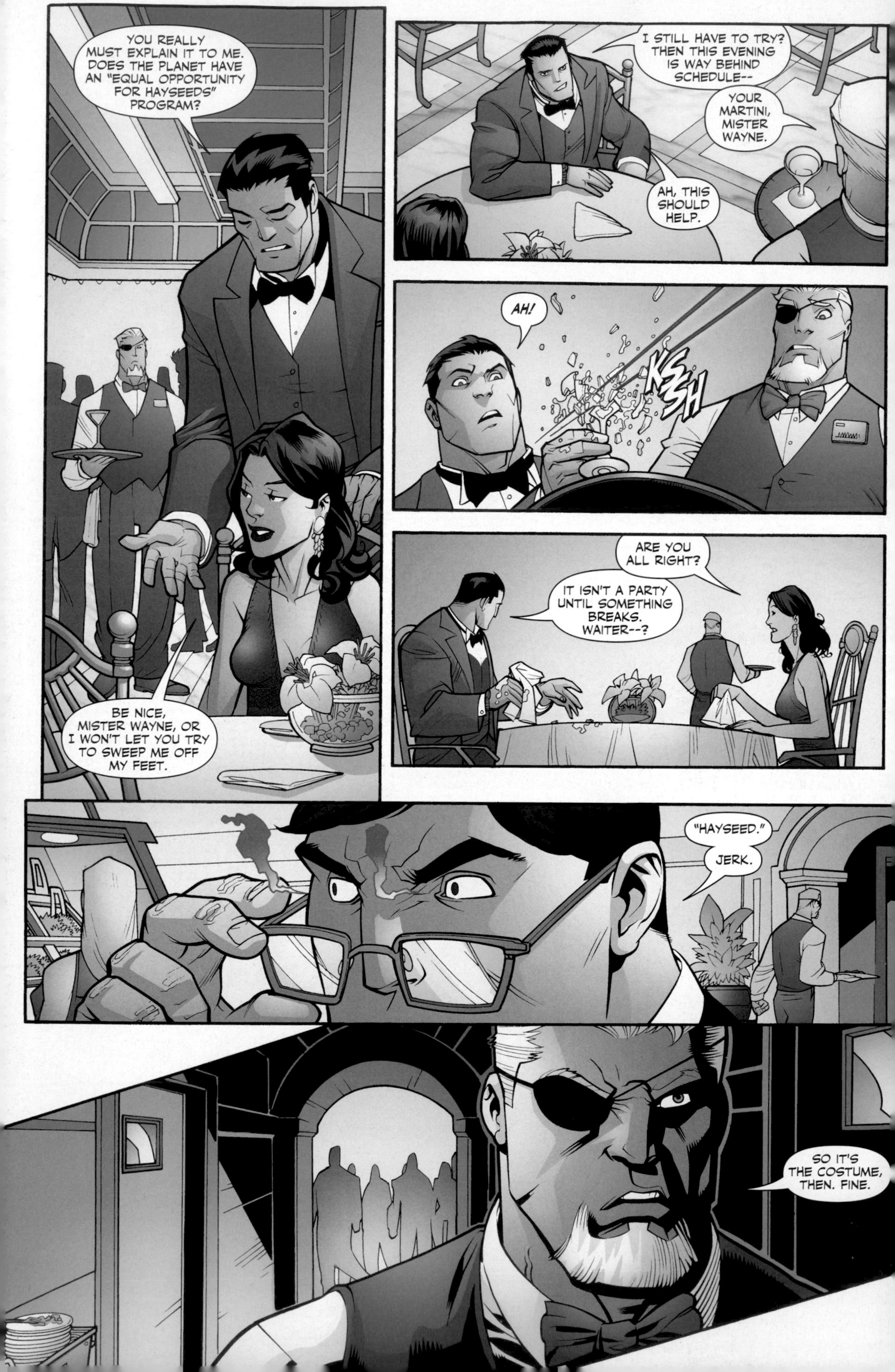
YOU REALLY MUST EXPLAIN IT TO ME. DOES THE PLANET HAVE AN "EQUAL OPPORTUNITY FOR HAYSEEDS" PROGRAM?
BE NICE, MISTER WAYNE, OR I WON'T LET YOU TRY TO SWEEP ME OFF MY FEET.
I STILL HAVE TO TRY? THEN THIS EVENING IS WAY BEHIND SCHEDULE--
YOUR MARTINI, MISTER WAYNE.
AH, THIS SHOULD HELP.
AH!
KSSH
ARE YOU ALL RIGHT?
IT ISN'T A PARTY UNTIL SOMETHING BREAKS. WAITER--?
"HAYSEED."
JERK.
SO IT'S THE COSTUME, THEN. FINE.

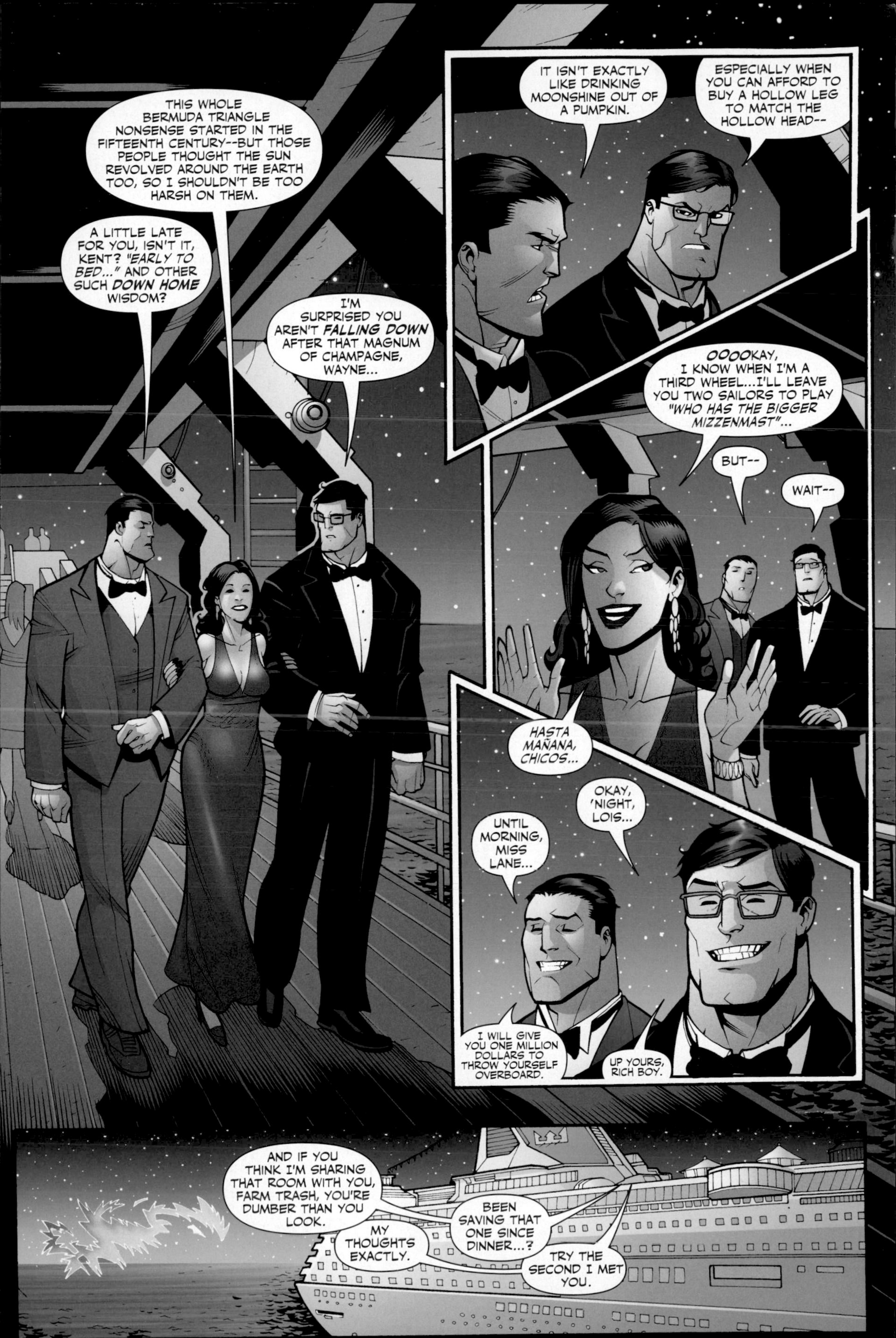
THIS WHOLE BERMUDA TRIANGLE NONSENSE STARTED IN THE FIFTEENTH CENTURY--BUT THOSE PEOPLE THOUGHT THE SUN REVOLVED AROUND THE EARTH TOO, SO I SHOULDN'T BE TOO HARSH ON THEM.
A LITTLE LATE FOR YOU, ISN'T IT, KENT? "EARLY TO BED..." AND OTHER SUCH DOWN HOME WISDOM?
I'M SURPRISED YOU AREN'T FALLING DOWN AFTER THAT MAGNUM OF CHAMPAGNE, WAYNE...
IT ISN'T EXACTLY LIKE DRINKING MOONSHINE OUT OF A PUMPKIN.
ESPECIALLY WHEN YOU CAN AFFORD TO BUY A HOLLOW LEG TO MATCH THE HOLLOW HEAD--
OOOOKAY, I KNOW WHEN I'M A THIRD WHEEL...I'LL LEAVE YOU TWO SAILORS TO PLAY "WHO HAS THE BIGGER MIZZENMAST"...
BUT--
WAIT--
HASTA MAÑANA, CHICOS...
UNTIL MORNING, MISS LANE...
OKAY, 'NIGHT, LOIS...
I WILL GIVE YOU ONE MILLION DOLLARS TO THROW YOURSELF OVERBOARD.
UP YOURS, RICH BOY.
AND IF YOU THINK I'M SHARING THAT ROOM WITH YOU, FARM TRASH, YOU'RE DUMBER THAN YOU LOOK.
MY THOUGHTS EXACTLY.
BEEN SAVING THAT ONE SINCE DINNER...?
TRY THE SECOND I MET YOU.

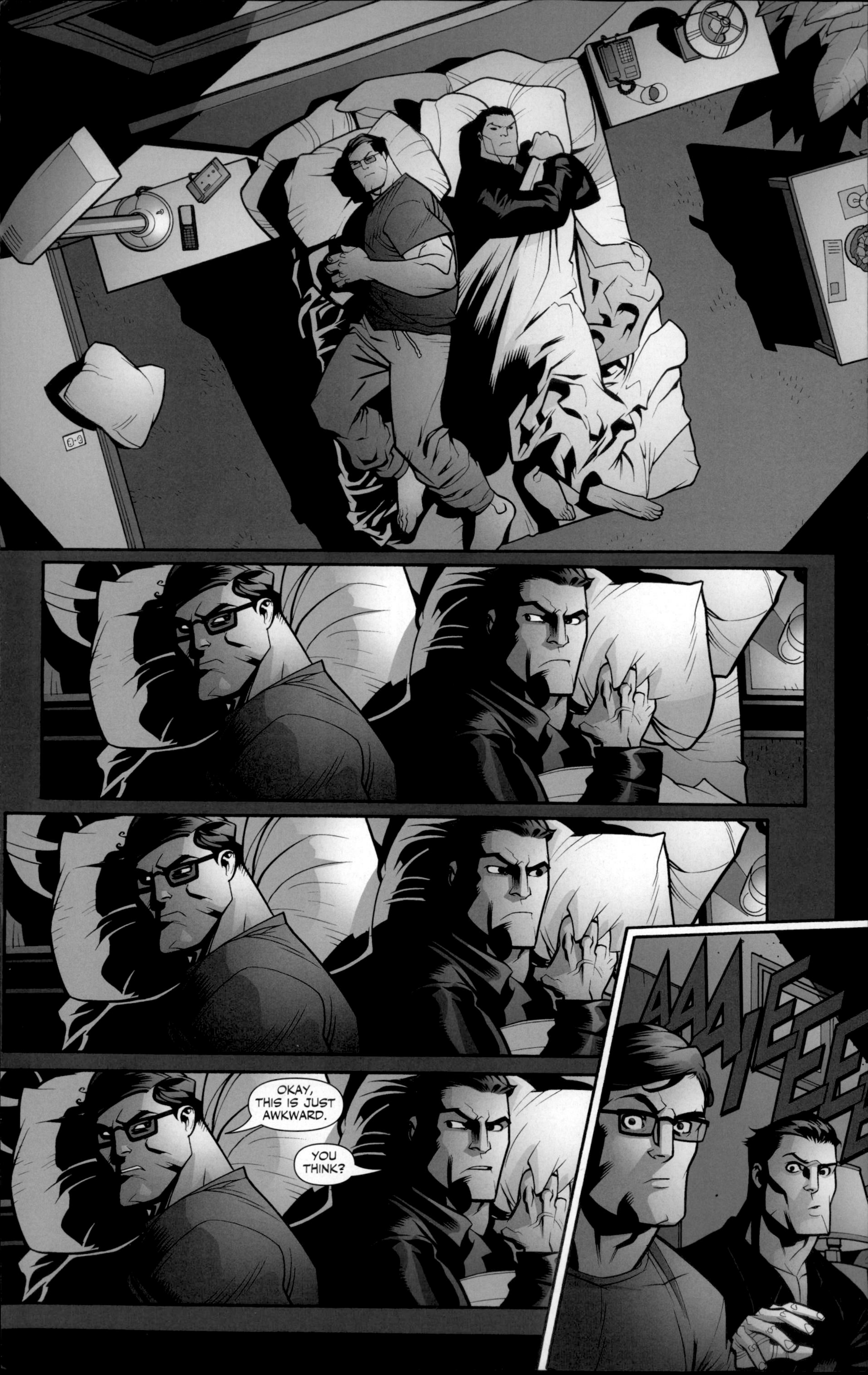
OKAY, THIS IS JUST AWKWARD.
YOU THINK?
AAAIEEE

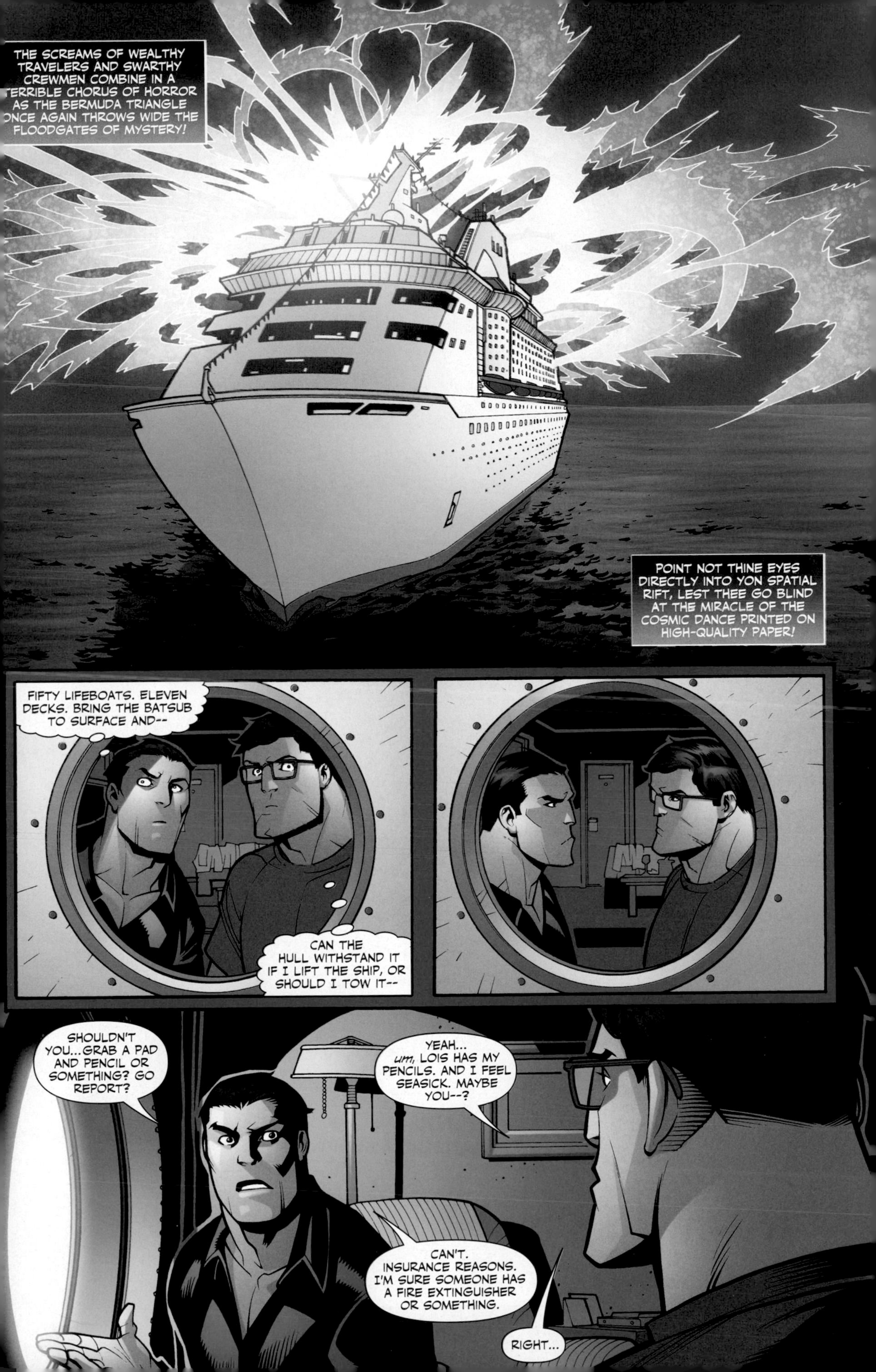
THE SCREAMS OF WEALTHY TRAVELERS AND SWARTHY CREWMEN COMBINE IN A TERRIBLE CHORUS OF HORROR AS THE BERMUDA TRIANGLE ONCE AGAIN THROWS WIDE THE FLOODGATES OF MYSTERY!
POINT NOT THINE EYES DIRECTLY INTO YON SPATIAL RIFT, LEST THEE GO BLIND AT THE MIRACLE OF THE COSMIC DANCE PRINTED ON HIGH-QUALITY PAPER!
FIFTY LIFEBOATS. ELEVEN DECKS. BRING THE BATSUB TO SURFACE AND--
CAN THE HULL WITHSTAND IT IF I LIFT THE SHIP, OR SHOULD I TOW IT--
SHOULDN'T YOU...GRAB A PAD AND PENCIL OR SOMETHING? GO REPORT?
YEAH... UM, LOIS HAS MY PENCILS. AND I FEEL SEASICK. MAYBE YOU--?
CAN'T. INSURANCE REASONS. I'M SURE SOMEONE HAS A FIRE EXTINGUISHER OR SOMETHING.
RIGHT...

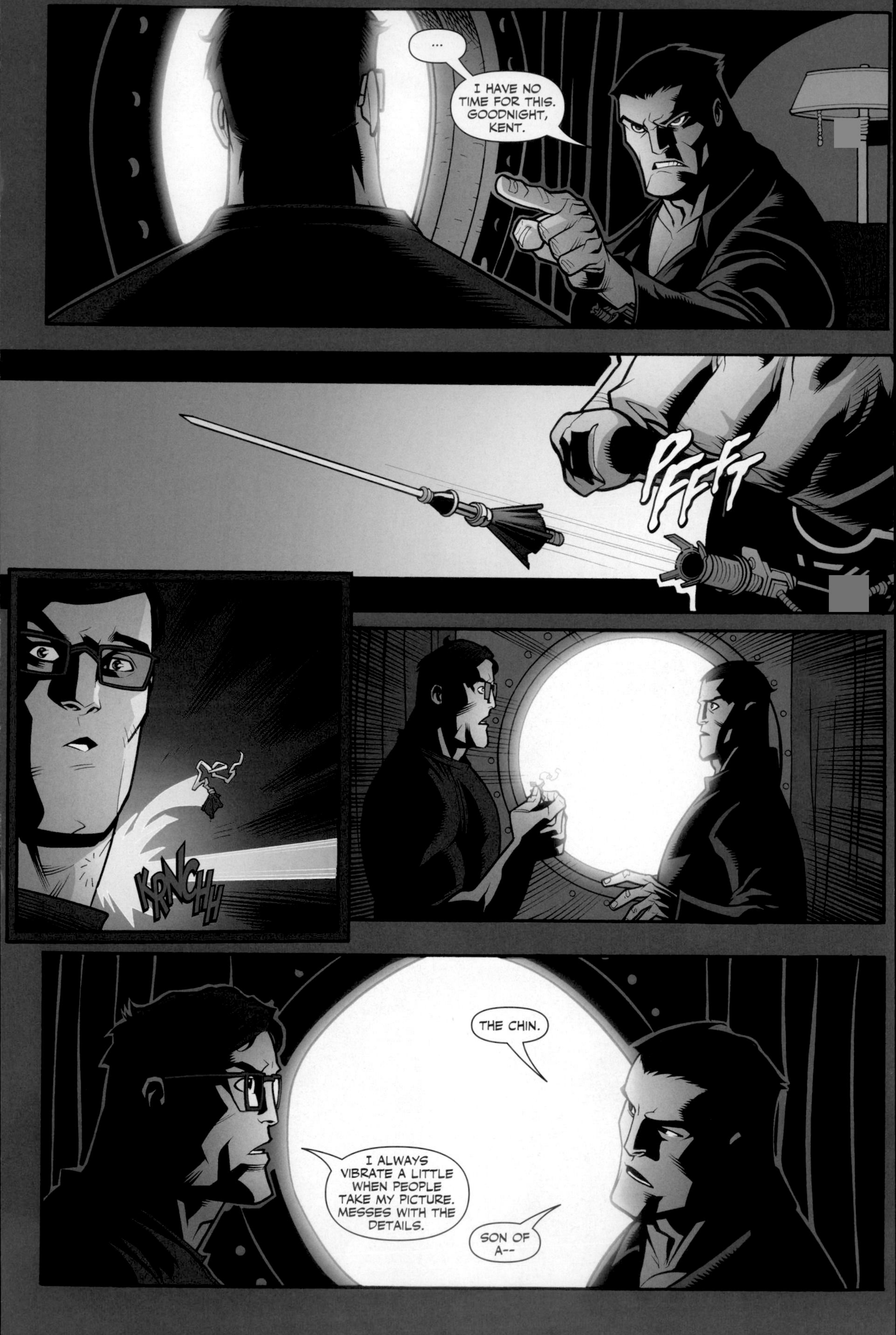
...
I HAVE NO TIME FOR THIS. GOODNIGHT, KENT.
PFFFT
KRNCHH
THE CHIN.
I ALWAYS VIBRATE A LITTLE WHEN PEOPLE TAKE MY PICTURE. MESSES WITH THE DETAILS.
SON OF A--

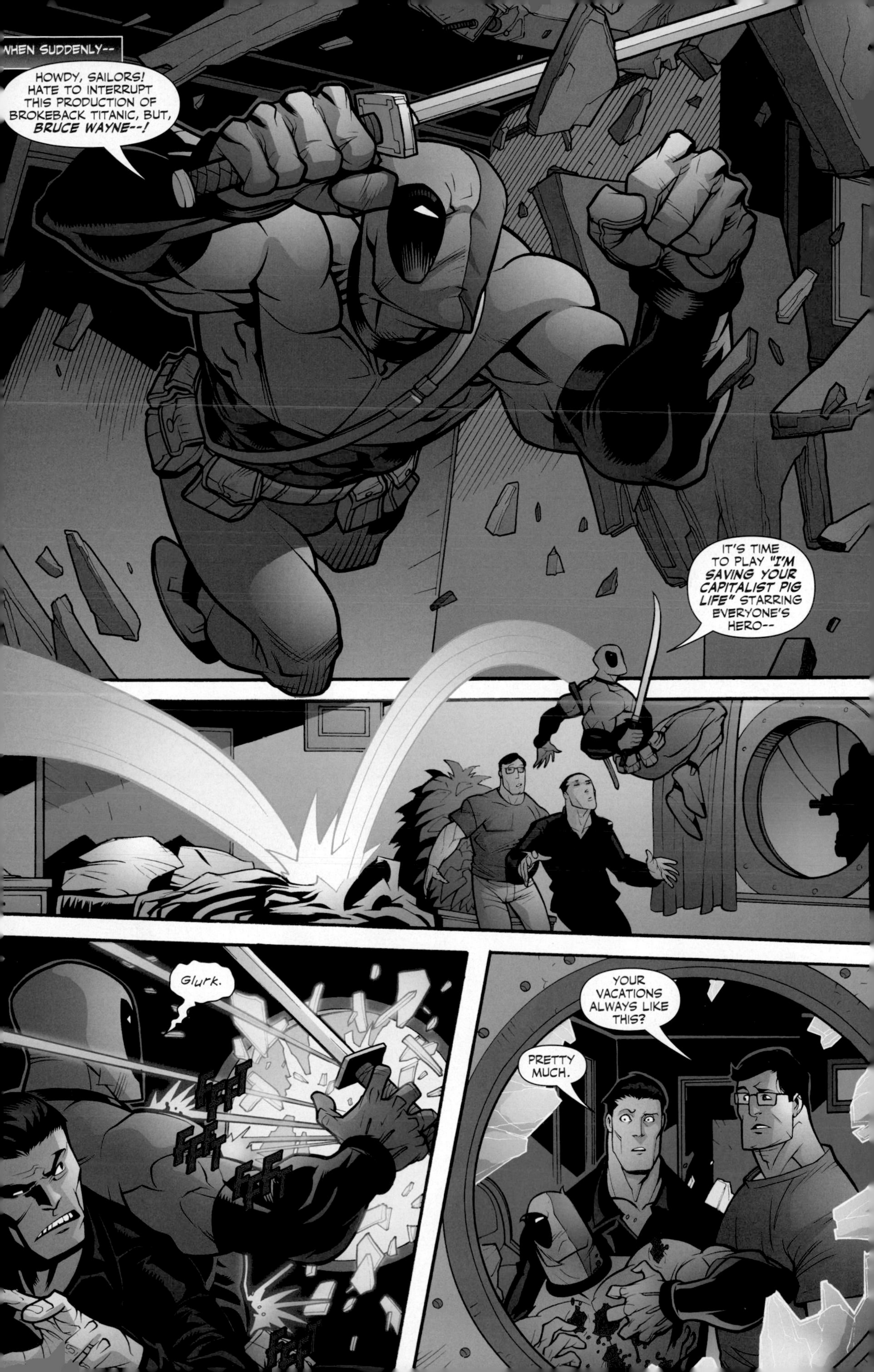
WHEN SUDDENLY--
HOWDY, SAILORS! HATE TO INTERRUPT THIS PRODUCTION OF BROKEBACK TITANIC, BUT, *BRUCE WAYNE--!*
IT'S TIME TO PLAY *"I'M SAVING YOUR CAPITALIST PIG LIFE"* STARRING EVERYONE'S HERO--
Glurk.
YOUR VACATIONS ALWAYS LIKE THIS?
PRETTY MUCH.

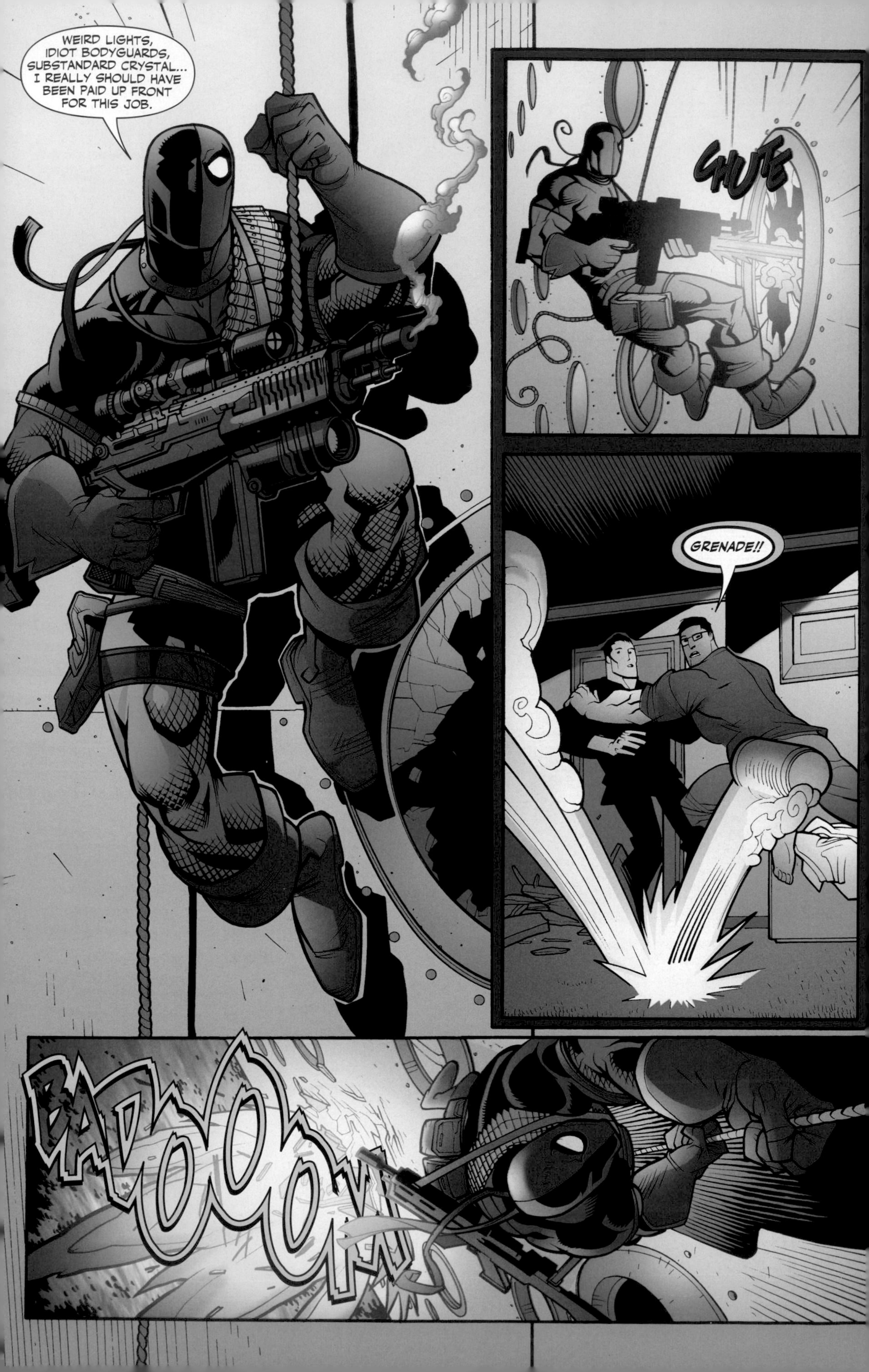

WEIRD LIGHTS, IDIOT BODYGUARDS, SUBSTANDARD CRYSTAL... I REALLY SHOULD HAVE BEEN PAID UP FRONT FOR THIS JOB.
CHUTE
GRENADE!!
BADOOOOM

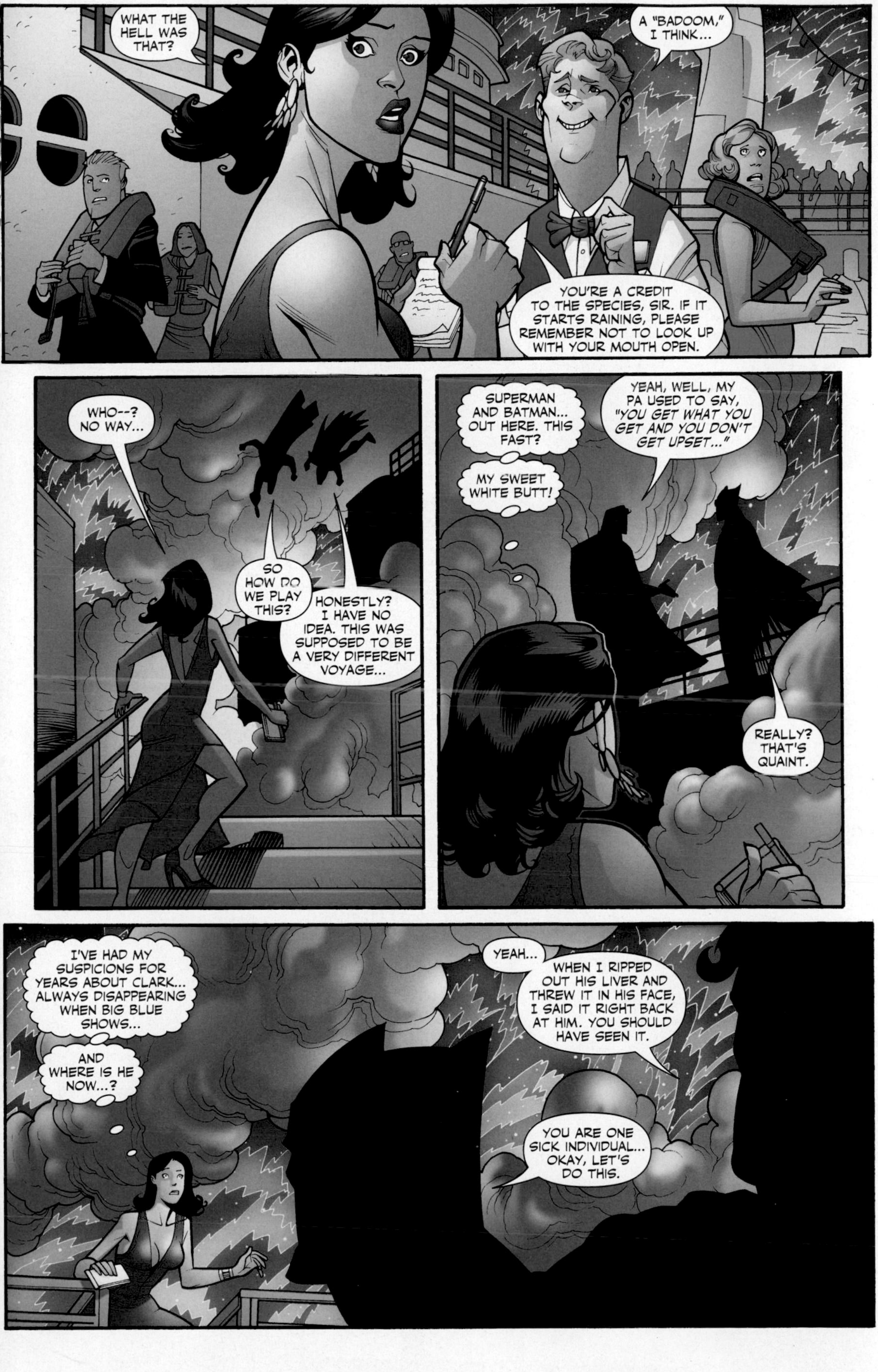
WHAT THE HELL WAS THAT?
A "BADOOM," I THINK...
YOU'RE A CREDIT TO THE SPECIES, SIR. IF IT STARTS RAINING, PLEASE REMEMBER NOT TO LOOK UP WITH YOUR MOUTH OPEN.
WHO--? NO WAY...
SO HOW DO WE PLAY THIS?
HONESTLY? I HAVE NO IDEA. THIS WAS SUPPOSED TO BE A VERY DIFFERENT VOYAGE...
SUPERMAN AND BATMAN... OUT HERE. THIS FAST?
MY SWEET WHITE BUTT!
YEAH, WELL, MY PA USED TO SAY, "YOU GET WHAT YOU GET AND YOU DON'T GET UPSET..."
REALLY? THAT'S QUAINT.
I'VE HAD MY SUSPICIONS FOR YEARS ABOUT CLARK... ALWAYS DISAPPEARING WHEN BIG BLUE SHOWS...
AND WHERE IS HE NOW...?
YEAH...
WHEN I RIPPED OUT HIS LIVER AND THREW IT IN HIS FACE, I SAID IT RIGHT BACK AT HIM. YOU SHOULD HAVE SEEN IT.
YOU ARE ONE SICK INDIVIDUAL... OKAY, LET'S DO THIS.

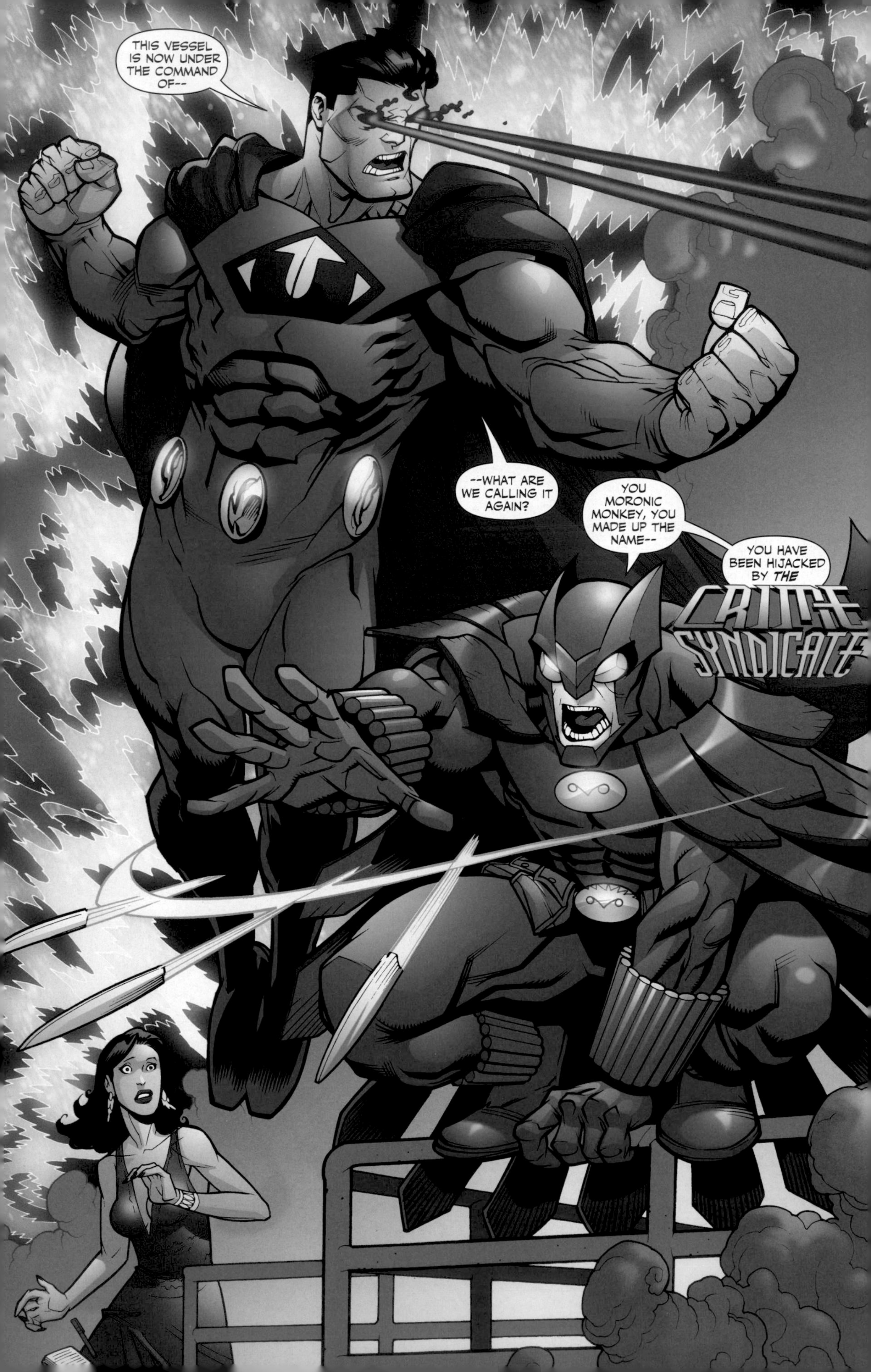
THIS VESSEL IS NOW UNDER THE COMMAND OF--
--WHAT ARE WE CALLING IT AGAIN?
YOU MORONIC MONKEY, YOU MADE UP THE NAME--
YOU HAVE BEEN HIJACKED BY *THE*
CRIME SYNDICATE

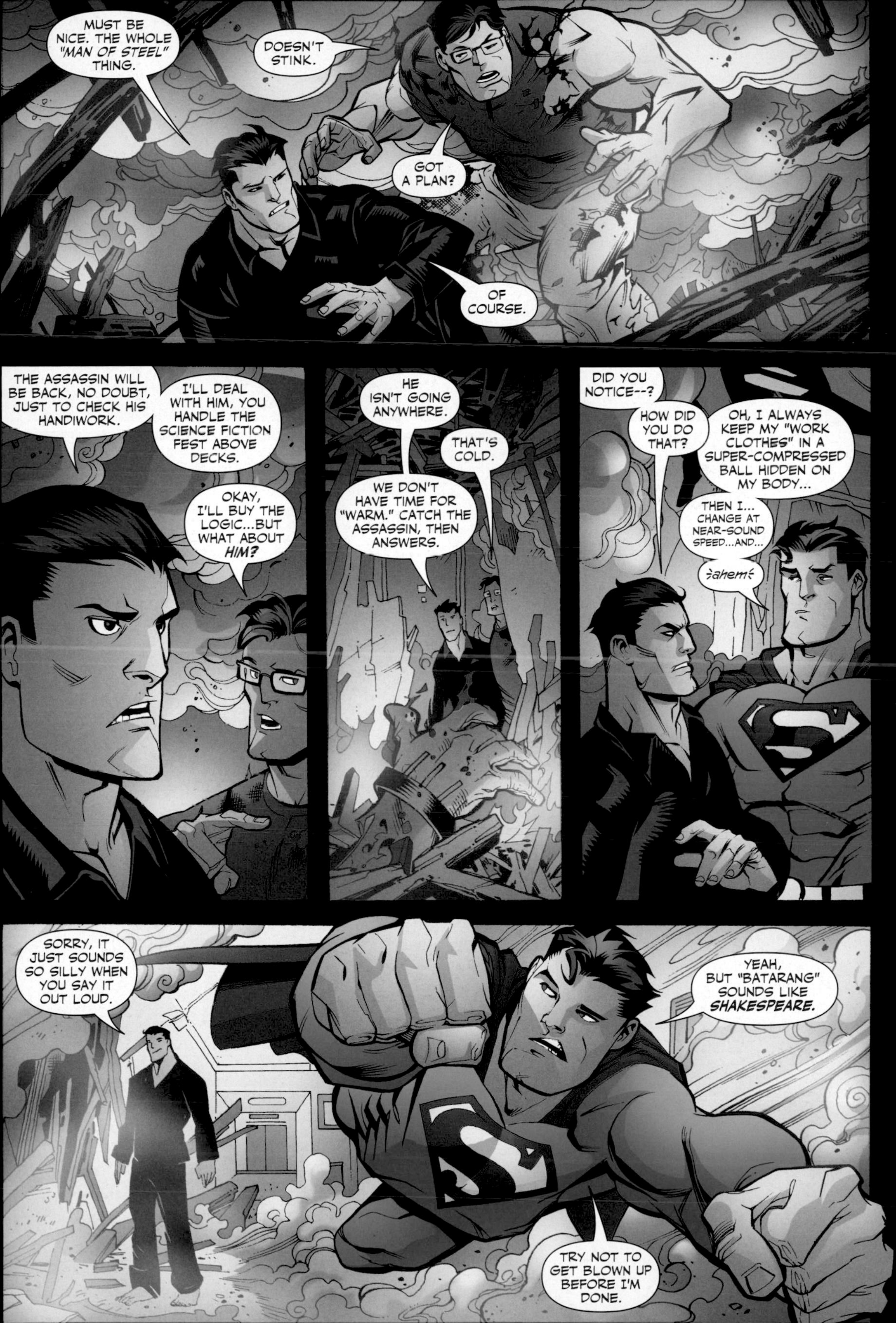
MUST BE NICE. THE WHOLE "MAN OF STEEL" THING.
DOESN'T STINK.
GOT A PLAN?
OF COURSE.
THE ASSASSIN WILL BE BACK, NO DOUBT, JUST TO CHECK HIS HANDIWORK.
I'LL DEAL WITH HIM, YOU HANDLE THE SCIENCE FICTION FEST ABOVE DECKS.
OKAY, I'LL BUY THE LOGIC...BUT WHAT ABOUT HIM?
HE ISN'T GOING ANYWHERE.
THAT'S COLD.
WE DON'T HAVE TIME FOR "WARM." CATCH THE ASSASSIN, THEN ANSWERS.
DID YOU NOTICE--?
HOW DID YOU DO THAT?
OH, I ALWAYS KEEP MY "WORK CLOTHES" IN A SUPER-COMPRESSED BALL HIDDEN ON MY BODY...
THEN I... CHANGE AT NEAR-SOUND SPEED...AND...
ahem
SORRY, IT JUST SOUNDS SO SILLY WHEN YOU SAY IT OUT LOUD.
YEAH, BUT "BATARANG" SOUNDS LIKE SHAKESPEARE.
TRY NOT TO GET BLOWN UP BEFORE I'M DONE.

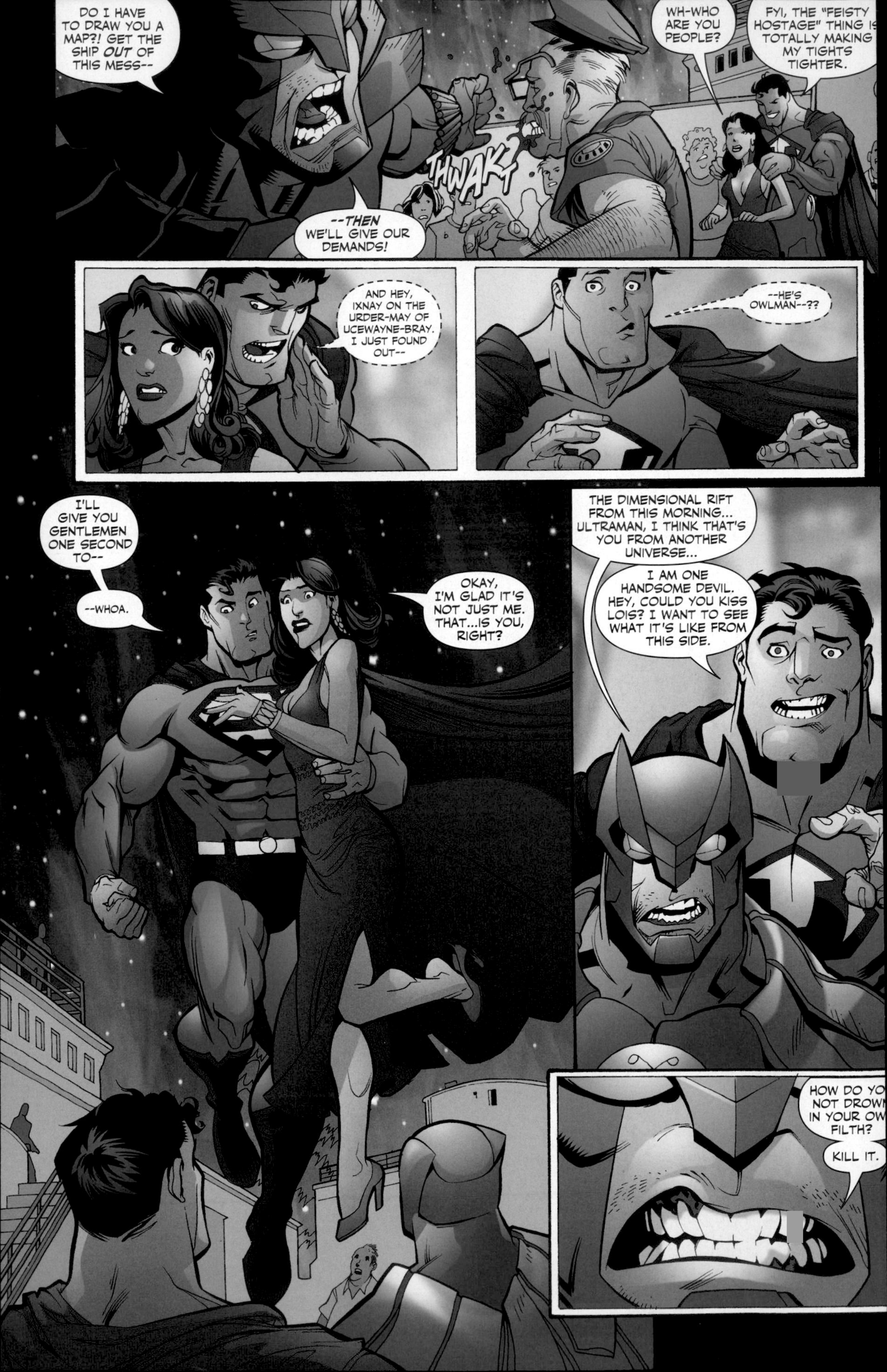
DO I HAVE TO DRAW YOU A MAP?! GET THE SHIP OUT OF THIS MESS--
THWAK!
--THEN WE'LL GIVE OUR DEMANDS!
WH-WHO ARE YOU PEOPLE?
FYI, THE "FEISTY HOSTAGE" THING IS TOTALLY MAKING MY TIGHTS TIGHTER.
AND HEY, IXNAY ON THE URDER-MAY OF UCEWAYNE-BRAY. I JUST FOUND OUT--
--HE'S OWLMAN--??
I'LL GIVE YOU GENTLEMEN ONE SECOND TO--
--WHOA.
OKAY, I'M GLAD IT'S NOT JUST ME. THAT...IS YOU, RIGHT?
THE DIMENSIONAL RIFT FROM THIS MORNING... ULTRAMAN, I THINK THAT'S YOU FROM ANOTHER UNIVERSE...
I AM ONE HANDSOME DEVIL. HEY, COULD YOU KISS LOIS? I WANT TO SEE WHAT IT'S LIKE FROM THIS SIDE.
HOW DO YO NOT DROWN IN YOUR OW FILTH?
KILL IT.

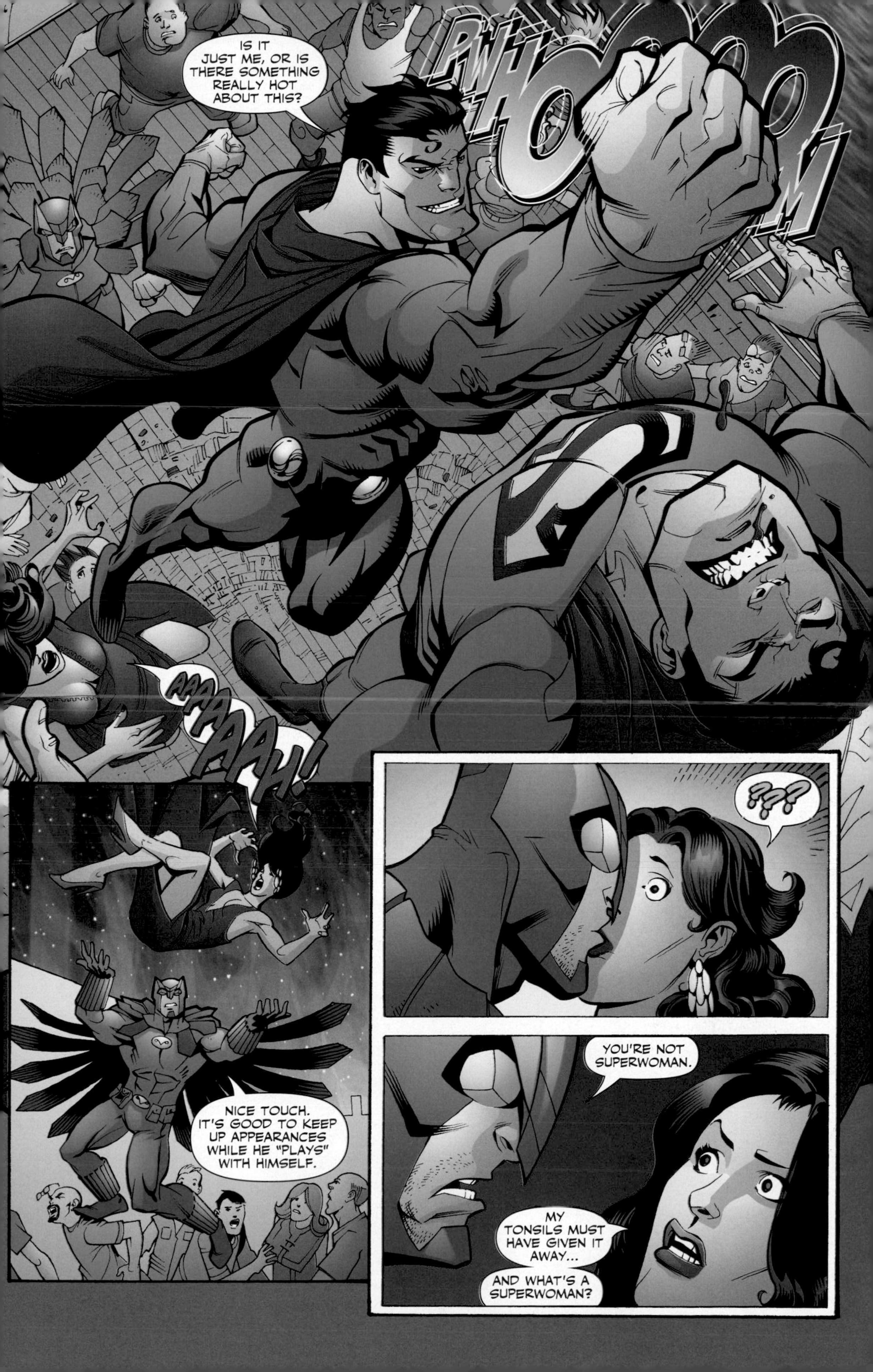
IS IT JUST ME, OR IS THERE SOMETHING REALLY HOT ABOUT THIS?
PWHOOOOM
AAAAAAAAAH!
???
NICE TOUCH. IT'S GOOD TO KEEP UP APPEARANCES WHILE HE "PLAYS" WITH HIMSELF.
YOU'RE NOT SUPERWOMAN.
MY TONSILS MUST HAVE GIVEN IT AWAY...
AND WHAT'S A SUPERWOMAN?

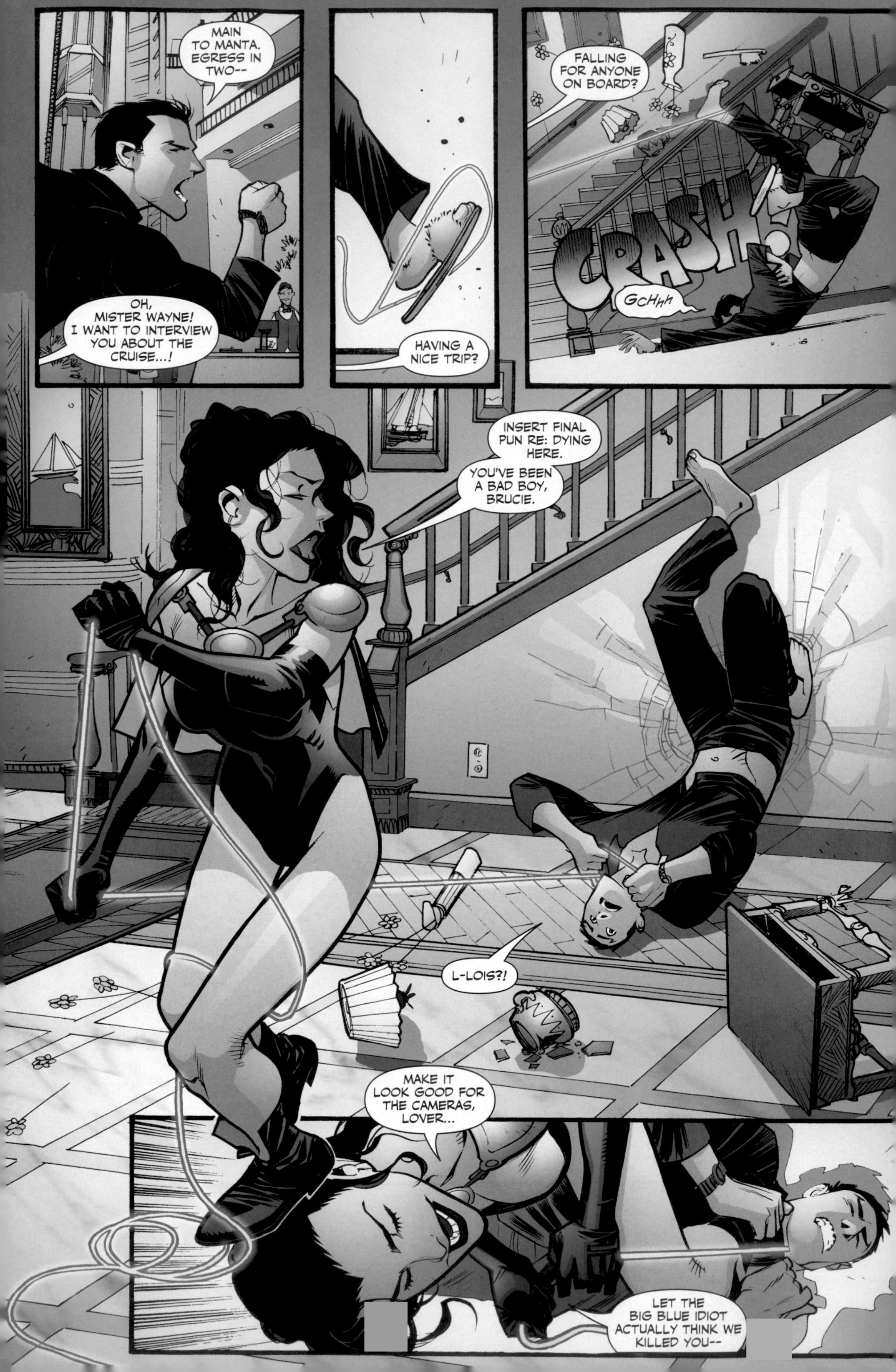
MAIN TO MANTA. EGRESS IN TWO--
OH, MISTER WAYNE! I WANT TO INTERVIEW YOU ABOUT THE CRUISE...!
HAVING A NICE TRIP?
FALLING FOR ANYONE ON BOARD?
CRASH!
GCHhh
INSERT FINAL PUN RE: DYING HERE.
YOU'VE BEEN A BAD BOY, BRUCIE.
L-LOIS?!
MAKE IT LOOK GOOD FOR THE CAMERAS, LOVER...
LET THE BIG BLUE IDIOT ACTUALLY THINK WE KILLED YOU--

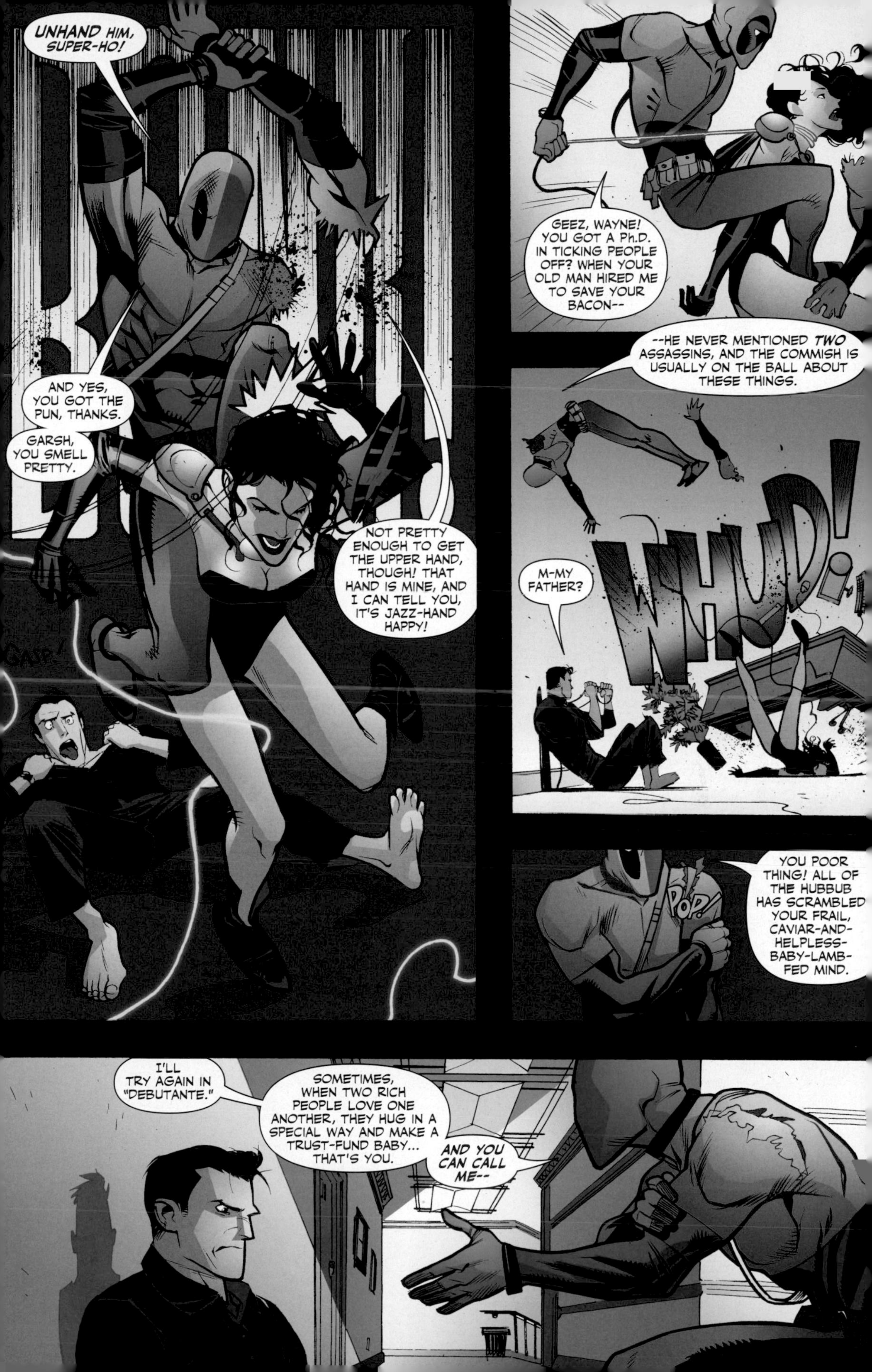
UNHAND HIM, SUPER-HO!
AND YES, YOU GOT THE PUN, THANKS.
GARSH, YOU SMELL PRETTY.
NOT PRETTY ENOUGH TO GET THE UPPER HAND, THOUGH! THAT HAND IS MINE, AND I CAN TELL YOU, IT'S JAZZ-HAND HAPPY!
GEEZ, WAYNE! YOU GOT A Ph.D. IN TICKING PEOPLE OFF? WHEN YOUR OLD MAN HIRED ME TO SAVE YOUR BACON--
--HE NEVER MENTIONED TWO ASSASSINS, AND THE COMMISH IS USUALLY ON THE BALL ABOUT THESE THINGS.
WHUD!
M-MY FATHER?
YOU POOR THING! ALL OF THE HUBBUB HAS SCRAMBLED YOUR FRAIL, CAVIAR-AND-HELPLESS-BABY-LAMB-FED MIND.
POP!
I'LL TRY AGAIN IN "DEBUTANTE."
SOMETIMES, WHEN TWO RICH PEOPLE LOVE ONE ANOTHER, THEY HUG IN A SPECIAL WAY AND MAKE A TRUST-FUND BABY... THAT'S YOU.
AND YOU CAN CALL ME--

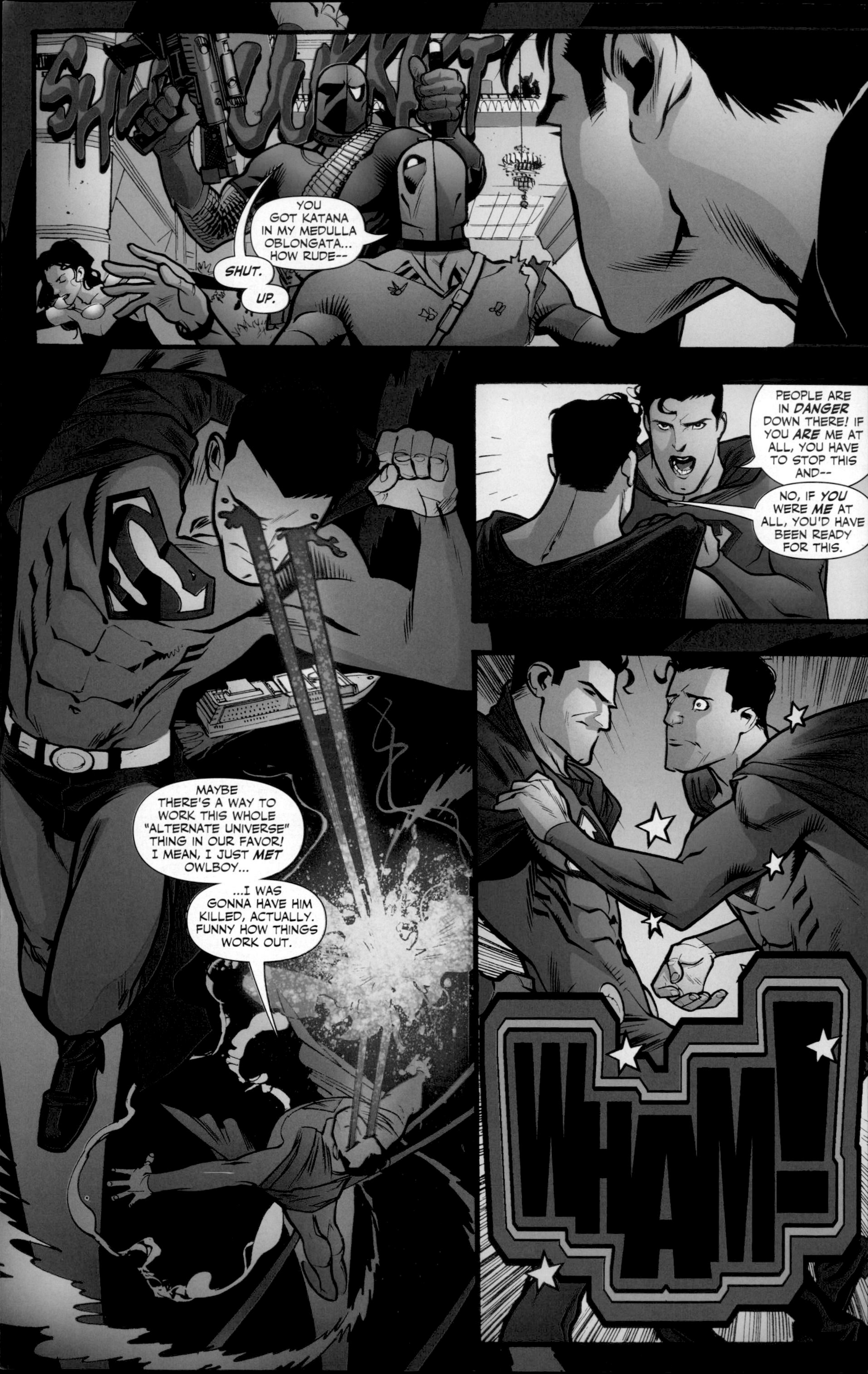
SHUUUKKT
YOU GOT KATANA IN MY MEDULLA OBLONGATA... HOW RUDE--
SHUT.
UP.
PEOPLE ARE IN DANGER DOWN THERE! IF YOU ARE ME AT ALL, YOU HAVE TO STOP THIS AND--
NO, IF YOU WERE ME AT ALL, YOU'D HAVE BEEN READY FOR THIS.
MAYBE THERE'S A WAY TO WORK THIS WHOLE "ALTERNATE UNIVERSE" THING IN OUR FAVOR! I MEAN, I JUST MET OWLBOY...
...I WAS GONNA HAVE HIM KILLED, ACTUALLY. FUNNY HOW THINGS WORK OUT.
WHAM!

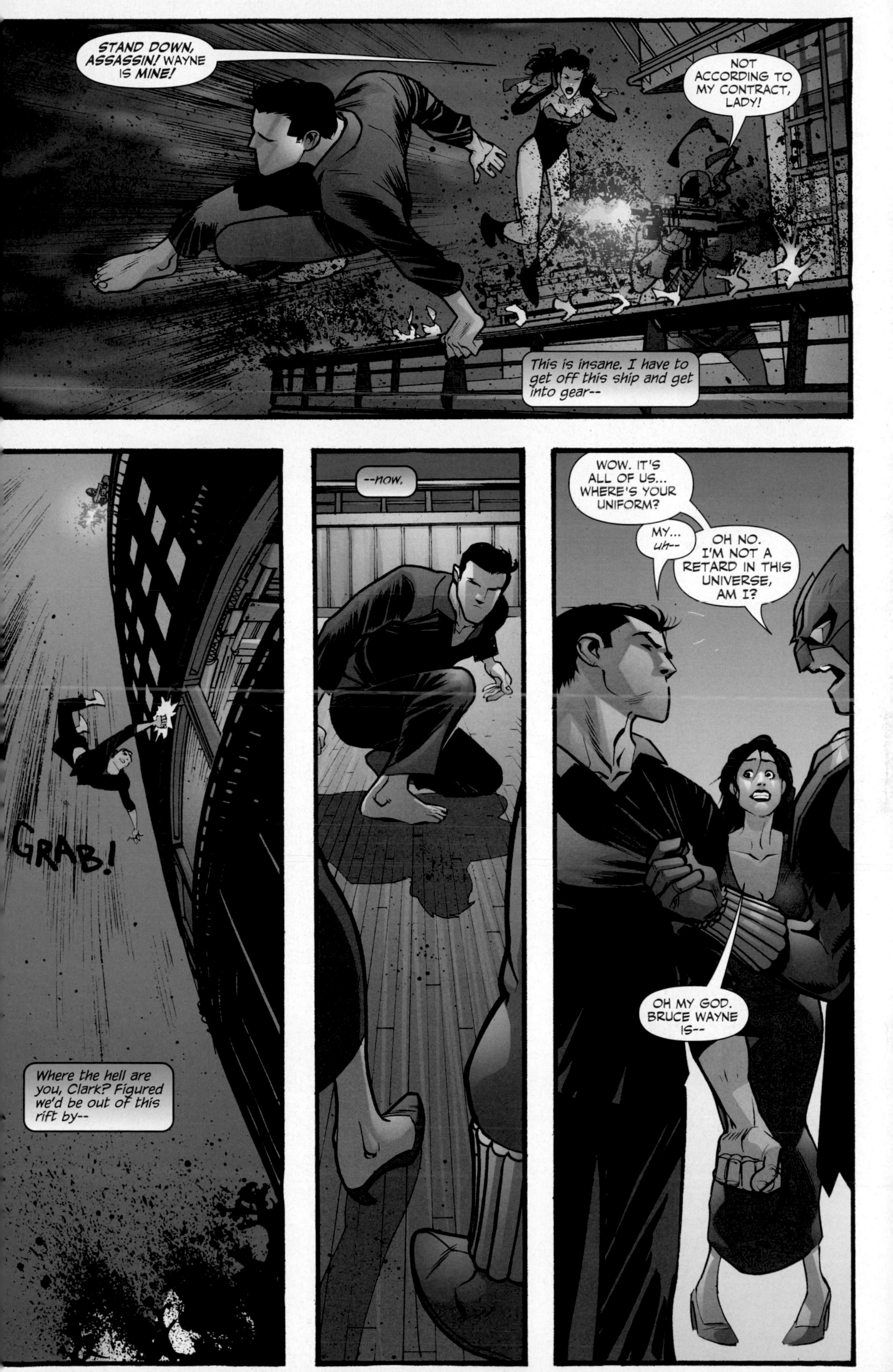
STAND DOWN, ASSASSIN! WAYNE IS MINE!
NOT ACCORDING TO MY CONTRACT, LADY!
This is insane. I have to get off this ship and get into gear--
GRAB!
Where the hell are you, Clark? Figured we'd be out of this rift by--
--now.
WOW. IT'S ALL OF US... WHERE'S YOUR UNIFORM?
MY... uh--
OH NO. I'M NOT A RETARD IN THIS UNIVERSE, AM I?
OH MY GOD. BRUCE WAYNE IS--

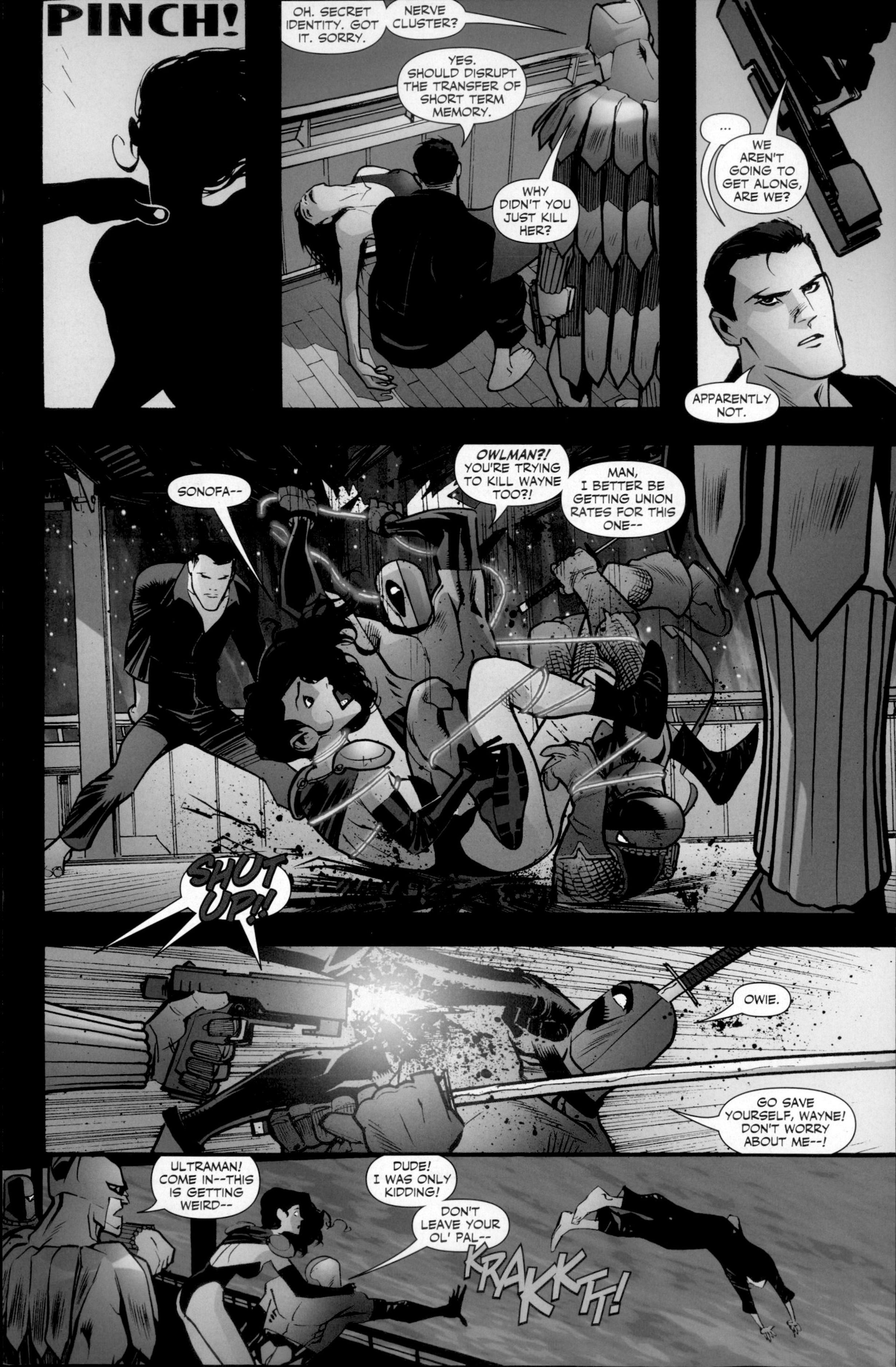
PINCH!
OH. SECRET IDENTITY. GOT IT. SORRY.
NERVE CLUSTER?
YES. SHOULD DISRUPT THE TRANSFER OF SHORT TERM MEMORY.
WHY DIDN'T YOU JUST KILL HER?
...
WE AREN'T GOING TO GET ALONG, ARE WE?
APPARENTLY NOT.
SONOFA--
OWLMAN?! YOU'RE TRYING TO KILL WAYNE TOO?!
MAN, I BETTER BE GETTING UNION RATES FOR THIS ONE--
SHUT UP!!
OWIE.
GO SAVE YOURSELF, WAYNE! DON'T WORRY ABOUT ME--!
ULTRAMAN! COME IN--THIS IS GETTING WEIRD--
DUDE! I WAS ONLY KIDDING!
DON'T LEAVE YOUR OL' PAL--
KRAKKTT!

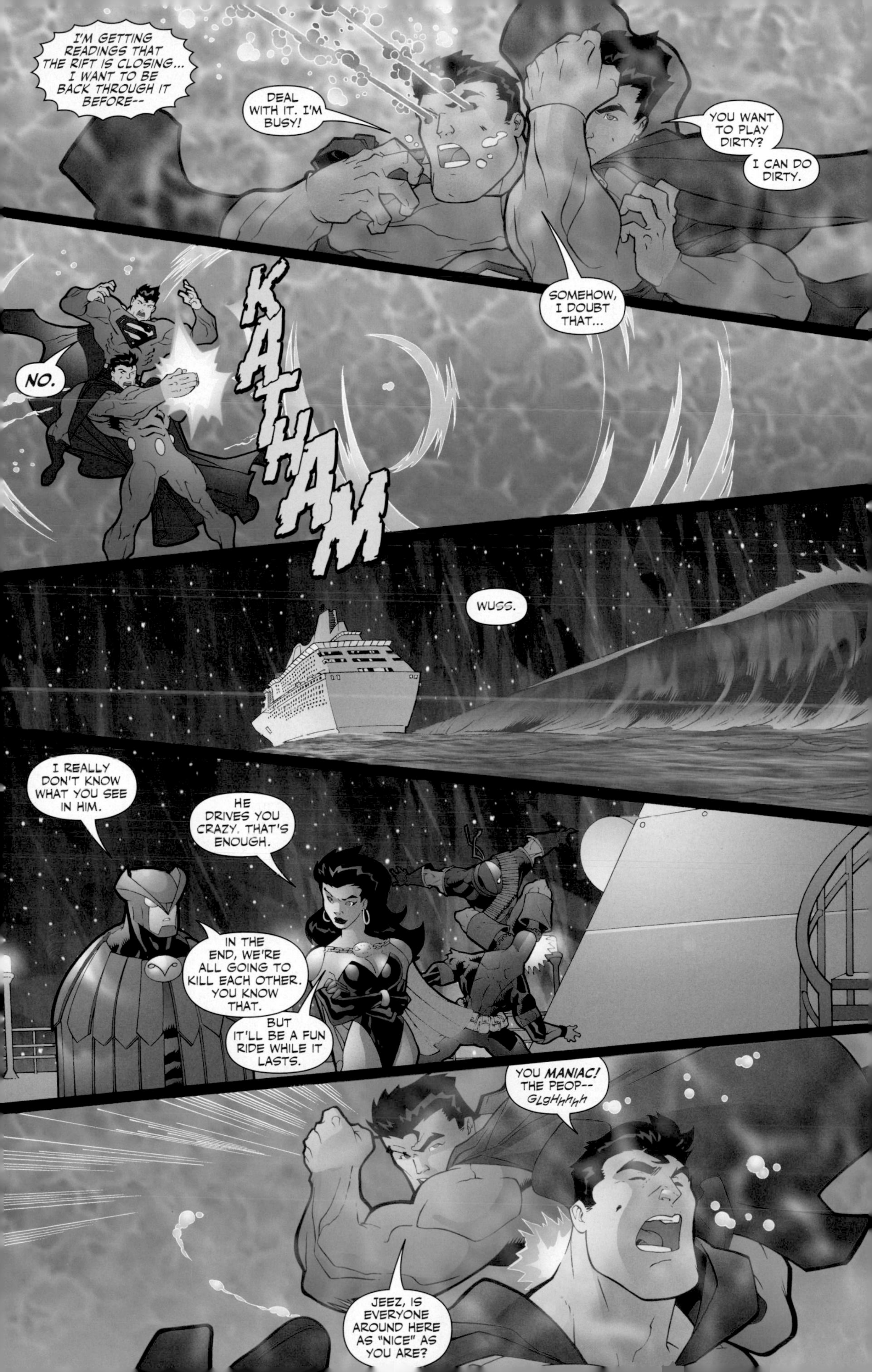
I'M GETTING READINGS THAT THE RIFT IS CLOSING... I WANT TO BE BACK THROUGH IT BEFORE--
DEAL WITH IT. I'M BUSY!
YOU WANT TO PLAY DIRTY?
I CAN DO DIRTY.
SOMEHOW, I DOUBT THAT...
NO.
KATHAM
WUSS.
I REALLY DON'T KNOW WHAT YOU SEE IN HIM.
HE DRIVES YOU CRAZY. THAT'S ENOUGH.
IN THE END, WE'RE ALL GOING TO KILL EACH OTHER. YOU KNOW THAT.
BUT IT'LL BE A FUN RIDE WHILE IT LASTS.
YOU MANIAC! THE PEOP-- GLGHhhhh
JEEZ, IS EVERYONE AROUND HERE AS "NICE" AS YOU ARE?

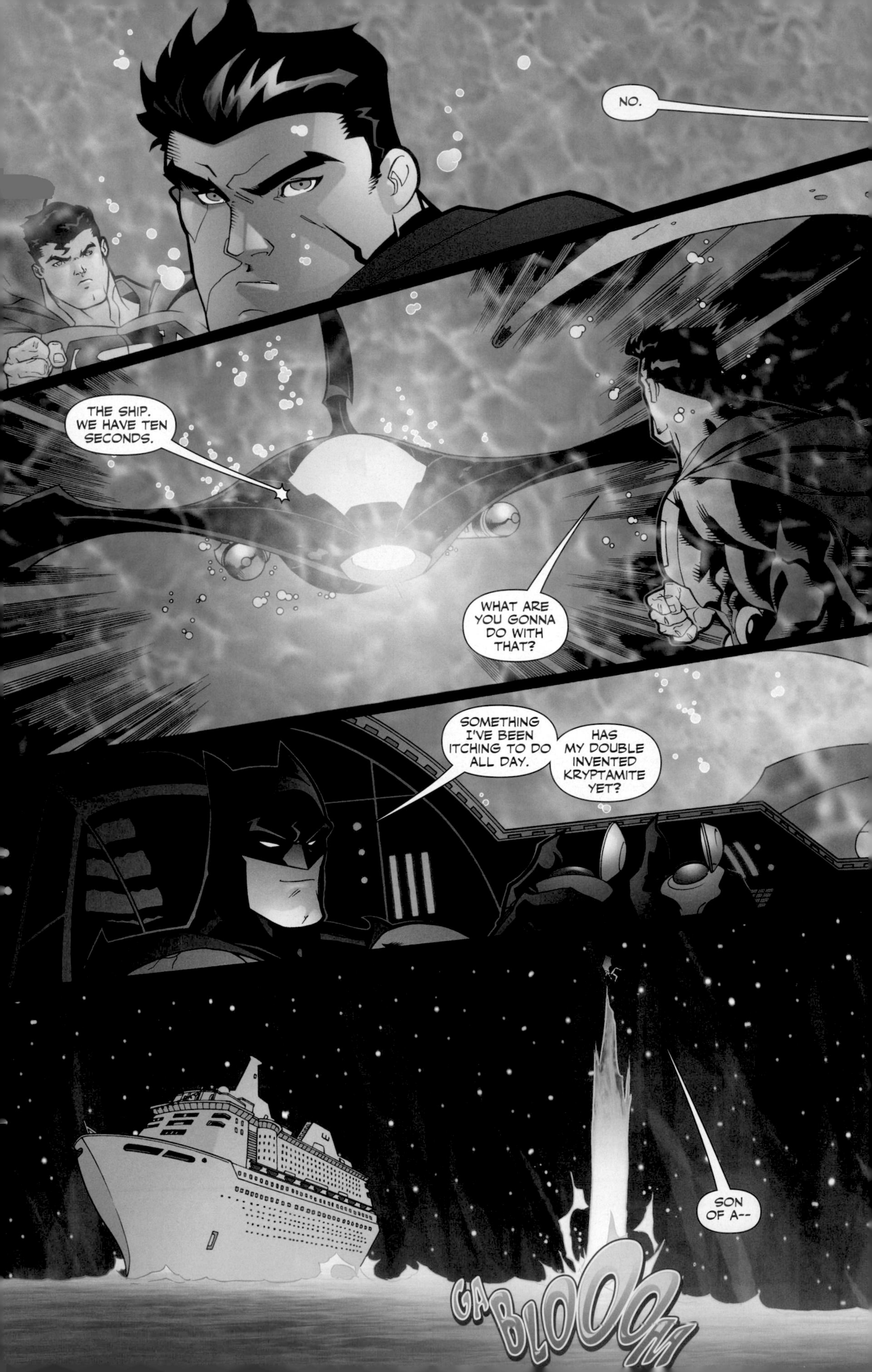
NO.
THE SHIP. WE HAVE TEN SECONDS.
WHAT ARE YOU GONNA DO WITH THAT?
SOMETHING I'VE BEEN ITCHING TO DO ALL DAY.
HAS MY DOUBLE INVENTED KRYPTAMITE YET?
SON OF A--
GABLOOOM

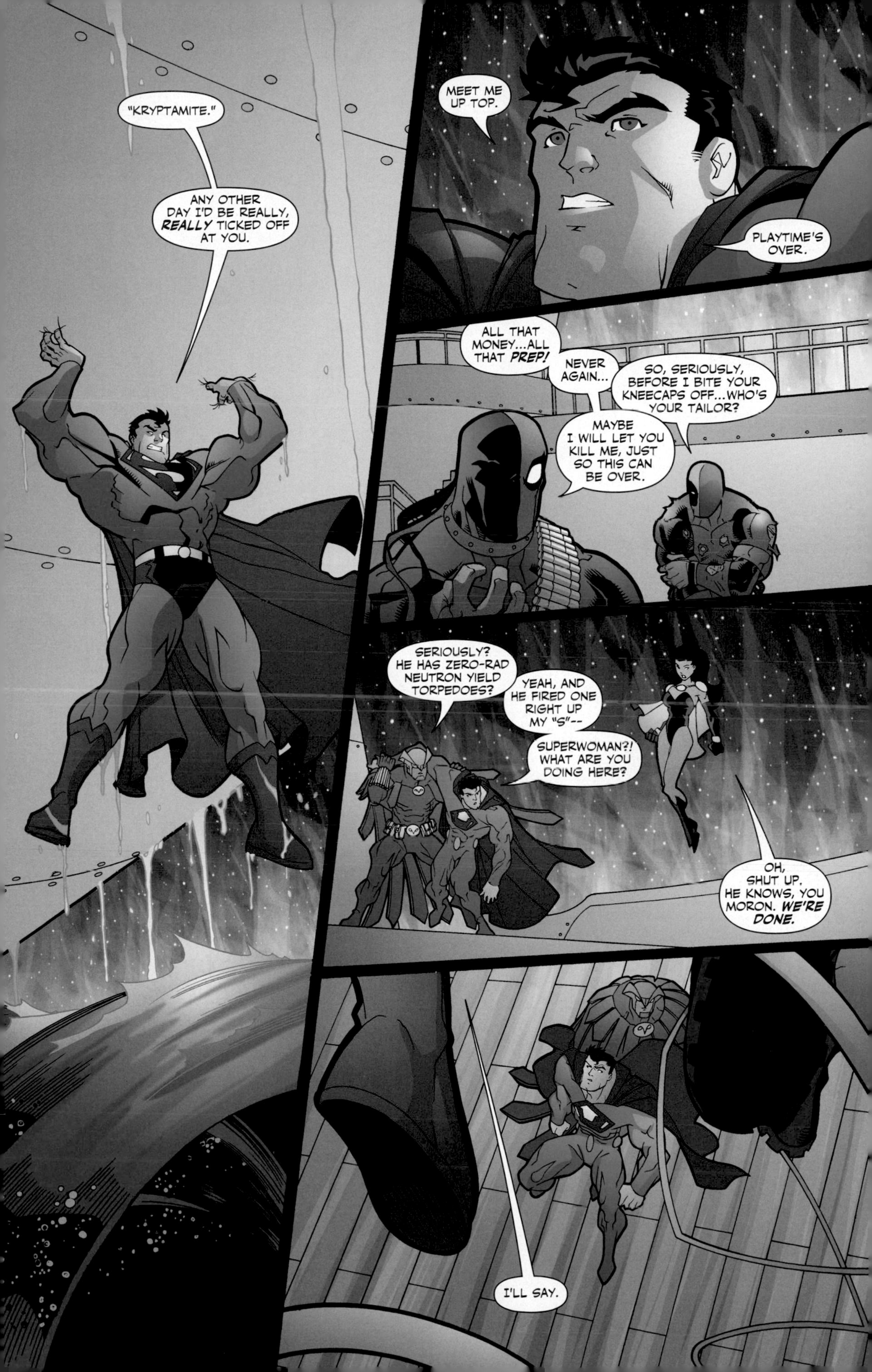
"KRYPTAMITE."
ANY OTHER DAY I'D BE REALLY, *REALLY* TICKED OFF AT YOU.
MEET ME UP TOP.
PLAYTIME'S OVER.
ALL THAT MONEY...ALL THAT *PREP!*
NEVER AGAIN...
MAYBE I WILL LET YOU KILL ME, JUST SO THIS CAN BE OVER.
SO, SERIOUSLY, BEFORE I BITE YOUR KNEECAPS OFF...WHO'S YOUR TAILOR?
SERIOUSLY? HE HAS ZERO-RAD NEUTRON YIELD TORPEDOES?
YEAH, AND HE FIRED ONE RIGHT UP MY "S"--
SUPERWOMAN?! WHAT ARE YOU DOING HERE?
OH, SHUT UP. HE KNOWS, YOU MORON. *WE'RE DONE.*
I'LL SAY.

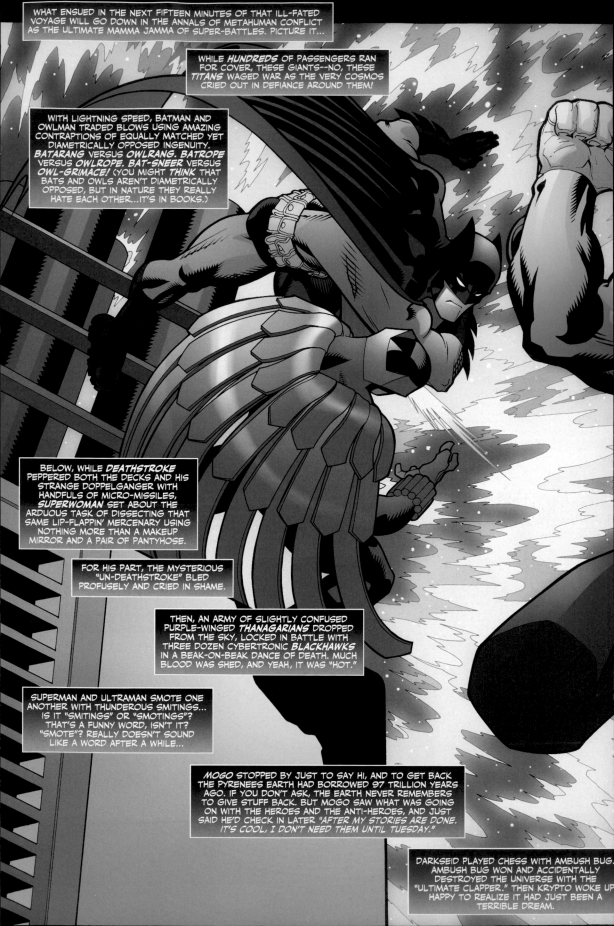

WHAT ENSUED IN THE NEXT FIFTEEN MINUTES OF THAT ILL-FATED VOYAGE WILL GO DOWN IN THE ANNALS OF METAHUMAN CONFLICT AS THE ULTIMATE MAMMA JAMMA OF SUPER-BATTLES. PICTURE IT...

WHILE *HUNDREDS* OF PASSENGERS RAN FOR COVER, THESE GIANTS--NO, THESE *TITANS* WAGED WAR AS THE VERY COSMOS CRIED OUT IN DEFIANCE AROUND THEM!

WITH LIGHTNING SPEED, BATMAN AND OWLMAN TRADED BLOWS USING AMAZING CONTRAPTIONS OF EQUALLY MATCHED YET DIAMETRICALLY OPPOSED INGENUITY. *BATARANG* VERSUS *OWLRANG*. *BATROPE* VERSUS *OWLROPE*. *BAT-SNEER* VERSUS *OWL-GRIMACE!* (YOU MIGHT *THINK* THAT BATS AND OWLS AREN'T DIAMETRICALLY OPPOSED, BUT IN NATURE THEY REALLY HATE EACH OTHER...IT'S IN BOOKS.)

BELOW, WHILE *DEATHSTROKE* PEPPERED BOTH THE DECKS AND HIS STRANGE DOPPELGANGER WITH HANDFULS OF MICRO-MISSILES, *SUPERWOMAN* SET ABOUT THE ARDUOUS TASK OF DISSECTING THAT SAME LIP-FLAPPIN' MERCENARY USING NOTHING MORE THAN A MAKEUP MIRROR AND A PAIR OF PANTYHOSE.

FOR HIS PART, THE MYSTERIOUS "UN-DEATHSTROKE" BLED PROFUSELY AND CRIED IN SHAME.

THEN, AN ARMY OF SLIGHTLY CONFUSED PURPLE-WINGED *THANAGARIANS* DROPPED FROM THE SKY, LOCKED IN BATTLE WITH THREE DOZEN CYBERTRONIC *BLACKHAWKS* IN A BEAK-ON-BEAK DANCE OF DEATH. MUCH BLOOD WAS SHED, AND YEAH, IT WAS "HOT."

SUPERMAN AND ULTRAMAN SMOTE ONE ANOTHER WITH THUNDEROUS SMITINGS... IS IT "SMITINGS" OR "SMOTINGS"? THAT'S A FUNNY WORD, ISN'T IT? "SMOTE"? REALLY DOESN'T SOUND LIKE A WORD AFTER A WHILE...

MOGO STOPPED BY JUST TO SAY HI, AND TO GET BACK THE PYRENEES EARTH HAD BORROWED 97 TRILLION YEARS AGO. IF YOU DON'T ASK, THE EARTH NEVER REMEMBERS TO GIVE STUFF BACK. BUT MOGO SAW WHAT WAS GOING ON WITH THE HEROES AND THE ANTI-HEROES, AND JUST SAID HE'D CHECK IN LATER *"AFTER MY STORIES ARE DONE. IT'S COOL, I DON'T NEED THEM UNTIL TUESDAY."*

DARKSEID PLAYED CHESS WITH AMBUSH BUG. AMBUSH BUG WON AND ACCIDENTALLY DESTROYED THE UNIVERSE WITH THE "ULTIMATE CLAPPER." THEN KRYPTO WOKE UP HAPPY TO REALIZE IT HAD JUST BEEN A TERRIBLE DREAM.

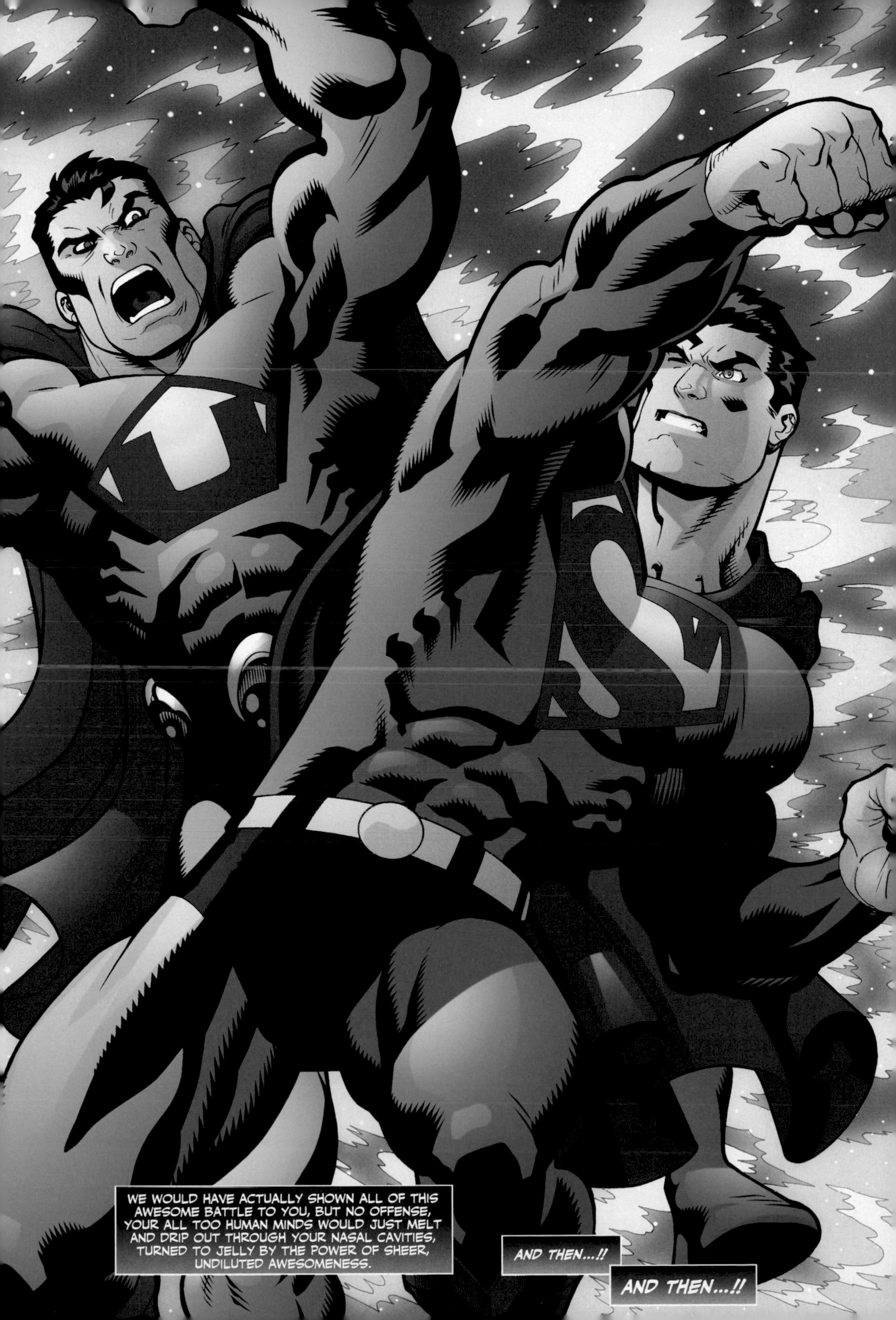
WE WOULD HAVE ACTUALLY SHOWN ALL OF THIS AWESOME BATTLE TO YOU, BUT NO OFFENSE, YOUR ALL TOO HUMAN MINDS WOULD JUST MELT AND DRIP OUT THROUGH YOUR NASAL CAVITIES, TURNED TO JELLY BY THE POWER OF SHEER, UNDILUTED AWESOMENESS.
AND THEN...!!
AND THEN...!!

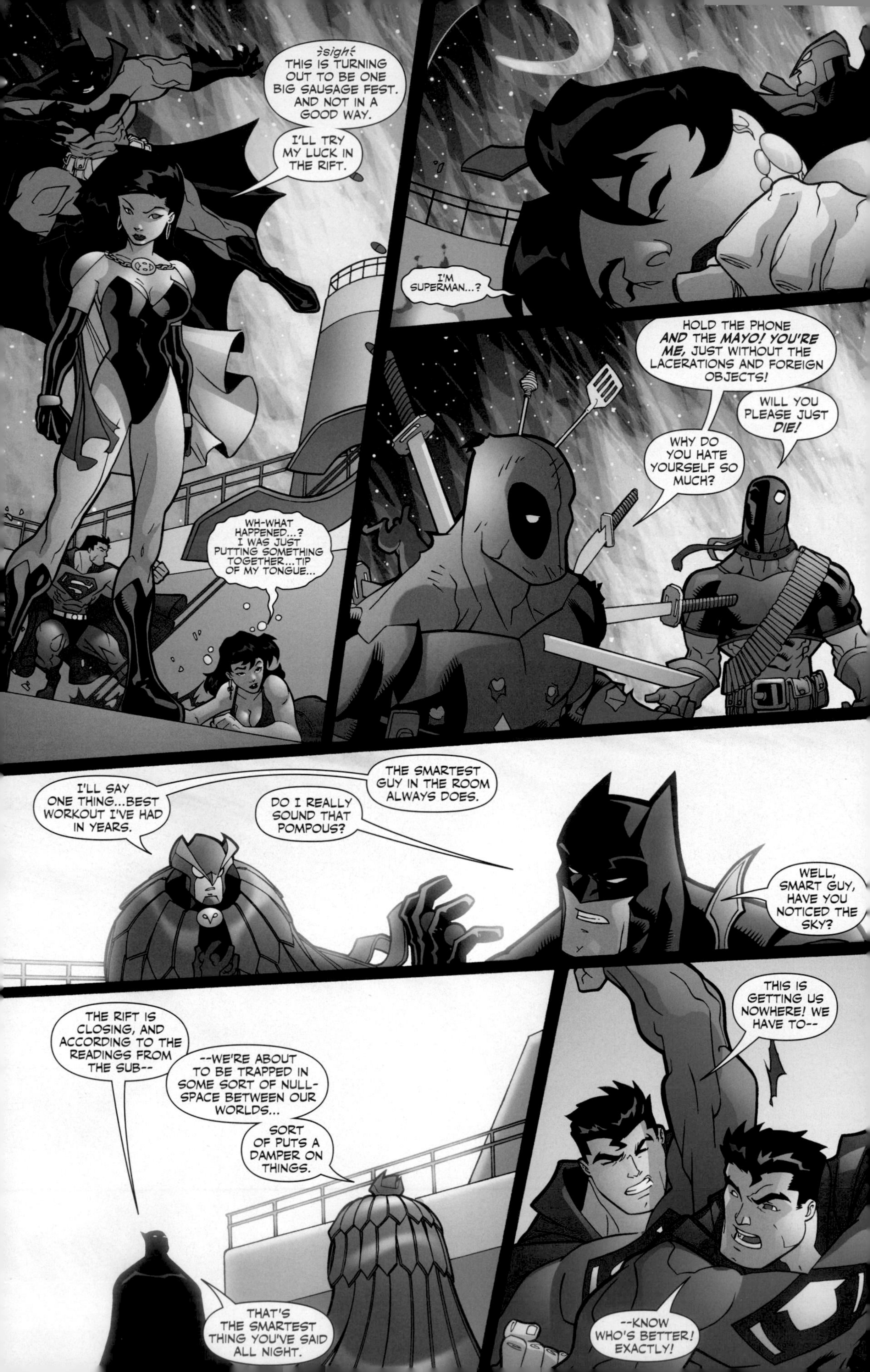

SIGH THIS IS TURNING OUT TO BE ONE BIG SAUSAGE FEST. AND NOT IN A GOOD WAY.
I'LL TRY MY LUCK IN THE RIFT.
WH-WHAT HAPPENED...? I WAS JUST PUTTING SOMETHING TOGETHER...TIP OF MY TONGUE...
I'M SUPERMAN...?
HOLD THE PHONE AND THE MAYO! YOU'RE ME, JUST WITHOUT THE LACERATIONS AND FOREIGN OBJECTS!
WHY DO YOU HATE YOURSELF SO MUCH?
WILL YOU PLEASE JUST DIE!
I'LL SAY ONE THING...BEST WORKOUT I'VE HAD IN YEARS.
THE SMARTEST GUY IN THE ROOM ALWAYS DOES.
DO I REALLY SOUND THAT POMPOUS?
WELL, SMART GUY, HAVE YOU NOTICED THE SKY?
THE RIFT IS CLOSING, AND ACCORDING TO THE READINGS FROM THE SUB--
--WE'RE ABOUT TO BE TRAPPED IN SOME SORT OF NULL-SPACE BETWEEN OUR WORLDS...
SORT OF PUTS A DAMPER ON THINGS.
THAT'S THE SMARTEST THING YOU'VE SAID ALL NIGHT.
THIS IS GETTING US NOWHERE! WE HAVE TO--
--KNOW WHO'S BETTER! EXACTLY!

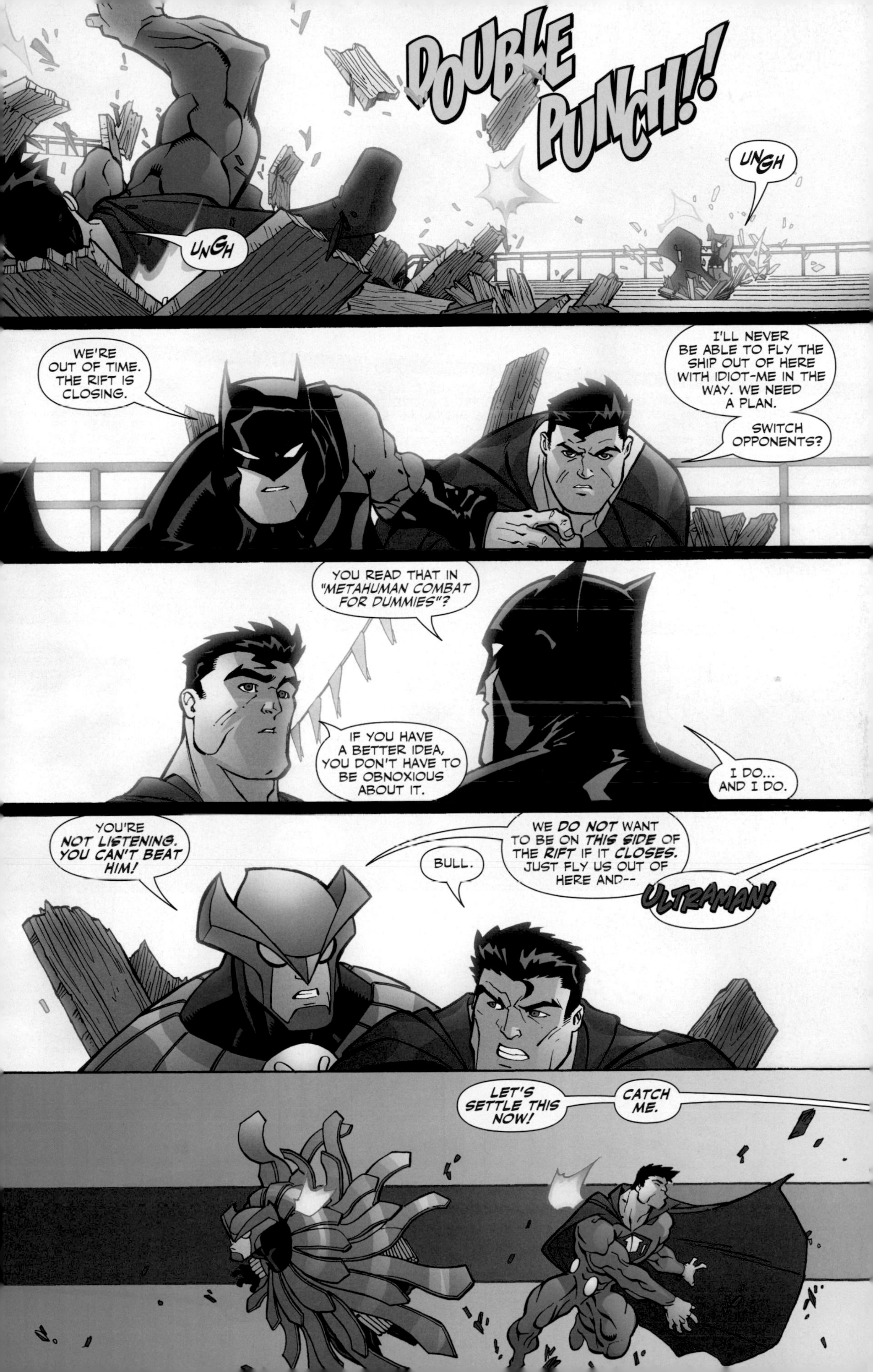
DOUBLE PUNCH!!
UNGH
UNGH
WE'RE OUT OF TIME. THE RIFT IS CLOSING.
I'LL NEVER BE ABLE TO FLY THE SHIP OUT OF HERE WITH IDIOT-ME IN THE WAY. WE NEED A PLAN.
SWITCH OPPONENTS?
YOU READ THAT IN "METAHUMAN COMBAT FOR DUMMIES"?
IF YOU HAVE A BETTER IDEA, YOU DON'T HAVE TO BE OBNOXIOUS ABOUT IT.
I DO... AND I DO.
YOU'RE NOT LISTENING. YOU CAN'T BEAT HIM!
BULL.
WE DO NOT WANT TO BE ON THIS SIDE OF THE RIFT IF IT CLOSES. JUST FLY US OUT OF HERE AND--
ULTRAMAN!
LET'S SETTLE THIS NOW!
CATCH ME.

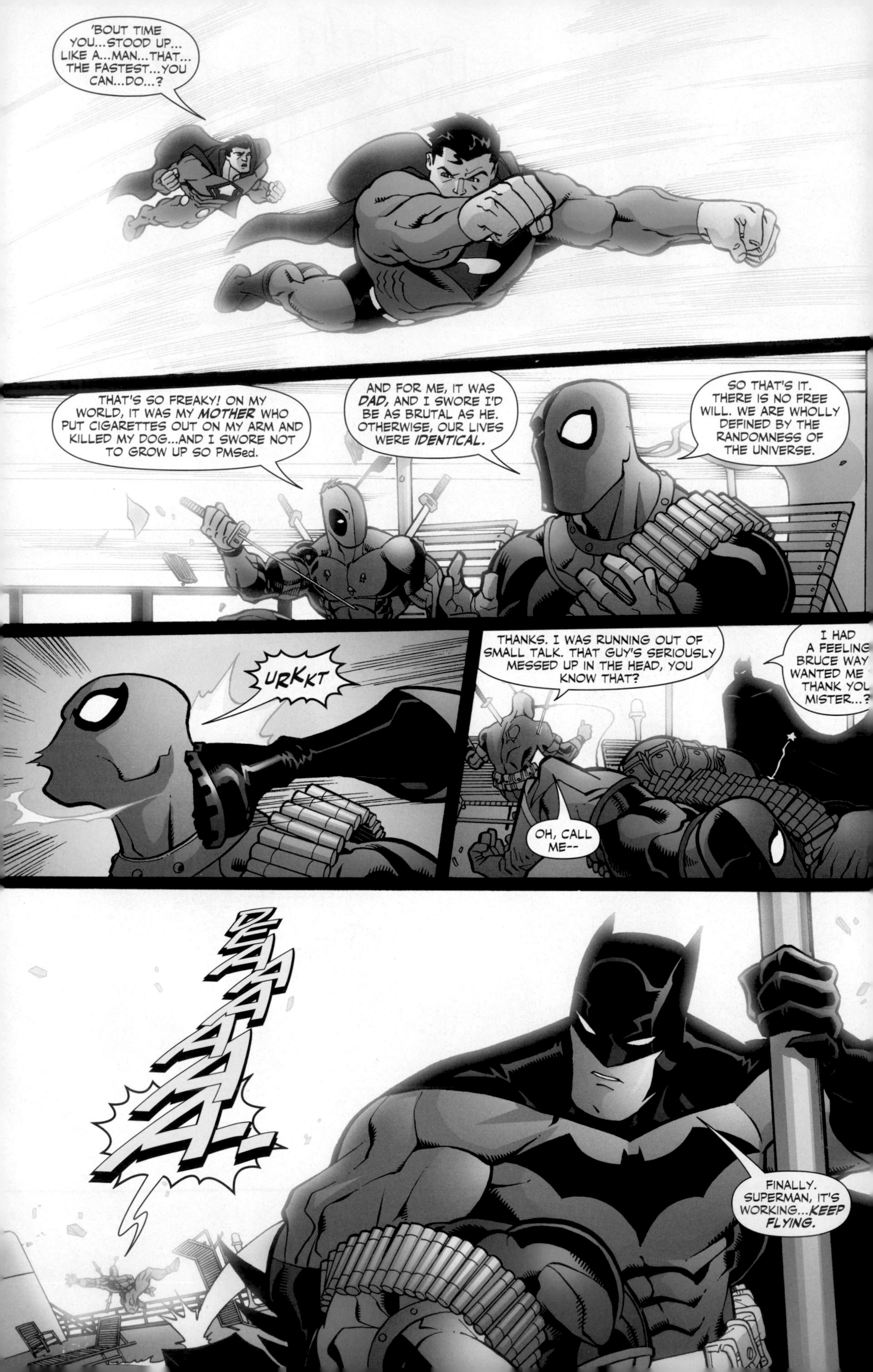
'BOUT TIME YOU...STOOD UP... LIKE A...MAN...THAT... THE FASTEST...YOU CAN...DO...?
THAT'S SO FREAKY! ON MY WORLD, IT WAS MY *MOTHER* WHO PUT CIGARETTES OUT ON MY ARM AND KILLED MY DOG...AND I SWORE NOT TO GROW UP SO PMSed.
AND FOR ME, IT WAS *DAD,* AND I SWORE I'D BE AS BRUTAL AS HE. OTHERWISE, OUR LIVES WERE *IDENTICAL.*
SO THAT'S IT. THERE IS NO FREE WILL. WE ARE WHOLLY DEFINED BY THE RANDOMNESS OF THE UNIVERSE.
URKKT
THANKS. I WAS RUNNING OUT OF SMALL TALK. THAT GUY'S SERIOUSLY MESSED UP IN THE HEAD, YOU KNOW THAT?
I HAD A FEELING BRUCE WAY WANTED ME THANK YOU MISTER...?
OH, CALL ME--
FINALLY. SUPERMAN, IT'S WORKING...*KEEP FLYING.*

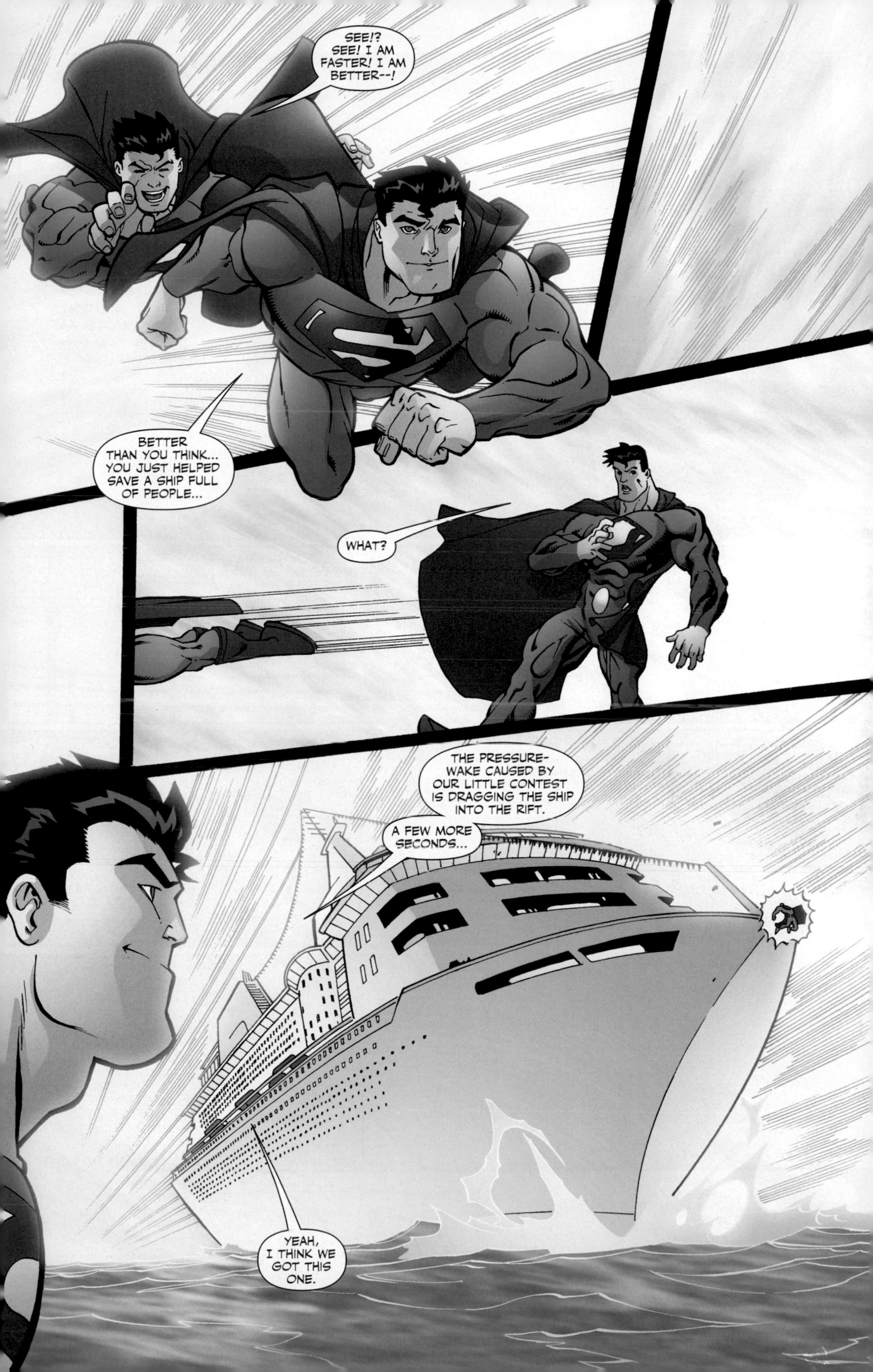
SEE!? SEE! I AM FASTER! I AM BETTER--!
BETTER THAN YOU THINK... YOU JUST HELPED SAVE A SHIP FULL OF PEOPLE...
WHAT?
THE PRESSURE-WAKE CAUSED BY OUR LITTLE CONTEST IS DRAGGING THE SHIP INTO THE RIFT.
A FEW MORE SECONDS...
YEAH, I THINK WE GOT THIS ONE.

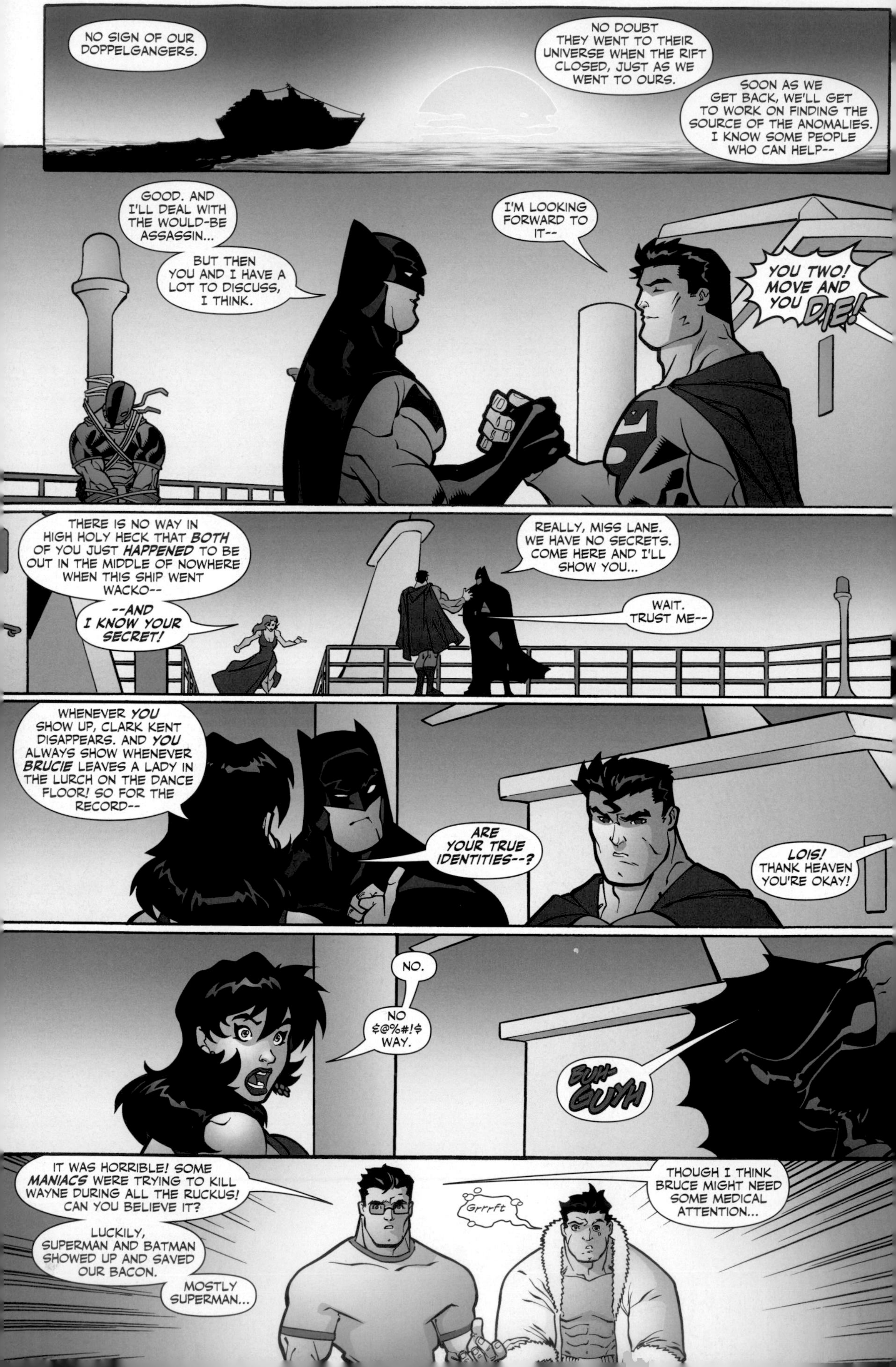
NO SIGN OF OUR DOPPELGANGERS.
NO DOUBT THEY WENT TO THEIR UNIVERSE WHEN THE RIFT CLOSED, JUST AS WE WENT TO OURS.
SOON AS WE GET BACK, WE'LL GET TO WORK ON FINDING THE SOURCE OF THE ANOMALIES. I KNOW SOME PEOPLE WHO CAN HELP--
GOOD. AND I'LL DEAL WITH THE WOULD-BE ASSASSIN...
BUT THEN YOU AND I HAVE A LOT TO DISCUSS, I THINK.
I'M LOOKING FORWARD TO IT--
YOU TWO! MOVE AND YOU DIE!
THERE IS NO WAY IN HIGH HOLY HECK THAT BOTH OF YOU JUST HAPPENED TO BE OUT IN THE MIDDLE OF NOWHERE WHEN THIS SHIP WENT WACKO--
--AND I KNOW YOUR SECRET!
REALLY, MISS LANE. WE HAVE NO SECRETS. COME HERE AND I'LL SHOW YOU...
WAIT. TRUST ME--
WHENEVER YOU SHOW UP, CLARK KENT DISAPPEARS. AND YOU ALWAYS SHOW WHENEVER BRUCIE LEAVES A LADY IN THE LURCH ON THE DANCE FLOOR! SO FOR THE RECORD--
ARE YOUR TRUE IDENTITIES--?
LOIS! THANK HEAVEN YOU'RE OKAY!
NO.
NO $@%#!$ WAY.
BUH-GUYH
IT WAS HORRIBLE! SOME MANIACS WERE TRYING TO KILL WAYNE DURING ALL THE RUCKUS! CAN YOU BELIEVE IT?
LUCKILY, SUPERMAN AND BATMAN SHOWED UP AND SAVED OUR BACON.
MOSTLY SUPERMAN...
Grrrft
THOUGH I THINK BRUCE MIGHT NEED SOME MEDICAL ATTENTION...

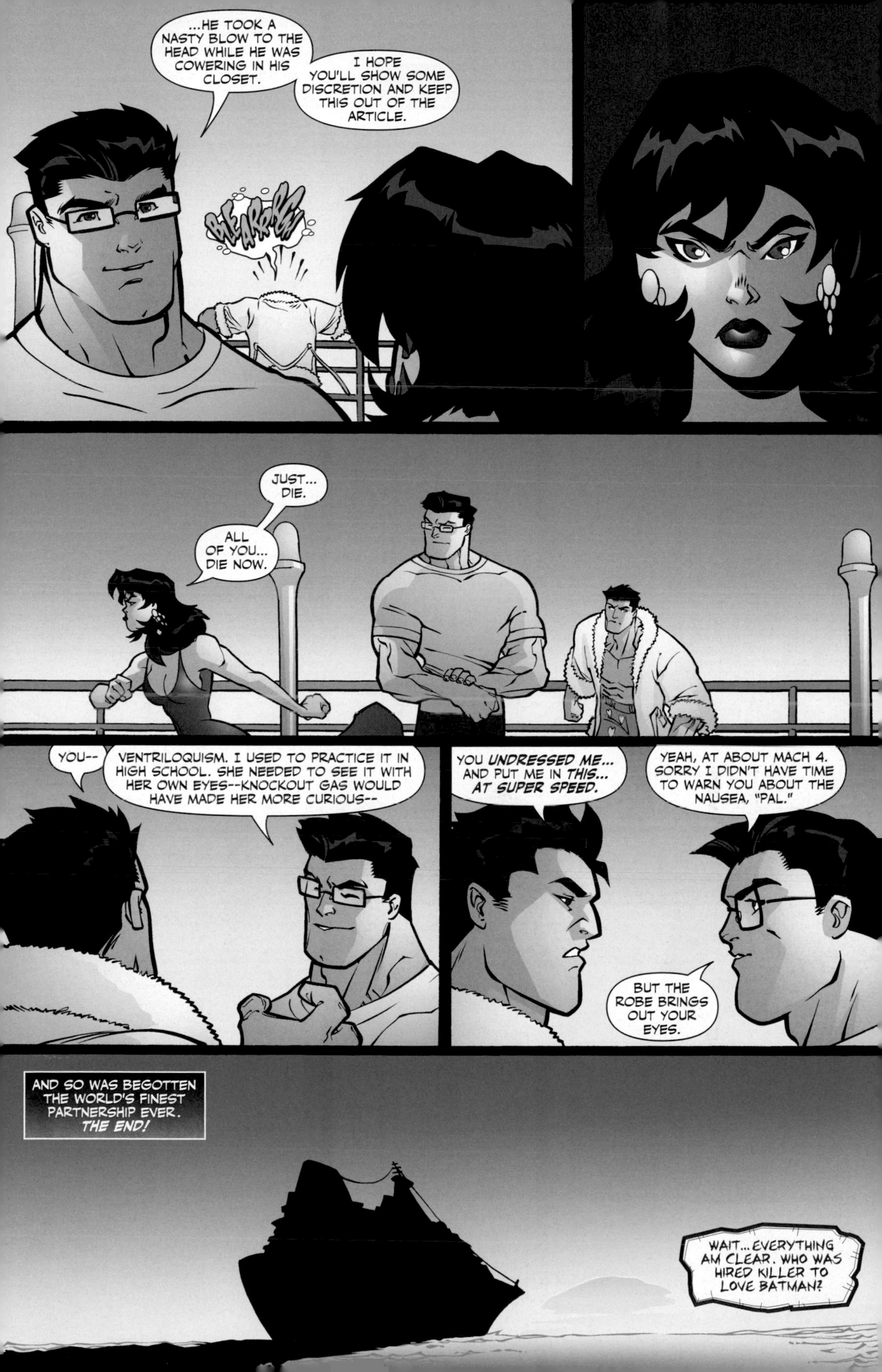

...HE TOOK A NASTY BLOW TO THE HEAD WHILE HE WAS COWERING IN HIS CLOSET.
I HOPE YOU'LL SHOW SOME DISCRETION AND KEEP THIS OUT OF THE ARTICLE.
BLEARRGH
JUST... DIE.
ALL OF YOU... DIE NOW.
YOU--
VENTRILOQUISM. I USED TO PRACTICE IT IN HIGH SCHOOL. SHE NEEDED TO SEE IT WITH HER OWN EYES--KNOCKOUT GAS WOULD HAVE MADE HER MORE CURIOUS--
YOU UNDRESSED ME... AND PUT ME IN THIS... AT SUPER SPEED.
YEAH, AT ABOUT MACH 4. SORRY I DIDN'T HAVE TIME TO WARN YOU ABOUT THE NAUSEA, "PAL."
BUT THE ROBE BRINGS OUT YOUR EYES.
AND SO WAS BEGOTTEN THE WORLD'S FINEST PARTNERSHIP EVER. THE END!
WAIT... EVERYTHING AM CLEAR. WHO WAS HIRED KILLER TO LOVE BATMAN?

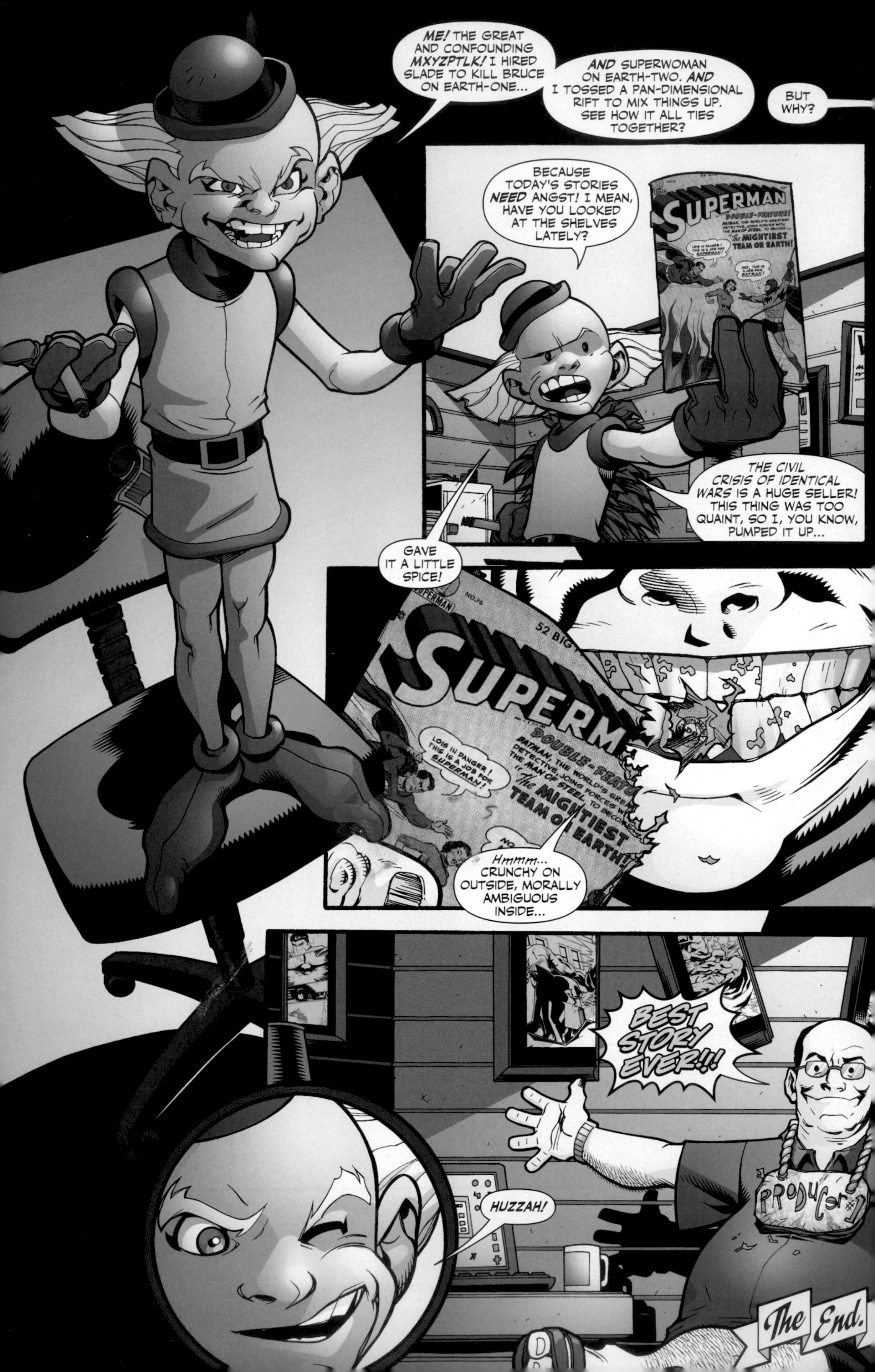
ME! THE GREAT AND CONFOUNDING MXYZPTLK! I HIRED SLADE TO KILL BRUCE ON EARTH-ONE...
AND SUPERWOMAN ON EARTH-TWO. AND I TOSSED A PAN-DIMENSIONAL RIFT TO MIX THINGS UP. SEE HOW IT ALL TIES TOGETHER?
BUT WHY?
BECAUSE TODAY'S STORIES NEED ANGST! I MEAN, HAVE YOU LOOKED AT THE SHELVES LATELY?
SUPERMAN
DOUBLE-FEATURE!
THE MIGHTIEST TEAM ON EARTH!
THE CIVIL CRISIS OF IDENTICAL WARS IS A HUGE SELLER! THIS THING WAS TOO QUAINT, SO I, YOU KNOW, PUMPED IT UP...
GAVE IT A LITTLE SPICE!
52 BIG
SUPERM
DOUBLE-FEATU
LOIS IN DANGER! THIS IS A JOB FOR SUPERMAN!
The MIGHTIEST TEAM ON EARTH!
Hmmm... CRUNCHY ON OUTSIDE, MORALLY AMBIGUOUS INSIDE...
BEST STORY EVER!!!
HUZZAH!
PRODUCER #1
The End.

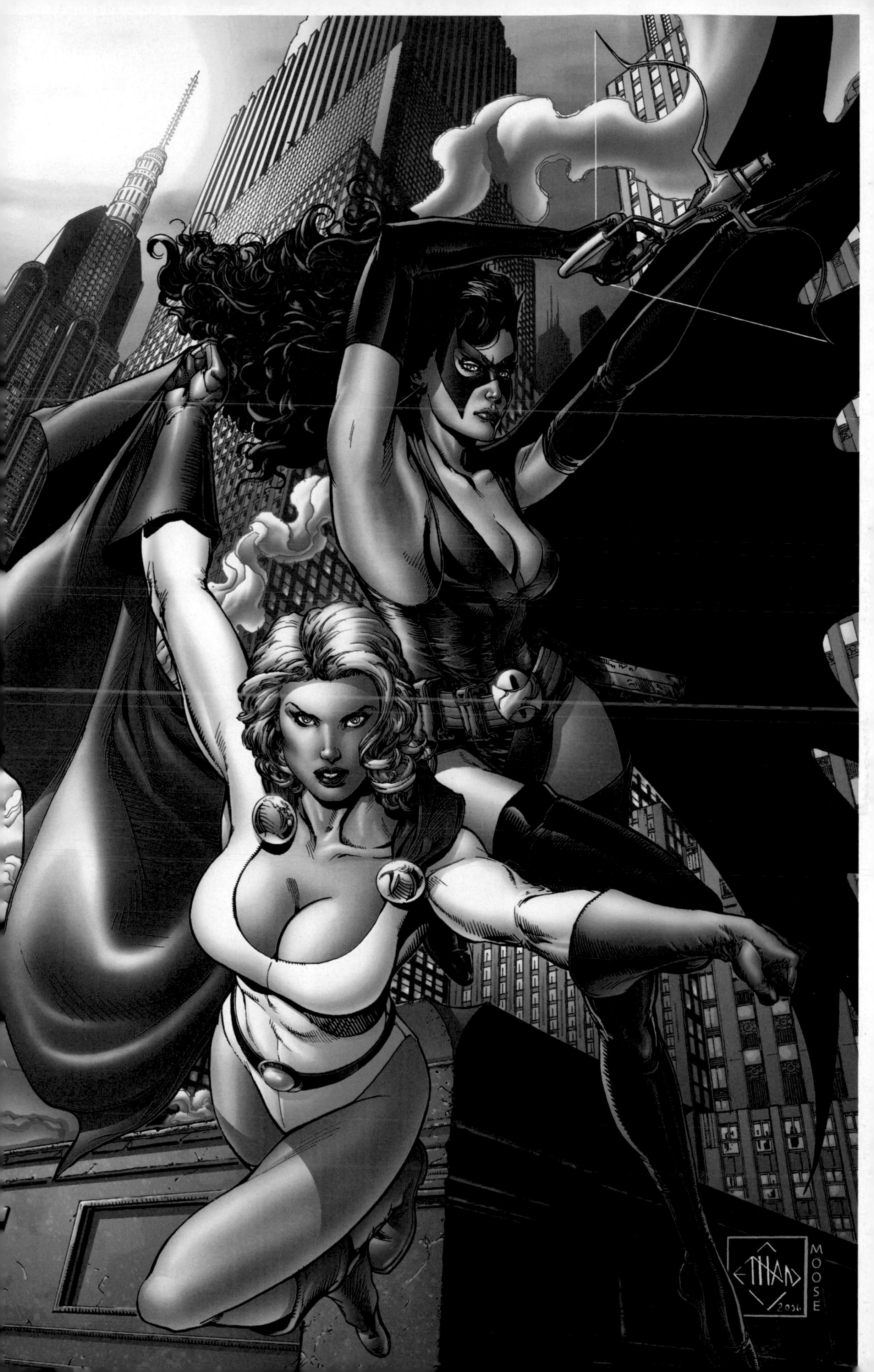
MOOSE

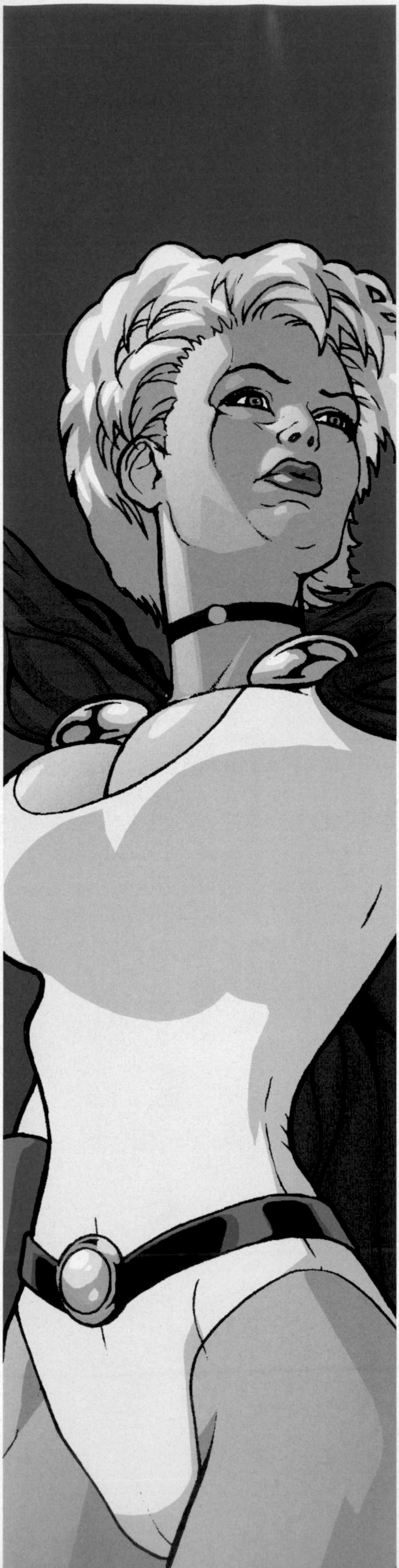

NEVERMIND

MARK VERHEIDEN
WRITER

KEVIN MAGUIRE
ARTIST

DAVE McCAIG
COLORIST

COMICRAFT
LETTERER

ETHAN VAN SCIVER
&
MOOSE BAUMANN
COVER

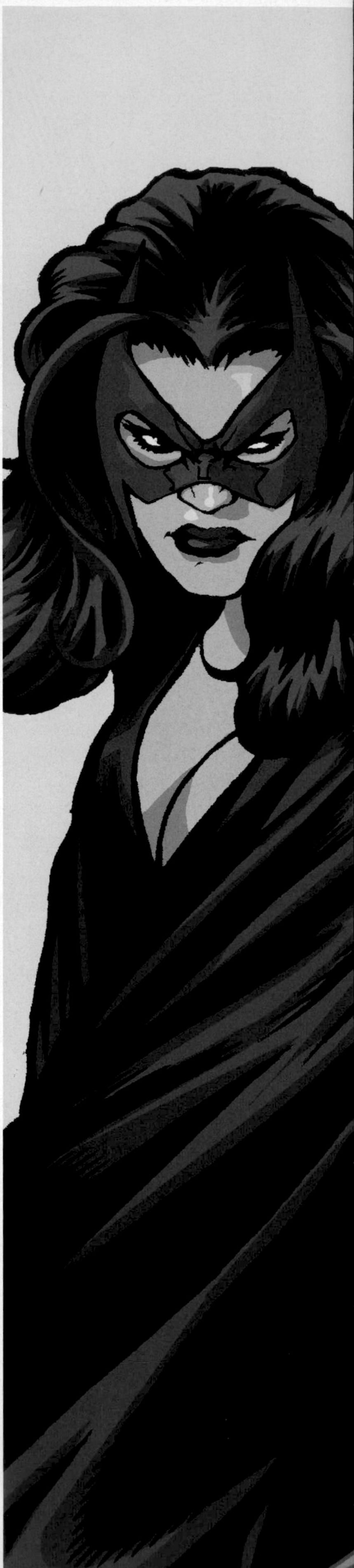

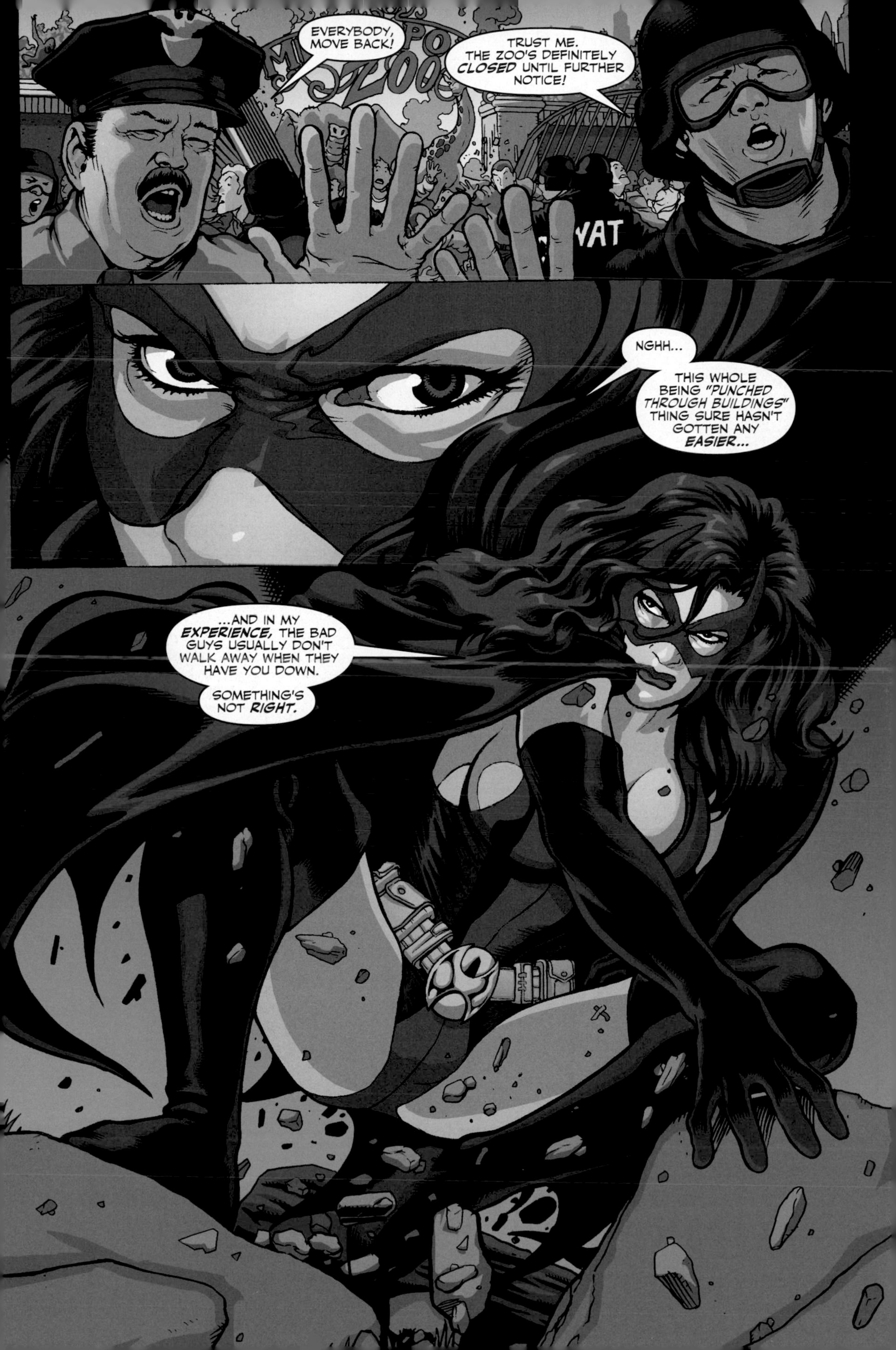
EVERYBODY, MOVE BACK!
TRUST ME. THE ZOO'S DEFINITELY CLOSED UNTIL FURTHER NOTICE!
SWAT
NGHH...
THIS WHOLE BEING "PUNCHED THROUGH BUILDINGS" THING SURE HASN'T GOTTEN ANY EASIER...
...AND IN MY EXPERIENCE, THE BAD GUYS USUALLY DON'T WALK AWAY WHEN THEY HAVE YOU DOWN.
SOMETHING'S NOT RIGHT.

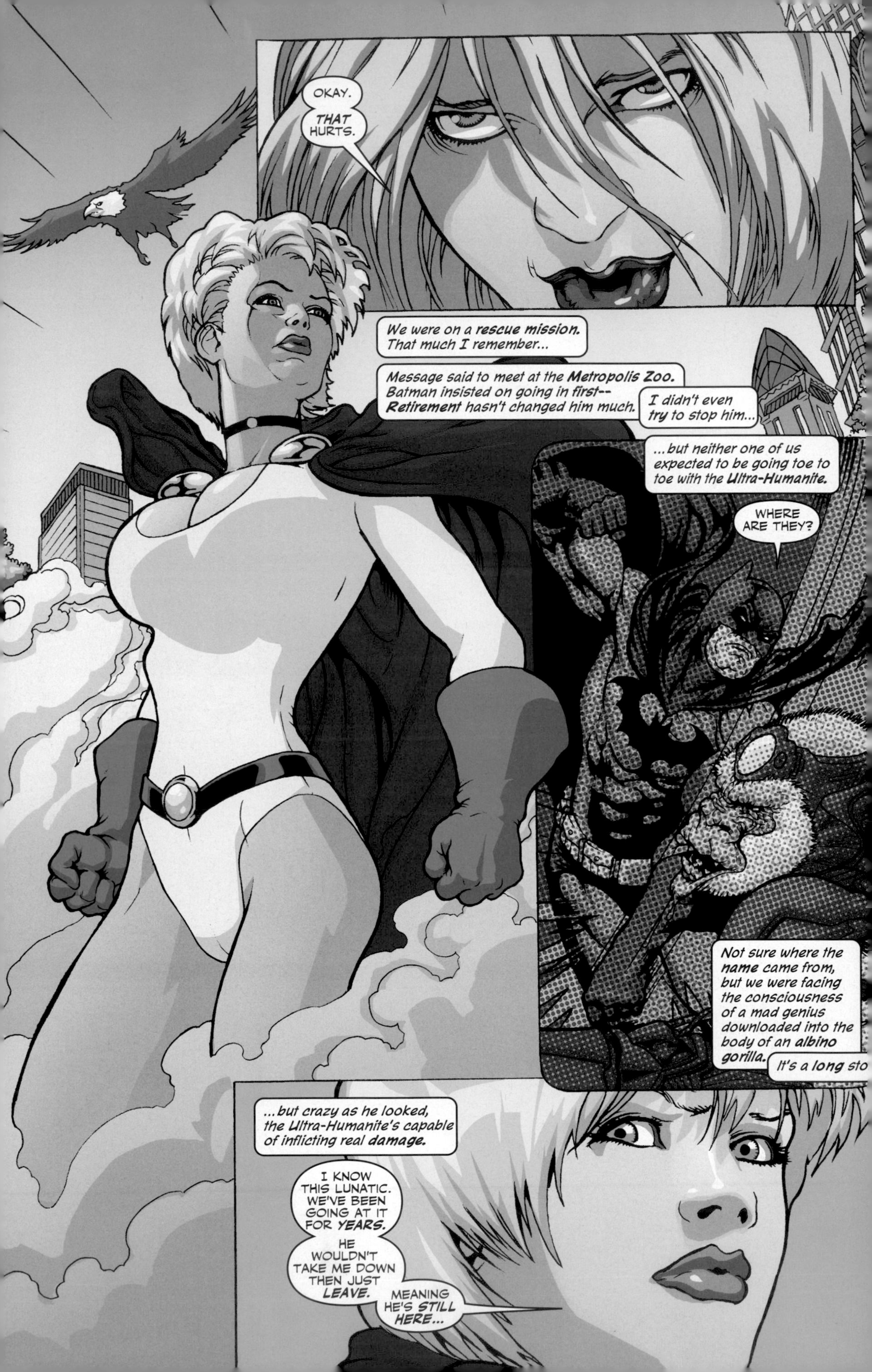
OKAY.
THAT HURTS.
We were on a rescue mission. That much I remember...
Message said to meet at the Metropolis Zoo. Batman insisted on going in first-- Retirement hasn't changed him much.
I didn't even try to stop him...
...but neither one of us expected to be going toe to toe with the Ultra-Humanite.
WHERE ARE THEY?
Not sure where the name came from, but we were facing the consciousness of a mad genius downloaded into the body of an albino gorilla.
It's a long sto
...but crazy as he looked, the Ultra-Humanite's capable of inflicting real damage.
I KNOW THIS LUNATIC. WE'VE BEEN GOING AT IT FOR YEARS.
HE WOULDN'T TAKE ME DOWN THEN JUST LEAVE.
MEANING HE'S STILL HERE...

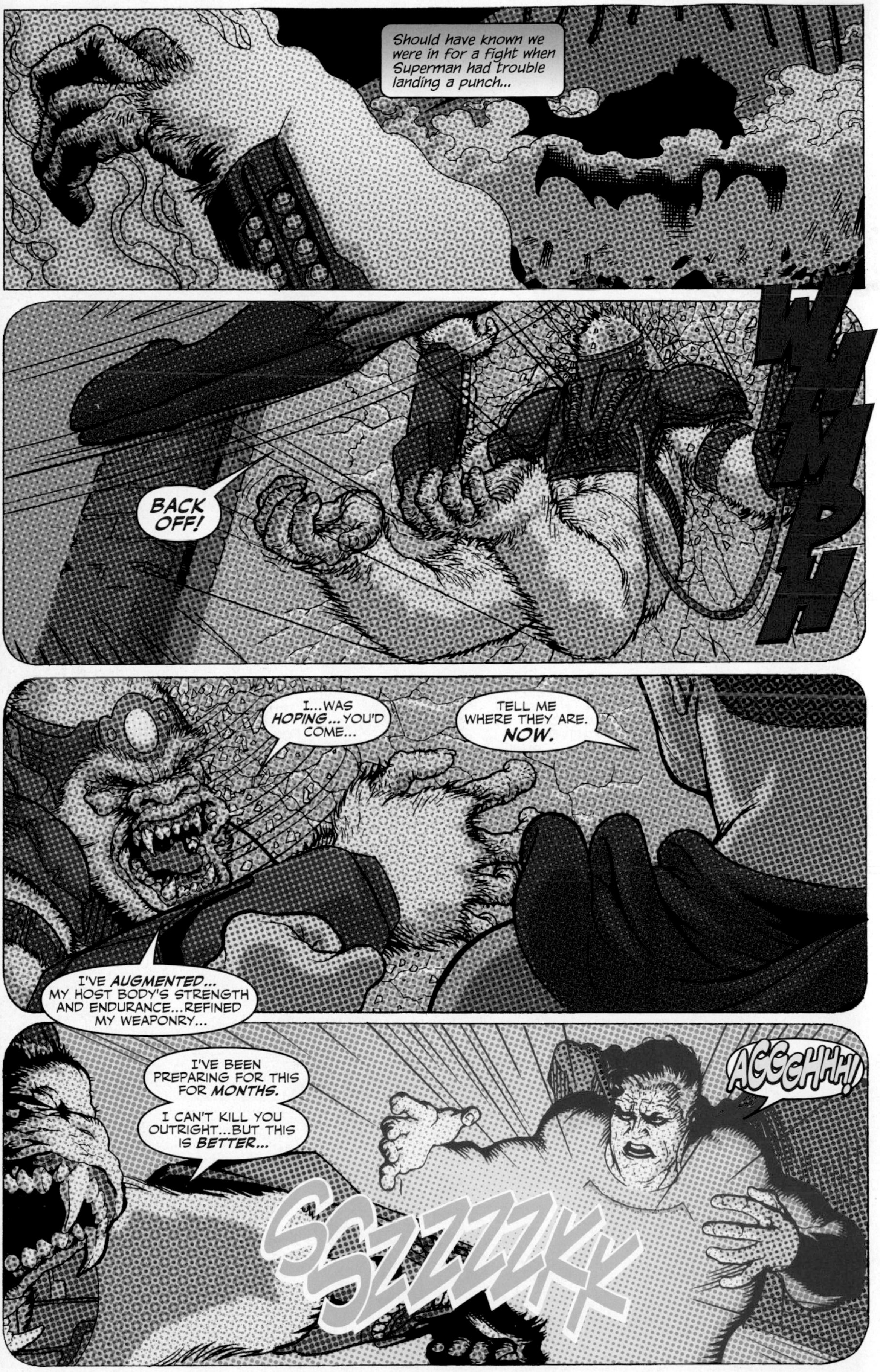
Should have known we were in for a fight when Superman had trouble landing a punch...
BACK OFF!
WMPH
I...WAS HOPING...YOU'D COME...
TELL ME WHERE THEY ARE. NOW.
I'VE AUGMENTED... MY HOST BODY'S STRENGTH AND ENDURANCE...REFINED MY WEAPONRY...
I'VE BEEN PREPARING FOR THIS FOR MONTHS.
I CAN'T KILL YOU OUTRIGHT...BUT THIS IS BETTER...
AGGGHHH!
SSZZZZK

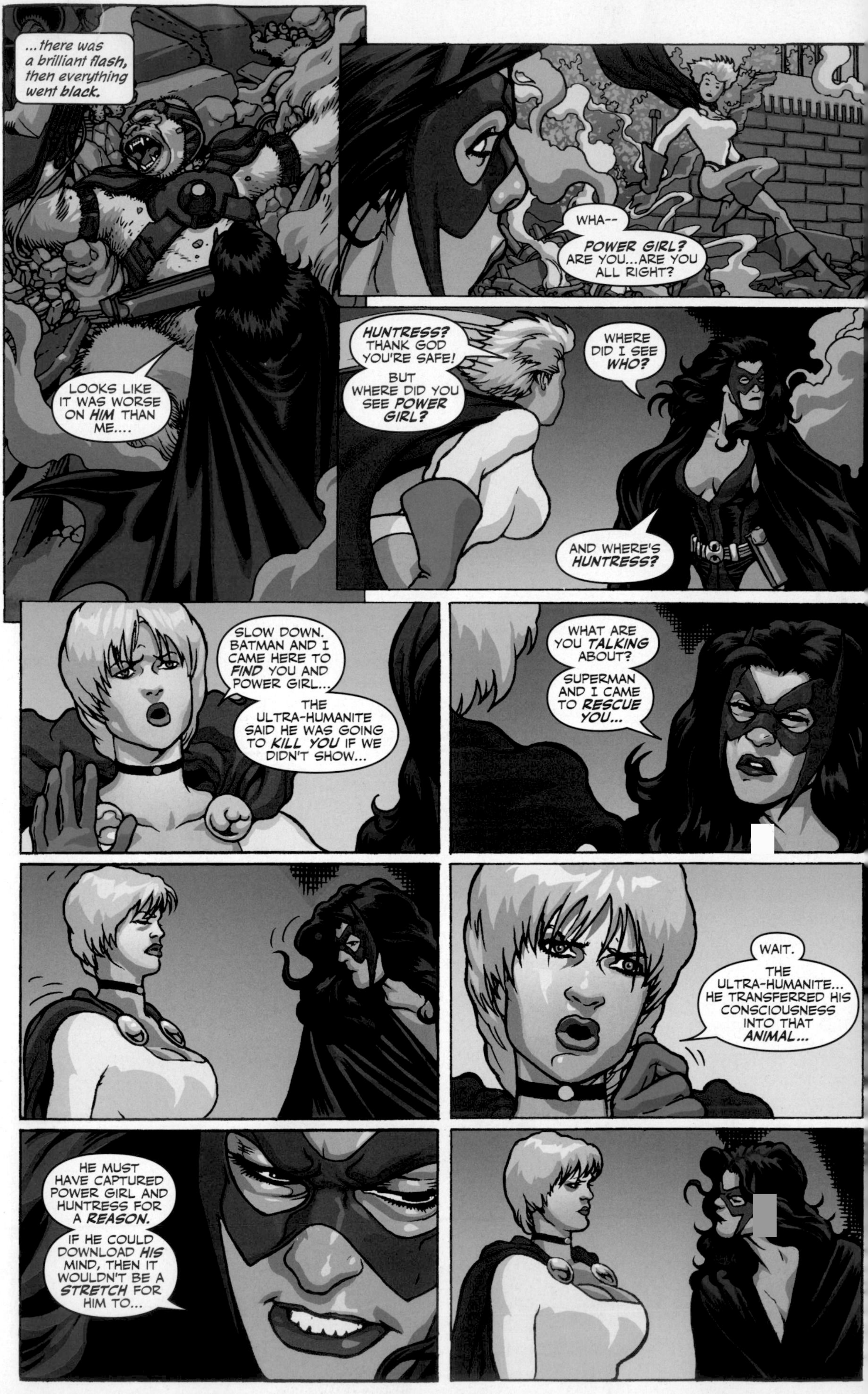
...there was a brilliant flash, then everything went black.
LOOKS LIKE IT WAS WORSE ON HIM THAN ME....
WHA--
POWER GIRL? ARE YOU...ARE YOU ALL RIGHT?
HUNTRESS? THANK GOD YOU'RE SAFE!
BUT WHERE DID YOU SEE POWER GIRL?
WHERE DID I SEE WHO?
AND WHERE'S HUNTRESS?
SLOW DOWN. BATMAN AND I CAME HERE TO FIND YOU AND POWER GIRL...
THE ULTRA-HUMANITE SAID HE WAS GOING TO KILL YOU IF WE DIDN'T SHOW...
WHAT ARE YOU TALKING ABOUT?
SUPERMAN AND I CAME TO RESCUE YOU...
WAIT.
THE ULTRA-HUMANITE... HE TRANSFERRED HIS CONSCIOUSNESS INTO THAT ANIMAL...
HE MUST HAVE CAPTURED POWER GIRL AND HUNTRESS FOR A REASON.
IF HE COULD DOWNLOAD HIS MIND, THEN IT WOULDN'T BE A STRETCH FOR HIM TO...

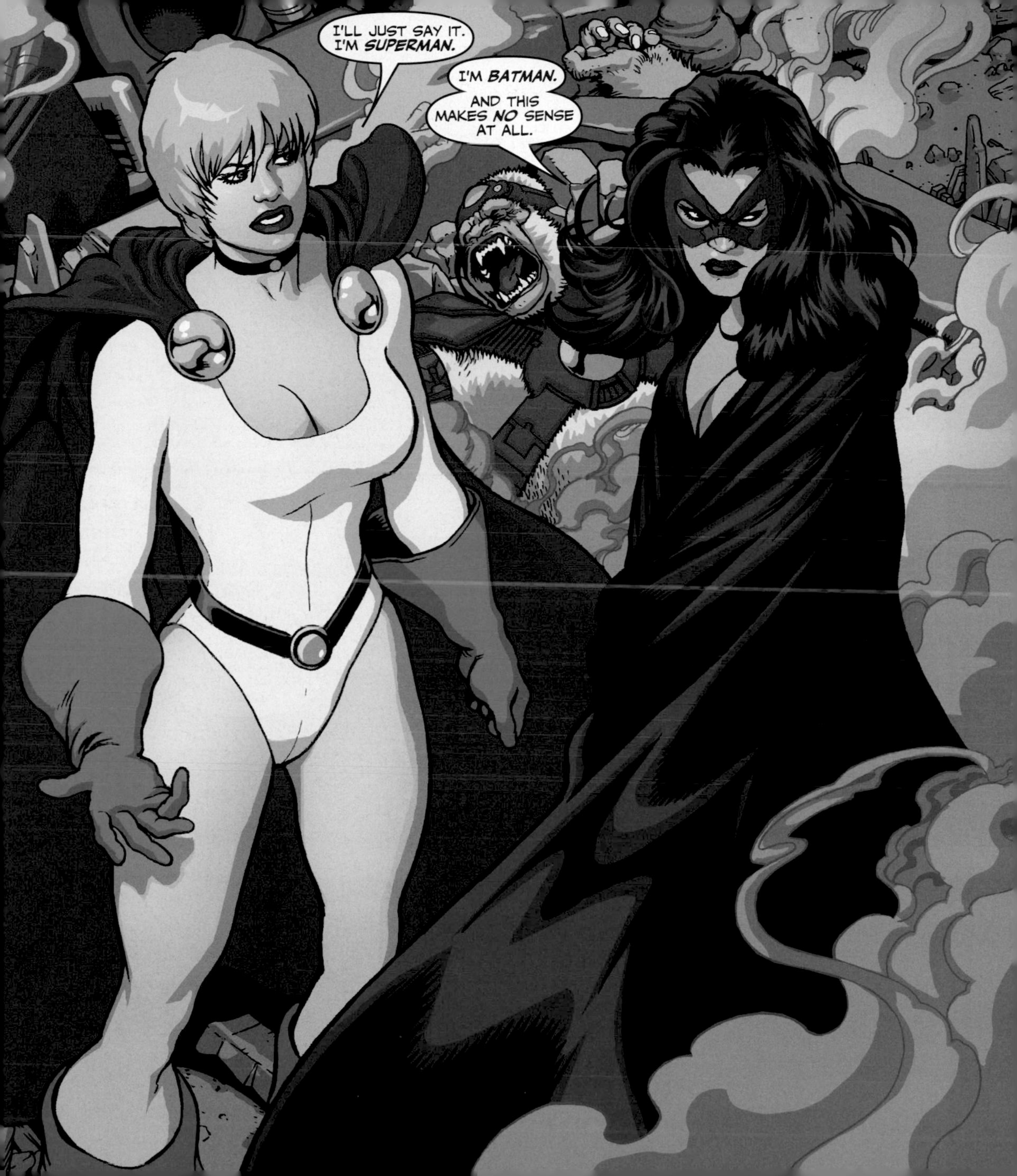
I'LL JUST SAY IT. I'M SUPERMAN.
I'M BATMAN.
AND THIS MAKES NO SENSE AT ALL.

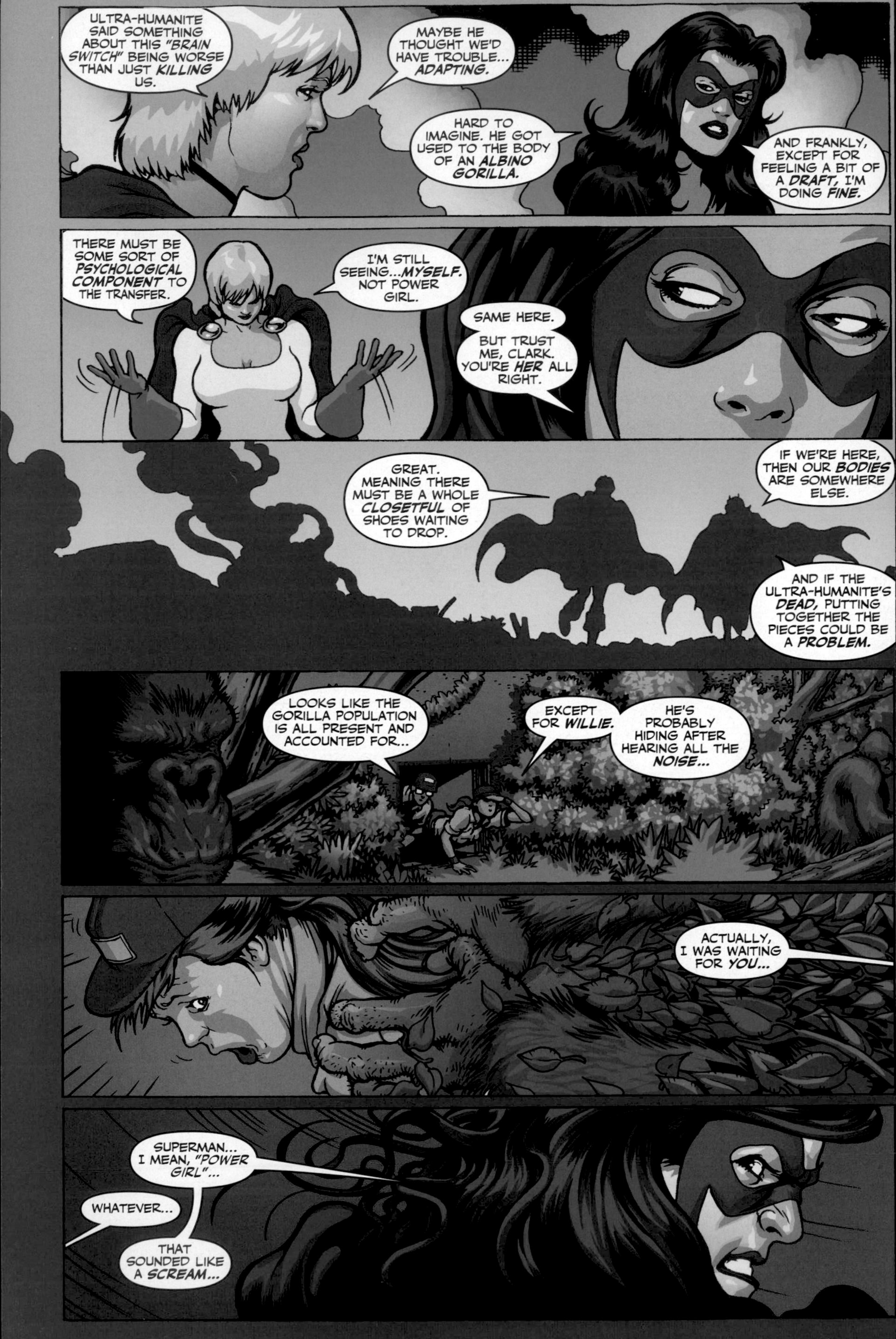

ULTRA-HUMANITE SAID SOMETHING ABOUT THIS "BRAIN SWITCH" BEING WORSE THAN JUST KILLING US.
MAYBE HE THOUGHT WE'D HAVE TROUBLE... ADAPTING.
HARD TO IMAGINE. HE GOT USED TO THE BODY OF AN ALBINO GORILLA.
AND FRANKLY, EXCEPT FOR FEELING A BIT OF A DRAFT, I'M DOING FINE.
THERE MUST BE SOME SORT OF PSYCHOLOGICAL COMPONENT TO THE TRANSFER.
I'M STILL SEEING...MYSELF. NOT POWER GIRL.
SAME HERE.
BUT TRUST ME, CLARK. YOU'RE HER ALL RIGHT.
GREAT. MEANING THERE MUST BE A WHOLE CLOSETFUL OF SHOES WAITING TO DROP.
IF WE'RE HERE, THEN OUR BODIES ARE SOMEWHERE ELSE.
AND IF THE ULTRA-HUMANITE'S DEAD, PUTTING TOGETHER THE PIECES COULD BE A PROBLEM.
LOOKS LIKE THE GORILLA POPULATION IS ALL PRESENT AND ACCOUNTED FOR...
EXCEPT FOR WILLIE.
HE'S PROBABLY HIDING AFTER HEARING ALL THE NOISE...
ACTUALLY, I WAS WAITING FOR YOU...
SUPERMAN... I MEAN, "POWER GIRL"...
WHATEVER...
THAT SOUNDED LIKE A SCREAM...

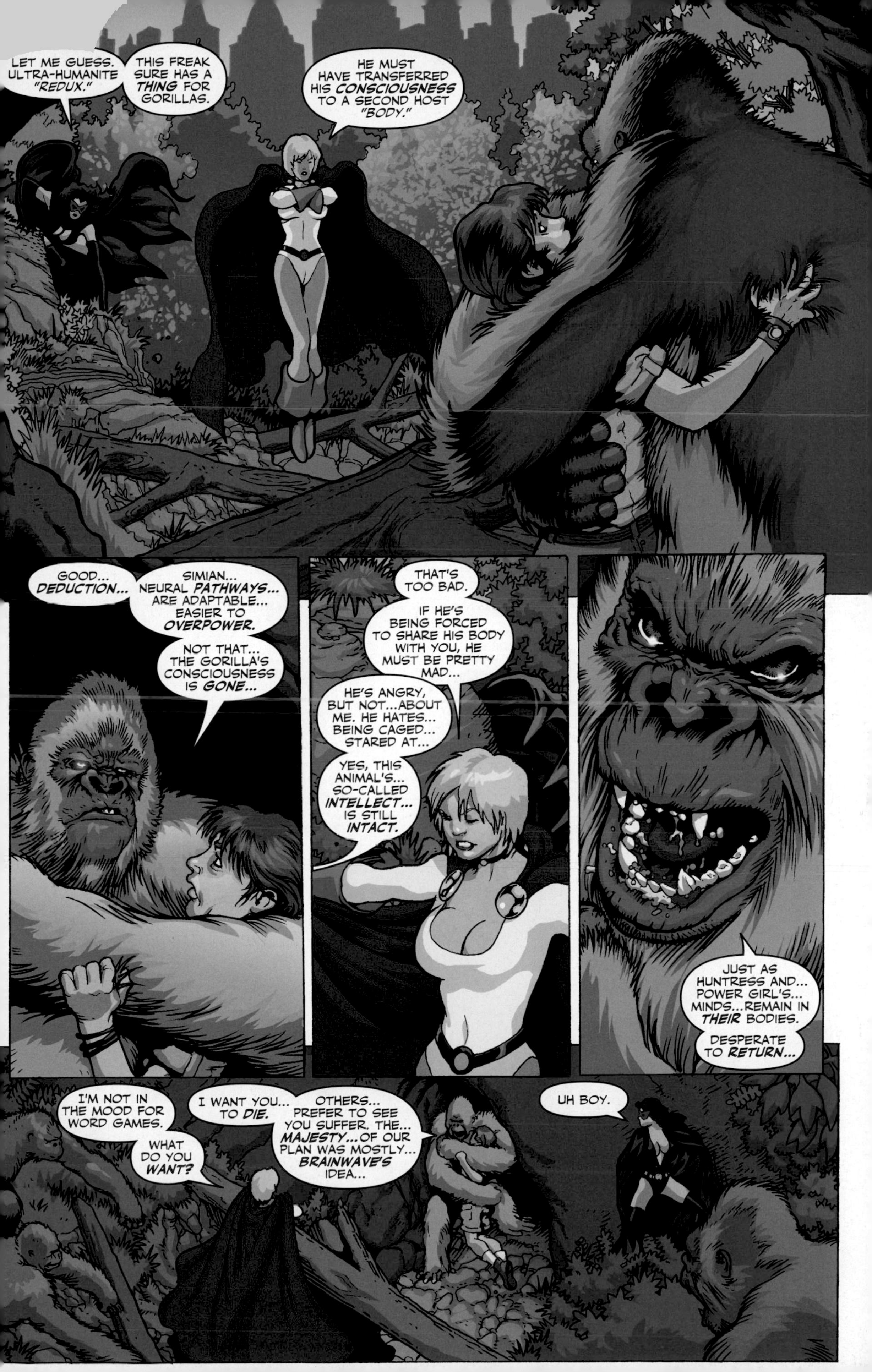
LET ME GUESS. ULTRA-HUMANITE "REDUX."
THIS FREAK SURE HAS A THING FOR GORILLAS.
HE MUST HAVE TRANSFERRED HIS CONSCIOUSNESS TO A SECOND HOST "BODY."
GOOD... DEDUCTION...
SIMIAN... NEURAL PATHWAYS... ARE ADAPTABLE... EASIER TO OVERPOWER.
NOT THAT... THE GORILLA'S CONSCIOUSNESS IS GONE...
THAT'S TOO BAD.
IF HE'S BEING FORCED TO SHARE HIS BODY WITH YOU, HE MUST BE PRETTY MAD...
HE'S ANGRY, BUT NOT...ABOUT ME. HE HATES... BEING CAGED... STARED AT...
YES, THIS ANIMAL'S... SO-CALLED INTELLECT... IS STILL INTACT.
JUST AS HUNTRESS AND... POWER GIRL'S... MINDS...REMAIN IN THEIR BODIES.
DESPERATE TO RETURN...
I'M NOT IN THE MOOD FOR WORD GAMES.
WHAT DO YOU WANT?
I WANT YOU... TO DIE.
OTHERS... PREFER TO SEE YOU SUFFER. THE... MAJESTY...OF OUR PLAN WAS MOSTLY... BRAINWAVE'S IDEA...
UH BOY.

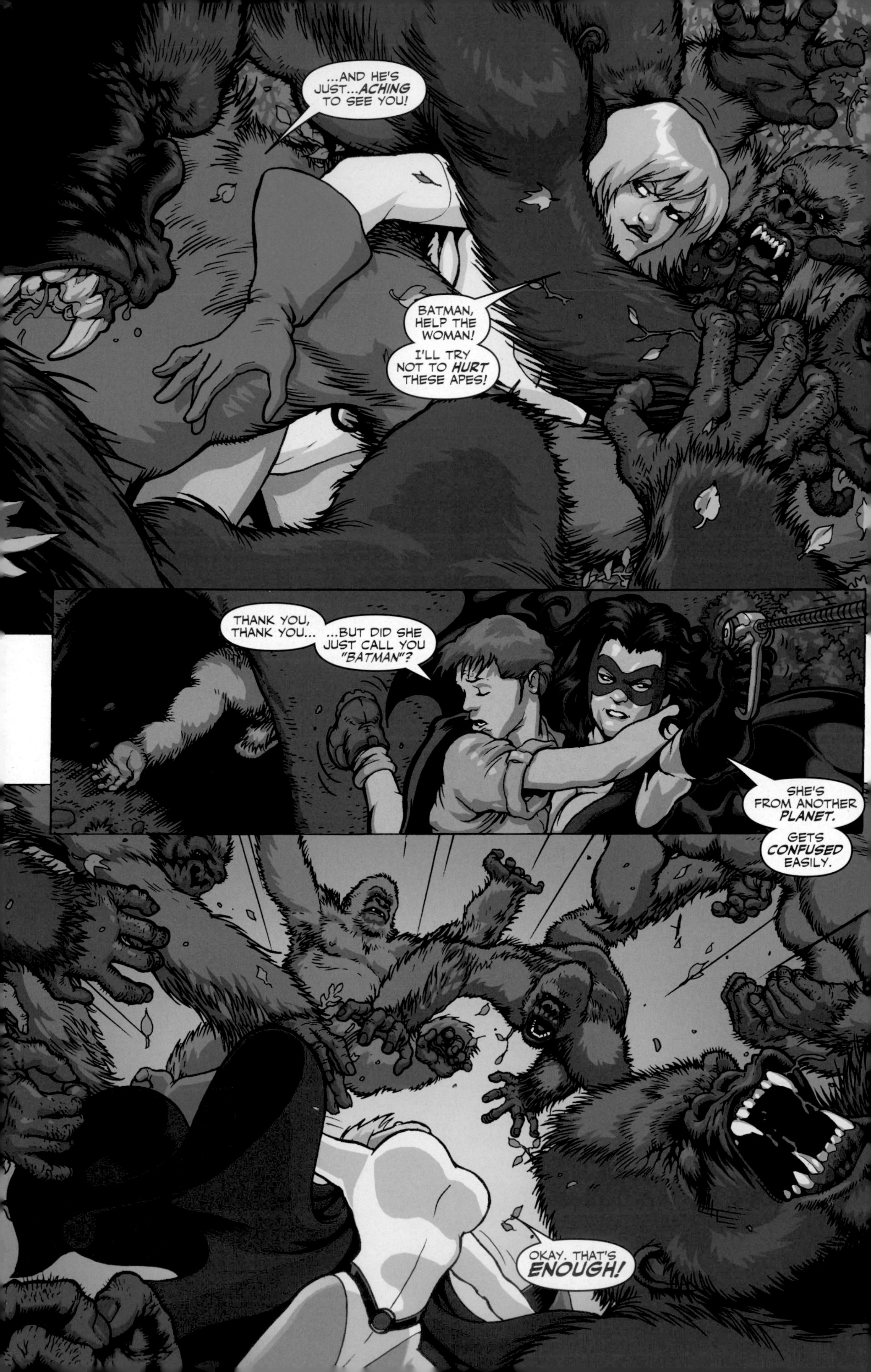
...AND HE'S JUST...ACHING TO SEE YOU!
BATMAN, HELP THE WOMAN!
I'LL TRY NOT TO HURT THESE APES!
THANK YOU, THANK YOU...
...BUT DID SHE JUST CALL YOU "BATMAN"?
SHE'S FROM ANOTHER PLANET.
GETS CONFUSED EASILY.
OKAY. THAT'S ENOUGH!

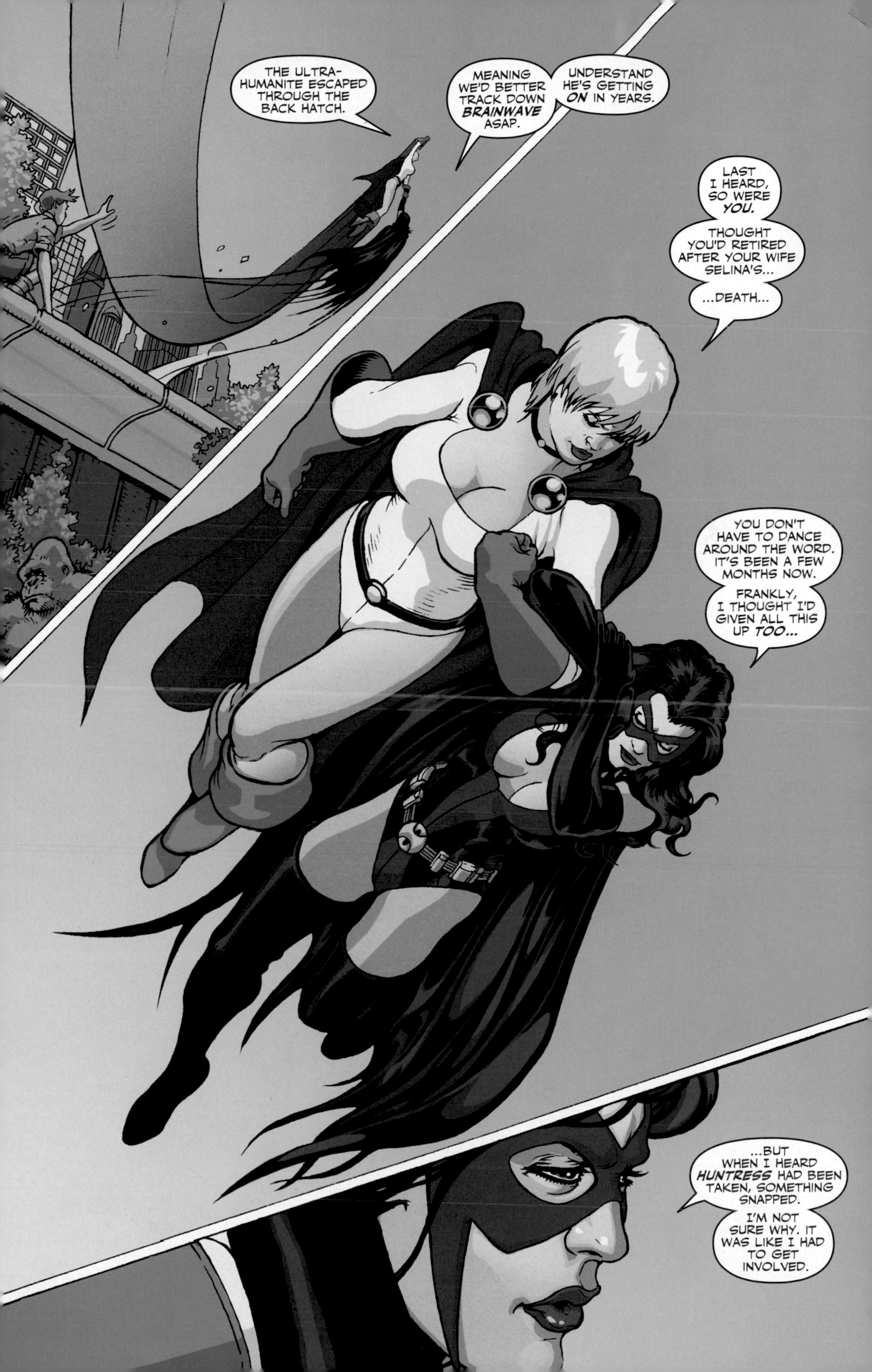
THE ULTRA-HUMANITE ESCAPED THROUGH THE BACK HATCH.
MEANING WE'D BETTER TRACK DOWN BRAINWAVE ASAP.
UNDERSTAND HE'S GETTING ON IN YEARS.
LAST I HEARD, SO WERE YOU.
THOUGHT YOU'D RETIRED AFTER YOUR WIFE SELINA'S...
...DEATH...
YOU DON'T HAVE TO DANCE AROUND THE WORD. IT'S BEEN A FEW MONTHS NOW.
FRANKLY, I THOUGHT I'D GIVEN ALL THIS UP TOO...
...BUT WHEN I HEARD HUNTRESS HAD BEEN TAKEN, SOMETHING SNAPPED.
I'M NOT SURE WHY. IT WAS LIKE I HAD TO GET INVOLVED.

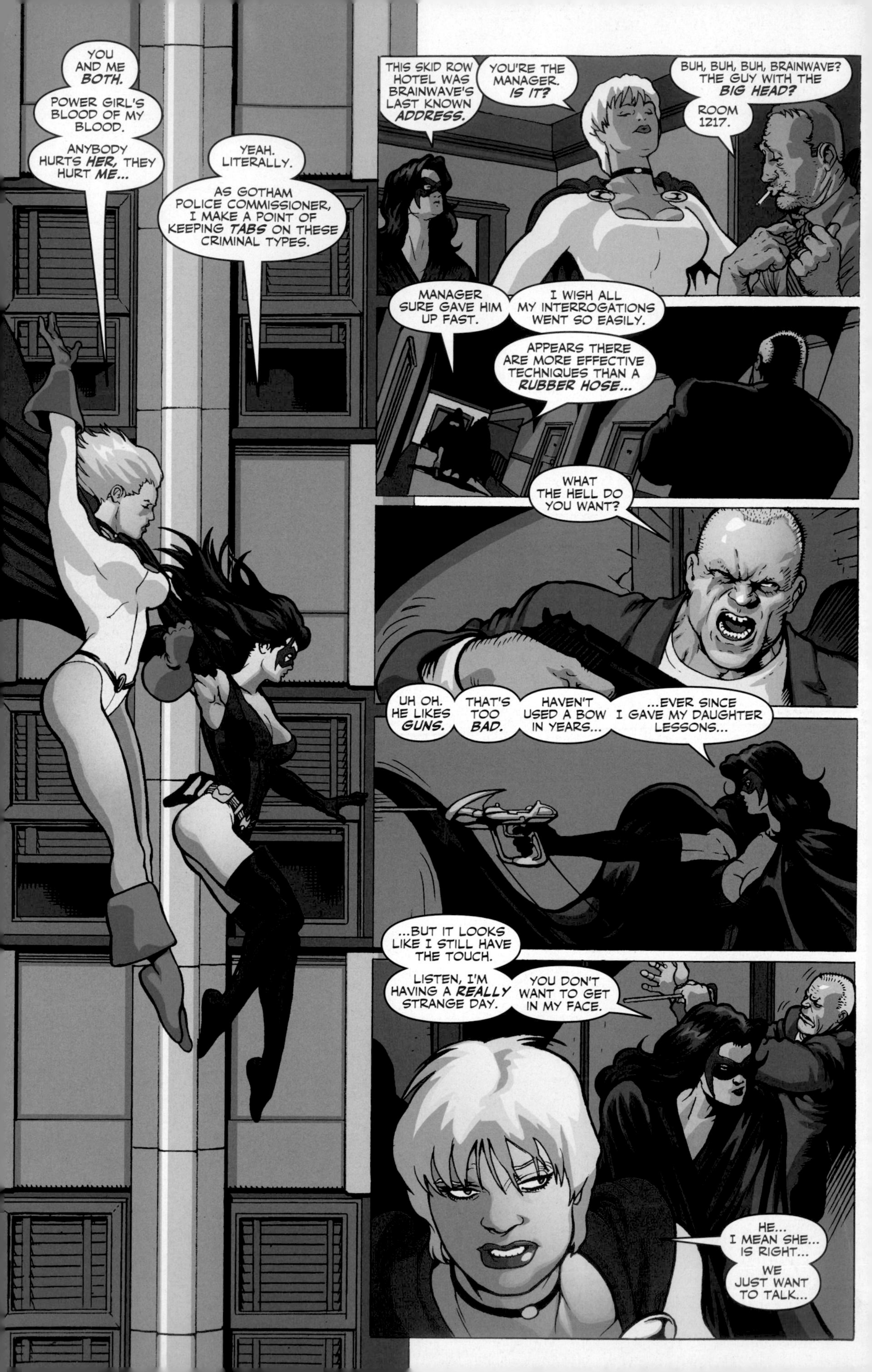
YOU AND ME BOTH.
POWER GIRL'S BLOOD OF MY BLOOD.
ANYBODY HURTS HER, THEY HURT ME...
YEAH. LITERALLY.
AS GOTHAM POLICE COMMISSIONER, I MAKE A POINT OF KEEPING TABS ON THESE CRIMINAL TYPES.
THIS SKID ROW HOTEL WAS BRAINWAVE'S LAST KNOWN ADDRESS.
YOU'RE THE MANAGER. IS IT?
BUH, BUH, BUH, BRAINWAVE? THE GUY WITH THE BIG HEAD?
ROOM 1217.
MANAGER SURE GAVE HIM UP FAST.
I WISH ALL MY INTERROGATIONS WENT SO EASILY.
APPEARS THERE ARE MORE EFFECTIVE TECHNIQUES THAN A RUBBER HOSE...
WHAT THE HELL DO YOU WANT?
UH OH. HE LIKES GUNS.
THAT'S TOO BAD.
HAVEN'T USED A BOW IN YEARS...
...EVER SINCE I GAVE MY DAUGHTER LESSONS...
...BUT IT LOOKS LIKE I STILL HAVE THE TOUCH.
LISTEN, I'M HAVING A REALLY STRANGE DAY.
YOU DON'T WANT TO GET IN MY FACE.
HE... I MEAN SHE... IS RIGHT...
WE JUST WANT TO TALK...

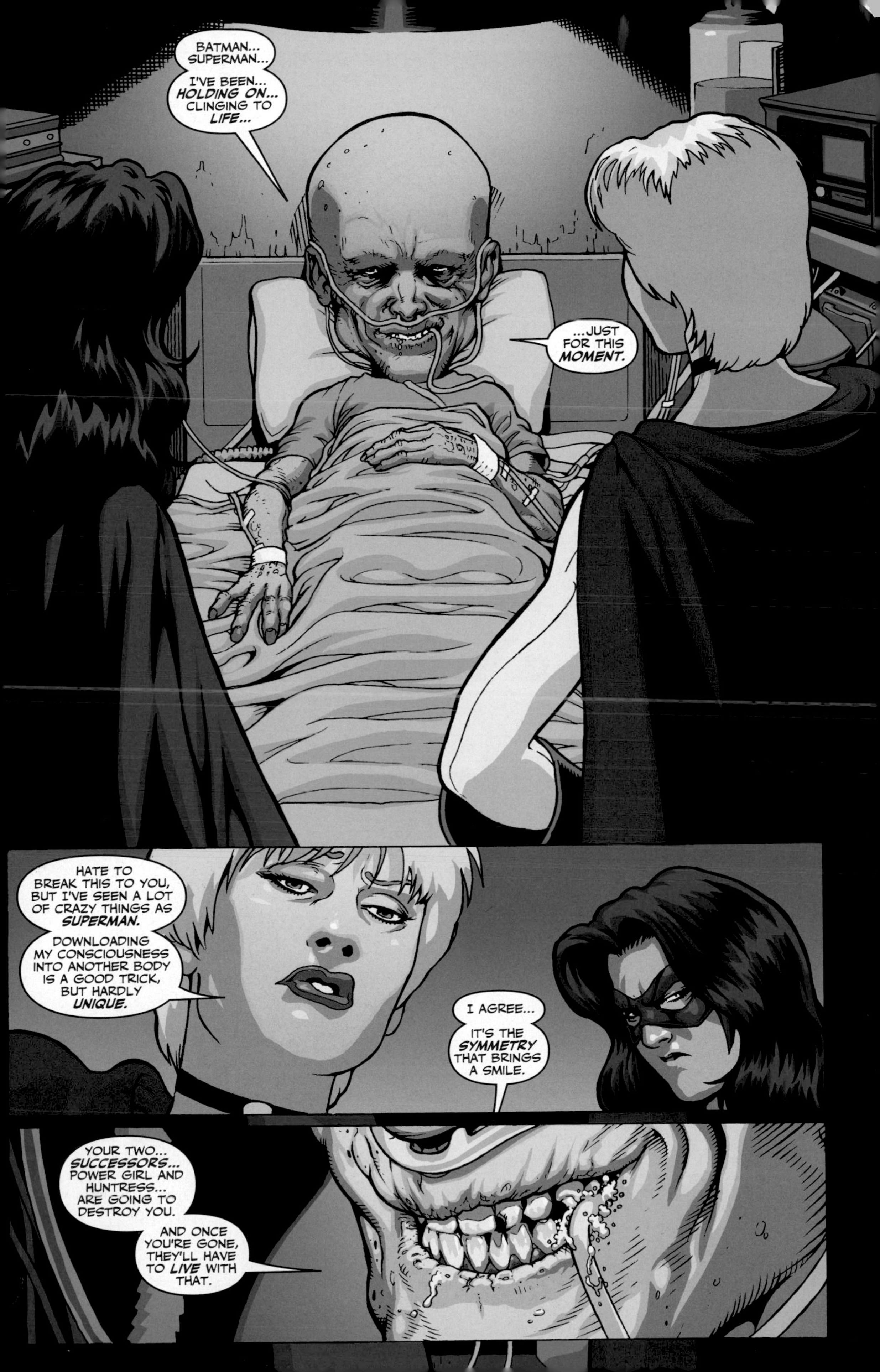

BATMAN... SUPERMAN...
I'VE BEEN... HOLDING ON... CLINGING TO LIFE...
...JUST FOR THIS MOMENT.
HATE TO BREAK THIS TO YOU, BUT I'VE SEEN A LOT OF CRAZY THINGS AS SUPERMAN.
DOWNLOADING MY CONSCIOUSNESS INTO ANOTHER BODY IS A GOOD TRICK, BUT HARDLY UNIQUE.
I AGREE...
IT'S THE SYMMETRY THAT BRINGS A SMILE.
YOUR TWO... SUCCESSORS... POWER GIRL AND HUNTRESS... ARE GOING TO DESTROY YOU.
AND ONCE YOU'RE GONE, THEY'LL HAVE TO LIVE WITH THAT.

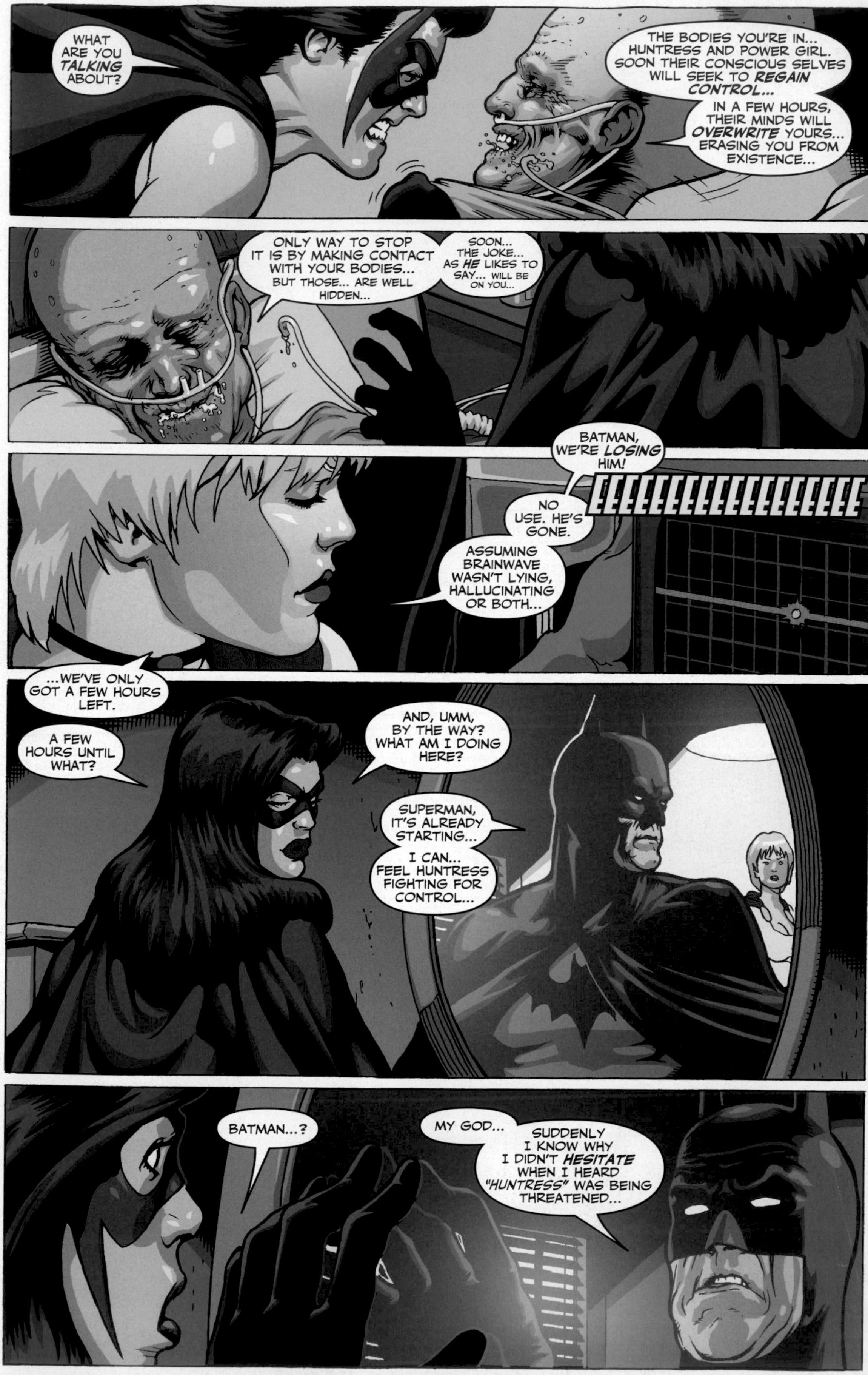

WHAT ARE YOU *TALKING* ABOUT?
THE BODIES YOU'RE IN... HUNTRESS AND POWER GIRL. SOON THEIR CONSCIOUS SELVES WILL SEEK TO *REGAIN CONTROL*...
IN A FEW HOURS, THEIR MINDS WILL *OVERWRITE* YOURS... ERASING YOU FROM EXISTENCE...
ONLY WAY TO STOP IT IS BY MAKING CONTACT WITH YOUR BODIES... BUT THOSE... ARE WELL HIDDEN...
SOON... THE JOKE... AS *HE* LIKES TO SAY... WILL BE ON YOU...
BATMAN, WE'RE *LOSING* HIM!
EEEEEEEEEEEEEEEEEE
NO USE. HE'S GONE.
ASSUMING BRAINWAVE WASN'T LYING, HALLUCINATING OR BOTH...
...WE'VE ONLY GOT A FEW HOURS LEFT.
A FEW HOURS UNTIL WHAT?
AND, UMM, BY THE WAY? WHAT AM I DOING HERE?
SUPERMAN, IT'S ALREADY STARTING...
I CAN... FEEL HUNTRESS FIGHTING FOR CONTROL...
BATMAN...?
MY GOD...
SUDDENLY I KNOW WHY I DIDN'T *HESITATE* WHEN I HEARD *"HUNTRESS"* WAS BEING THREATENED...

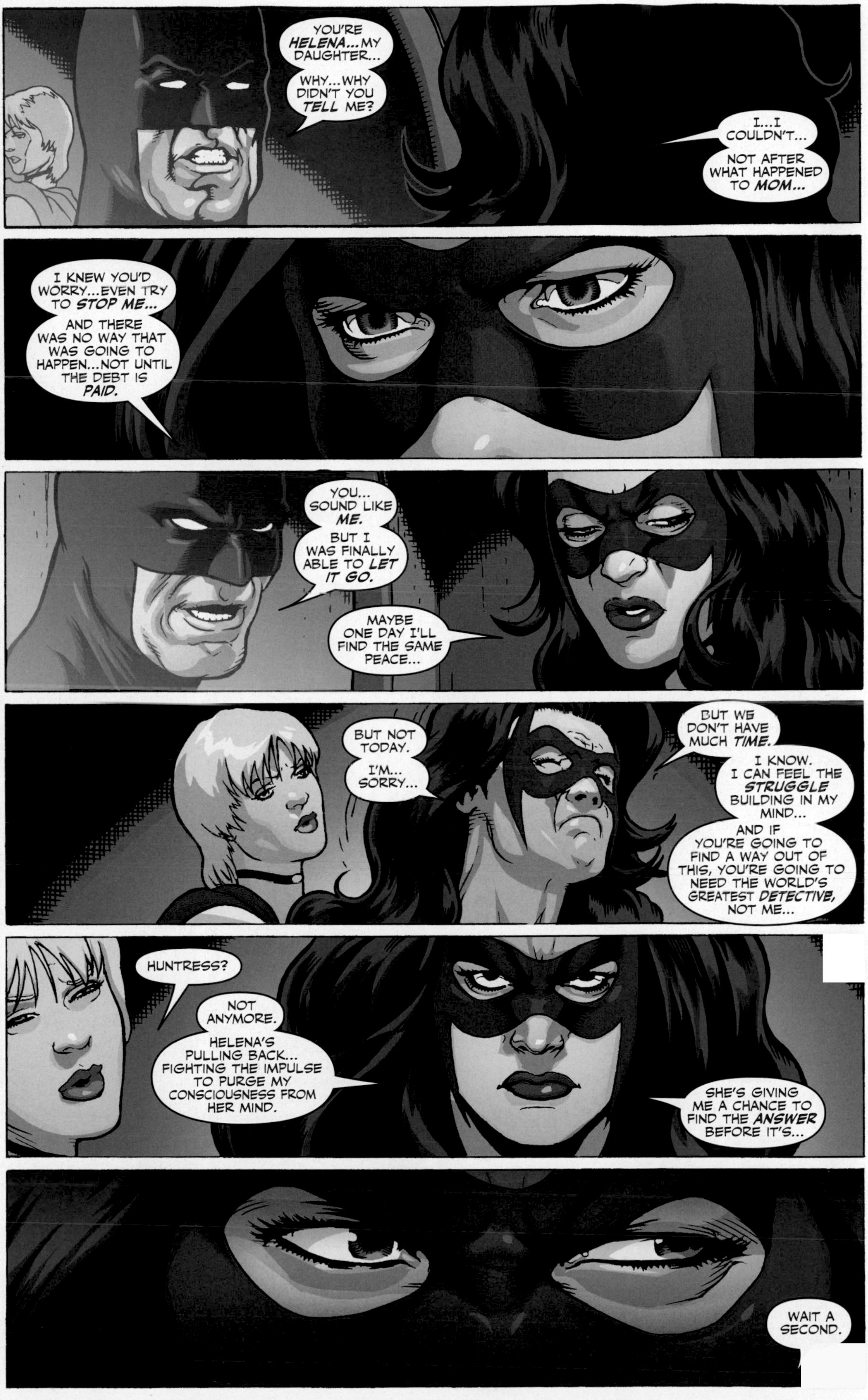

YOU'RE HELENA...MY DAUGHTER...
WHY...WHY DIDN'T YOU TELL ME?
I...I COULDN'T...
NOT AFTER WHAT HAPPENED TO MOM...
I KNEW YOU'D WORRY...EVEN TRY TO STOP ME...
AND THERE WAS NO WAY THAT WAS GOING TO HAPPEN...NOT UNTIL THE DEBT IS PAID.
YOU... SOUND LIKE ME.
BUT I WAS FINALLY ABLE TO LET IT GO.
MAYBE ONE DAY I'LL FIND THE SAME PEACE...
BUT NOT TODAY.
I'M... SORRY...
BUT WE DON'T HAVE MUCH TIME.
I KNOW. I CAN FEEL THE STRUGGLE BUILDING IN MY MIND...
AND IF YOU'RE GOING TO FIND A WAY OUT OF THIS, YOU'RE GOING TO NEED THE WORLD'S GREATEST DETECTIVE, NOT ME...
HUNTRESS?
NOT ANYMORE.
HELENA'S PULLING BACK... FIGHTING THE IMPULSE TO PURGE MY CONSCIOUSNESS FROM HER MIND.
SHE'S GIVING ME A CHANCE TO FIND THE ANSWER BEFORE IT'S...
WAIT A SECOND.

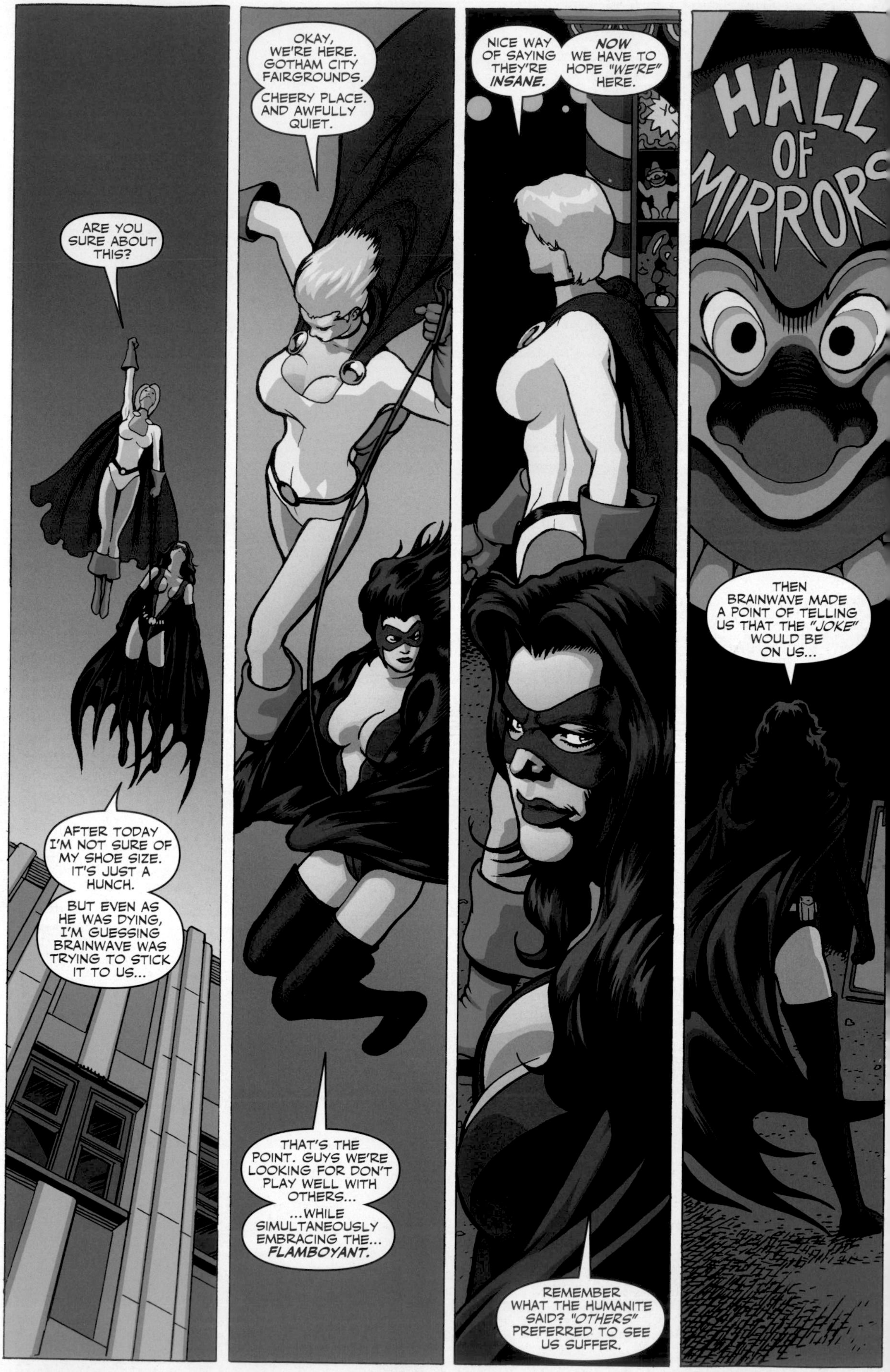
ARE YOU SURE ABOUT THIS?
AFTER TODAY I'M NOT SURE OF MY SHOE SIZE. IT'S JUST A HUNCH.
BUT EVEN AS HE WAS DYING, I'M GUESSING BRAINWAVE WAS TRYING TO STICK IT TO US...
OKAY, WE'RE HERE. GOTHAM CITY FAIRGROUNDS.
CHEERY PLACE. AND AWFULLY QUIET.
THAT'S THE POINT. GUYS WE'RE LOOKING FOR DON'T PLAY WELL WITH OTHERS...
...WHILE SIMULTANEOUSLY EMBRACING THE... *FLAMBOYANT.*
NICE WAY OF SAYING THEY'RE *INSANE.*
NOW WE HAVE TO HOPE *"WE'RE"* HERE.
REMEMBER WHAT THE HUMANITE SAID? *"OTHERS"* PREFERRED TO SEE US SUFFER.
HALL OF MIRRORS
THEN BRAINWAVE MADE A POINT OF TELLING US THAT THE *"JOKE"* WOULD BE ON US...

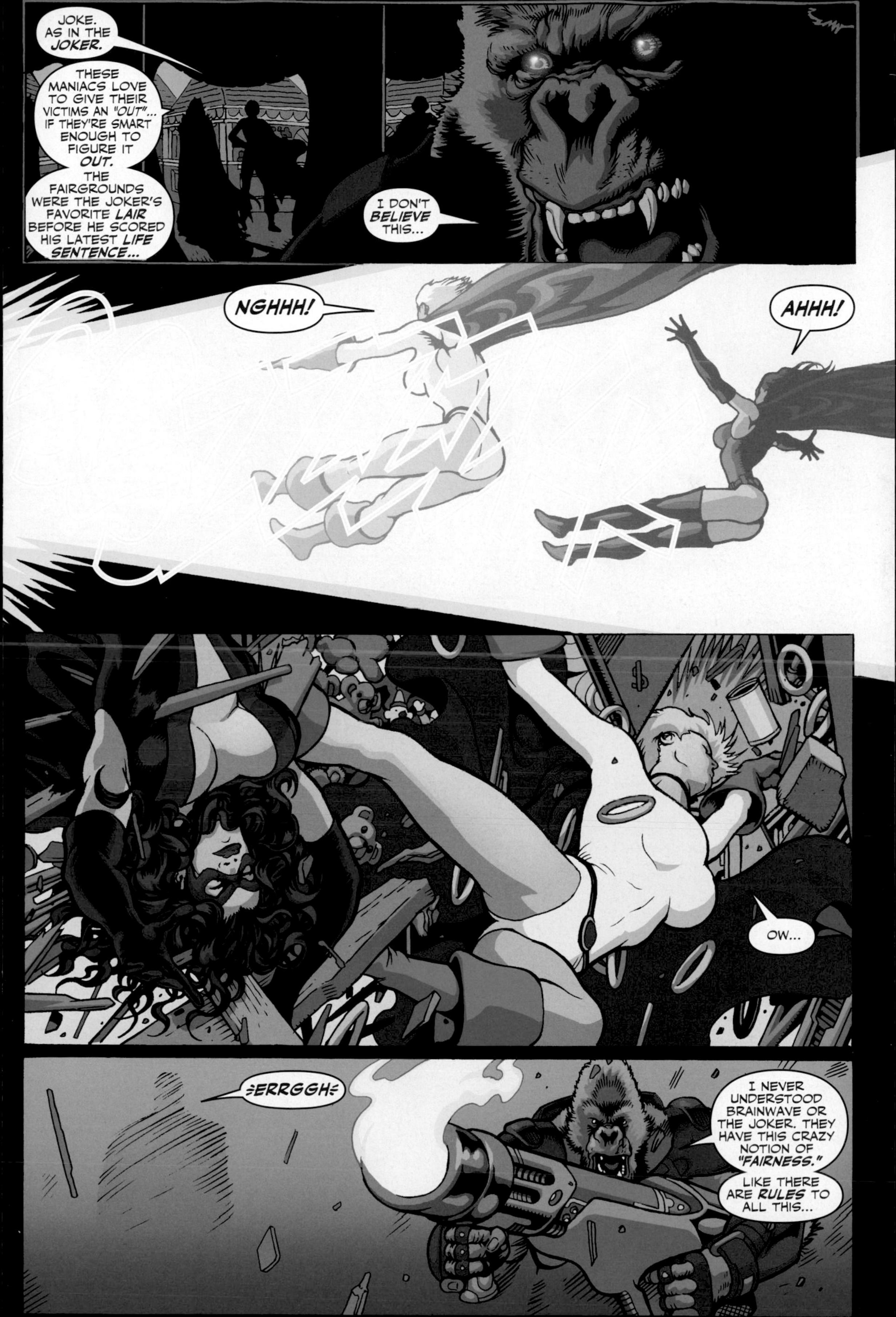
JOKE. AS IN THE JOKER.
THESE MANIACS LOVE TO GIVE THEIR VICTIMS AN "OUT"... IF THEY'RE SMART ENOUGH TO FIGURE IT OUT.
THE FAIRGROUNDS WERE THE JOKER'S FAVORITE LAIR BEFORE HE SCORED HIS LATEST LIFE SENTENCE...
I DON'T BELIEVE THIS...
NGHHH!
AHHH!
OW...
ERRGGH
I NEVER UNDERSTOOD BRAINWAVE OR THE JOKER. THEY HAVE THIS CRAZY NOTION OF "FAIRNESS."
LIKE THERE ARE RULES TO ALL THIS...

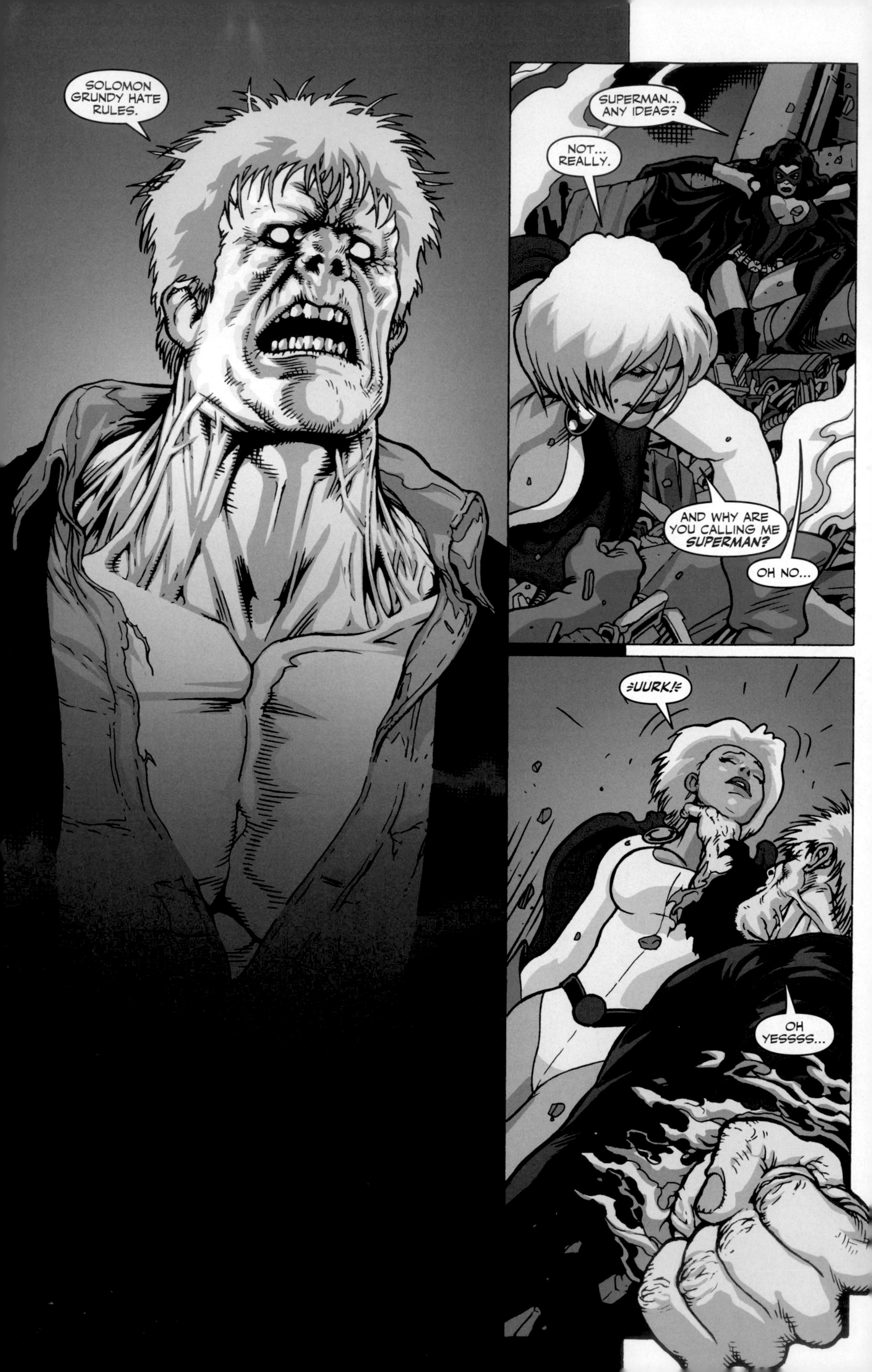
SOLOMON GRUNDY HATE RULES.
SUPERMAN... ANY IDEAS?
NOT... REALLY.
AND WHY ARE YOU CALLING ME SUPERMAN?
OH NO...
UURK!
OH YESSSS...

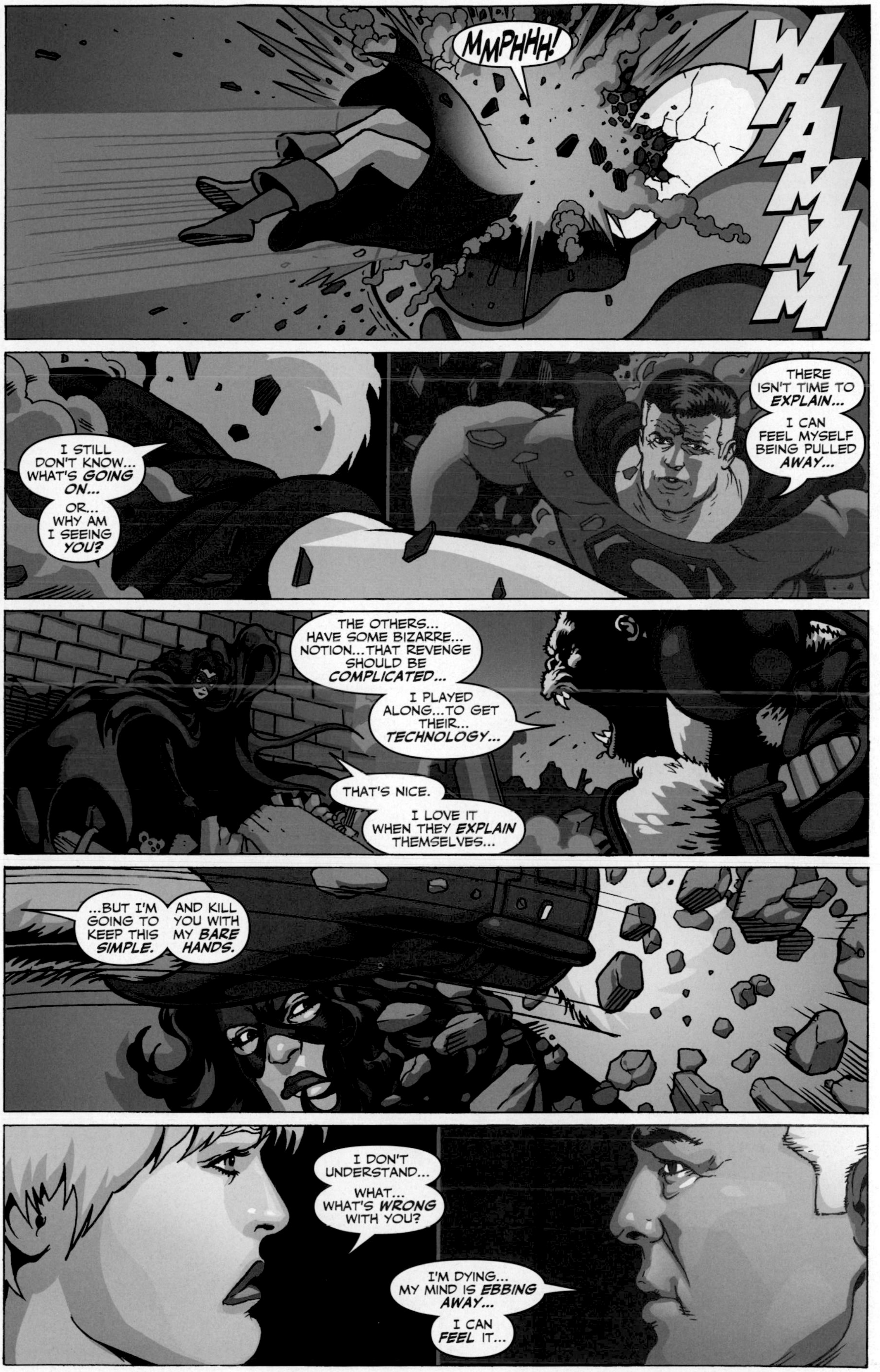
MMPHHH!
WHAMMM
I STILL DON'T KNOW... WHAT'S GOING ON...
OR... WHY AM I SEEING YOU?
THERE ISN'T TIME TO EXPLAIN...
I CAN FEEL MYSELF BEING PULLED AWAY...
THE OTHERS... HAVE SOME BIZARRE... NOTION...THAT REVENGE SHOULD BE COMPLICATED...
I PLAYED ALONG...TO GET THEIR... TECHNOLOGY...
THAT'S NICE.
I LOVE IT WHEN THEY EXPLAIN THEMSELVES...
...BUT I'M GOING TO KEEP THIS SIMPLE.
AND KILL YOU WITH MY BARE HANDS.
I DON'T UNDERSTAND...
WHAT... WHAT'S WRONG WITH YOU?
I'M DYING... MY MIND IS EBBING AWAY...
I CAN FEEL IT...

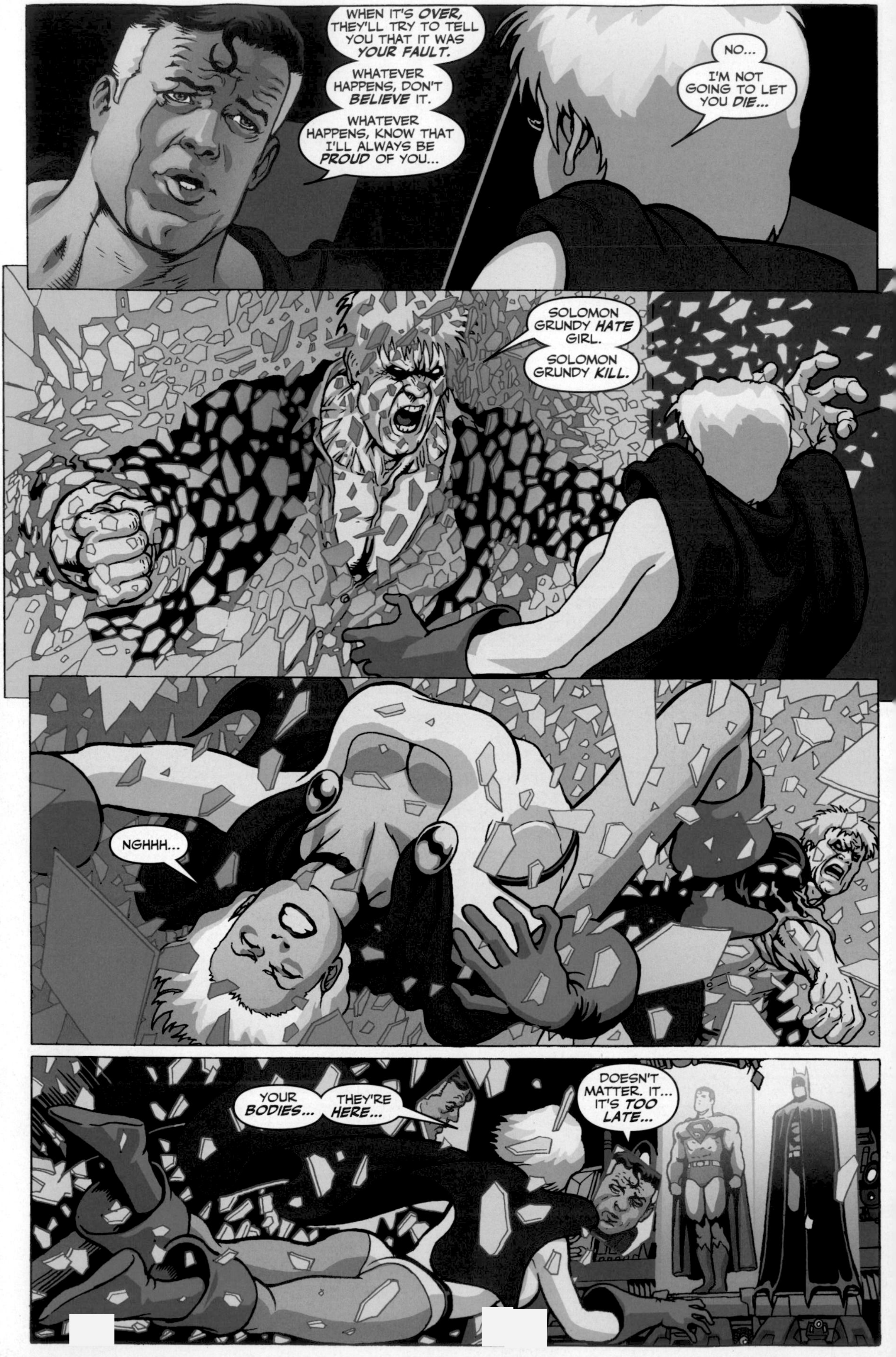
WHEN IT'S OVER, THEY'LL TRY TO TELL YOU THAT IT WAS YOUR FAULT.
WHATEVER HAPPENS, DON'T BELIEVE IT.
WHATEVER HAPPENS, KNOW THAT I'LL ALWAYS BE PROUD OF YOU...
NO...
I'M NOT GOING TO LET YOU DIE...
SOLOMON GRUNDY HATE GIRL.
SOLOMON GRUNDY KILL.
NGHHH...
YOUR BODIES...
THEY'RE HERE...
DOESN'T MATTER. IT... IT'S TOO LATE...

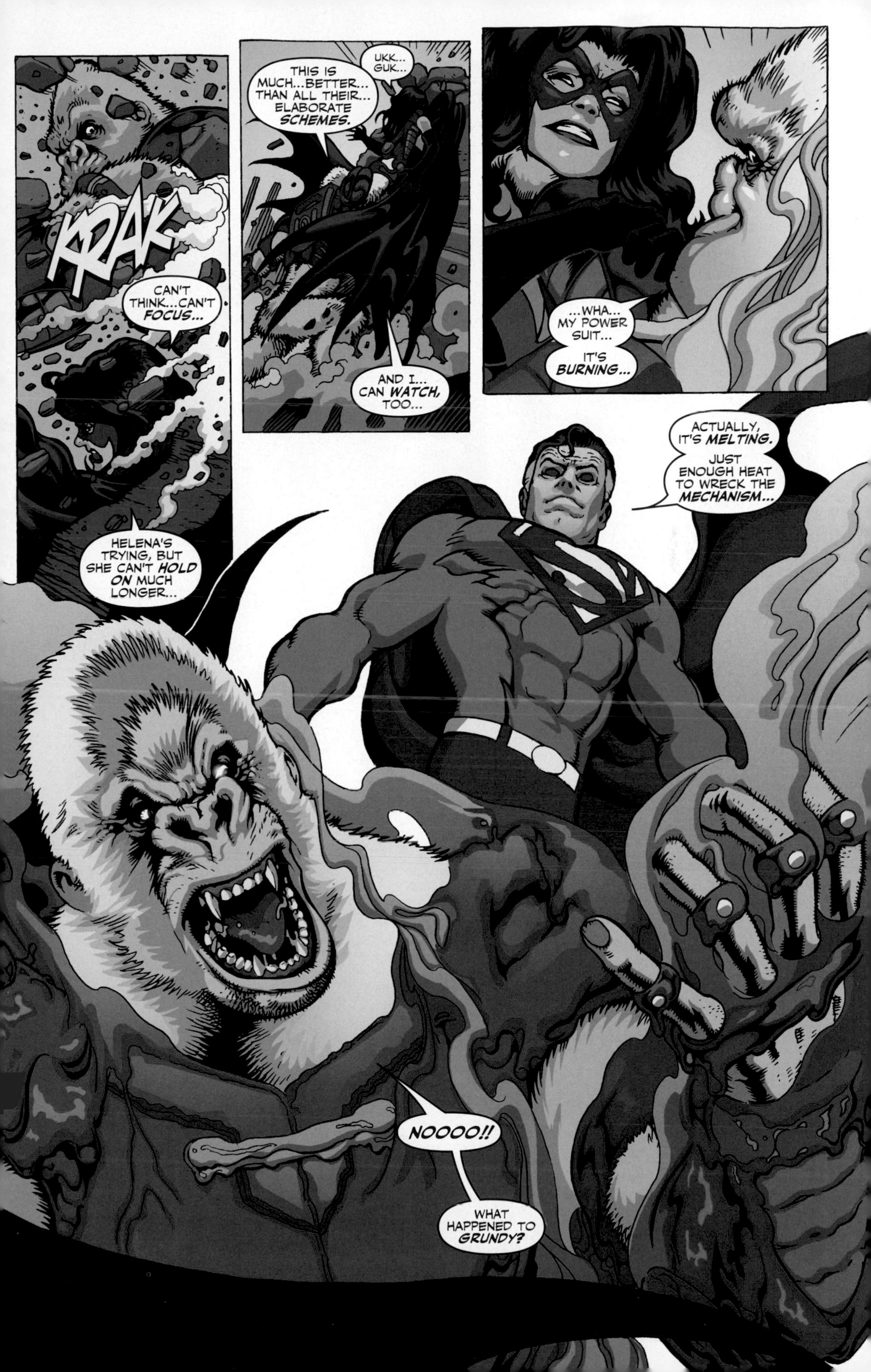
KRAK
CAN'T THINK...CAN'T FOCUS...
HELENA'S TRYING, BUT SHE CAN'T HOLD ON MUCH LONGER...
UKK... GUK...
THIS IS MUCH...BETTER... THAN ALL THEIR... ELABORATE SCHEMES.
AND I... CAN WATCH, TOO...
...WHA... MY POWER SUIT...
IT'S BURNING...
ACTUALLY, IT'S MELTING.
JUST ENOUGH HEAT TO WRECK THE MECHANISM...
NOOOO!!
WHAT HAPPENED TO GRUNDY?

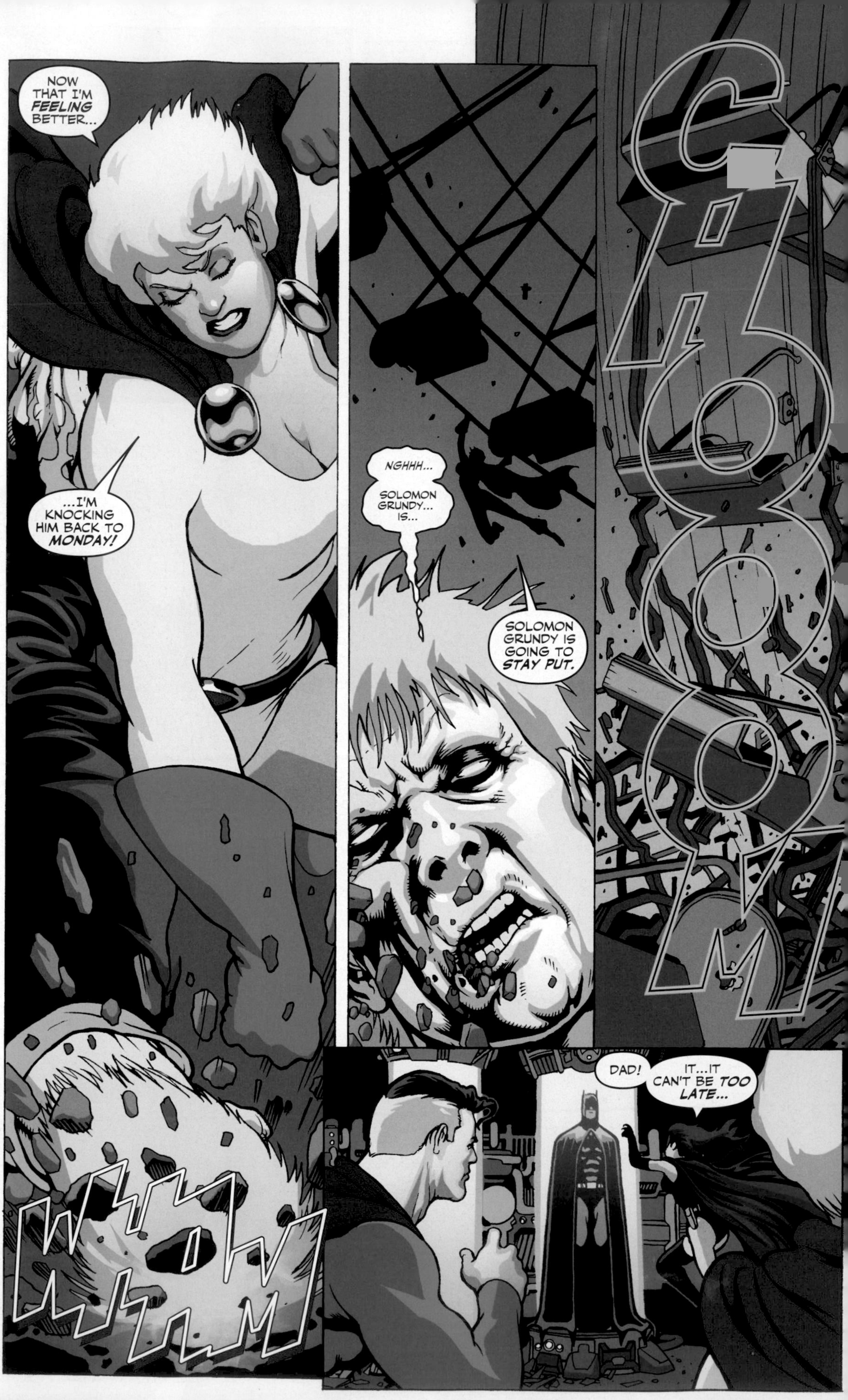
NOW THAT I'M *FEELING* BETTER...
...I'M KNOCKING HIM BACK TO *MONDAY!*
NGHHH...
SOLOMON GRUNDY... IS...
SOLOMON GRUNDY IS GOING TO *STAY PUT.*
DAD!
IT...IT CAN'T BE *TOO LATE...*

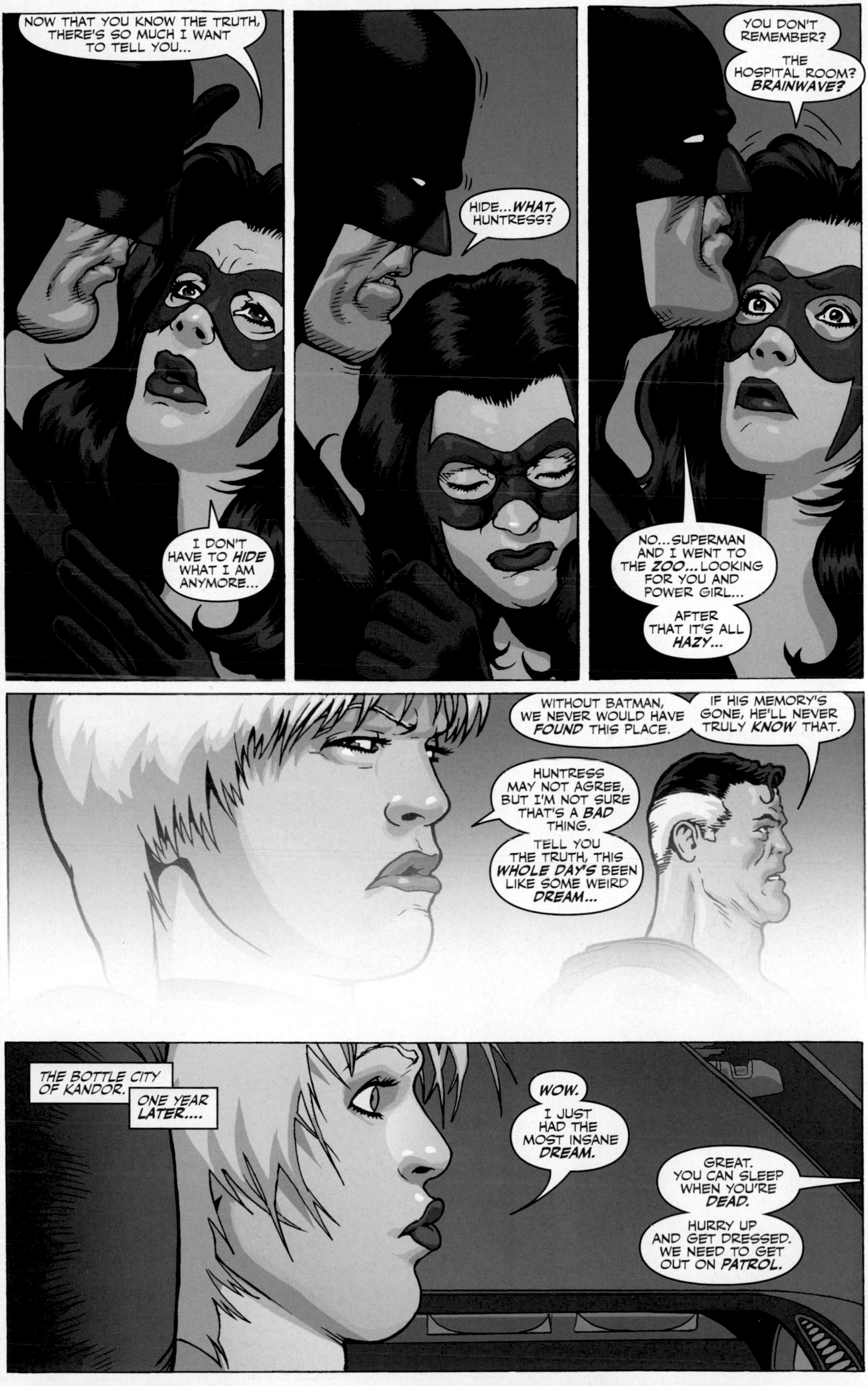
NOW THAT YOU KNOW THE TRUTH, THERE'S SO MUCH I WANT TO TELL YOU...
I DON'T HAVE TO HIDE WHAT I AM ANYMORE...
HIDE...WHAT, HUNTRESS?
YOU DON'T REMEMBER?
THE HOSPITAL ROOM? BRAINWAVE?
NO...SUPERMAN AND I WENT TO THE ZOO...LOOKING FOR YOU AND POWER GIRL...
AFTER THAT IT'S ALL HAZY...
WITHOUT BATMAN, WE NEVER WOULD HAVE FOUND THIS PLACE.
IF HIS MEMORY'S GONE, HE'LL NEVER TRULY KNOW THAT.
HUNTRESS MAY NOT AGREE, BUT I'M NOT SURE THAT'S A BAD THING.
TELL YOU THE TRUTH, THIS WHOLE DAY'S BEEN LIKE SOME WEIRD DREAM...
THE BOTTLE CITY OF KANDOR.
ONE YEAR LATER....
WOW.
I JUST HAD THE MOST INSANE DREAM.
GREAT. YOU CAN SLEEP WHEN YOU'RE DEAD.
HURRY UP AND GET DRESSED. WE NEED TO GET OUT ON PATROL.

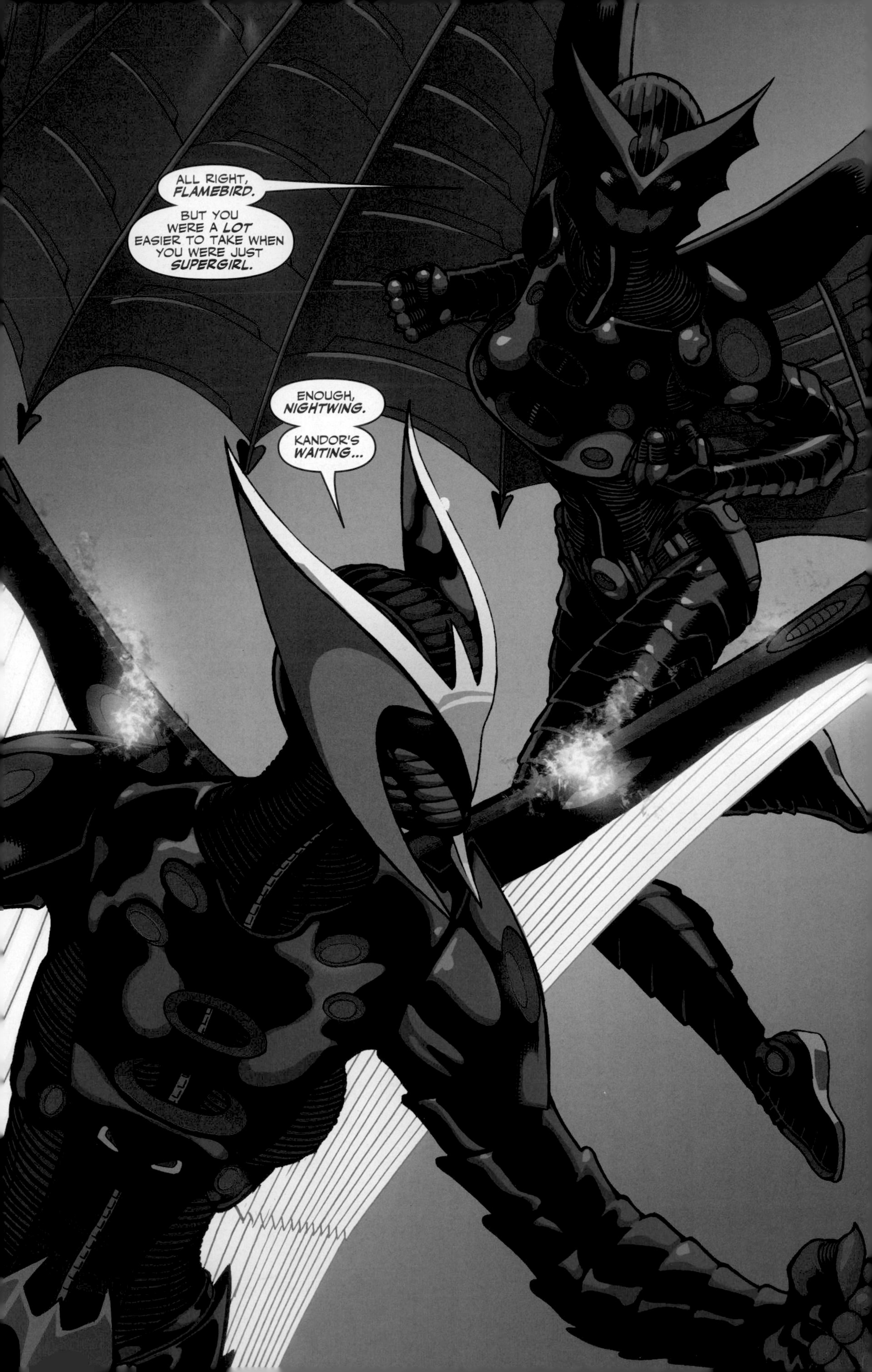
ALL RIGHT, *FLAMEBIRD.*
BUT YOU WERE A *LOT* EASIER TO TAKE WHEN YOU WERE JUST *SUPERGIRL.*
ENOUGH, *NIGHTWING.*
KANDOR'S *WAITING...*

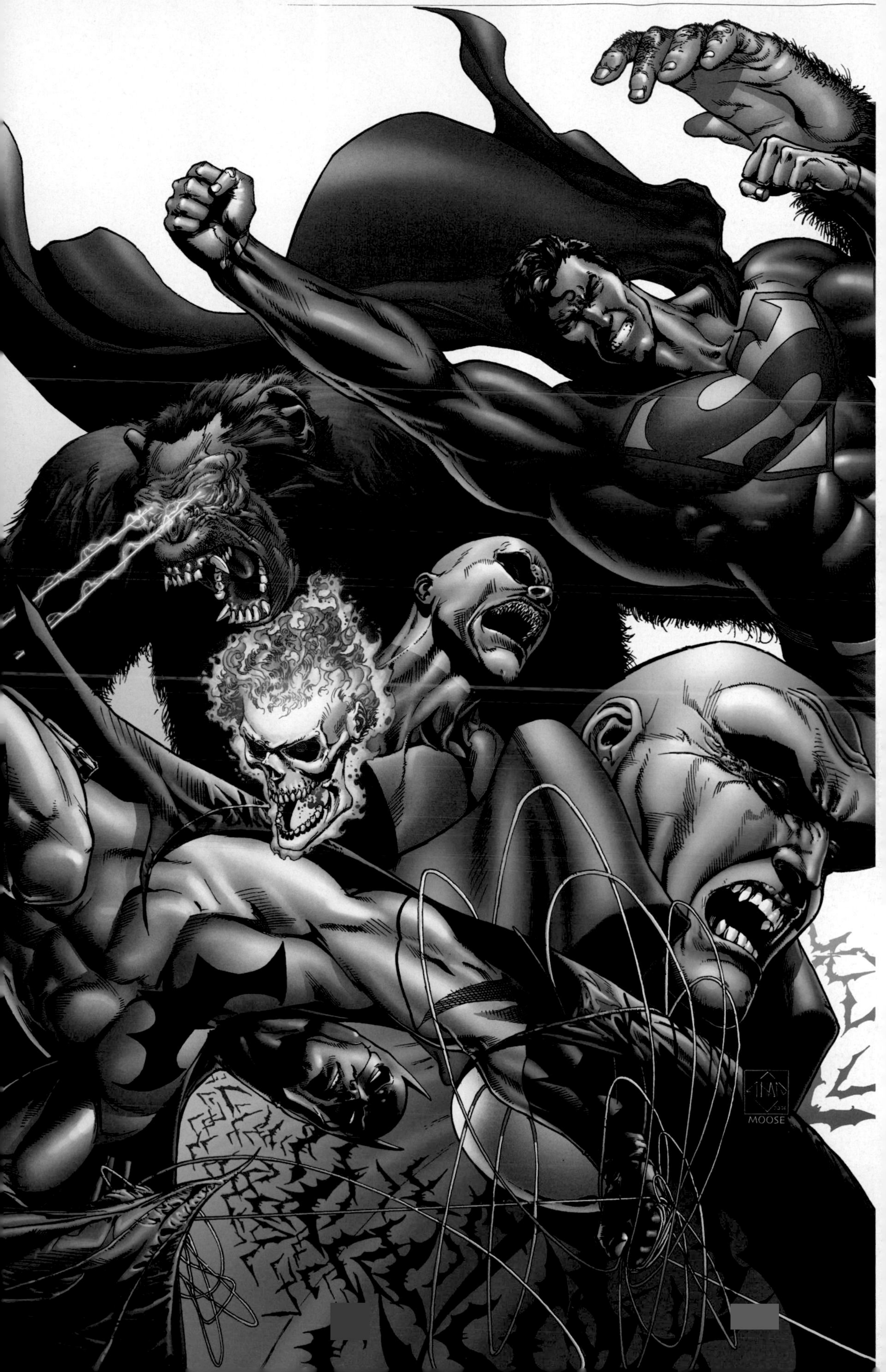
MOOSE

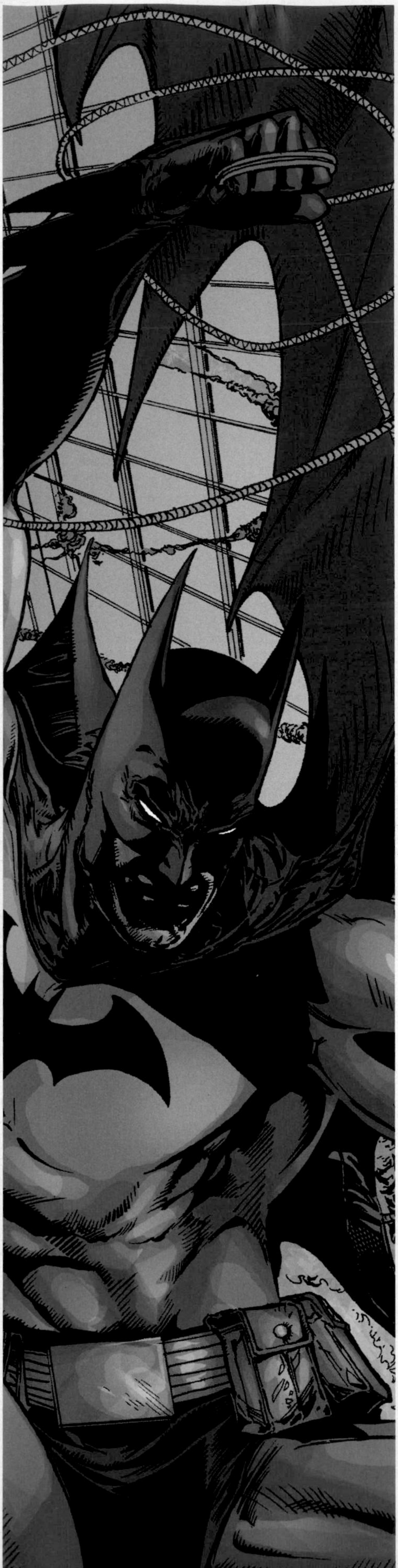

THE ENEMIES AMONG US

PART 1

MARK VERHEIDEN
WRITER

ETHAN VAN SCIVER
PENCILLER

CHRIS CHUCKRY
COLORIST

ROB LEIGH
LETTERER

ETHAN VAN SCIVER
&
MOOSE BAUMANN
COVER

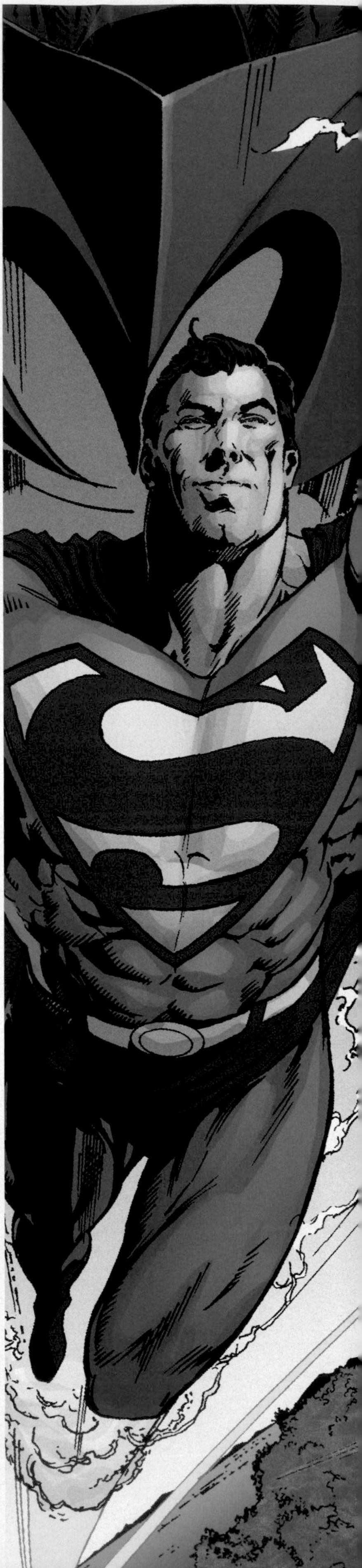

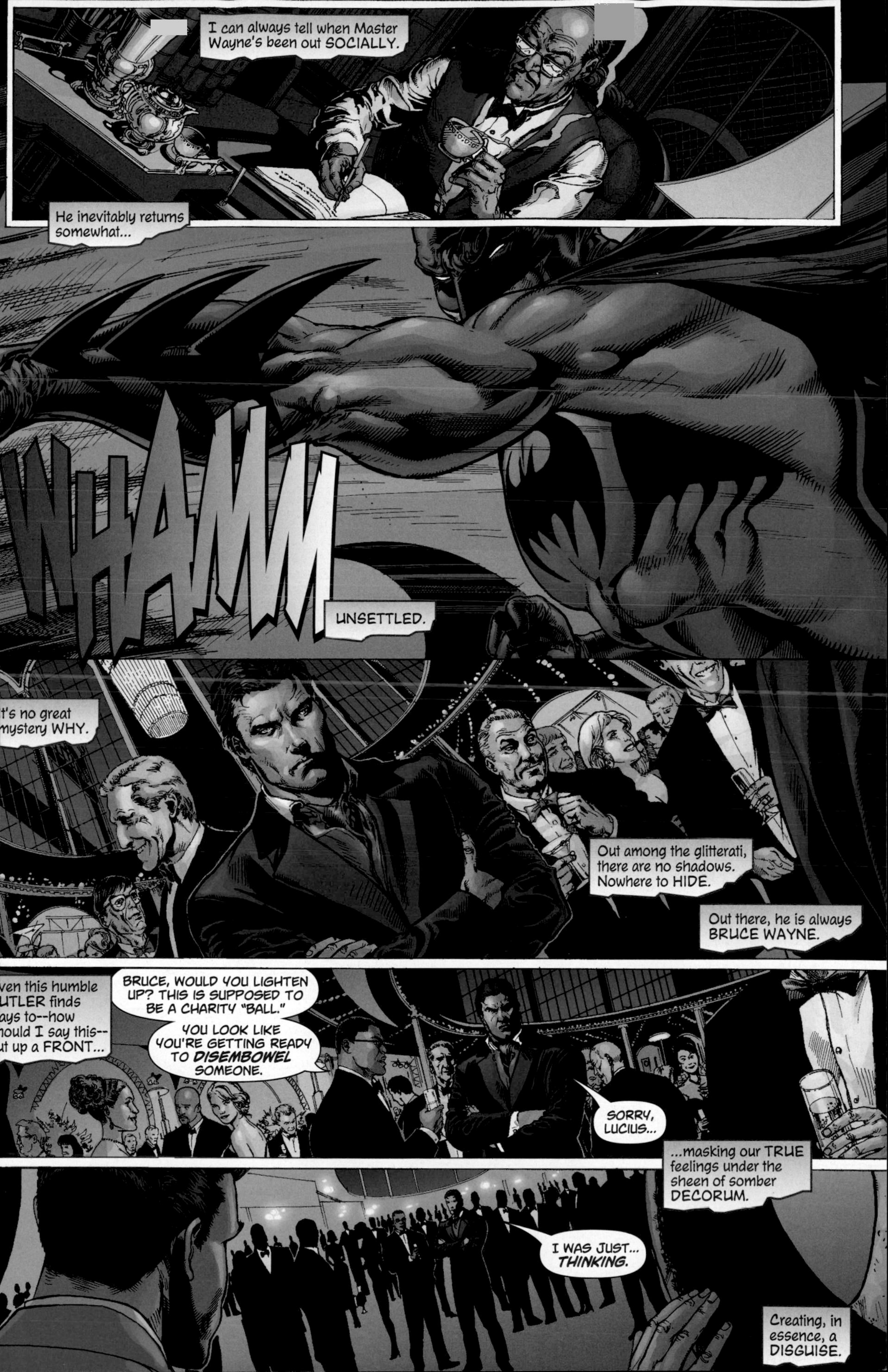
I can always tell when Master Wayne's been out SOCIALLY.
He inevitably returns somewhat...
WHAMM
UNSETTLED.
t's no great mystery WHY.
Out among the glitterati, there are no shadows. Nowhere to HIDE.
Out there, he is always BRUCE WAYNE.
ven this humble UTLER finds ays to--how hould I say this-- ut up a FRONT...
BRUCE, WOULD YOU LIGHTEN UP? THIS IS SUPPOSED TO BE A CHARITY "BALL."
YOU LOOK LIKE YOU'RE GETTING READY TO DISEMBOWEL SOMEONE.
SORRY, LUCIUS...
...masking our TRUE feelings under the sheen of somber DECORUM.
I WAS JUST... THINKING.
Creating, in essence, a DISGUISE.

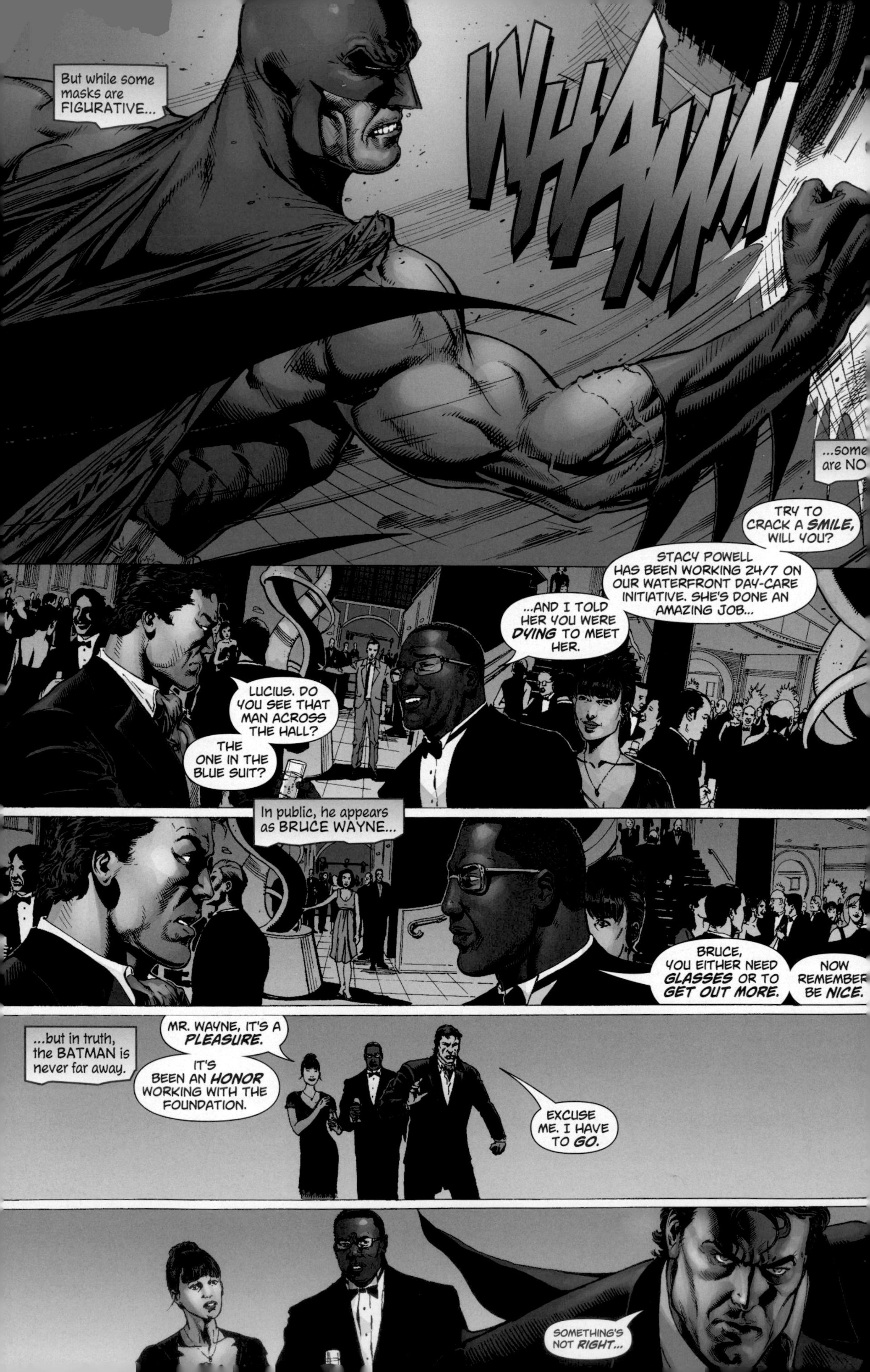
But while some masks are FIGURATIVE...
WHAMM
...some are NO
TRY TO CRACK A SMILE, WILL YOU?
STACY POWELL HAS BEEN WORKING 24/7 ON OUR WATERFRONT DAY-CARE INITIATIVE. SHE'S DONE AN AMAZING JOB...
...AND I TOLD HER YOU WERE DYING TO MEET HER.
LUCIUS. DO YOU SEE THAT MAN ACROSS THE HALL?
THE ONE IN THE BLUE SUIT?
In public, he appears as BRUCE WAYNE...
BRUCE, YOU EITHER NEED GLASSES OR TO GET OUT MORE.
NOW REMEMBER BE NICE.
...but in truth, the BATMAN is never far away.
MR. WAYNE, IT'S A PLEASURE.
IT'S BEEN AN HONOR WORKING WITH THE FOUNDATION.
EXCUSE ME. I HAVE TO GO.
SOMETHING'S NOT RIGHT...

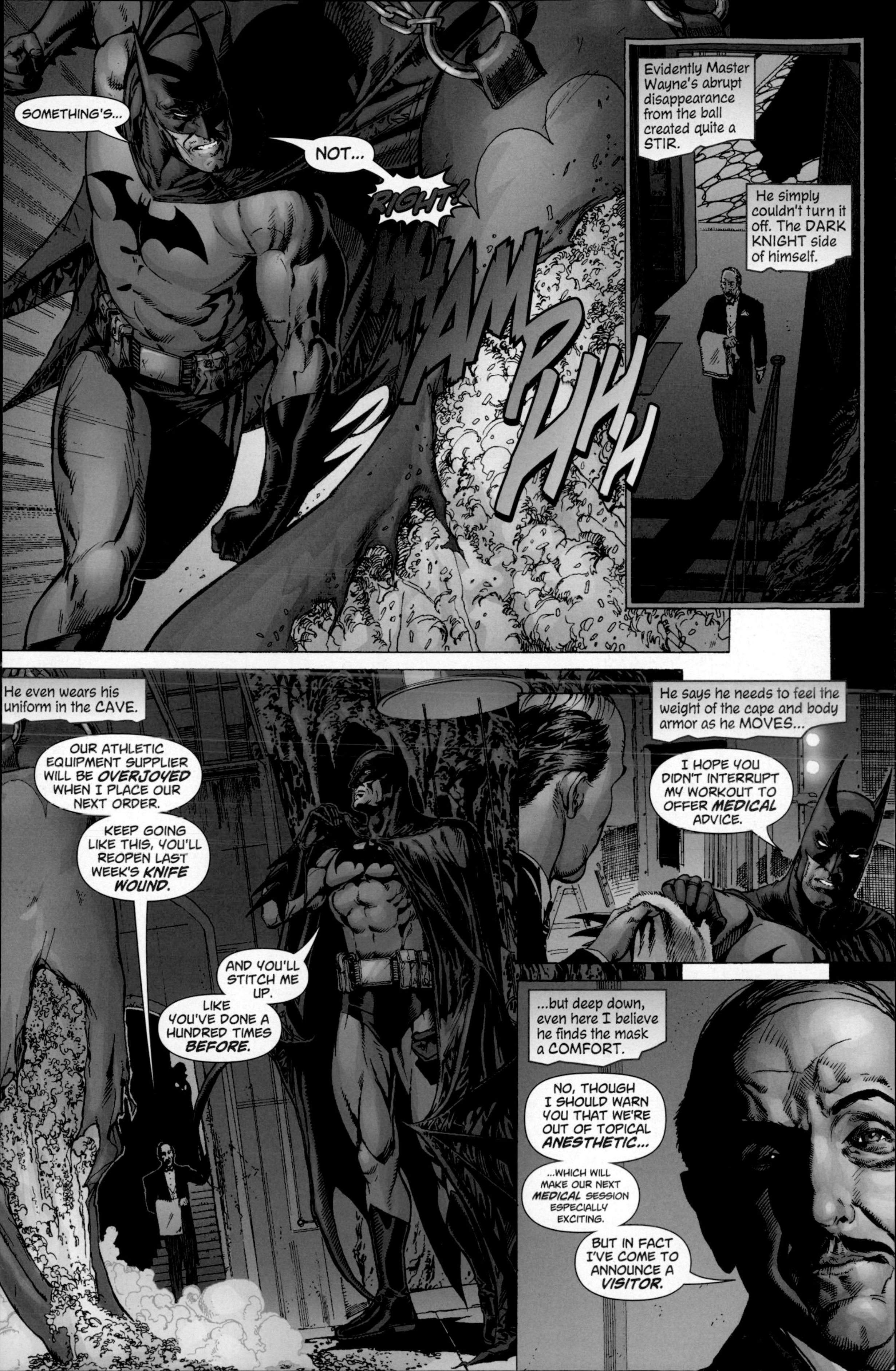
SOMETHING'S...
NOT...
RIGHT!
WHAM
PUHHH
Evidently Master Wayne's abrupt disappearance from the ball created quite a STIR.
He simply couldn't turn it off. The DARK KNIGHT side of himself.
He even wears his uniform in the CAVE.
OUR ATHLETIC EQUIPMENT SUPPLIER WILL BE OVERJOYED WHEN I PLACE OUR NEXT ORDER.
KEEP GOING LIKE THIS, YOU'LL REOPEN LAST WEEK'S KNIFE WOUND.
AND YOU'LL STITCH ME UP.
LIKE YOU'VE DONE A HUNDRED TIMES BEFORE.
He says he needs to feel the weight of the cape and body armor as he MOVES...
I HOPE YOU DIDN'T INTERRUPT MY WORKOUT TO OFFER MEDICAL ADVICE.
...but deep down, even here I believe he finds the mask a COMFORT.
NO, THOUGH I SHOULD WARN YOU THAT WE'RE OUT OF TOPICAL ANESTHETIC...
...WHICH WILL MAKE OUR NEXT MEDICAL SESSION ESPECIALLY EXCITING.
BUT IN FACT I'VE COME TO ANNOUNCE A VISITOR.

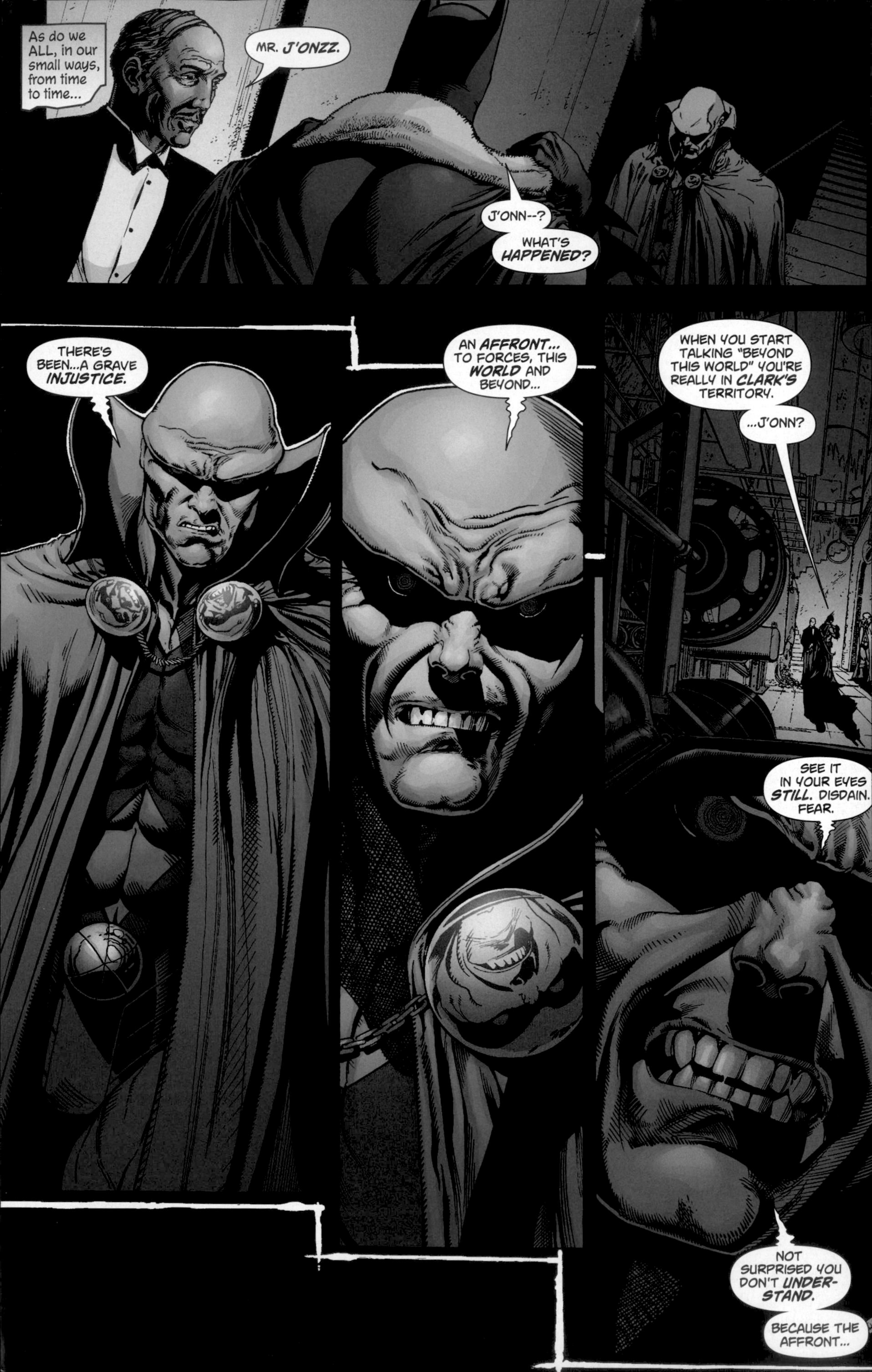
As do we ALL, in our small ways, from time to time...
MR. J'ONZZ.
J'ONN--?
WHAT'S HAPPENED?
THERE'S BEEN...A GRAVE INJUSTICE.
AN AFFRONT... TO FORCES, THIS WORLD AND BEYOND...
WHEN YOU START TALKING "BEYOND THIS WORLD" YOU'RE REALLY IN CLARK'S TERRITORY.
...J'ONN?
SEE IT IN YOUR EYES STILL. DISDAIN. FEAR.
NOT SURPRISED YOU DON'T UNDER-STAND.
BECAUSE THE AFFRONT...

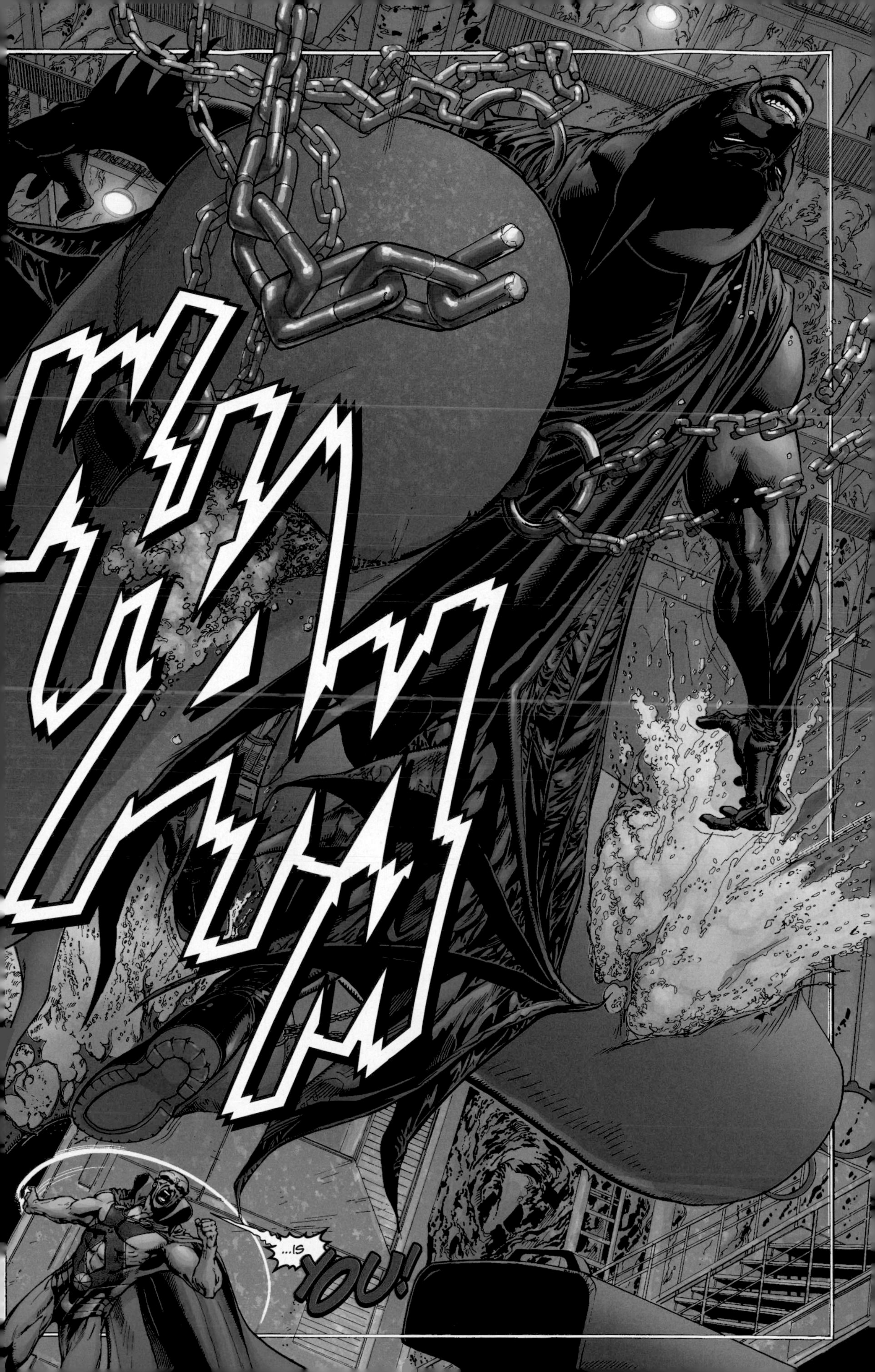
...IS
YOU!

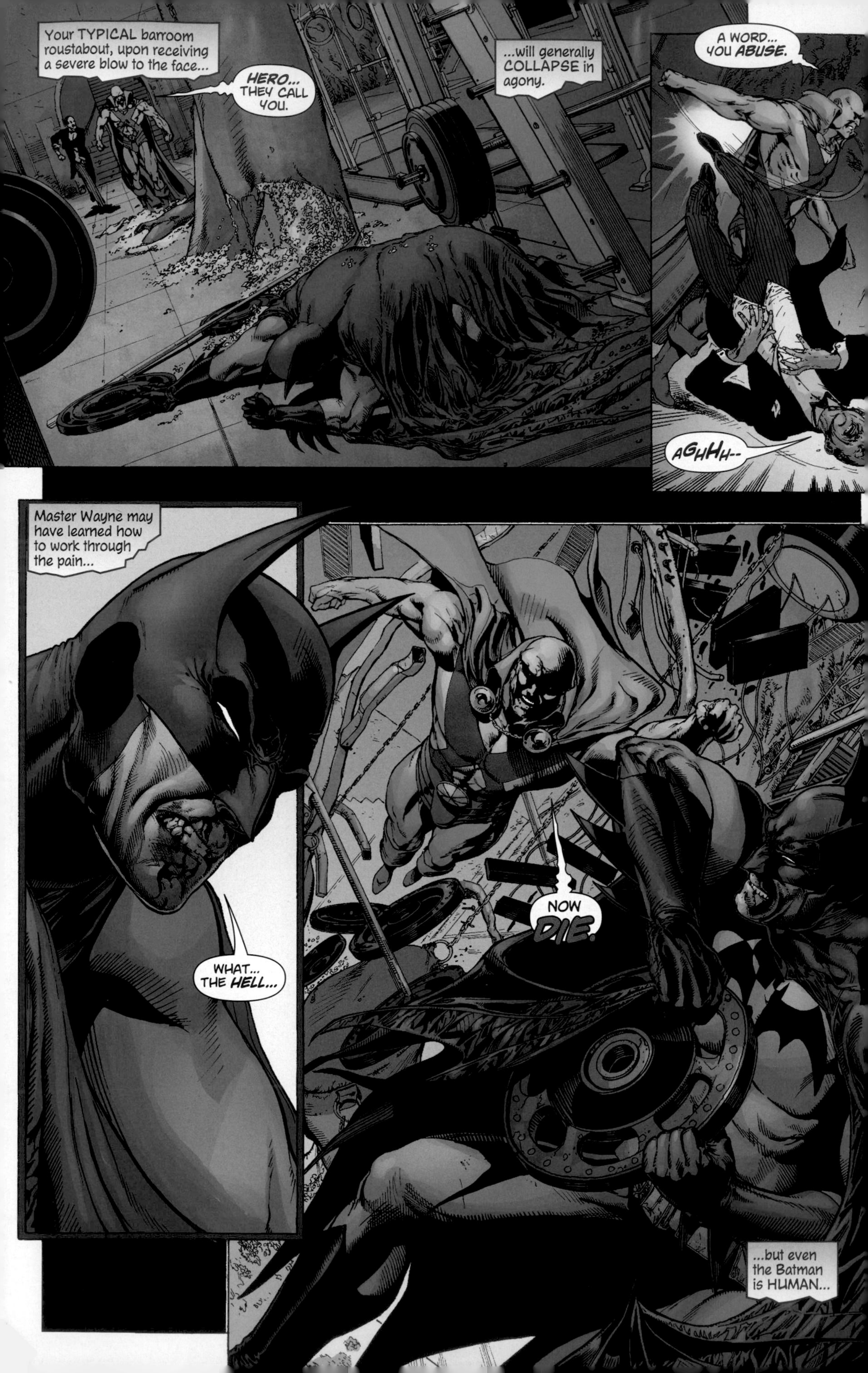

Your TYPICAL barroom roustabout, upon receiving a severe blow to the face...
HERO... THEY CALL YOU.
...will generally COLLAPSE in agony.
A WORD... YOU ABUSE.
AGHHH--
Master Wayne may have learned how to work through the pain...
WHAT... THE HELL...
NOW DIE.
...but even the Batman is HUMAN...

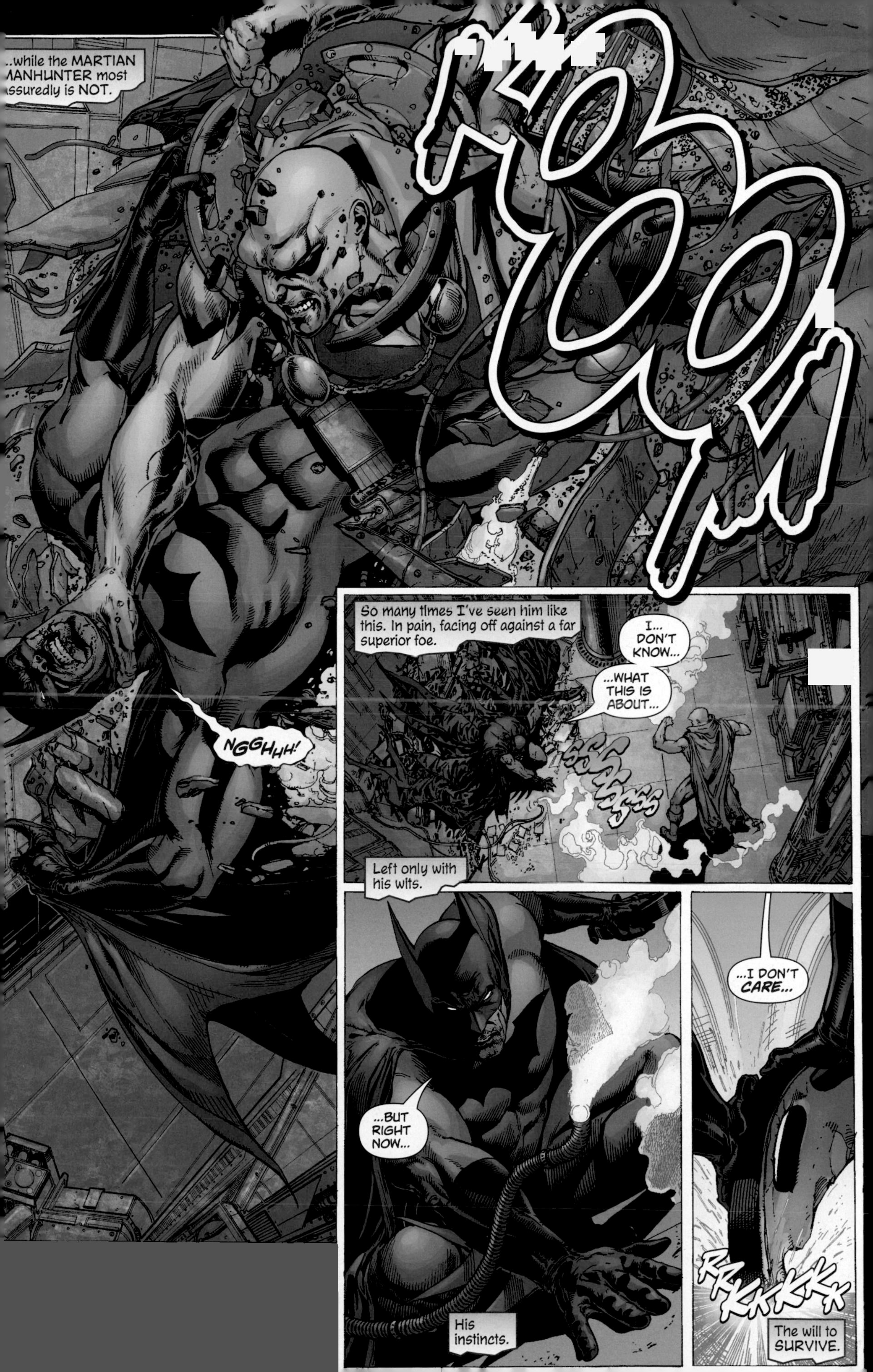

...while the MARTIAN MANHUNTER most assuredly is NOT.
NGGHHH!
So many times I've seen him like this. In pain, facing off against a far superior foe.
I... DON'T KNOW...
...WHAT THIS IS ABOUT...
Left only with his wits.
...BUT RIGHT NOW...
His instincts.
...I DON'T CARE...
RRKKKKKK
The will to SURVIVE.

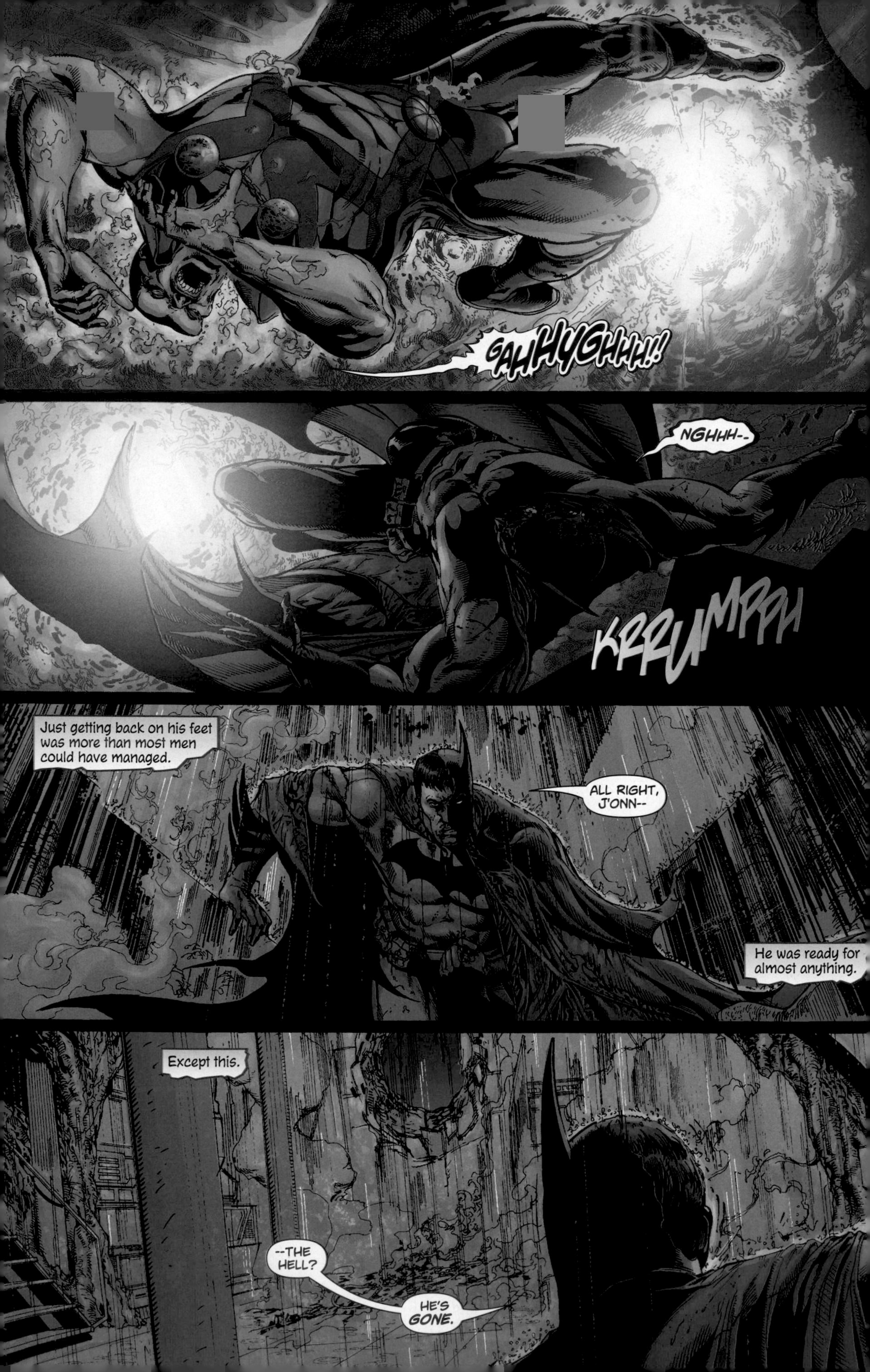
GAHHYGHHH!!
NGHHH--
KRRUMPPH
Just getting back on his feet was more than most men could have managed.
ALL RIGHT, J'ONN--
He was ready for almost anything.
Except this.
--THE HELL?
HE'S GONE.

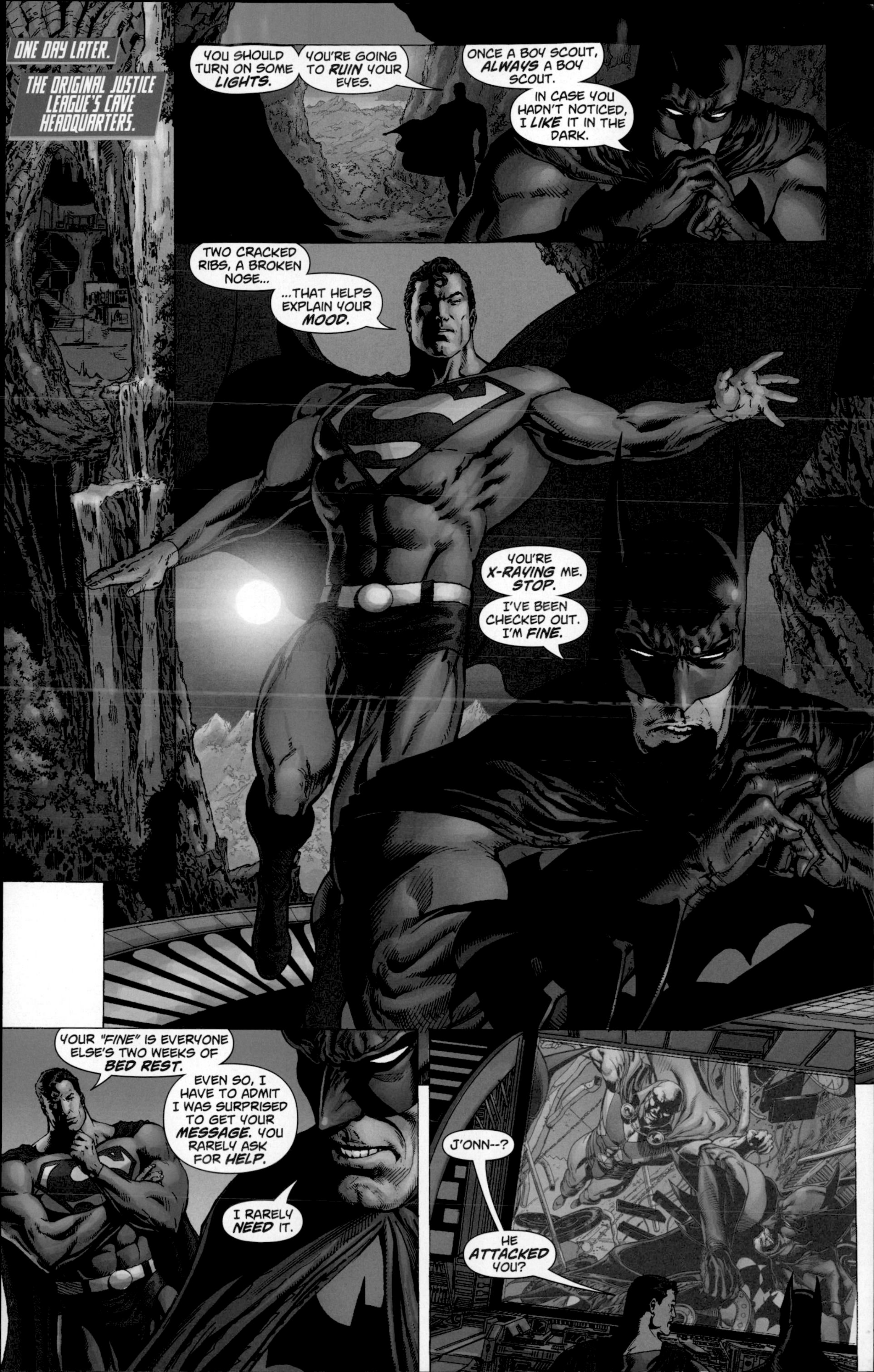
ONE DAY LATER.
THE ORIGINAL JUSTICE LEAGUE'S CAVE HEADQUARTERS.
YOU SHOULD TURN ON SOME LIGHTS.
YOU'RE GOING TO RUIN YOUR EYES.
ONCE A BOY SCOUT, ALWAYS A BOY SCOUT.
IN CASE YOU HADN'T NOTICED, I LIKE IT IN THE DARK.
TWO CRACKED RIBS, A BROKEN NOSE...
...THAT HELPS EXPLAIN YOUR MOOD.
YOU'RE X-RAYING ME. STOP.
I'VE BEEN CHECKED OUT. I'M FINE.
YOUR "FINE" IS EVERYONE ELSE'S TWO WEEKS OF BED REST.
EVEN SO, I HAVE TO ADMIT I WAS SURPRISED TO GET YOUR MESSAGE. YOU RARELY ASK FOR HELP.
I RARELY NEED IT.
J'ONN--?
HE ATTACKED YOU?

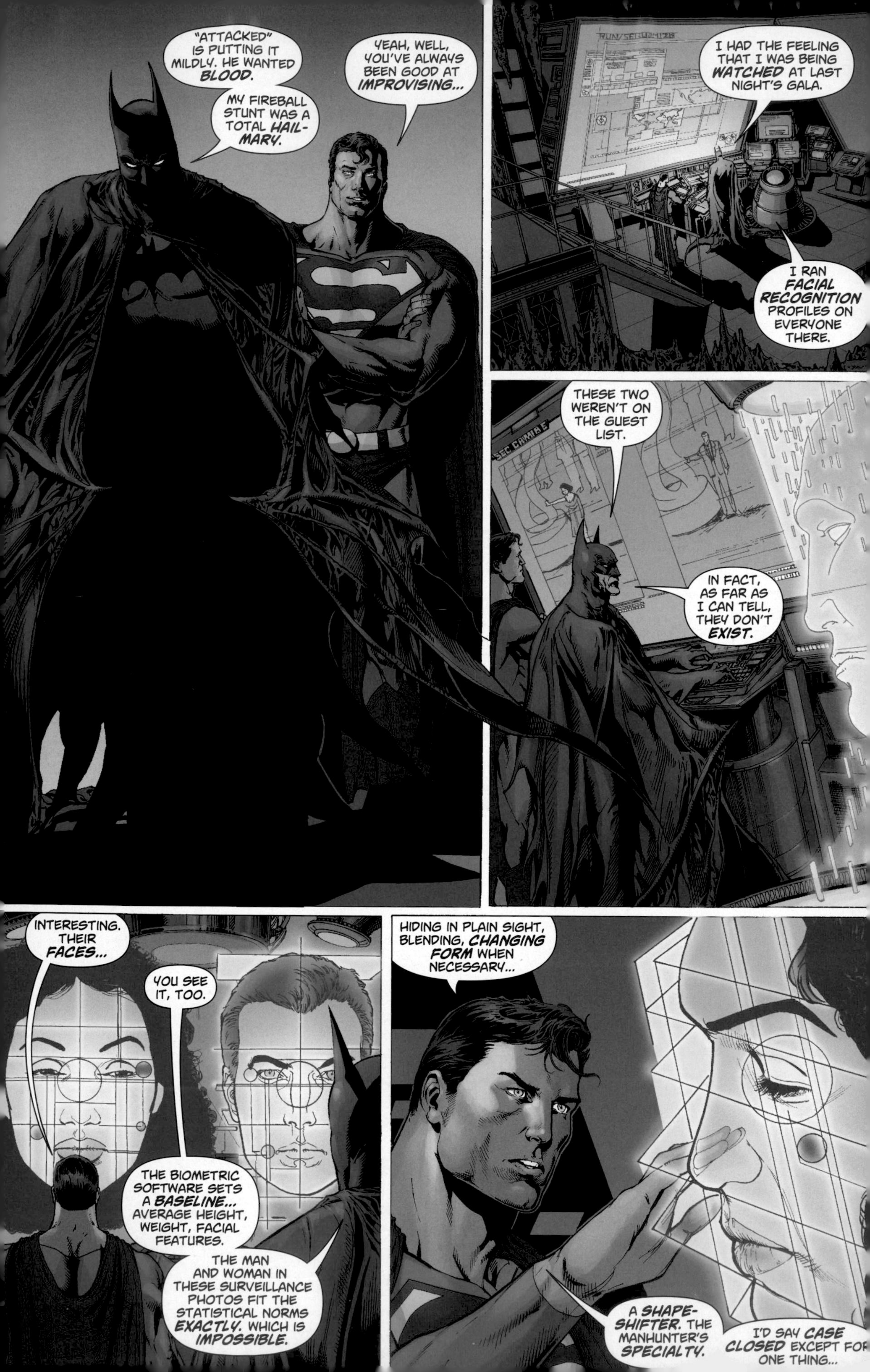
"ATTACKED" IS PUTTING IT MILDLY. HE WANTED BLOOD.
MY FIREBALL STUNT WAS A TOTAL HAIL-MARY.
YEAH, WELL, YOU'VE ALWAYS BEEN GOOD AT IMPROVISING...
I HAD THE FEELING THAT I WAS BEING WATCHED AT LAST NIGHT'S GALA.
I RAN FACIAL RECOGNITION PROFILES ON EVERYONE THERE.
THESE TWO WEREN'T ON THE GUEST LIST.
IN FACT, AS FAR AS I CAN TELL, THEY DON'T EXIST.
INTERESTING. THEIR FACES...
YOU SEE IT, TOO.
THE BIOMETRIC SOFTWARE SETS A BASELINE... AVERAGE HEIGHT, WEIGHT, FACIAL FEATURES.
THE MAN AND WOMAN IN THESE SURVEILLANCE PHOTOS FIT THE STATISTICAL NORMS EXACTLY. WHICH IS IMPOSSIBLE.
HIDING IN PLAIN SIGHT, BLENDING, CHANGING FORM WHEN NECESSARY...
A SHAPE-SHIFTER. THE MANHUNTER'S SPECIALTY.
I'D SAY CASE CLOSED EXCEPT FOR ONE THING...

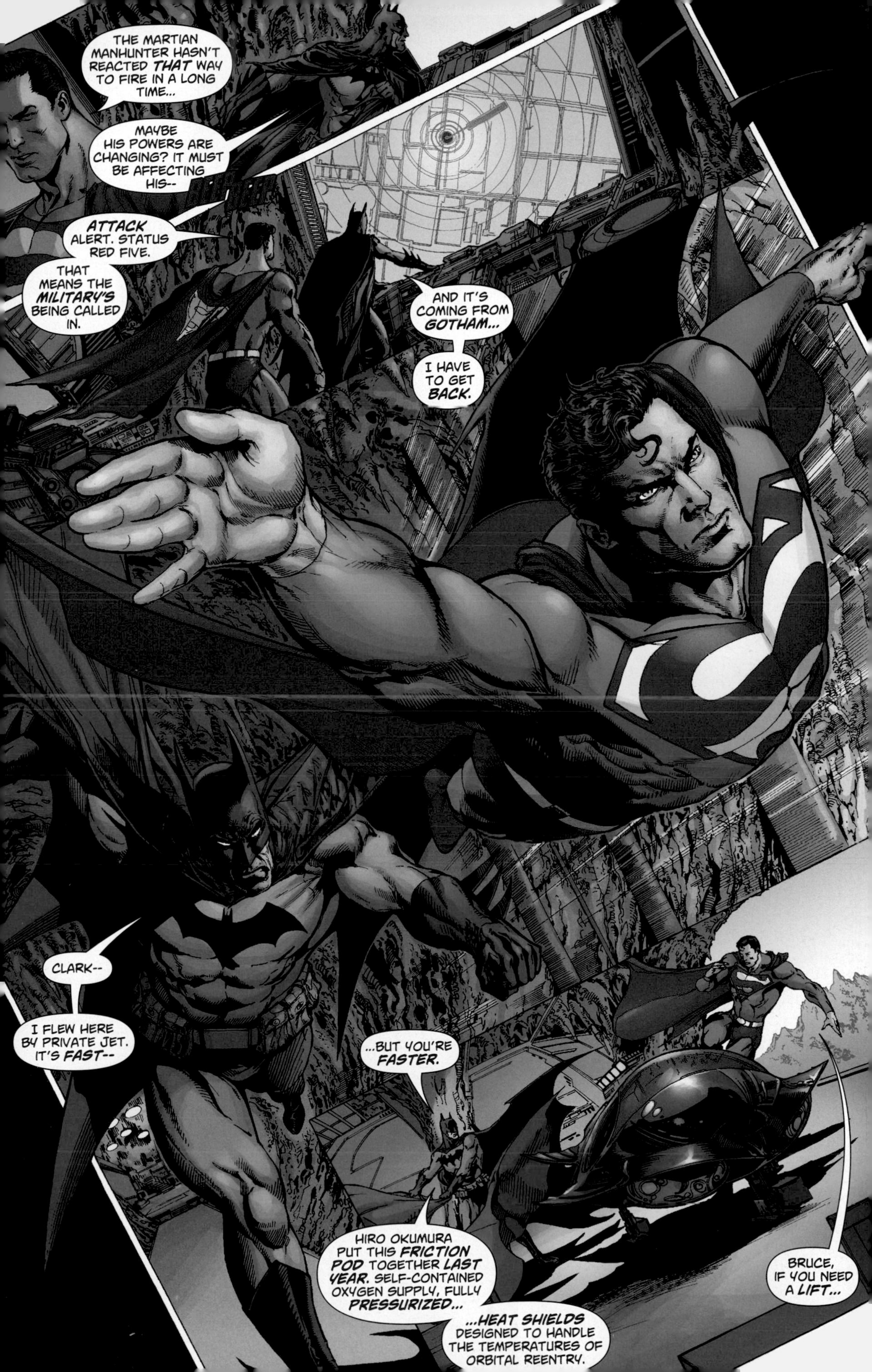
THE MARTIAN MANHUNTER HASN'T REACTED THAT WAY TO FIRE IN A LONG TIME...
MAYBE HIS POWERS ARE CHANGING? IT MUST BE AFFECTING HIS--
ATTACK ALERT. STATUS RED FIVE.
THAT MEANS THE MILITARY'S BEING CALLED IN.
AND IT'S COMING FROM GOTHAM...
I HAVE TO GET BACK.
CLARK--
I FLEW HERE BY PRIVATE JET. IT'S FAST--
...BUT YOU'RE FASTER.
HIRO OKUMURA PUT THIS FRICTION POD TOGETHER LAST YEAR. SELF-CONTAINED OXYGEN SUPPLY, FULLY PRESSURIZED...
...HEAT SHIELDS DESIGNED TO HANDLE THE TEMPERATURES OF ORBITAL REENTRY.
BRUCE, IF YOU NEED A LIFT...

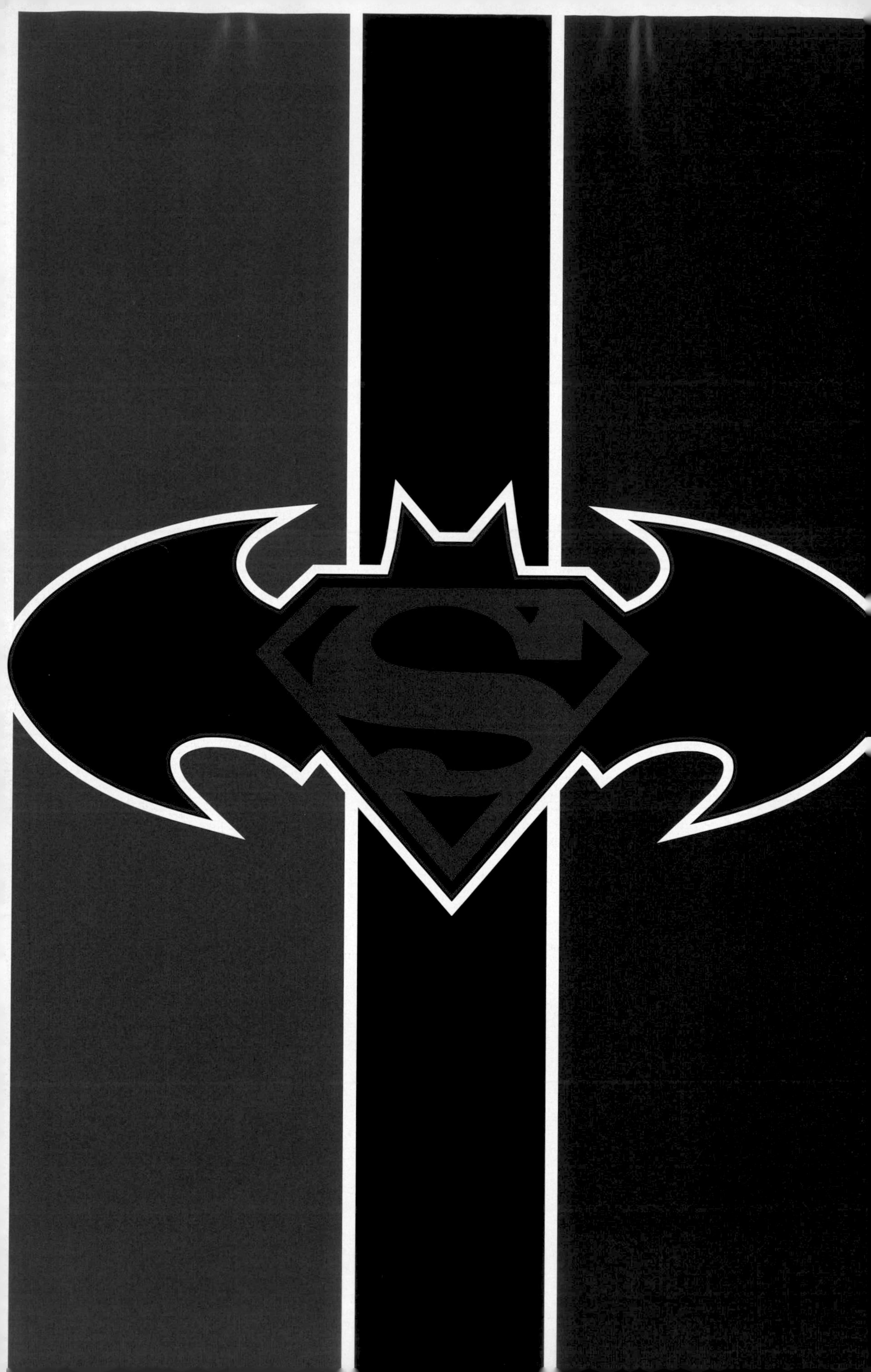

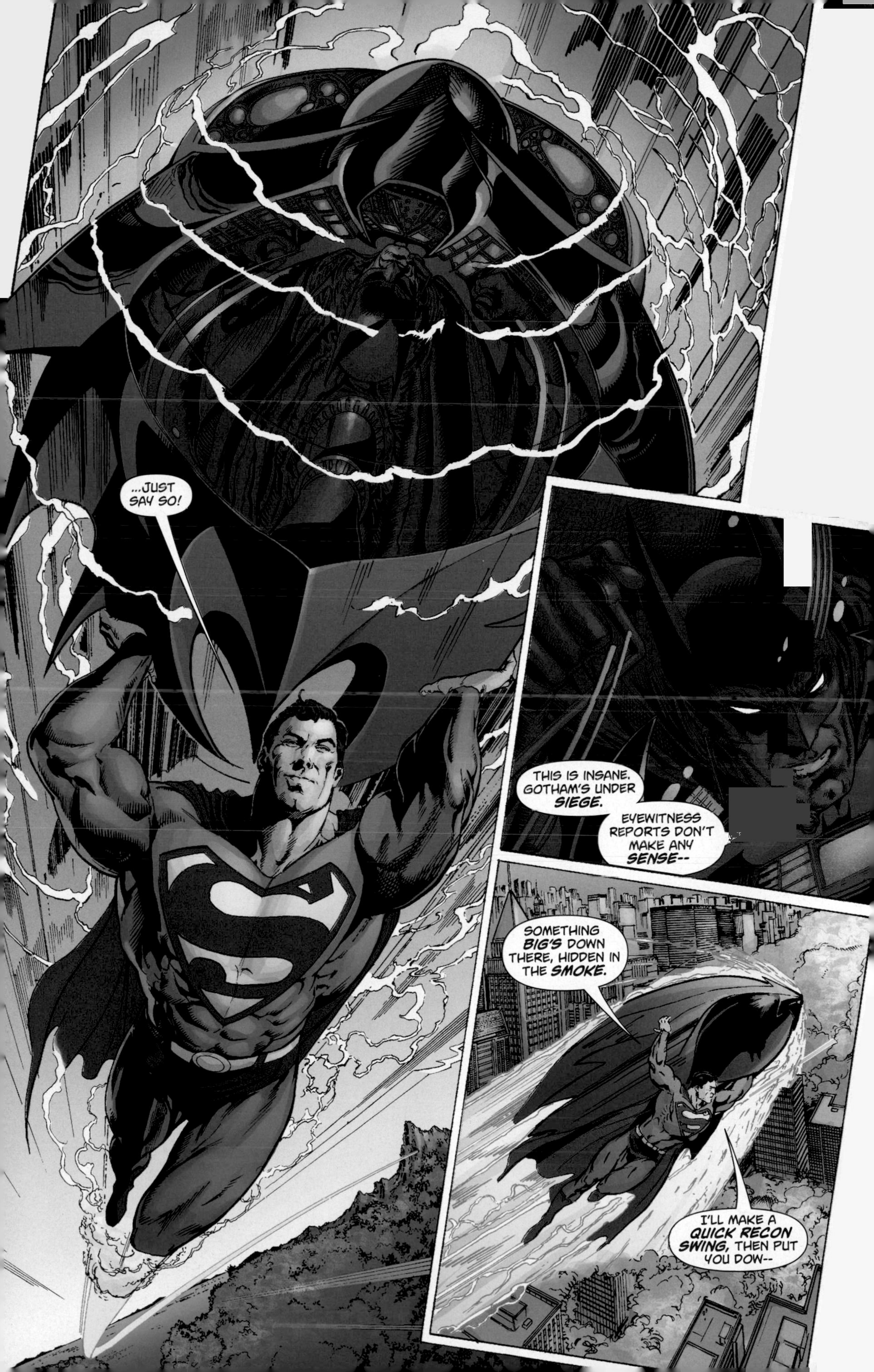
...JUST SAY SO!
THIS IS INSANE. GOTHAM'S UNDER SIEGE.
EYEWITNESS REPORTS DON'T MAKE ANY SENSE--
SOMETHING BIG'S DOWN THERE, HIDDEN IN THE SMOKE.
I'LL MAKE A QUICK RECON SWING, THEN PUT YOU DOW--

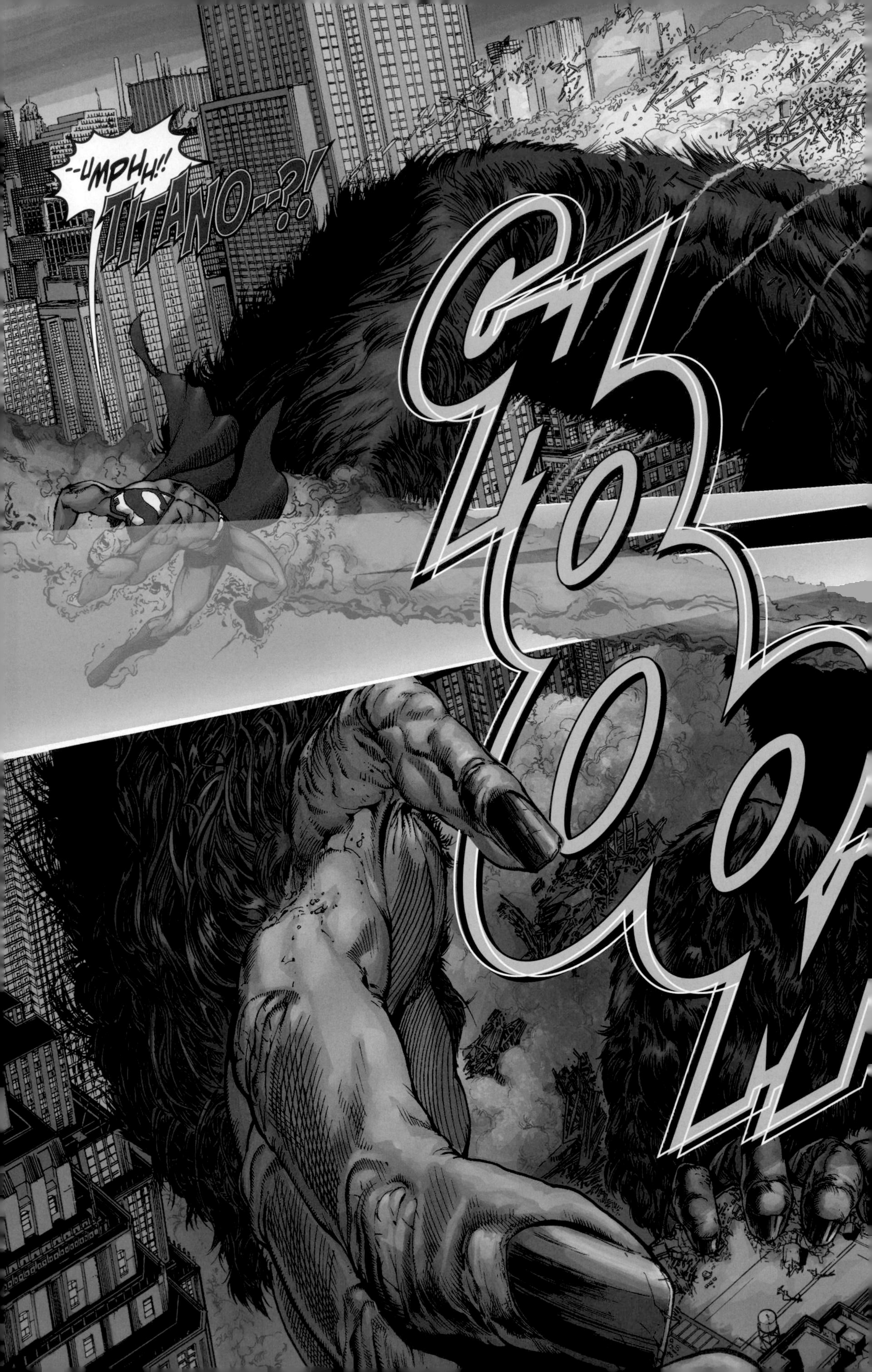
--UMPHH!! TITANO--?!

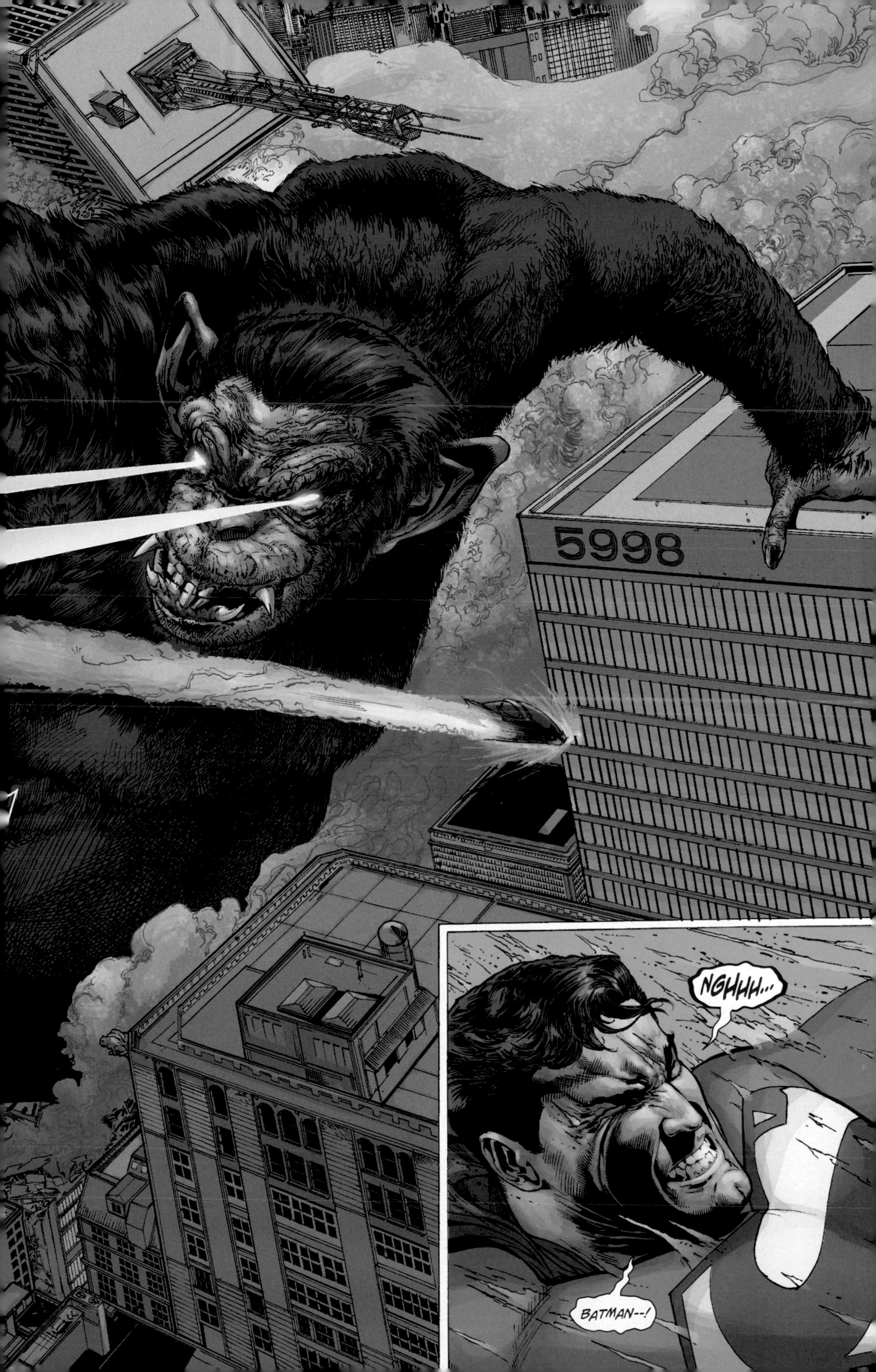
5998
NGHHH...
BATMAN--!

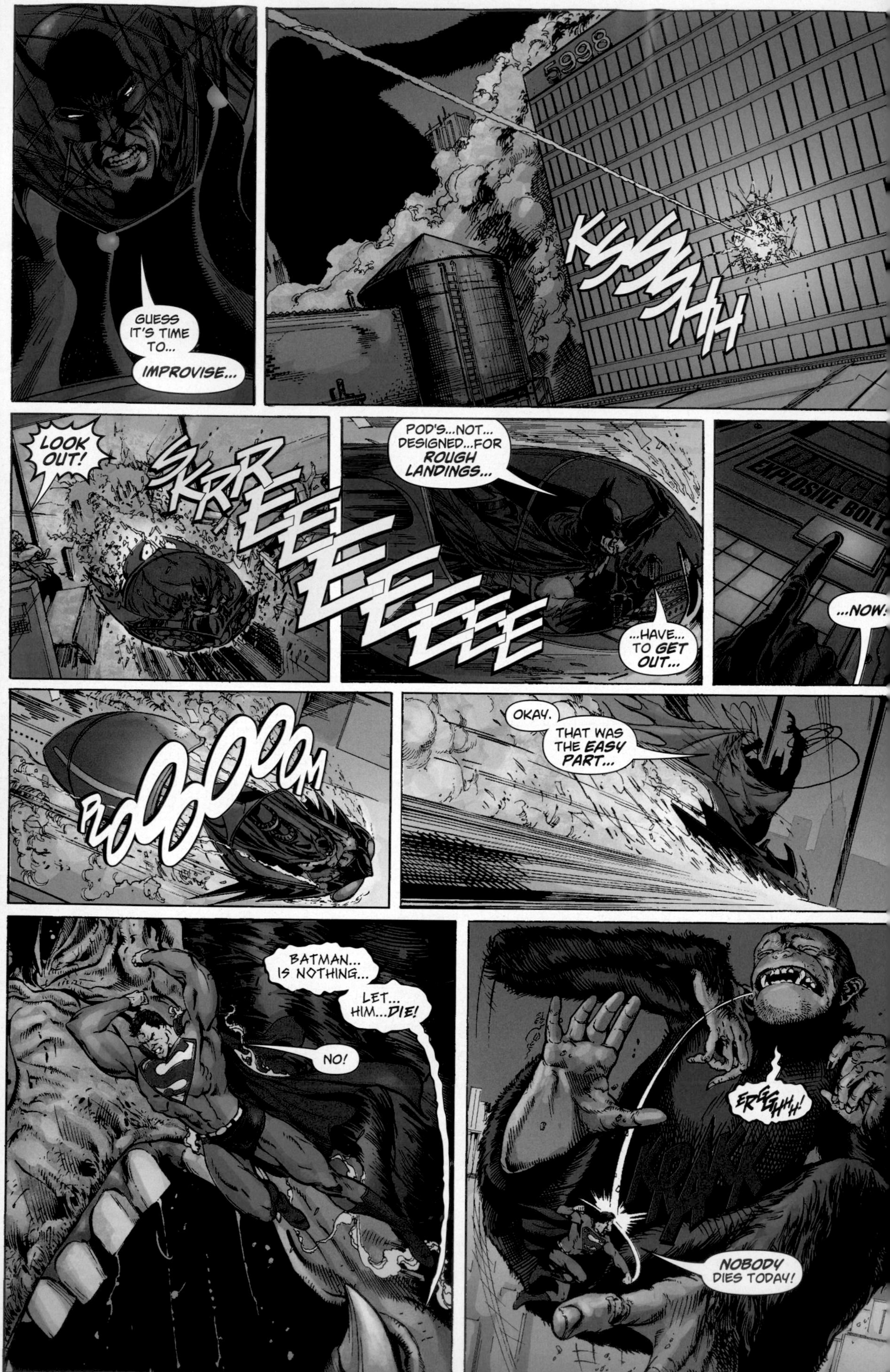
GUESS IT'S TIME TO...
IMPROVISE...
KSSSHHH
5998
LOOK OUT!
SKRREEEEEEEEE
POD'S...NOT... DESIGNED...FOR ROUGH LANDINGS...
...HAVE... TO GET OUT...
EXPLOSIVE BOLTS
...NOW!
POOOOOOOM
OKAY.
THAT WAS THE EASY PART...
BATMAN... IS NOTHING...
LET... HIM...DIE!
NO!
ERGGHHH!
NOBODY DIES TODAY!

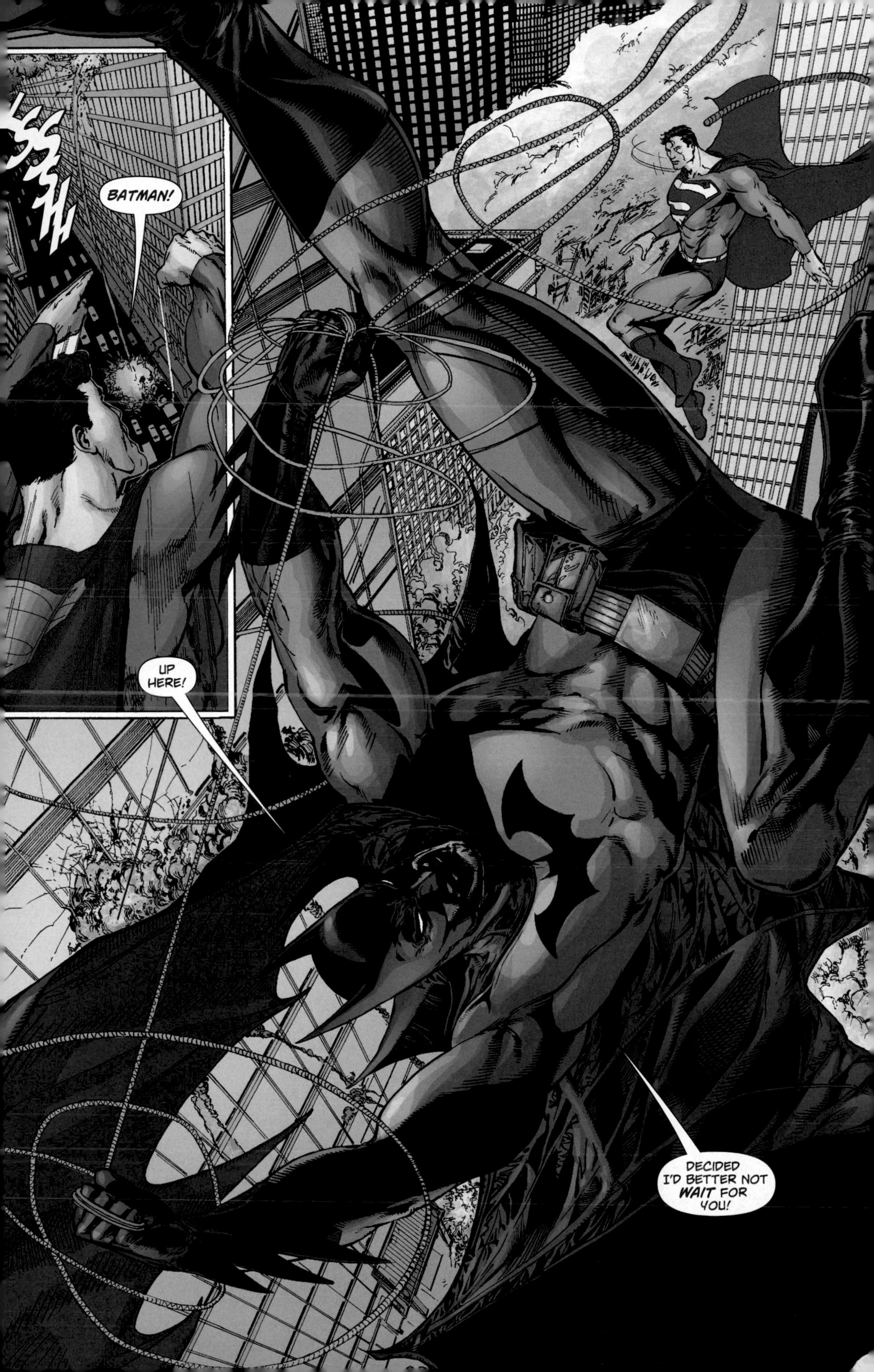
BATMAN!
UP HERE!
DECIDED I'D BETTER NOT WAIT FOR YOU!

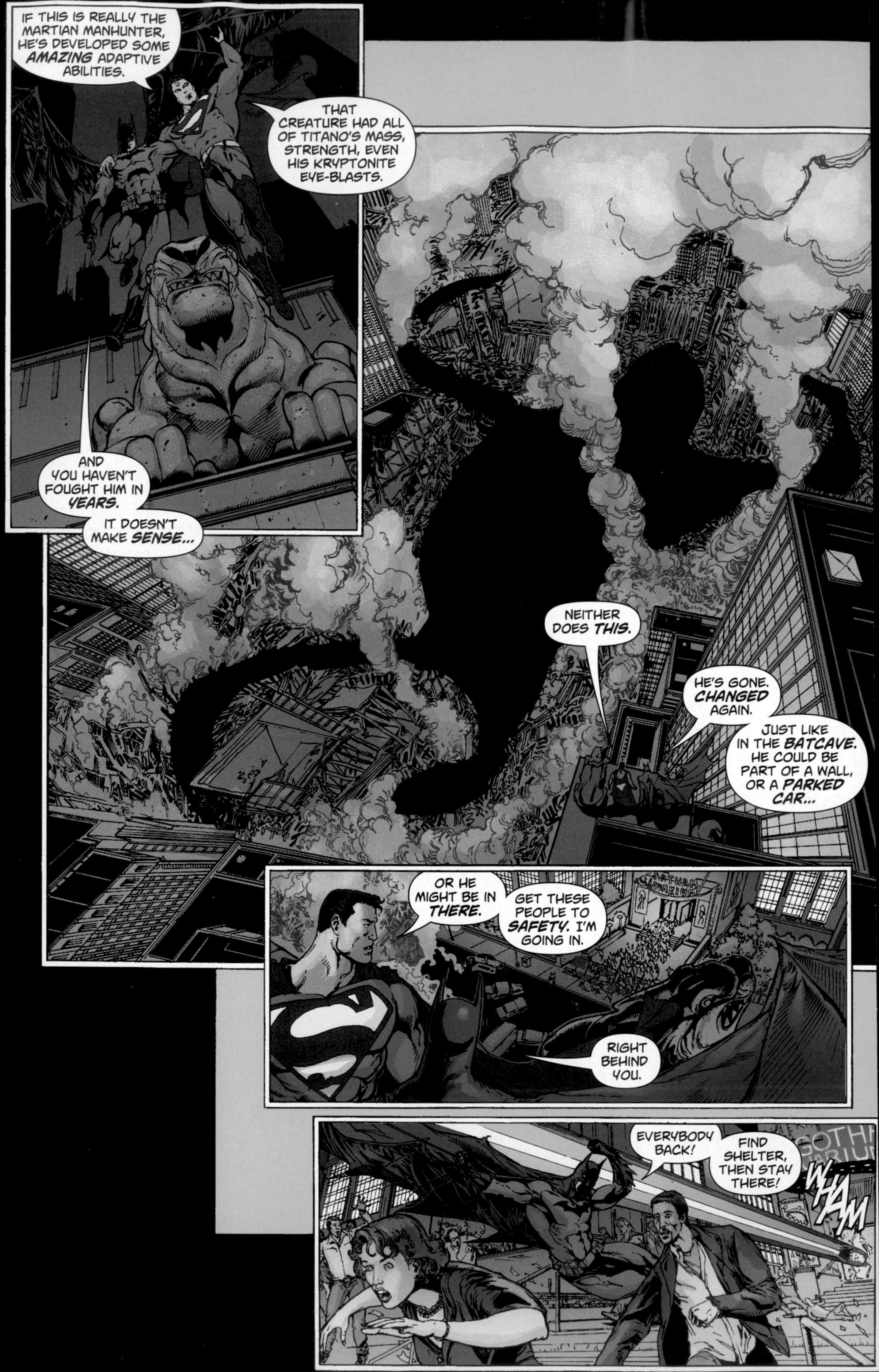
IF THIS IS REALLY THE MARTIAN MANHUNTER, HE'S DEVELOPED SOME AMAZING ADAPTIVE ABILITIES.
THAT CREATURE HAD ALL OF TITANO'S MASS, STRENGTH, EVEN HIS KRYPTONITE EYE-BLASTS.
AND YOU HAVEN'T FOUGHT HIM IN YEARS.
IT DOESN'T MAKE SENSE...
NEITHER DOES THIS.
HE'S GONE. CHANGED AGAIN.
JUST LIKE IN THE BATCAVE. HE COULD BE PART OF A WALL, OR A PARKED CAR...
OR HE MIGHT BE IN THERE.
GET THESE PEOPLE TO SAFETY. I'M GOING IN.
RIGHT BEHIND YOU.
EVERYBODY BACK!
FIND SHELTER, THEN STAY THERE!
WHAM

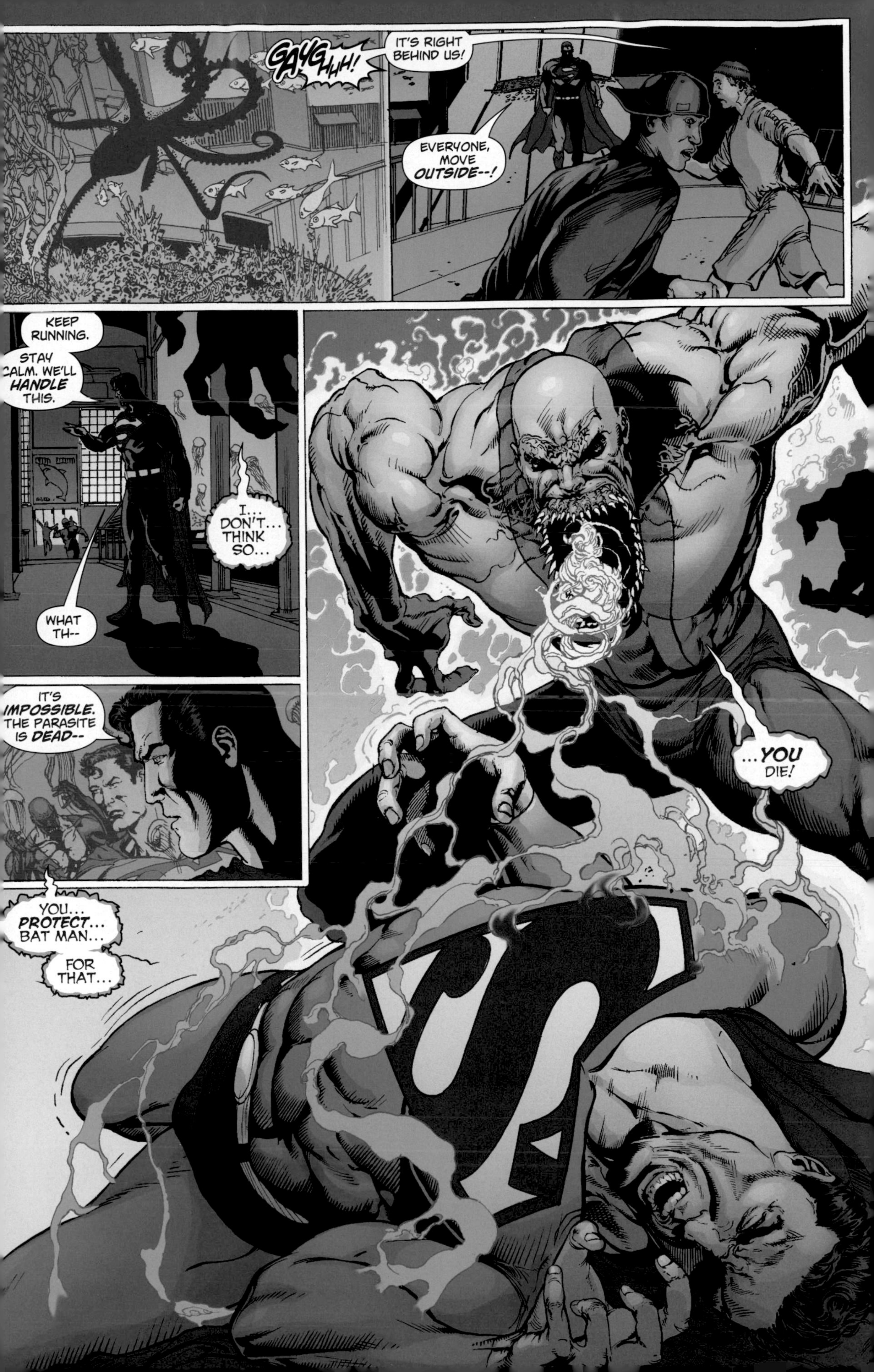
GAYGHHH!
IT'S RIGHT BEHIND US!
EVERYONE, MOVE OUTSIDE--!
KEEP RUNNING.
STAY CALM. WE'LL HANDLE THIS.
I... DON'T... THINK SO...
WHAT TH--
IT'S IMPOSSIBLE. THE PARASITE IS DEAD--
YOU... PROTECT... BAT MAN...
FOR THAT...
...YOU DIE!

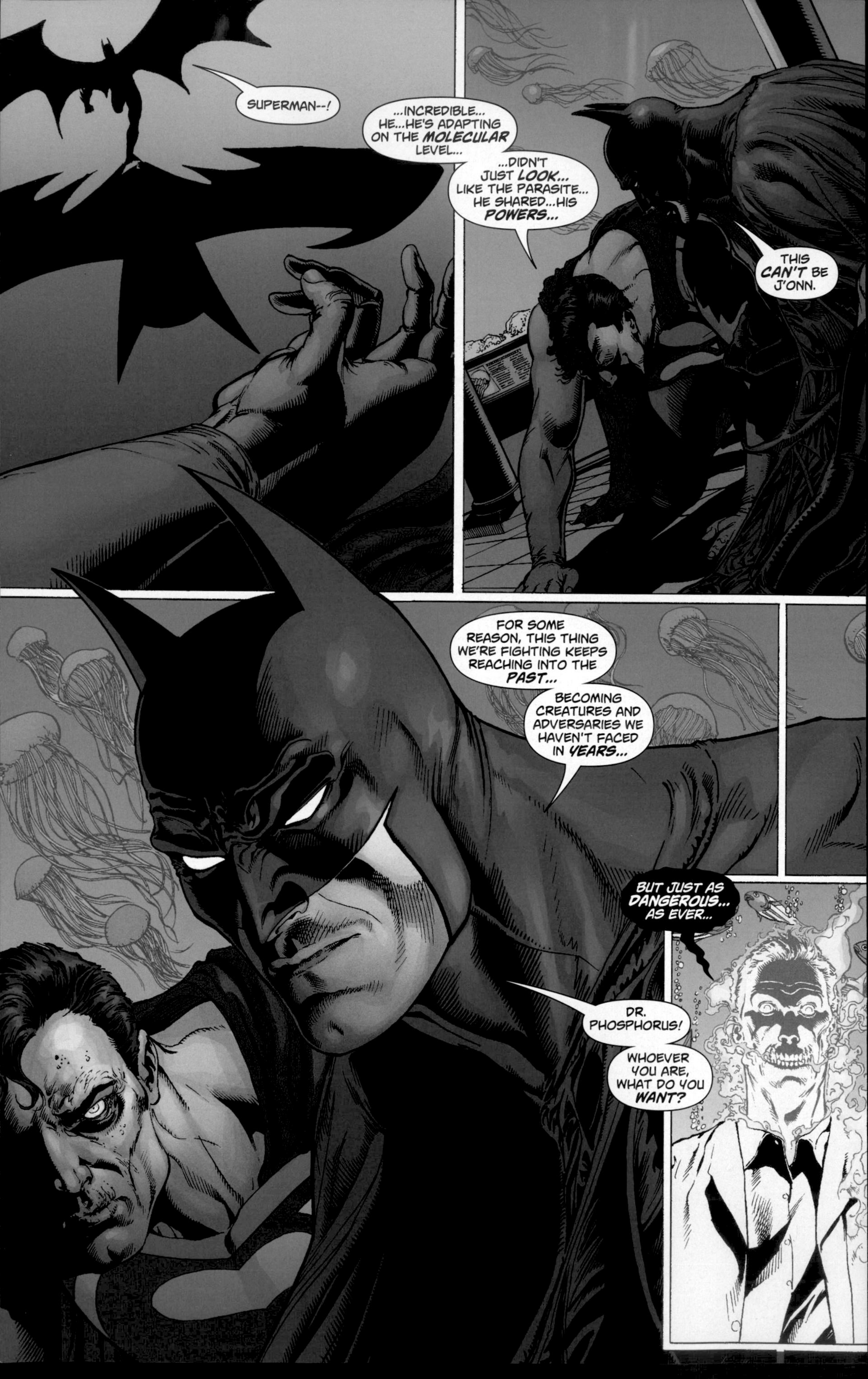
SUPERMAN--!
...INCREDIBLE... HE...HE'S ADAPTING ON THE MOLECULAR LEVEL...
...DIDN'T JUST LOOK... LIKE THE PARASITE... HE SHARED...HIS POWERS...
THIS CAN'T BE J'ONN.
FOR SOME REASON, THIS THING WE'RE FIGHTING KEEPS REACHING INTO THE PAST...
BECOMING CREATURES AND ADVERSARIES WE HAVEN'T FACED IN YEARS...
BUT JUST AS DANGEROUS... AS EVER...
DR. PHOSPHORUS!
WHOEVER YOU ARE, WHAT DO YOU WANT?

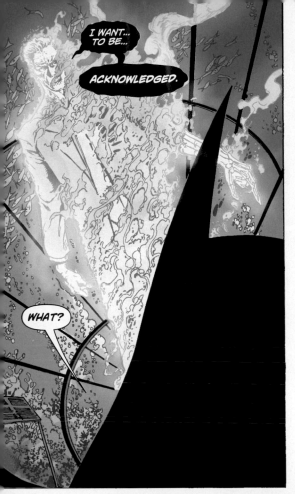

I WANT... TO BE...

ACKNOWLEDGED.

WHAT?

SO LONG... WAS I IGNORED...

...ABUSED...

...THEN FORGOTTEN...

WHICH ONE OF YOU, DAMMIT?

WHO WAS FORGOTTEN?

BATMAN--

HOLD YOUR BREATH.

CTNK

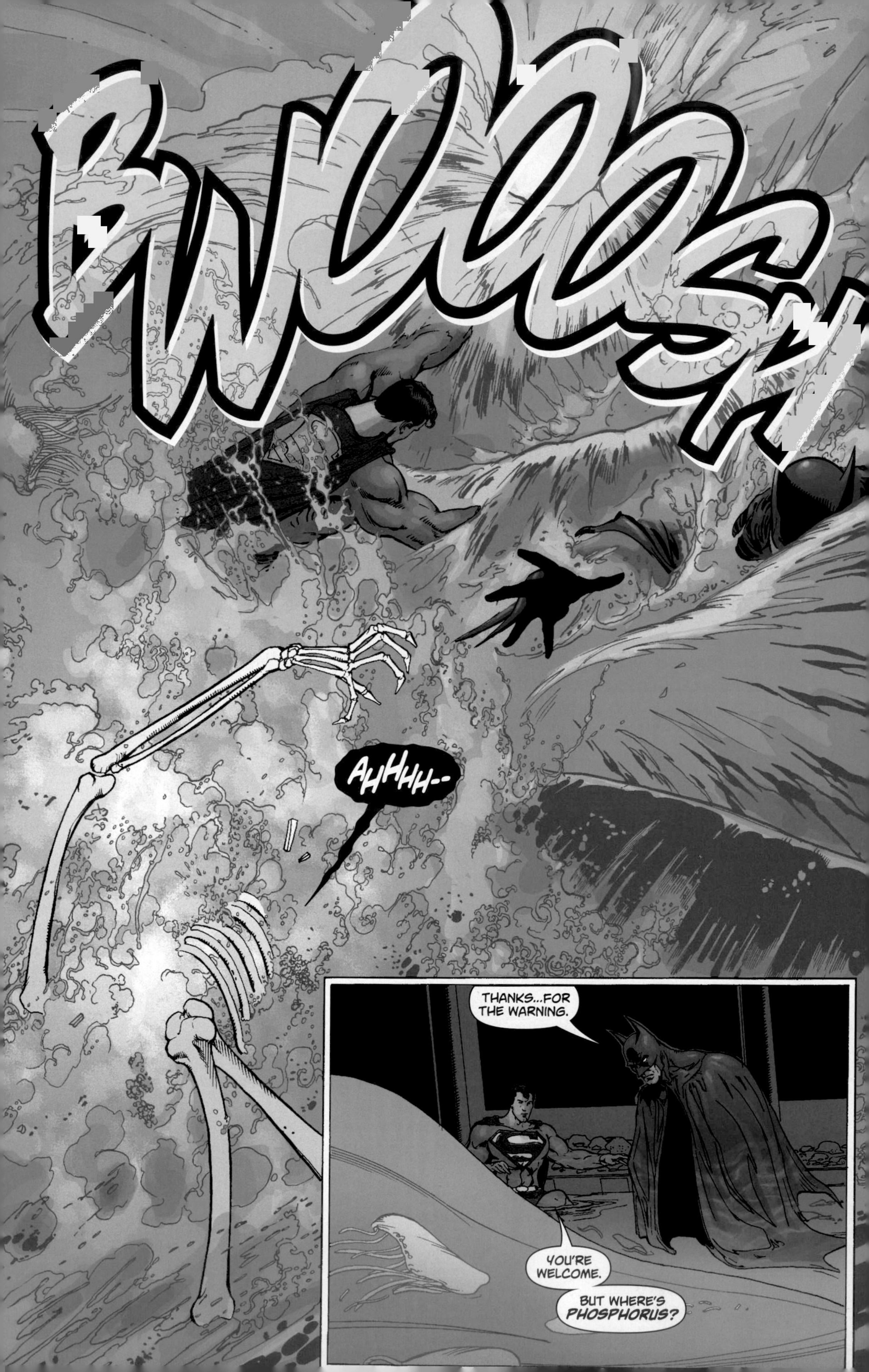
BWOOSH
AHHHH--
THANKS...FOR THE WARNING.
YOU'RE WELCOME.
BUT WHERE'S PHOSPHORUS?

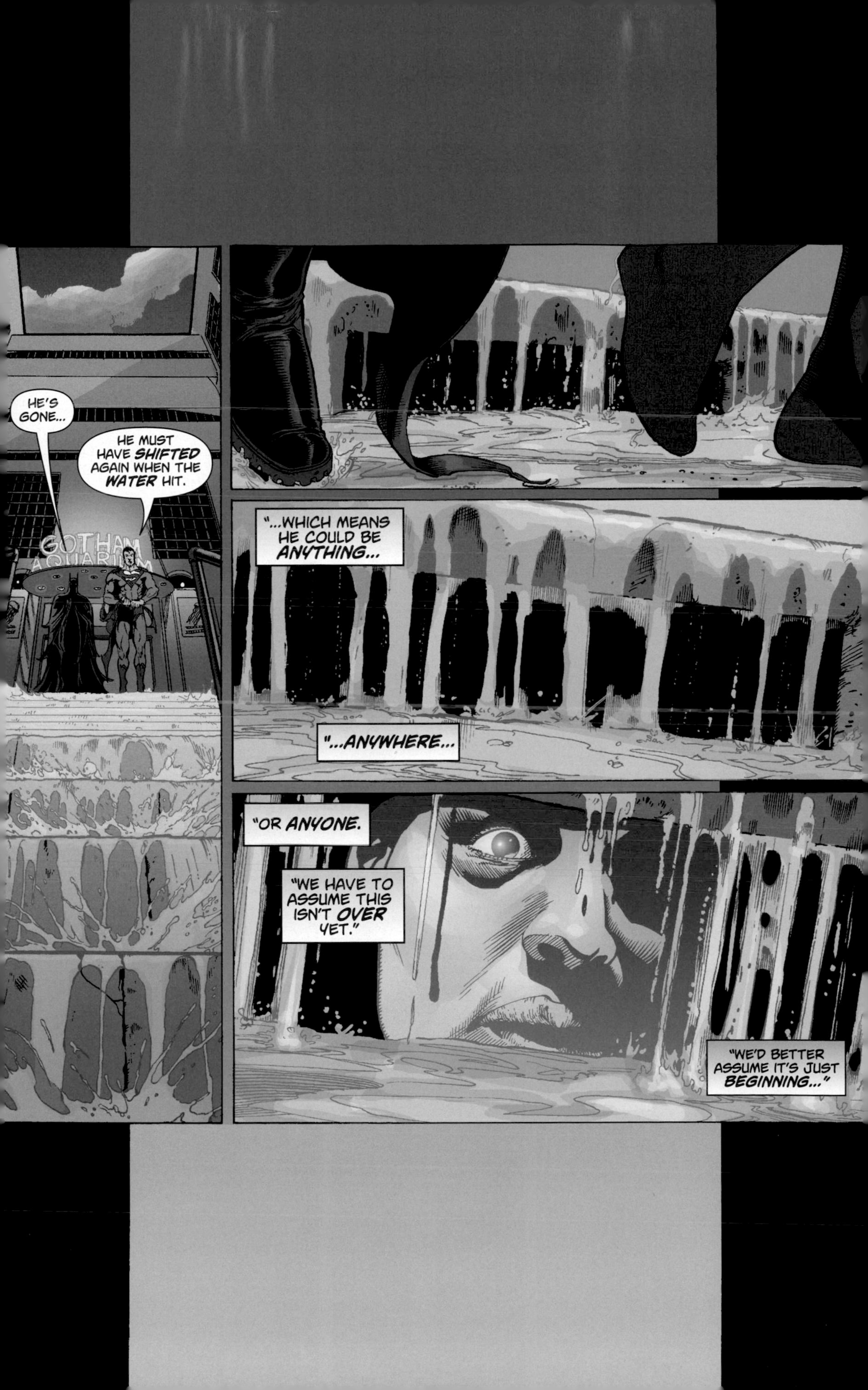
HE'S GONE...
HE MUST HAVE SHIFTED AGAIN WHEN THE WATER HIT.
GOTHAM AQUARIUM
"...WHICH MEANS HE COULD BE ANYTHING...
"...ANYWHERE...
"OR ANYONE.
"WE HAVE TO ASSUME THIS ISN'T OVER YET."
"WE'D BETTER ASSUME IT'S JUST BEGINNING..."

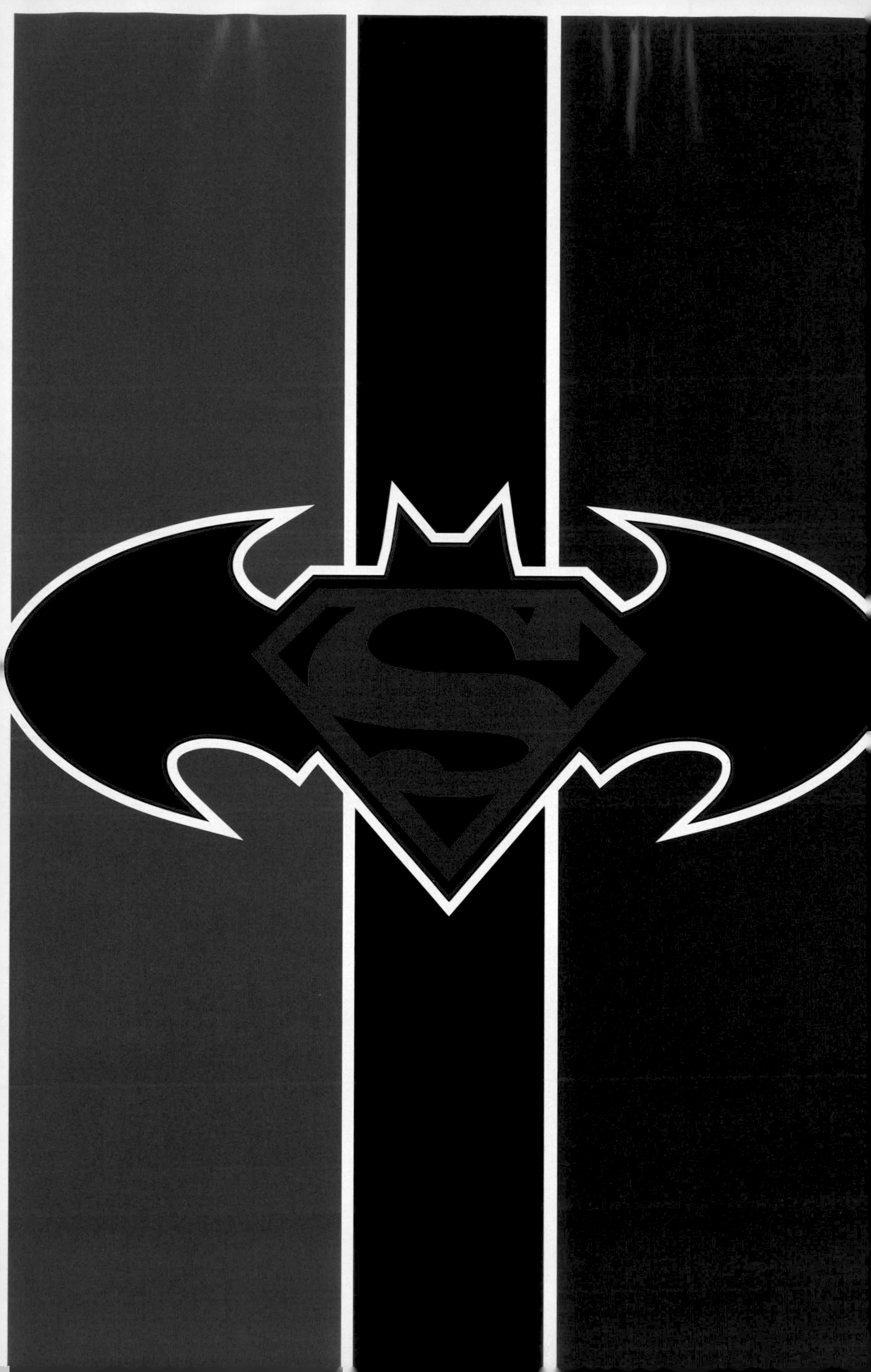

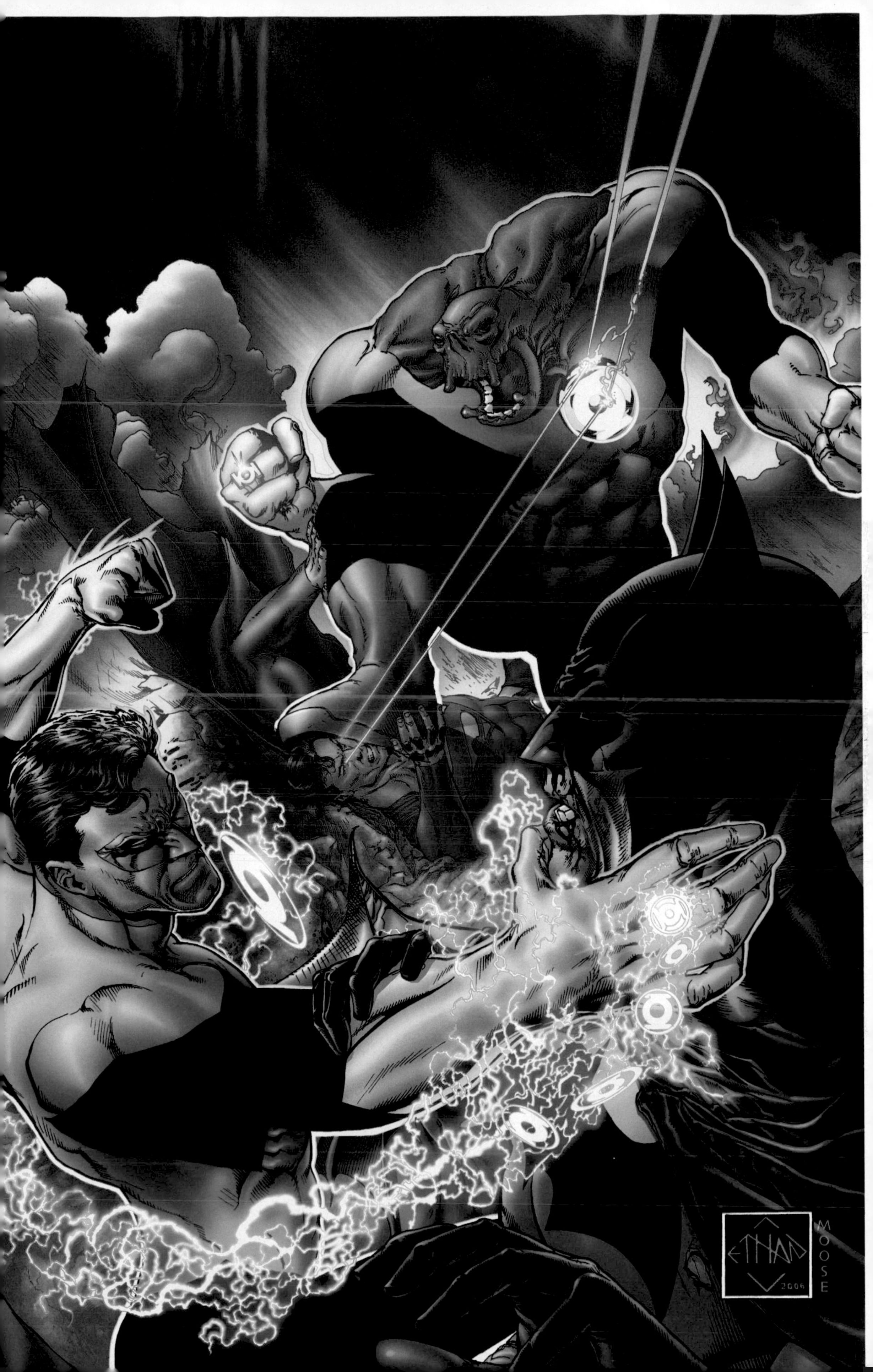
ETHAN
MOOSE
2006

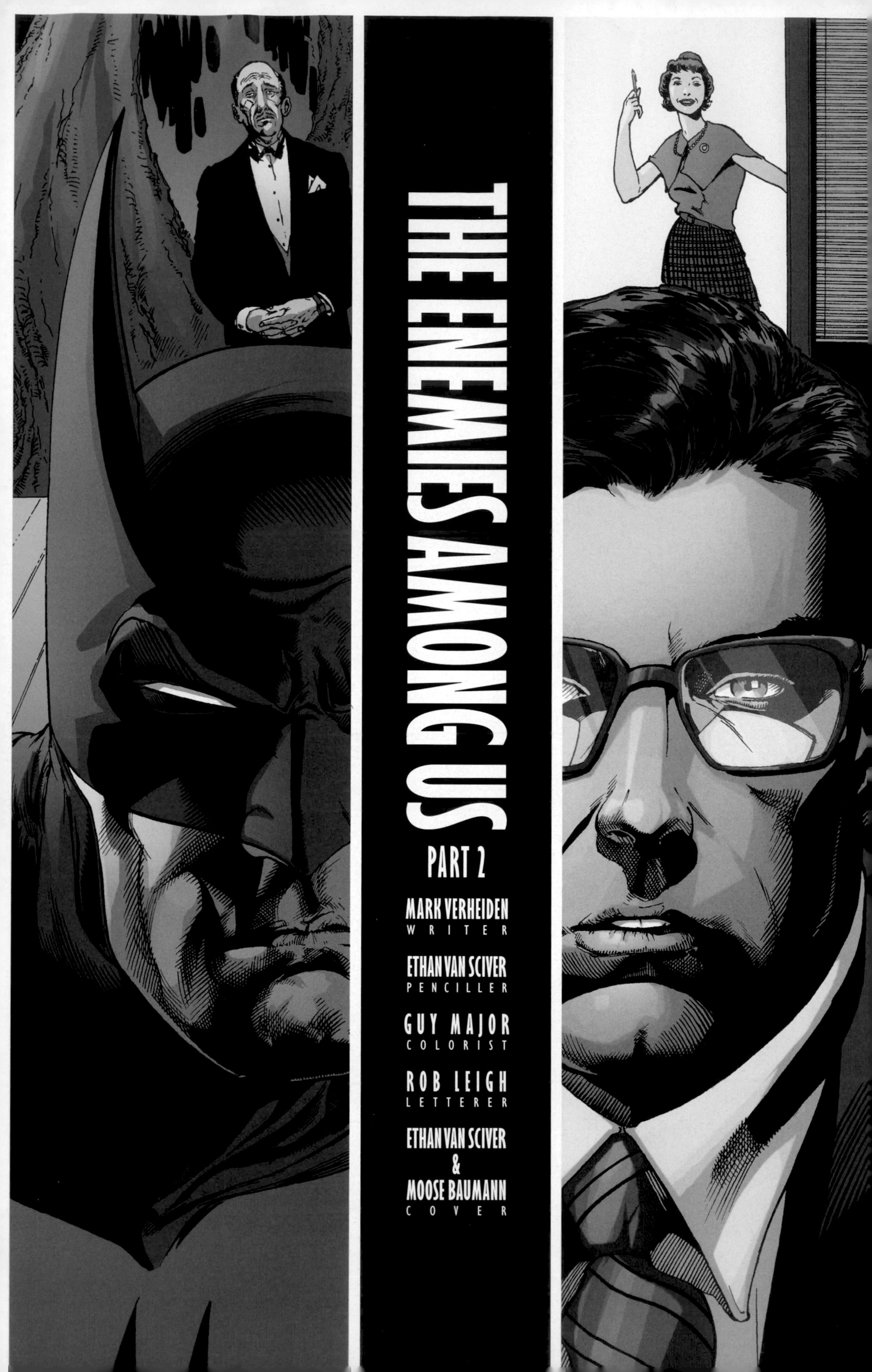
THE ENEMIES AMONG US
PART 2
MARK VERHEIDEN
WRITER
ETHAN VAN SCIVER
PENCILLER
GUY MAJOR
COLORIST
ROB LEIGH
LETTERER
ETHAN VAN SCIVER
&
MOOSE BAUMANN
COVER

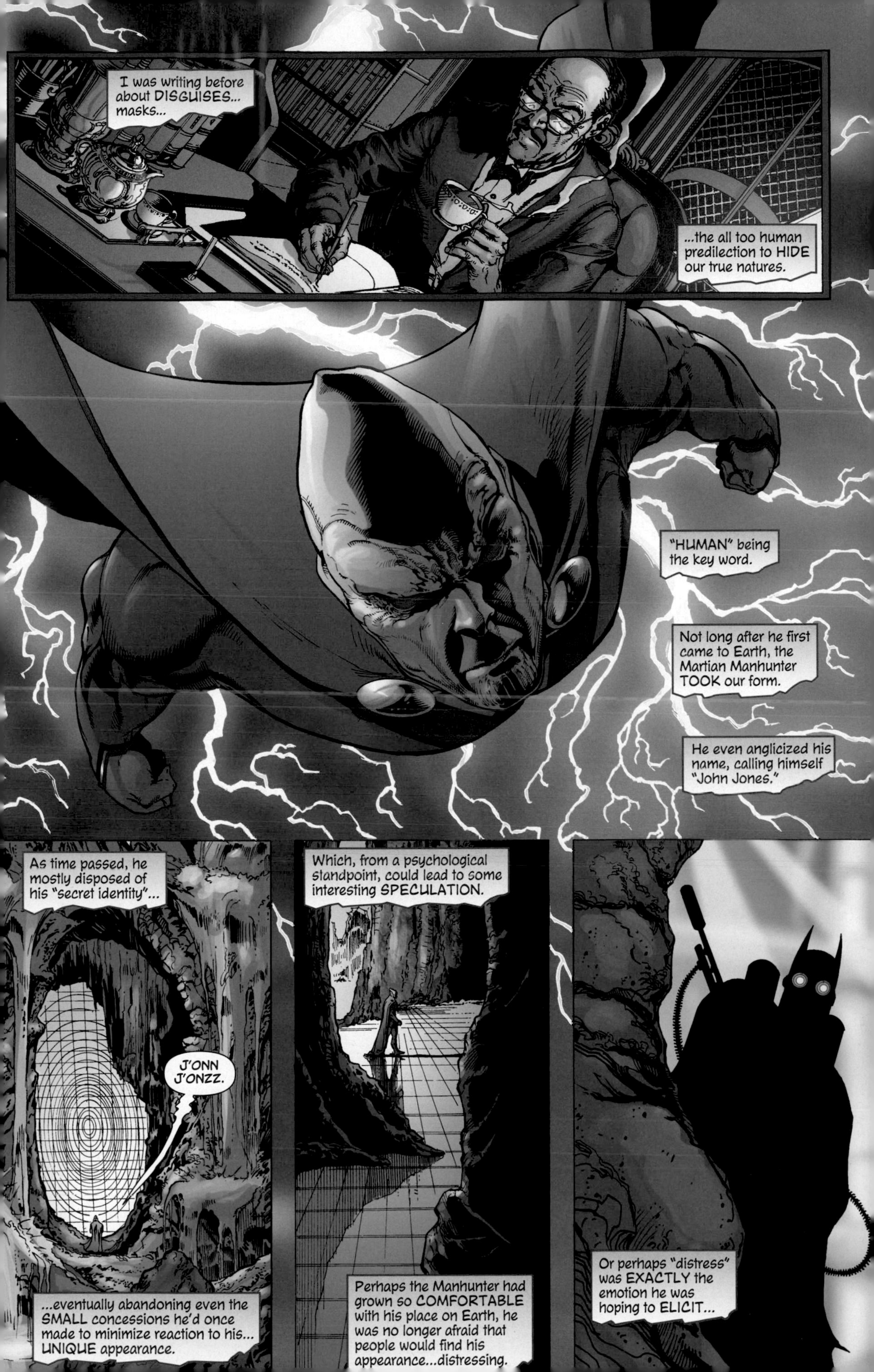
I was writing before about DISGUISES... masks...
...the all too human predilection to HIDE our true natures.
"HUMAN" being the key word.
Not long after he first came to Earth, the Martian Manhunter TOOK our form.
He even anglicized his name, calling himself "John Jones."
As time passed, he mostly disposed of his "secret identity"...
J'ONN J'ONZZ.
...eventually abandoning even the SMALL concessions he'd once made to minimize reaction to his... UNIQUE appearance.
Which, from a psychological standpoint, could lead to some interesting SPECULATION.
Perhaps the Manhunter had grown so COMFORTABLE with his place on Earth, he was no longer afraid that people would find his appearance...distressing.
Or perhaps "distress" was EXACTLY the emotion he was hoping to ELICIT...

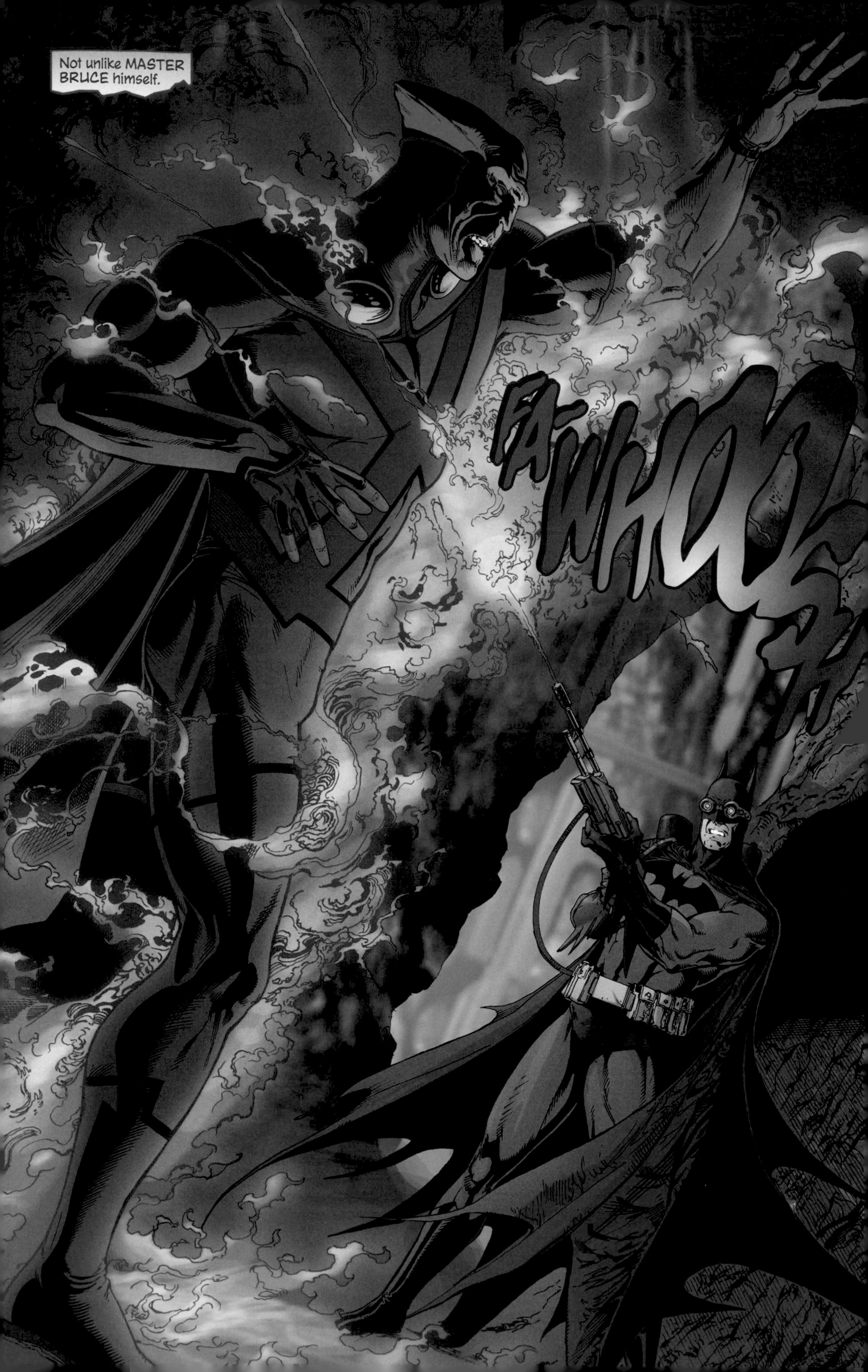
Not unlike MASTER BRUCE himself.
FA-WHOOSH

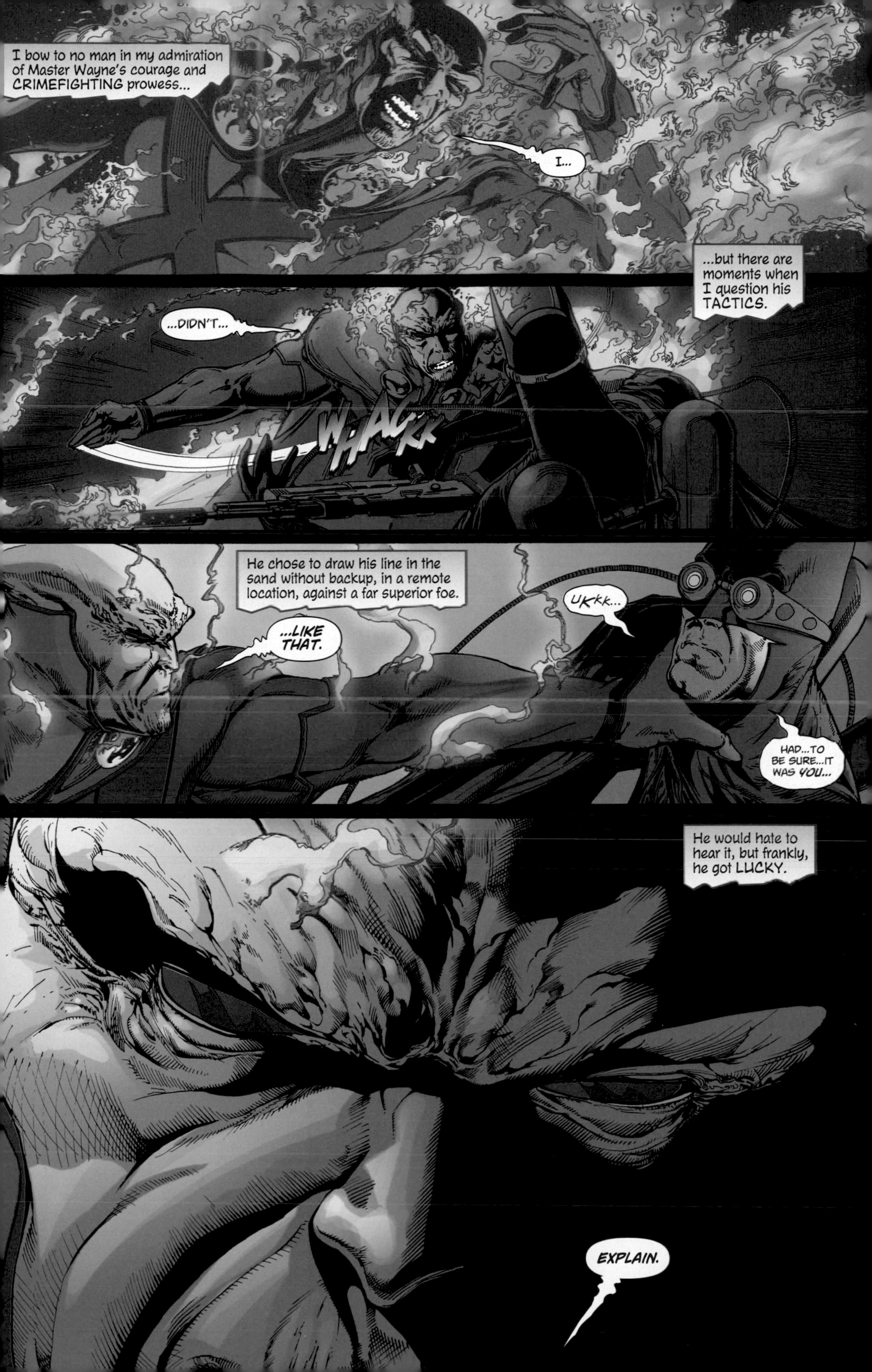

I bow to no man in my admiration of Master Wayne's courage and CRIMEFIGHTING prowess...
I...
...but there are moments when I question his TACTICS.
...DIDN'T...
WHACKK
He chose to draw his line in the sand without backup, in a remote location, against a far superior foe.
UKKK...
...LIKE THAT.
HAD...TO BE SURE...IT WAS YOU...
He would hate to hear it, but frankly, he got LUCKY.
EXPLAIN.

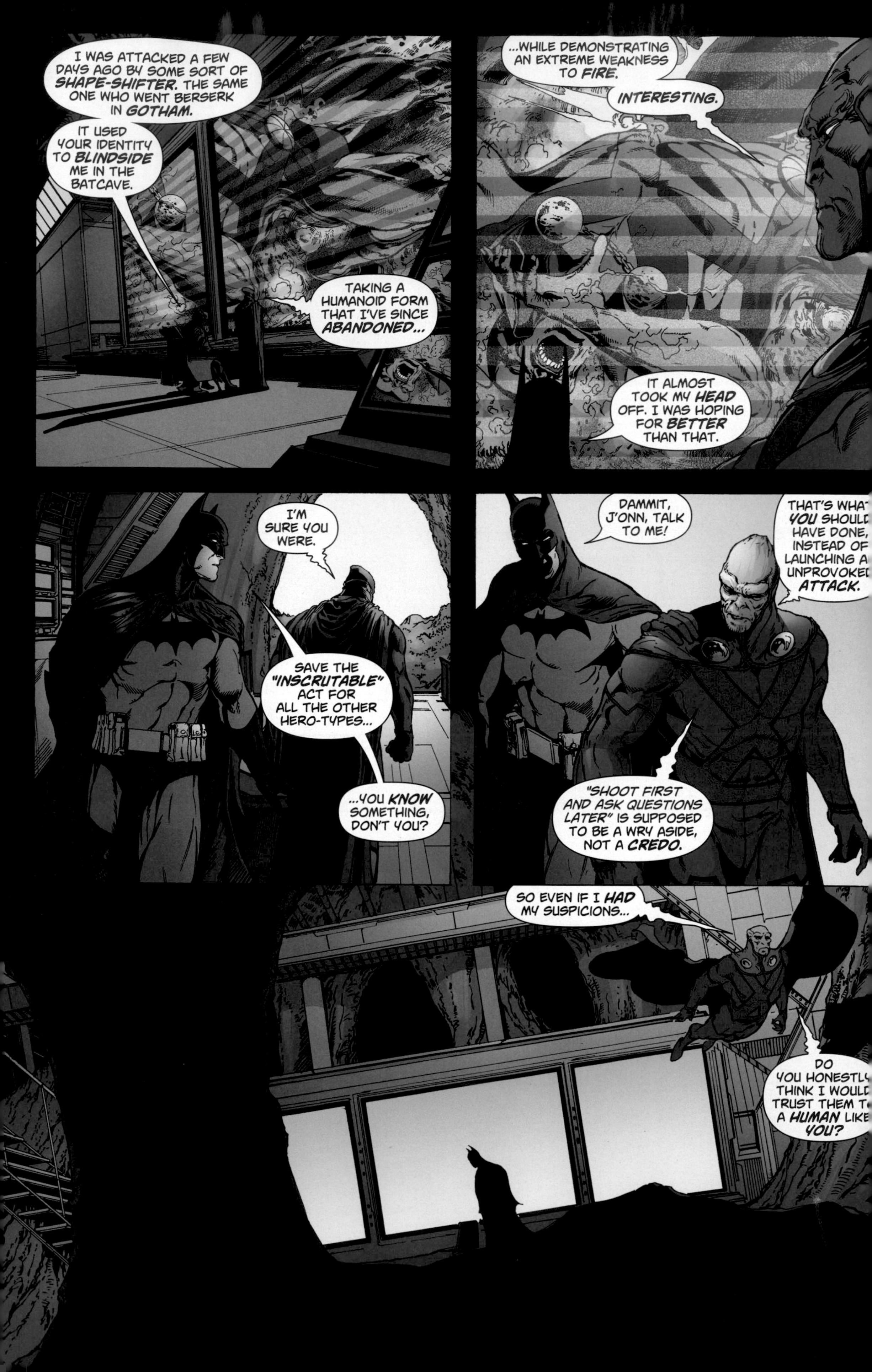
I WAS ATTACKED A FEW DAYS AGO BY SOME SORT OF SHAPE-SHIFTER. THE SAME ONE WHO WENT BERSERK IN GOTHAM.
IT USED YOUR IDENTITY TO BLINDSIDE ME IN THE BATCAVE.
TAKING A HUMANOID FORM THAT I'VE SINCE ABANDONED...
...WHILE DEMONSTRATING AN EXTREME WEAKNESS TO FIRE.
INTERESTING.
IT ALMOST TOOK MY HEAD OFF. I WAS HOPING FOR BETTER THAN THAT.
I'M SURE YOU WERE.
SAVE THE "INSCRUTABLE" ACT FOR ALL THE OTHER HERO-TYPES...
...YOU KNOW SOMETHING, DON'T YOU?
DAMMIT, J'ONN, TALK TO ME!
THAT'S WHAT YOU SHOULD HAVE DONE, INSTEAD OF LAUNCHING AN UNPROVOKED ATTACK.
"SHOOT FIRST AND ASK QUESTIONS LATER" IS SUPPOSED TO BE A WRY ASIDE, NOT A CREDO.
SO EVEN IF I HAD MY SUSPICIONS...
DO YOU HONESTLY THINK I WOULD TRUST THEM TO A HUMAN LIKE YOU?

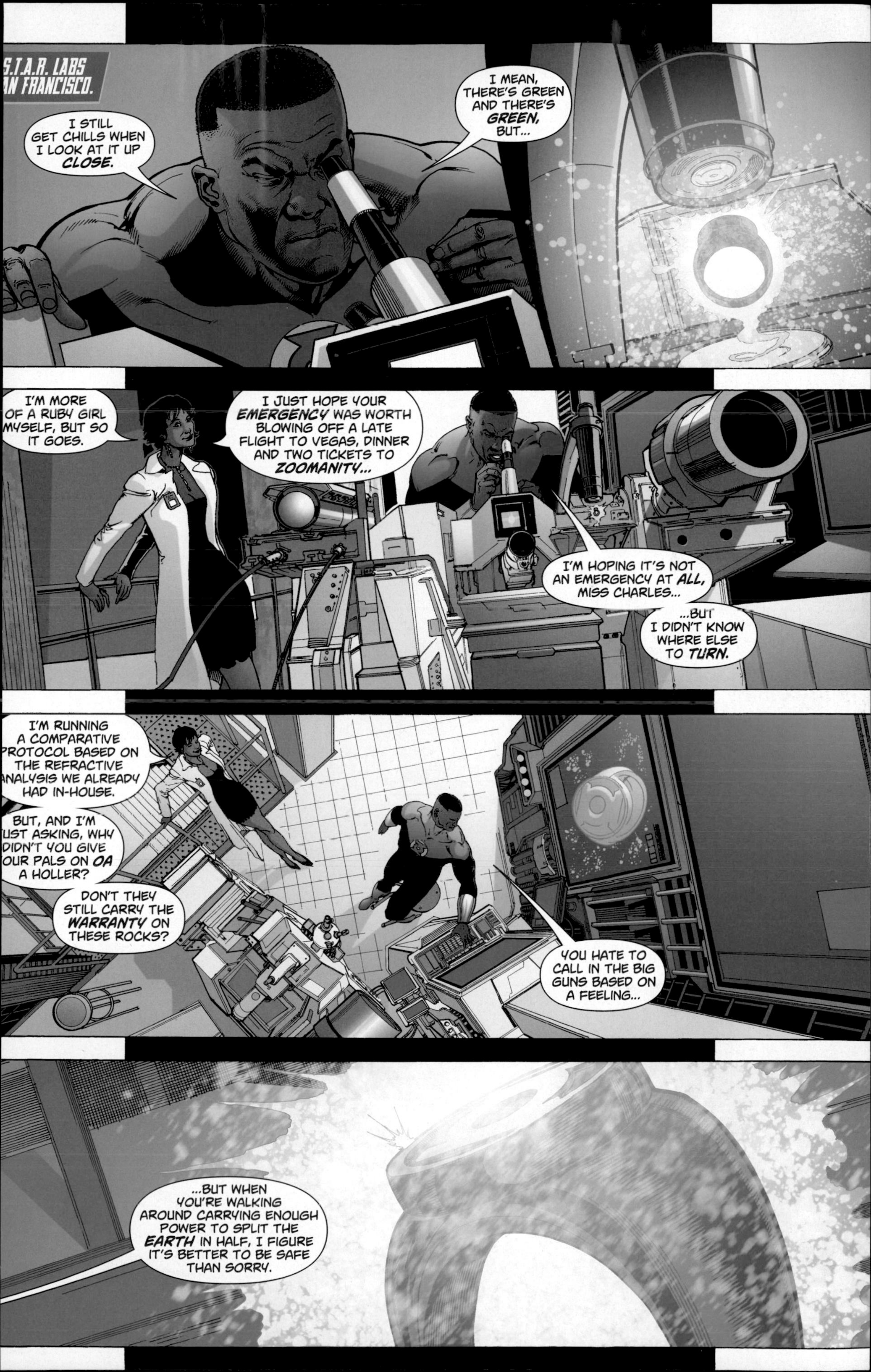
S.T.A.R. LABS
AN FRANCISCO.
I STILL GET CHILLS WHEN I LOOK AT IT UP CLOSE.
I MEAN, THERE'S GREEN AND THERE'S GREEN, BUT...
I'M MORE OF A RUBY GIRL MYSELF, BUT SO IT GOES.
I JUST HOPE YOUR EMERGENCY WAS WORTH BLOWING OFF A LATE FLIGHT TO VEGAS, DINNER AND TWO TICKETS TO ZOOMANITY...
I'M HOPING IT'S NOT AN EMERGENCY AT ALL, MISS CHARLES...
...BUT I DIDN'T KNOW WHERE ELSE TO TURN.
I'M RUNNING A COMPARATIVE PROTOCOL BASED ON THE REFRACTIVE ANALYSIS WE ALREADY HAD IN-HOUSE.
BUT, AND I'M JUST ASKING, WHY DIDN'T YOU GIVE YOUR PALS ON OA A HOLLER?
DON'T THEY STILL CARRY THE WARRANTY ON THESE ROCKS?
YOU HATE TO CALL IN THE BIG GUNS BASED ON A FEELING...
...BUT WHEN YOU'RE WALKING AROUND CARRYING ENOUGH POWER TO SPLIT THE EARTH IN HALF, I FIGURE IT'S BETTER TO BE SAFE THAN SORRY.

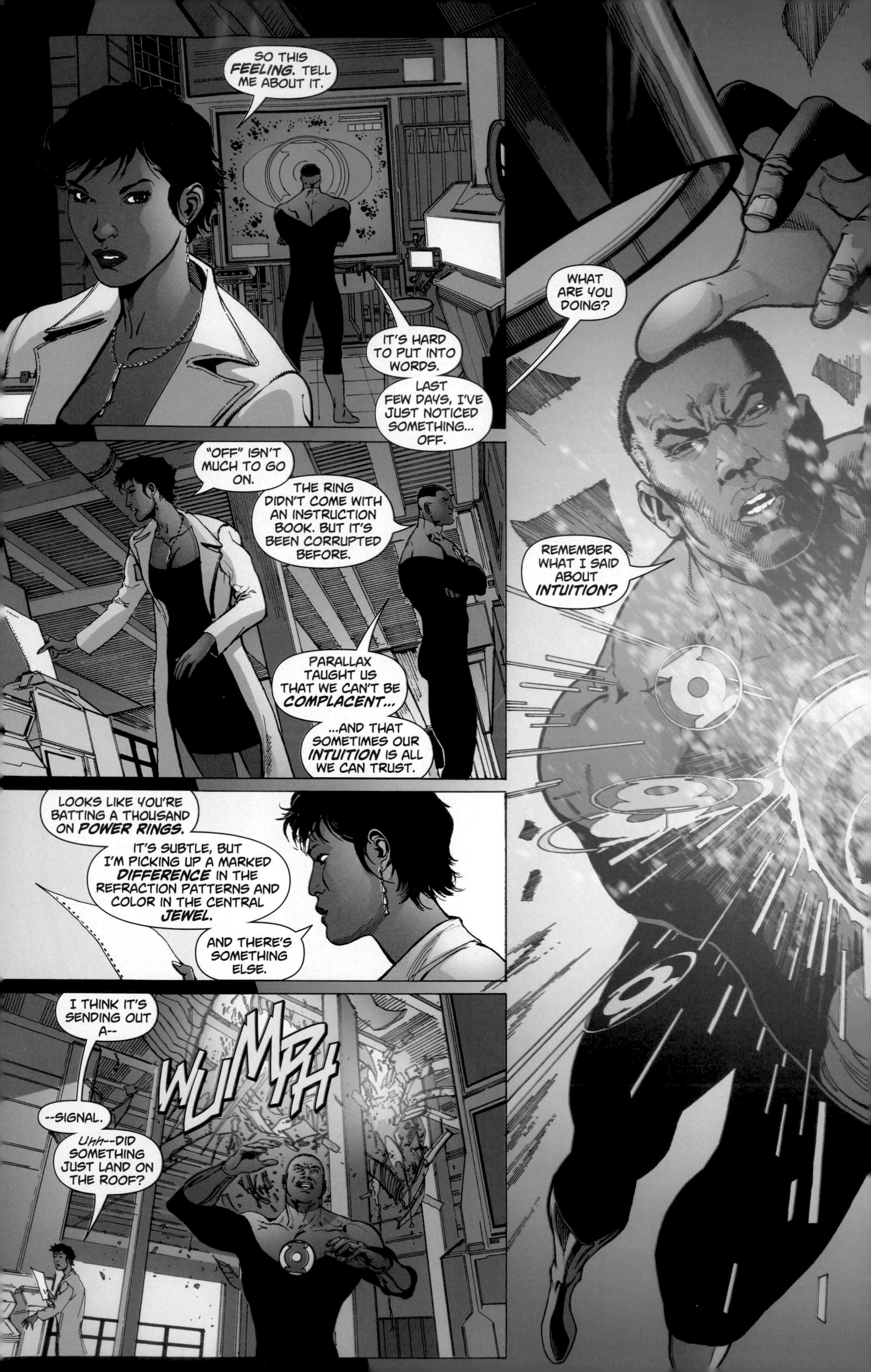

SO THIS FEELING. TELL ME ABOUT IT.
IT'S HARD TO PUT INTO WORDS.
LAST FEW DAYS, I'VE JUST NOTICED SOMETHING... OFF.
"OFF" ISN'T MUCH TO GO ON.
THE RING DIDN'T COME WITH AN INSTRUCTION BOOK. BUT IT'S BEEN CORRUPTED BEFORE.
PARALLAX TAUGHT US THAT WE CAN'T BE COMPLACENT...
...AND THAT SOMETIMES OUR INTUITION IS ALL WE CAN TRUST.
LOOKS LIKE YOU'RE BATTING A THOUSAND ON POWER RINGS.
IT'S SUBTLE, BUT I'M PICKING UP A MARKED DIFFERENCE IN THE REFRACTION PATTERNS AND COLOR IN THE CENTRAL JEWEL.
AND THERE'S SOMETHING ELSE.
I THINK IT'S SENDING OUT A--
WUMPH
--SIGNAL.
Uhh--DID SOMETHING JUST LAND ON THE ROOF?
WHAT ARE YOU DOING?
REMEMBER WHAT I SAID ABOUT INTUITION?

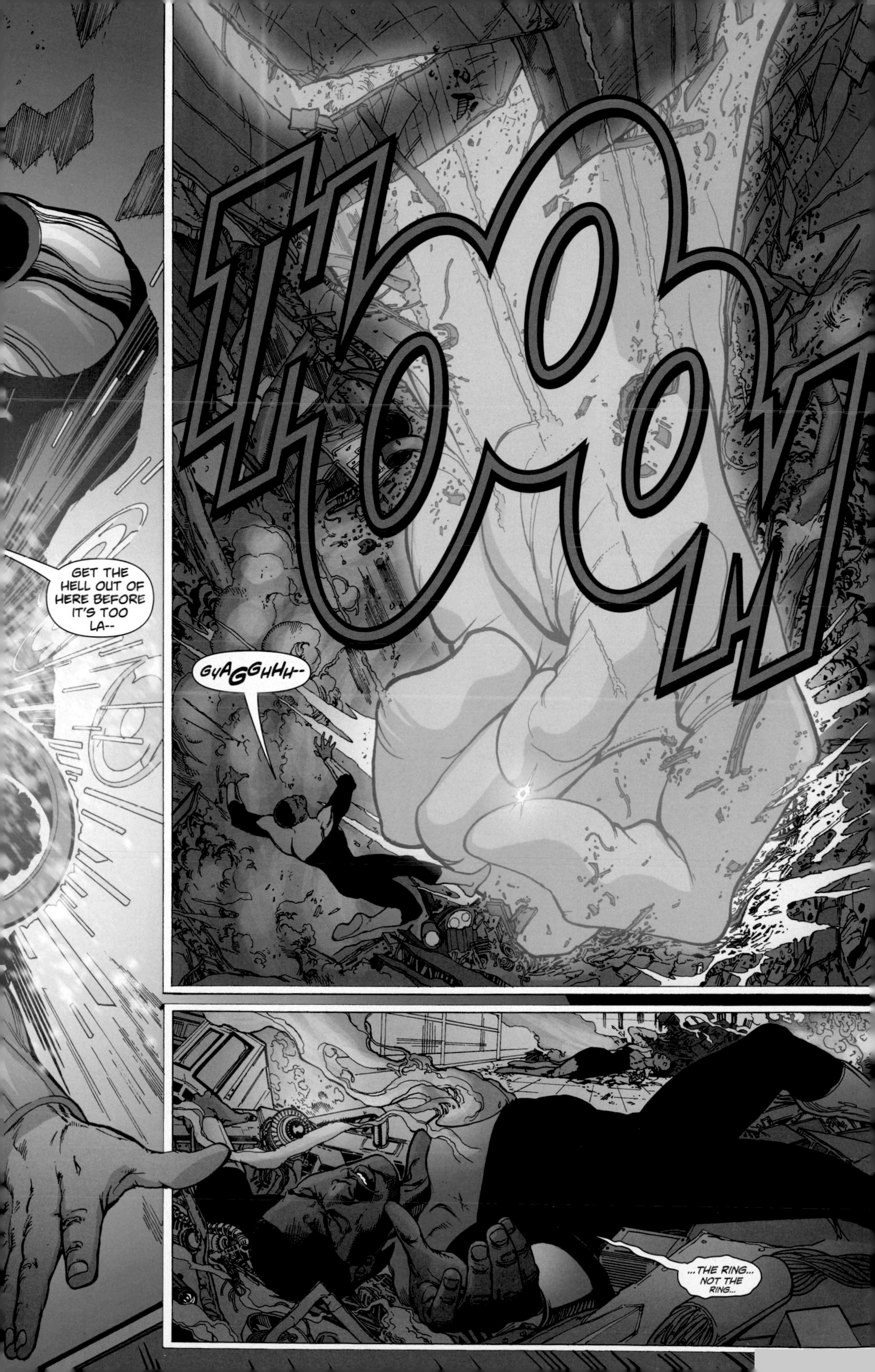

THOOM
GET THE HELL OUT OF HERE BEFORE IT'S TOO LA--
GYAGGHHH--
...THE RING... NOT THE RING...

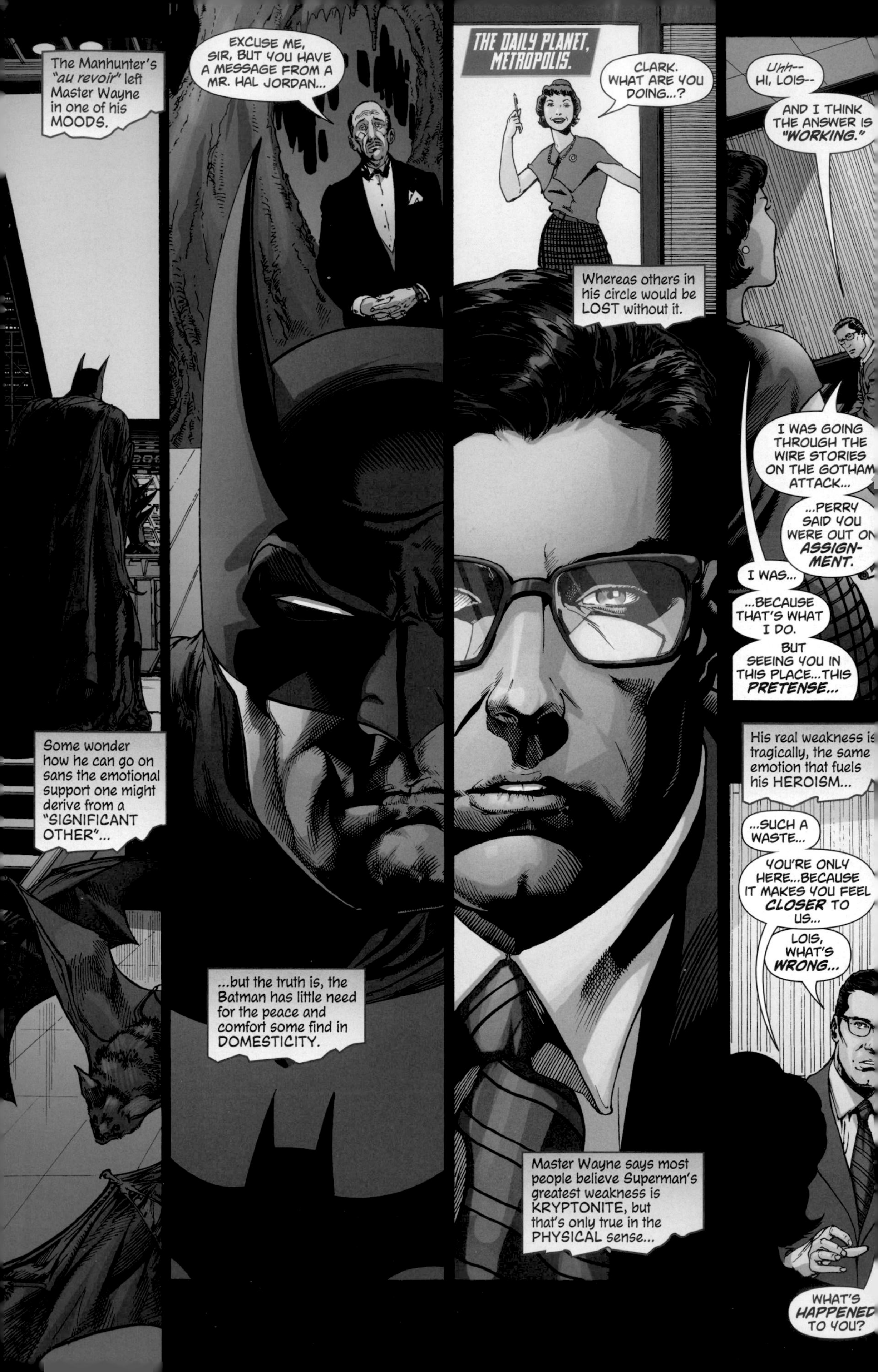

The Manhunter's "au revoir" left Master Wayne in one of his MOODS.
EXCUSE ME, SIR, BUT YOU HAVE A MESSAGE FROM A MR. HAL JORDAN...
THE DAILY PLANET, METROPOLIS.
CLARK. WHAT ARE YOU DOING...?
Uhh-- HI, LOIS--
AND I THINK THE ANSWER IS "WORKING."
Whereas others in his circle would be LOST without it.
I WAS GOING THROUGH THE WIRE STORIES ON THE GOTHAM ATTACK...
...PERRY SAID YOU WERE OUT ON ASSIGN-MENT.
I WAS...
...BECAUSE THAT'S WHAT I DO.
BUT SEEING YOU IN THIS PLACE...THIS PRETENSE...
Some wonder how he can go on sans the emotional support one might derive from a "SIGNIFICANT OTHER"...
His real weakness is tragically, the same emotion that fuels his HEROISM...
...SUCH A WASTE...
YOU'RE ONLY HERE...BECAUSE IT MAKES YOU FEEL CLOSER TO US...
LOIS, WHAT'S WRONG...
...but the truth is, the Batman has little need for the peace and comfort some find in DOMESTICITY.
Master Wayne says most people believe Superman's greatest weakness is KRYPTONITE, but that's only true in the PHYSICAL sense...
WHAT'S HAPPENED TO YOU?

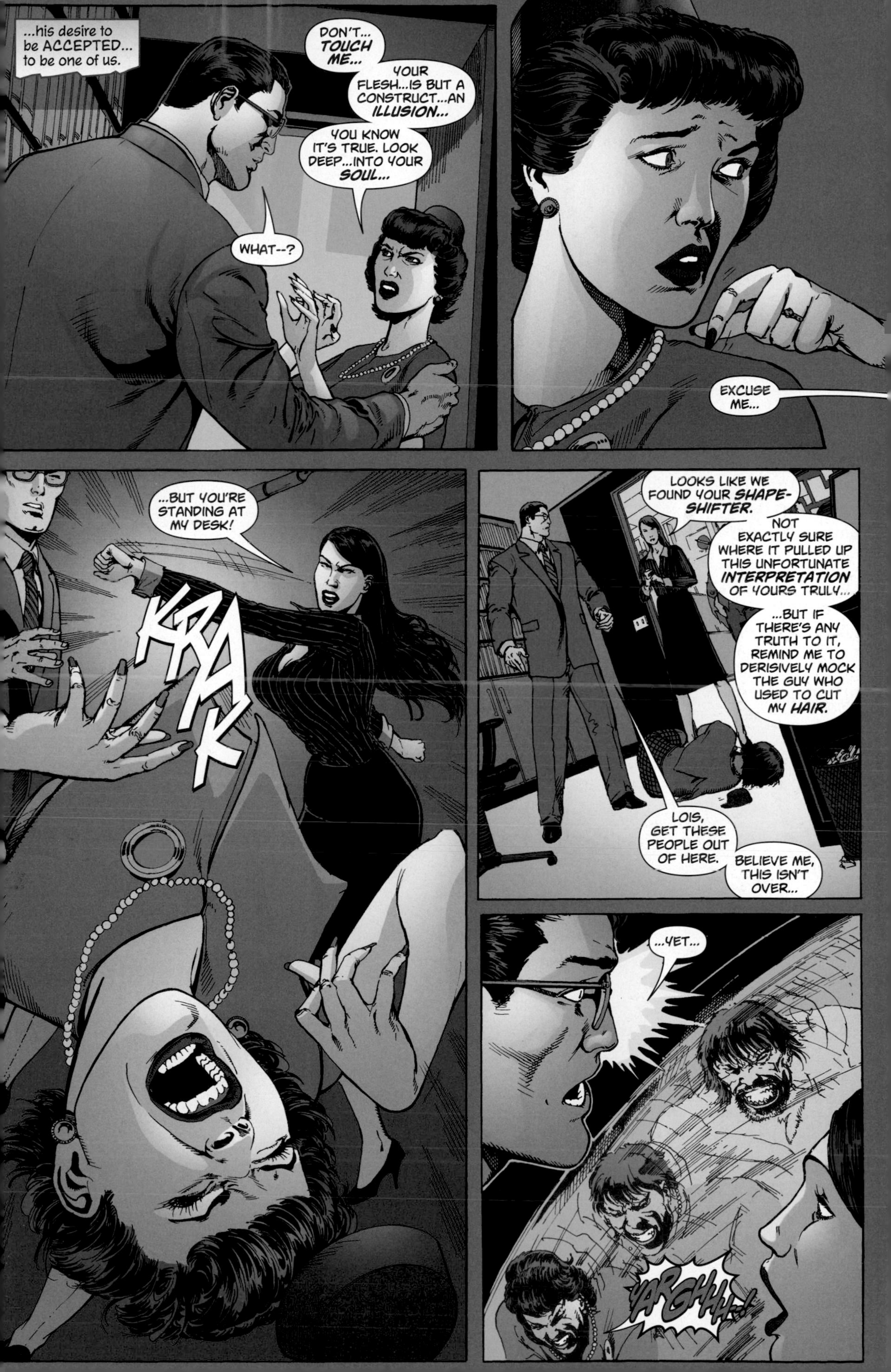
...his desire to be ACCEPTED... to be one of us.
DON'T... TOUCH ME...
YOUR FLESH...IS BUT A CONSTRUCT...AN ILLUSION...
YOU KNOW IT'S TRUE. LOOK DEEP...INTO YOUR SOUL...
WHAT--?
EXCUSE ME...
...BUT YOU'RE STANDING AT MY DESK!
KRAK
LOOKS LIKE WE FOUND YOUR SHAPE-SHIFTER.
NOT EXACTLY SURE WHERE IT PULLED UP THIS UNFORTUNATE INTERPRETATION OF YOURS TRULY...
...BUT IF THERE'S ANY TRUTH TO IT, REMIND ME TO DERISIVELY MOCK THE GUY WHO USED TO CUT MY HAIR.
LOIS, GET THESE PEOPLE OUT OF HERE.
BELIEVE ME, THIS ISN'T OVER...
...YET...
YARGHHH--!

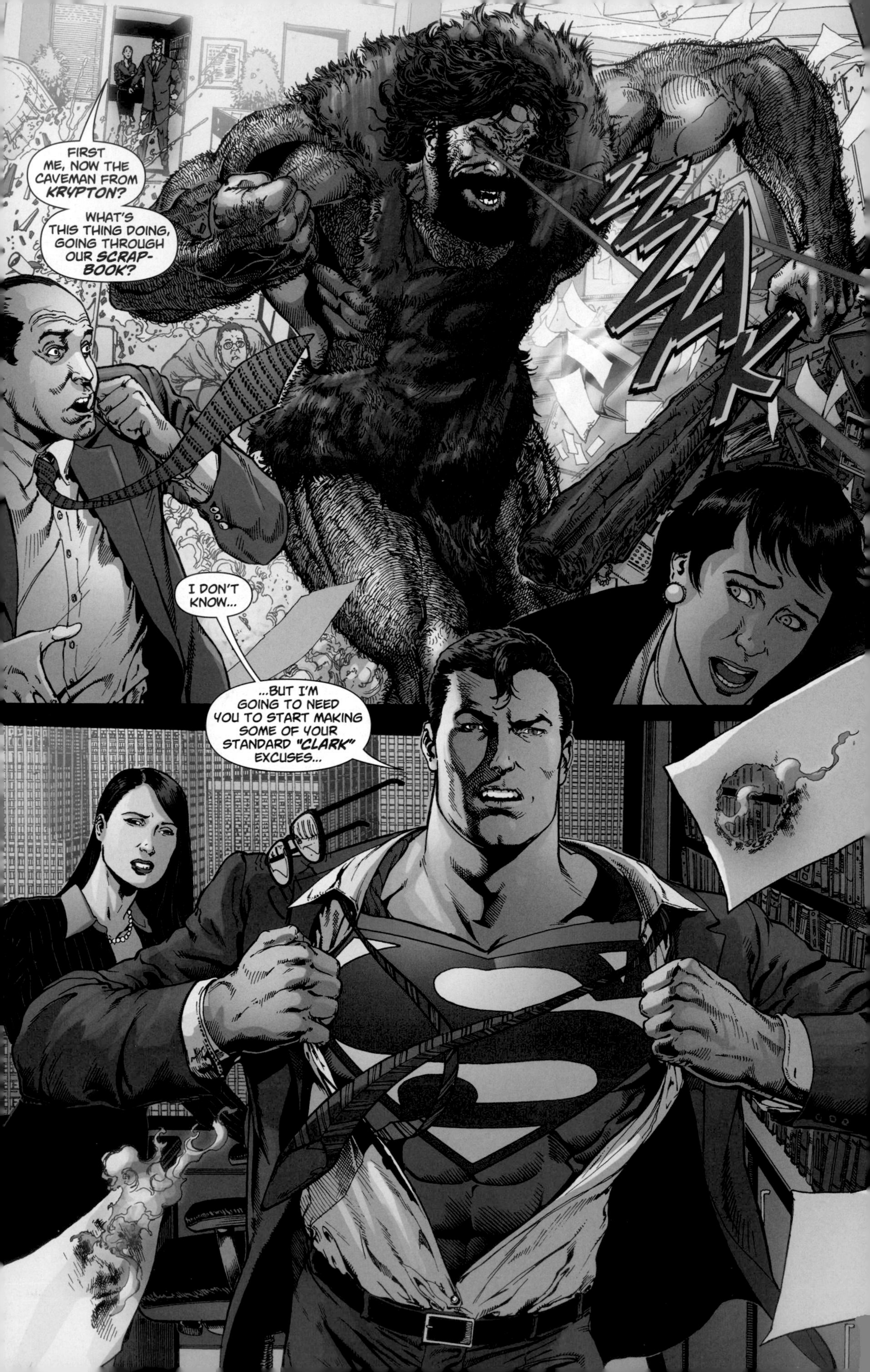
FIRST ME, NOW THE CAVEMAN FROM KRYPTON?
WHAT'S THIS THING DOING, GOING THROUGH OUR SCRAPBOOK?
WAK
I DON'T KNOW...
...BUT I'M GOING TO NEED YOU TO START MAKING SOME OF YOUR STANDARD "CLARK" EXCUSES...

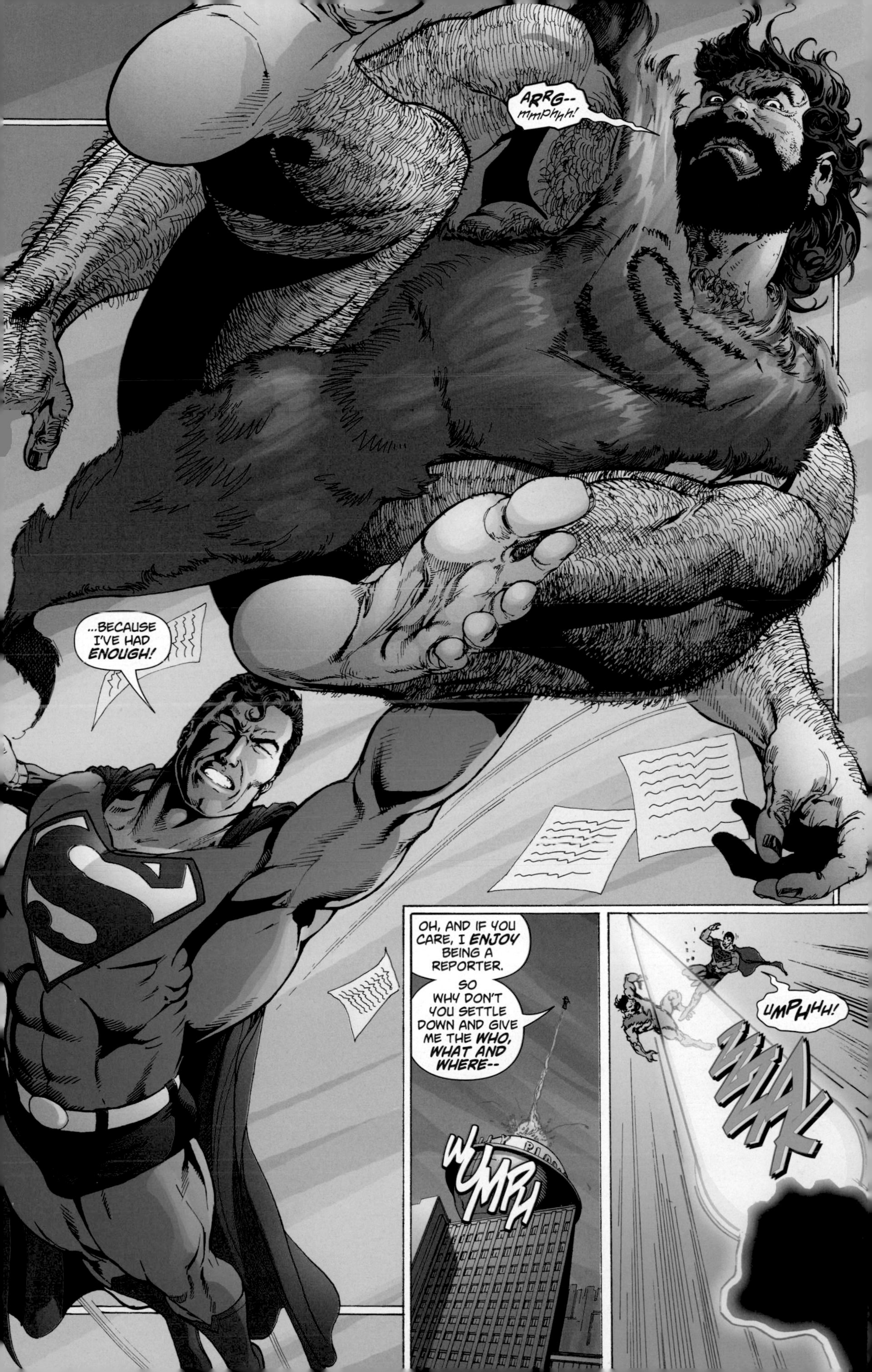
ARRG--
mmphhh!
...BECAUSE I'VE HAD ENOUGH!
OH, AND IF YOU CARE, I ENJOY BEING A REPORTER.
SO WHY DON'T YOU SETTLE DOWN AND GIVE ME THE WHO, WHAT AND WHERE--
WUMPH
UMPHHH!
WHAK

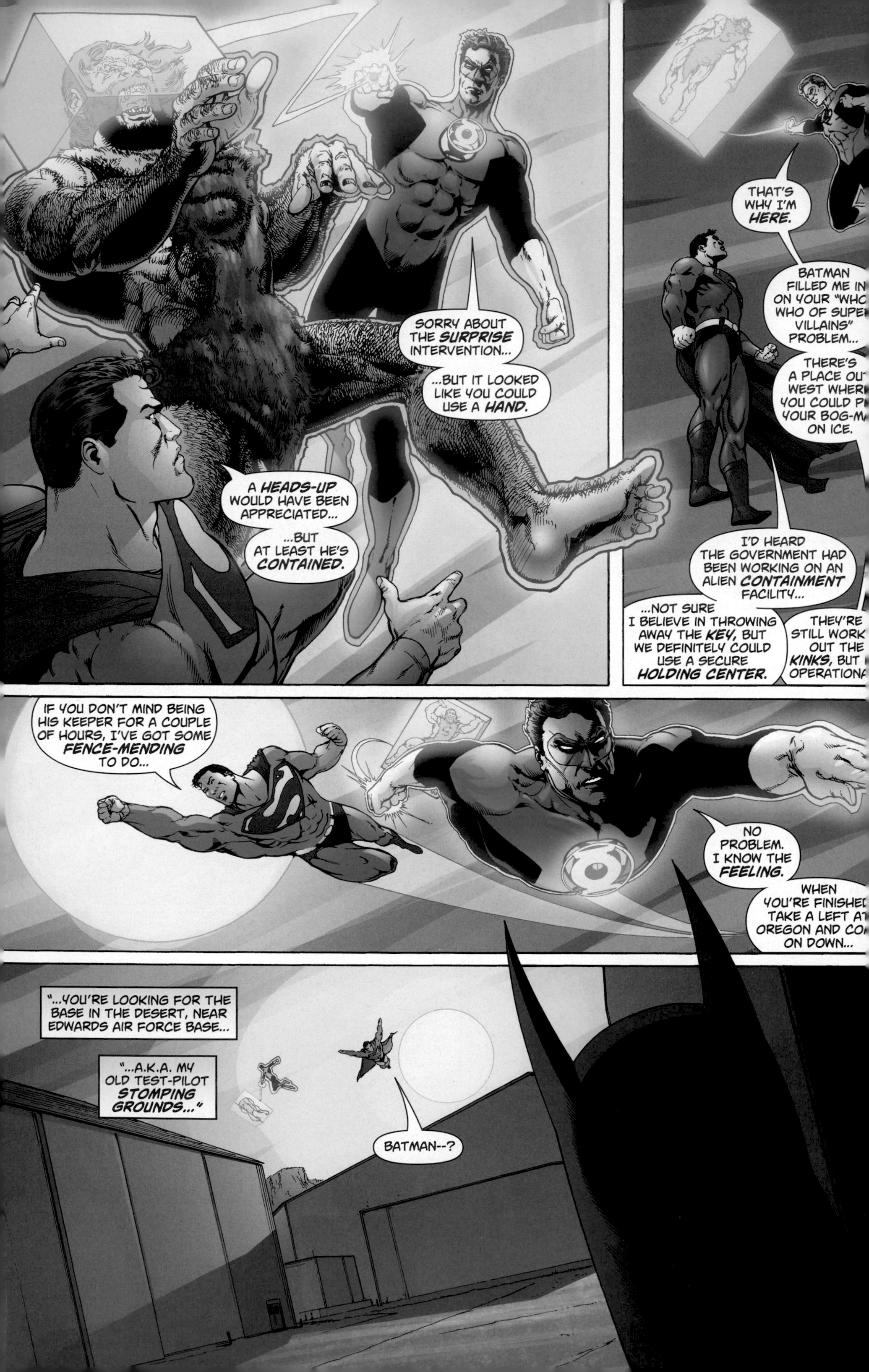
SORRY ABOUT THE SURPRISE INTERVENTION...
...BUT IT LOOKED LIKE YOU COULD USE A HAND.
A HEADS-UP WOULD HAVE BEEN APPRECIATED...
...BUT AT LEAST HE'S CONTAINED.
THAT'S WHY I'M HERE.
BATMAN FILLED ME IN ON YOUR "WHO WHO OF SUPE VILLAINS" PROBLEM...
THERE'S A PLACE OU WEST WHER YOU COULD P YOUR BOG-M ON ICE.
I'D HEARD THE GOVERNMENT HAD BEEN WORKING ON AN ALIEN CONTAINMENT FACILITY...
THEY'RE STILL WORK OUT THE KINKS, BUT OPERATIONA
...NOT SURE I BELIEVE IN THROWING AWAY THE KEY, BUT WE DEFINITELY COULD USE A SECURE HOLDING CENTER.
IF YOU DON'T MIND BEING HIS KEEPER FOR A COUPLE OF HOURS, I'VE GOT SOME FENCE-MENDING TO DO...
NO PROBLEM. I KNOW THE FEELING.
WHEN YOU'RE FINISHED TAKE A LEFT AT OREGON AND CO ON DOWN...
"...YOU'RE LOOKING FOR THE BASE IN THE DESERT, NEAR EDWARDS AIR FORCE BASE...
"...A.K.A. MY OLD TEST-PILOT STOMPING GROUNDS..."
BATMAN--?

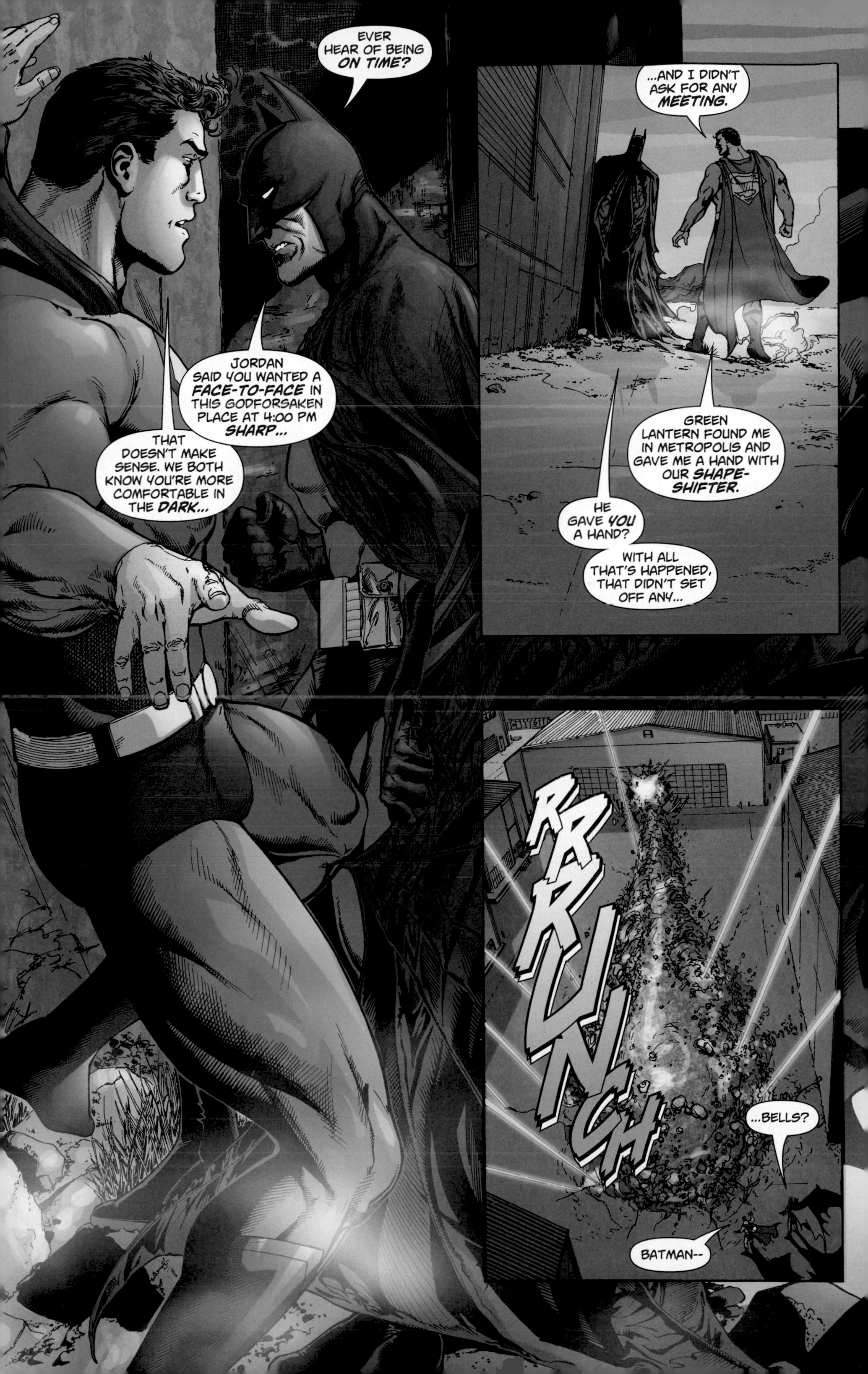
EVER HEAR OF BEING ON TIME?
JORDAN SAID YOU WANTED A FACE-TO-FACE IN THIS GODFORSAKEN PLACE AT 4:00 PM SHARP...
THAT DOESN'T MAKE SENSE. WE BOTH KNOW YOU'RE MORE COMFORTABLE IN THE DARK...
...AND I DIDN'T ASK FOR ANY MEETING.
GREEN LANTERN FOUND ME IN METROPOLIS AND GAVE ME A HAND WITH OUR SHAPE-SHIFTER.
HE GAVE YOU A HAND?
WITH ALL THAT'S HAPPENED, THAT DIDN'T SET OFF ANY...
RRRUNCH
...BELLS?
BATMAN--

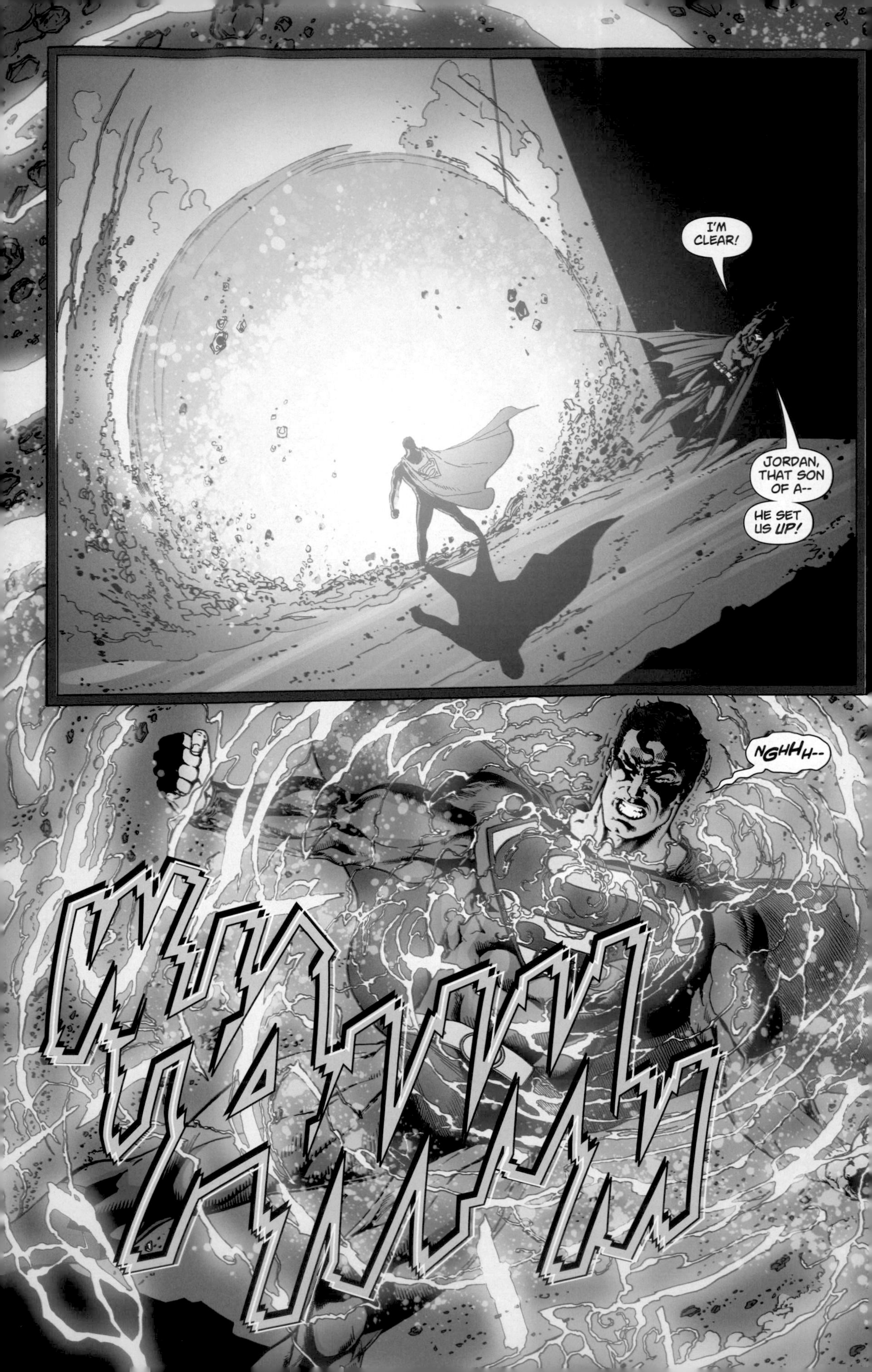
I'M CLEAR!
JORDAN, THAT SON OF A--
HE SET US UP!
NGHHH--

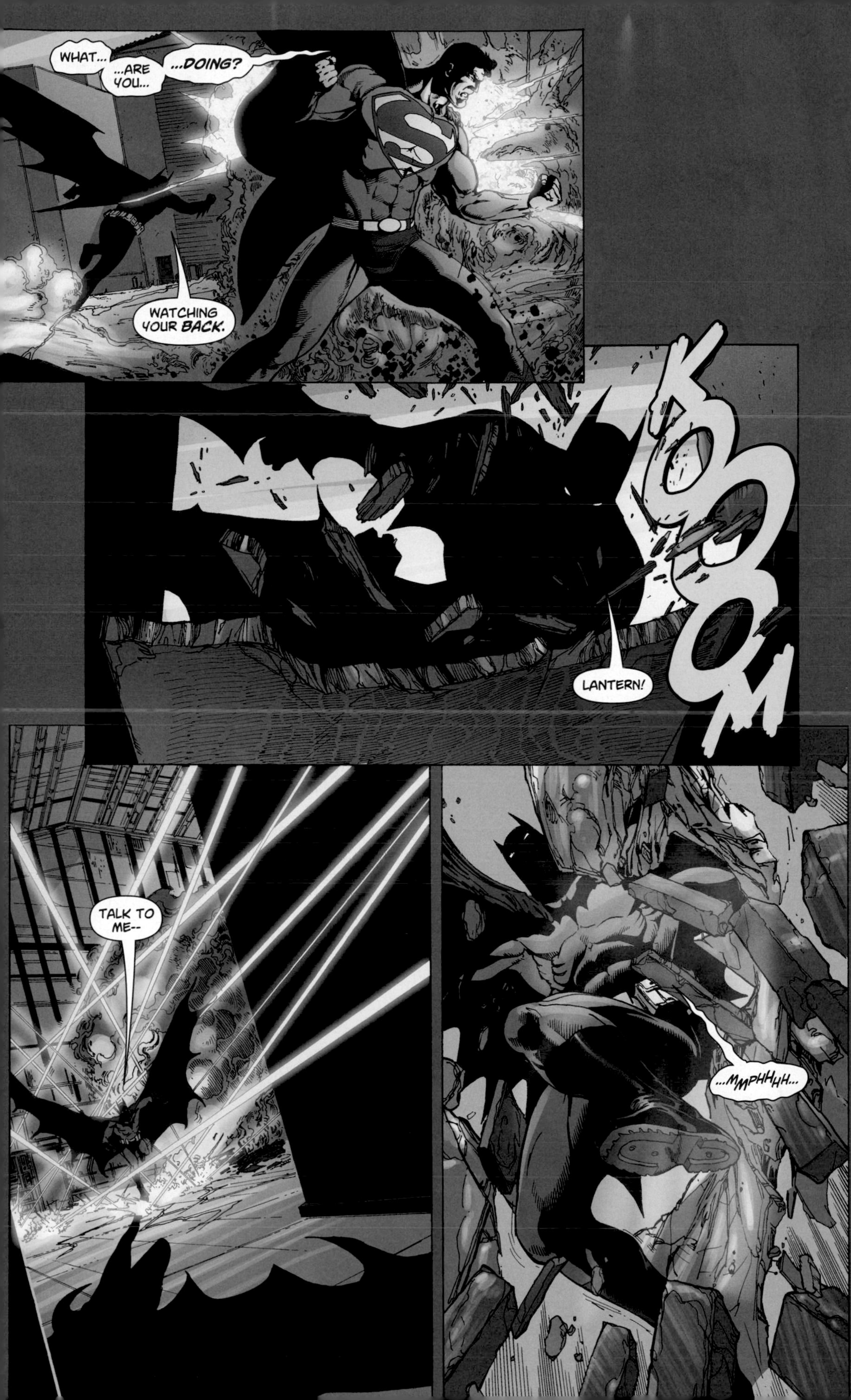
WHAT...
...ARE YOU...
...DOING?
WATCHING YOUR BACK.
KOOOM
LANTERN!
TALK TO ME--
...MMPHHHH...

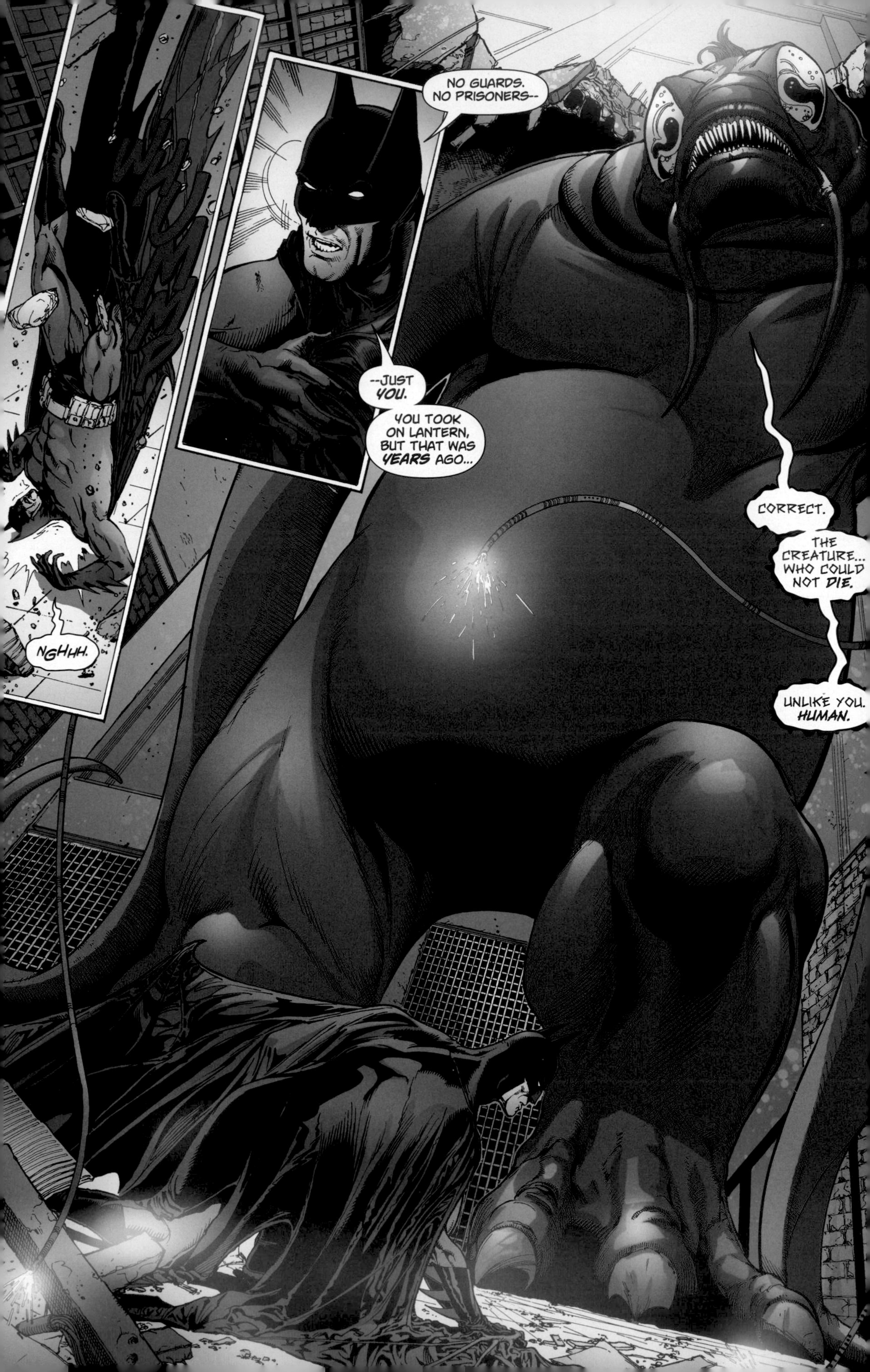
NO GUARDS. NO PRISONERS--
--JUST YOU.
YOU TOOK ON LANTERN, BUT THAT WAS YEARS AGO...
NGHHH.
CORRECT.
THE CREATURE... WHO COULD NOT DIE.
UNLIKE YOU. HUMAN.

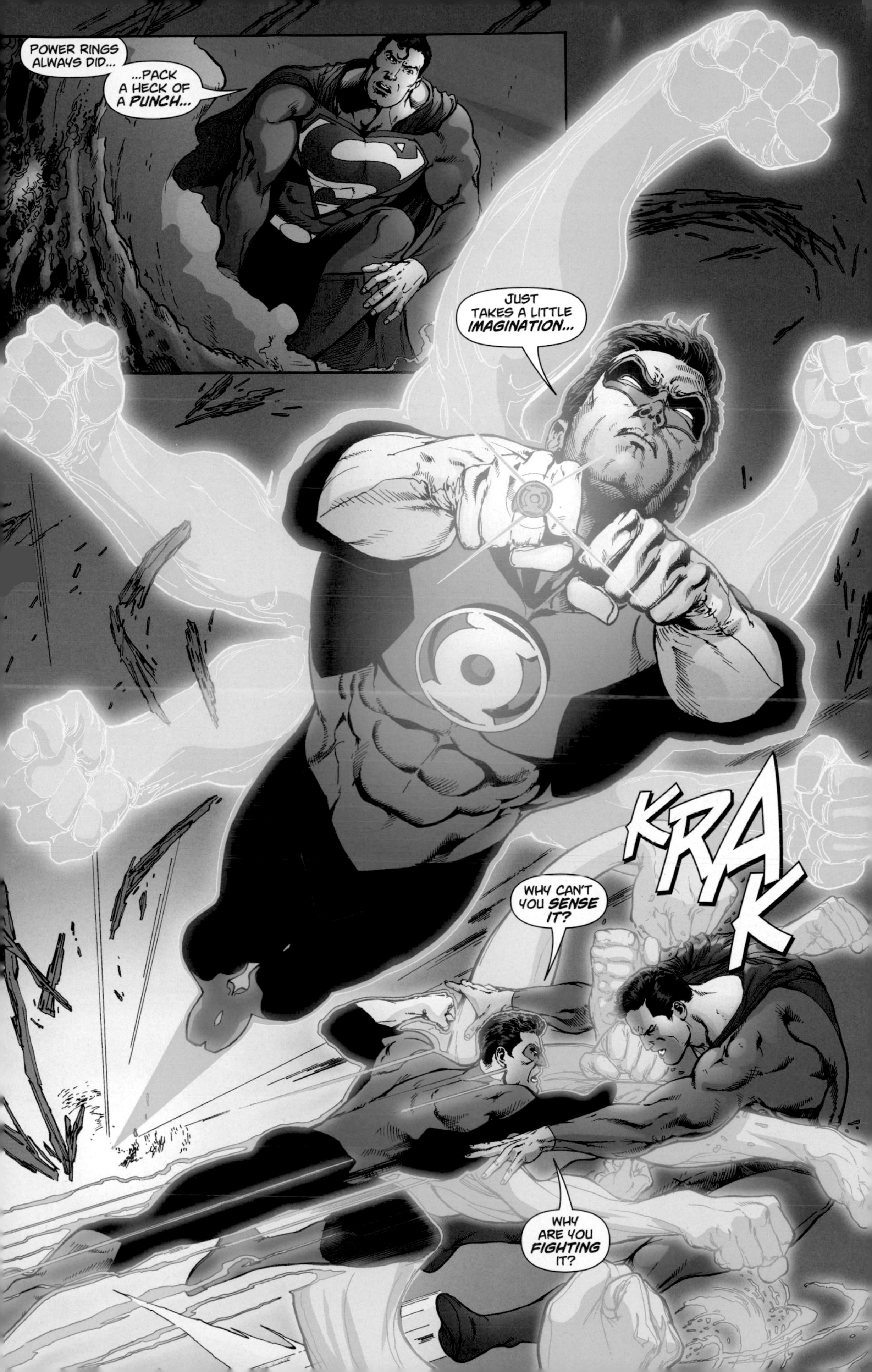
POWER RINGS ALWAYS DID...
...PACK A HECK OF A PUNCH...
JUST TAKES A LITTLE IMAGINATION...
KRAK
WHY CAN'T YOU SENSE IT?
WHY ARE YOU FIGHTING IT?

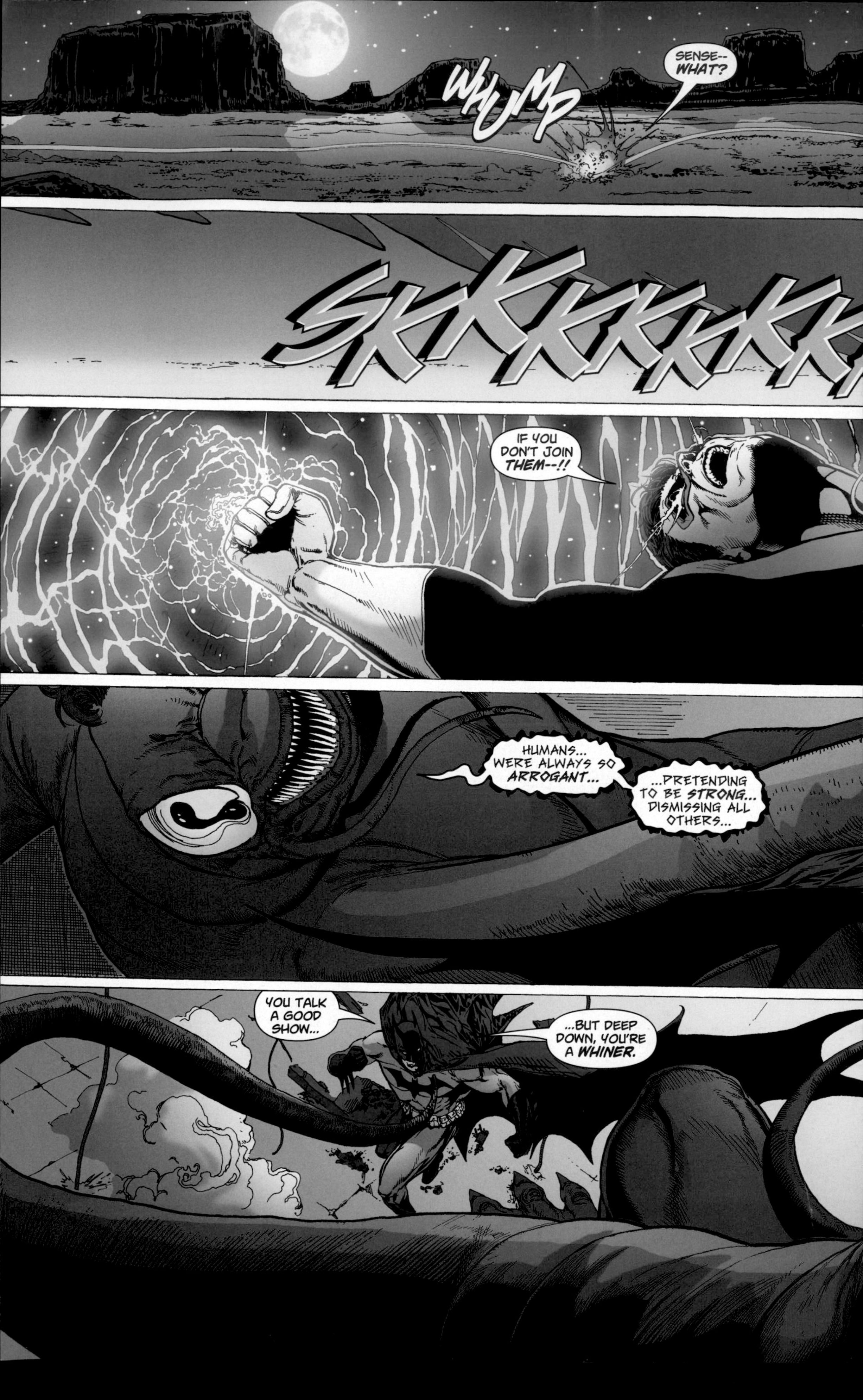
WHUMP
SENSE-- WHAT?
SKKKKKKK
IF YOU DON'T JOIN THEM--!!
HUMANS... WERE ALWAYS SO ARROGANT...
...PRETENDING TO BE STRONG... DISMISSING ALL OTHERS...
YOU TALK A GOOD SHOW...
...BUT DEEP DOWN, YOU'RE A WHINER.

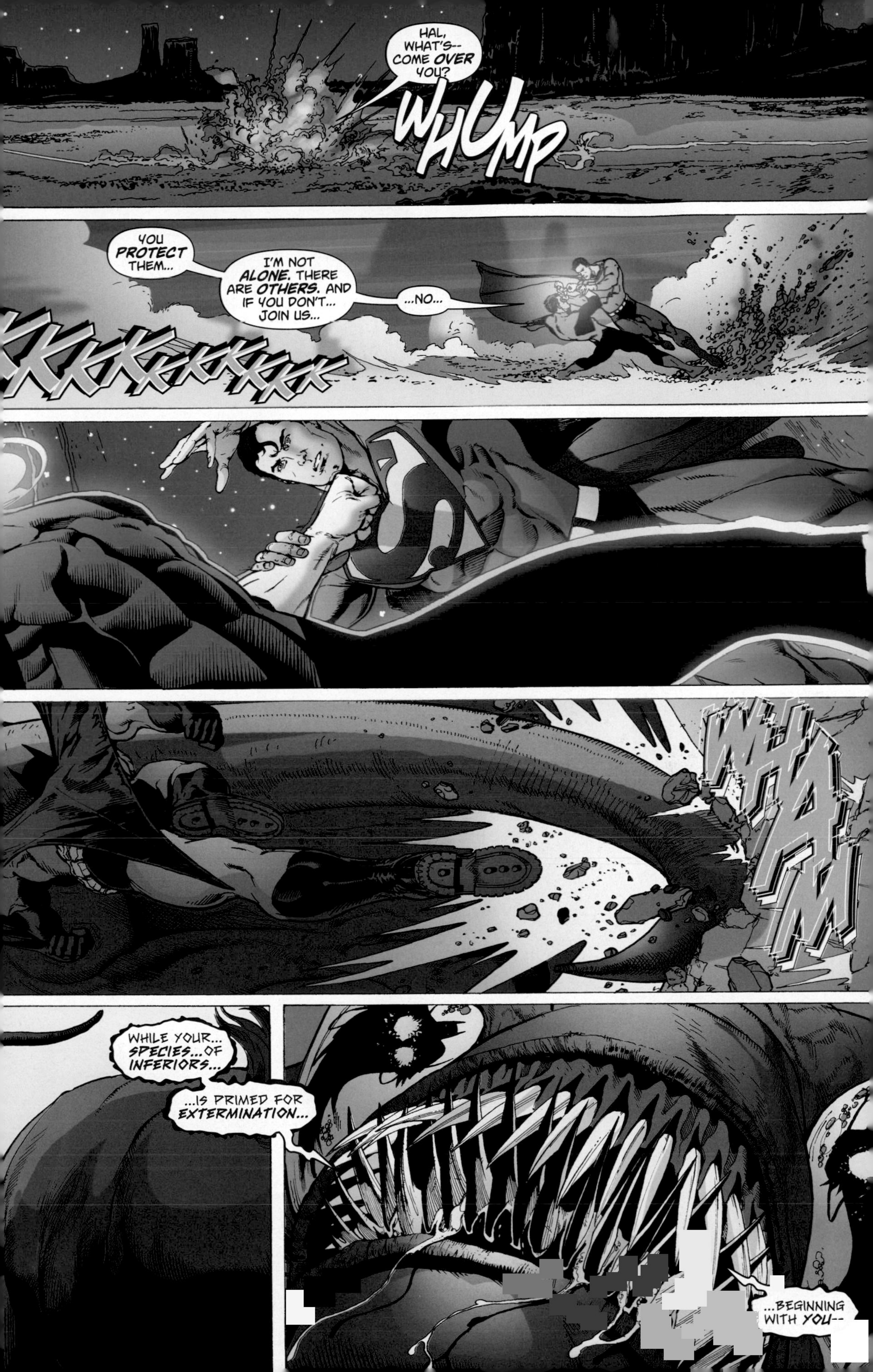
HAL, WHAT'S-- COME OVER YOU?
WHUMP
YOU PROTECT THEM...
I'M NOT ALONE. THERE ARE OTHERS. AND IF YOU DON'T... JOIN US...
...NO...
KKKKKKKKKKKK
WHAM
WHILE YOUR... SPECIES... OF INFERIORS...
...IS PRIMED FOR EXTERMINATION...
...BEGINNING WITH YOU--

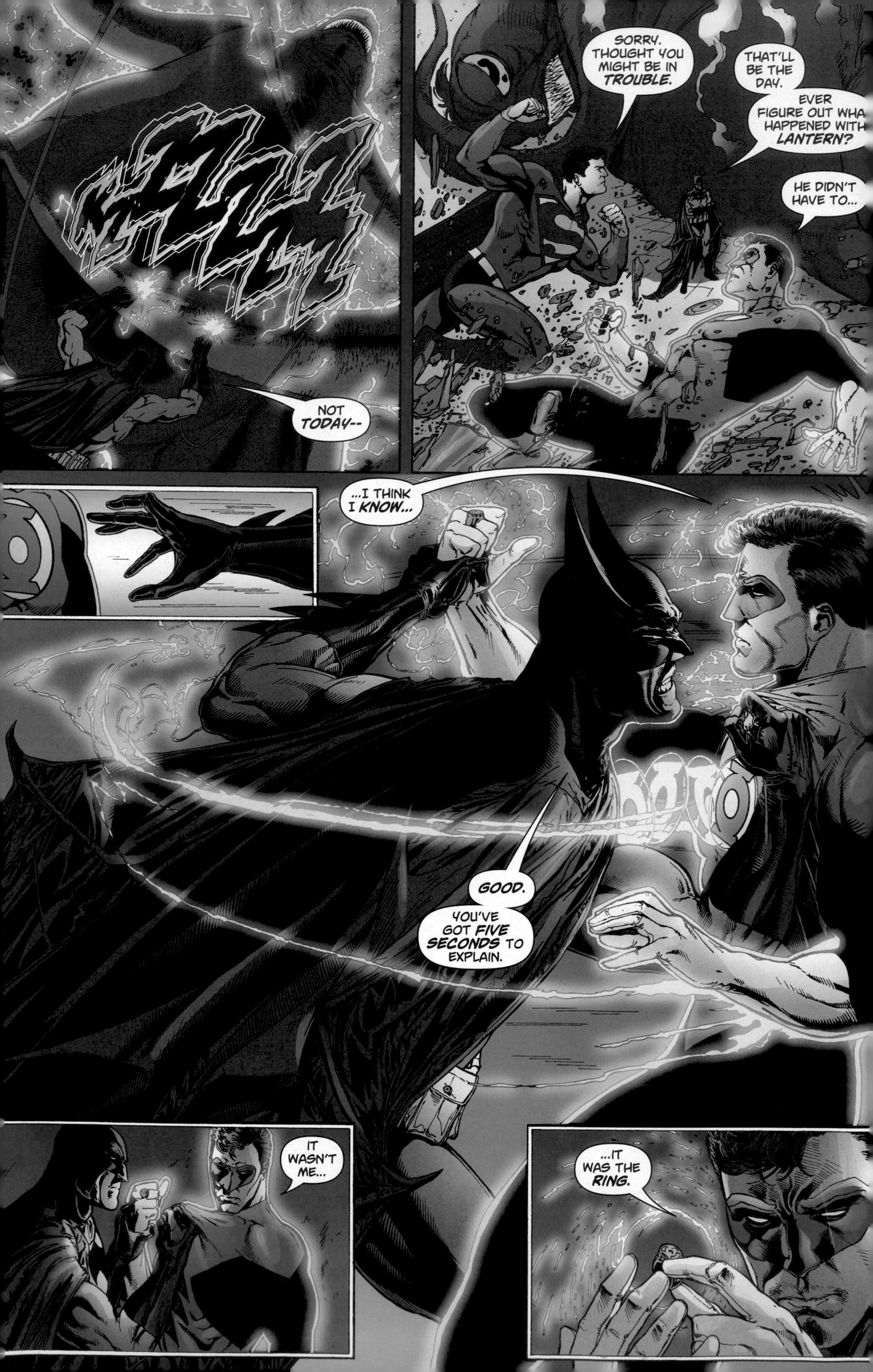
NOT TODAY--
SORRY. THOUGHT YOU MIGHT BE IN TROUBLE.
THAT'LL BE THE DAY.
EVER FIGURE OUT WHA HAPPENED WITH LANTERN?
HE DIDN'T HAVE TO...
...I THINK I KNOW...
GOOD.
YOU'VE GOT FIVE SECONDS TO EXPLAIN.
IT WASN'T ME...
...IT WAS THE RING.

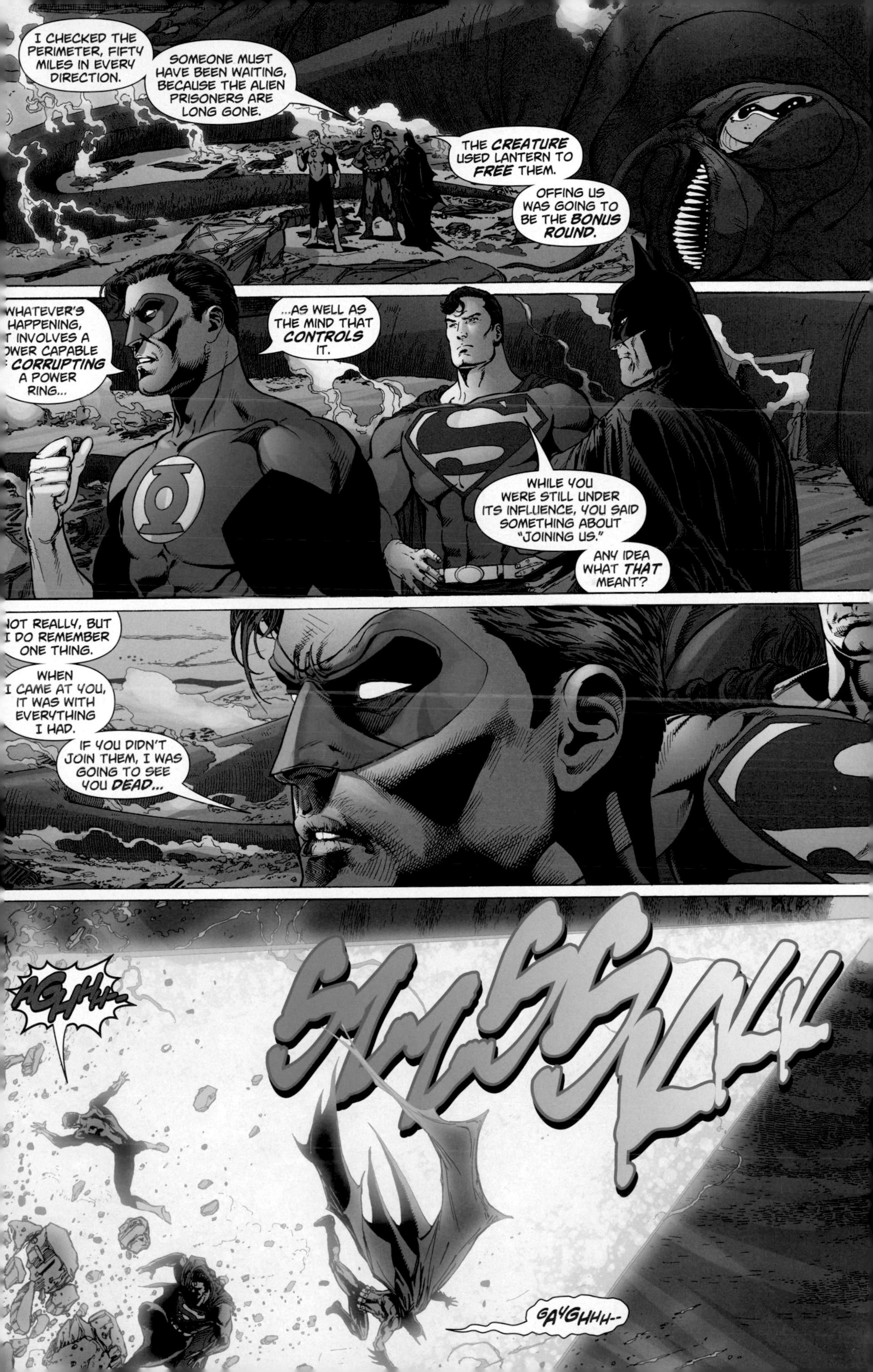
I CHECKED THE PERIMETER, FIFTY MILES IN EVERY DIRECTION.
SOMEONE MUST HAVE BEEN WAITING, BECAUSE THE ALIEN PRISONERS ARE LONG GONE.
THE CREATURE USED LANTERN TO FREE THEM.
OFFING US WAS GOING TO BE THE BONUS ROUND.
WHATEVER'S HAPPENING, IT INVOLVES A POWER CAPABLE OF CORRUPTING A POWER RING...
...AS WELL AS THE MIND THAT CONTROLS IT.
WHILE YOU WERE STILL UNDER ITS INFLUENCE, YOU SAID SOMETHING ABOUT "JOINING US."
ANY IDEA WHAT THAT MEANT?
NOT REALLY, BUT I DO REMEMBER ONE THING.
WHEN I CAME AT YOU, IT WAS WITH EVERYTHING I HAD.
IF YOU DIDN'T JOIN THEM, I WAS GOING TO SEE YOU DEAD...
AGHHH--
SMASSKK
GAYGHHH--

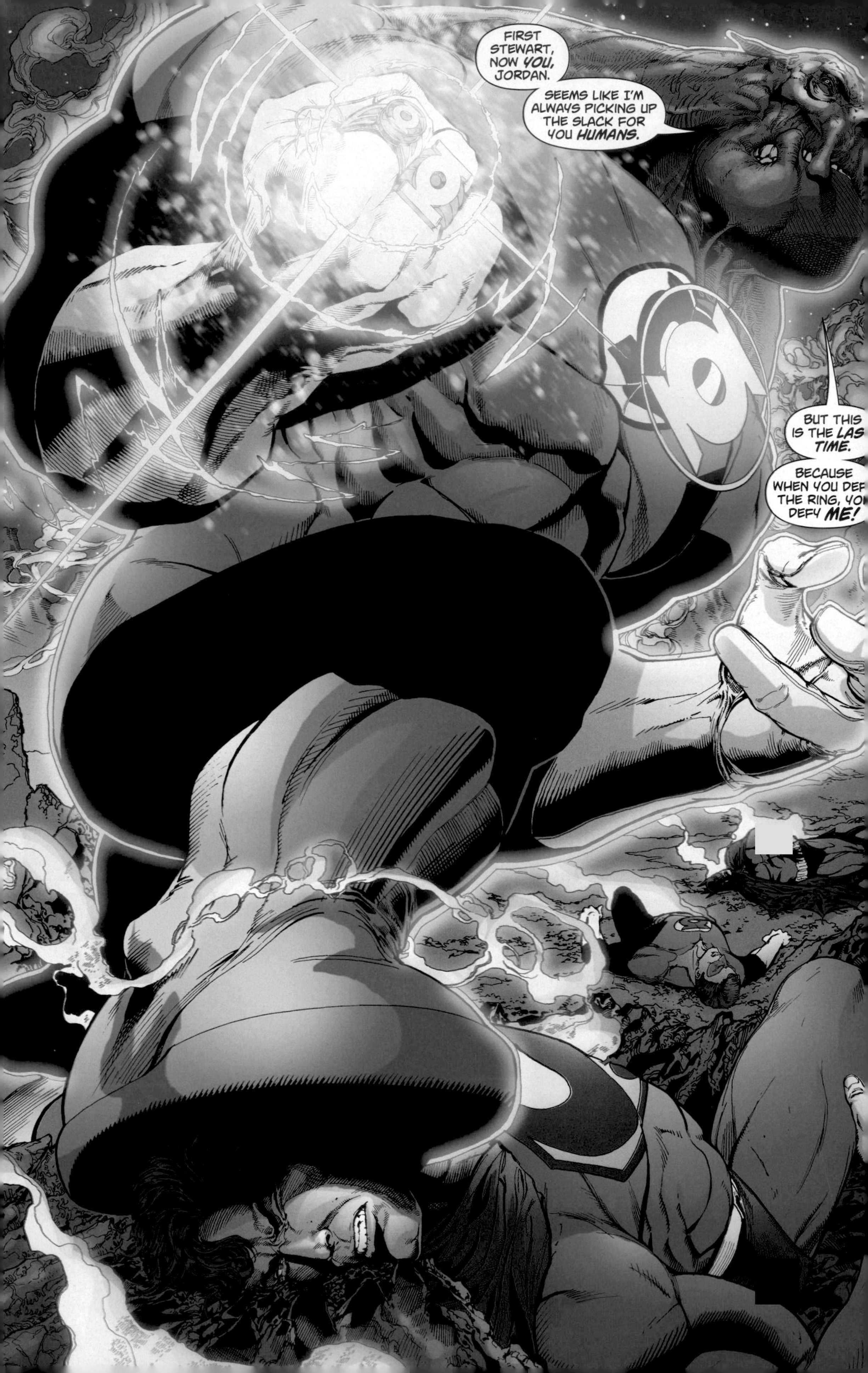
FIRST STEWART, NOW YOU, JORDAN.
SEEMS LIKE I'M ALWAYS PICKING UP THE SLACK FOR YOU HUMANS.
BUT THIS IS THE LAS TIME.
BECAUSE WHEN YOU DEF THE RING, YO DEFY ME!

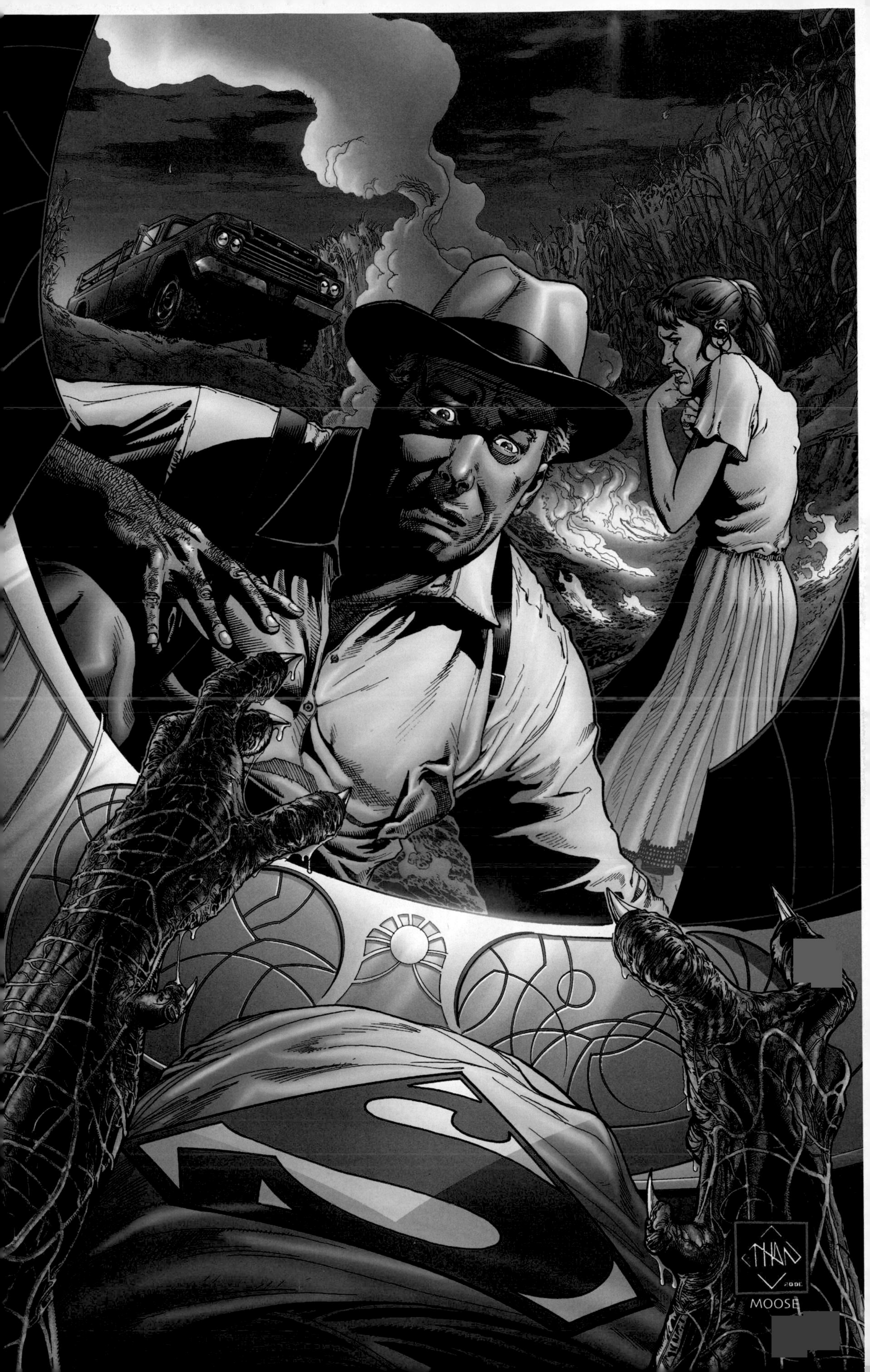
MOOSE

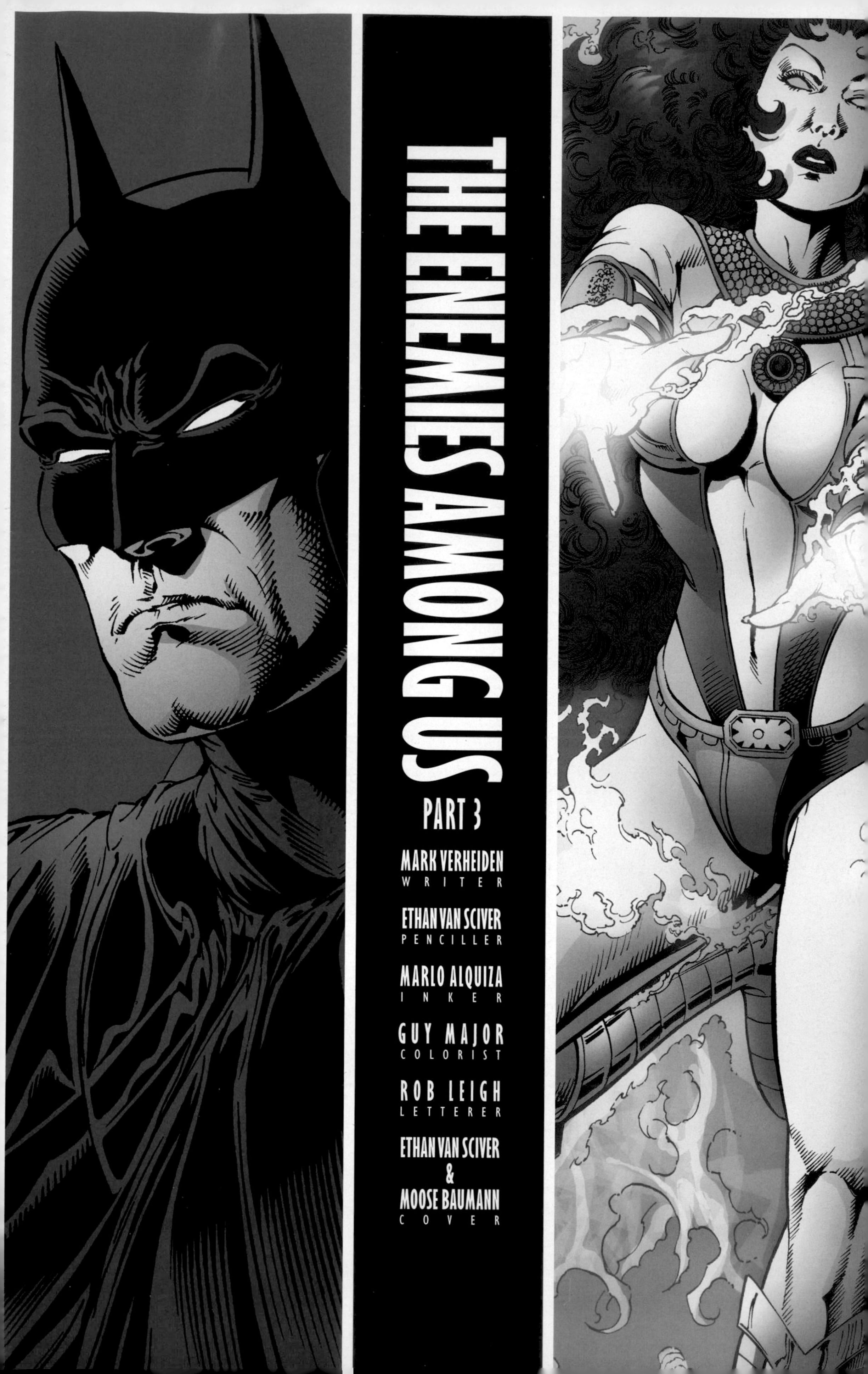
THE ENEMIES AMONG US
PART 3
MARK VERHEIDEN
WRITER
ETHAN VAN SCIVER
PENCILLER
MARLO ALQUIZA
INKER
GUY MAJOR
COLORIST
ROB LEIGH
LETTERER
ETHAN VAN SCIVER
&
MOOSE BAUMANN
COVER

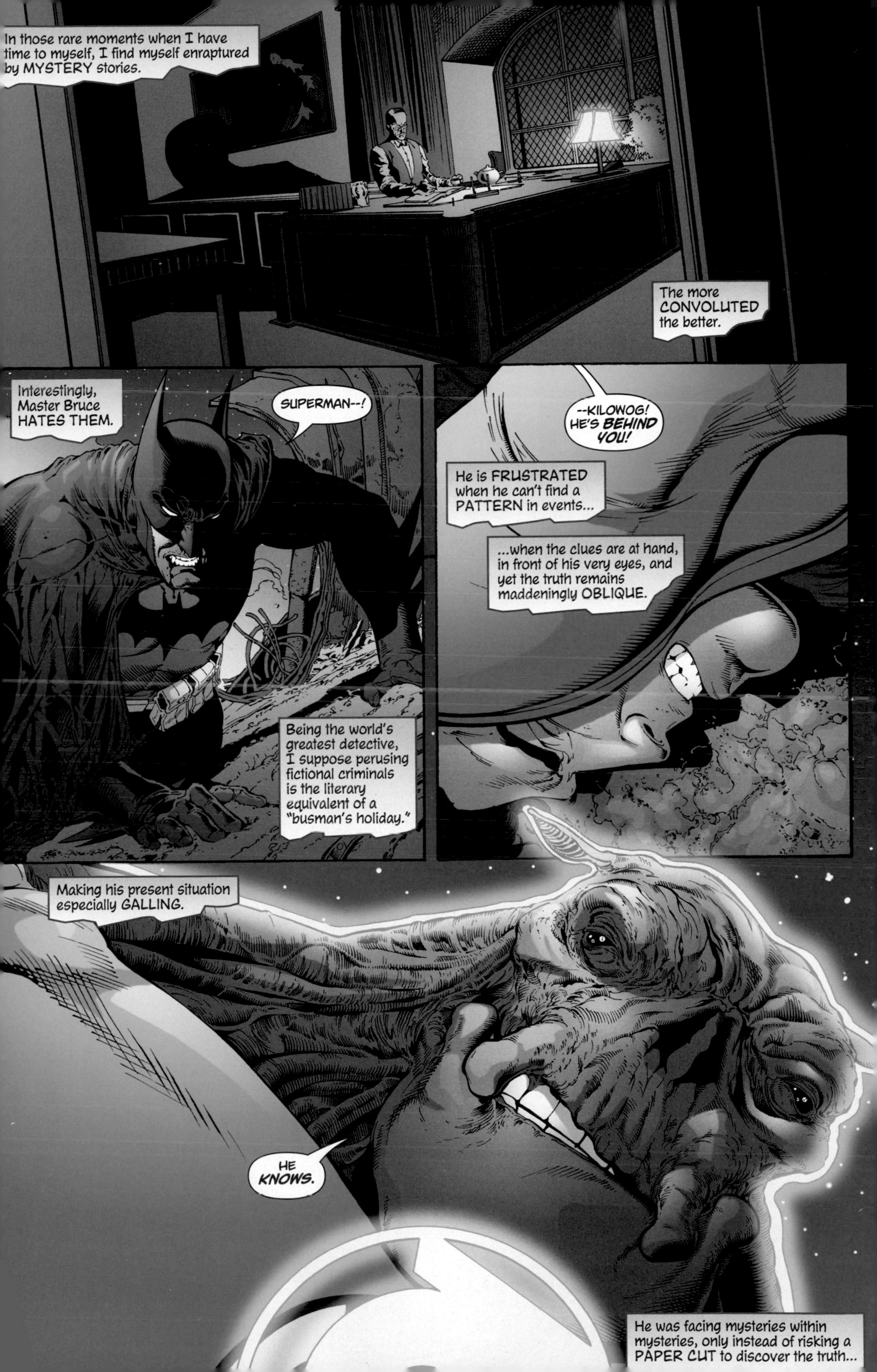
In those rare moments when I have time to myself, I find myself enraptured by MYSTERY stories.
The more CONVOLUTED the better.
Interestingly, Master Bruce HATES THEM.
SUPERMAN--!
Being the world's greatest detective, I suppose perusing fictional criminals is the literary equivalent of a "busman's holiday."
--KILOWOG! HE'S BEHIND YOU!
He is FRUSTRATED when he can't find a PATTERN in events...
...when the clues are at hand, in front of his very eyes, and yet the truth remains maddeningly OBLIQUE.
Making his present situation especially GALLING.
HE KNOWS.
He was facing mysteries within mysteries, only instead of risking a PAPER CUT to discover the truth...

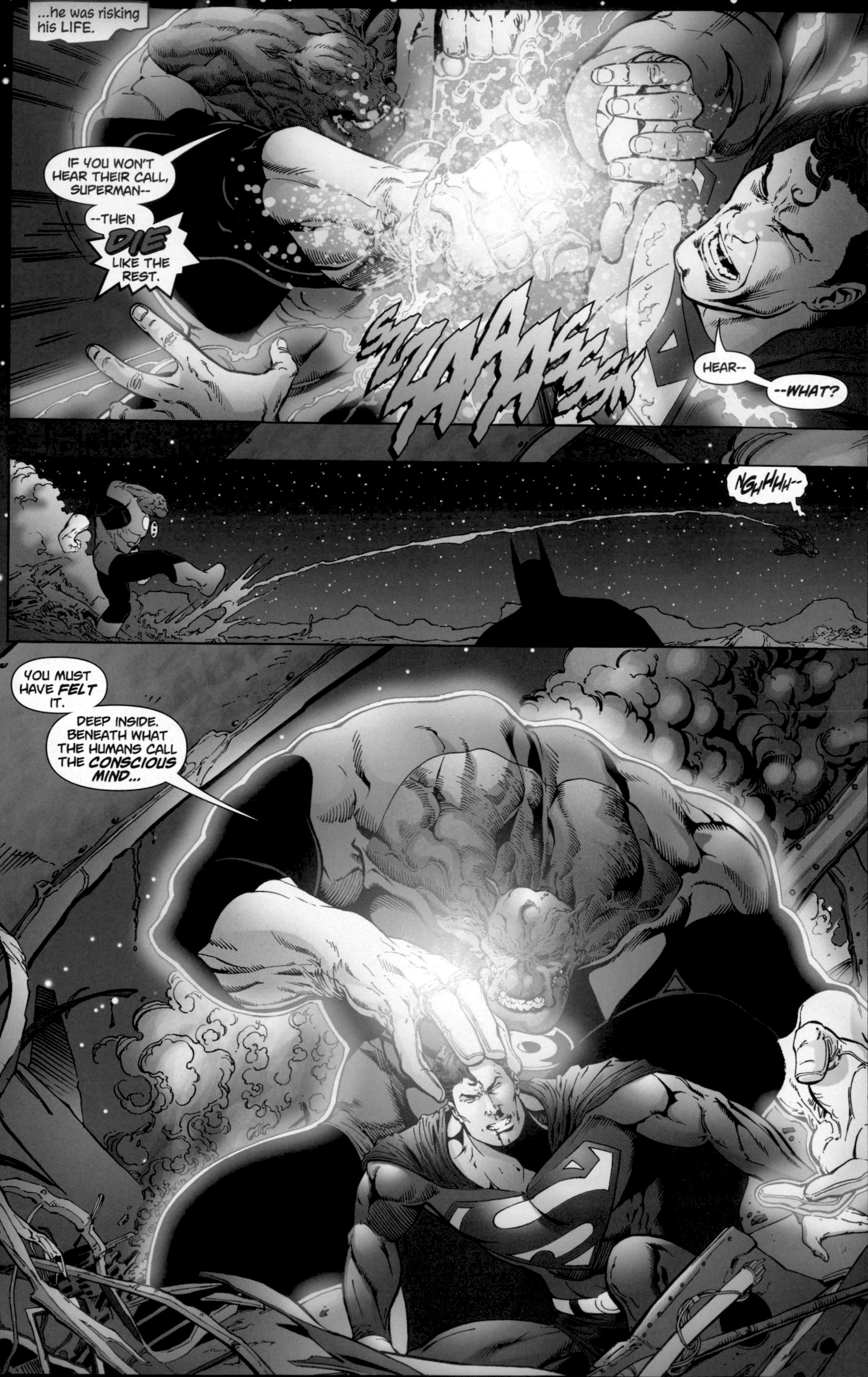
...he was risking his LIFE.
IF YOU WON'T HEAR THEIR CALL, SUPERMAN--
--THEN DIE LIKE THE REST.
HEAR--
--WHAT?
NGHHH--
YOU MUST HAVE FELT IT.
DEEP INSIDE. BENEATH WHAT THE HUMANS CALL THE CONSCIOUS MIND...

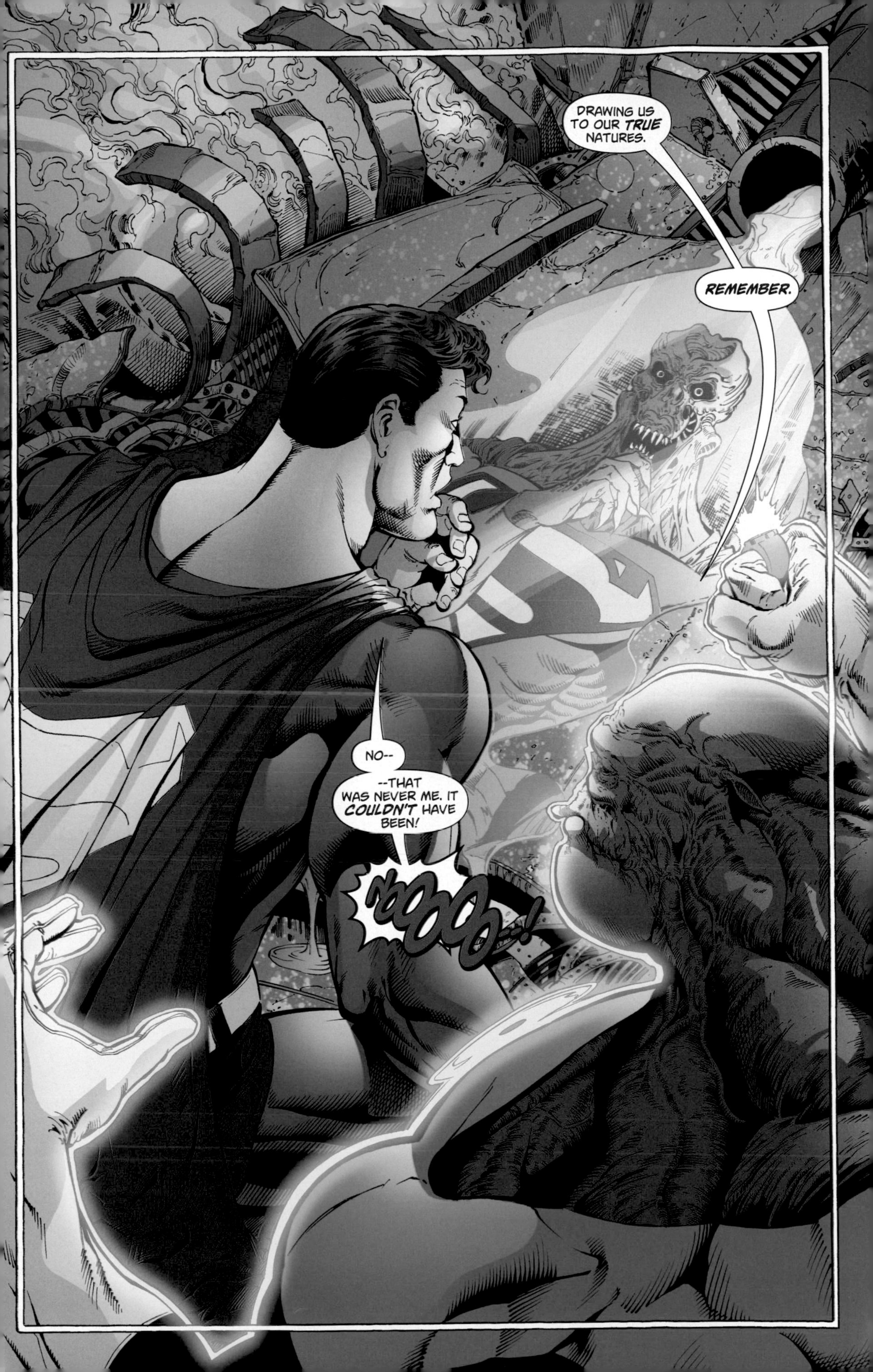
DRAWING US TO OUR TRUE NATURES.
REMEMBER.
NO--
--THAT WAS NEVER ME. IT COULDN'T HAVE BEEN!
NOOOOO--!

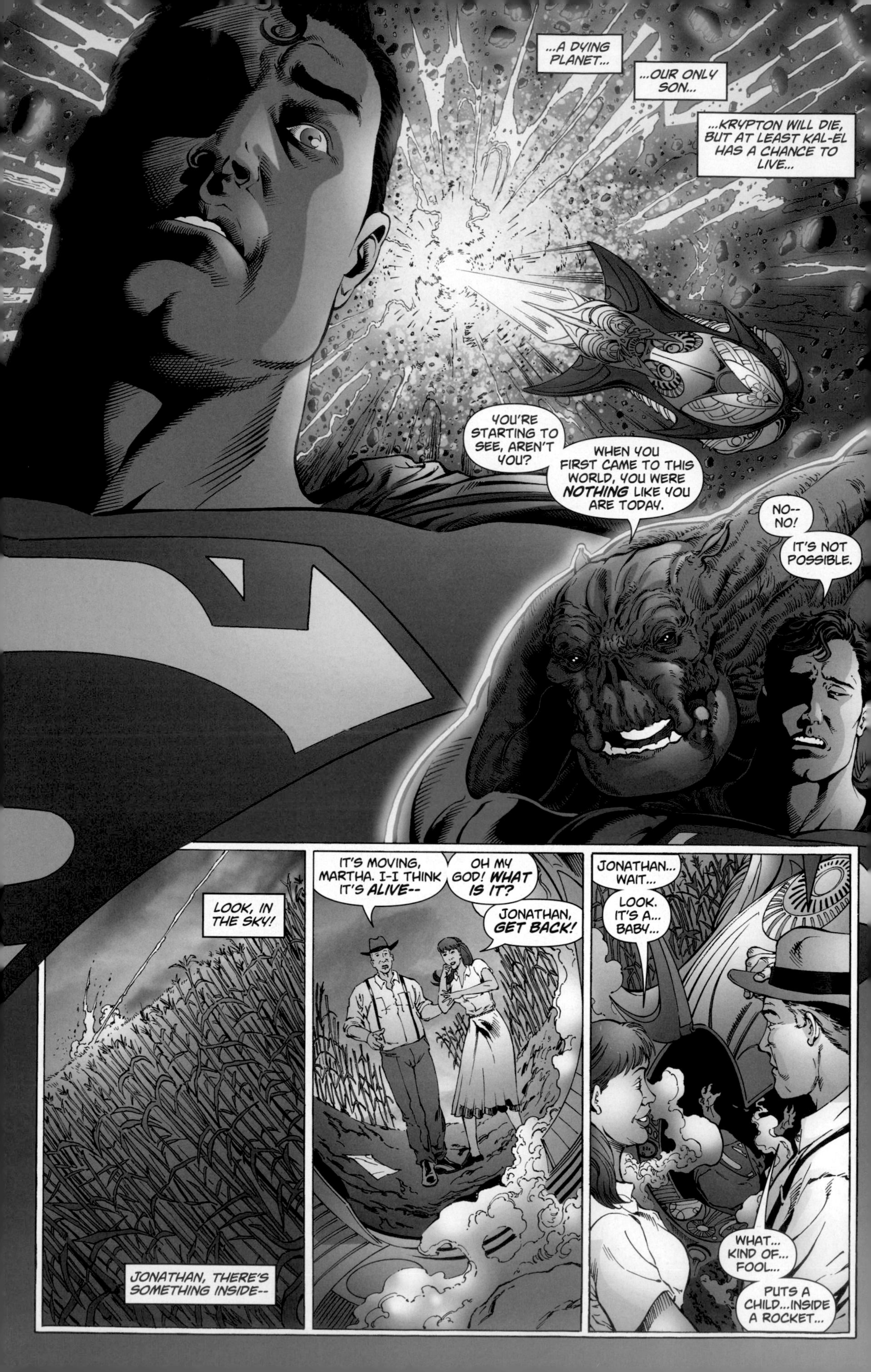
...A DYING PLANET...
...OUR ONLY SON...
...KRYPTON WILL DIE, BUT AT LEAST KAL-EL HAS A CHANCE TO LIVE...
YOU'RE STARTING TO SEE, AREN'T YOU?
WHEN YOU FIRST CAME TO THIS WORLD, YOU WERE NOTHING LIKE YOU ARE TODAY.
NO-- NO!
IT'S NOT POSSIBLE.
LOOK, IN THE SKY!
JONATHAN, THERE'S SOMETHING INSIDE--
IT'S MOVING, MARTHA. I-I THINK IT'S ALIVE--
OH MY GOD! WHAT IS IT?
JONATHAN, GET BACK!
JONATHAN... WAIT...
LOOK. IT'S A... BABY...
WHAT... KIND OF... FOOL...
PUTS A CHILD...INSIDE A ROCKET...

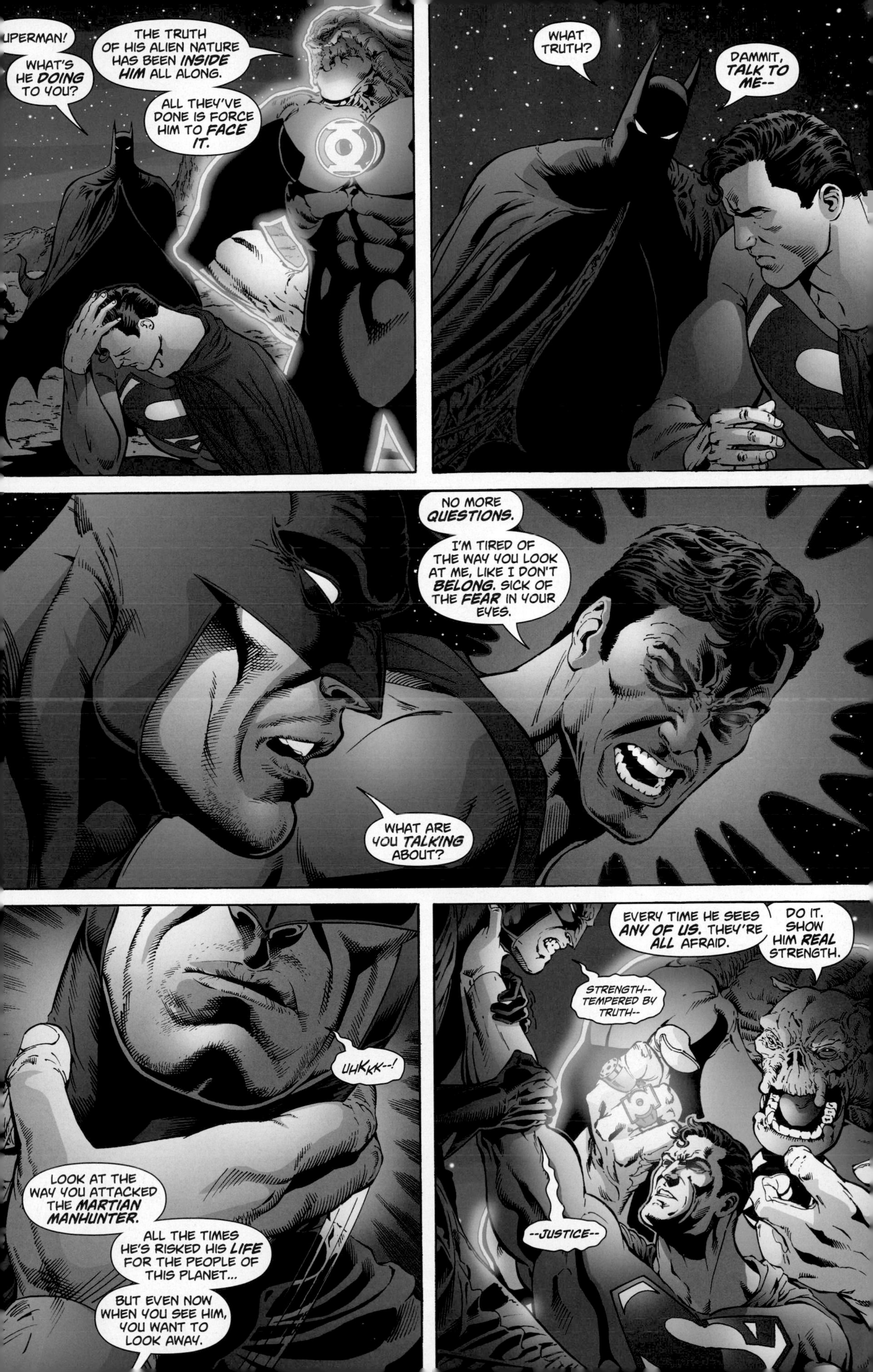
UPERMAN!
WHAT'S HE DOING TO YOU?
THE TRUTH OF HIS ALIEN NATURE HAS BEEN INSIDE HIM ALL ALONG.
ALL THEY'VE DONE IS FORCE HIM TO FACE IT.
WHAT TRUTH?
DAMMIT, TALK TO ME--
NO MORE QUESTIONS.
I'M TIRED OF THE WAY YOU LOOK AT ME, LIKE I DON'T BELONG. SICK OF THE FEAR IN YOUR EYES.
WHAT ARE YOU TALKING ABOUT?
UHKKK--!
LOOK AT THE WAY YOU ATTACKED THE MARTIAN MANHUNTER.
ALL THE TIMES HE'S RISKED HIS LIFE FOR THE PEOPLE OF THIS PLANET...
BUT EVEN NOW WHEN YOU SEE HIM, YOU WANT TO LOOK AWAY.
EVERY TIME HE SEES ANY OF US. THEY'RE ALL AFRAID.
DO IT. SHOW HIM REAL STRENGTH.
STRENGTH-- TEMPERED BY TRUTH--
--JUSTICE--

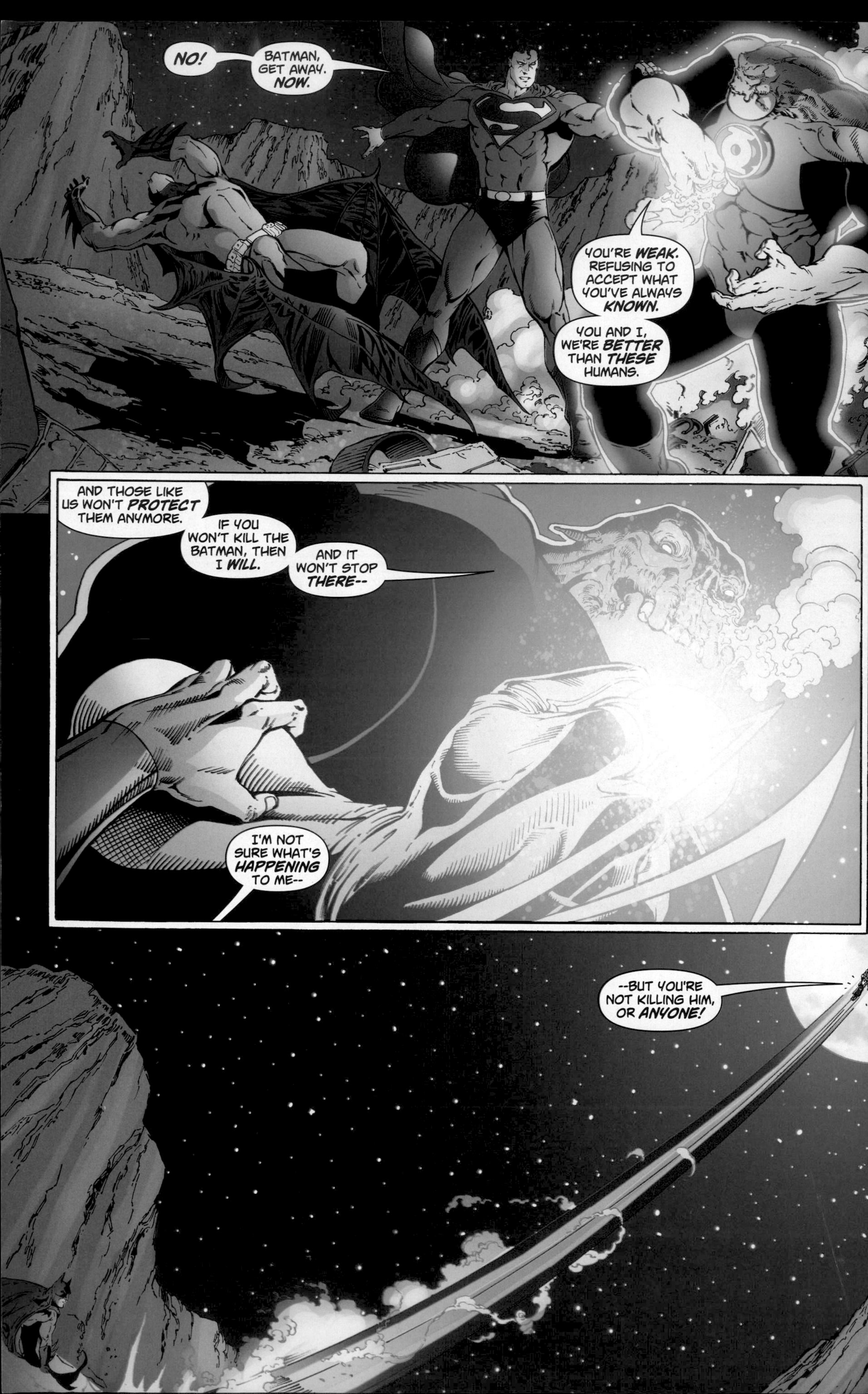
NO!
BATMAN, GET AWAY. NOW.
YOU'RE WEAK. REFUSING TO ACCEPT WHAT YOU'VE ALWAYS KNOWN.
YOU AND I, WE'RE BETTER THAN THESE HUMANS.
AND THOSE LIKE US WON'T PROTECT THEM ANYMORE.
IF YOU WON'T KILL THE BATMAN, THEN I WILL.
AND IT WON'T STOP THERE--
I'M NOT SURE WHAT'S HAPPENING TO ME--
--BUT YOU'RE NOT KILLING HIM, OR ANYONE!

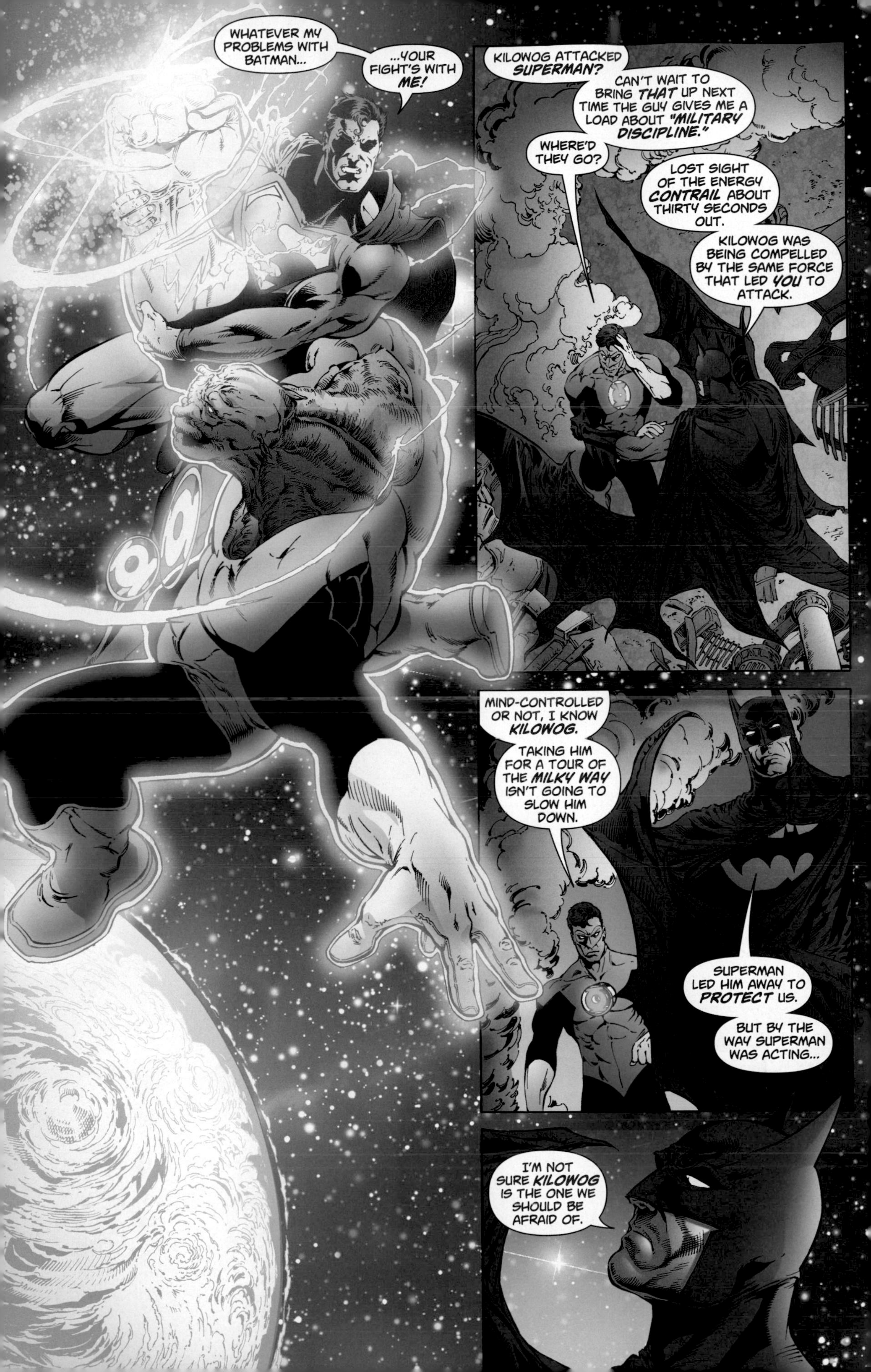
WHATEVER MY PROBLEMS WITH BATMAN...
...YOUR FIGHT'S WITH ME!
KILOWOG ATTACKED SUPERMAN?
CAN'T WAIT TO BRING THAT UP NEXT TIME THE GUY GIVES ME A LOAD ABOUT "MILITARY DISCIPLINE."
WHERE'D THEY GO?
LOST SIGHT OF THE ENERGY CONTRAIL ABOUT THIRTY SECONDS OUT.
KILOWOG WAS BEING COMPELLED BY THE SAME FORCE THAT LED YOU TO ATTACK.
MIND-CONTROLLED OR NOT, I KNOW KILOWOG.
TAKING HIM FOR A TOUR OF THE MILKY WAY ISN'T GOING TO SLOW HIM DOWN.
SUPERMAN LED HIM AWAY TO PROTECT US.
BUT BY THE WAY SUPERMAN WAS ACTING...
I'M NOT SURE KILOWOG IS THE ONE WE SHOULD BE AFRAID OF.

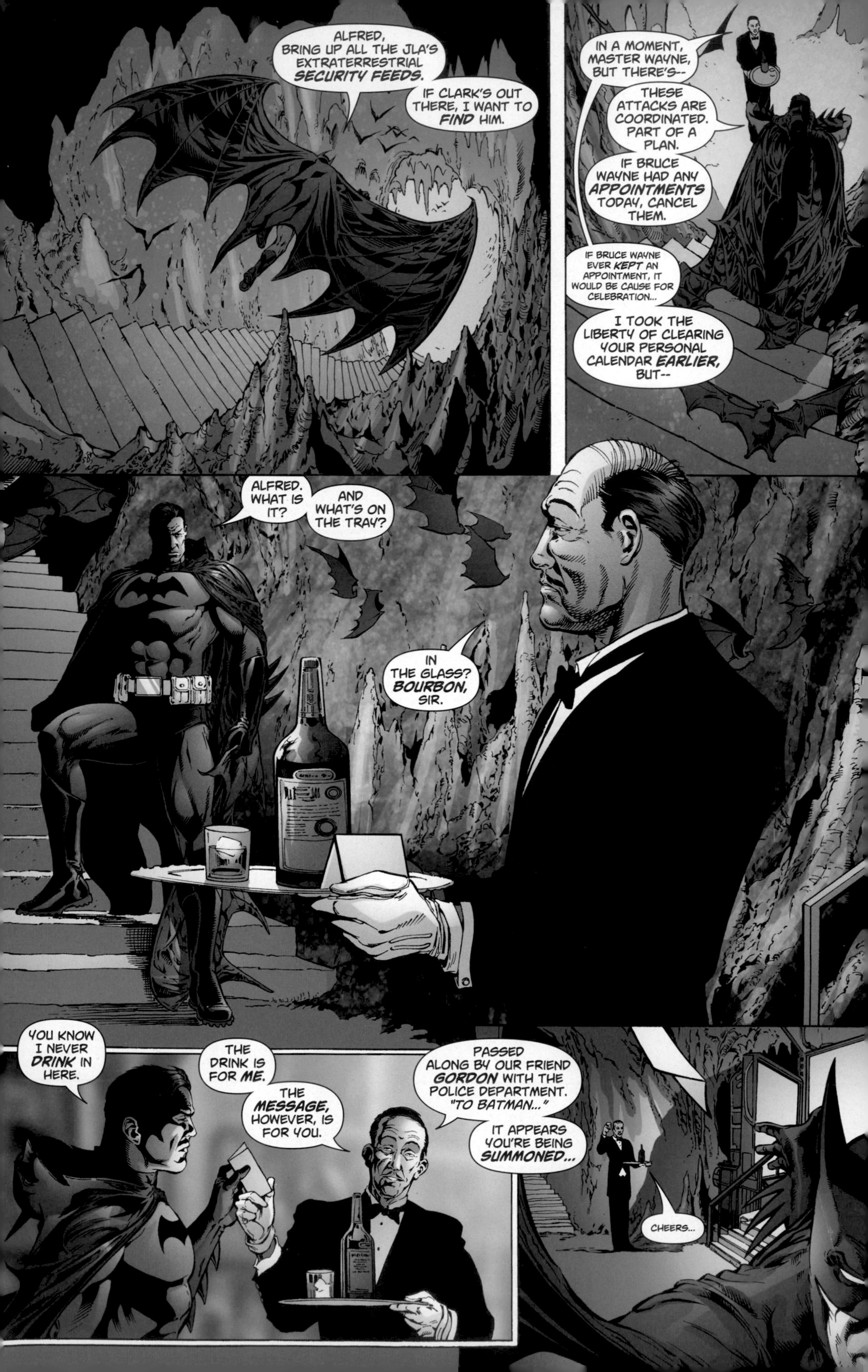
ALFRED, BRING UP ALL THE JLA'S EXTRATERRESTRIAL SECURITY FEEDS.
IF CLARK'S OUT THERE, I WANT TO FIND HIM.
IN A MOMENT, MASTER WAYNE, BUT THERE'S--
THESE ATTACKS ARE COORDINATED. PART OF A PLAN.
IF BRUCE WAYNE HAD ANY APPOINTMENTS TODAY, CANCEL THEM.
IF BRUCE WAYNE EVER KEPT AN APPOINTMENT, IT WOULD BE CAUSE FOR CELEBRATION...
I TOOK THE LIBERTY OF CLEARING YOUR PERSONAL CALENDAR EARLIER, BUT--
ALFRED. WHAT IS IT?
AND WHAT'S ON THE TRAY?
IN THE GLASS? BOURBON, SIR.
YOU KNOW I NEVER DRINK IN HERE.
THE DRINK IS FOR ME.
THE MESSAGE, HOWEVER, IS FOR YOU.
PASSED ALONG BY OUR FRIEND GORDON WITH THE POLICE DEPARTMENT. "TO BATMAN..."
IT APPEARS YOU'RE BEING SUMMONED...
CHEERS...

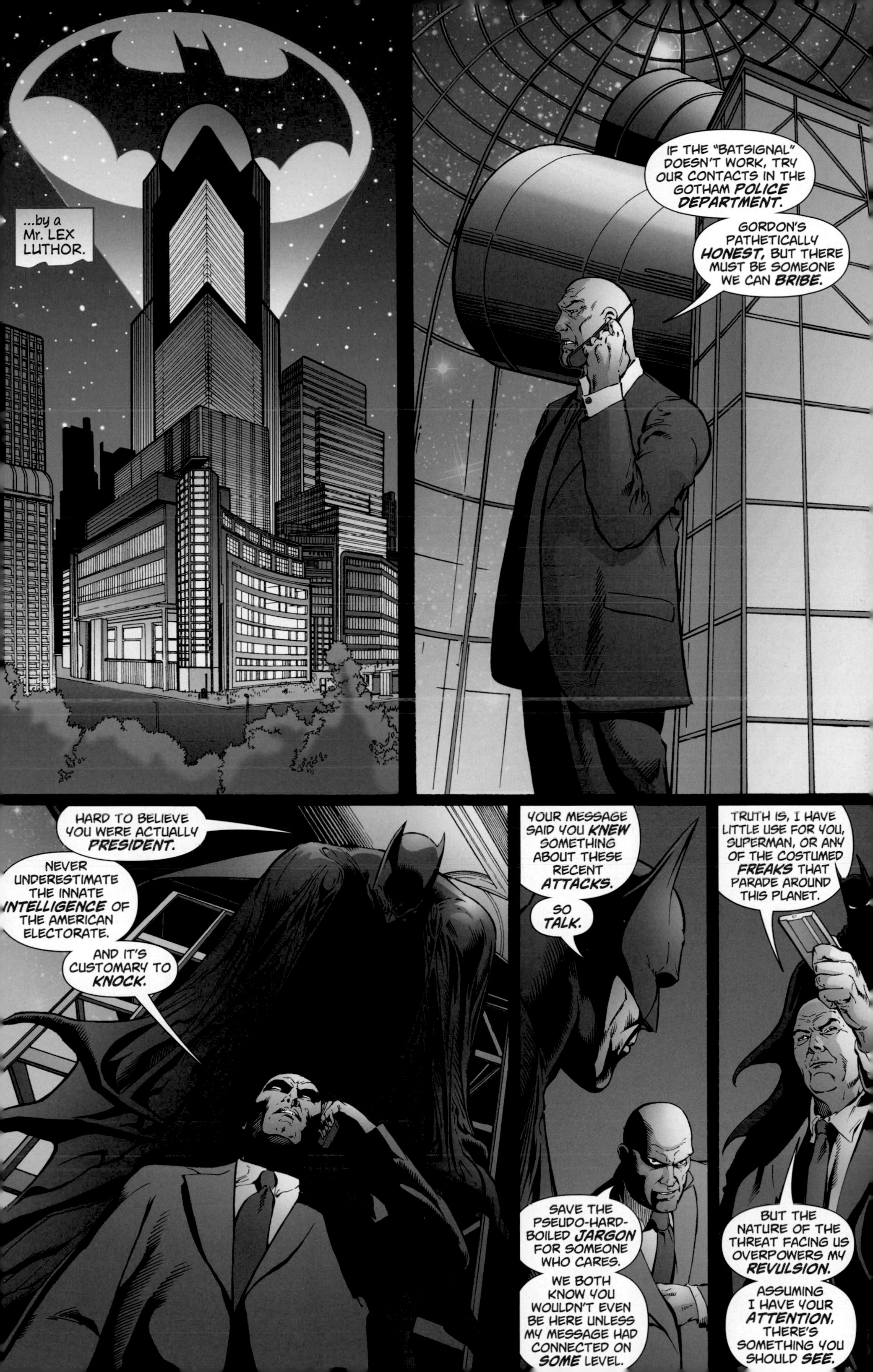
...by a Mr. LEX LUTHOR.
IF THE "BATSIGNAL" DOESN'T WORK, TRY OUR CONTACTS IN THE GOTHAM POLICE DEPARTMENT.
GORDON'S PATHETICALLY HONEST, BUT THERE MUST BE SOMEONE WE CAN BRIBE.
HARD TO BELIEVE YOU WERE ACTUALLY PRESIDENT.
NEVER UNDERESTIMATE THE INNATE INTELLIGENCE OF THE AMERICAN ELECTORATE.
AND IT'S CUSTOMARY TO KNOCK.
YOUR MESSAGE SAID YOU KNEW SOMETHING ABOUT THESE RECENT ATTACKS.
SO TALK.
SAVE THE PSEUDO-HARD-BOILED JARGON FOR SOMEONE WHO CARES.
WE BOTH KNOW YOU WOULDN'T EVEN BE HERE UNLESS MY MESSAGE HAD CONNECTED ON SOME LEVEL.
TRUTH IS, I HAVE LITTLE USE FOR YOU, SUPERMAN, OR ANY OF THE COSTUMED FREAKS THAT PARADE AROUND THIS PLANET.
BUT THE NATURE OF THE THREAT FACING US OVERPOWERS MY REVULSION.
ASSUMING I HAVE YOUR ATTENTION, THERE'S SOMETHING YOU SHOULD SEE.

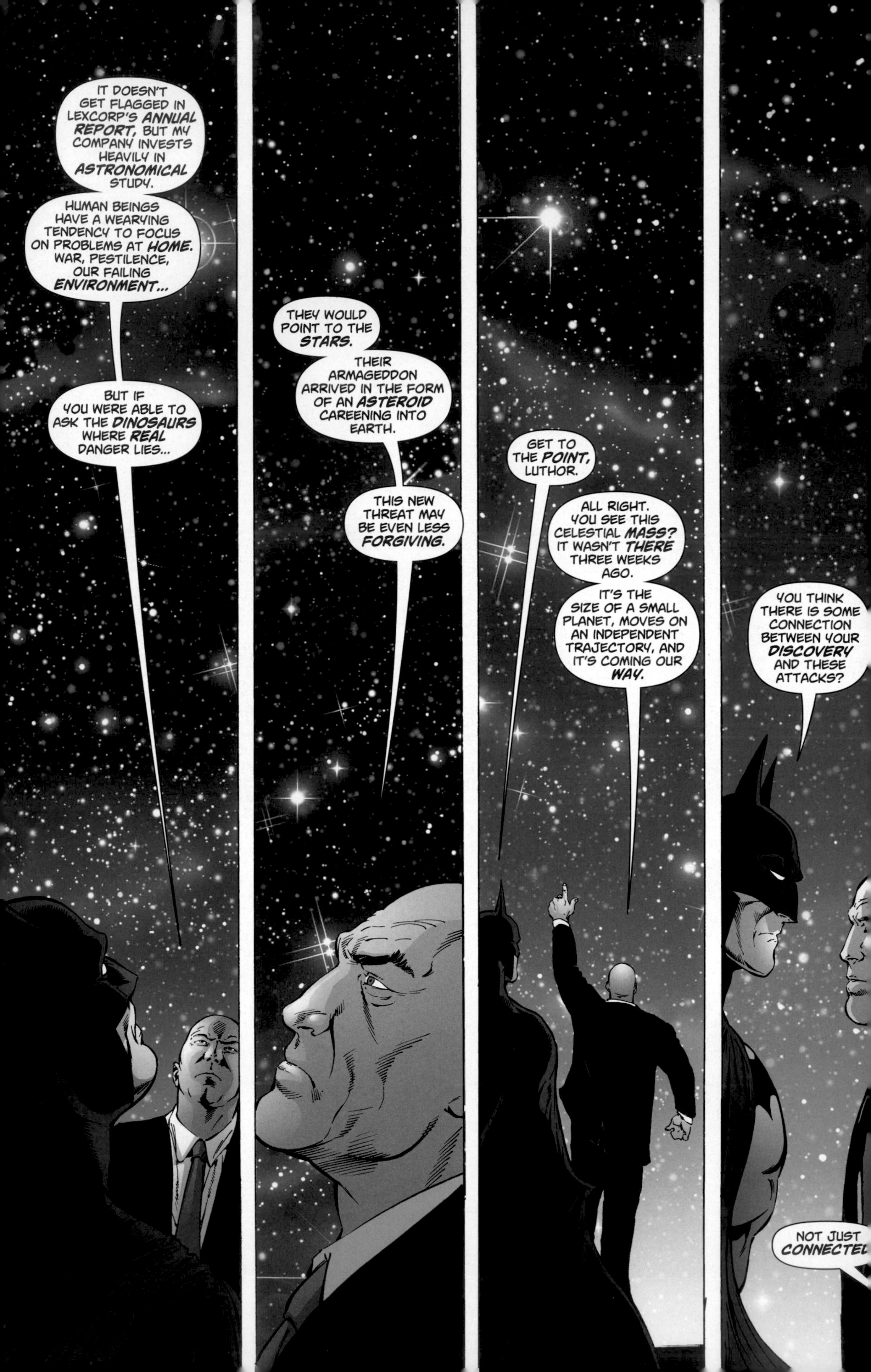

IT DOESN'T GET FLAGGED IN LEXCORP'S ANNUAL REPORT, BUT MY COMPANY INVESTS HEAVILY IN ASTRONOMICAL STUDY.
HUMAN BEINGS HAVE A WEARYING TENDENCY TO FOCUS ON PROBLEMS AT HOME. WAR, PESTILENCE, OUR FAILING ENVIRONMENT...
BUT IF YOU WERE ABLE TO ASK THE DINOSAURS WHERE REAL DANGER LIES...
THEY WOULD POINT TO THE STARS.
THEIR ARMAGEDDON ARRIVED IN THE FORM OF AN ASTEROID CAREENING INTO EARTH.
THIS NEW THREAT MAY BE EVEN LESS FORGIVING.
GET TO THE POINT, LUTHOR.
ALL RIGHT. YOU SEE THIS CELESTIAL MASS? IT WASN'T THERE THREE WEEKS AGO.
IT'S THE SIZE OF A SMALL PLANET, MOVES ON AN INDEPENDENT TRAJECTORY, AND IT'S COMING OUR WAY.
YOU THINK THERE IS SOME CONNECTION BETWEEN YOUR DISCOVERY AND THESE ATTACKS?
NOT JUST CONNECTE

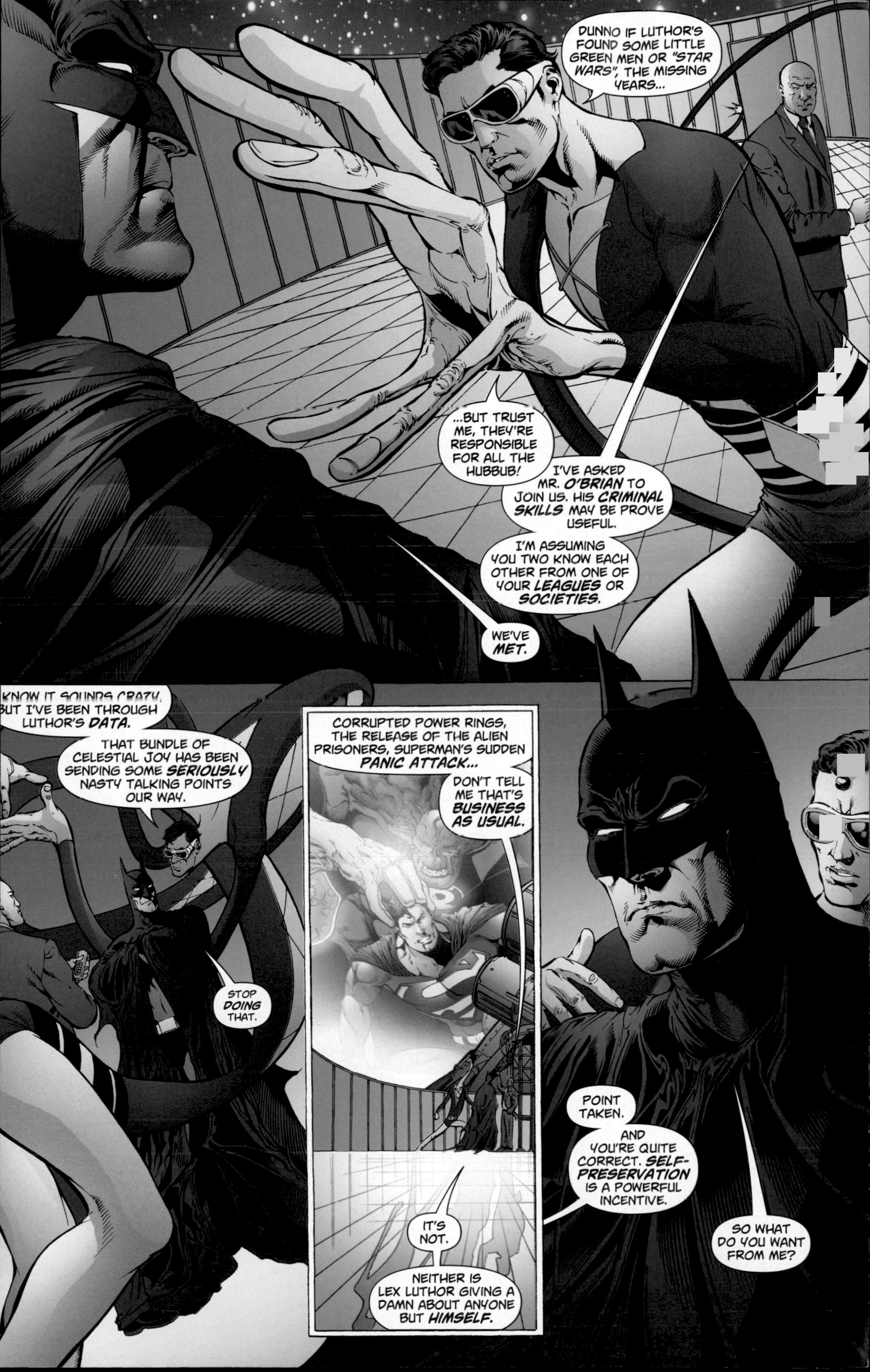
DUNNO IF LUTHOR'S FOUND SOME LITTLE GREEN MEN OR "STAR WARS", THE MISSING YEARS...
...BUT TRUST ME, THEY'RE RESPONSIBLE FOR ALL THE HUBBUB!
I'VE ASKED MR. O'BRIAN TO JOIN US. HIS CRIMINAL SKILLS MAY BE PROVE USEFUL.
I'M ASSUMING YOU TWO KNOW EACH OTHER FROM ONE OF YOUR LEAGUES OR SOCIETIES.
WE'VE MET.
KNOW IT SOUNDS CRAZY, BUT I'VE BEEN THROUGH LUTHOR'S DATA.
THAT BUNDLE OF CELESTIAL JOY HAS BEEN SENDING SOME SERIOUSLY NASTY TALKING POINTS OUR WAY.
STOP DOING THAT.
CORRUPTED POWER RINGS, THE RELEASE OF THE ALIEN PRISONERS, SUPERMAN'S SUDDEN PANIC ATTACK...
DON'T TELL ME THAT'S BUSINESS AS USUAL.
IT'S NOT.
NEITHER IS LEX LUTHOR GIVING A DAMN ABOUT ANYONE BUT HIMSELF.
POINT TAKEN.
AND YOU'RE QUITE CORRECT. SELF-PRESERVATION IS A POWERFUL INCENTIVE.
SO WHAT DO YOU WANT FROM ME?

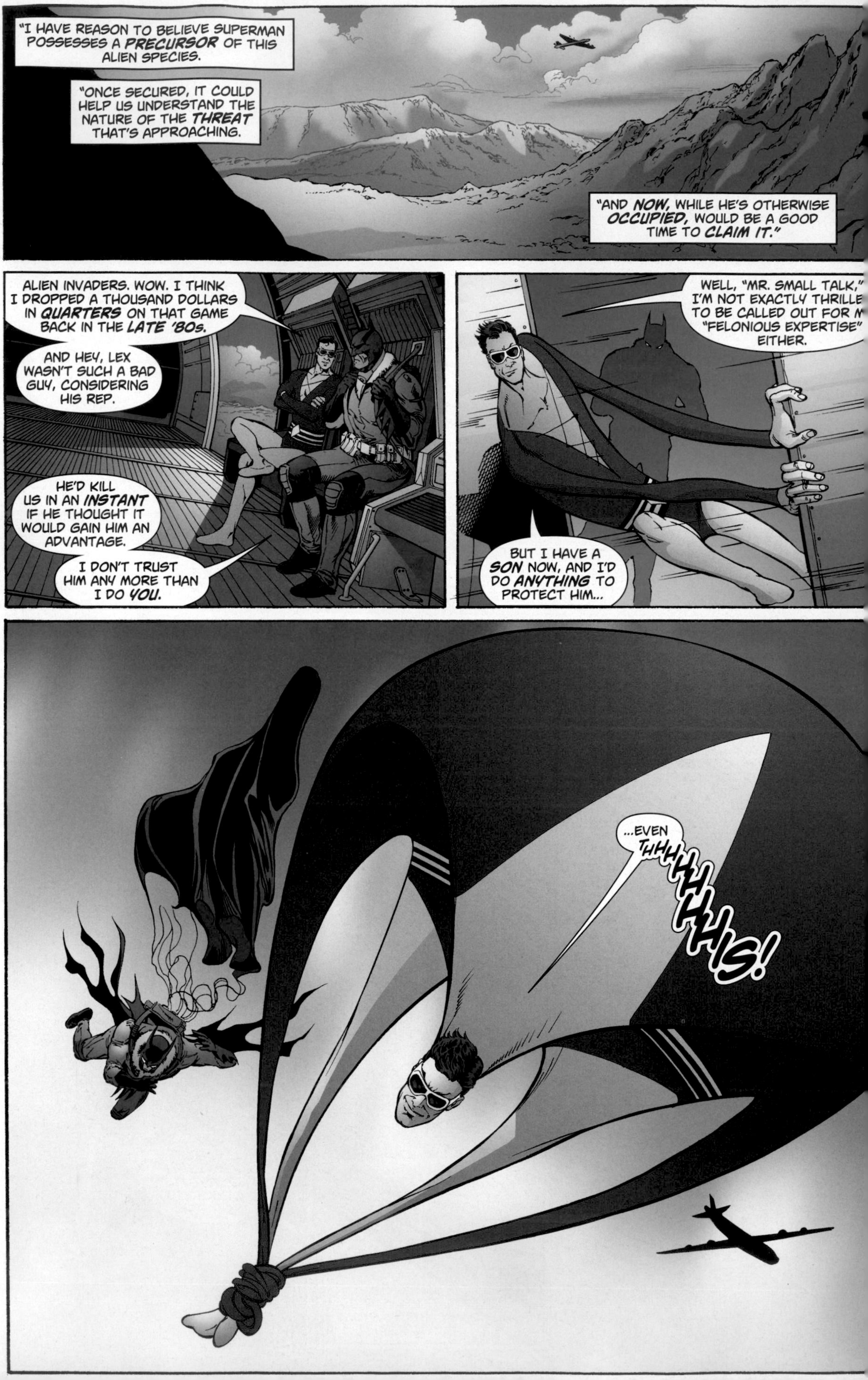
"I HAVE REASON TO BELIEVE SUPERMAN POSSESSES A PRECURSOR OF THIS ALIEN SPECIES.
"ONCE SECURED, IT COULD HELP US UNDERSTAND THE NATURE OF THE THREAT THAT'S APPROACHING.
"AND NOW, WHILE HE'S OTHERWISE OCCUPIED, WOULD BE A GOOD TIME TO CLAIM IT."
ALIEN INVADERS. WOW. I THINK I DROPPED A THOUSAND DOLLARS IN QUARTERS ON THAT GAME BACK IN THE LATE '80s.
AND HEY, LEX WASN'T SUCH A BAD GUY, CONSIDERING HIS REP.
HE'D KILL US IN AN INSTANT IF HE THOUGHT IT WOULD GAIN HIM AN ADVANTAGE.
I DON'T TRUST HIM ANY MORE THAN I DO YOU.
WELL, "MR. SMALL TALK," I'M NOT EXACTLY THRILLE TO BE CALLED OUT FOR M "FELONIOUS EXPERTISE" EITHER.
BUT I HAVE A SON NOW, AND I'D DO ANYTHING TO PROTECT HIM...
...EVEN THHHHHHIS!

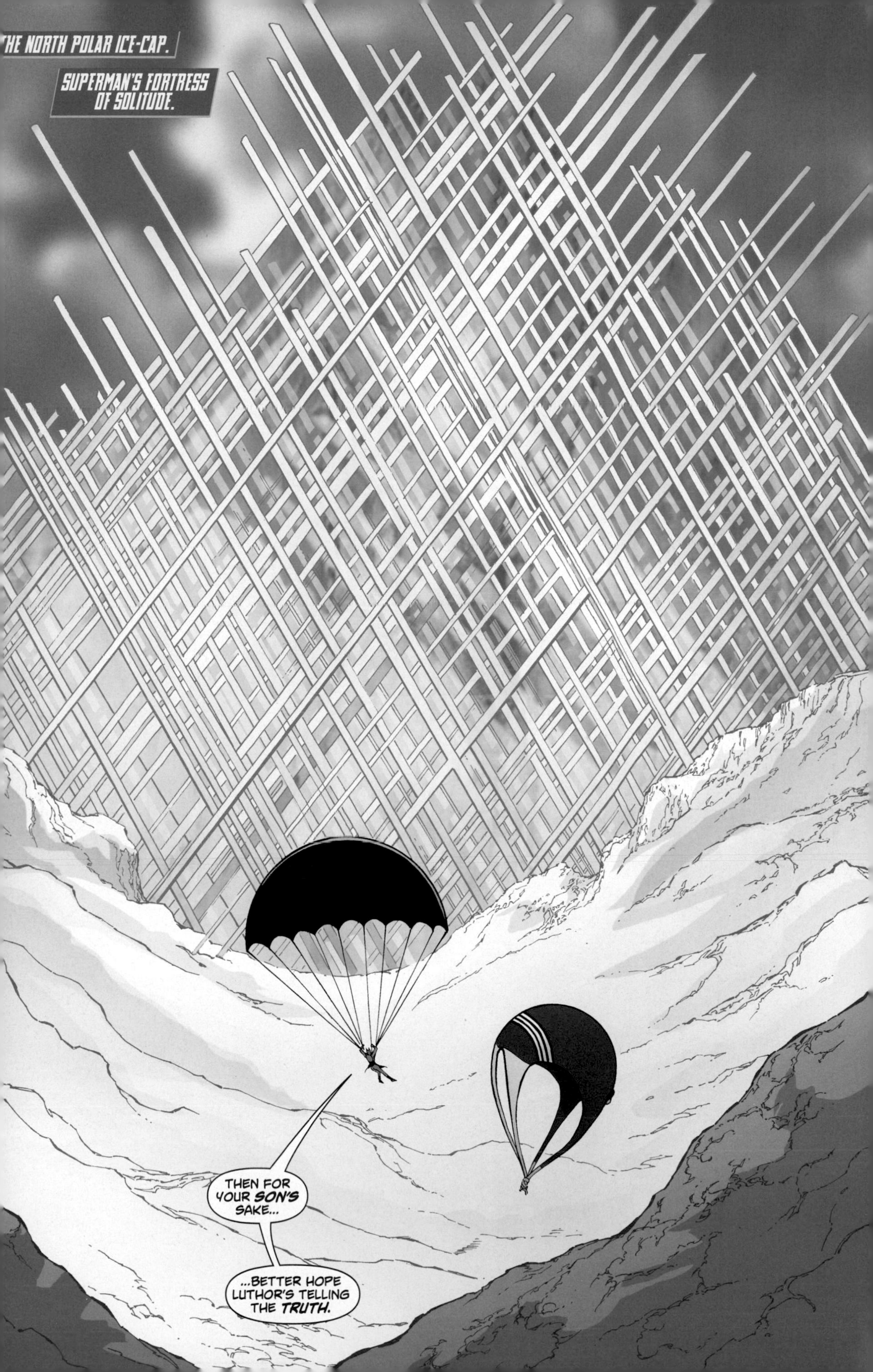
THE NORTH POLAR ICE-CAP.
SUPERMAN'S FORTRESS OF SOLITUDE.
THEN FOR YOUR SON'S SAKE...
...BETTER HOPE LUTHOR'S TELLING THE TRUTH.

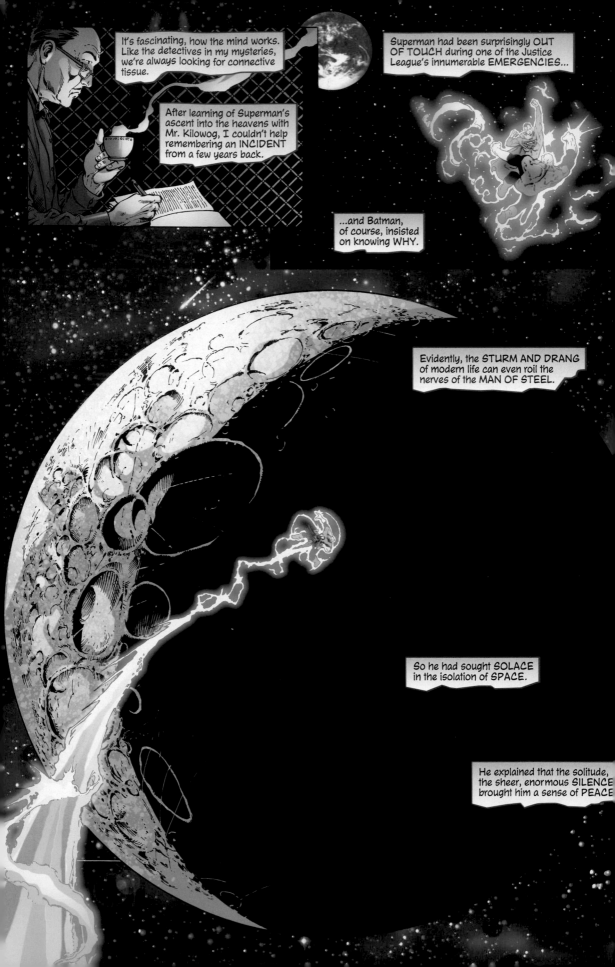

It's fascinating, how the mind works. Like the detectives in my mysteries, we're always looking for connective tissue.

After learning of Superman's ascent into the heavens with Mr. Kilowog, I couldn't help remembering an INCIDENT from a few years back.

Superman had been surprisingly OUT OF TOUCH during one of the Justice League's innumerable EMERGENCIES...

...and Batman, of course, insisted on knowing WHY.

Evidently, the STURM AND DRANG of modern life can even roil the nerves of the MAN OF STEEL.

So he had sought SOLACE in the isolation of SPACE.

He explained that the solitude, the sheer, enormous SILENCE brought him a sense of PEACE.

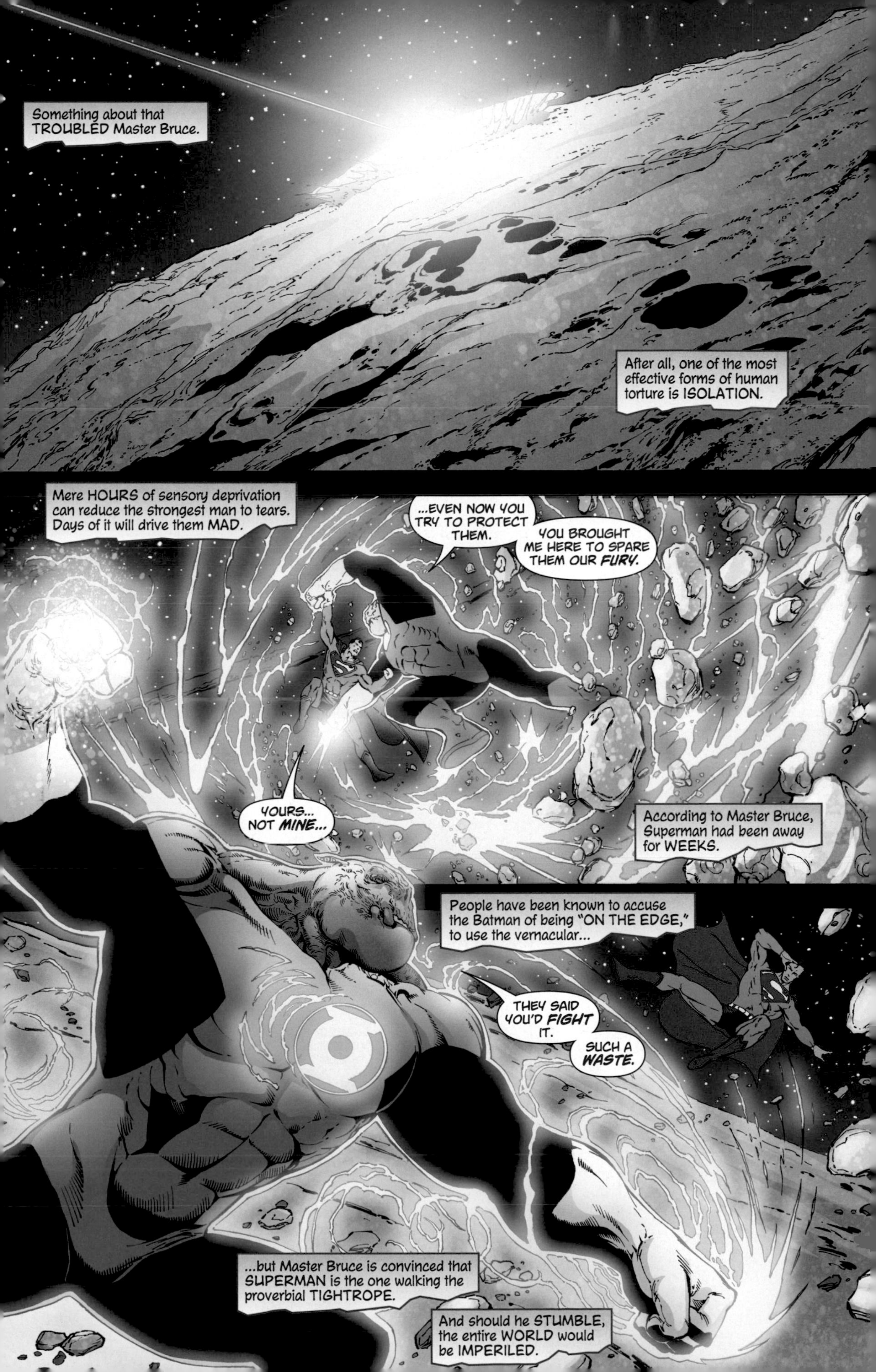
Something about that TROUBLED Master Bruce.
After all, one of the most effective forms of human torture is ISOLATION.
Mere HOURS of sensory deprivation can reduce the strongest man to tears. Days of it will drive them MAD.
...EVEN NOW YOU TRY TO PROTECT THEM.
YOU BROUGHT ME HERE TO SPARE THEM OUR FURY.
YOURS... NOT MINE...
According to Master Bruce, Superman had been away for WEEKS.
People have been known to accuse the Batman of being "ON THE EDGE," to use the vernacular...
THEY SAID YOU'D FIGHT IT.
SUCH A WASTE.
...but Master Bruce is convinced that SUPERMAN is the one walking the proverbial TIGHTROPE.
And should he STUMBLE, the entire WORLD would be IMPERILED.

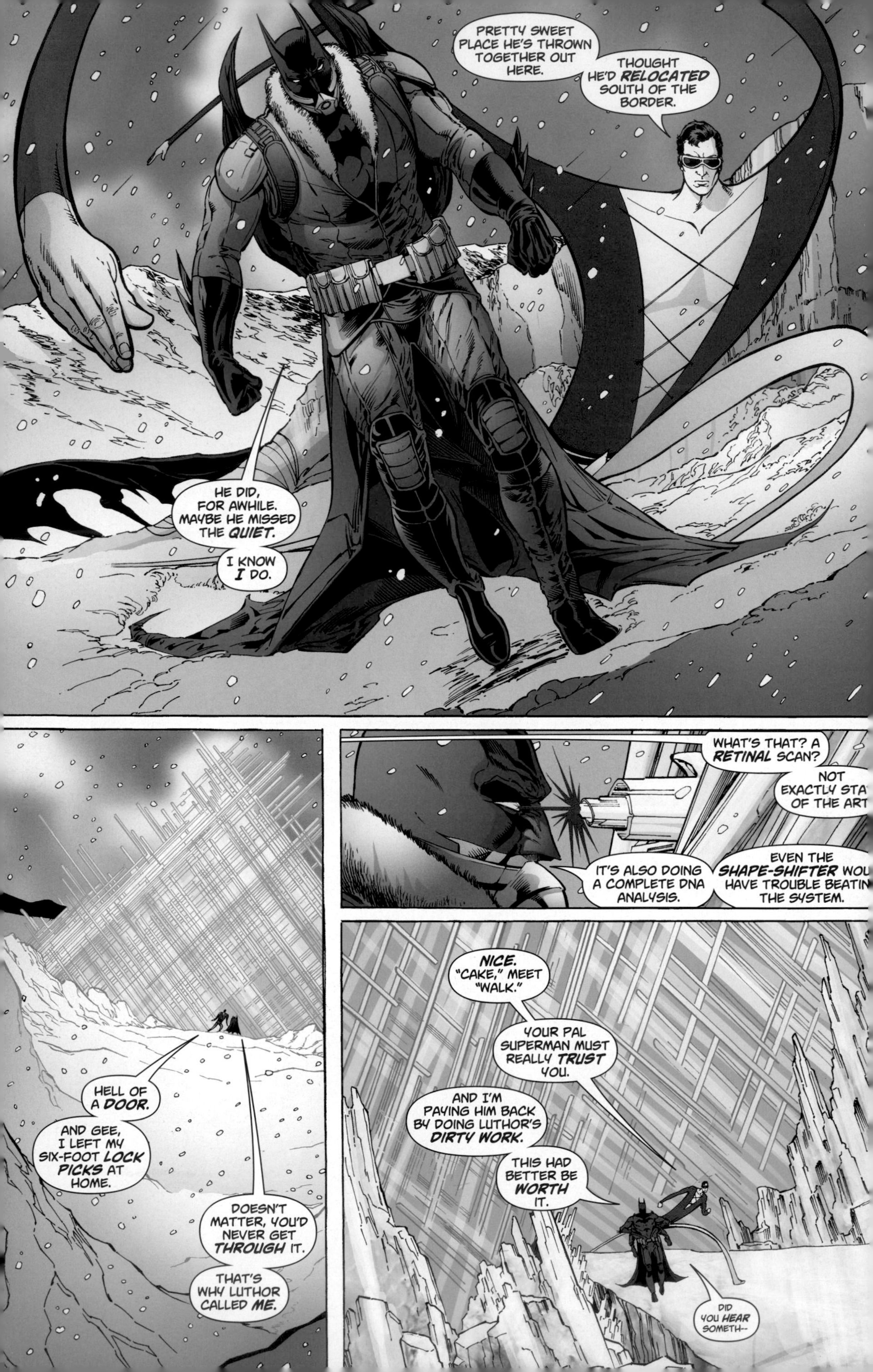
PRETTY SWEET PLACE HE'S THROWN TOGETHER OUT HERE.
THOUGHT HE'D RELOCATED SOUTH OF THE BORDER.
HE DID, FOR AWHILE. MAYBE HE MISSED THE QUIET.
I KNOW I DO.
HELL OF A DOOR.
AND GEE, I LEFT MY SIX-FOOT LOCK PICKS AT HOME.
DOESN'T MATTER, YOU'D NEVER GET THROUGH IT.
THAT'S WHY LUTHOR CALLED ME.
WHAT'S THAT? A RETINAL SCAN?
NOT EXACTLY STA OF THE ART
IT'S ALSO DOING A COMPLETE DNA ANALYSIS.
EVEN THE SHAPE-SHIFTER WOU HAVE TROUBLE BEATIN THE SYSTEM.
NICE. "CAKE," MEET "WALK."
YOUR PAL SUPERMAN MUST REALLY TRUST YOU.
AND I'M PAYING HIM BACK BY DOING LUTHOR'S DIRTY WORK.
THIS HAD BETTER BE WORTH IT.
DID YOU HEAR SOMETH--

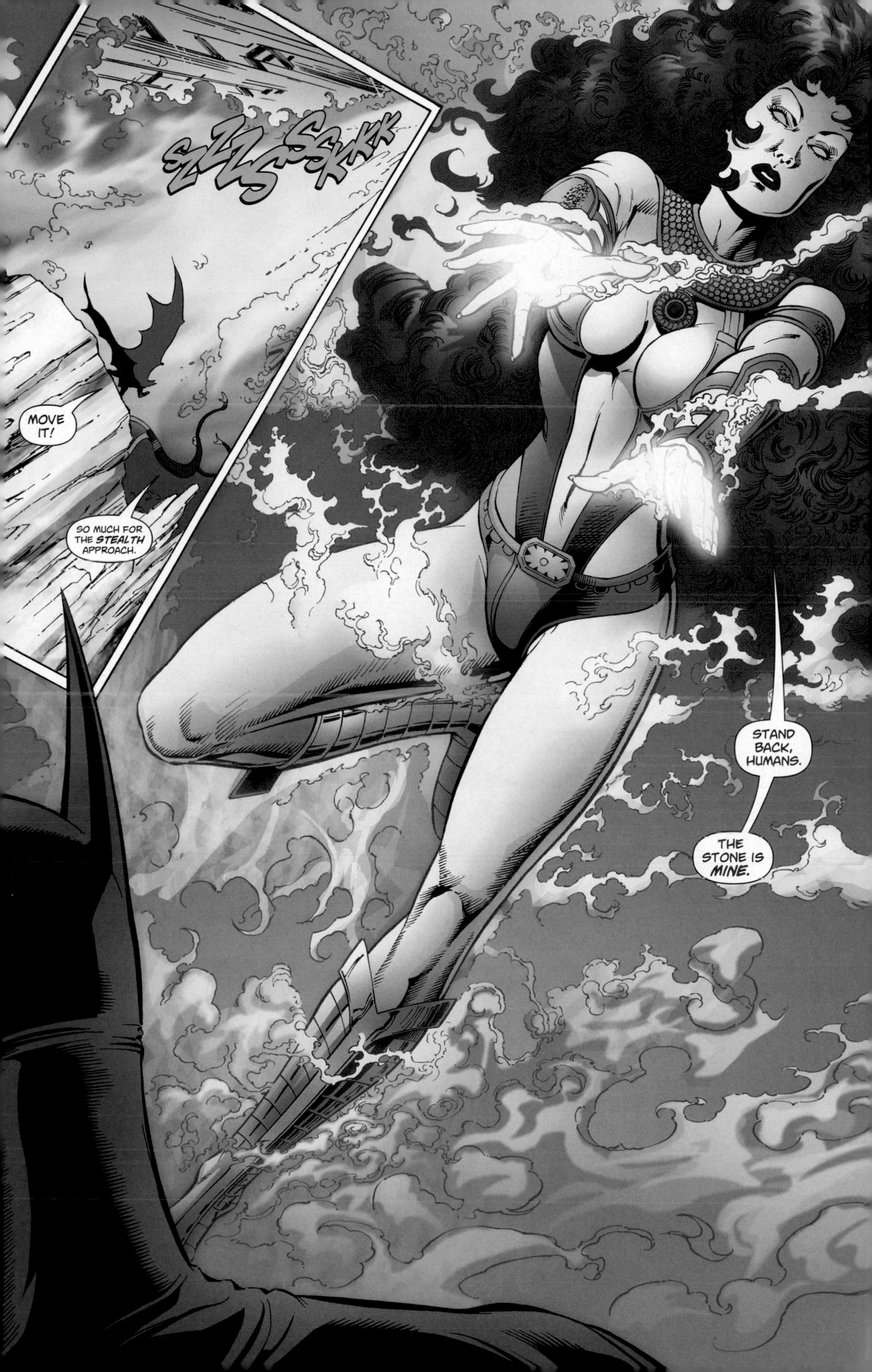
SZZZSSKKKK
MOVE IT!
SO MUCH FOR THE STEALTH APPROACH.
STAND BACK, HUMANS.
THE STONE IS MINE.

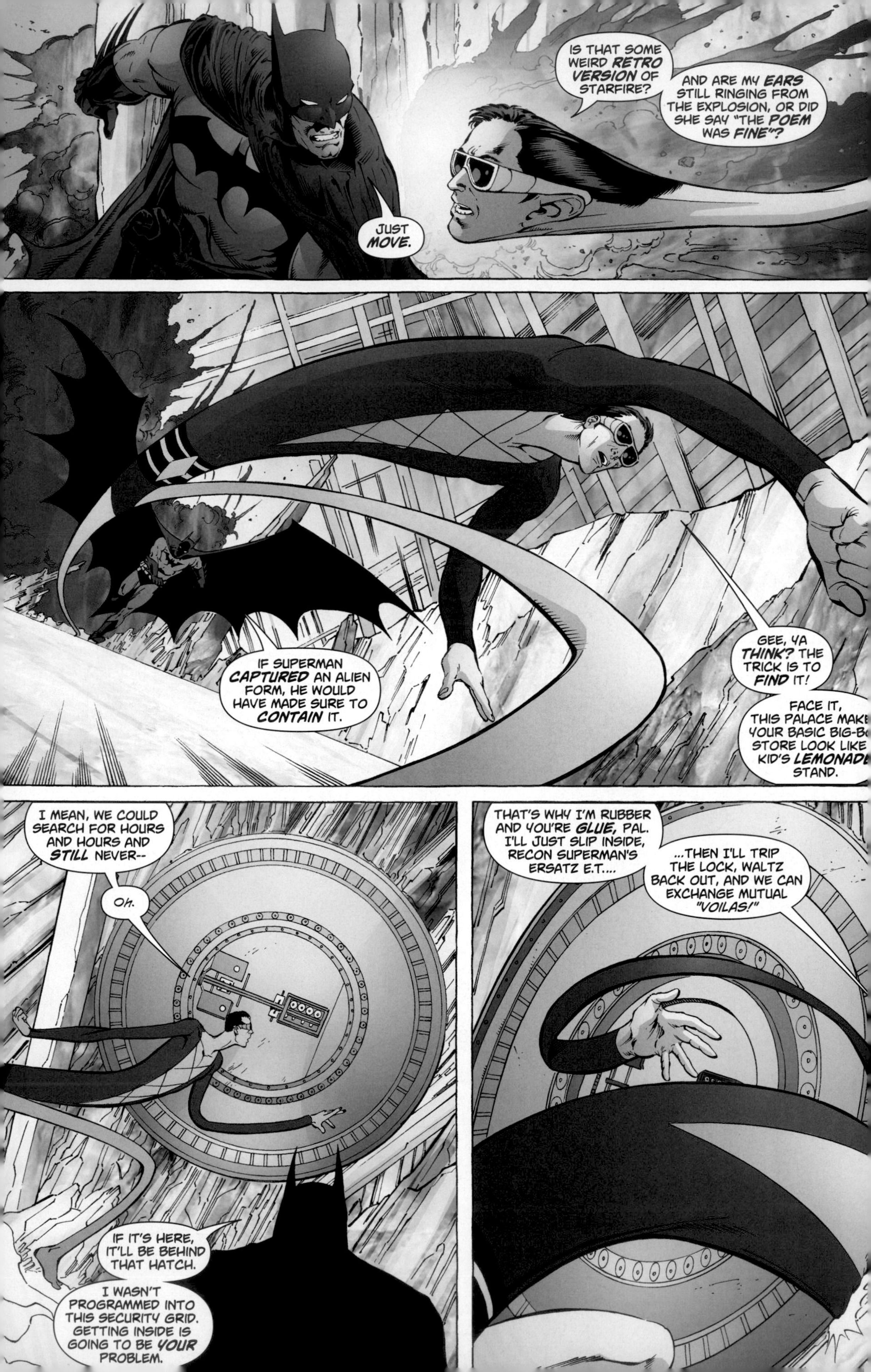
IS THAT SOME WEIRD RETRO VERSION OF STARFIRE?
AND ARE MY EARS STILL RINGING FROM THE EXPLOSION, OR DID SHE SAY "THE POEM WAS FINE"?
JUST MOVE.
IF SUPERMAN CAPTURED AN ALIEN FORM, HE WOULD HAVE MADE SURE TO CONTAIN IT.
GEE, YA THINK? THE TRICK IS TO FIND IT!
FACE IT, THIS PALACE MAKE YOUR BASIC BIG-BO STORE LOOK LIKE KID'S LEMONADE STAND.
I MEAN, WE COULD SEARCH FOR HOURS AND HOURS AND STILL NEVER--
Oh.
IF IT'S HERE, IT'LL BE BEHIND THAT HATCH.
I WASN'T PROGRAMMED INTO THIS SECURITY GRID. GETTING INSIDE IS GOING TO BE YOUR PROBLEM.
THAT'S WHY I'M RUBBER AND YOU'RE GLUE, PAL. I'LL JUST SLIP INSIDE, RECON SUPERMAN'S ERSATZ E.T....
...THEN I'LL TRIP THE LOCK, WALTZ BACK OUT, AND WE CAN EXCHANGE MUTUAL "VOILAS!"

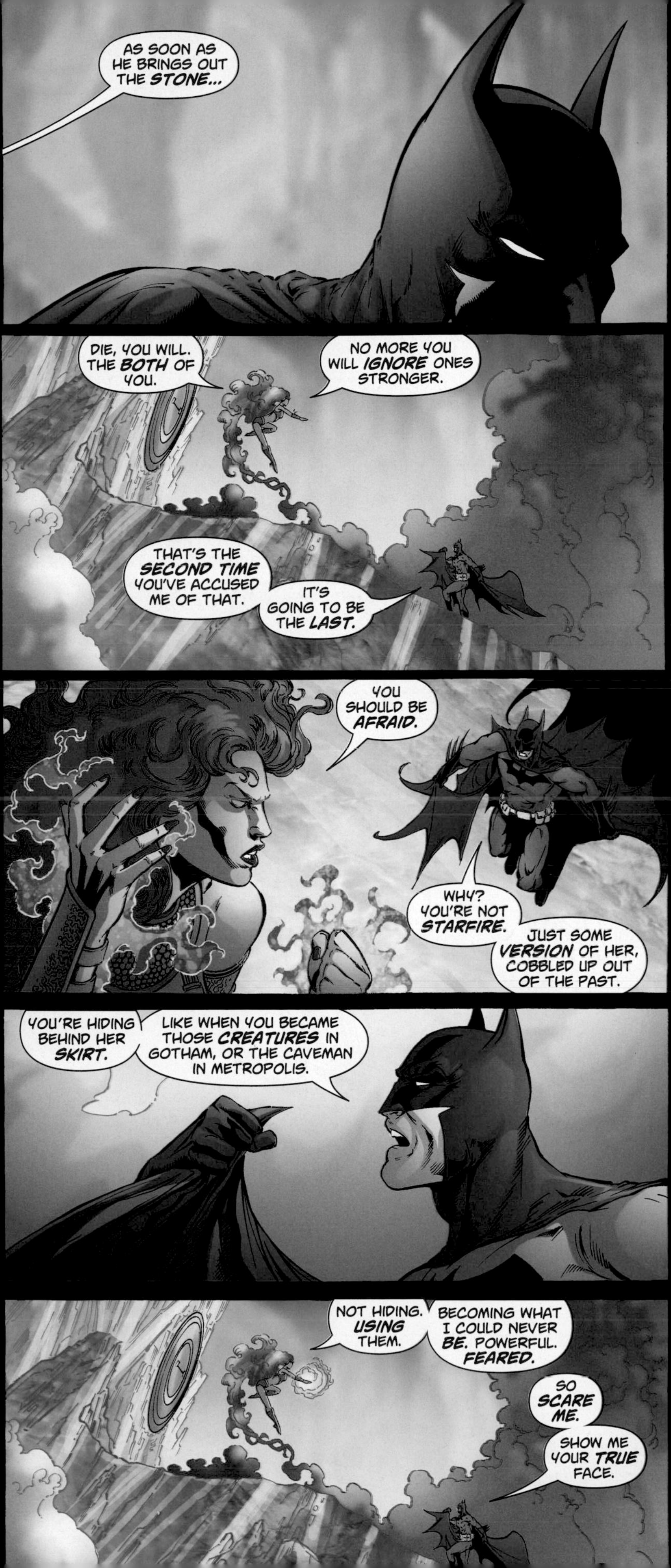
AS SOON AS HE BRINGS OUT THE STONE...
DIE, YOU WILL. THE BOTH OF YOU.
NO MORE YOU WILL IGNORE ONES STRONGER.
THAT'S THE SECOND TIME YOU'VE ACCUSED ME OF THAT.
IT'S GOING TO BE THE LAST.
YOU SHOULD BE AFRAID.
WHY? YOU'RE NOT STARFIRE.
JUST SOME VERSION OF HER, COBBLED UP OUT OF THE PAST.
YOU'RE HIDING BEHIND HER SKIRT.
LIKE WHEN YOU BECAME THOSE CREATURES IN GOTHAM, OR THE CAVEMAN IN METROPOLIS.
NOT HIDING. USING THEM.
BECOMING WHAT I COULD NEVER BE. POWERFUL. FEARED.
SO SCARE ME.
SHOW ME YOUR TRUE FACE.

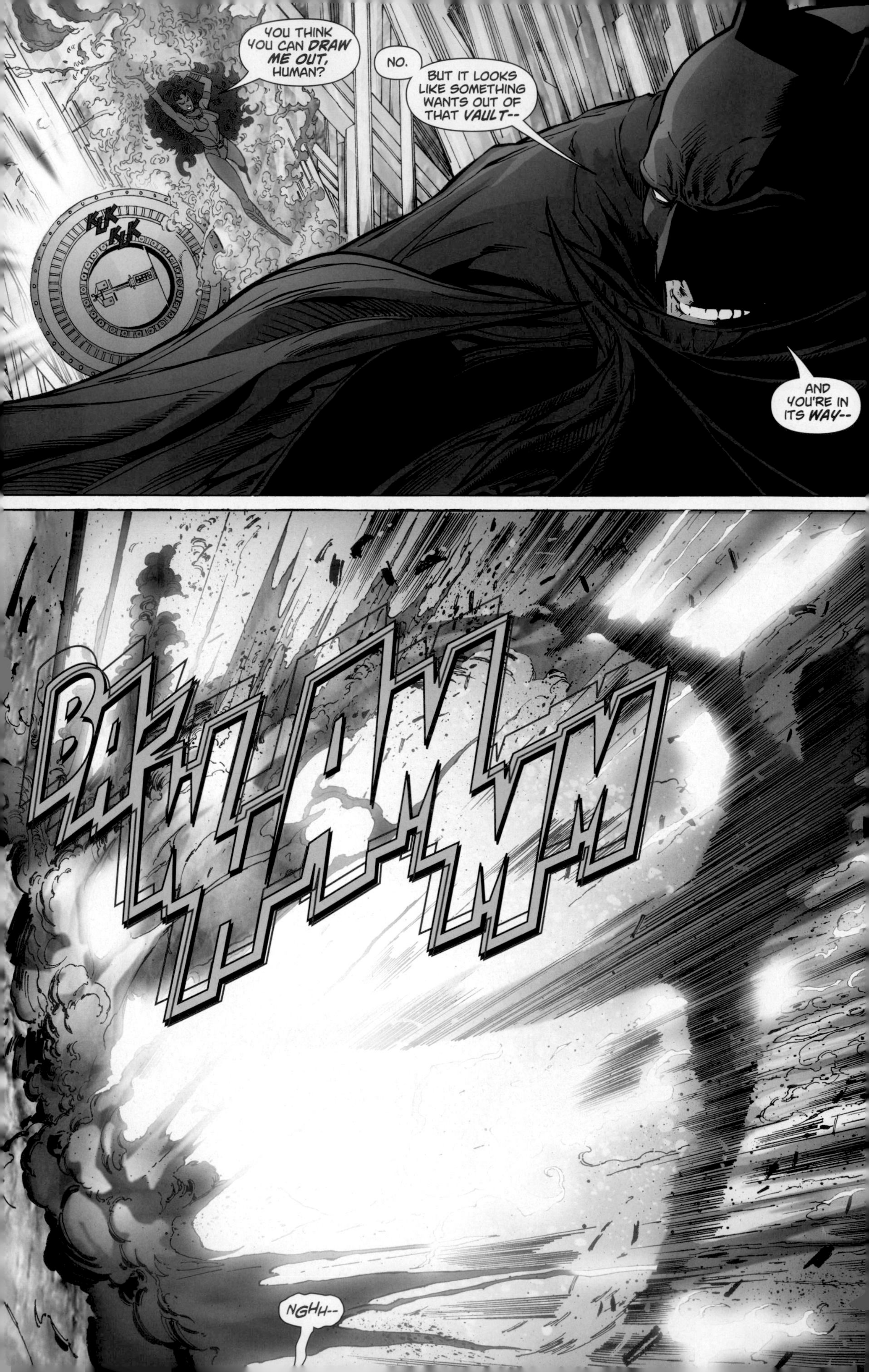
YOU THINK YOU CAN DRAW ME OUT, HUMAN?
NO.
BUT IT LOOKS LIKE SOMETHING WANTS OUT OF THAT VAULT--
KLIK KLIK
AND YOU'RE IN ITS WAY--
BAWHAMM
NGHH--

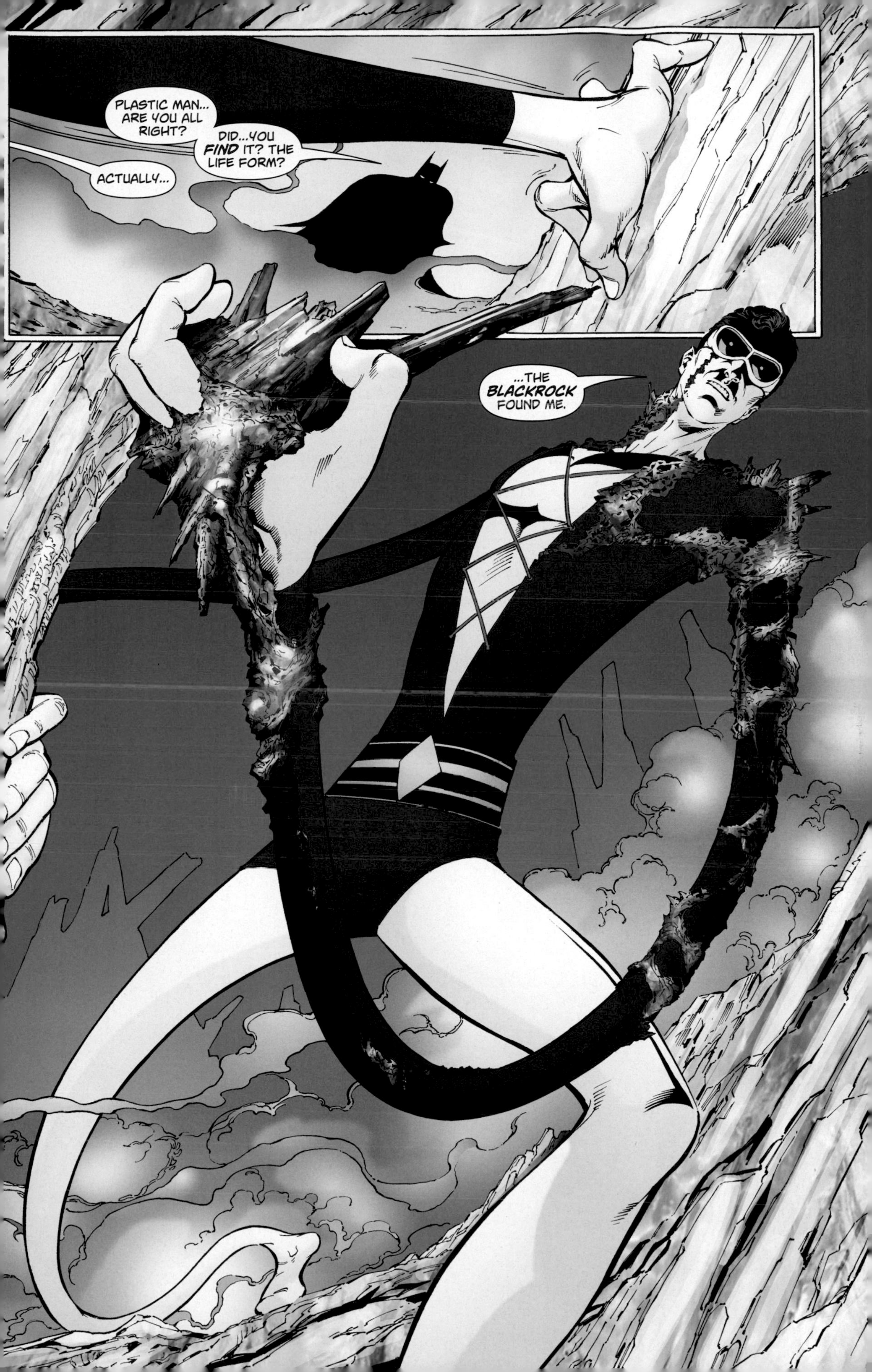
PLASTIC MAN... ARE YOU ALL RIGHT?
DID...YOU FIND IT? THE LIFE FORM?
ACTUALLY...
...THE BLACKROCK FOUND ME.

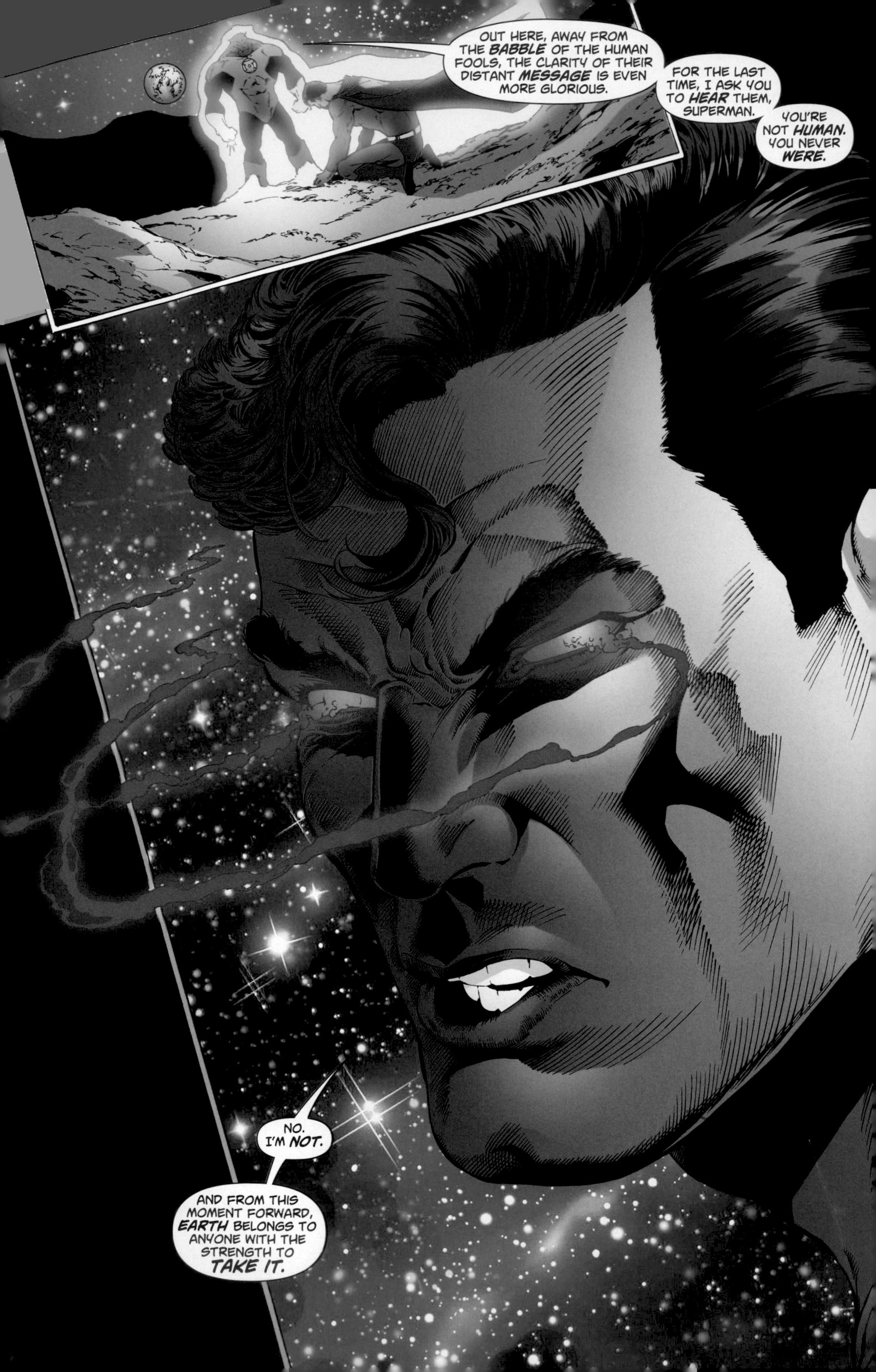

OUT HERE, AWAY FROM THE BABBLE OF THE HUMAN FOOLS, THE CLARITY OF THEIR DISTANT MESSAGE IS EVEN MORE GLORIOUS.
FOR THE LAST TIME, I ASK YOU TO HEAR THEM, SUPERMAN.
YOU'RE NOT HUMAN. YOU NEVER WERE.
NO. I'M NOT.
AND FROM THIS MOMENT FORWARD, EARTH BELONGS TO ANYONE WITH THE STRENGTH TO TAKE IT.

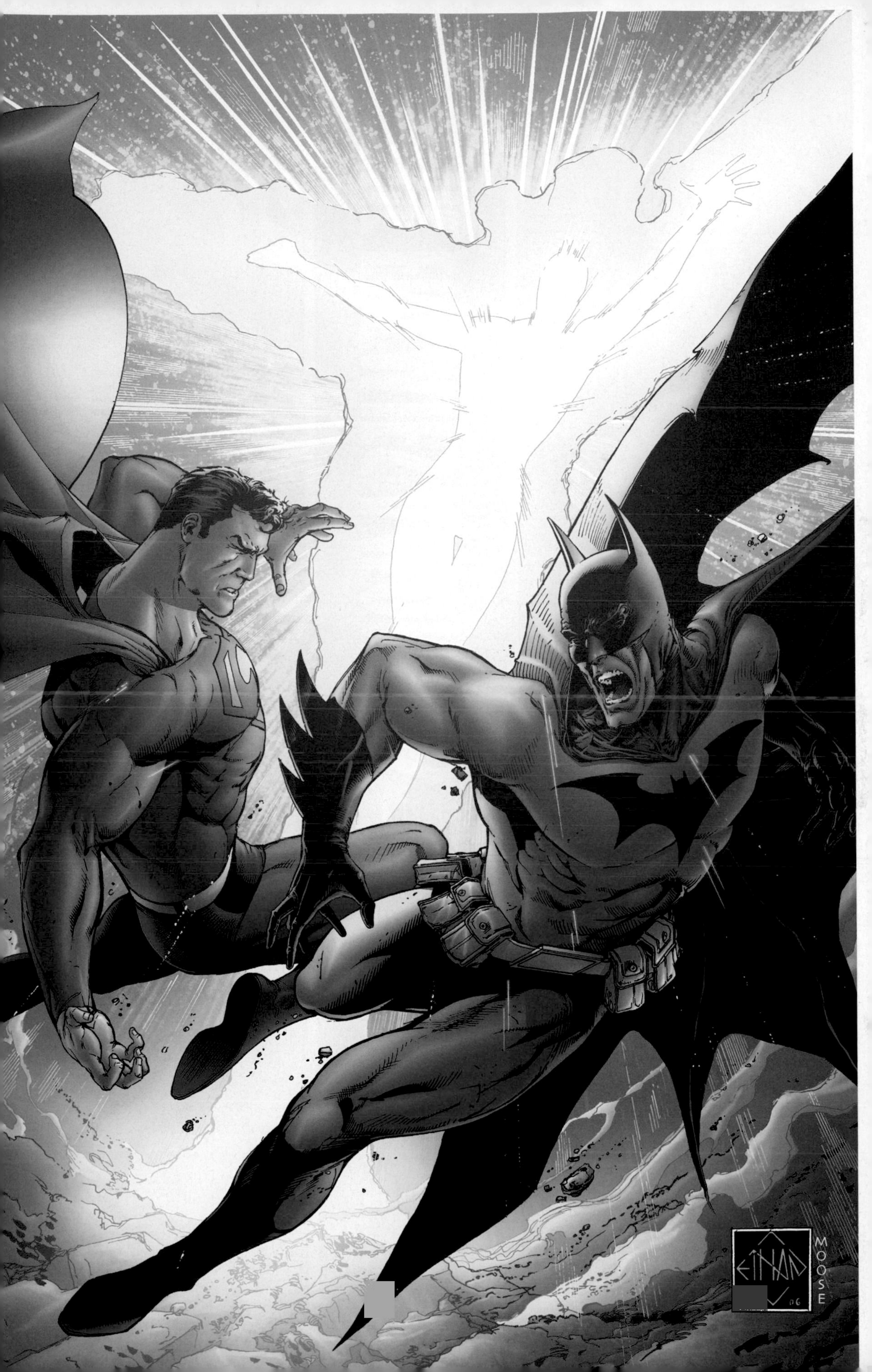
MOOSE

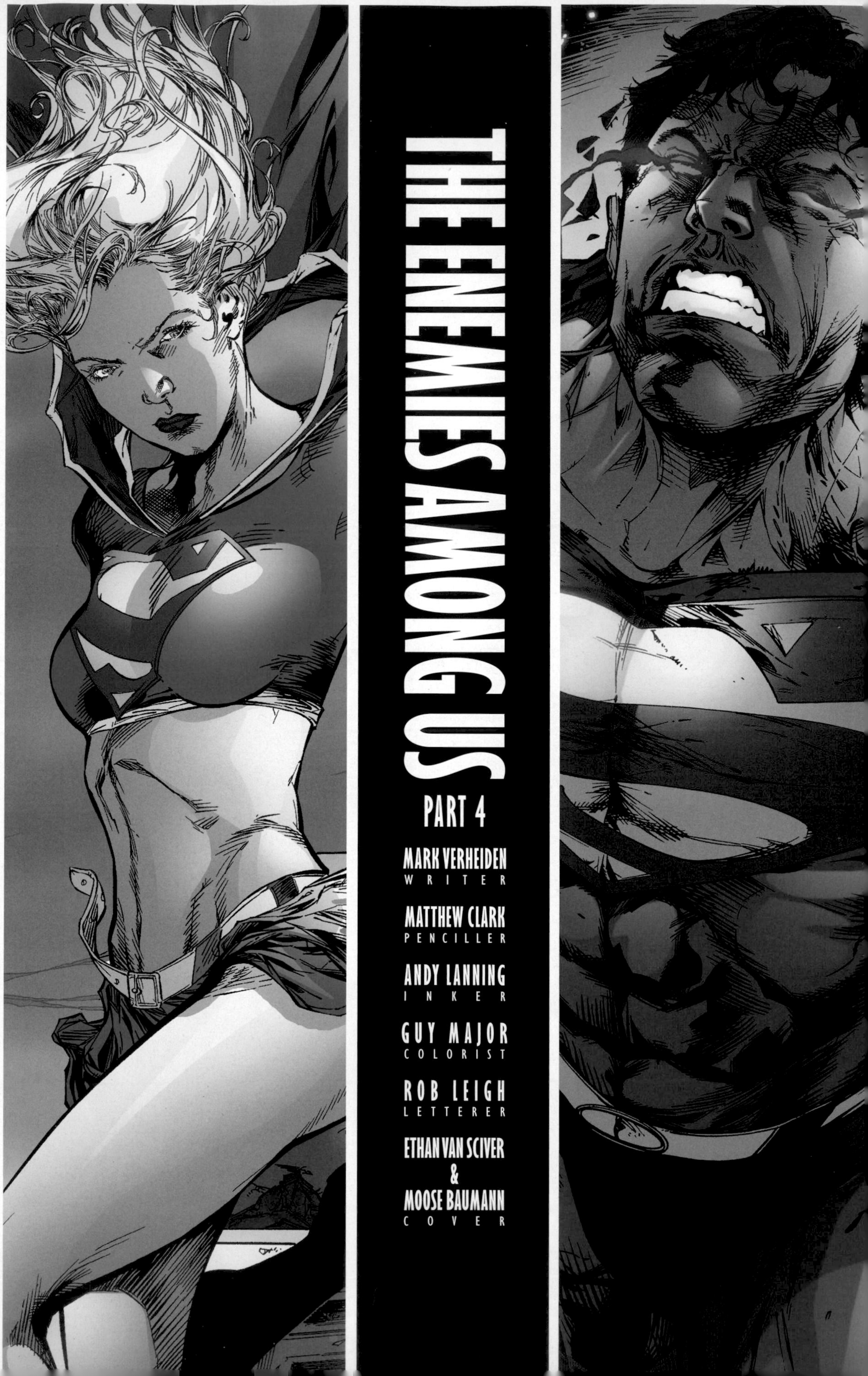
THE ENEMIES AMONG US
PART 4
MARK VERHEIDEN
WRITER
MATTHEW CLARK
PENCILLER
ANDY LANNING
INKER
GUY MAJOR
COLORIST
ROB LEIGH
LETTERER
ETHAN VAN SCIVER
&
MOOSE BAUMANN
COVER

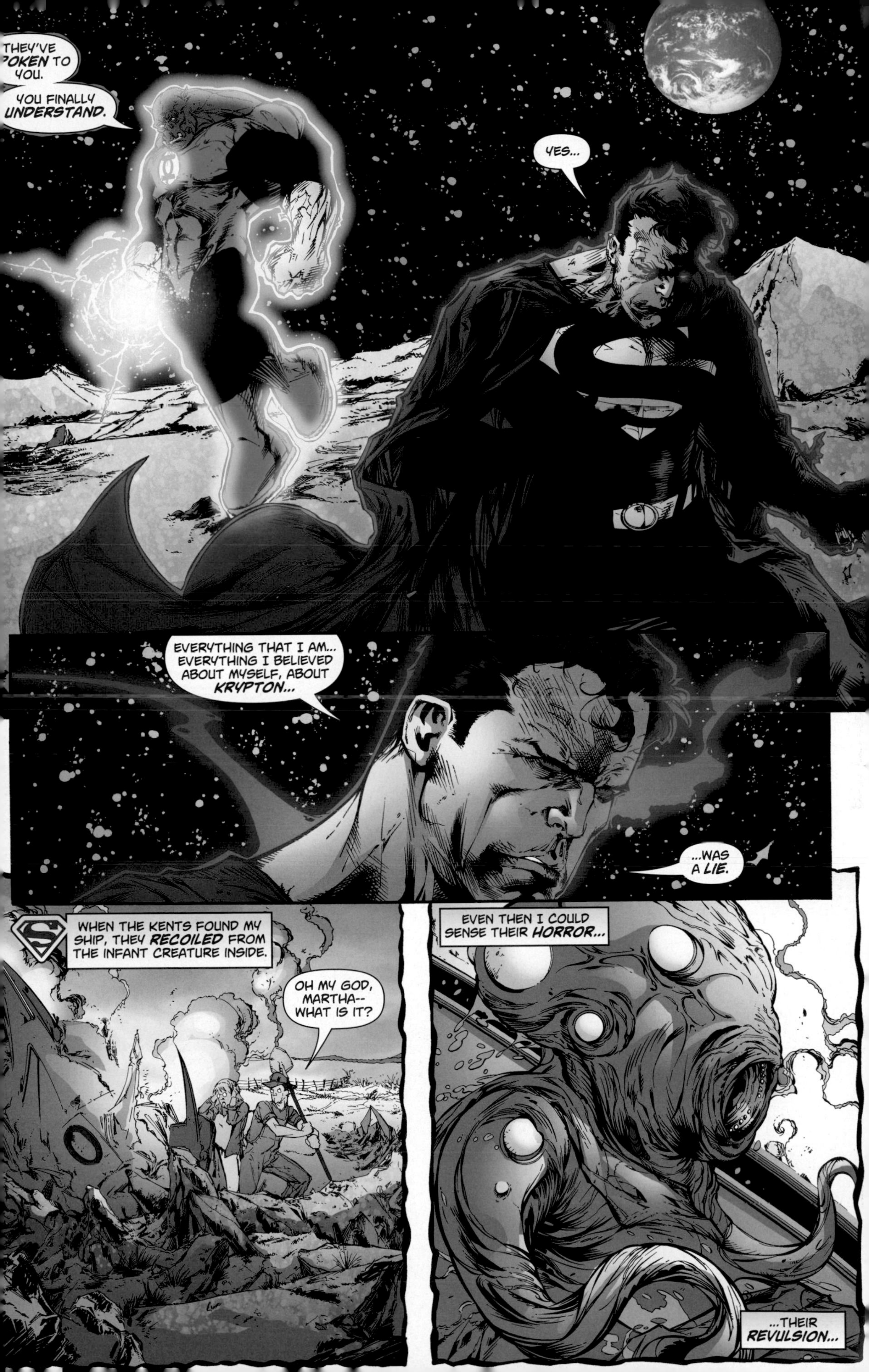
THEY'VE SPOKEN TO YOU.
YOU FINALLY UNDERSTAND.
YES...
EVERYTHING THAT I AM... EVERYTHING I BELIEVED ABOUT MYSELF, ABOUT KRYPTON...
...WAS A LIE.
WHEN THE KENTS FOUND MY SHIP, THEY RECOILED FROM THE INFANT CREATURE INSIDE.
OH MY GOD, MARTHA-- WHAT IS IT?
EVEN THEN I COULD SENSE THEIR HORROR...
...THEIR REVULSION...

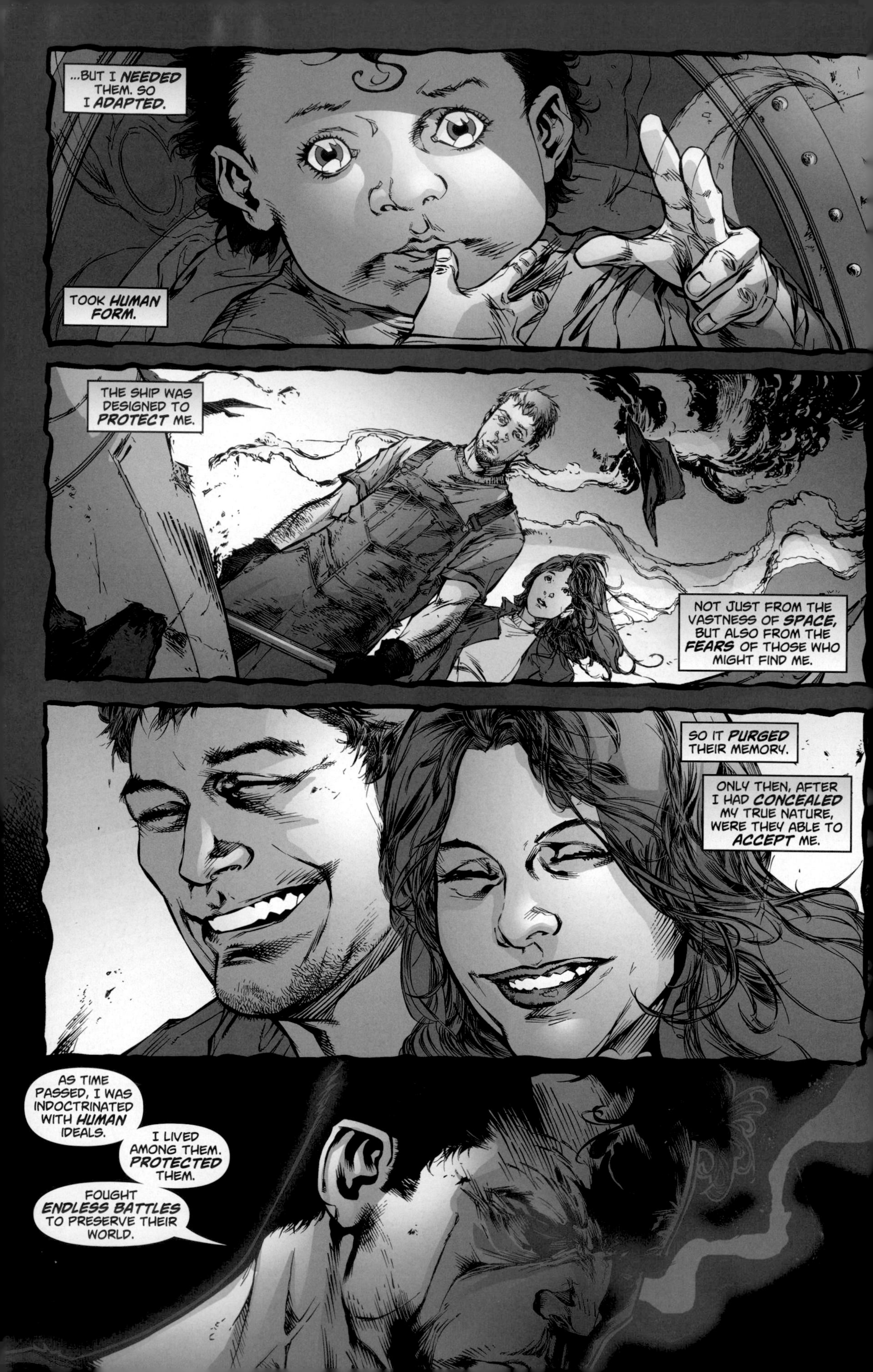
...BUT I NEEDED THEM. SO I ADAPTED.
TOOK HUMAN FORM.
THE SHIP WAS DESIGNED TO PROTECT ME.
NOT JUST FROM THE VASTNESS OF SPACE, BUT ALSO FROM THE FEARS OF THOSE WHO MIGHT FIND ME.
SO IT PURGED THEIR MEMORY.
ONLY THEN, AFTER I HAD CONCEALED MY TRUE NATURE, WERE THEY ABLE TO ACCEPT ME.
AS TIME PASSED, I WAS INDOCTRINATED WITH HUMAN IDEALS.
I LIVED AMONG THEM. PROTECTED THEM.
FOUGHT ENDLESS BATTLES TO PRESERVE THEIR WORLD.

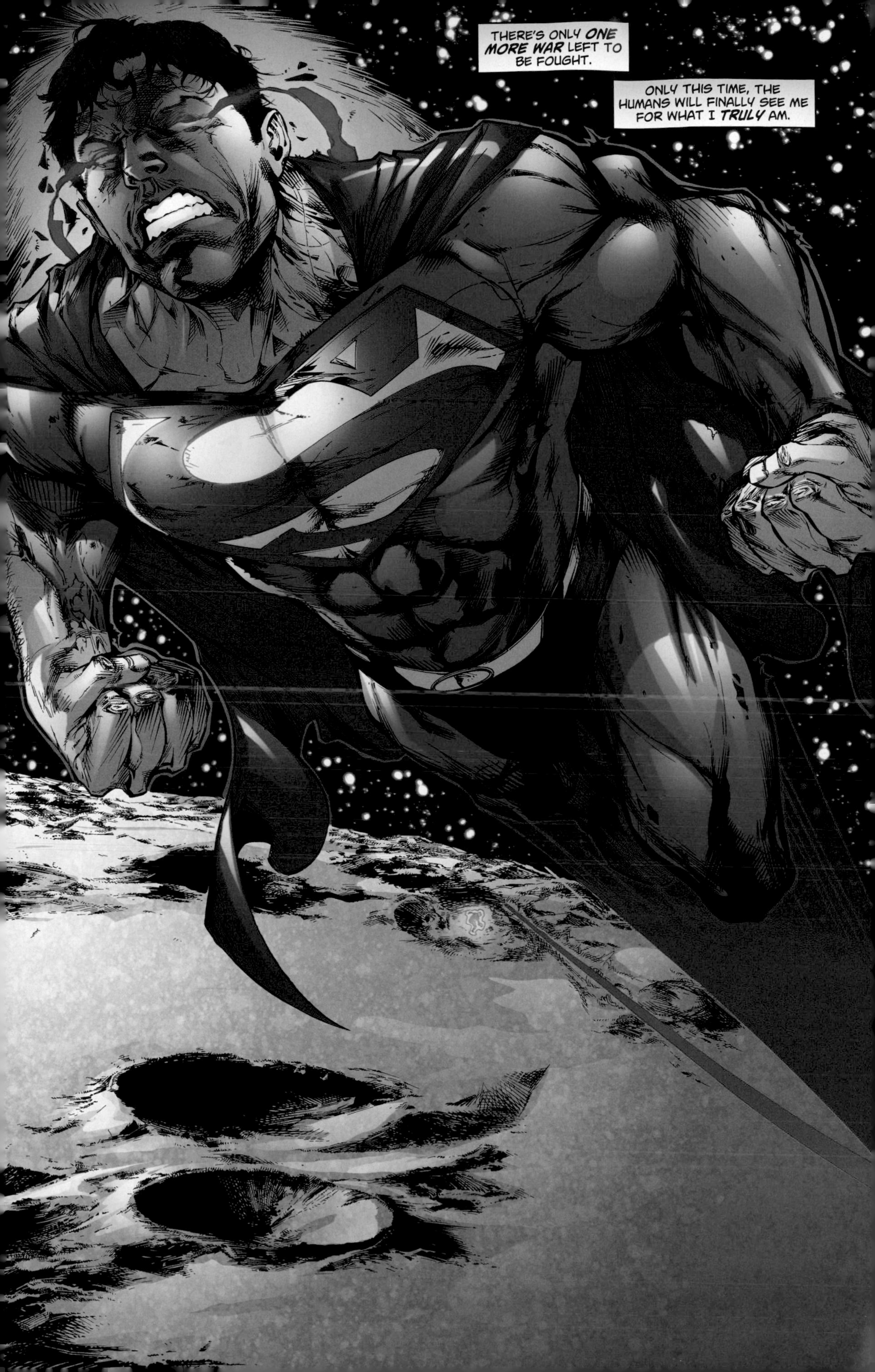
THERE'S ONLY ONE MORE WAR LEFT TO BE FOUGHT.
ONLY THIS TIME, THE HUMANS WILL FINALLY SEE ME FOR WHAT I TRULY AM.

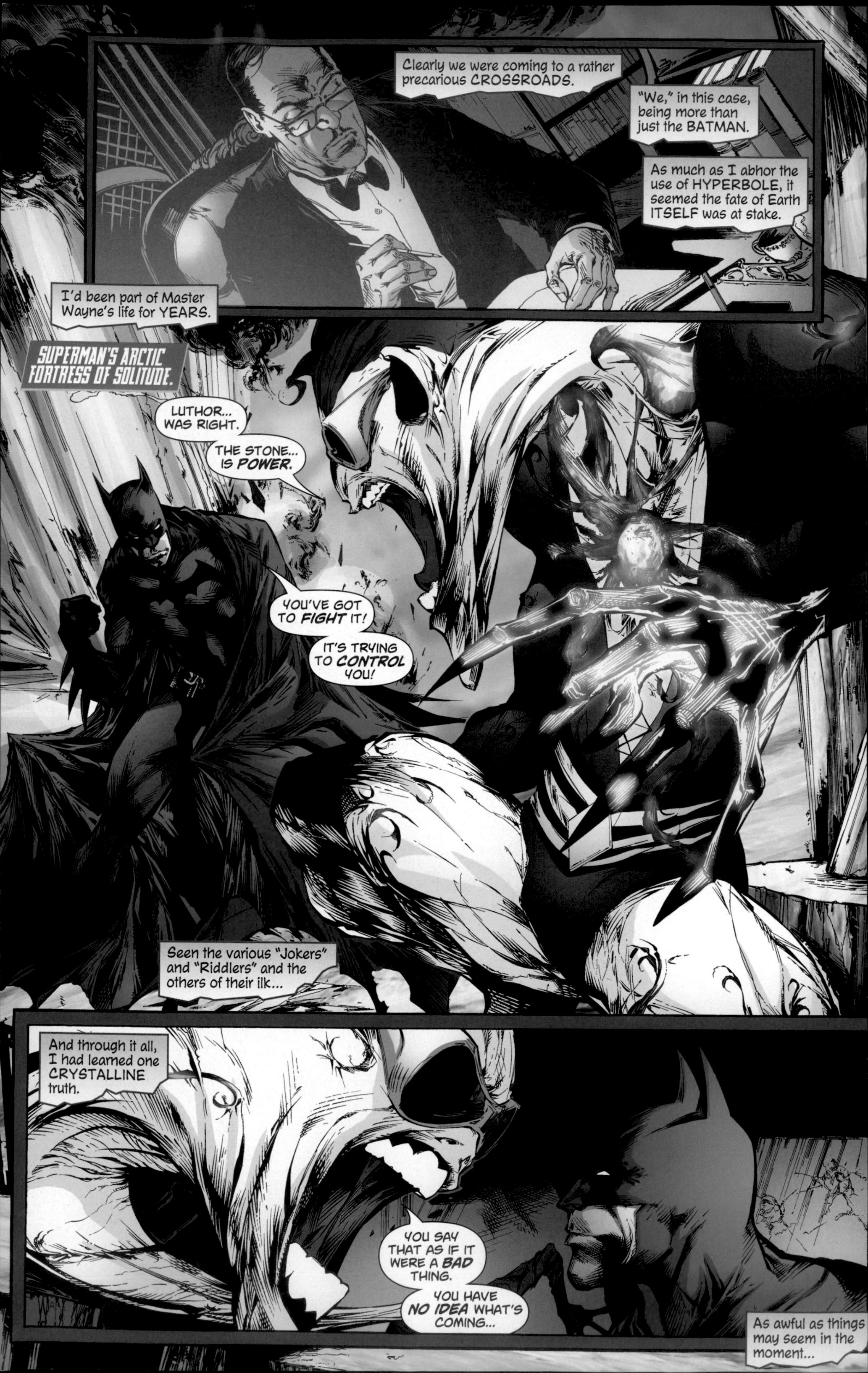
Clearly we were coming to a rather precarious CROSSROADS.
"We," in this case, being more than just the BATMAN.
As much as I abhor the use of HYPERBOLE, it seemed the fate of Earth ITSELF was at stake.
I'd been part of Master Wayne's life for YEARS.
SUPERMAN'S ARCTIC FORTRESS OF SOLITUDE.
LUTHOR... WAS RIGHT.
THE STONE... IS POWER.
YOU'VE GOT TO FIGHT IT!
IT'S TRYING TO CONTROL YOU!
Seen the various "Jokers" and "Riddlers" and the others of their ilk...
And through it all, I had learned one CRYSTALLINE truth.
YOU SAY THAT AS IF IT WERE A BAD THING.
YOU HAVE NO IDEA WHAT'S COMING...
As awful as things may seem in the moment...

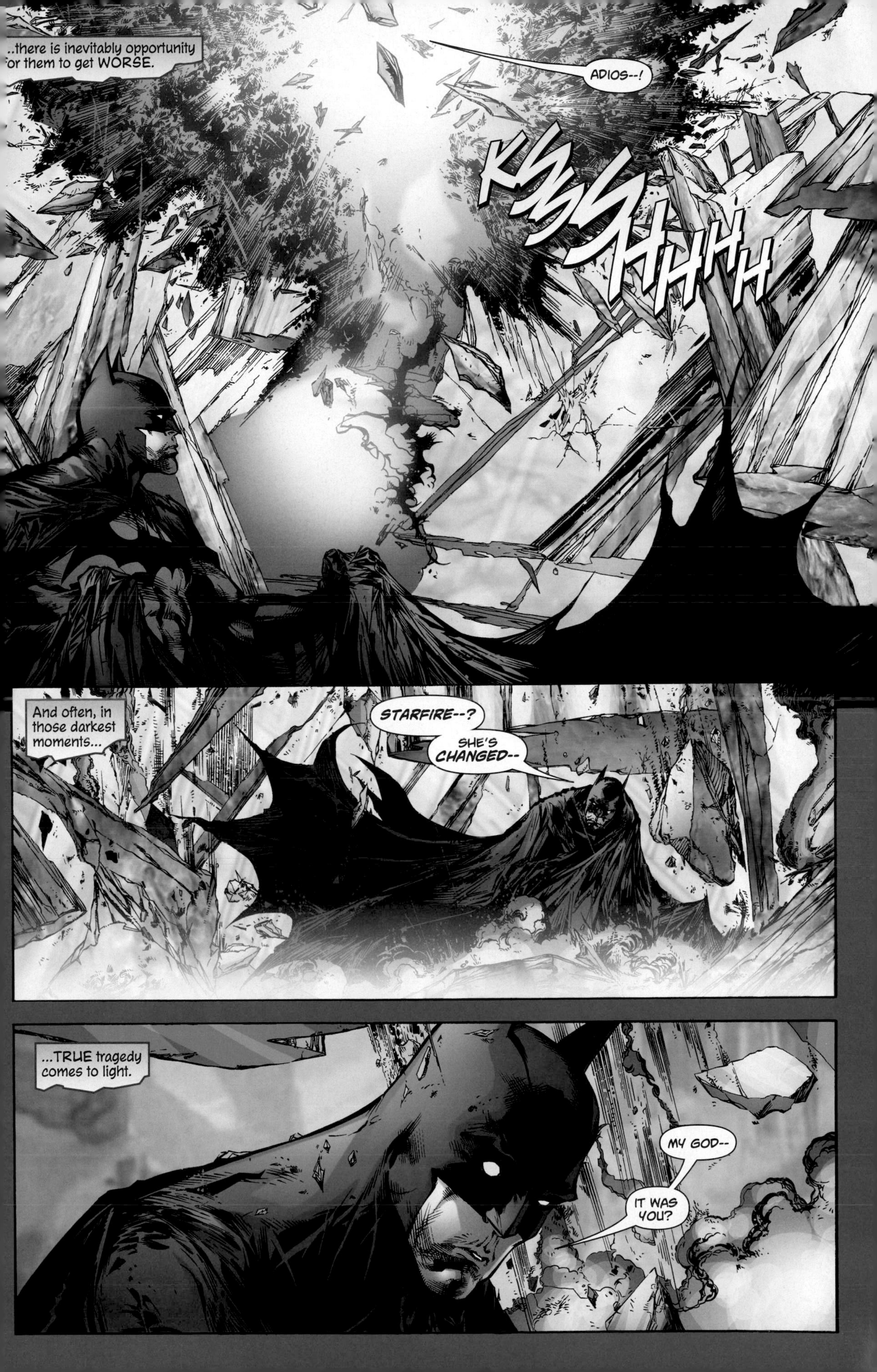

..there is inevitably opportunity for them to get WORSE.
ADIOS--!
KSSSHHHH
And often, in those darkest moments...
STARFIRE--?
SHE'S CHANGED--
...TRUE tragedy comes to light.
MY GOD--
IT WAS YOU?

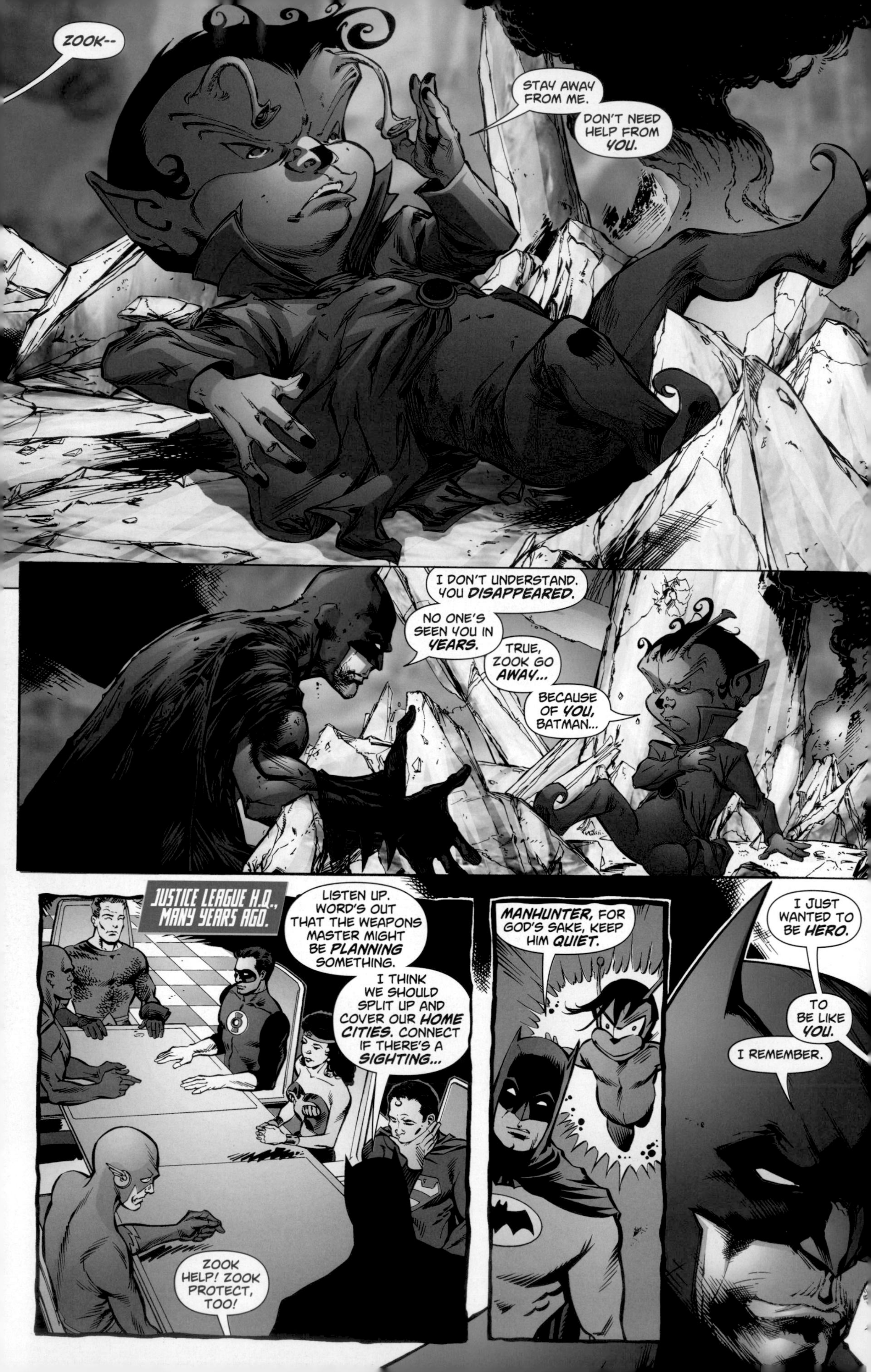
ZOOK--
STAY AWAY FROM ME.
DON'T NEED HELP FROM YOU.
I DON'T UNDERSTAND. YOU DISAPPEARED.
NO ONE'S SEEN YOU IN YEARS.
TRUE, ZOOK GO AWAY...
BECAUSE OF YOU, BATMAN...
JUSTICE LEAGUE H.Q., MANY YEARS AGO.
LISTEN UP. WORD'S OUT THAT THE WEAPONS MASTER MIGHT BE PLANNING SOMETHING.
I THINK WE SHOULD SPLIT UP AND COVER OUR HOME CITIES. CONNECT IF THERE'S A SIGHTING...
ZOOK HELP! ZOOK PROTECT, TOO!
MANHUNTER, FOR GOD'S SAKE, KEEP HIM QUIET.
I JUST WANTED TO BE HERO.
TO BE LIKE YOU.
I REMEMBER.

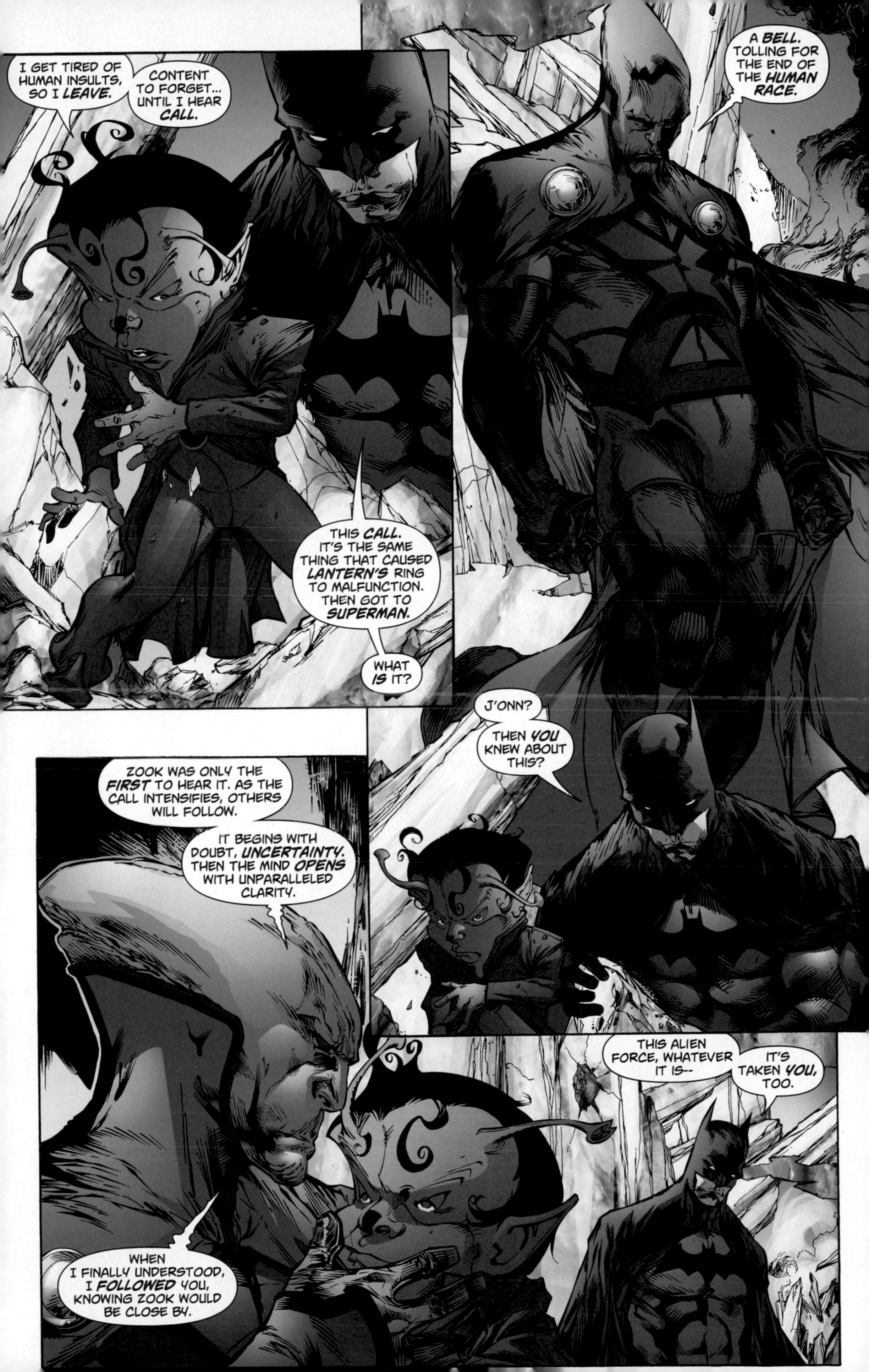
I GET TIRED OF HUMAN INSULTS, SO I LEAVE.
CONTENT TO FORGET... UNTIL I HEAR CALL.
A BELL. TOLLING FOR THE END OF THE HUMAN RACE.
THIS CALL. IT'S THE SAME THING THAT CAUSED LANTERN'S RING TO MALFUNCTION. THEN GOT TO SUPERMAN.
WHAT IS IT?
ZOOK WAS ONLY THE FIRST TO HEAR IT. AS THE CALL INTENSIFIES, OTHERS WILL FOLLOW.
IT BEGINS WITH DOUBT, UNCERTAINTY. THEN THE MIND OPENS WITH UNPARALLELED CLARITY.
J'ONN?
THEN YOU KNEW ABOUT THIS?
WHEN I FINALLY UNDERSTOOD, I FOLLOWED YOU, KNOWING ZOOK WOULD BE CLOSE BY.
THIS ALIEN FORCE, WHATEVER IT IS--
IT'S TAKEN YOU, TOO.

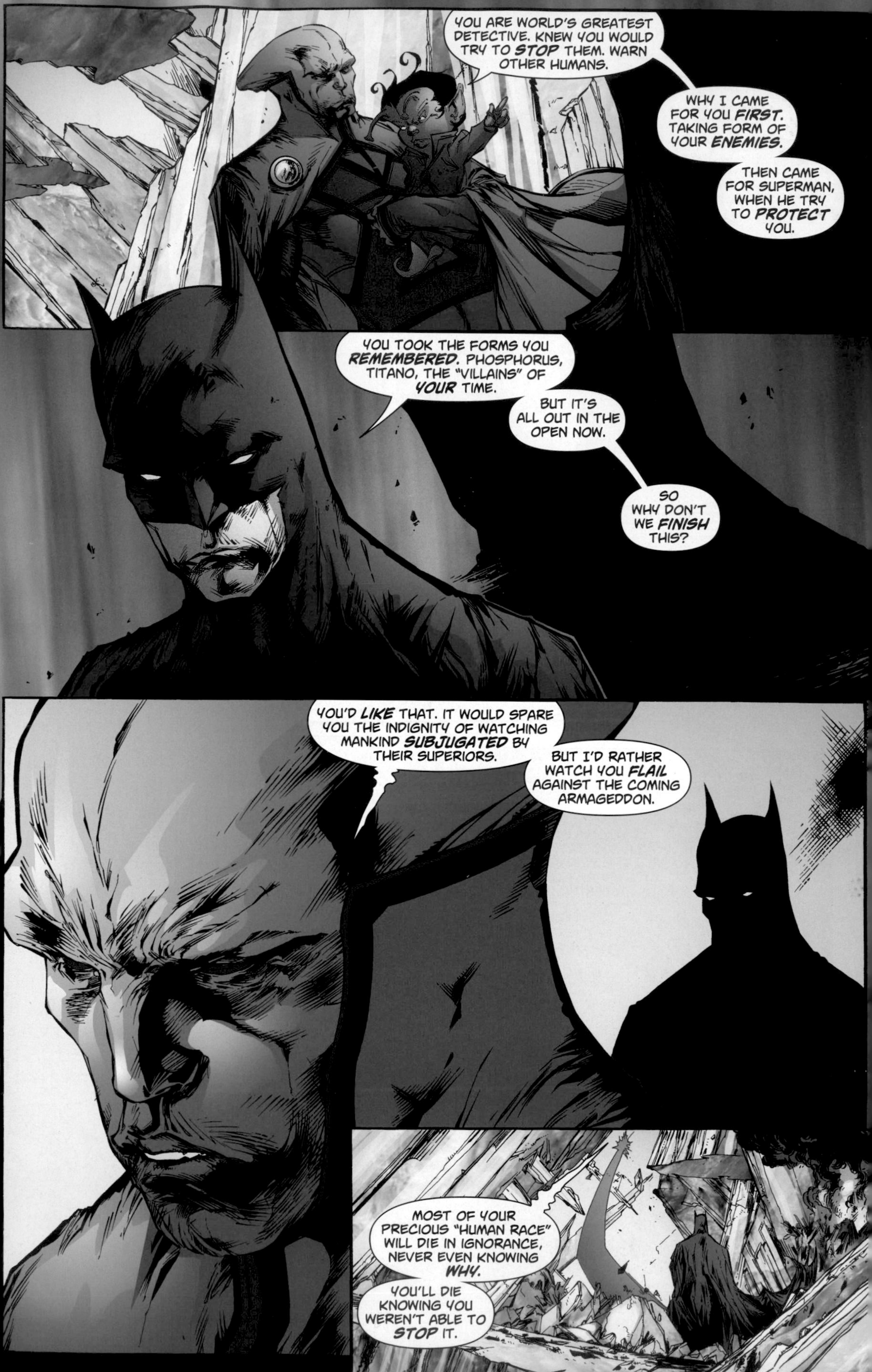

YOU ARE WORLD'S GREATEST DETECTIVE. KNEW YOU WOULD TRY TO STOP THEM. WARN OTHER HUMANS.
WHY I CAME FOR YOU FIRST. TAKING FORM OF YOUR ENEMIES.
THEN CAME FOR SUPERMAN, WHEN HE TRY TO PROTECT YOU.
YOU TOOK THE FORMS YOU REMEMBERED. PHOSPHORUS, TITANO, THE "VILLAINS" OF YOUR TIME.
BUT IT'S ALL OUT IN THE OPEN NOW.
SO WHY DON'T WE FINISH THIS?
YOU'D LIKE THAT. IT WOULD SPARE YOU THE INDIGNITY OF WATCHING MANKIND SUBJUGATED BY THEIR SUPERIORS.
BUT I'D RATHER WATCH YOU FLAIL AGAINST THE COMING ARMAGEDDON.
MOST OF YOUR PRECIOUS "HUMAN RACE" WILL DIE IN IGNORANCE, NEVER EVEN KNOWING WHY.
YOU'LL DIE KNOWING YOU WEREN'T ABLE TO STOP IT.

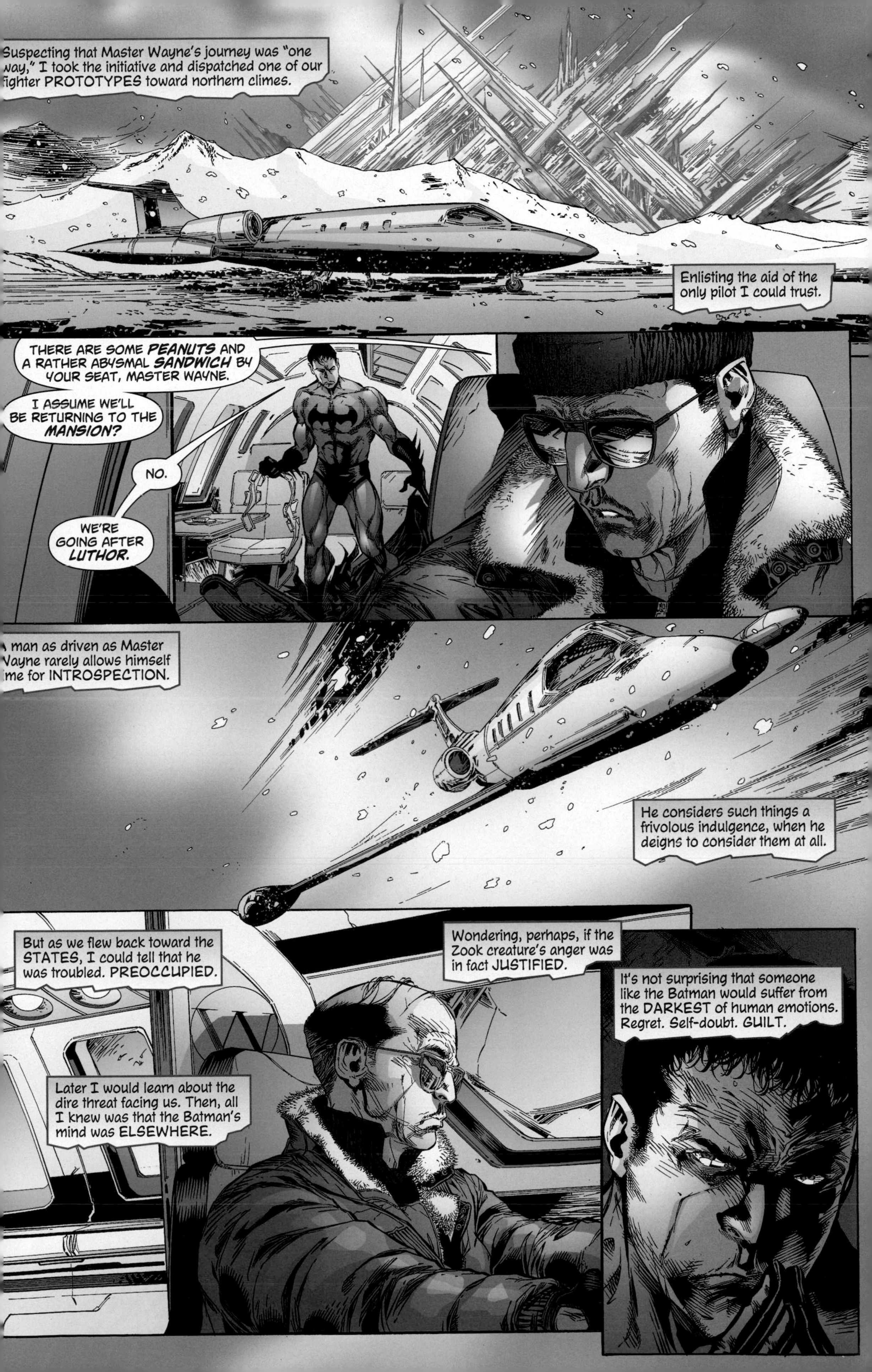

Suspecting that Master Wayne's journey was "one way," I took the initiative and dispatched one of our fighter PROTOTYPES toward northern climes.
Enlisting the aid of the only pilot I could trust.
THERE ARE SOME PEANUTS AND A RATHER ABYSMAL SANDWICH BY YOUR SEAT, MASTER WAYNE.
I ASSUME WE'LL BE RETURNING TO THE MANSION?
NO.
WE'RE GOING AFTER LUTHOR.
man as driven as Master Vayne rarely allows himself me for INTROSPECTION.
He considers such things a frivolous indulgence, when he deigns to consider them at all.
But as we flew back toward the STATES, I could tell that he was troubled. PREOCCUPIED.
Wondering, perhaps, if the Zook creature's anger was in fact JUSTIFIED.
It's not surprising that someone like the Batman would suffer from the DARKEST of human emotions. Regret. Self-doubt. GUILT.
Later I would learn about the dire threat facing us. Then, all I knew was that the Batman's mind was ELSEWHERE.

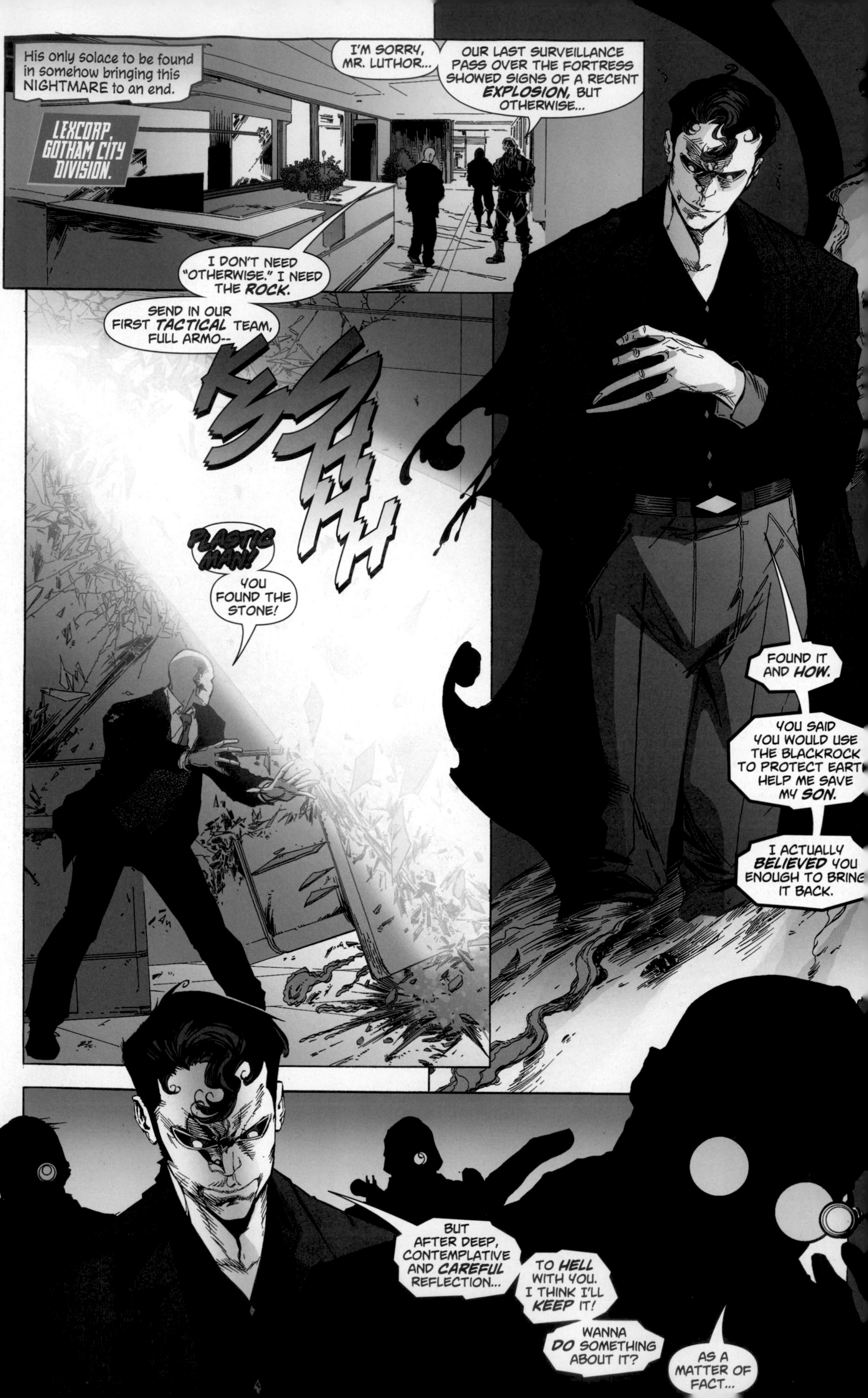

His only solace to be found in somehow bringing this NIGHTMARE to an end.
LEXCORP, GOTHAM CITY DIVISION.
I'M SORRY, MR. LUTHOR...
OUR LAST SURVEILLANCE PASS OVER THE FORTRESS SHOWED SIGNS OF A RECENT EXPLOSION, BUT OTHERWISE...
I DON'T NEED "OTHERWISE." I NEED THE ROCK.
SEND IN OUR FIRST TACTICAL TEAM, FULL ARMO--
KSSHHH
PLASTIC MAN!
YOU FOUND THE STONE!
FOUND IT AND HOW.
YOU SAID YOU WOULD USE THE BLACKROCK TO PROTECT EARTH
HELP ME SAVE MY SON.
I ACTUALLY BELIEVED YOU ENOUGH TO BRING IT BACK.
BUT AFTER DEEP, CONTEMPLATIVE AND CAREFUL REFLECTION...
TO HELL WITH YOU. I THINK I'LL KEEP IT!
WANNA DO SOMETHING ABOUT IT?
AS A MATTER OF FACT...

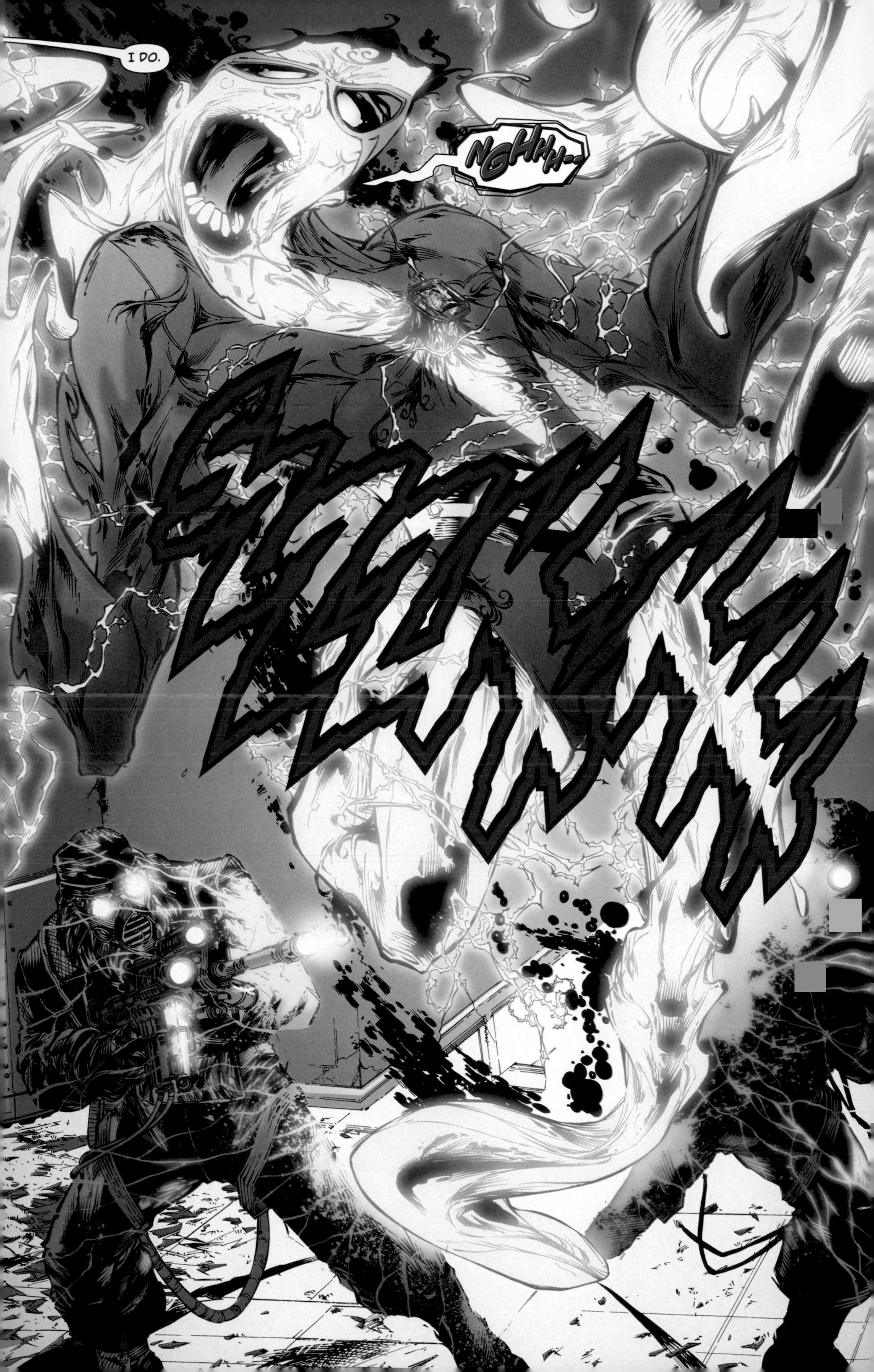
I DO.
NGHHH--

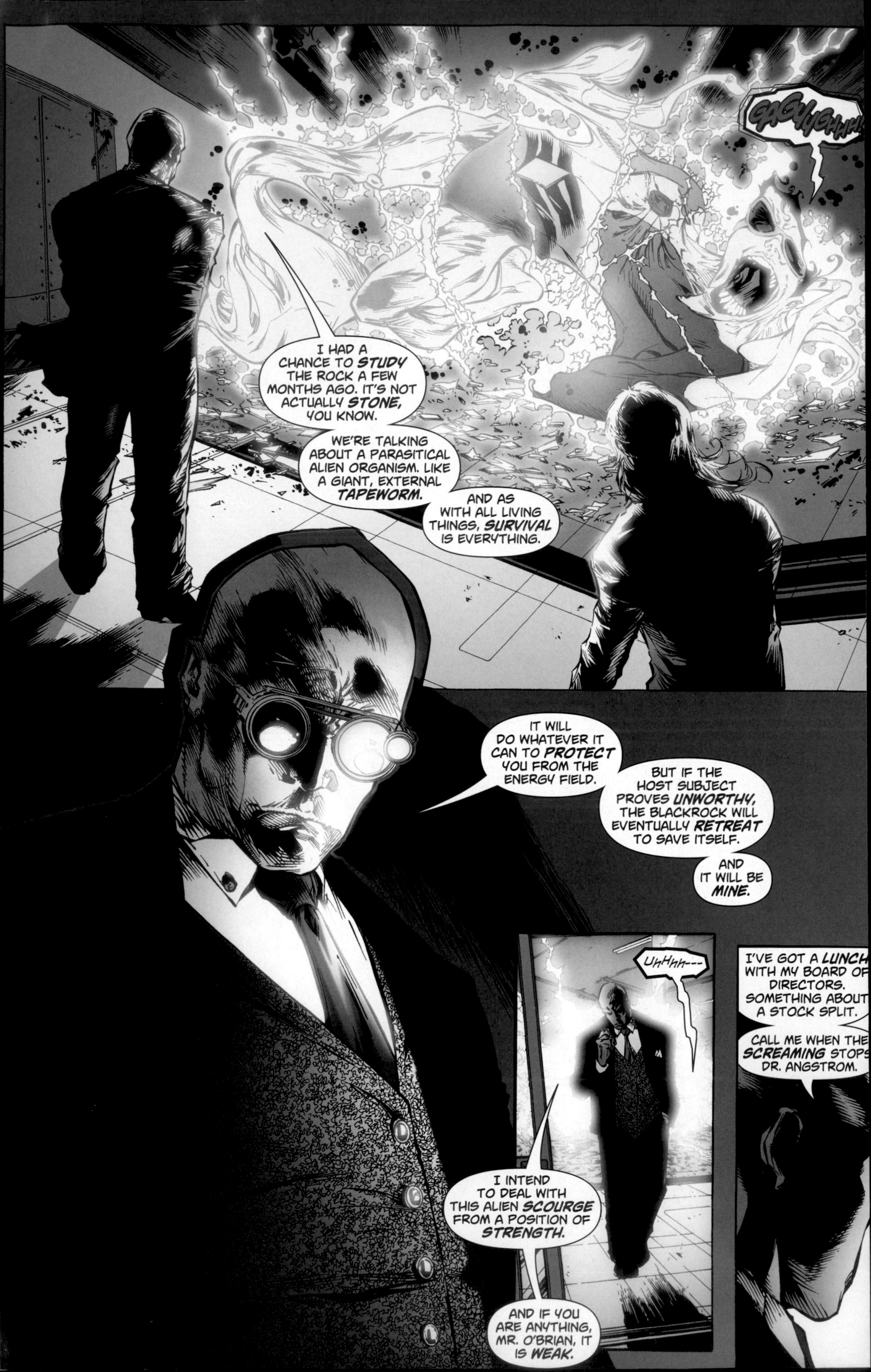
GAGUYGHHH
I HAD A CHANCE TO STUDY THE ROCK A FEW MONTHS AGO. IT'S NOT ACTUALLY STONE, YOU KNOW.
WE'RE TALKING ABOUT A PARASITICAL ALIEN ORGANISM. LIKE A GIANT, EXTERNAL TAPEWORM.
AND AS WITH ALL LIVING THINGS, SURVIVAL IS EVERYTHING.
IT WILL DO WHATEVER IT CAN TO PROTECT YOU FROM THE ENERGY FIELD.
BUT IF THE HOST SUBJECT PROVES UNWORTHY, THE BLACKROCK WILL EVENTUALLY RETREAT TO SAVE ITSELF.
AND IT WILL BE MINE.
UHHhh---
I INTEND TO DEAL WITH THIS ALIEN SCOURGE FROM A POSITION OF STRENGTH.
AND IF YOU ARE ANYTHING, MR. O'BRIAN, IT IS WEAK.
I'VE GOT A LUNCH WITH MY BOARD OF DIRECTORS. SOMETHING ABOUT A STOCK SPLIT.
CALL ME WHEN THE SCREAMING STOPS DR. ANGSTROM.

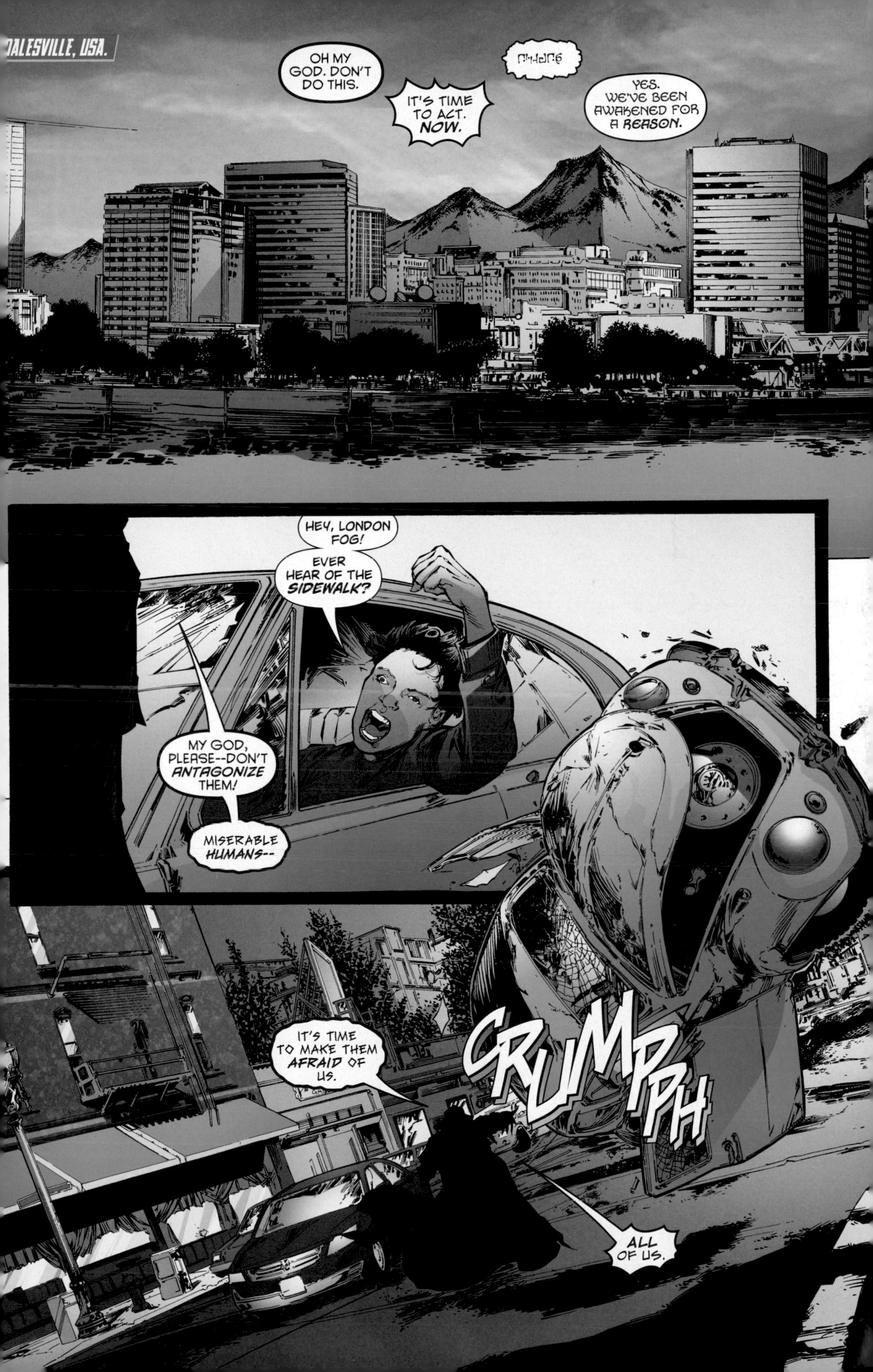
DALESVILLE, USA.
OH MY GOD. DON'T DO THIS.
IT'S TIME TO ACT. NOW.
YES. WE'VE BEEN AWAKENED FOR A REASON.
HEY, LONDON FOG!
EVER HEAR OF THE SIDEWALK?
MY GOD, PLEASE--DON'T ANTAGONIZE THEM!
MISERABLE HUMANS--
IT'S TIME TO MAKE THEM AFRAID OF US.
CRUMPH
ALL OF US.

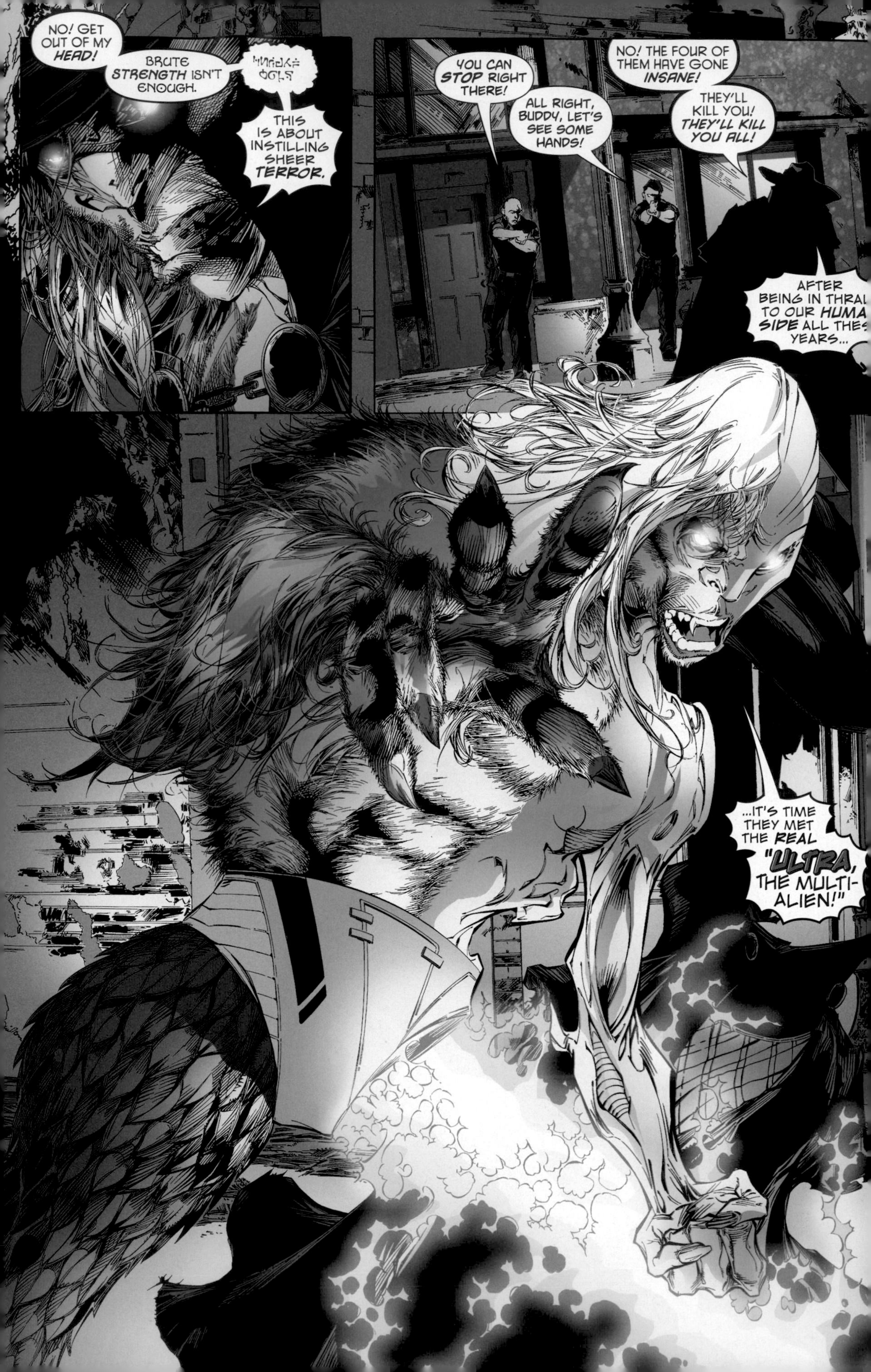

NO! GET OUT OF MY HEAD!
BRUTE STRENGTH ISN'T ENOUGH.
THIS IS ABOUT INSTILLING SHEER TERROR.
YOU CAN STOP RIGHT THERE!
ALL RIGHT, BUDDY, LET'S SEE SOME HANDS!
NO! THE FOUR OF THEM HAVE GONE INSANE!
THEY'LL KILL YOU! THEY'LL KILL YOU ALL!
AFTER BEING IN THRAL TO OUR HUMA SIDE ALL THES YEARS...
...IT'S TIME THEY MET THE REAL "ULTRA, THE MULTI-ALIEN!"

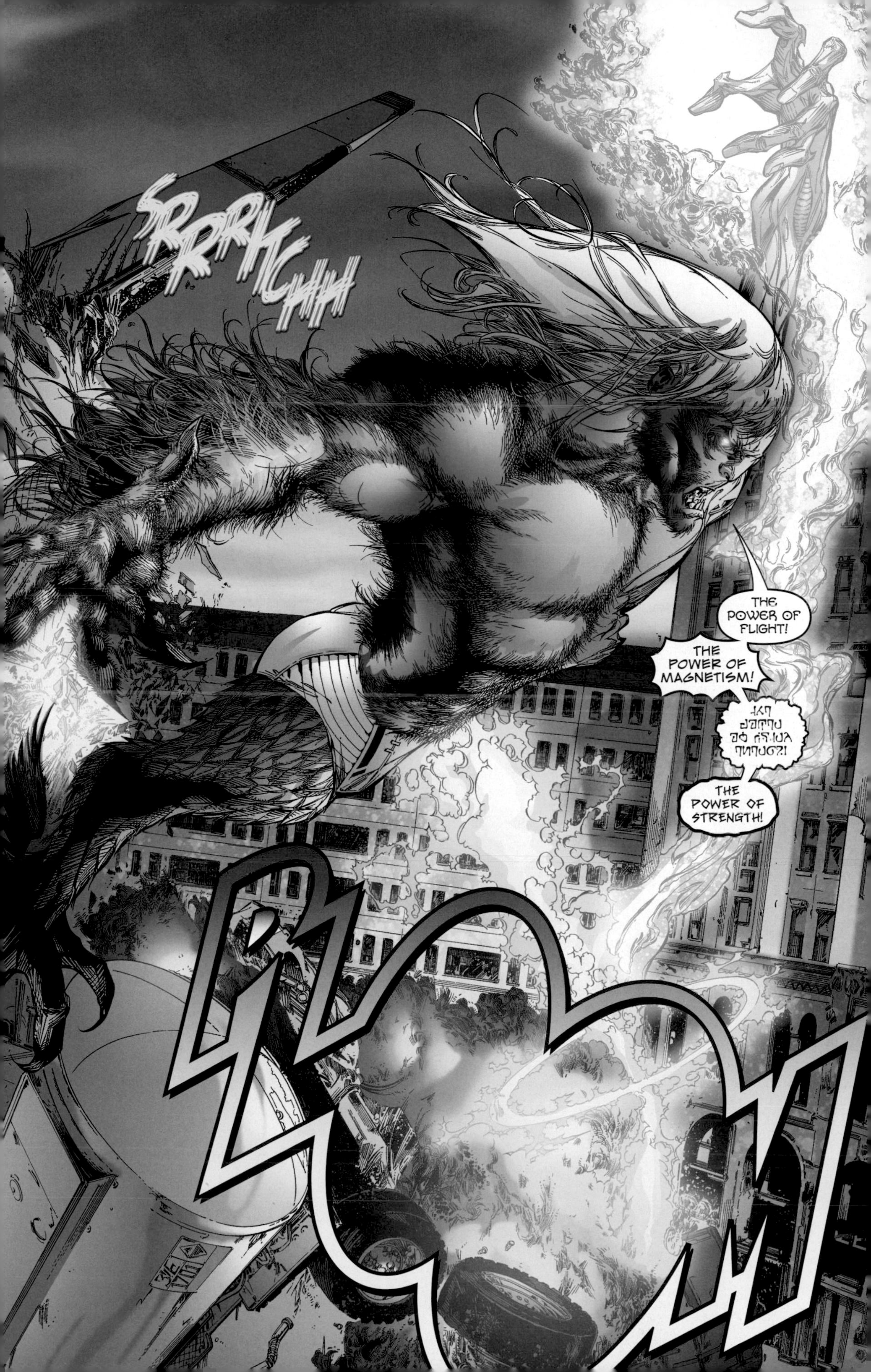
THE POWER OF FLIGHT!
THE POWER OF MAGNETISM!
THE POWER OF STRENGTH!

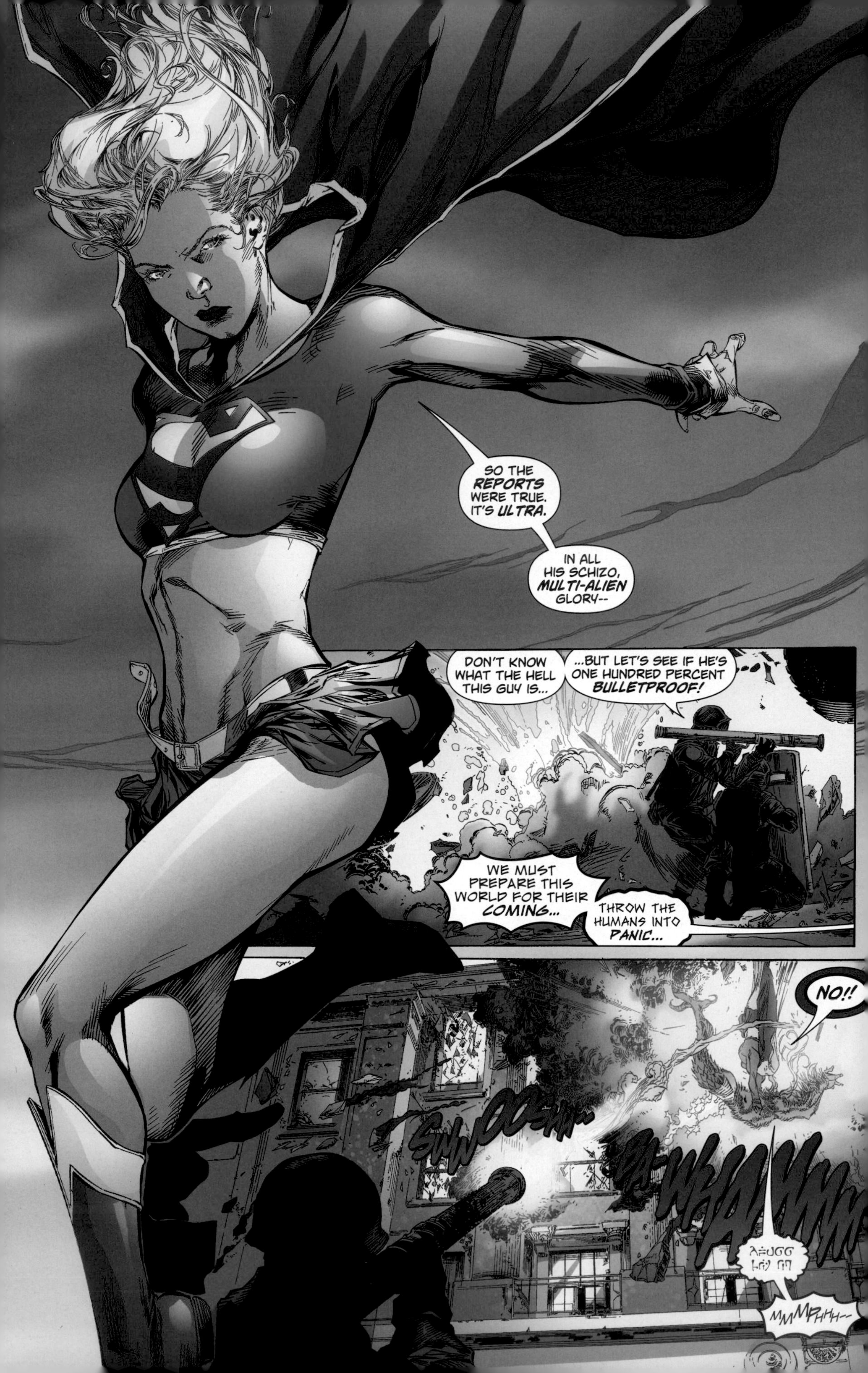

SO THE REPORTS WERE TRUE. IT'S ULTRA.
IN ALL HIS SCHIZO, MULTI-ALIEN GLORY--
DON'T KNOW WHAT THE HELL THIS GUY IS...
...BUT LET'S SEE IF HE'S ONE HUNDRED PERCENT BULLETPROOF!
WE MUST PREPARE THIS WORLD FOR THEIR COMING...
THROW THE HUMANS INTO PANIC...
NO!!
SWOOSH--
MMMPHHH--

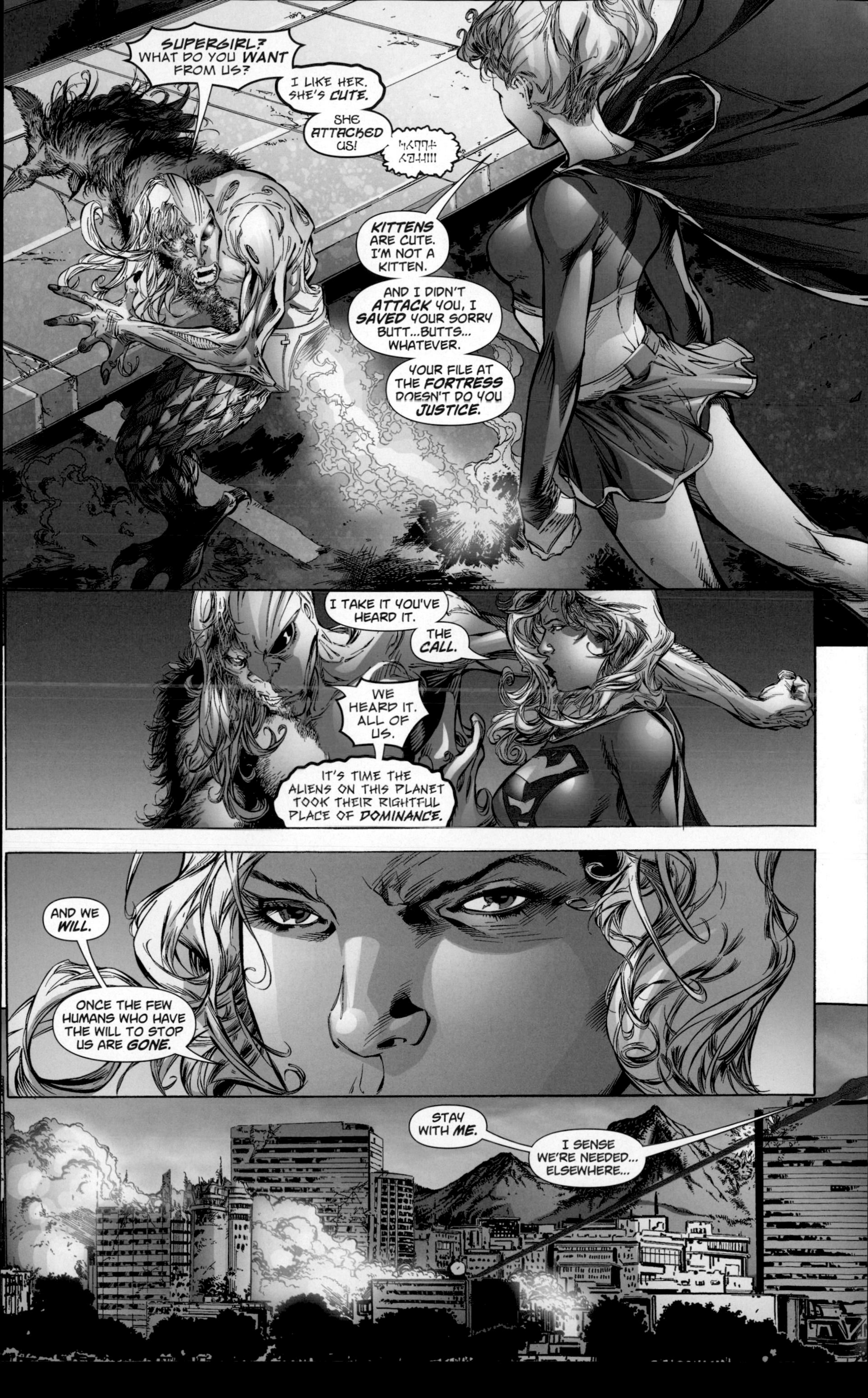
SUPERGIRL? WHAT DO YOU WANT FROM US?
I LIKE HER. SHE'S CUTE.
SHE ATTACKED US!
KITTENS ARE CUTE. I'M NOT A KITTEN.
AND I DIDN'T ATTACK YOU, I SAVED YOUR SORRY BUTT...BUTTS... WHATEVER.
YOUR FILE AT THE FORTRESS DOESN'T DO YOU JUSTICE.
I TAKE IT YOU'VE HEARD IT.
THE CALL.
WE HEARD IT. ALL OF US.
IT'S TIME THE ALIENS ON THIS PLANET TOOK THEIR RIGHTFUL PLACE OF DOMINANCE.
AND WE WILL.
ONCE THE FEW HUMANS WHO HAVE THE WILL TO STOP US ARE GONE.
STAY WITH ME.
I SENSE WE'RE NEEDED... ELSEWHERE...

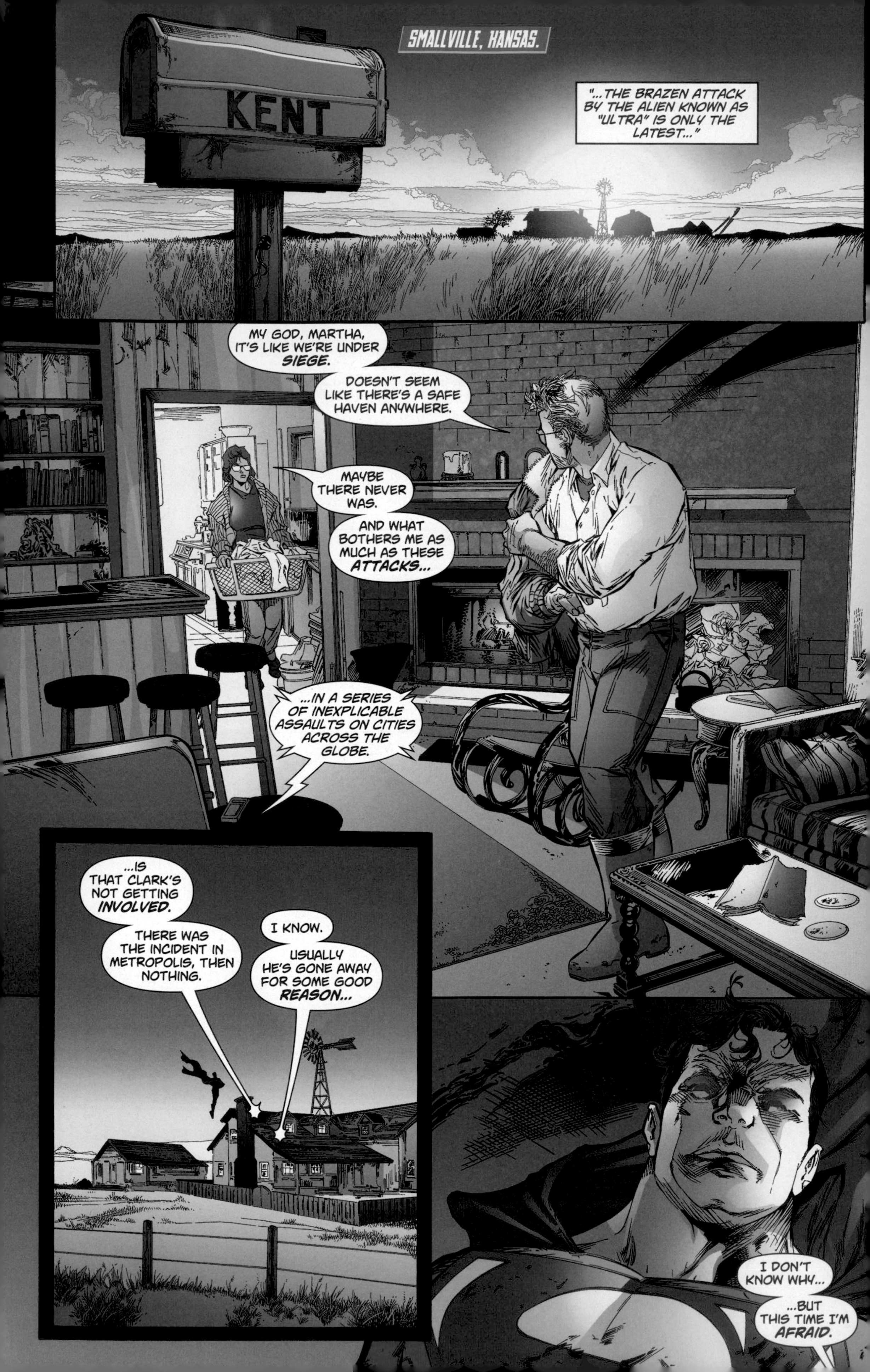
SMALLVILLE, KANSAS.
"...THE BRAZEN ATTACK BY THE ALIEN KNOWN AS "ULTRA" IS ONLY THE LATEST..."
KENT
MY GOD, MARTHA, IT'S LIKE WE'RE UNDER SIEGE.
DOESN'T SEEM LIKE THERE'S A SAFE HAVEN ANYWHERE.
MAYBE THERE NEVER WAS.
AND WHAT BOTHERS ME AS MUCH AS THESE ATTACKS...
...IN A SERIES OF INEXPLICABLE ASSAULTS ON CITIES ACROSS THE GLOBE.
...IS THAT CLARK'S NOT GETTING INVOLVED.
THERE WAS THE INCIDENT IN METROPOLIS, THEN NOTHING.
I KNOW.
USUALLY HE'S GONE AWAY FOR SOME GOOD REASON...
I DON'T KNOW WHY...
...BUT THIS TIME I'M AFRAID.

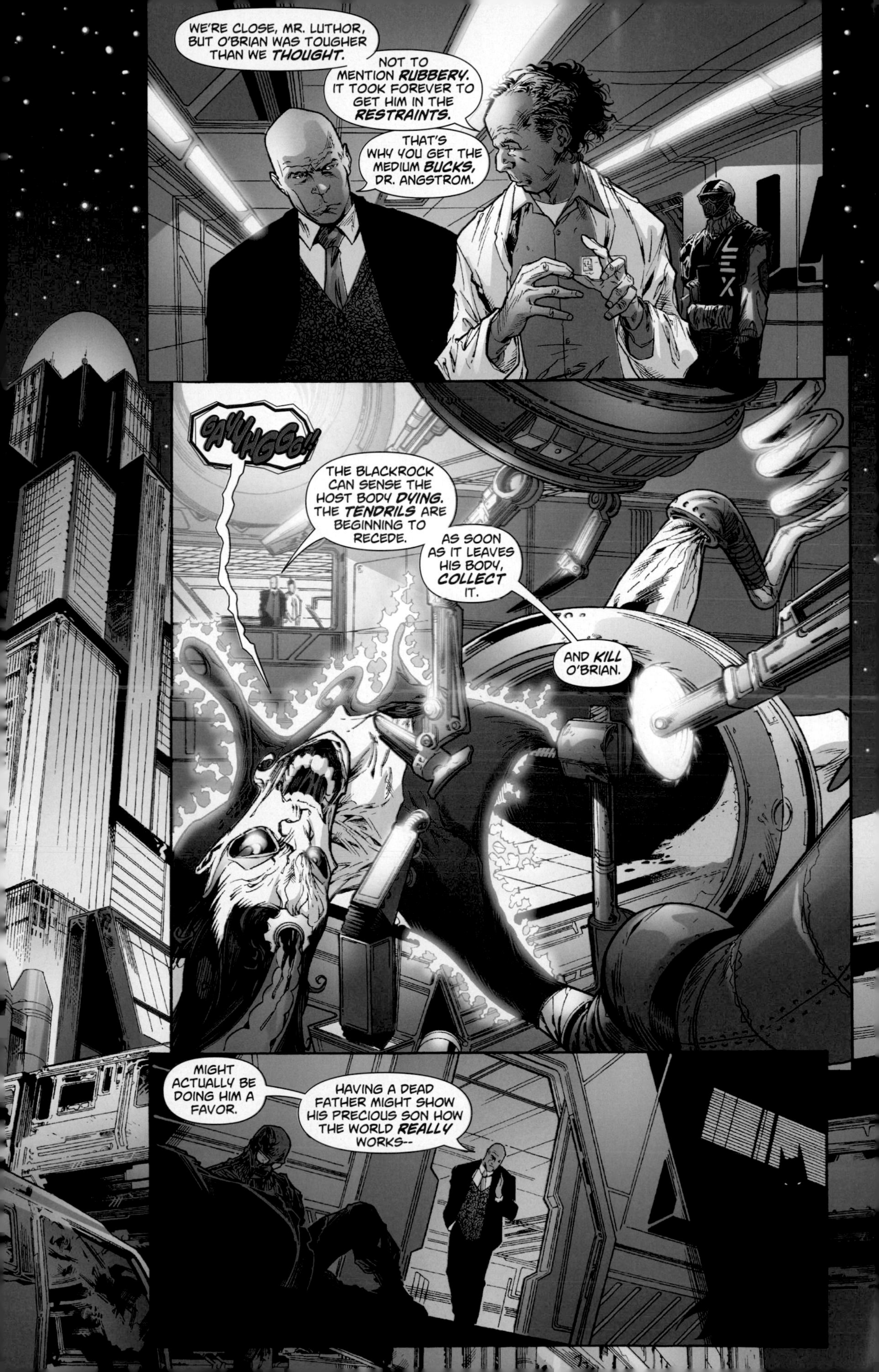
WE'RE CLOSE, MR. LUTHOR, BUT O'BRIAN WAS TOUGHER THAN WE THOUGHT.
NOT TO MENTION RUBBERY. IT TOOK FOREVER TO GET HIM IN THE RESTRAINTS.
THAT'S WHY YOU GET THE MEDIUM BUCKS, DR. ANGSTROM.
LEX
GAAAHGGG!!
THE BLACKROCK CAN SENSE THE HOST BODY DYING. THE TENDRILS ARE BEGINNING TO RECEDE.
AS SOON AS IT LEAVES HIS BODY, COLLECT IT.
AND KILL O'BRIAN.
MIGHT ACTUALLY BE DOING HIM A FAVOR.
HAVING A DEAD FATHER MIGHT SHOW HIS PRECIOUS SON HOW THE WORLD REALLY WORKS--

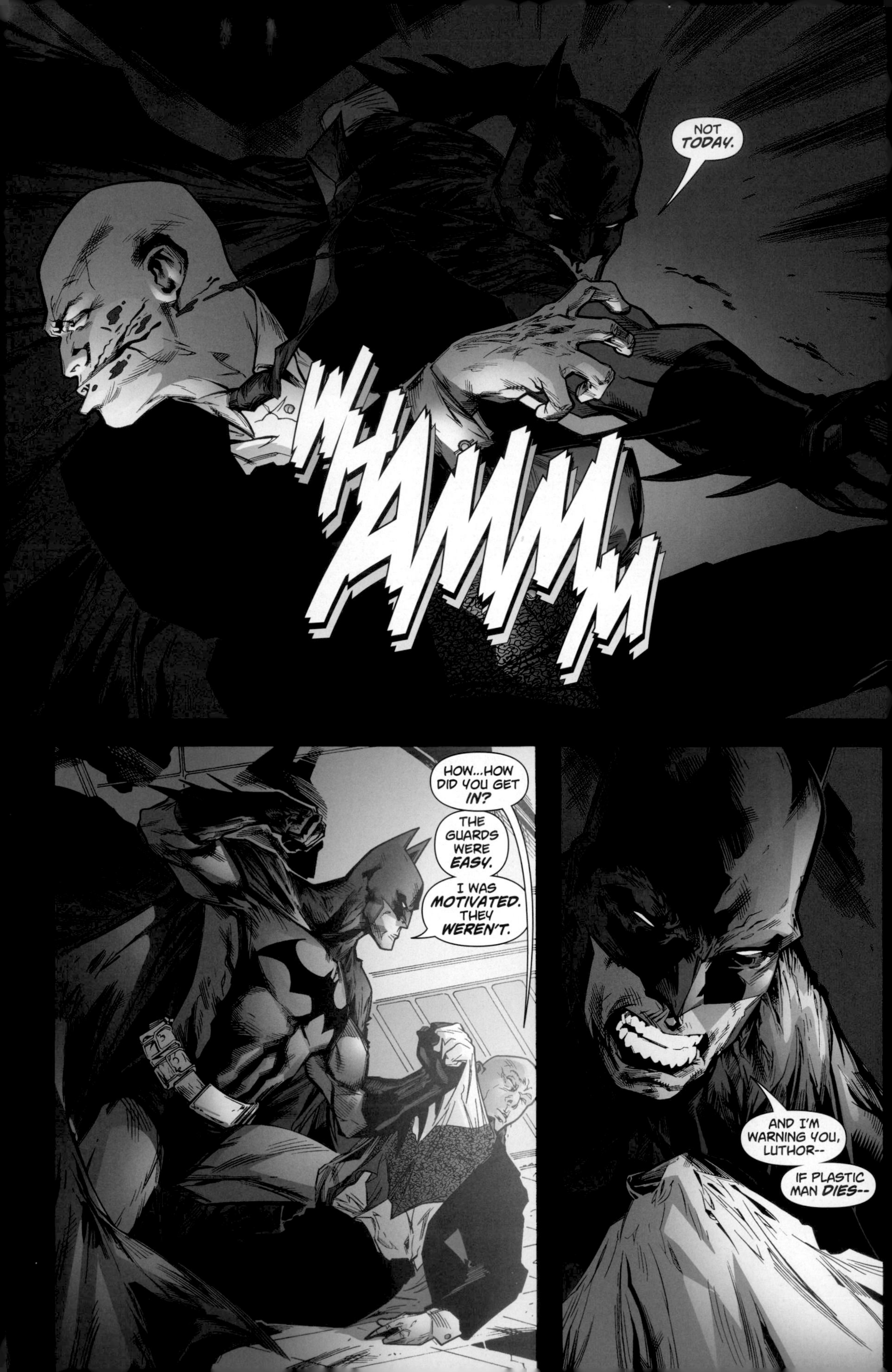
NOT TODAY.
WHAMMM
HOW...HOW DID YOU GET IN?
THE GUARDS WERE EASY.
I WAS MOTIVATED. THEY WEREN'T.
AND I'M WARNING YOU, LUTHOR--
IF PLASTIC MAN DIES--

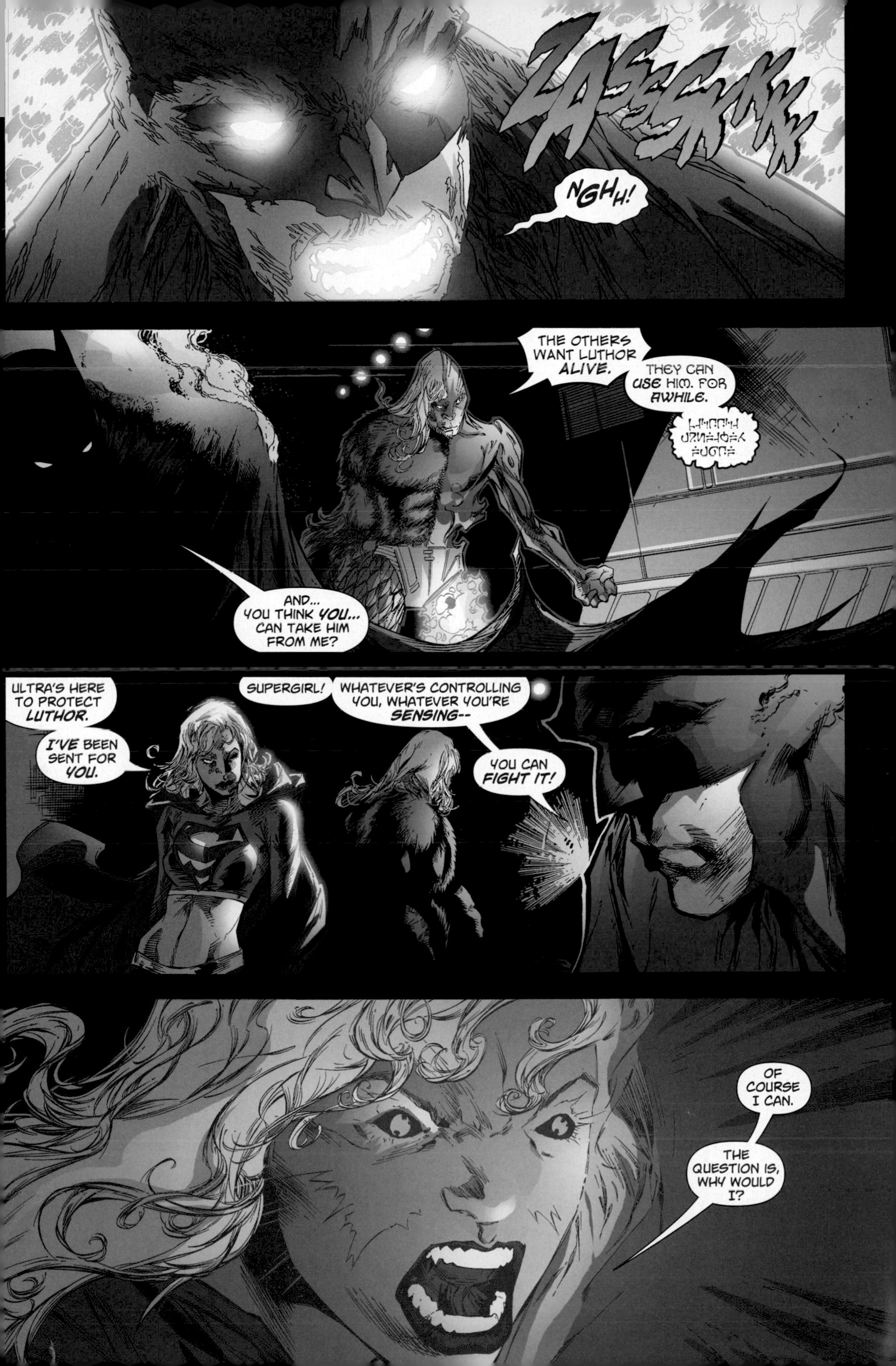
ZASSSKKK
NGHH!
THE OTHERS WANT LUTHOR ALIVE.
THEY CAN USE HIM. FOR AWHILE.
AND... YOU THINK YOU... CAN TAKE HIM FROM ME?
ULTRA'S HERE TO PROTECT LUTHOR.
I'VE BEEN SENT FOR YOU.
SUPERGIRL!
WHATEVER'S CONTROLLING YOU, WHATEVER YOU'RE SENSING--
YOU CAN FIGHT IT!
OF COURSE I CAN.
THE QUESTION IS, WHY WOULD I?

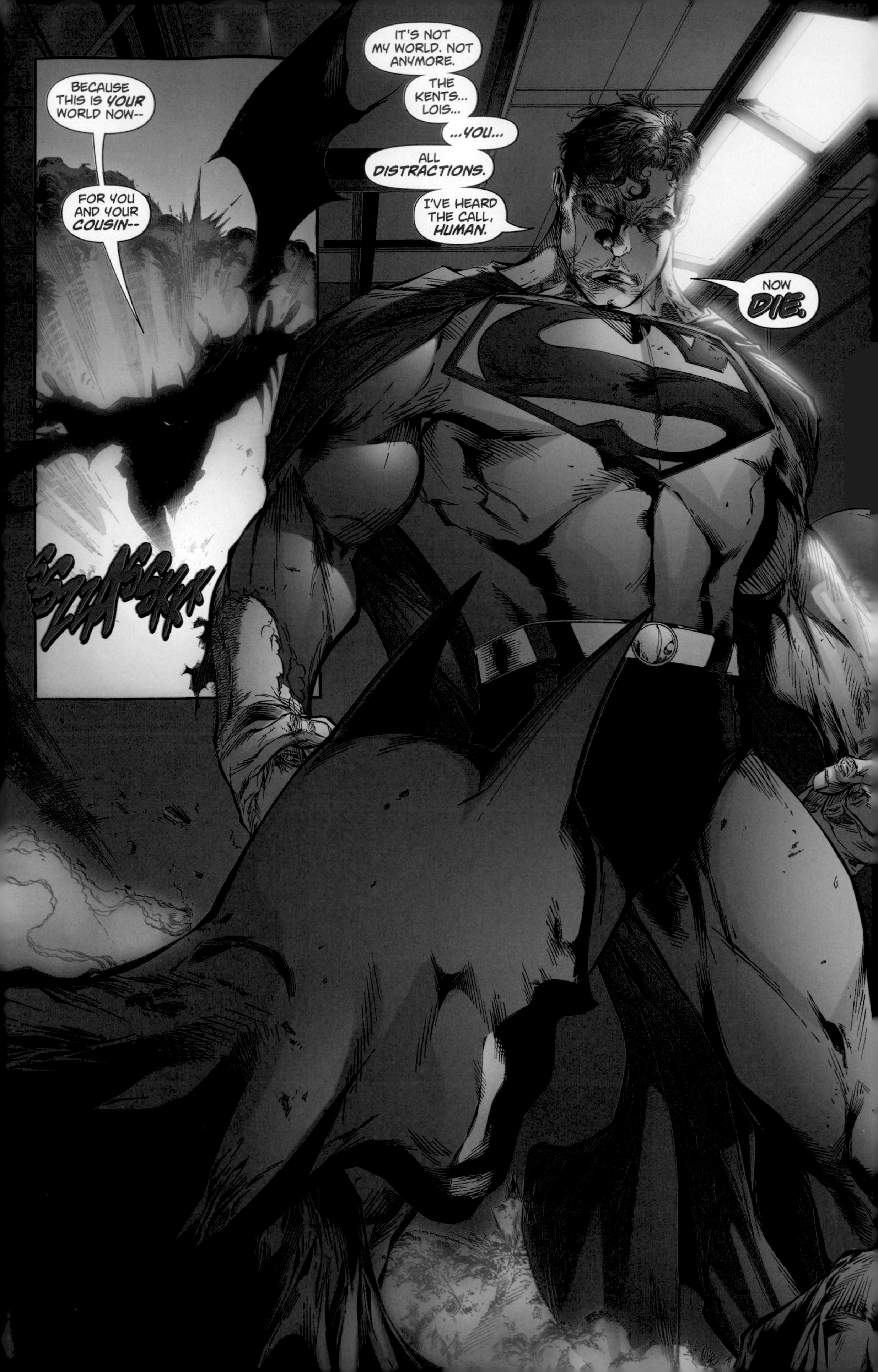
BECAUSE THIS IS *YOUR* WORLD NOW--
FOR YOU AND YOUR *COUSIN*--
IT'S NOT MY WORLD. NOT ANYMORE.
THE KENTS... LOIS...
...*YOU*...
ALL *DISTRACTIONS*.
I'VE HEARD THE CALL, *HUMAN*.
NOW *DIE*.

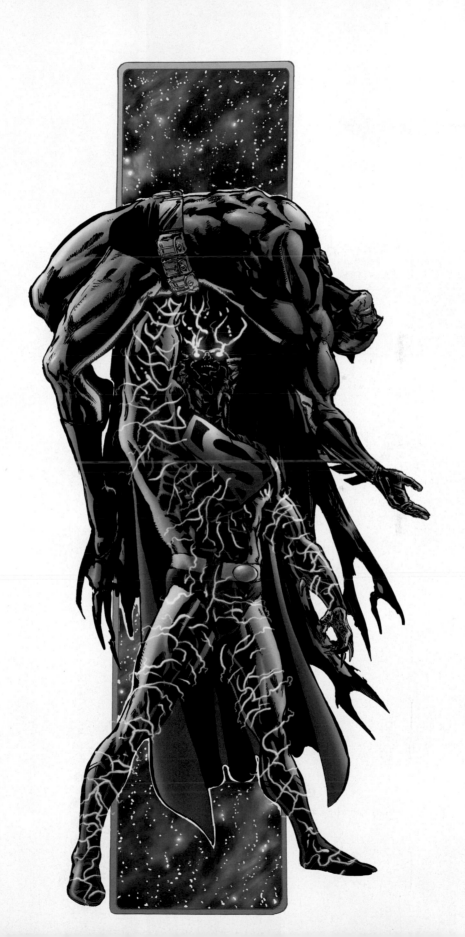

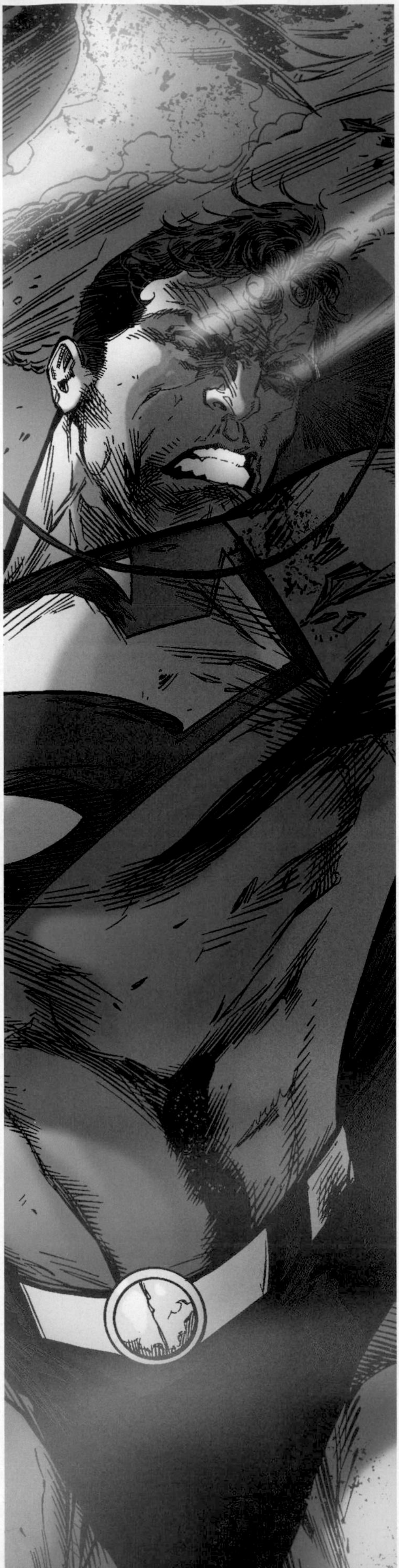

THE ENEMIES AMONG US

PART 5

MARK VERHEIDEN
WRITER

MATTHEW CLARK
& RON RANDALL
PENCILLERS

ANDY LANNING
&
DON HILLSMAN II
INKER

GUY MAJOR
COLORIST

ROB LEIGH
LETTERER

PHIL JIMENEZ,
ANDY LANNING
&
MOOSE BAUMANN
COVER

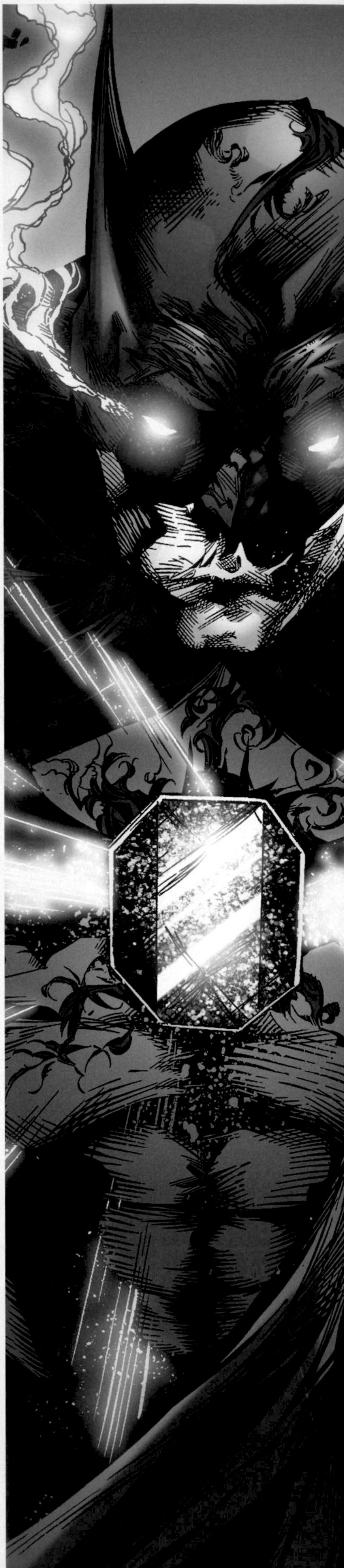

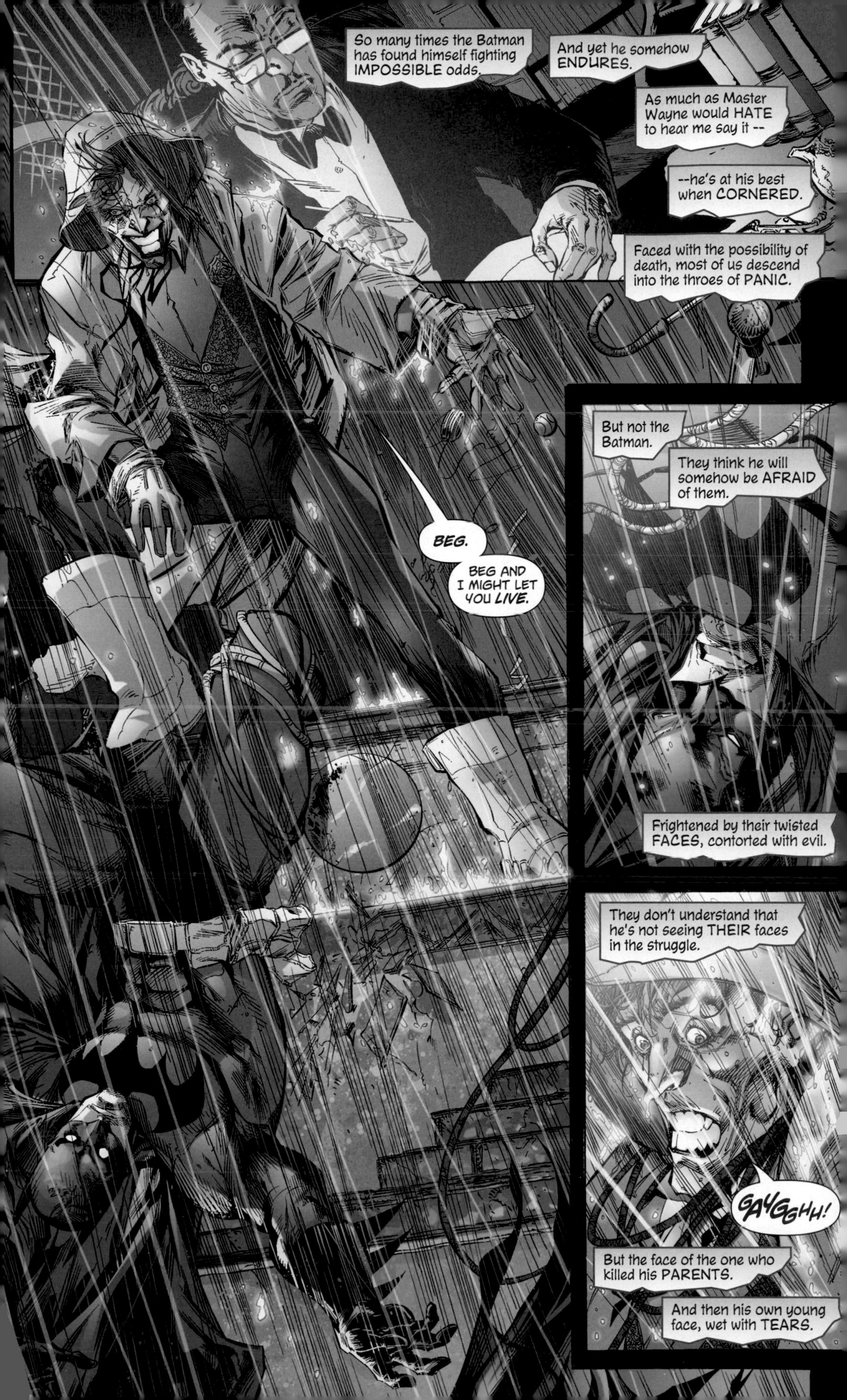
So many times the Batman has found himself fighting IMPOSSIBLE odds.
And yet he somehow ENDURES.
As much as Master Wayne would HATE to hear me say it --
--he's at his best when CORNERED.
Faced with the possibility of death, most of us descend into the throes of PANIC.
BEG.
BEG AND I MIGHT LET YOU LIVE.
But not the Batman.
They think he will somehow be AFRAID of them.
Frightened by their twisted FACES, contorted with evil.
They don't understand that he's not seeing THEIR faces in the struggle.
GAYGGHH!
But the face of the one who killed his PARENTS.
And then his own young face, wet with TEARS.

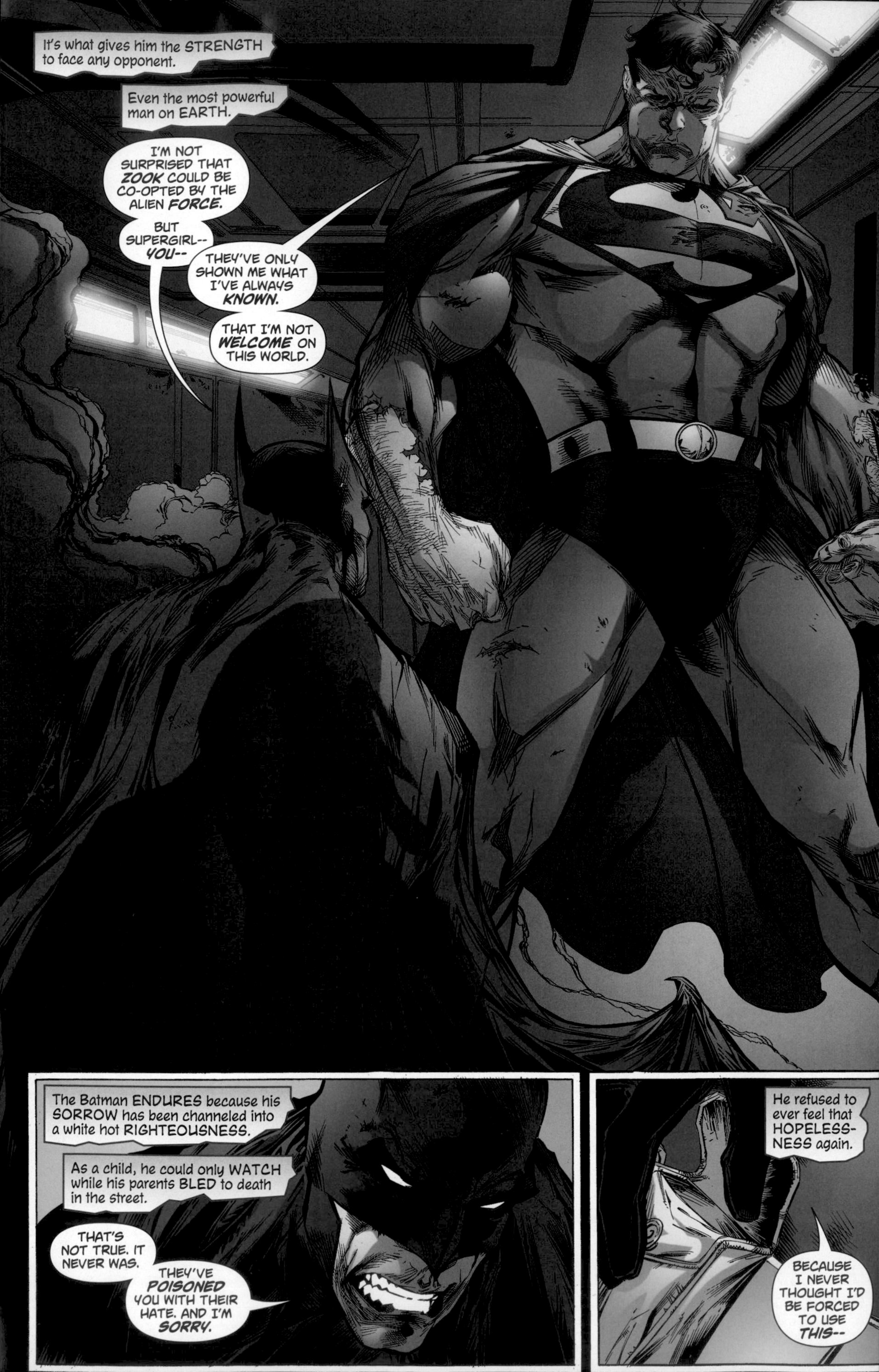

It's what gives him the STRENGTH to face any opponent.
Even the most powerful man on EARTH.
I'M NOT SURPRISED THAT ZOOK COULD BE CO-OPTED BY THE ALIEN FORCE.
BUT SUPERGIRL-- YOU--
THEY'VE ONLY SHOWN ME WHAT I'VE ALWAYS KNOWN.
THAT I'M NOT WELCOME ON THIS WORLD.
The Batman ENDURES because his SORROW has been channeled into a white hot RIGHTEOUSNESS.
As a child, he could only WATCH while his parents BLED to death in the street.
THAT'S NOT TRUE. IT NEVER WAS.
THEY'VE POISONED YOU WITH THEIR HATE. AND I'M SORRY.
He refused to ever feel that HOPELESS-NESS again.
BECAUSE I NEVER THOUGHT I'D BE FORCED TO USE THIS--

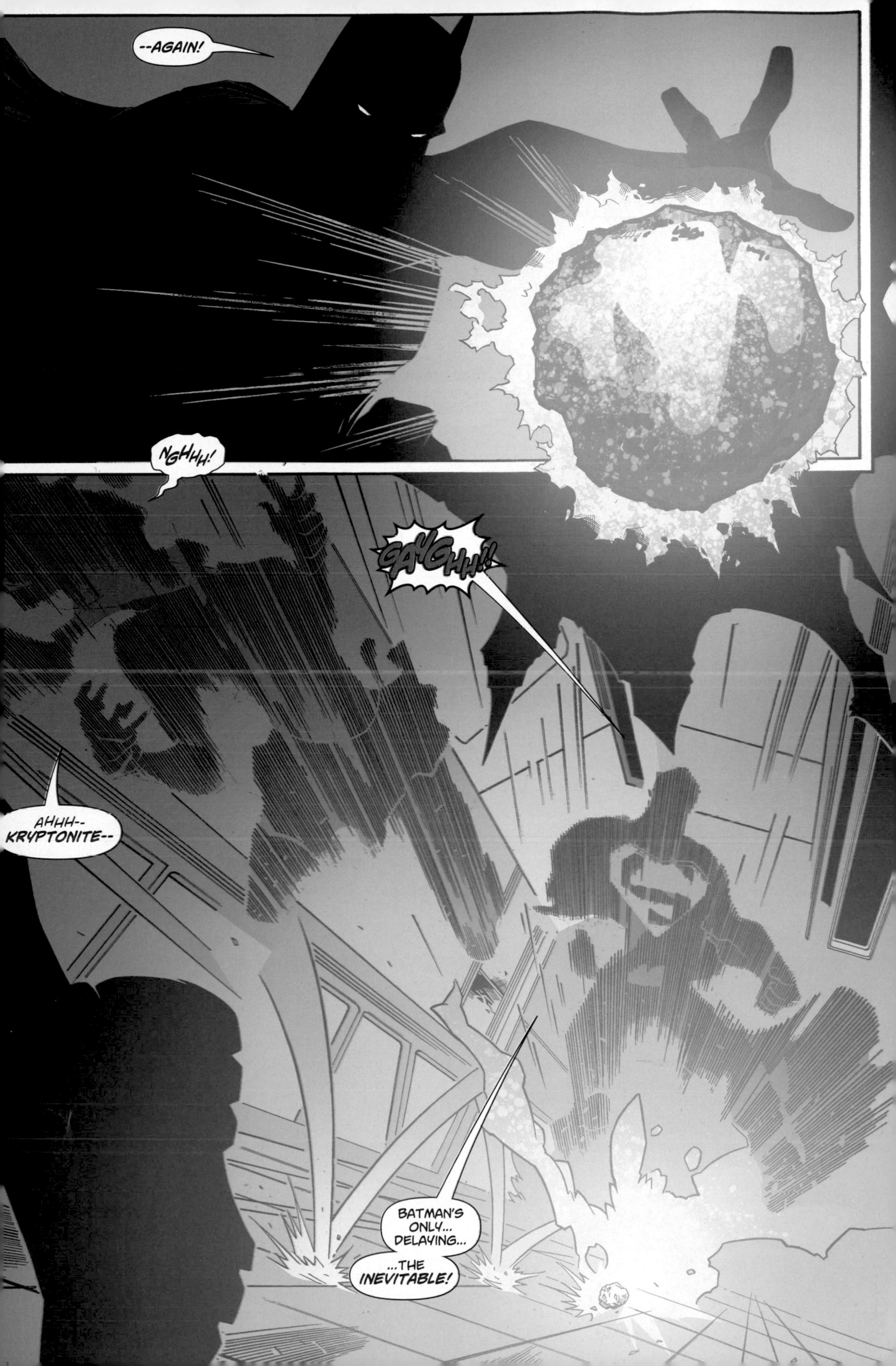
--AGAIN!
NGHHH!
GAUGHHH!!
AHHH-- KRYPTONITE--
BATMAN'S ONLY... DELAYING...
...THE INEVITABLE!

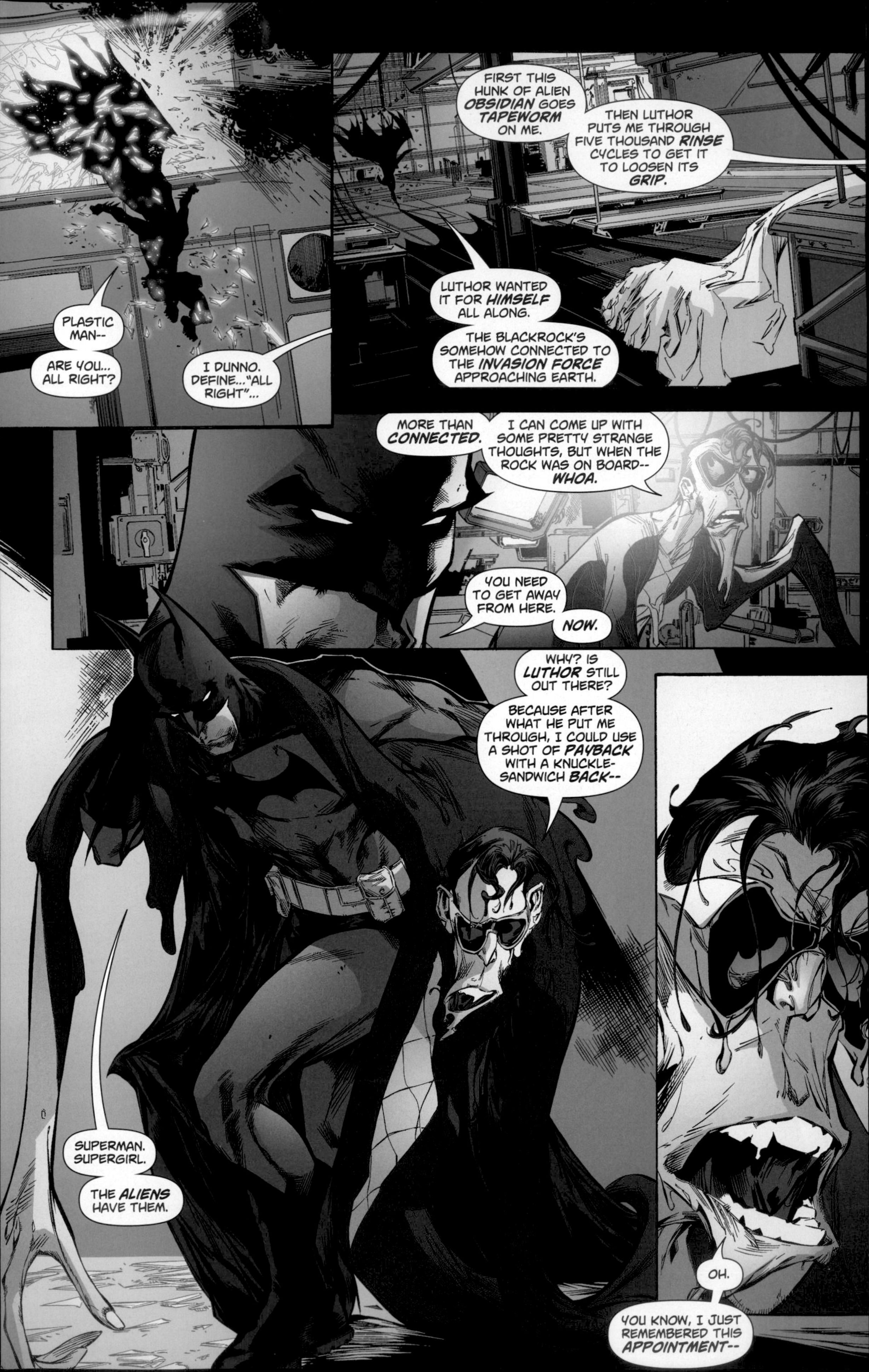
PLASTIC MAN--
ARE YOU... ALL RIGHT?
I DUNNO. DEFINE..."ALL RIGHT"...
FIRST THIS HUNK OF ALIEN OBSIDIAN GOES TAPEWORM ON ME.
THEN LUTHOR PUTS ME THROUGH FIVE THOUSAND RINSE CYCLES TO GET IT TO LOOSEN ITS GRIP.
LUTHOR WANTED IT FOR HIMSELF ALL ALONG.
THE BLACKROCK'S SOMEHOW CONNECTED TO THE INVASION FORCE APPROACHING EARTH.
MORE THAN CONNECTED.
I CAN COME UP WITH SOME PRETTY STRANGE THOUGHTS, BUT WHEN THE ROCK WAS ON BOARD-- WHOA.
YOU NEED TO GET AWAY FROM HERE.
NOW.
WHY? IS LUTHOR STILL OUT THERE?
BECAUSE AFTER WHAT HE PUT ME THROUGH, I COULD USE A SHOT OF PAYBACK WITH A KNUCKLE-SANDWICH BACK--
SUPERMAN. SUPERGIRL.
THE ALIENS HAVE THEM.
OH.
YOU KNOW, I JUST REMEMBERED THIS APPOINTMENT--

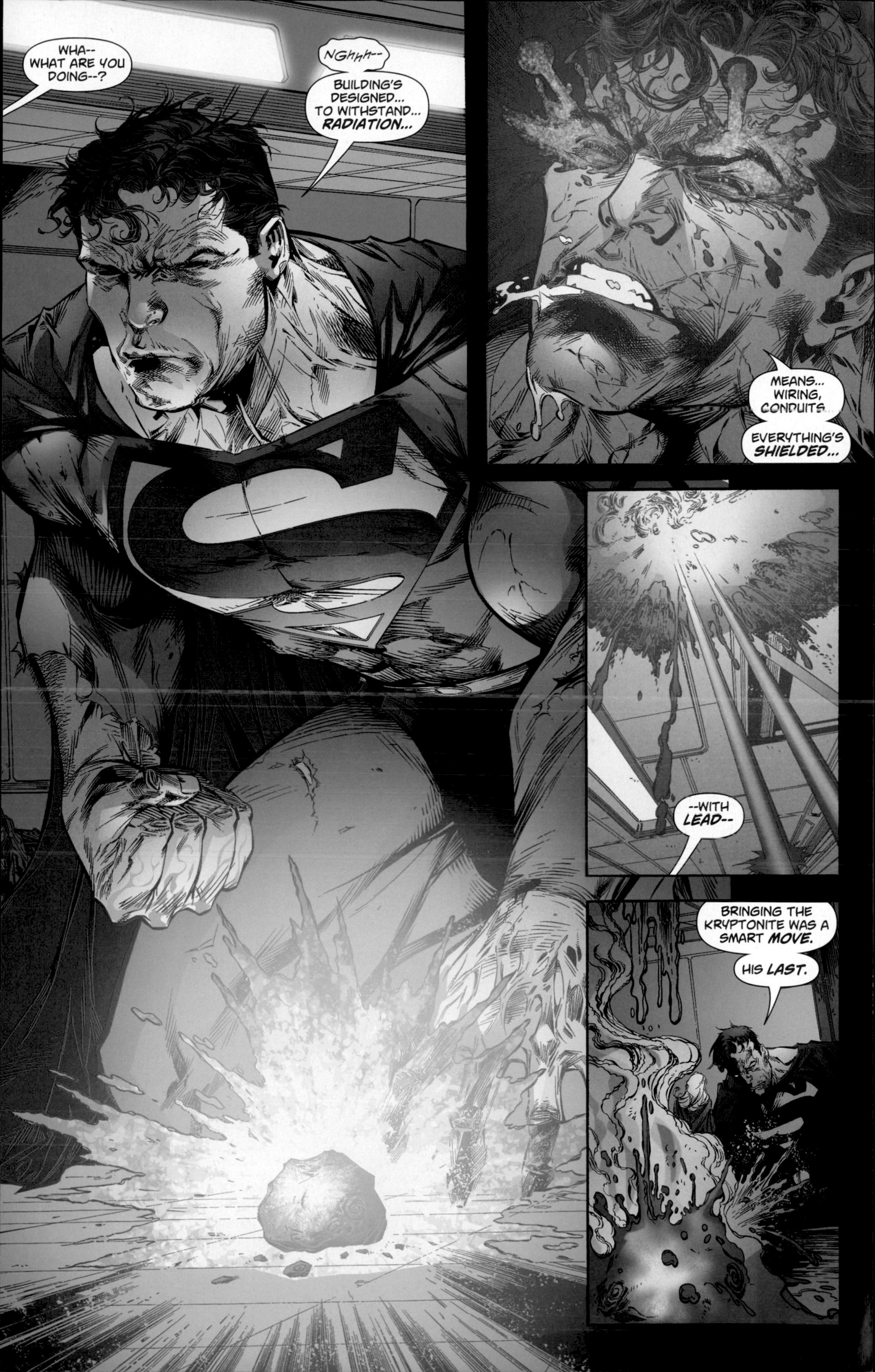
WHA--
WHAT ARE YOU DOING--?
NGhhh--
BUILDING'S DESIGNED... TO WITHSTAND... RADIATION...
MEANS... WIRING, CONDUITS...
EVERYTHING'S SHIELDED...
--WITH LEAD--
BRINGING THE KRYPTONITE WAS A SMART MOVE.
HIS LAST.

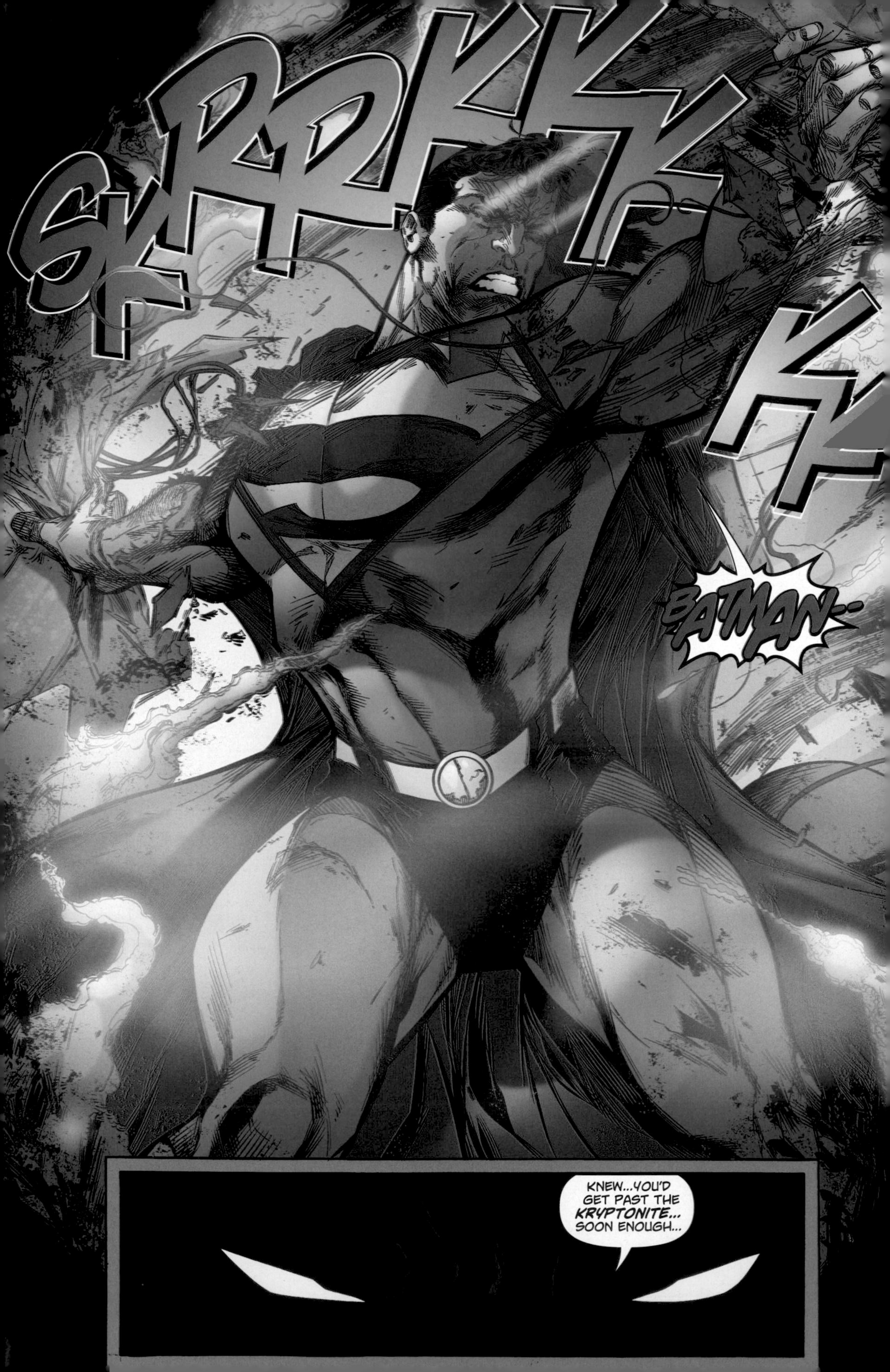
SKRAKK
KKK
BATMAN--
KNEW...YOU'D GET PAST THE KRYPTONITE... SOON ENOUGH...

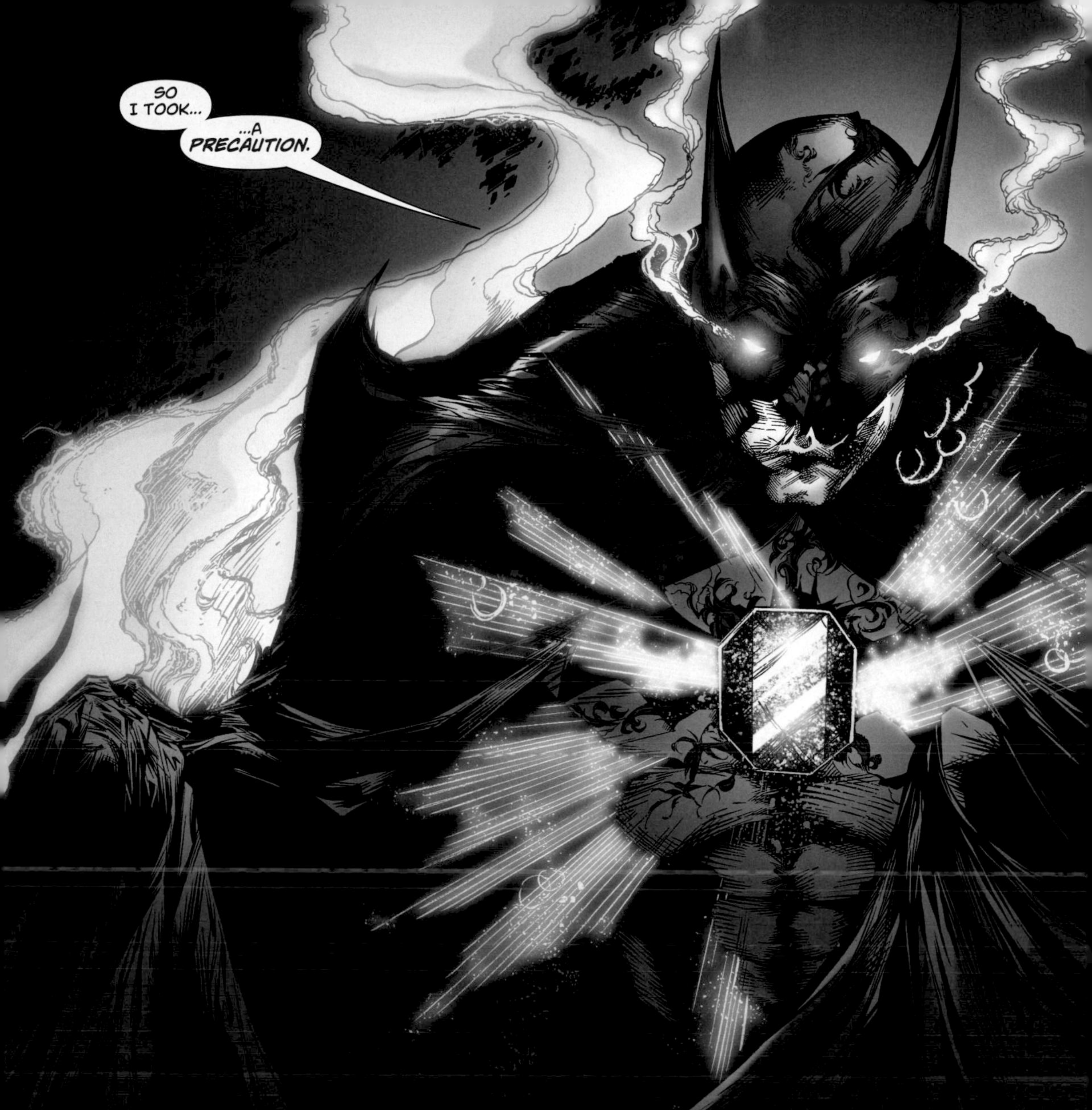
SO I TOOK...
...A PRECAUTION.
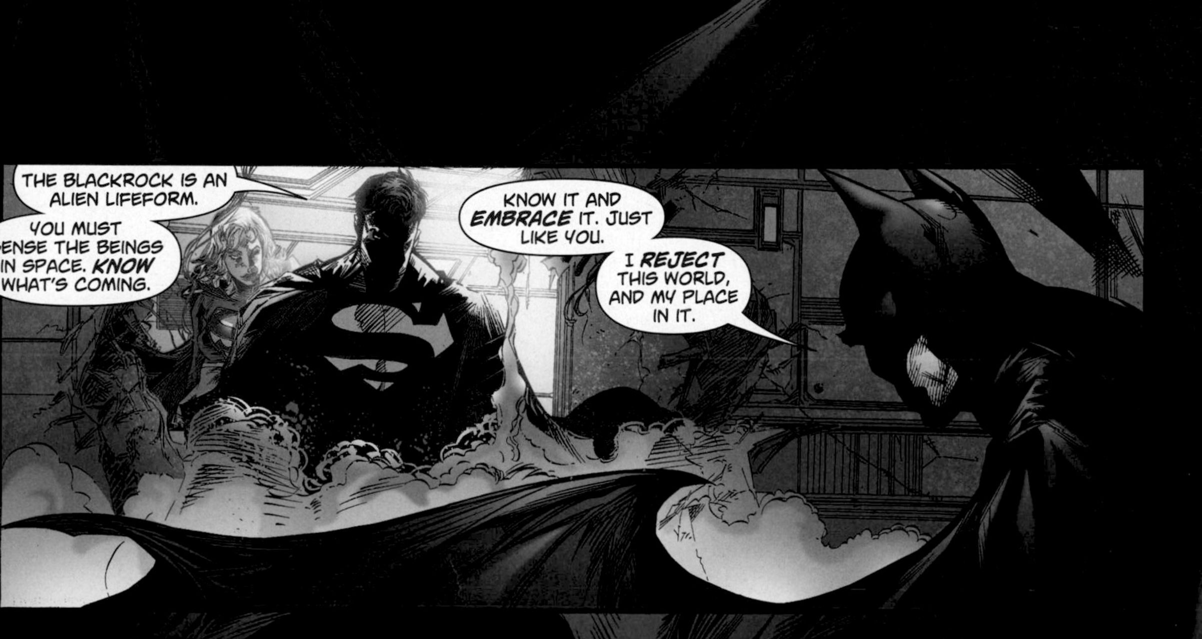
THE BLACKROCK IS AN ALIEN LIFEFORM.
YOU MUST SENSE THE BEINGS IN SPACE. KNOW WHAT'S COMING.
KNOW IT AND EMBRACE IT. JUST LIKE YOU.
I REJECT THIS WORLD, AND MY PLACE IN IT.

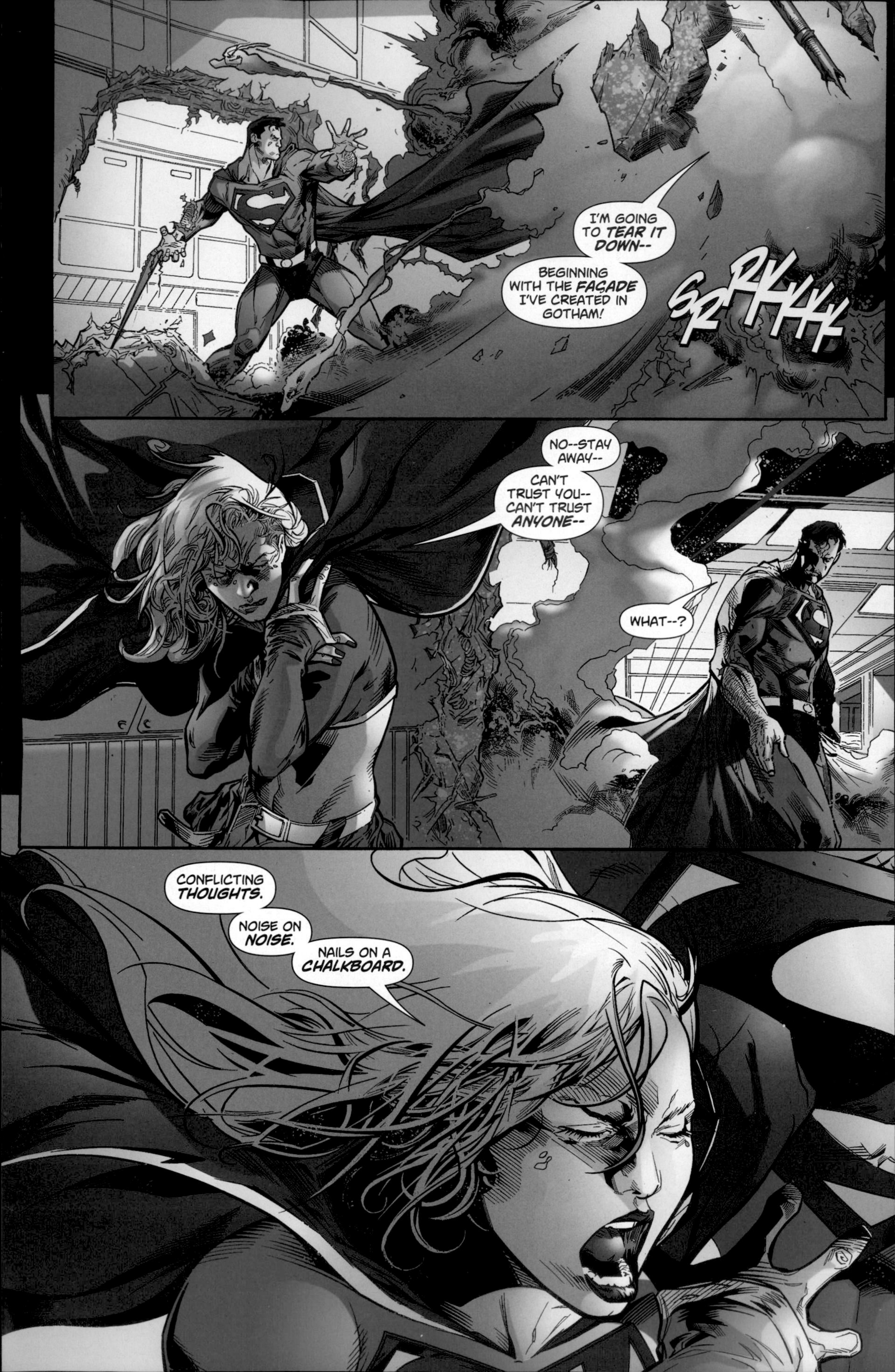
I'M GOING TO TEAR IT DOWN--
BEGINNING WITH THE FAÇADE I'VE CREATED IN GOTHAM!
SRRKKKK
NO--STAY AWAY--
CAN'T TRUST YOU-- CAN'T TRUST ANYONE--
WHAT--?
CONFLICTING THOUGHTS.
NOISE ON NOISE.
NAILS ON A CHALKBOARD.

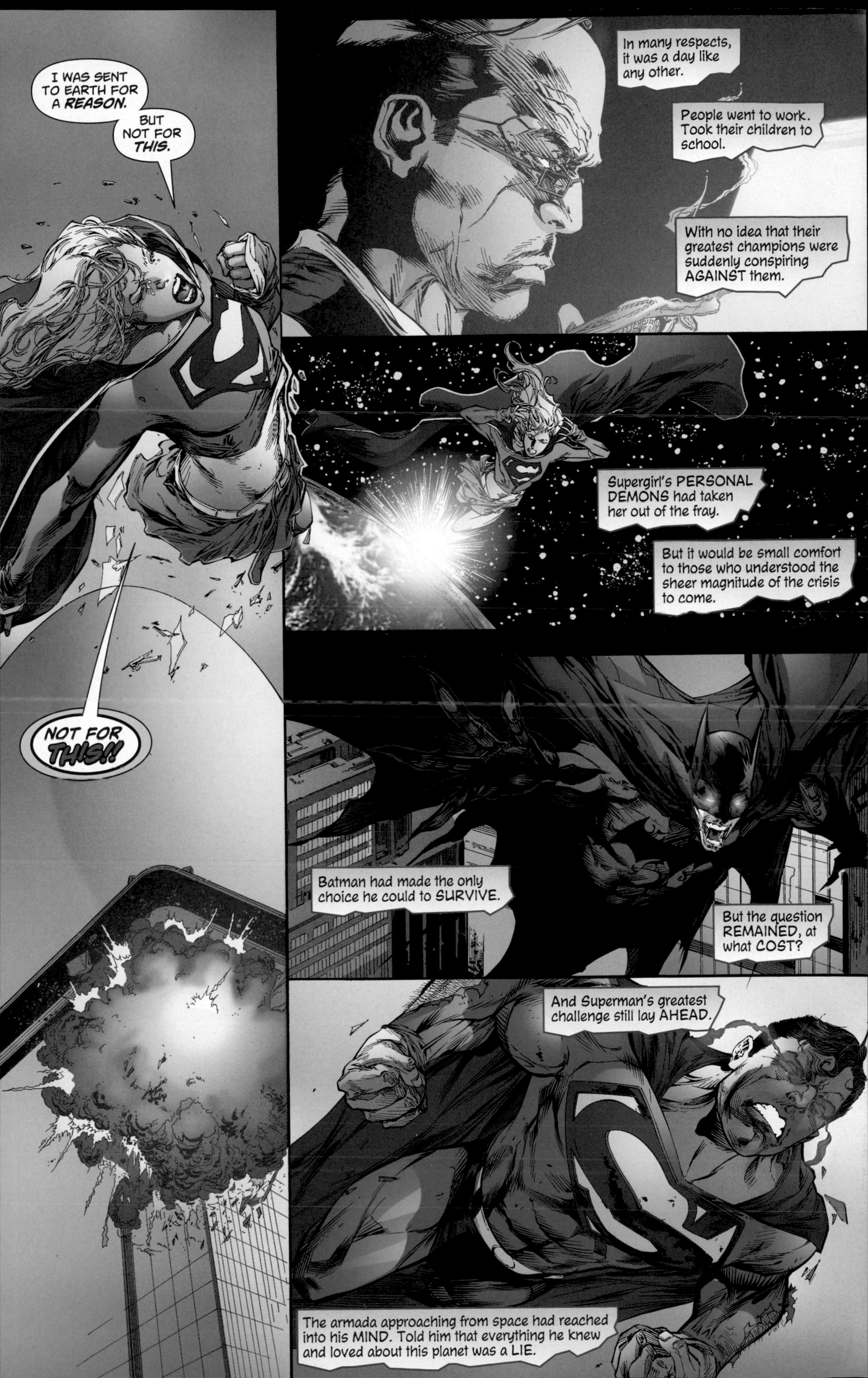

I WAS SENT TO EARTH FOR A REASON.
BUT NOT FOR THIS.
NOT FOR THIS!!
In many respects, it was a day like any other.
People went to work. Took their children to school.
With no idea that their greatest champions were suddenly conspiring AGAINST them.
Supergirl's PERSONAL DEMONS had taken her out of the fray.
But it would be small comfort to those who understood the sheer magnitude of the crisis to come.
Batman had made the only choice he could to SURVIVE.
But the question REMAINED, at what COST?
And Superman's greatest challenge still lay AHEAD.
The armada approaching from space had reached into his MIND. Told him that everything he knew and loved about this planet was a LIE.

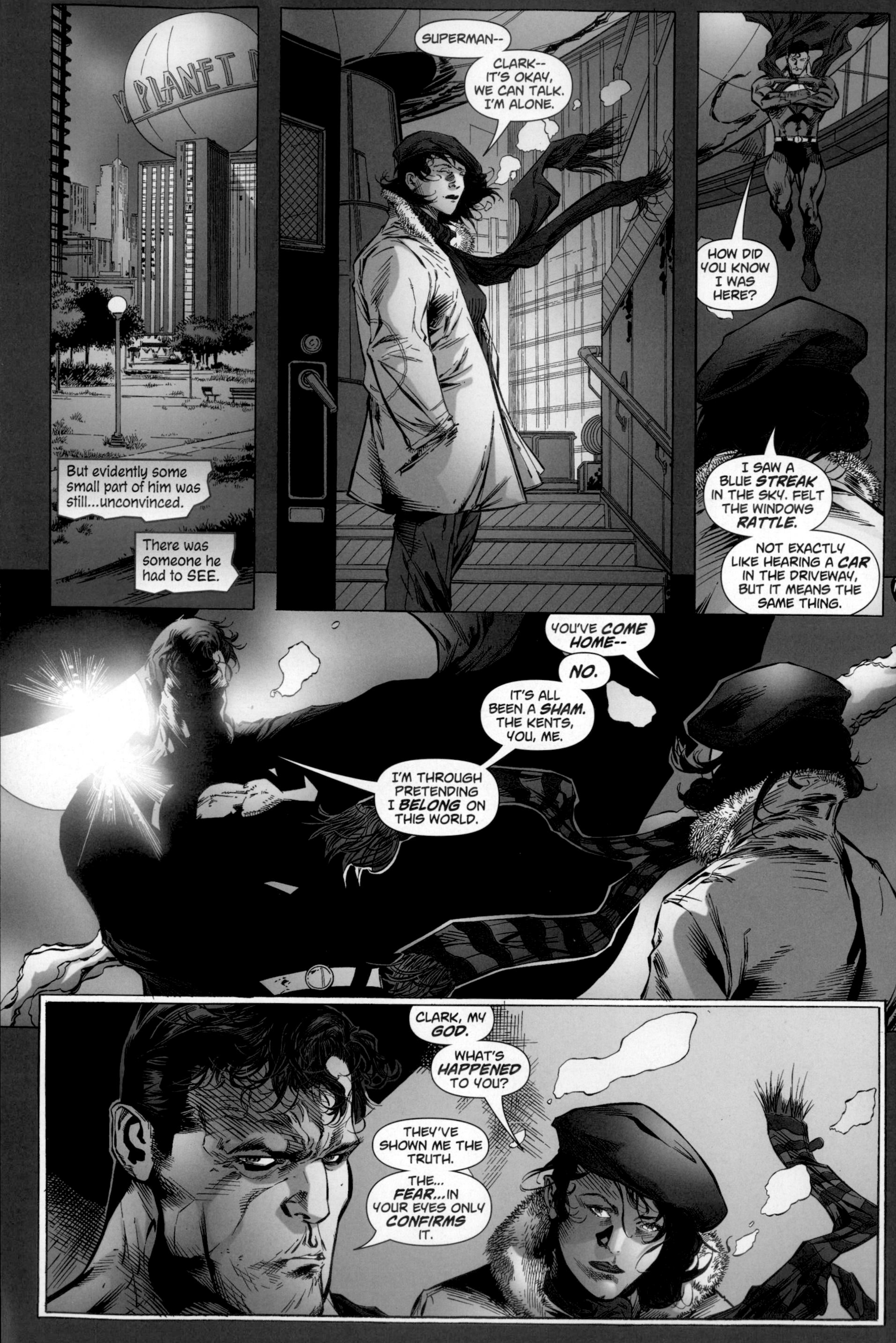
PLANET
But evidently some small part of him was still...unconvinced.
There was someone he had to SEE.
SUPERMAN--
CLARK-- IT'S OKAY, WE CAN TALK. I'M ALONE.
HOW DID YOU KNOW I WAS HERE?
I SAW A BLUE STREAK IN THE SKY. FELT THE WINDOWS RATTLE.
NOT EXACTLY LIKE HEARING A CAR IN THE DRIVEWAY, BUT IT MEANS THE SAME THING.
YOU'VE COME HOME--
NO.
IT'S ALL BEEN A SHAM. THE KENTS, YOU, ME.
I'M THROUGH PRETENDING I BELONG ON THIS WORLD.
CLARK, MY GOD.
WHAT'S HAPPENED TO YOU?
THEY'VE SHOWN ME THE TRUTH.
THE... FEAR...IN YOUR EYES ONLY CONFIRMS IT.

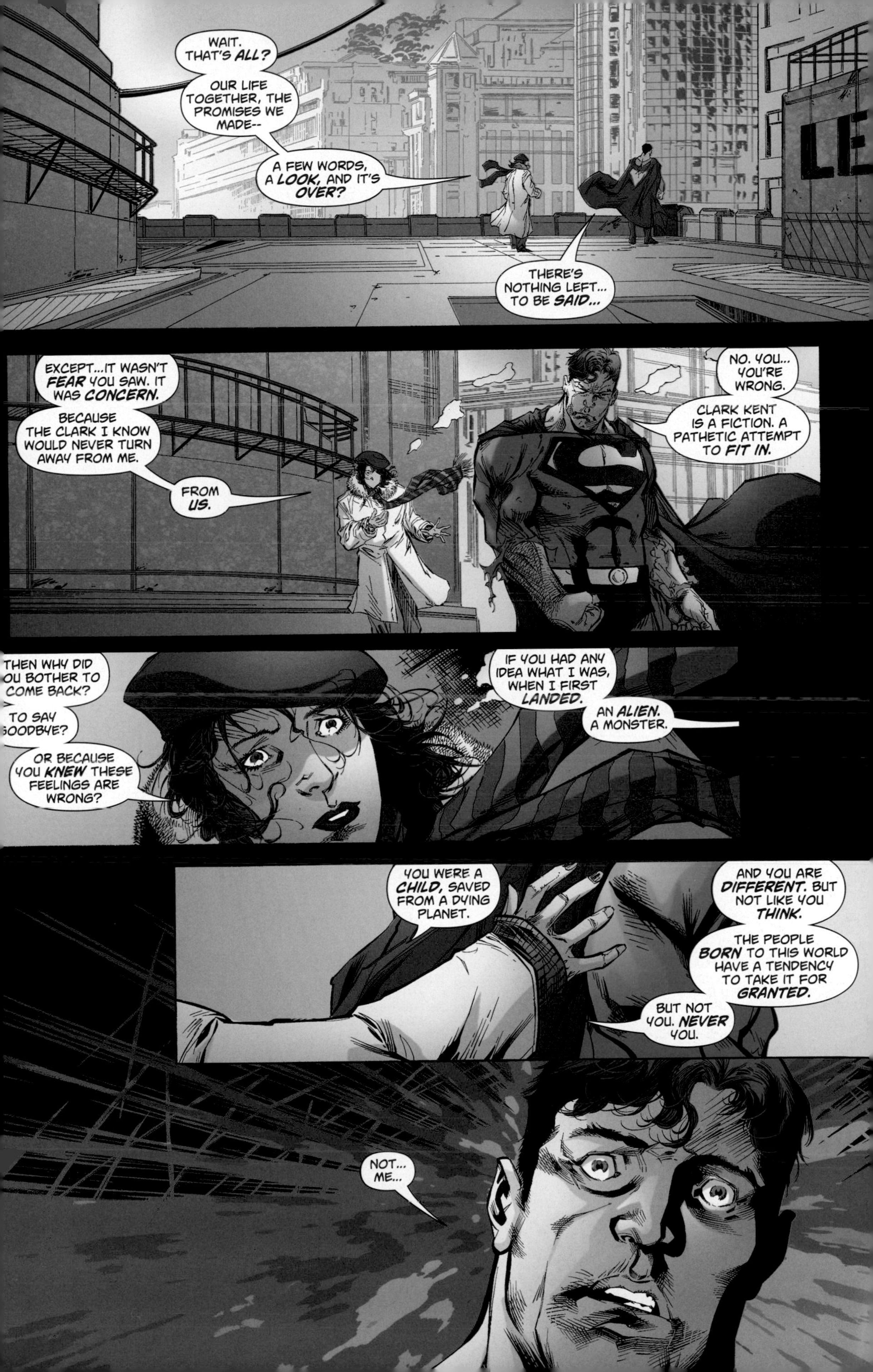
WAIT. THAT'S ALL?
OUR LIFE TOGETHER, THE PROMISES WE MADE--
A FEW WORDS, A LOOK, AND IT'S OVER?
THERE'S NOTHING LEFT... TO BE SAID...
EXCEPT...IT WASN'T FEAR YOU SAW. IT WAS CONCERN.
BECAUSE THE CLARK I KNOW WOULD NEVER TURN AWAY FROM ME.
FROM US.
NO. YOU... YOU'RE WRONG.
CLARK KENT IS A FICTION. A PATHETIC ATTEMPT TO FIT IN.
THEN WHY DID OU BOTHER TO COME BACK?
TO SAY OODBYE?
OR BECAUSE YOU KNEW THESE FEELINGS ARE WRONG?
IF YOU HAD ANY IDEA WHAT I WAS, WHEN I FIRST LANDED.
AN ALIEN. A MONSTER.
YOU WERE A CHILD, SAVED FROM A DYING PLANET.
AND YOU ARE DIFFERENT. BUT NOT LIKE YOU THINK.
THE PEOPLE BORN TO THIS WORLD HAVE A TENDENCY TO TAKE IT FOR GRANTED.
BUT NOT YOU. NEVER YOU.
NOT... ME...

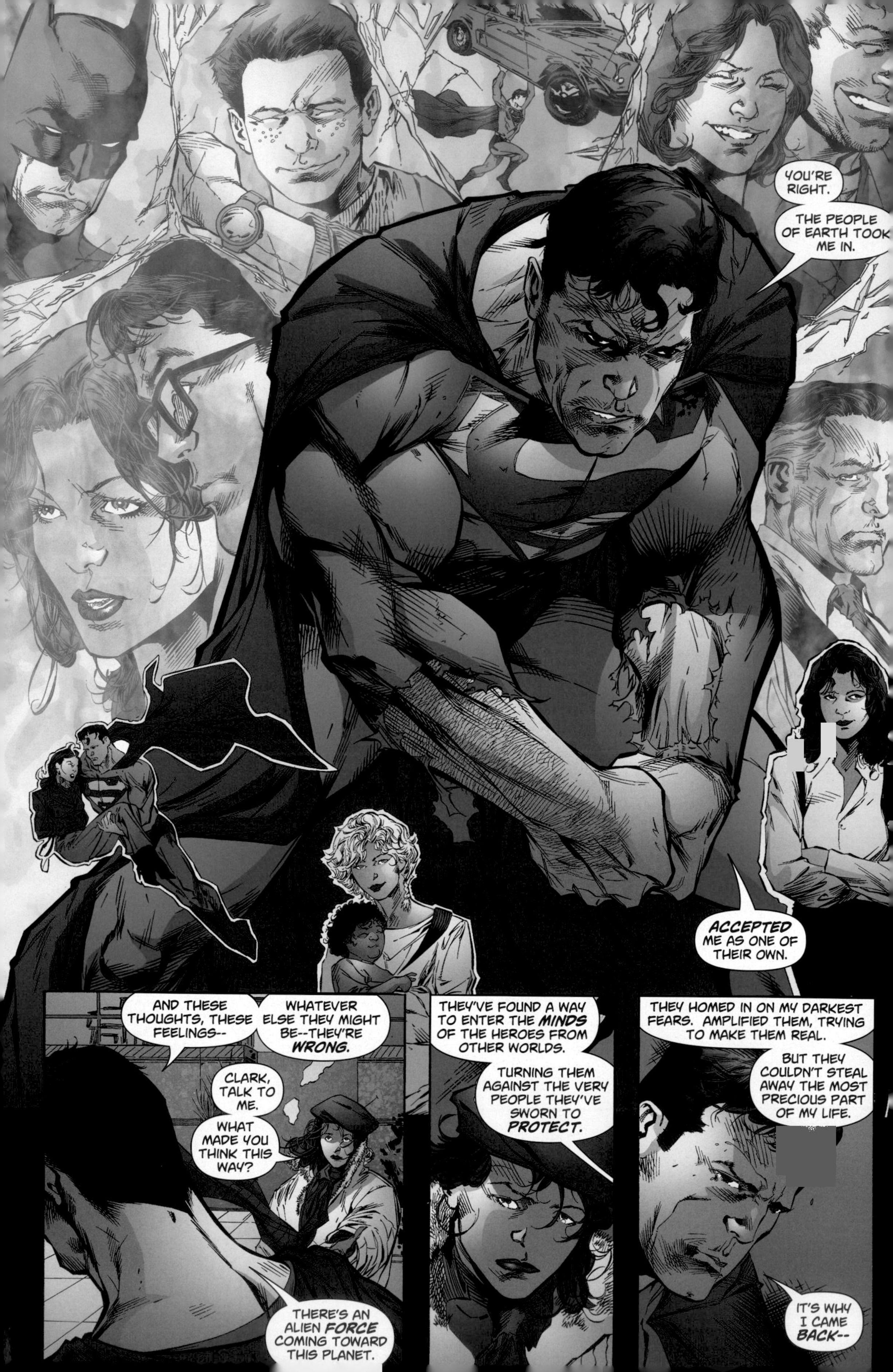
YOU'RE RIGHT.
THE PEOPLE OF EARTH TOOK ME IN.
ACCEPTED ME AS ONE OF THEIR OWN.
AND THESE THOUGHTS, THESE FEELINGS--
WHATEVER ELSE THEY MIGHT BE--THEY'RE WRONG.
CLARK, TALK TO ME.
WHAT MADE YOU THINK THIS WAY?
THERE'S AN ALIEN FORCE COMING TOWARD THIS PLANET.
THEY'VE FOUND A WAY TO ENTER THE MINDS OF THE HEROES FROM OTHER WORLDS.
TURNING THEM AGAINST THE VERY PEOPLE THEY'VE SWORN TO PROTECT.
THEY HOMED IN ON MY DARKEST FEARS. AMPLIFIED THEM, TRYING TO MAKE THEM REAL.
BUT THEY COULDN'T STEAL AWAY THE MOST PRECIOUS PART OF MY LIFE.
IT'S WHY I CAME BACK--

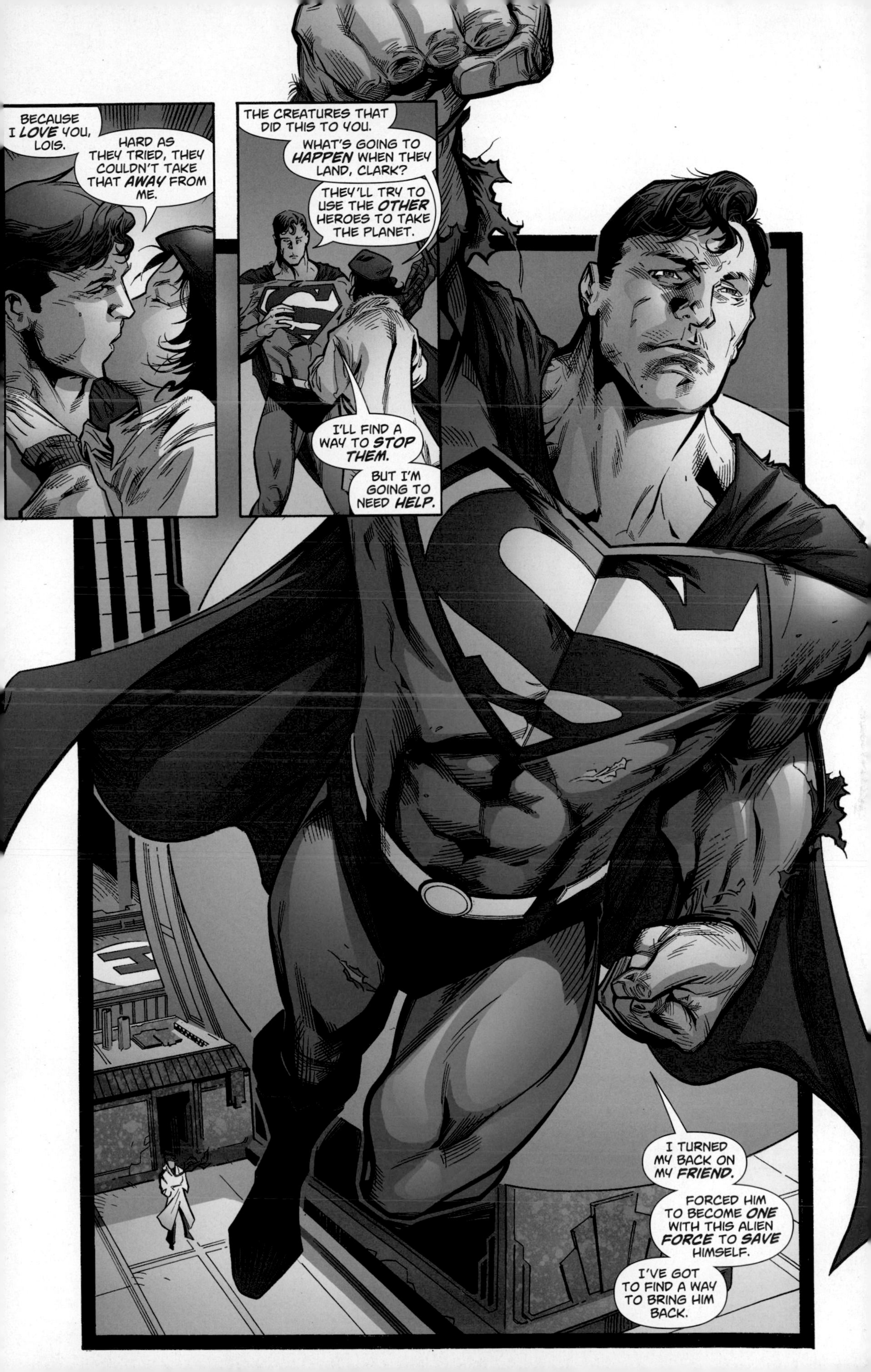

BECAUSE I LOVE YOU, LOIS.
HARD AS THEY TRIED, THEY COULDN'T TAKE THAT AWAY FROM ME.
THE CREATURES THAT DID THIS TO YOU.
WHAT'S GOING TO HAPPEN WHEN THEY LAND, CLARK?
THEY'LL TRY TO USE THE OTHER HEROES TO TAKE THE PLANET.
I'LL FIND A WAY TO STOP THEM.
BUT I'M GOING TO NEED HELP.
I TURNED MY BACK ON MY FRIEND.
FORCED HIM TO BECOME ONE WITH THIS ALIEN FORCE TO SAVE HIMSELF.
I'VE GOT TO FIND A WAY TO BRING HIM BACK.

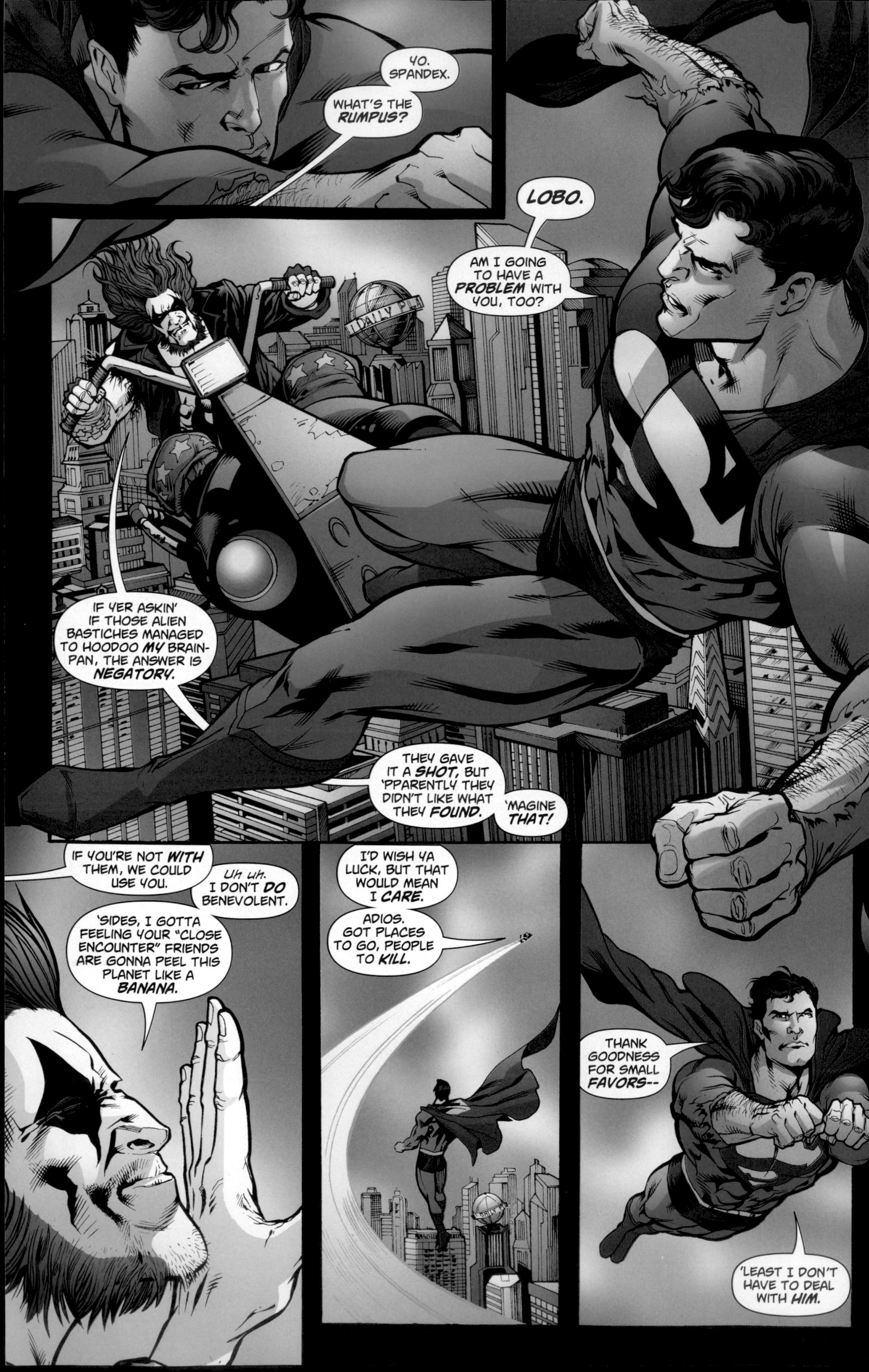
YO. SPANDEX.
WHAT'S THE RUMPUS?
LOBO.
AM I GOING TO HAVE A PROBLEM WITH YOU, TOO?
IF YER ASKIN' IF THOSE ALIEN BASTICHES MANAGED TO HOODOO MY BRAIN-PAN, THE ANSWER IS NEGATORY.
THEY GAVE IT A SHOT, BUT 'PPARENTLY THEY DIDN'T LIKE WHAT THEY FOUND.
'MAGINE THAT!
IF YOU'RE NOT WITH THEM, WE COULD USE YOU.
Uh uh. I DON'T DO BENEVOLENT.
'SIDES, I GOTTA FEELING YOUR "CLOSE ENCOUNTER" FRIENDS ARE GONNA PEEL THIS PLANET LIKE A BANANA.
I'D WISH YA LUCK, BUT THAT WOULD MEAN I CARE.
ADIOS. GOT PLACES TO GO, PEOPLE TO KILL.
THANK GOODNESS FOR SMALL FAVORS--
'LEAST I DON'T HAVE TO DEAL WITH HIM.

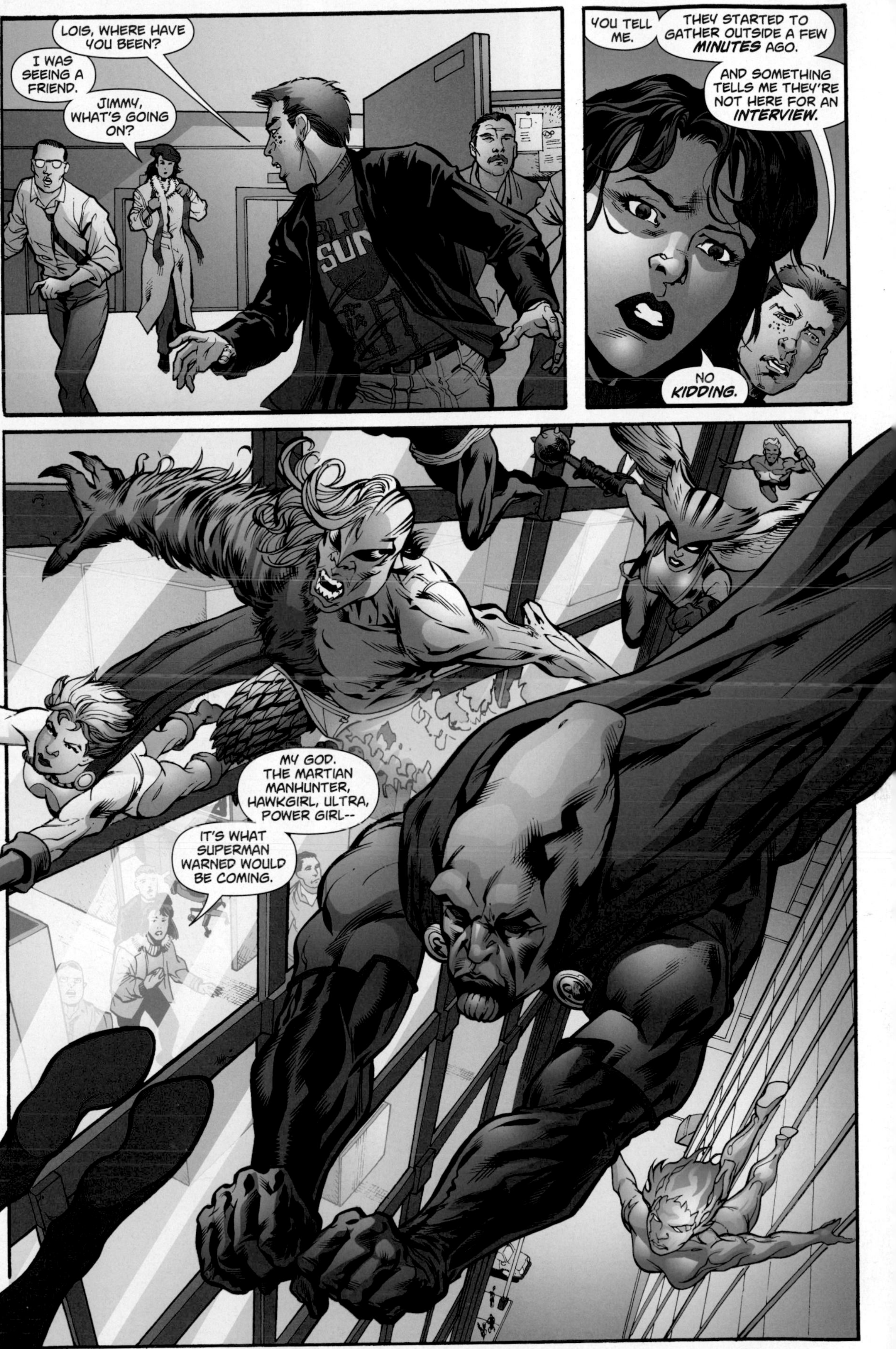
LOIS, WHERE HAVE YOU BEEN?
I WAS SEEING A FRIEND.
JIMMY, WHAT'S GOING ON?
BLUE SUN
YOU TELL ME.
THEY STARTED TO GATHER OUTSIDE A FEW MINUTES AGO.
AND SOMETHING TELLS ME THEY'RE NOT HERE FOR AN INTERVIEW.
NO KIDDING.
MY GOD. THE MARTIAN MANHUNTER, HAWKGIRL, ULTRA, POWER GIRL--
IT'S WHAT SUPERMAN WARNED WOULD BE COMING.

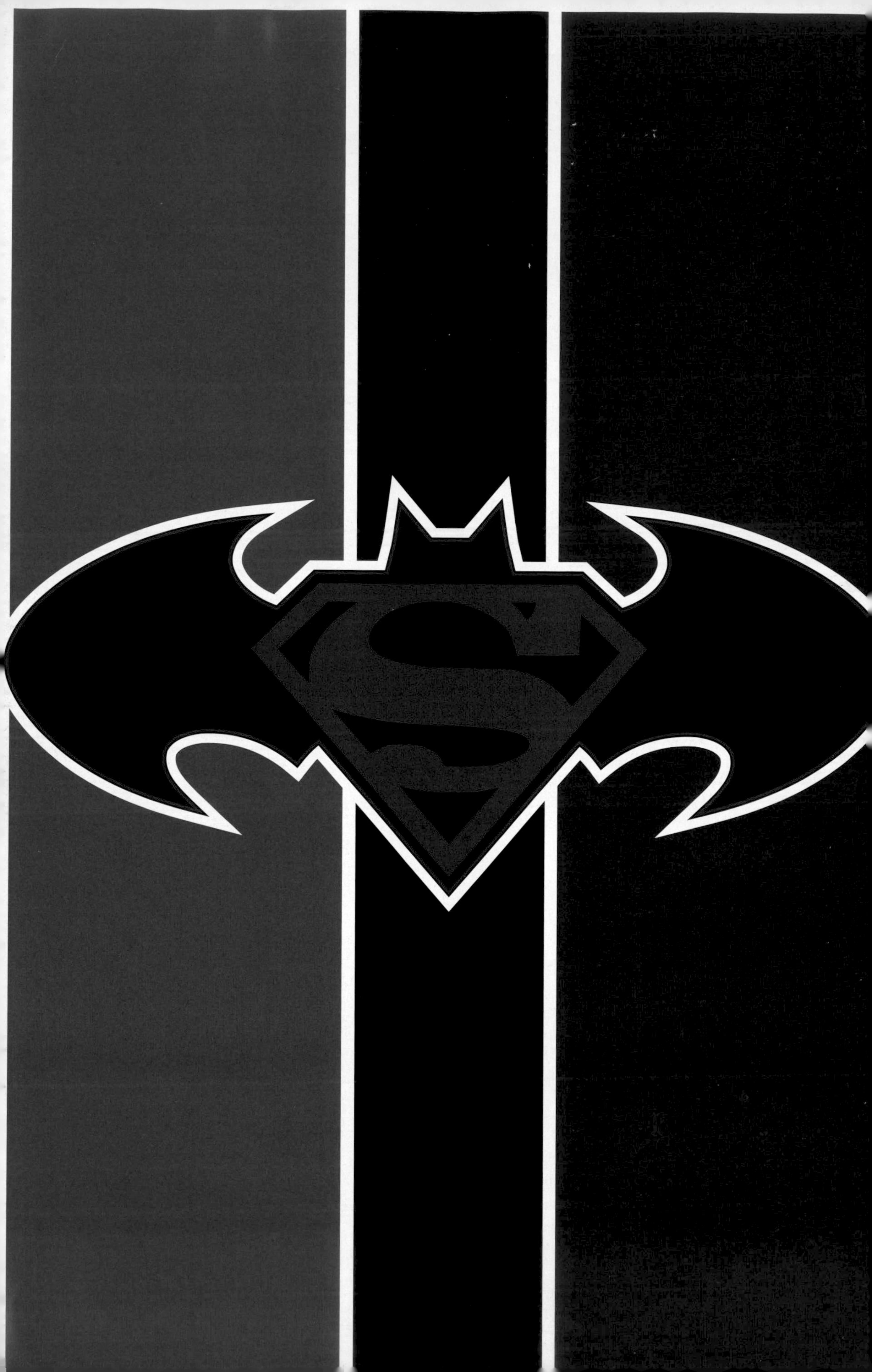

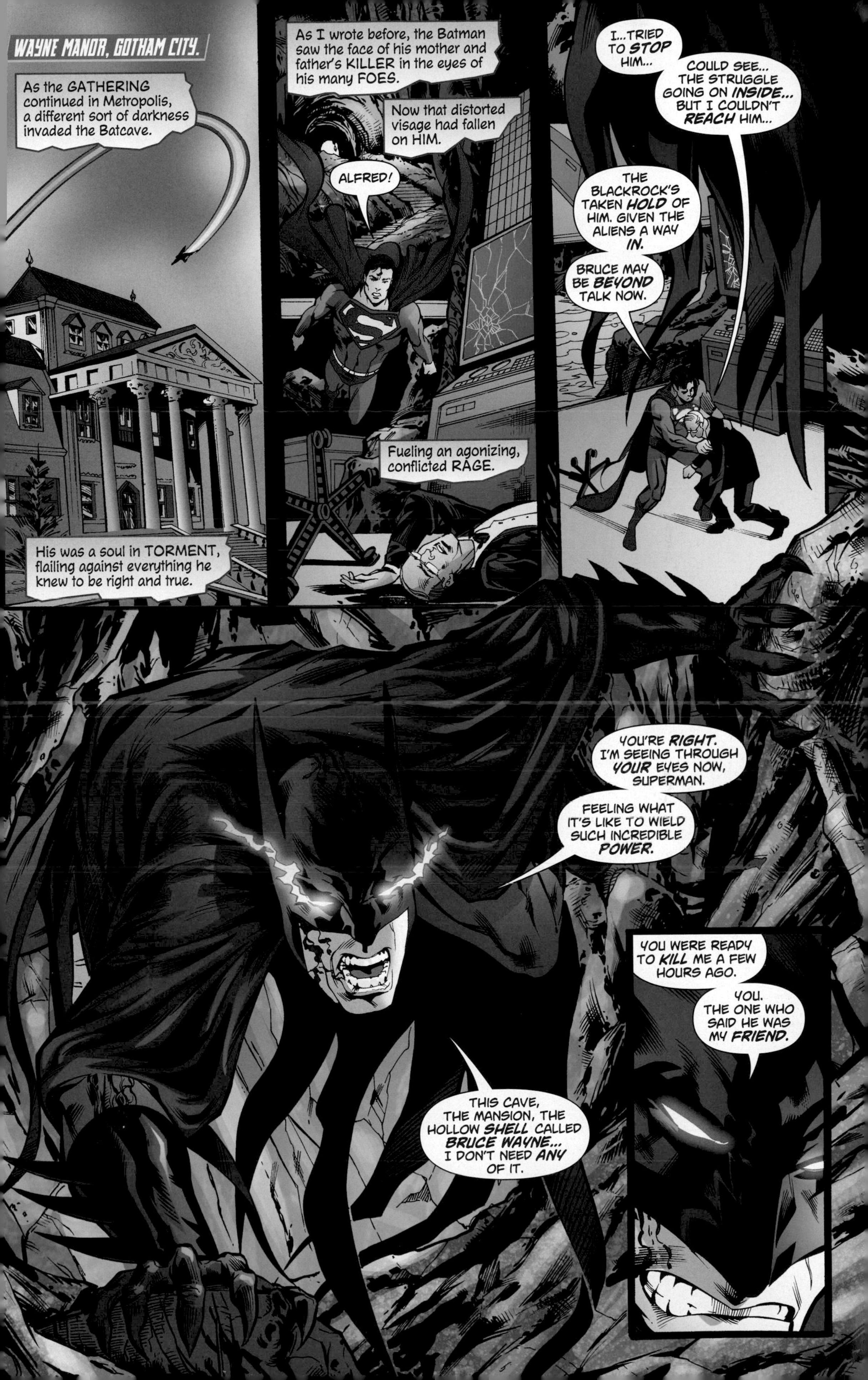
WAYNE MANOR, GOTHAM CITY.
As the GATHERING continued in Metropolis, a different sort of darkness invaded the Batcave.
His was a soul in TORMENT, flailing against everything he knew to be right and true.
As I wrote before, the Batman saw the face of his mother and father's KILLER in the eyes of his many FOES.
Now that distorted visage had fallen on HIM.
ALFRED!
Fueling an agonizing, conflicted RAGE.
I...TRIED TO STOP HIM...
COULD SEE... THE STRUGGLE GOING ON INSIDE... BUT I COULDN'T REACH HIM...
THE BLACKROCK'S TAKEN HOLD OF HIM. GIVEN THE ALIENS A WAY IN.
BRUCE MAY BE BEYOND TALK NOW.
YOU'RE RIGHT. I'M SEEING THROUGH YOUR EYES NOW, SUPERMAN.
FEELING WHAT IT'S LIKE TO WIELD SUCH INCREDIBLE POWER.
THIS CAVE, THE MANSION, THE HOLLOW SHELL CALLED BRUCE WAYNE... I DON'T NEED ANY OF IT.
YOU WERE READY TO KILL ME A FEW HOURS AGO.
YOU. THE ONE WHO SAID HE WAS MY FRIEND.

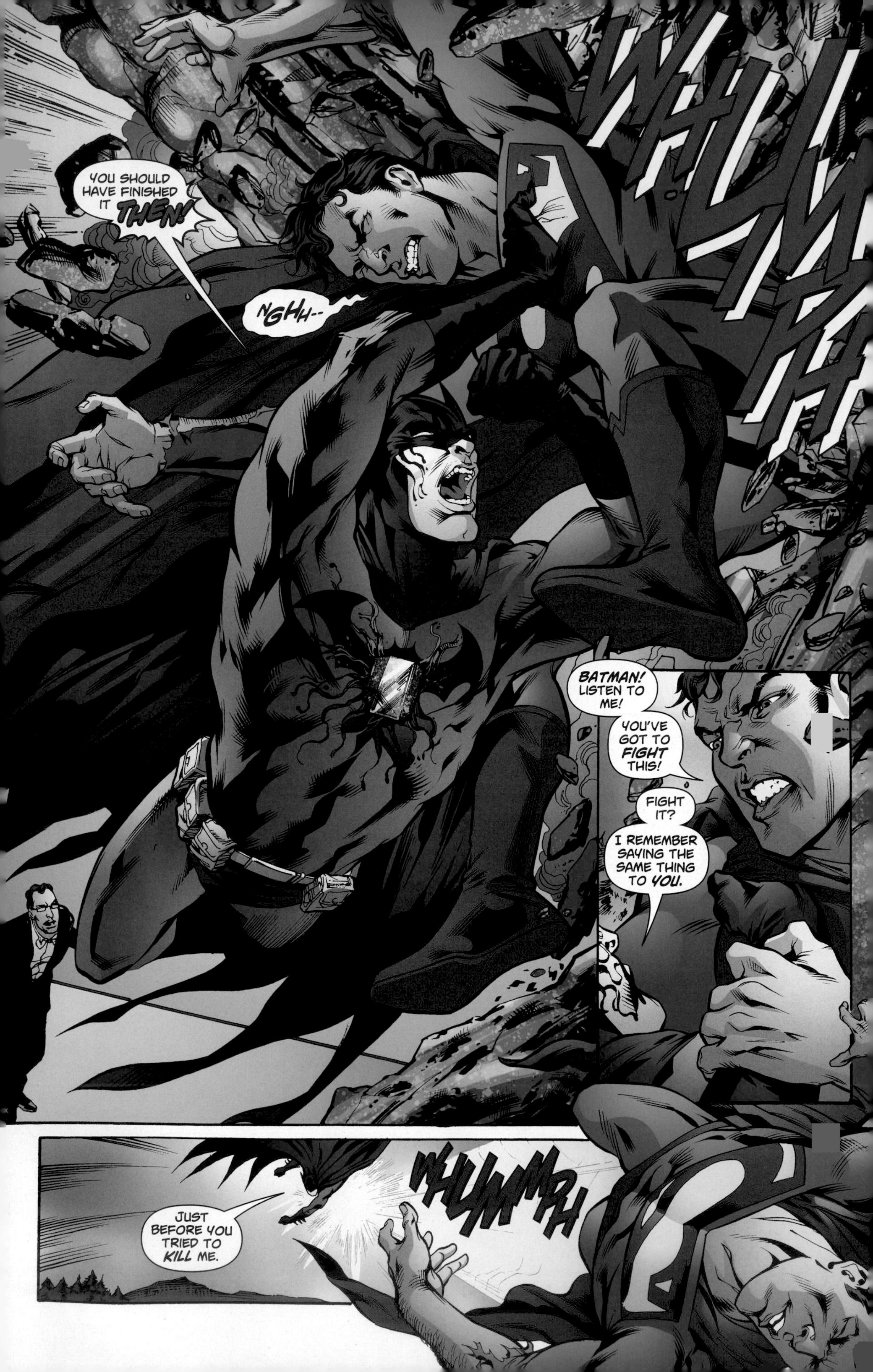
WHUMP
YOU SHOULD HAVE FINISHED IT THEN!
NGHH--
BATMAN! LISTEN TO ME!
YOU'VE GOT TO FIGHT THIS!
FIGHT IT?
I REMEMBER SAYING THE SAME THING TO YOU.
WHUMMPH
JUST BEFORE YOU TRIED TO KILL ME.

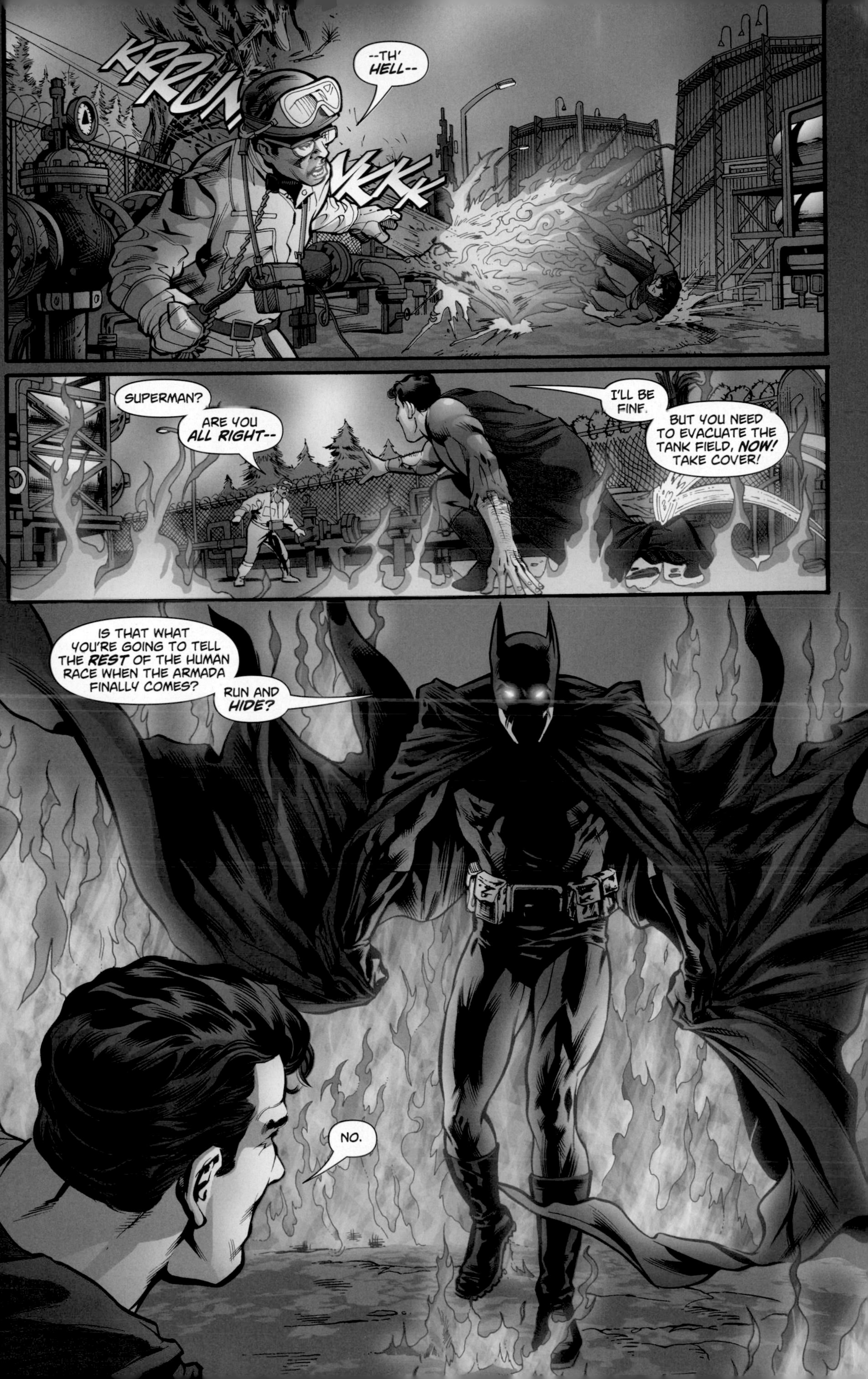
KRRUNKKK
--TH' HELL--
SUPERMAN?
ARE YOU ALL RIGHT--
I'LL BE FINE.
BUT YOU NEED TO EVACUATE THE TANK FIELD, NOW! TAKE COVER!
IS THAT WHAT YOU'RE GOING TO TELL THE REST OF THE HUMAN RACE WHEN THE ARMADA FINALLY COMES?
RUN AND HIDE?
NO.

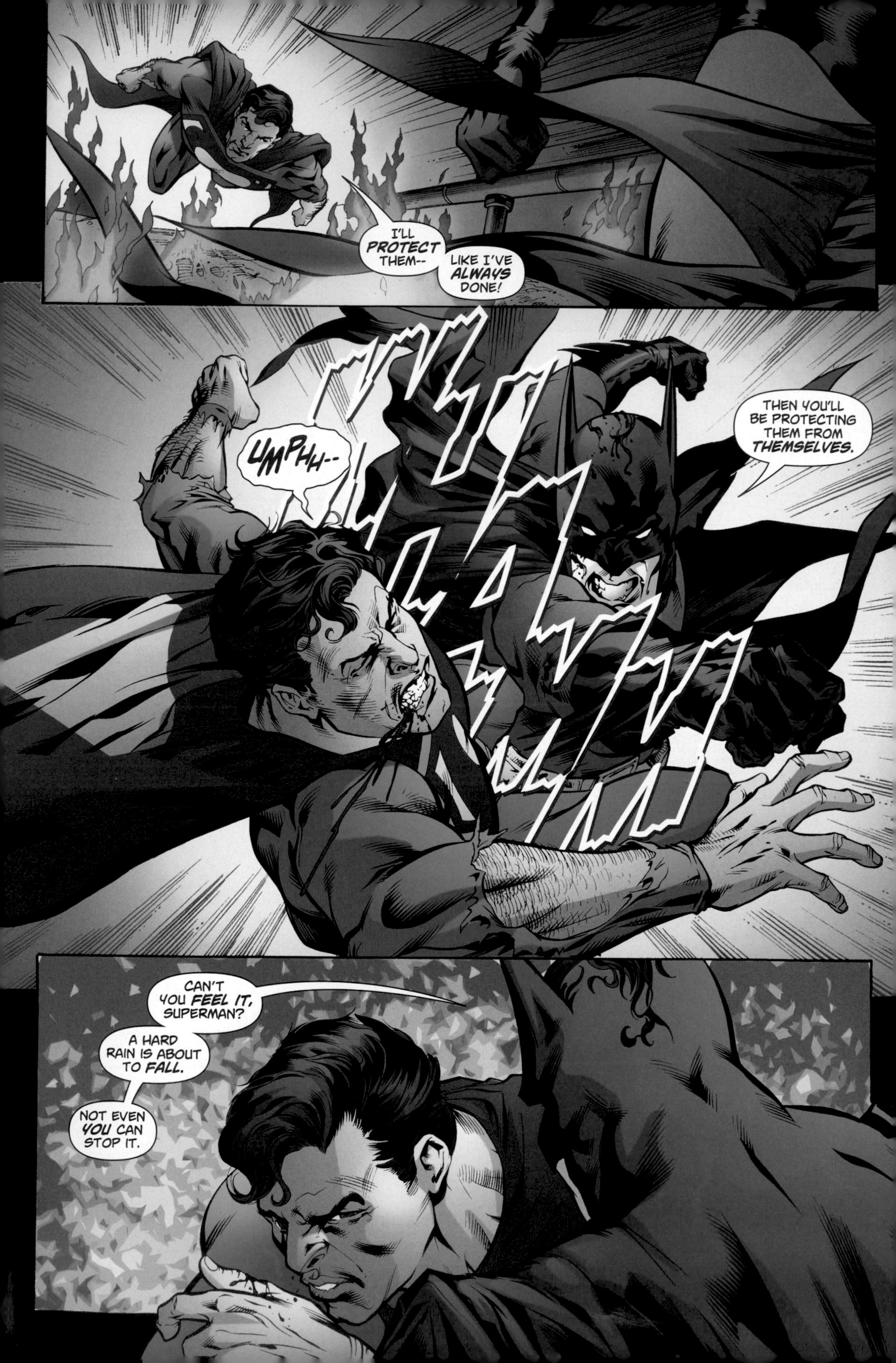
I'LL PROTECT THEM--
LIKE I'VE ALWAYS DONE!
UMPHH--
THEN YOU'LL BE PROTECTING THEM FROM THEMSELVES.
CAN'T YOU FEEL IT, SUPERMAN?
A HARD RAIN IS ABOUT TO FALL.
NOT EVEN YOU CAN STOP IT.

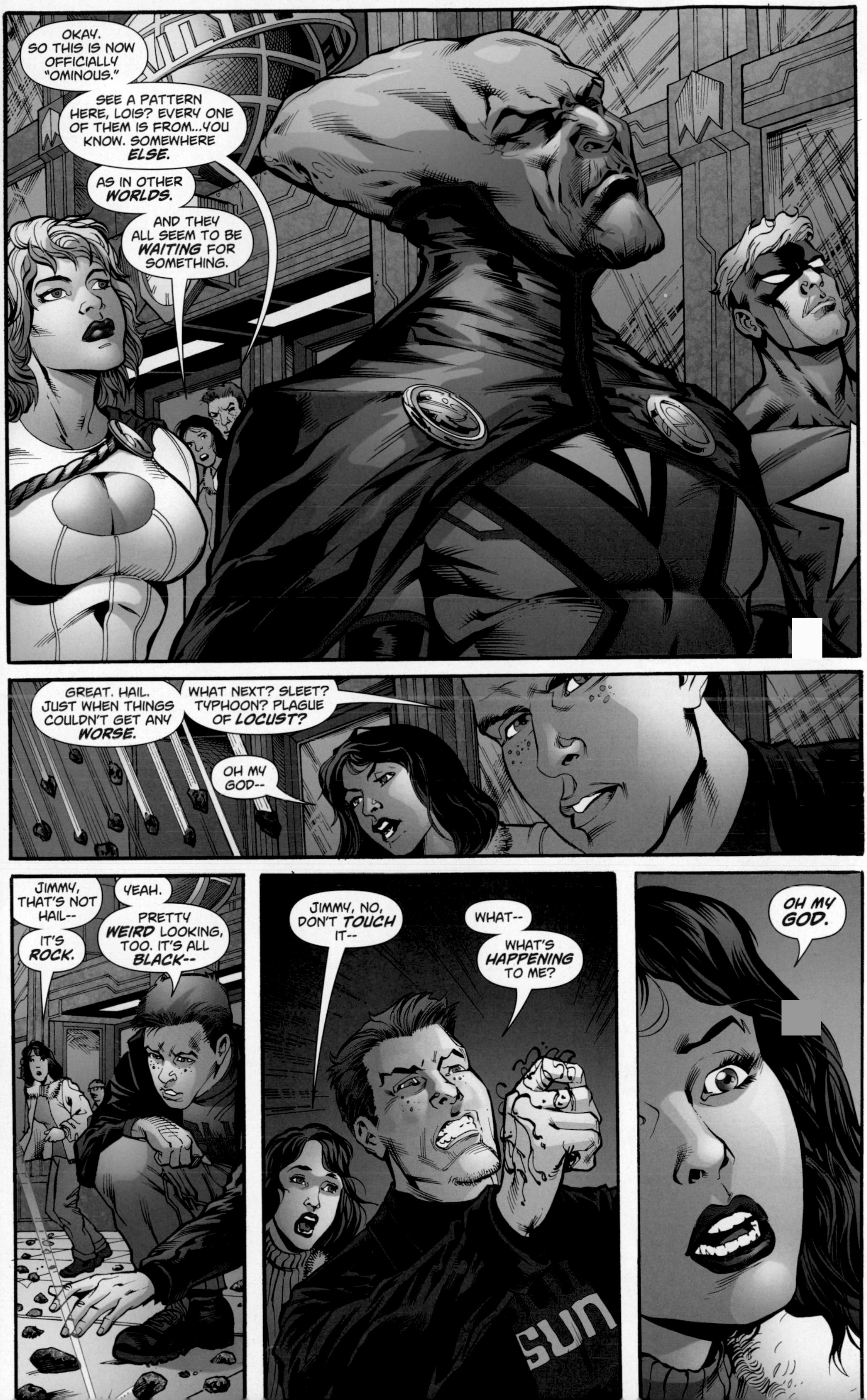
OKAY. SO THIS IS NOW OFFICIALLY "OMINOUS."
SEE A PATTERN HERE, LOIS? EVERY ONE OF THEM IS FROM...YOU KNOW. SOMEWHERE ELSE.
AS IN OTHER WORLDS.
AND THEY ALL SEEM TO BE WAITING FOR SOMETHING.
GREAT. HAIL. JUST WHEN THINGS COULDN'T GET ANY WORSE.
WHAT NEXT? SLEET? TYPHOON? PLAGUE OF LOCUST?
OH MY GOD--
JIMMY, THAT'S NOT HAIL--
IT'S ROCK.
YEAH.
PRETTY WEIRD LOOKING, TOO. IT'S ALL BLACK--
JIMMY, NO, DON'T TOUCH IT--
WHAT--
WHAT'S HAPPENING TO ME?
OH MY GOD.
SUN

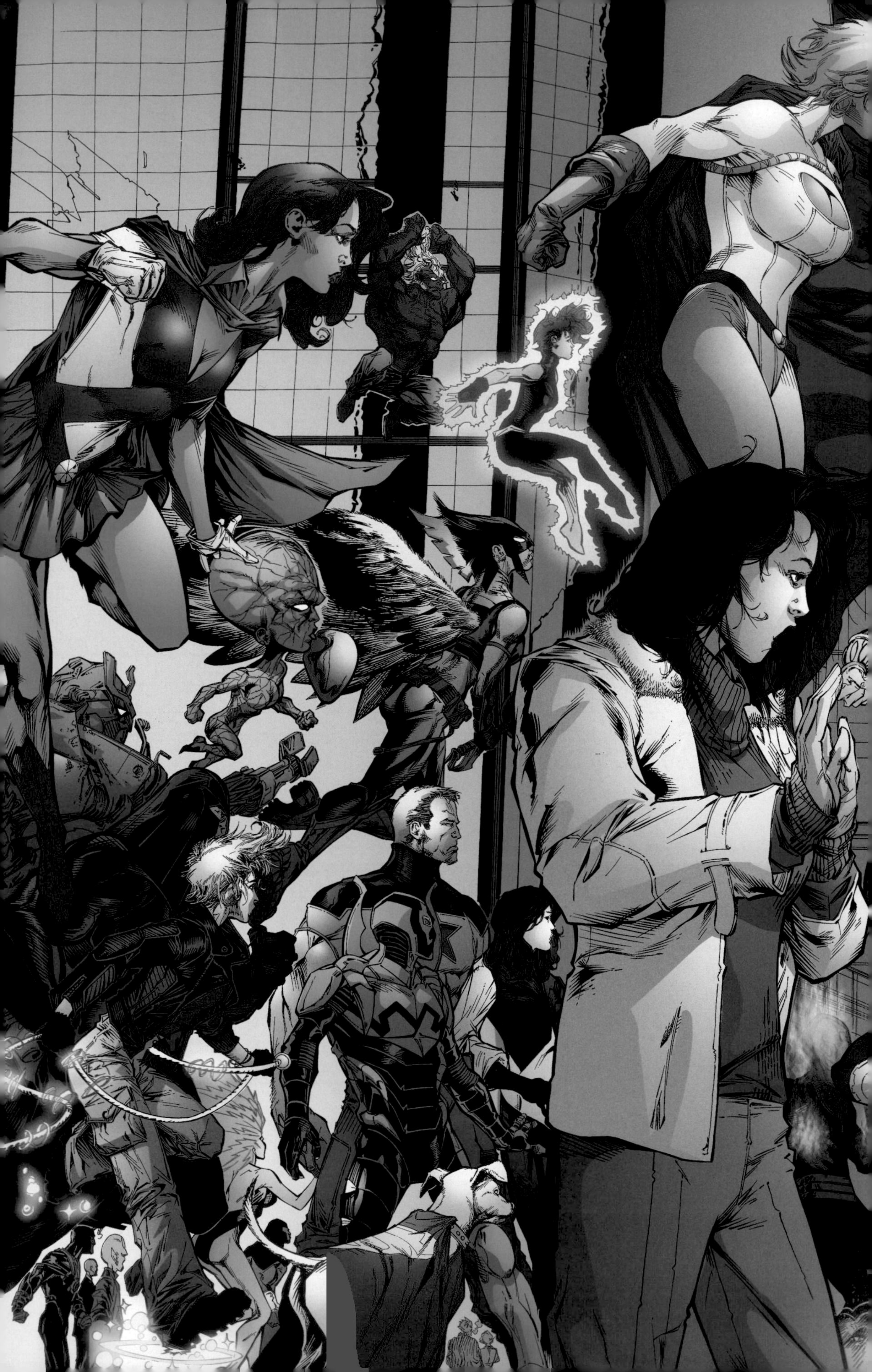

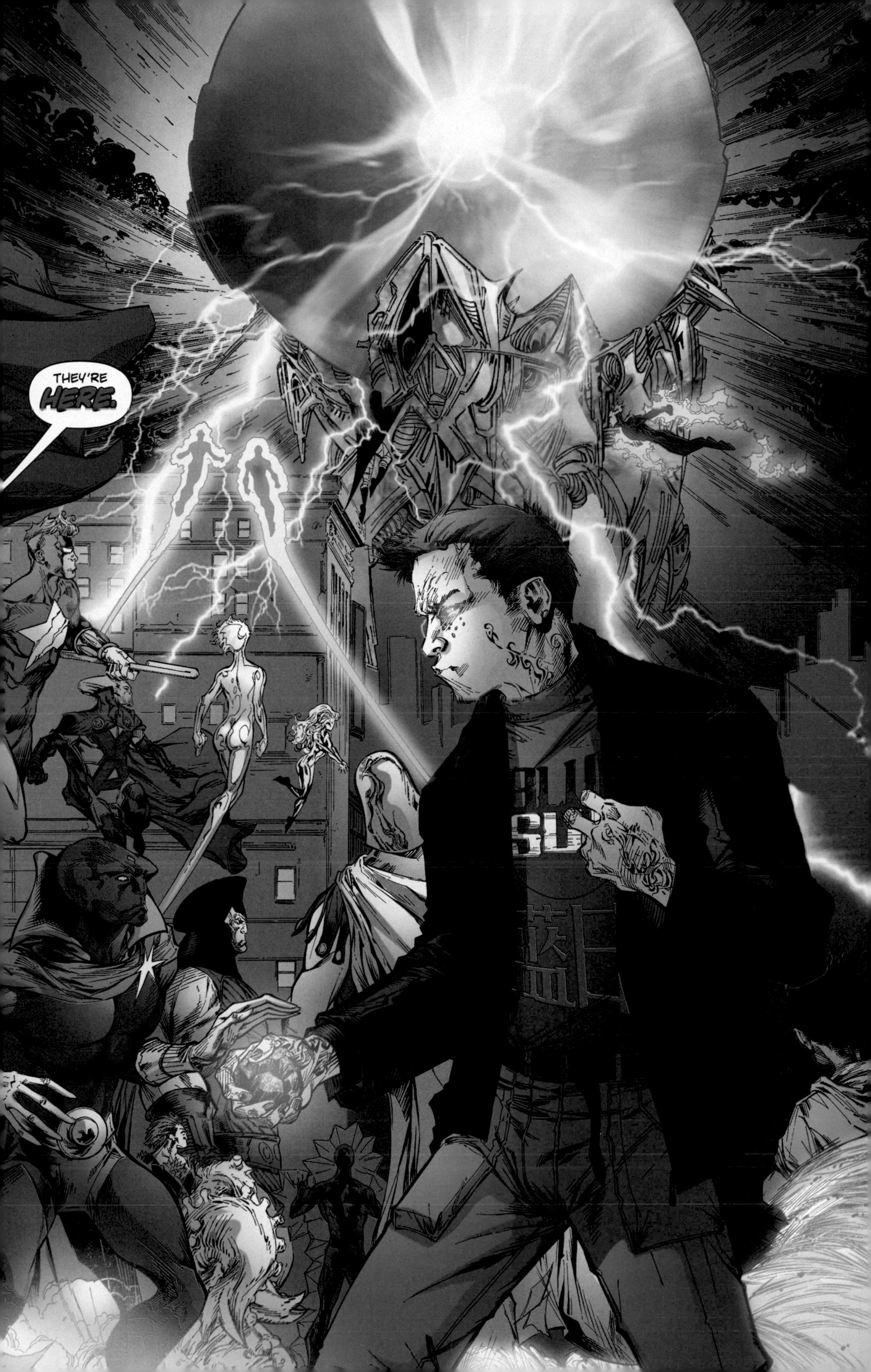
THEY'RE HERE.

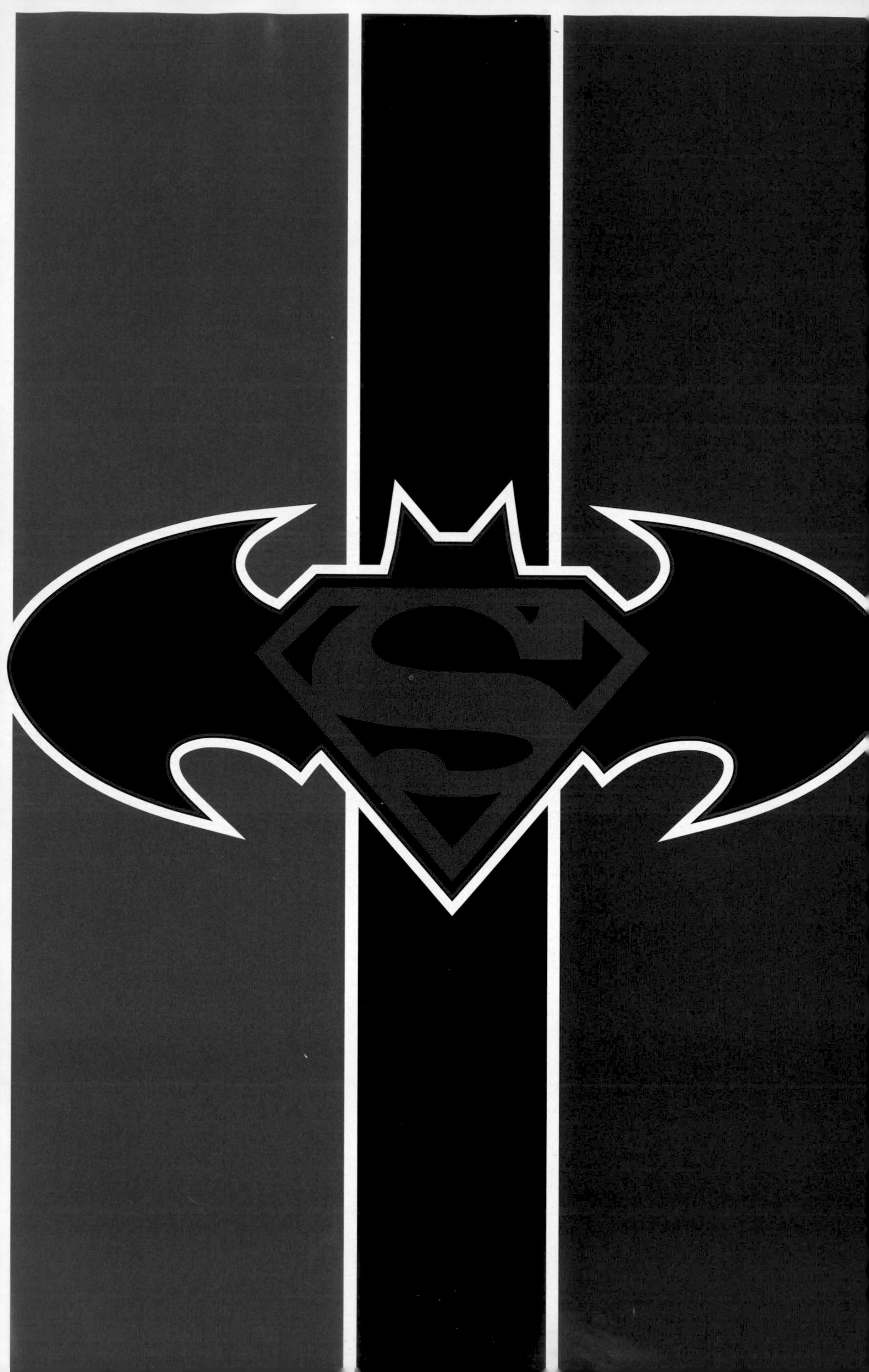

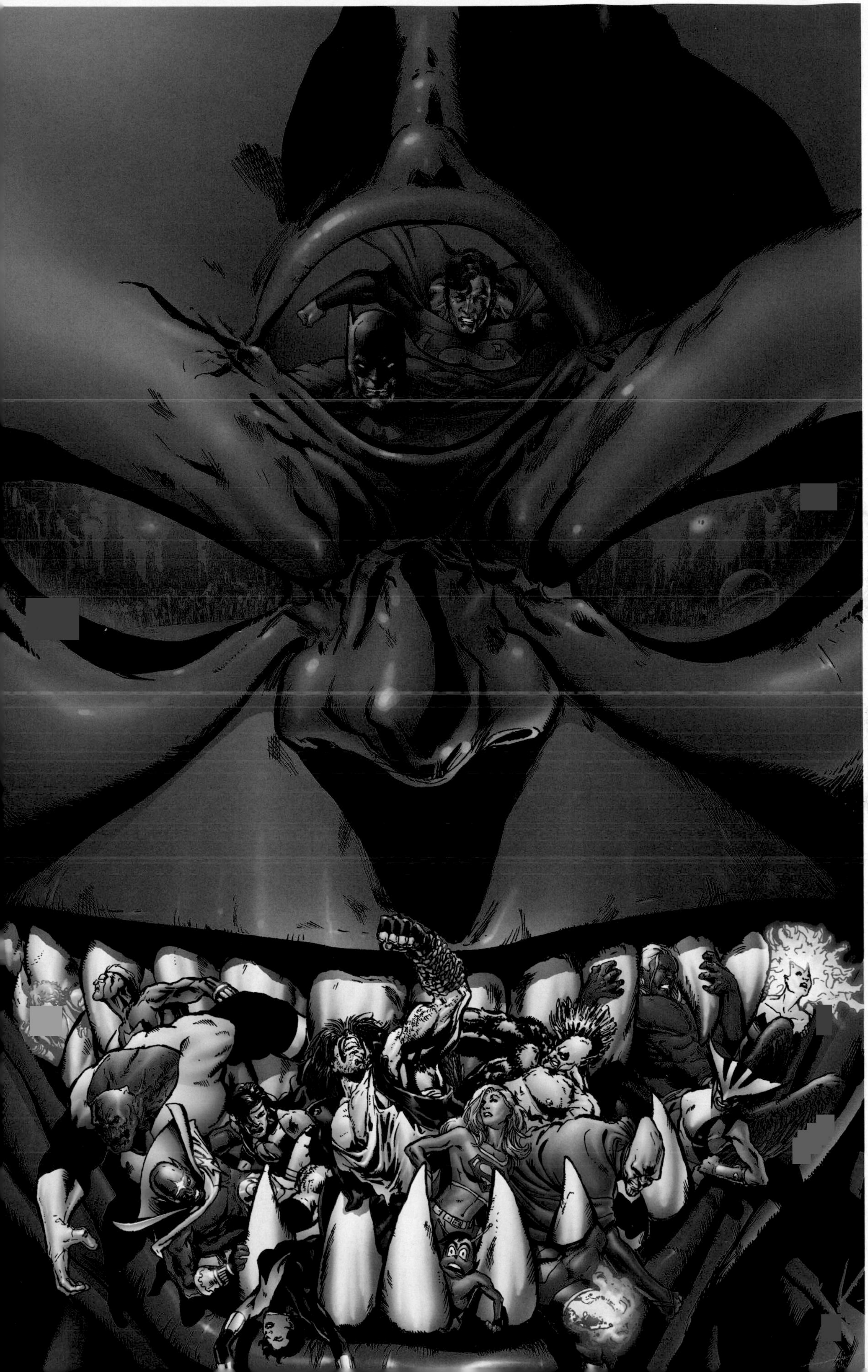

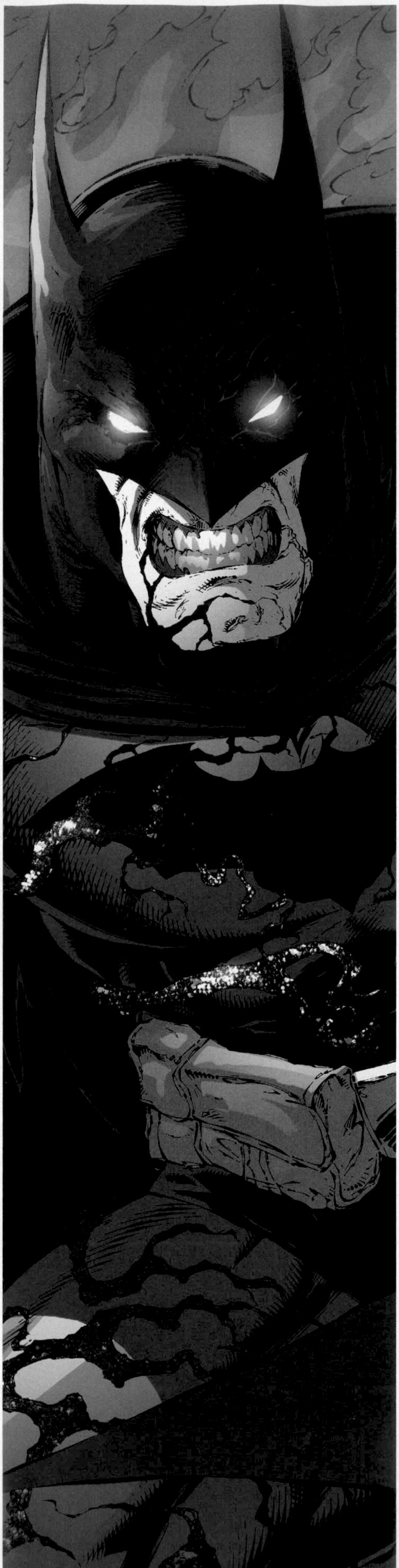

THE ENEMIES AMONG US

PART 6

MARK VERHEIDEN
WRITER

JOE BENITEZ
PENCILLER

VICTOR LLAMAS
INKER

GUY MAJOR
COLORIST

ROB LEIGH
LETTERER

PHIL JIMENEZ, ANDY LANNING & MOOSE BAUMANN
COVER

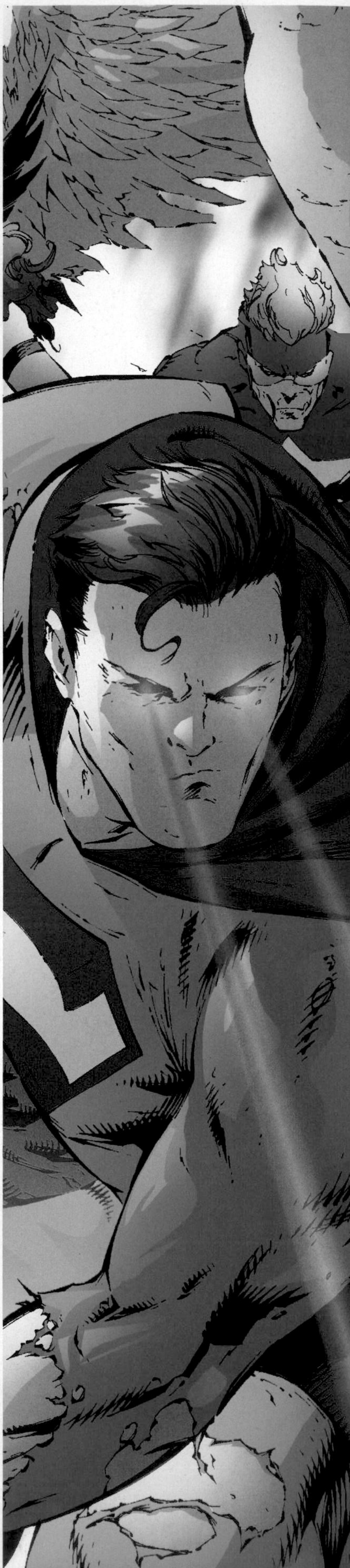

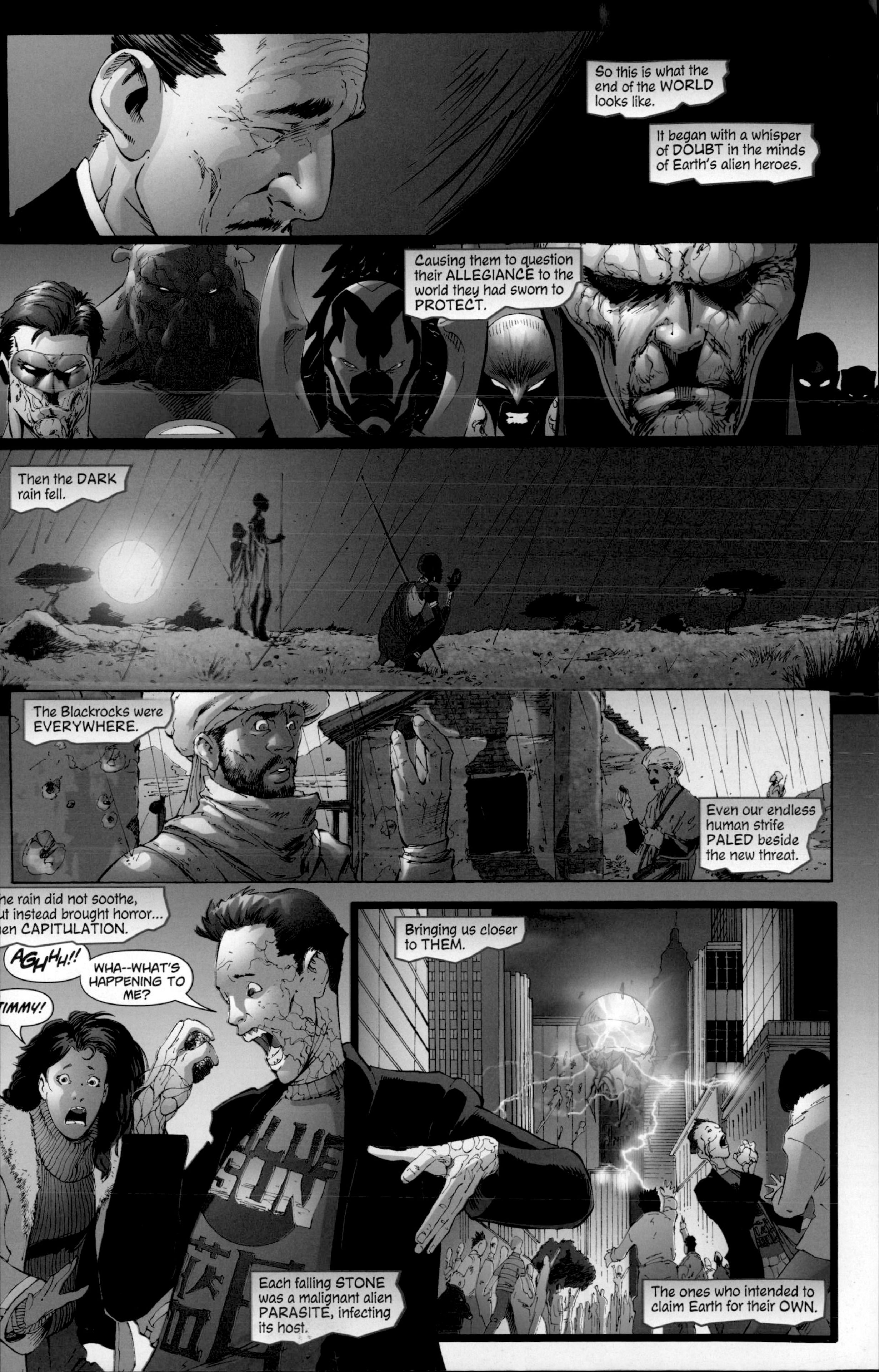

So this is what the end of the WORLD looks like.
It began with a whisper of DOUBT in the minds of Earth's alien heroes.
Causing them to question their ALLEGIANCE to the world they had sworn to PROTECT.
Then the DARK rain fell.
The Blackrocks were EVERYWHERE.
Even our endless human strife PALED beside the new threat.
he rain did not soothe, ut instead brought horror... en CAPITULATION.
AGHHH!!
WHA--WHAT'S HAPPENING TO ME?
IMMY!
Bringing us closer to THEM.
Each falling STONE was a malignant alien PARASITE, infecting its host.
The ones who intended to claim Earth for their OWN.

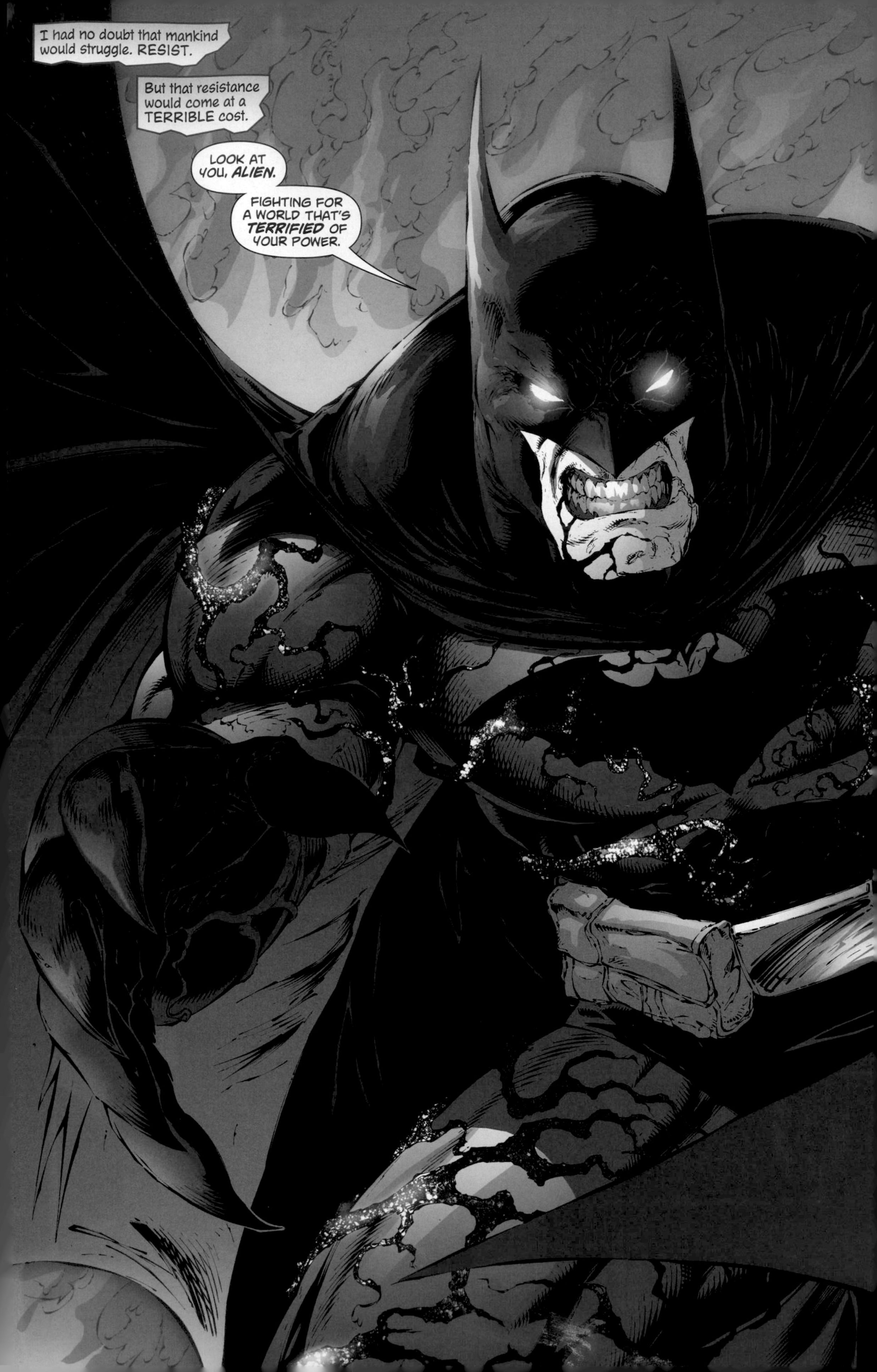
I had no doubt that mankind would struggle. RESIST.
But that resistance would come at a TERRIBLE cost.
LOOK AT YOU, ALIEN.
FIGHTING FOR A WORLD THAT'S TERRIFIED OF YOUR POWER.

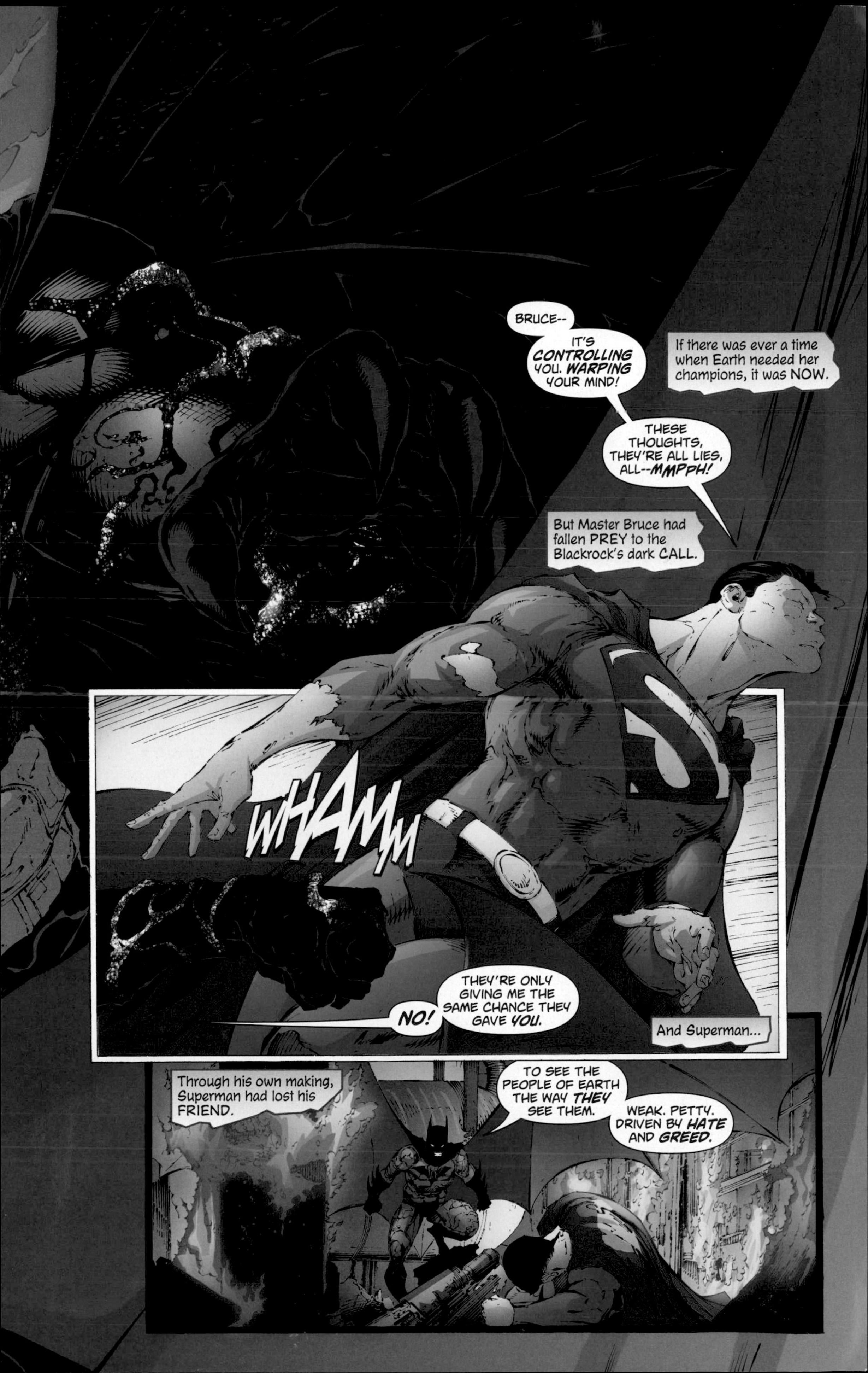

BRUCE--
IT'S CONTROLLING YOU. WARPING YOUR MIND!
If there was ever a time when Earth needed her champions, it was NOW.
THESE THOUGHTS, THEY'RE ALL LIES, ALL--MMPPH!
But Master Bruce had fallen PREY to the Blackrock's dark CALL.
WHAMM
NO!
THEY'RE ONLY GIVING ME THE SAME CHANCE THEY GAVE YOU.
And Superman...
Through his own making, Superman had lost his FRIEND.
TO SEE THE PEOPLE OF EARTH THE WAY THEY SEE THEM.
WEAK. PETTY. DRIVEN BY HATE AND GREED.

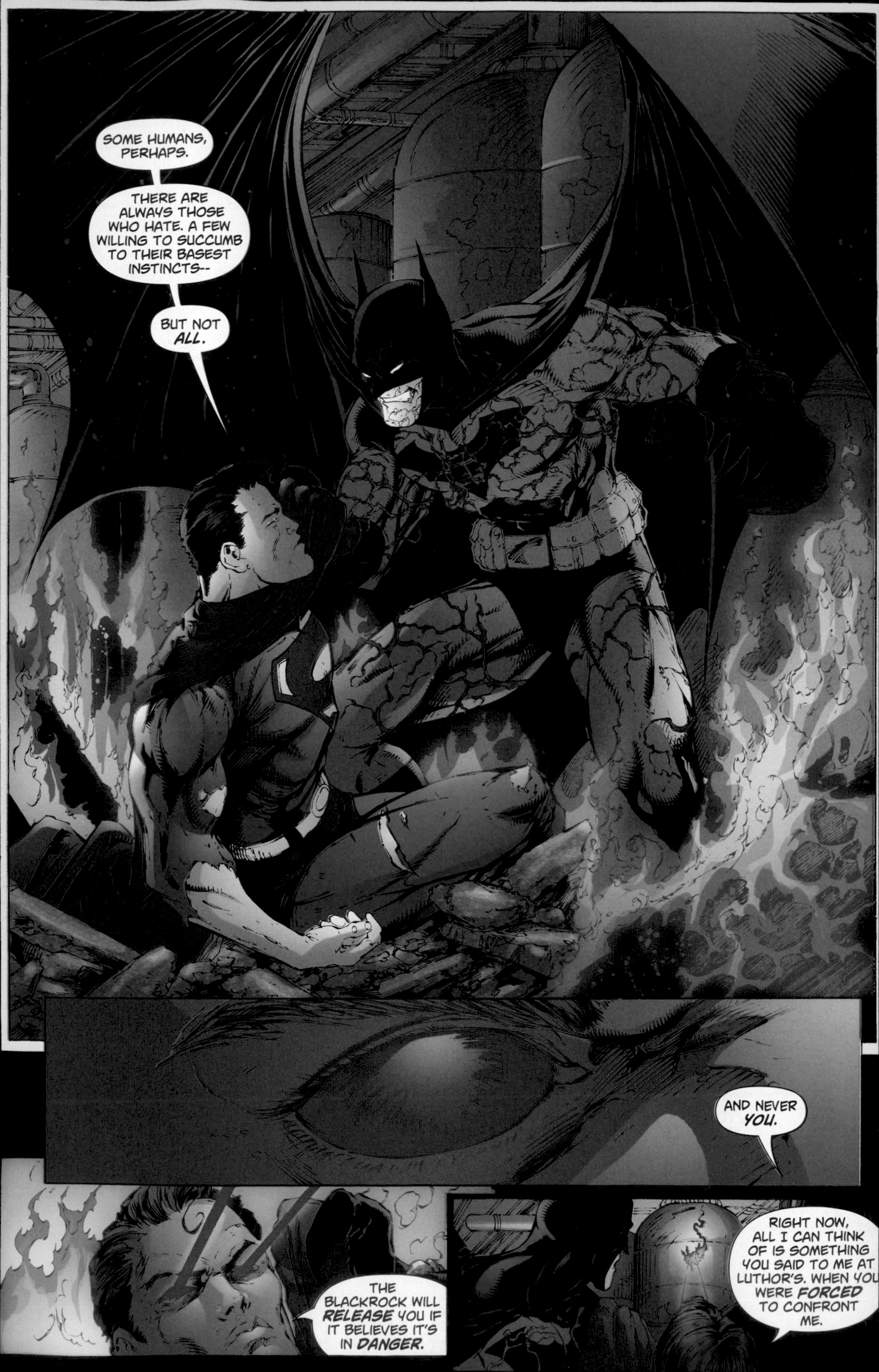
SOME HUMANS, PERHAPS.
THERE ARE ALWAYS THOSE WHO HATE. A FEW WILLING TO SUCCUMB TO THEIR BASEST INSTINCTS--
BUT NOT ALL.
AND NEVER YOU.
THE BLACKROCK WILL RELEASE YOU IF IT BELIEVES IT'S IN DANGER.
RIGHT NOW, ALL I CAN THINK OF IS SOMETHING YOU SAID TO ME AT LUTHOR'S. WHEN YOU WERE FORCED TO CONFRONT ME.

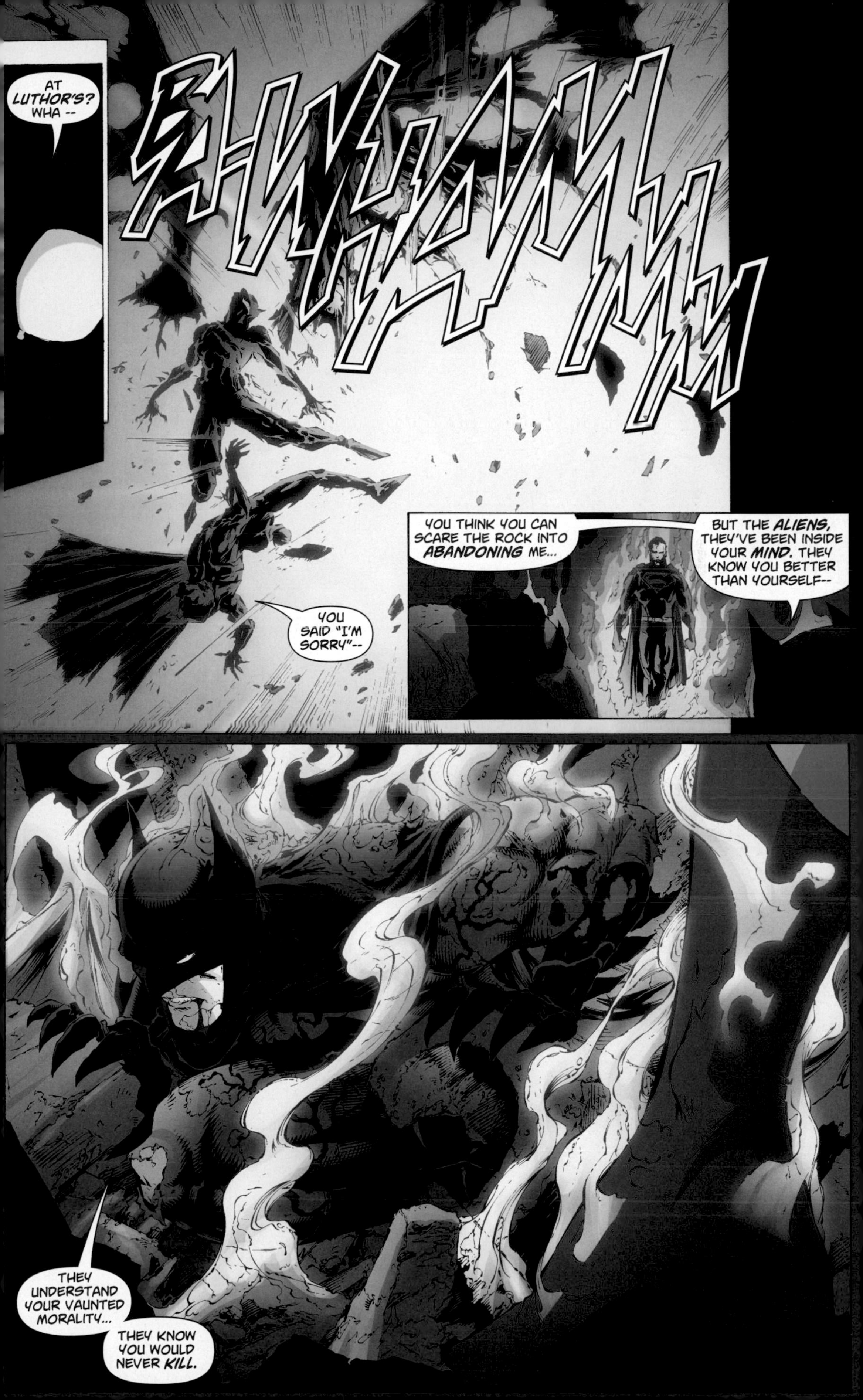
AT LUTHOR'S? WHA --
YOU SAID "I'M SORRY"--
YOU THINK YOU CAN SCARE THE ROCK INTO ABANDONING ME...
BUT THE ALIENS, THEY'VE BEEN INSIDE YOUR MIND. THEY KNOW YOU BETTER THAN YOURSELF--
THEY UNDERSTAND YOUR VAUNTED MORALITY...
THEY KNOW YOU WOULD NEVER KILL.

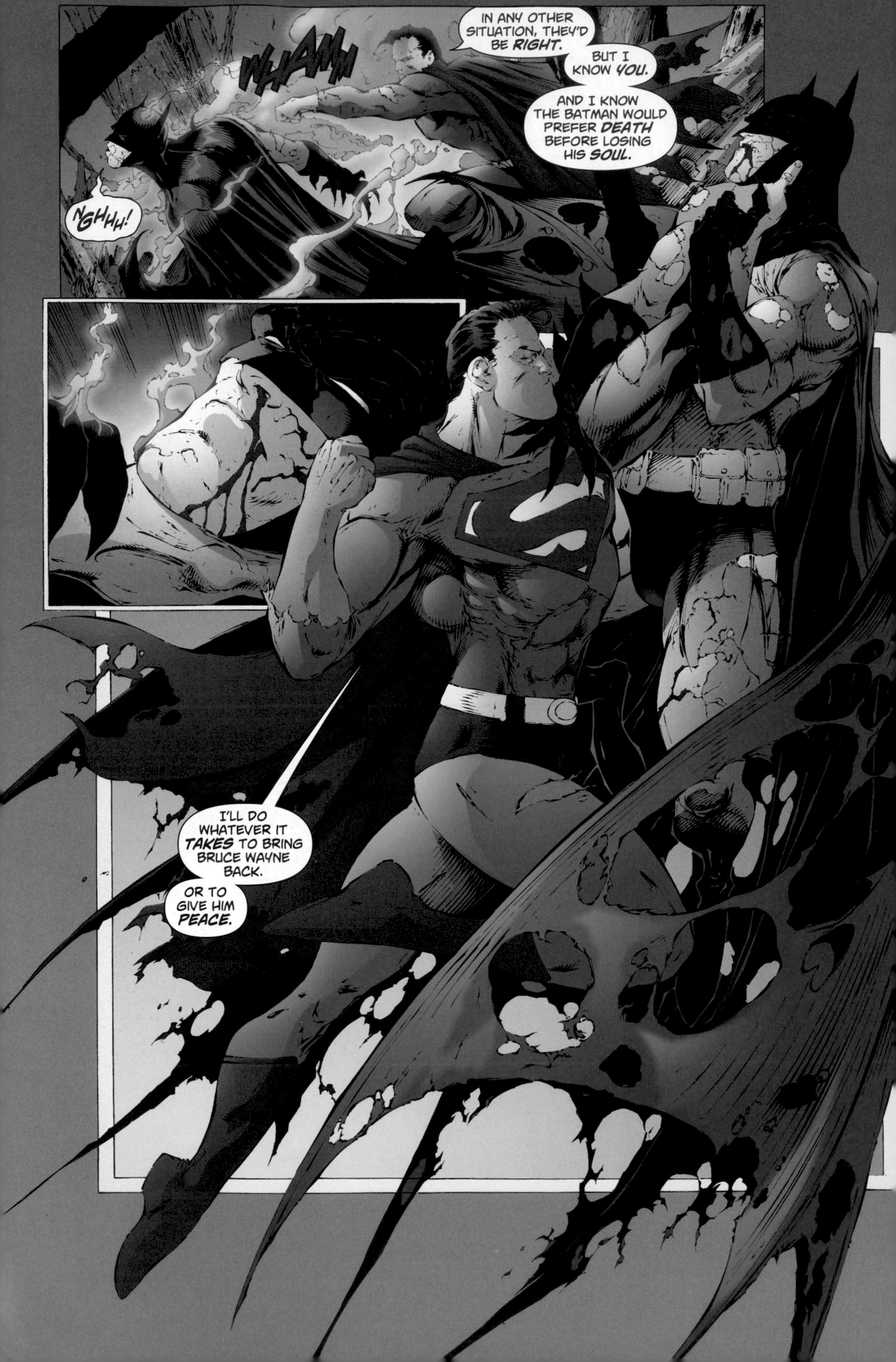
IN ANY OTHER SITUATION, THEY'D BE RIGHT.
WHAMM
BUT I KNOW YOU.
AND I KNOW THE BATMAN WOULD PREFER DEATH BEFORE LOSING HIS SOUL.
NGHHH!
I'LL DO WHATEVER IT TAKES TO BRING BRUCE WAYNE BACK.
OR TO GIVE HIM PEACE.

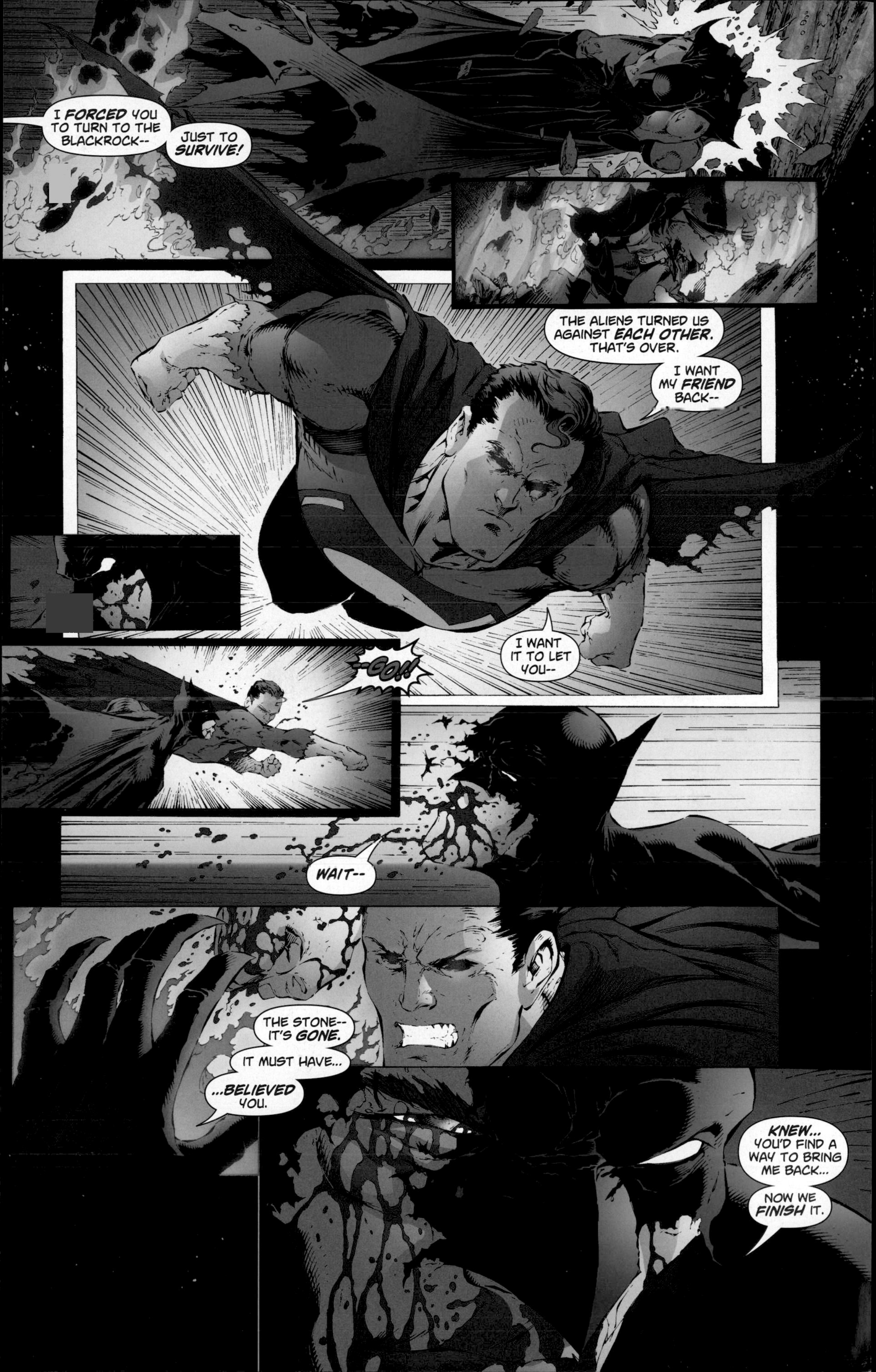
I FORCED YOU TO TURN TO THE BLACKROCK--
JUST TO SURVIVE!
THE ALIENS TURNED US AGAINST EACH OTHER. THAT'S OVER.
I WANT MY FRIEND BACK--
I WANT IT TO LET YOU--
--GO!!
WAIT--
THE STONE-- IT'S GONE.
IT MUST HAVE...
...BELIEVED YOU.
KNEW... YOU'D FIND A WAY TO BRING ME BACK...
NOW WE FINISH IT.

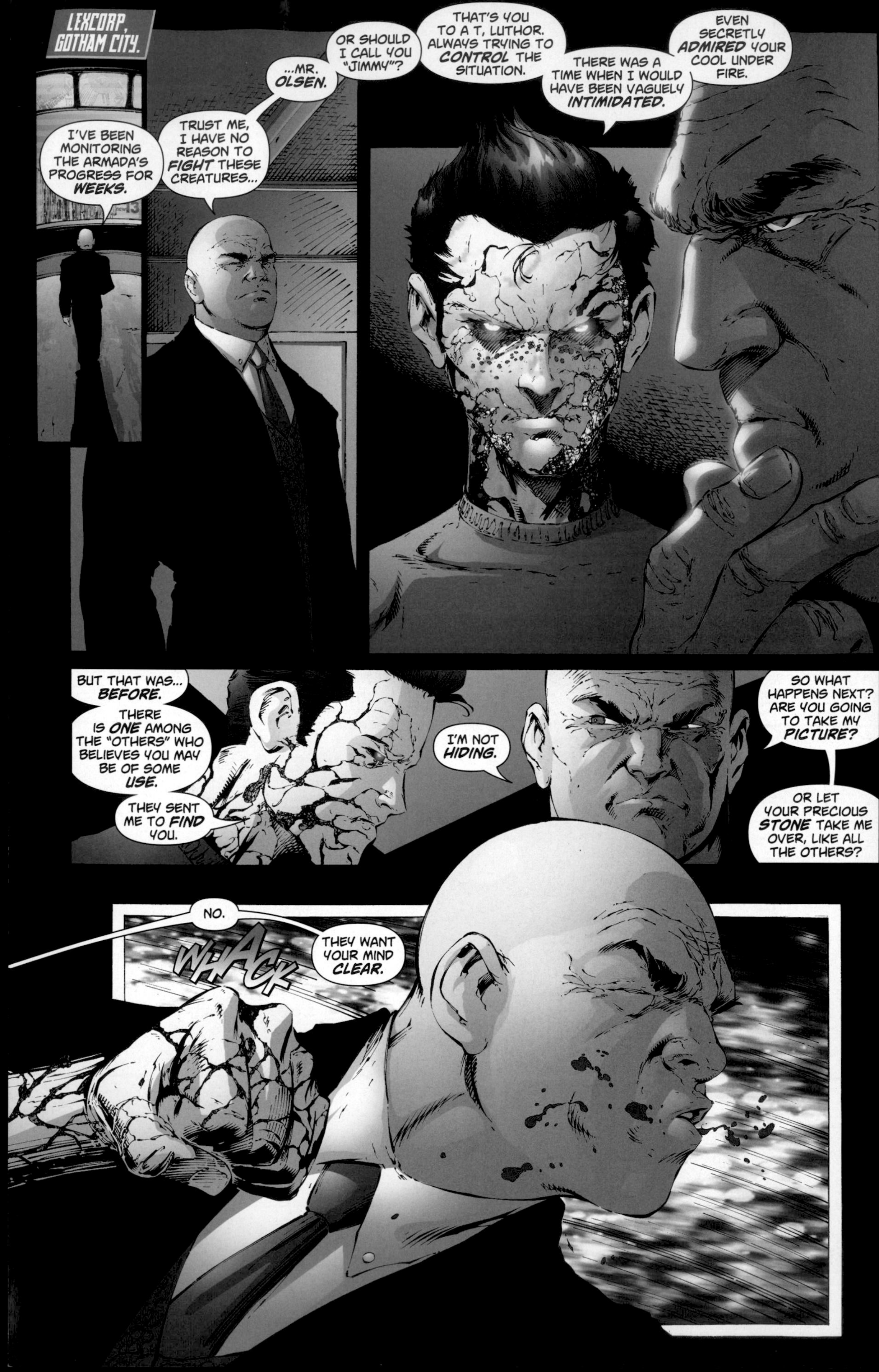
LEXCORP, GOTHAM CITY.
I'VE BEEN MONITORING THE ARMADA'S PROGRESS FOR WEEKS.
TRUST ME, I HAVE NO REASON TO FIGHT THESE CREATURES...
...MR. OLSEN.
OR SHOULD I CALL YOU "JIMMY"?
THAT'S YOU TO A T, LUTHOR. ALWAYS TRYING TO CONTROL THE SITUATION.
THERE WAS A TIME WHEN I WOULD HAVE BEEN VAGUELY INTIMIDATED.
EVEN SECRETLY ADMIRED YOUR COOL UNDER FIRE.
BUT THAT WAS... BEFORE.
THERE IS ONE AMONG THE "OTHERS" WHO BELIEVES YOU MAY BE OF SOME USE.
THEY SENT ME TO FIND YOU.
I'M NOT HIDING.
SO WHAT HAPPENS NEXT? ARE YOU GOING TO TAKE MY PICTURE?
OR LET YOUR PRECIOUS STONE TAKE ME OVER, LIKE ALL THE OTHERS?
NO.
THEY WANT YOUR MIND CLEAR.
WHACK

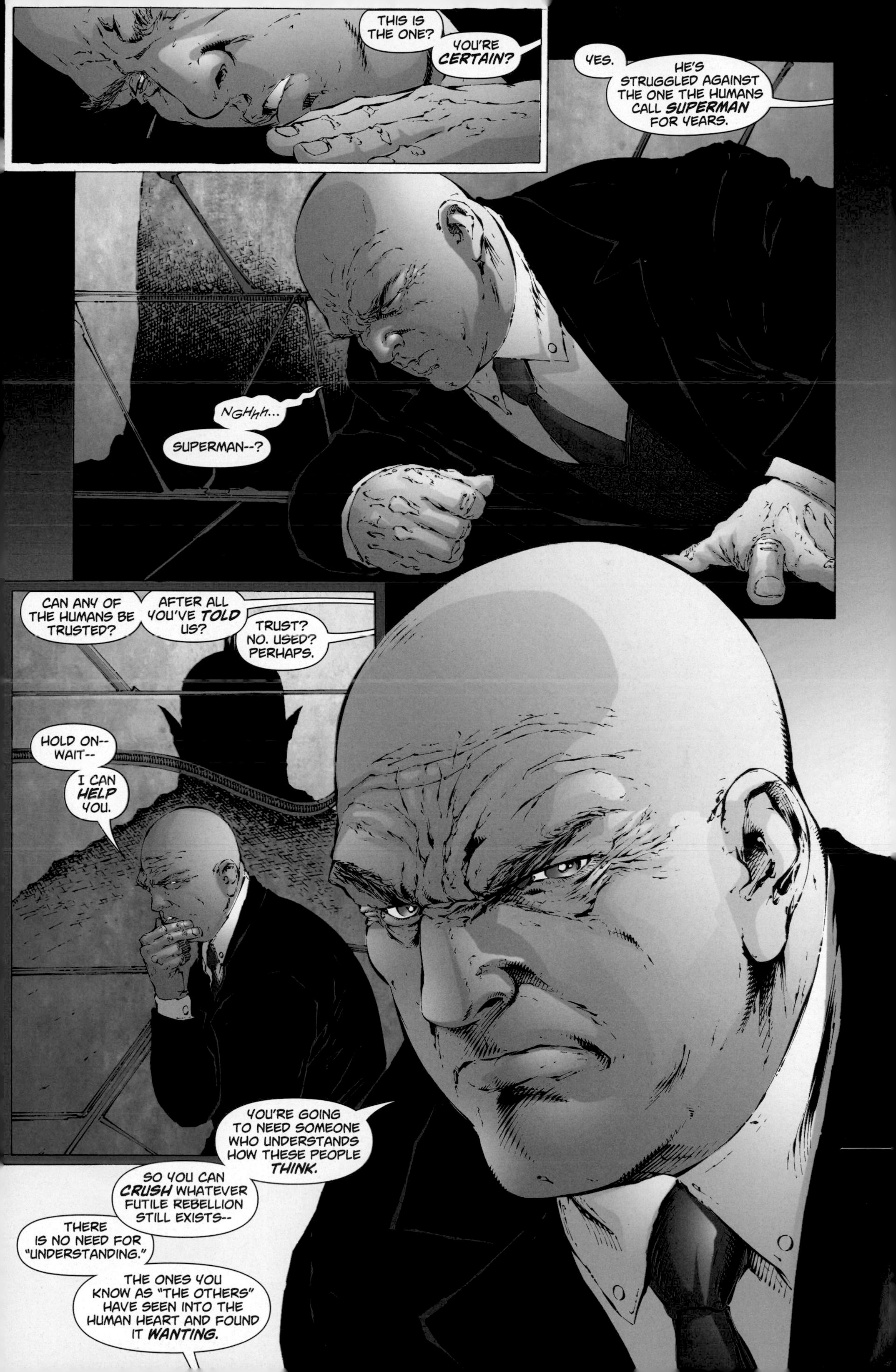

THIS IS THE ONE?
YOU'RE CERTAIN?
YES.
HE'S STRUGGLED AGAINST THE ONE THE HUMANS CALL SUPERMAN FOR YEARS.
NGHhh...
SUPERMAN--?
CAN ANY OF THE HUMANS BE TRUSTED?
AFTER ALL YOU'VE TOLD US?
TRUST? NO. USED? PERHAPS.
HOLD ON-- WAIT--
I CAN HELP YOU.
YOU'RE GOING TO NEED SOMEONE WHO UNDERSTANDS HOW THESE PEOPLE THINK.
SO YOU CAN CRUSH WHATEVER FUTILE REBELLION STILL EXISTS--
THERE IS NO NEED FOR "UNDERSTANDING."
THE ONES YOU KNOW AS "THE OTHERS" HAVE SEEN INTO THE HUMAN HEART AND FOUND IT WANTING.

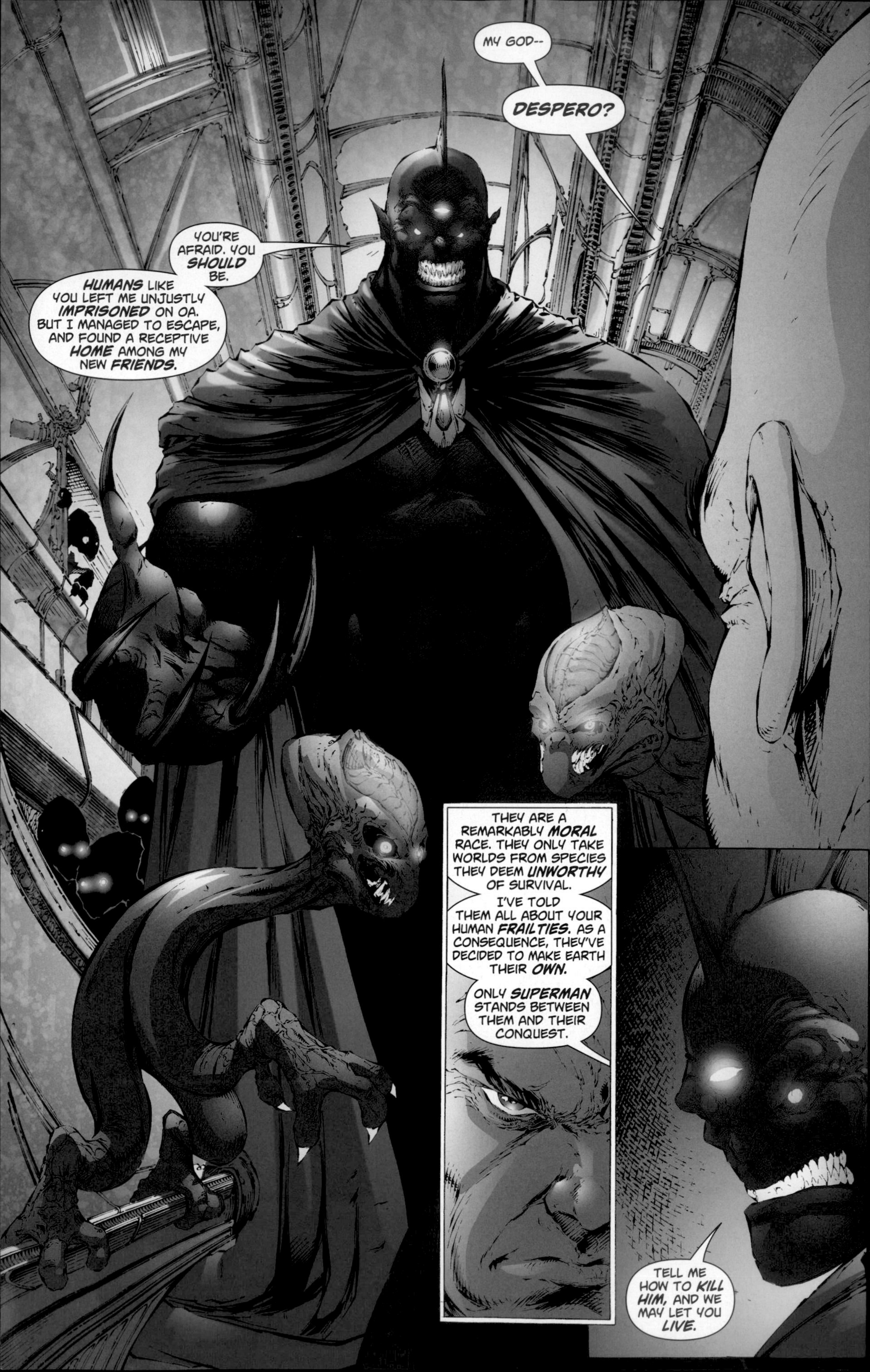
MY GOD--
DESPERO?
YOU'RE AFRAID. YOU SHOULD BE.
HUMANS LIKE YOU LEFT ME UNJUSTLY IMPRISONED ON OA. BUT I MANAGED TO ESCAPE, AND FOUND A RECEPTIVE HOME AMONG MY NEW FRIENDS.
THEY ARE A REMARKABLY MORAL RACE. THEY ONLY TAKE WORLDS FROM SPECIES THEY DEEM UNWORTHY OF SURVIVAL.
I'VE TOLD THEM ALL ABOUT YOUR HUMAN FRAILTIES. AS A CONSEQUENCE, THEY'VE DECIDED TO MAKE EARTH THEIR OWN.
ONLY SUPERMAN STANDS BETWEEN THEM AND THEIR CONQUEST.
TELL ME HOW TO KILL HIM, AND WE MAY LET YOU LIVE.

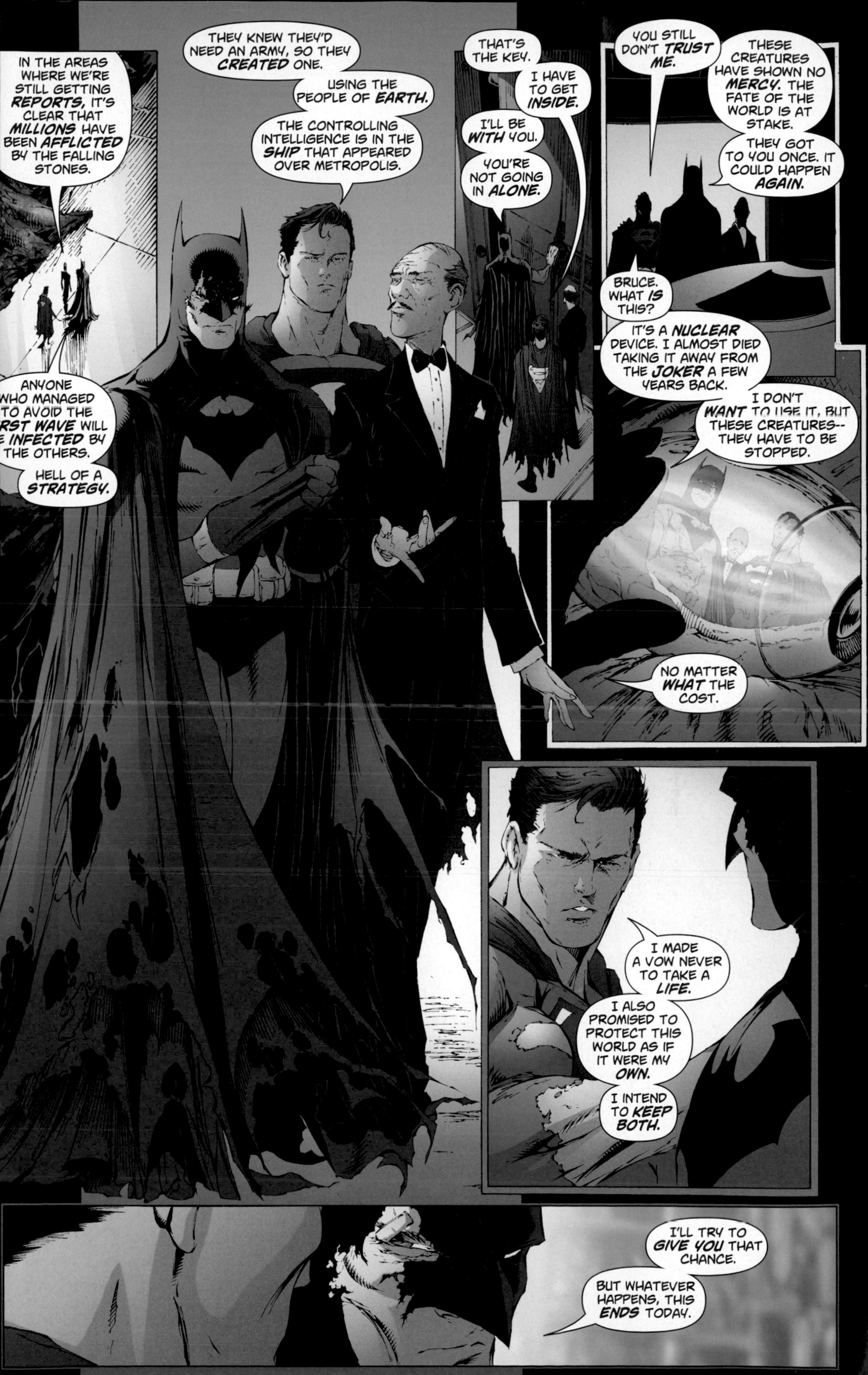
IN THE AREAS WHERE WE'RE STILL GETTING REPORTS, IT'S CLEAR THAT MILLIONS HAVE BEEN AFFLICTED BY THE FALLING STONES.
ANYONE WHO MANAGED TO AVOID THE RST WAVE WILL E INFECTED BY THE OTHERS.
HELL OF A STRATEGY.
THEY KNEW THEY'D NEED AN ARMY, SO THEY CREATED ONE.
USING THE PEOPLE OF EARTH.
THE CONTROLLING INTELLIGENCE IS IN THE SHIP THAT APPEARED OVER METROPOLIS.
THAT'S THE KEY.
I HAVE TO GET INSIDE.
I'LL BE WITH YOU.
YOU'RE NOT GOING IN ALONE.
YOU STILL DON'T TRUST ME.
THESE CREATURES HAVE SHOWN NO MERCY. THE FATE OF THE WORLD IS AT STAKE.
THEY GOT TO YOU ONCE. IT COULD HAPPEN AGAIN.
BRUCE. WHAT IS THIS?
IT'S A NUCLEAR DEVICE. I ALMOST DIED TAKING IT AWAY FROM THE JOKER A FEW YEARS BACK.
I DON'T WANT TO USE IT, BUT THESE CREATURES-- THEY HAVE TO BE STOPPED.
NO MATTER WHAT THE COST.
I MADE A VOW NEVER TO TAKE A LIFE.
I ALSO PROMISED TO PROTECT THIS WORLD AS IF IT WERE MY OWN.
I INTEND TO KEEP BOTH.
I'LL TRY TO GIVE YOU THAT CHANCE.
BUT WHATEVER HAPPENS, THIS ENDS TODAY.

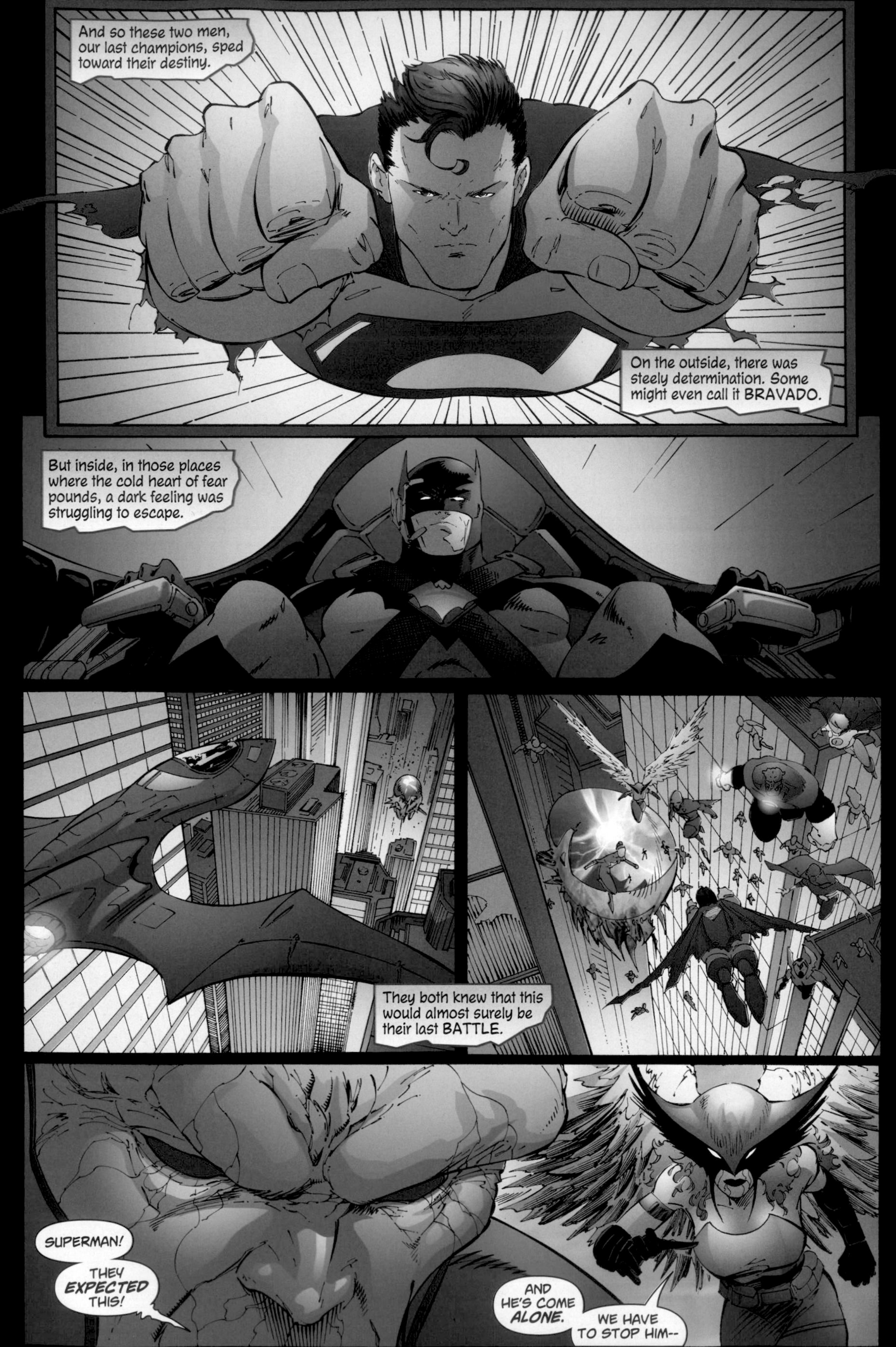
And so these two men, our last champions, sped toward their destiny.
On the outside, there was steely determination. Some might even call it BRAVADO.
But inside, in those places where the cold heart of fear pounds, a dark feeling was struggling to escape.
They both knew that this would almost surely be their last BATTLE.
SUPERMAN!
THEY EXPECTED THIS!
AND HE'S COME ALONE.
WE HAVE TO STOP HIM--

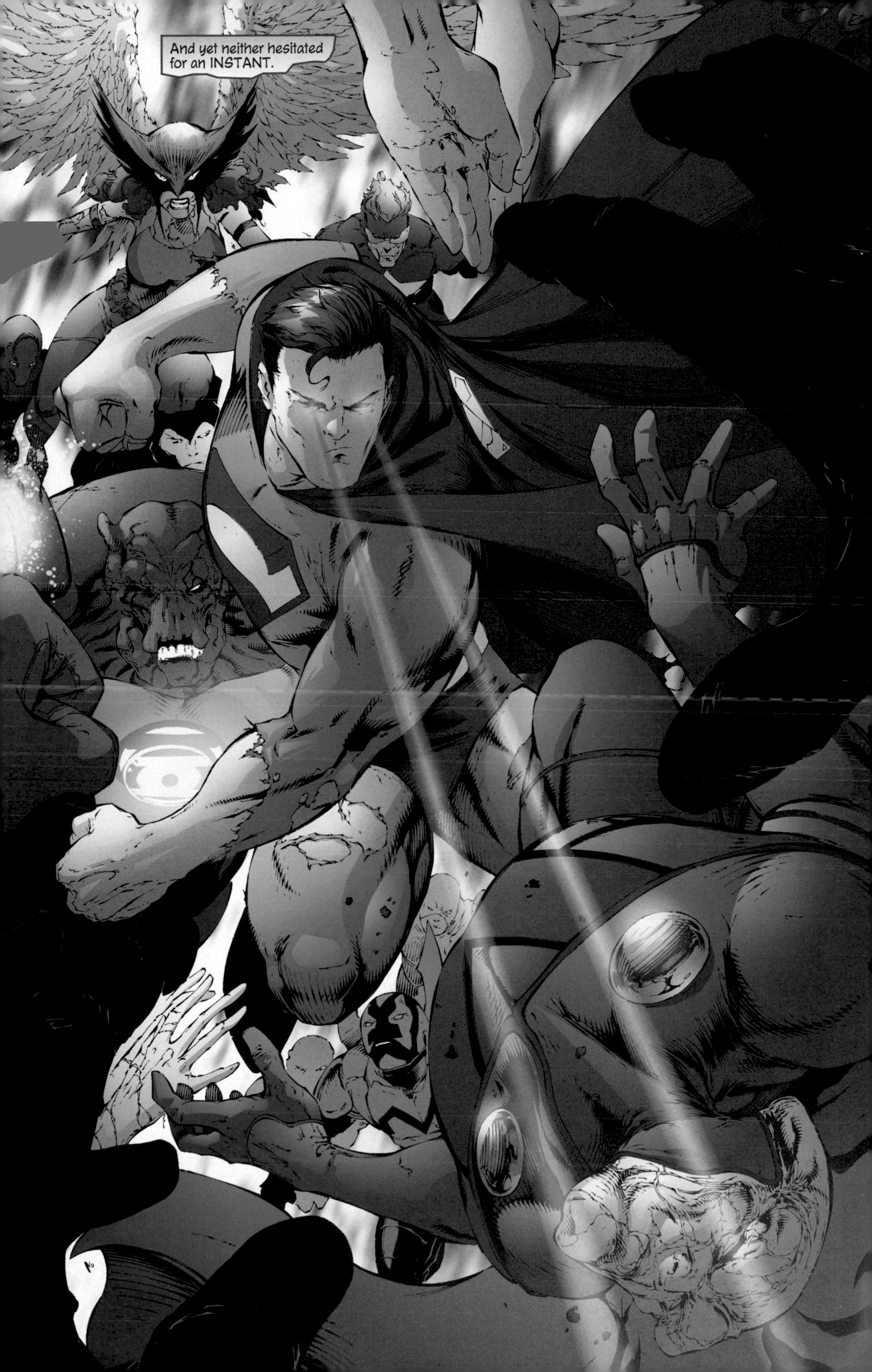
And yet neither hesitated for an INSTANT.

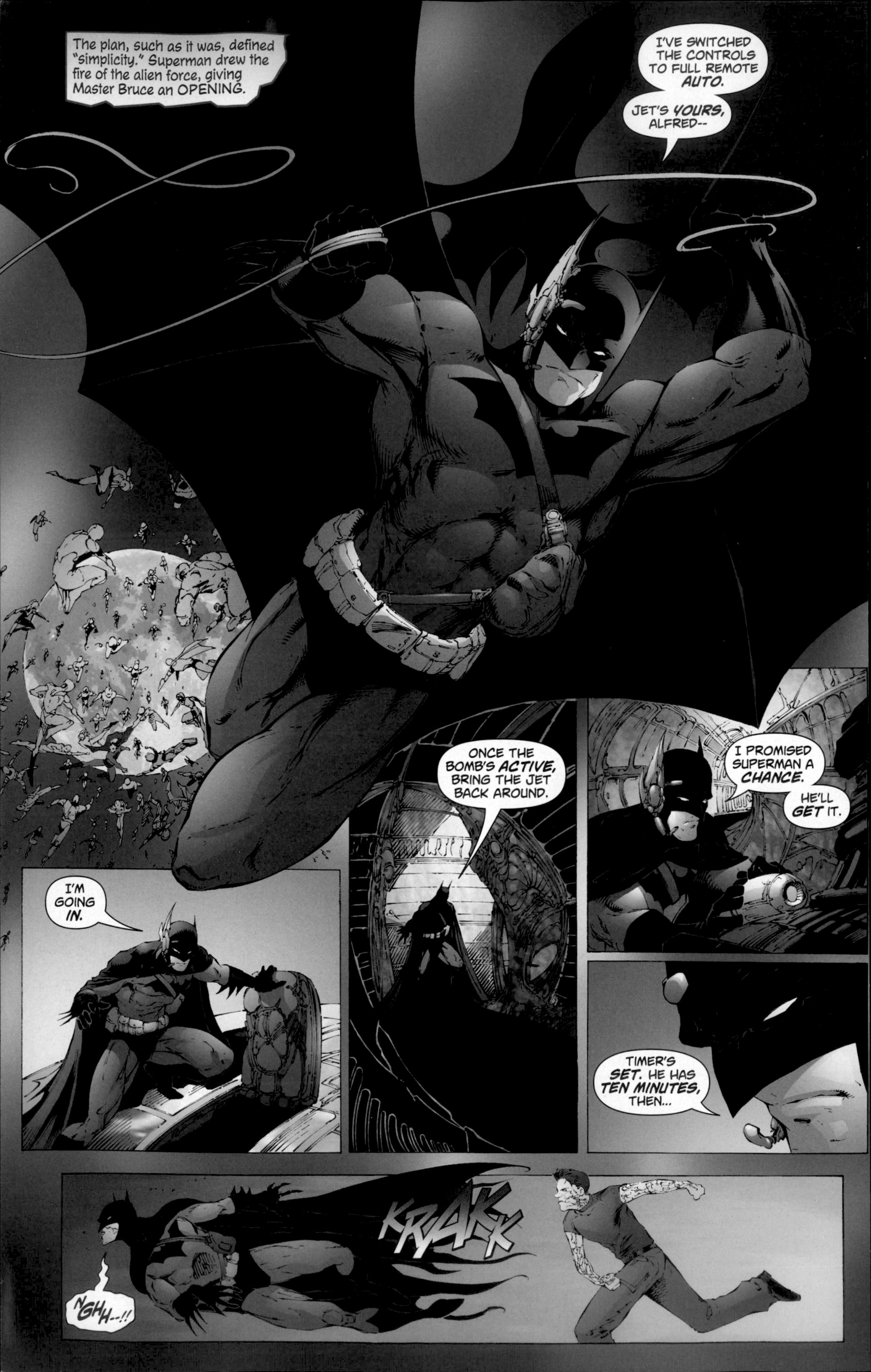

The plan, such as it was, defined "simplicity." Superman drew the fire of the alien force, giving Master Bruce an OPENING.
I'VE SWITCHED THE CONTROLS TO FULL REMOTE AUTO.
JET'S YOURS, ALFRED--
I'M GOING IN.
ONCE THE BOMB'S ACTIVE, BRING THE JET BACK AROUND.
I PROMISED SUPERMAN A CHANCE.
HE'LL GET IT.
TIMER'S SET. HE HAS TEN MINUTES, THEN...
KRAKK
NGHH--!!

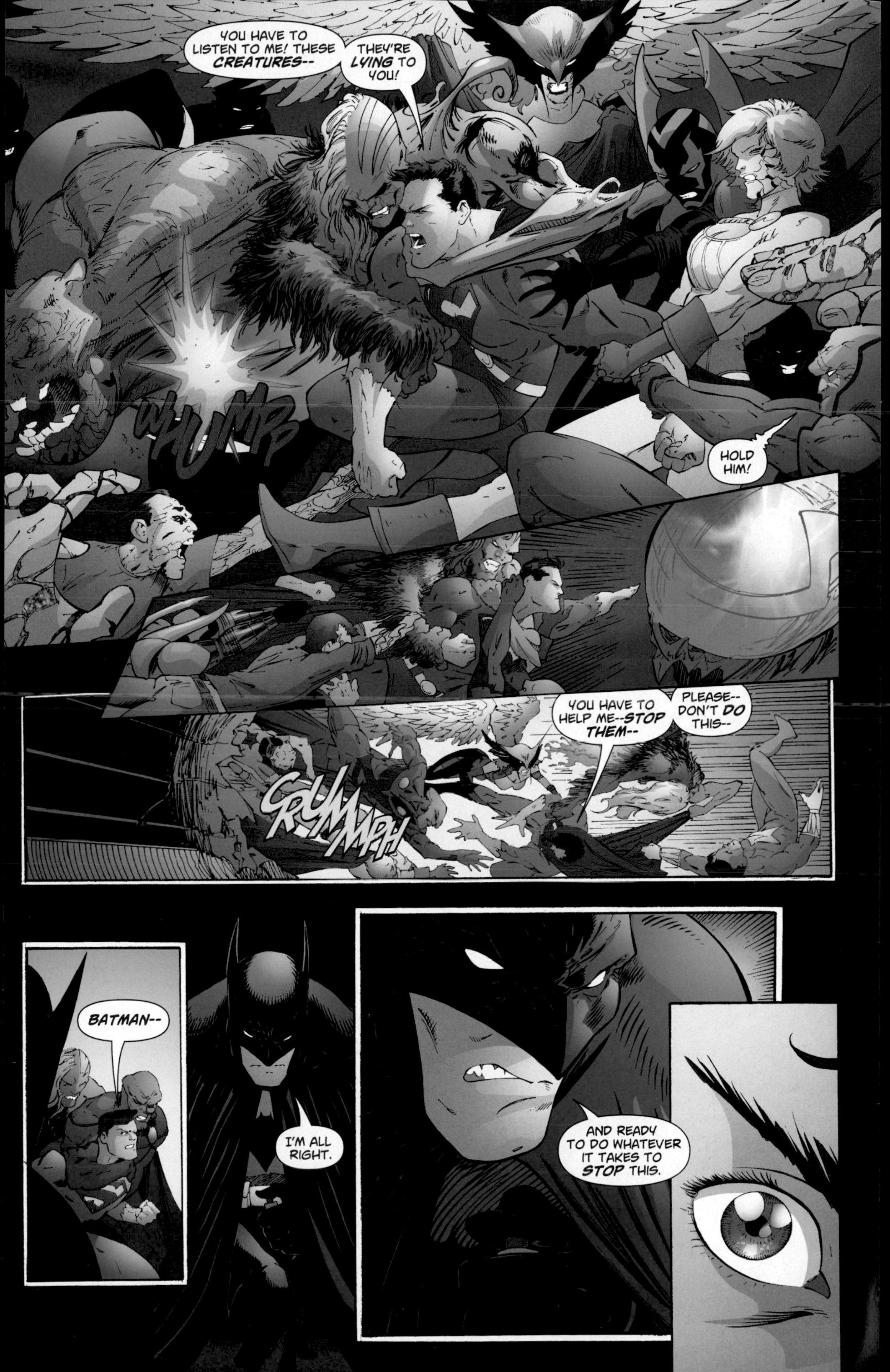
YOU HAVE TO LISTEN TO ME! THESE CREATURES--
THEY'RE LYING TO YOU!
WHUMP
HOLD HIM!
YOU HAVE TO HELP ME--STOP THEM--
PLEASE--DON'T DO THIS--
CRUMMPH
BATMAN--
I'M ALL RIGHT.
AND READY TO DO WHATEVER IT TAKES TO STOP THIS.

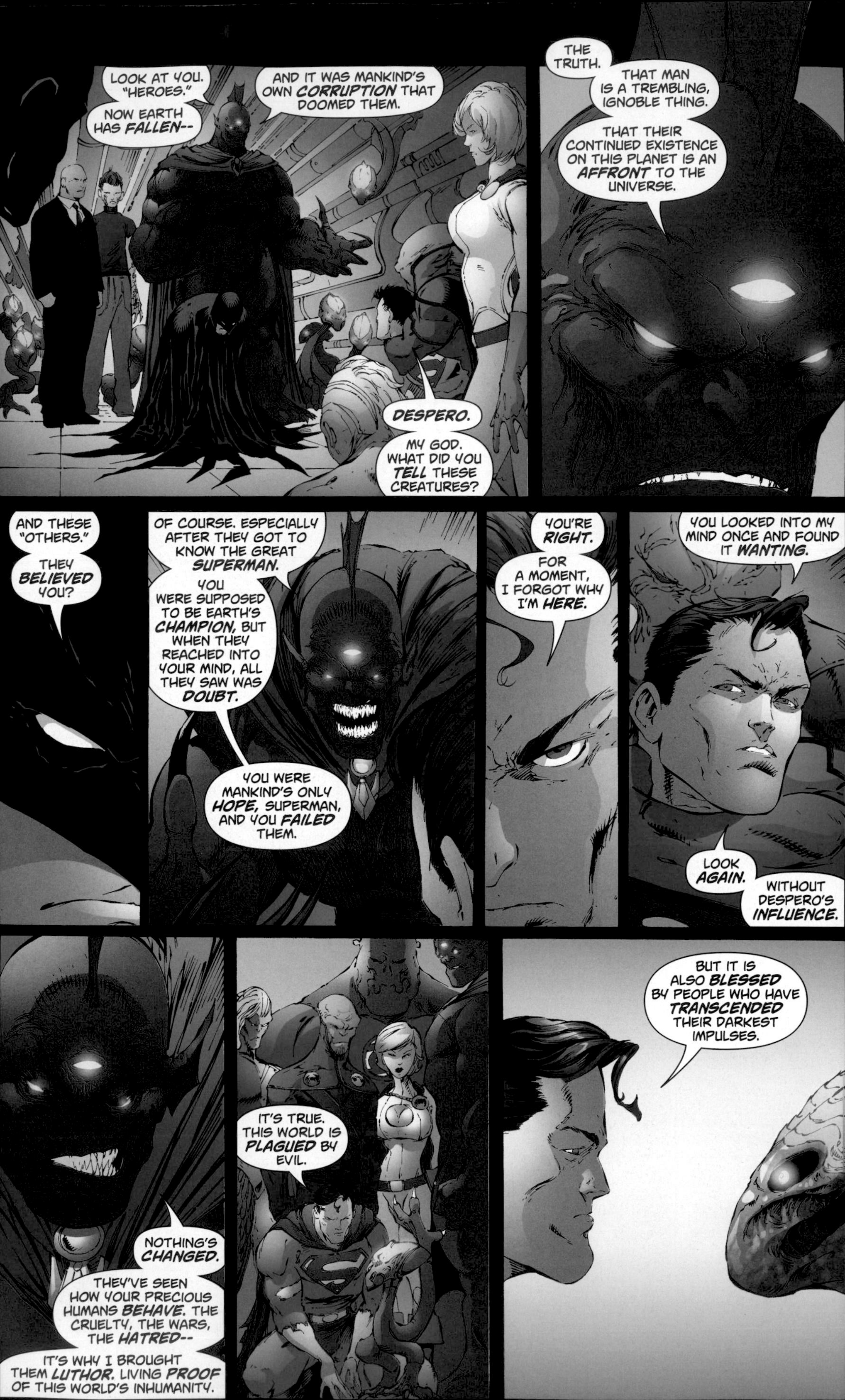
LOOK AT YOU. "HEROES."
NOW EARTH HAS FALLEN--
AND IT WAS MANKIND'S OWN CORRUPTION THAT DOOMED THEM.
DESPERO.
MY GOD. WHAT DID YOU TELL THESE CREATURES?
THE TRUTH.
THAT MAN IS A TREMBLING, IGNOBLE THING.
THAT THEIR CONTINUED EXISTENCE ON THIS PLANET IS AN AFFRONT TO THE UNIVERSE.
AND THESE "OTHERS."
THEY BELIEVED YOU?
OF COURSE. ESPECIALLY AFTER THEY GOT TO KNOW THE GREAT SUPERMAN.
YOU WERE SUPPOSED TO BE EARTH'S CHAMPION, BUT WHEN THEY REACHED INTO YOUR MIND, ALL THEY SAW WAS DOUBT.
YOU WERE MANKIND'S ONLY HOPE, SUPERMAN, AND YOU FAILED THEM.
YOU'RE RIGHT.
FOR A MOMENT, I FORGOT WHY I'M HERE.
YOU LOOKED INTO MY MIND ONCE AND FOUND IT WANTING.
LOOK AGAIN.
WITHOUT DESPERO'S INFLUENCE.
NOTHING'S CHANGED.
THEY'VE SEEN HOW YOUR PRECIOUS HUMANS BEHAVE. THE CRUELTY, THE WARS, THE HATRED--
IT'S WHY I BROUGHT THEM LUTHOR. LIVING PROOF OF THIS WORLD'S INHUMANITY.
IT'S TRUE. THIS WORLD IS PLAGUED BY EVIL.
BUT IT IS ALSO BLESSED BY PEOPLE WHO HAVE TRANSCENDED THEIR DARKEST IMPULSES.

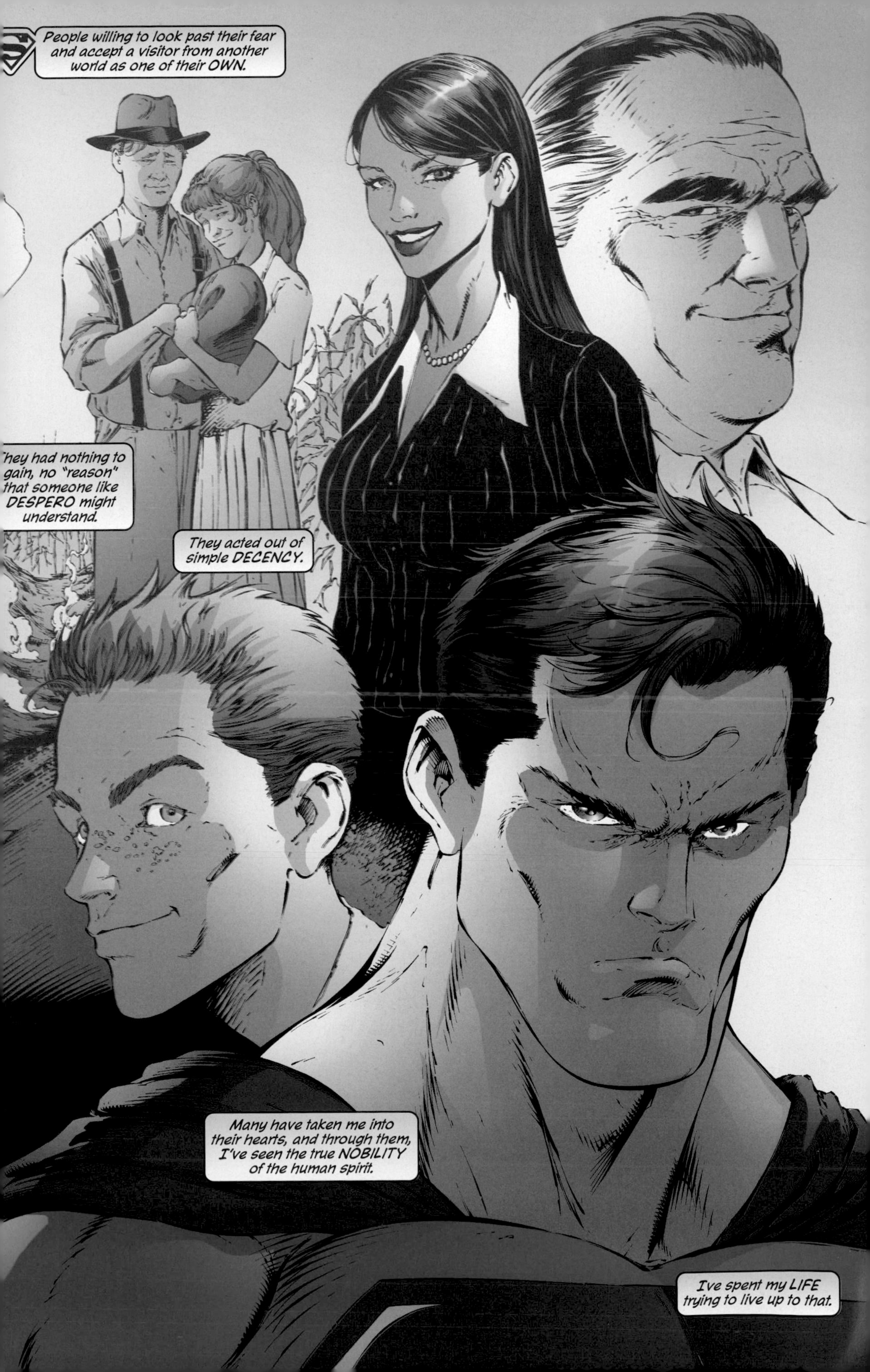
People willing to look past their fear and accept a visitor from another world as one of their OWN.
They had nothing to gain, no "reason" that someone like DESPERO might understand.
They acted out of simple DECENCY.
Many have taken me into their hearts, and through them, I've seen the true NOBILITY of the human spirit.
I've spent my LIFE trying to live up to that.

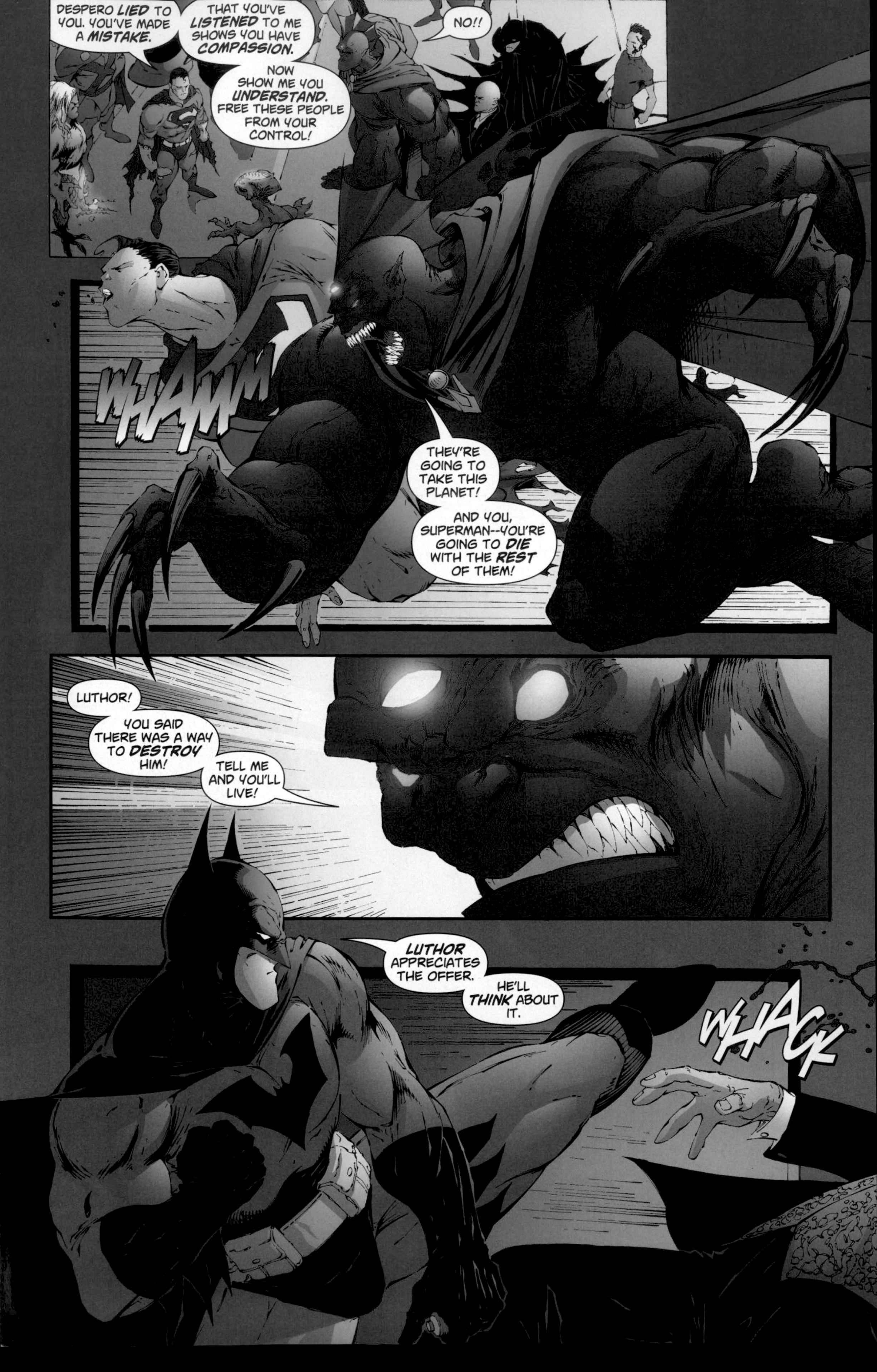
DESPERO LIED TO YOU. YOU'VE MADE A MISTAKE.
THAT YOU'VE LISTENED TO ME SHOWS YOU HAVE COMPASSION.
NOW SHOW ME YOU UNDERSTAND. FREE THESE PEOPLE FROM YOUR CONTROL!
NO!!
WHAMM
THEY'RE GOING TO TAKE THIS PLANET!
AND YOU, SUPERMAN--YOU'RE GOING TO DIE WITH THE REST OF THEM!
LUTHOR!
YOU SAID THERE WAS A WAY TO DESTROY HIM!
TELL ME AND YOU'LL LIVE!
LUTHOR APPRECIATES THE OFFER.
HE'LL THINK ABOUT IT.
WHACK

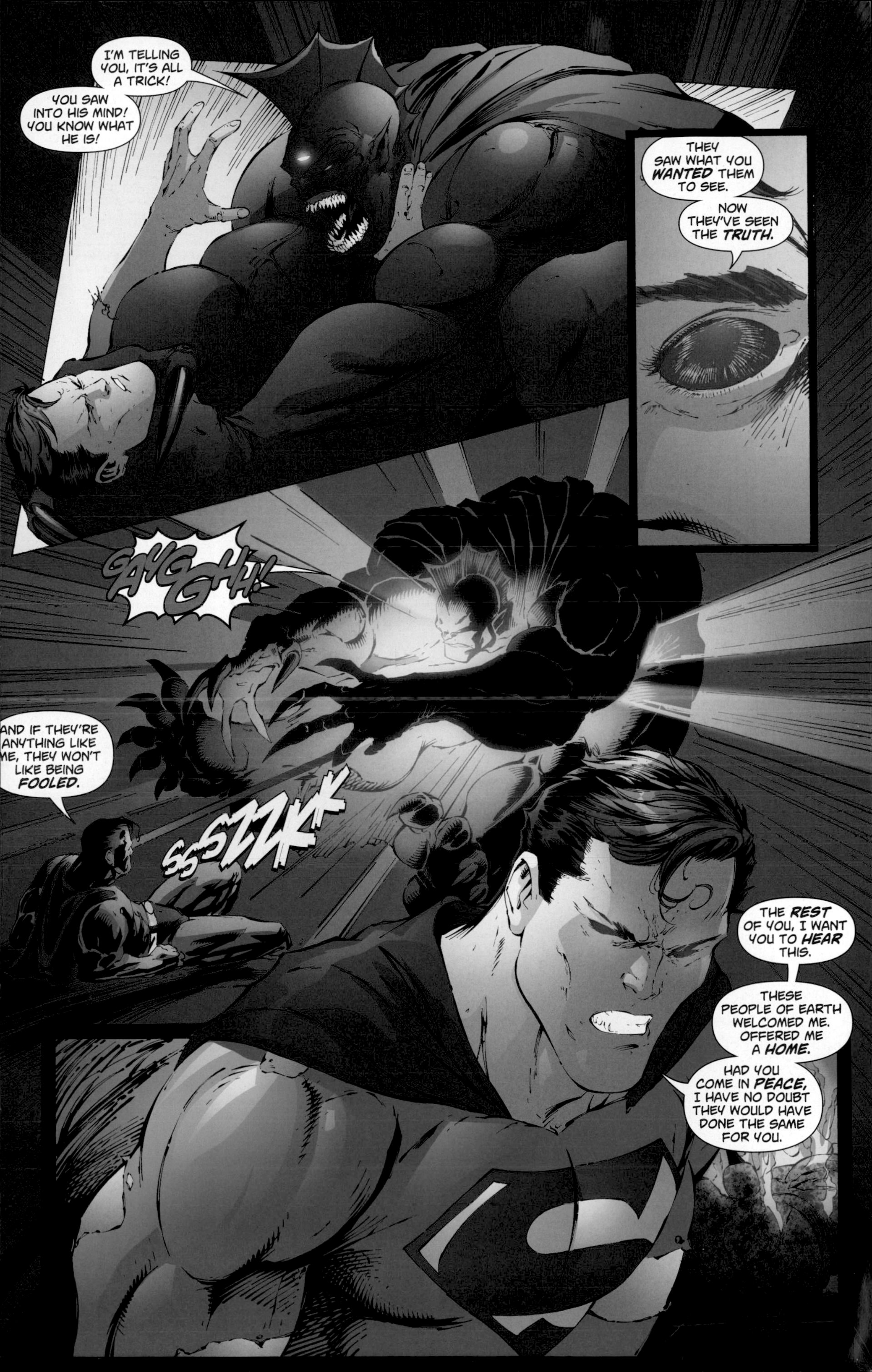

I'M TELLING YOU, IT'S ALL A TRICK!
YOU SAW INTO HIS MIND! YOU KNOW WHAT HE IS!
THEY SAW WHAT YOU WANTED THEM TO SEE.
NOW THEY'VE SEEN THE TRUTH.
GAUGGHH!
AND IF THEY'RE ANYTHING LIKE ME, THEY WON'T LIKE BEING FOOLED.
SSSZZKK
THE REST OF YOU, I WANT YOU TO HEAR THIS.
THESE PEOPLE OF EARTH WELCOMED ME. OFFERED ME A HOME.
HAD YOU COME IN PEACE, I HAVE NO DOUBT THEY WOULD HAVE DONE THE SAME FOR YOU.

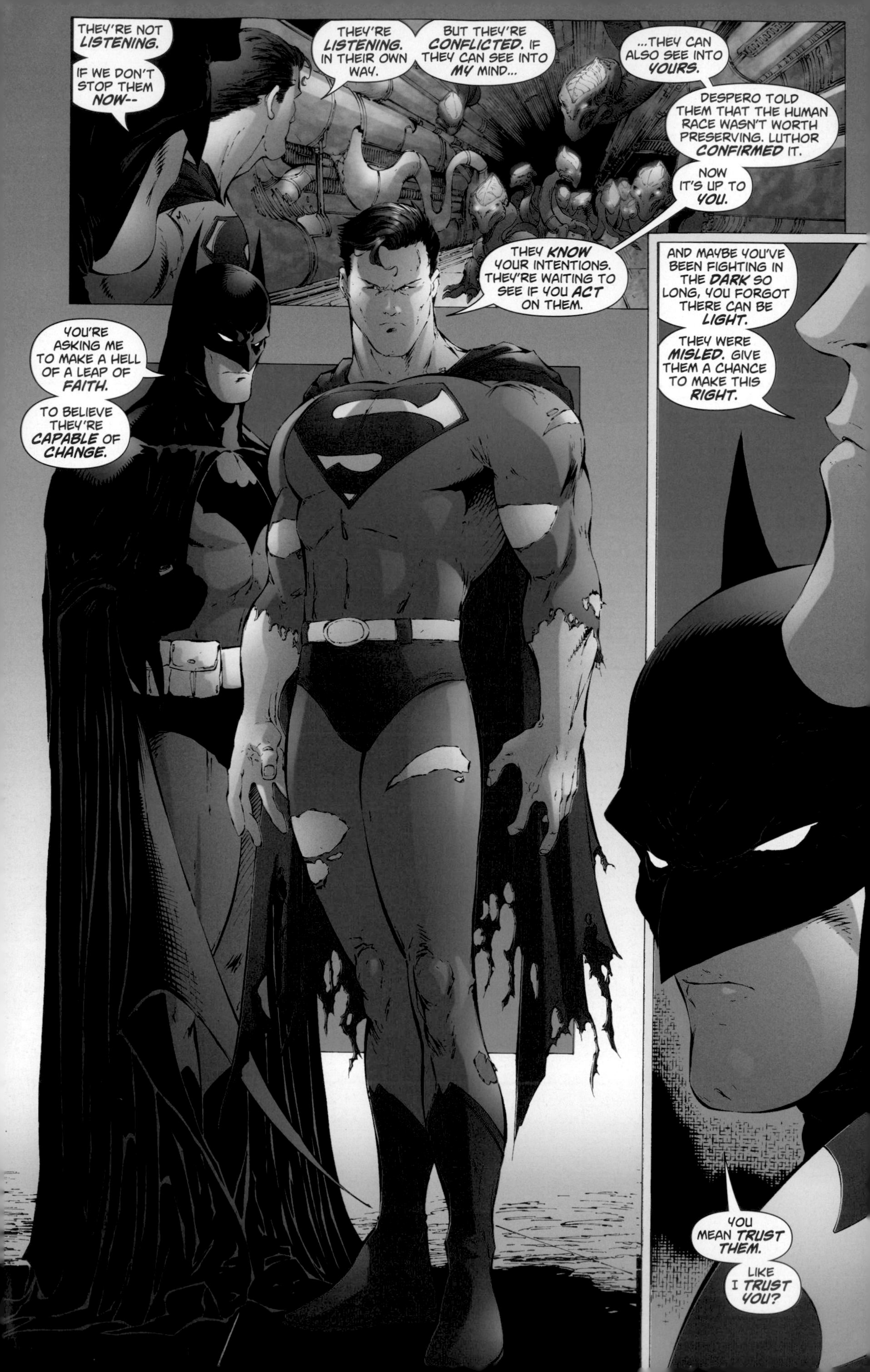
THEY'RE NOT LISTENING.
IF WE DON'T STOP THEM NOW--
THEY'RE LISTENING. IN THEIR OWN WAY.
BUT THEY'RE CONFLICTED. IF THEY CAN SEE INTO MY MIND...
...THEY CAN ALSO SEE INTO YOURS.
DESPERO TOLD THEM THAT THE HUMAN RACE WASN'T WORTH PRESERVING. LUTHOR CONFIRMED IT.
NOW IT'S UP TO YOU.
THEY KNOW YOUR INTENTIONS. THEY'RE WAITING TO SEE IF YOU ACT ON THEM.
YOU'RE ASKING ME TO MAKE A HELL OF A LEAP OF FAITH.
TO BELIEVE THEY'RE CAPABLE OF CHANGE.
AND MAYBE YOU'VE BEEN FIGHTING IN THE DARK SO LONG, YOU FORGOT THERE CAN BE LIGHT.
THEY WERE MISLED. GIVE THEM A CHANCE TO MAKE THIS RIGHT.
YOU MEAN TRUST THEM.
LIKE I TRUST YOU?

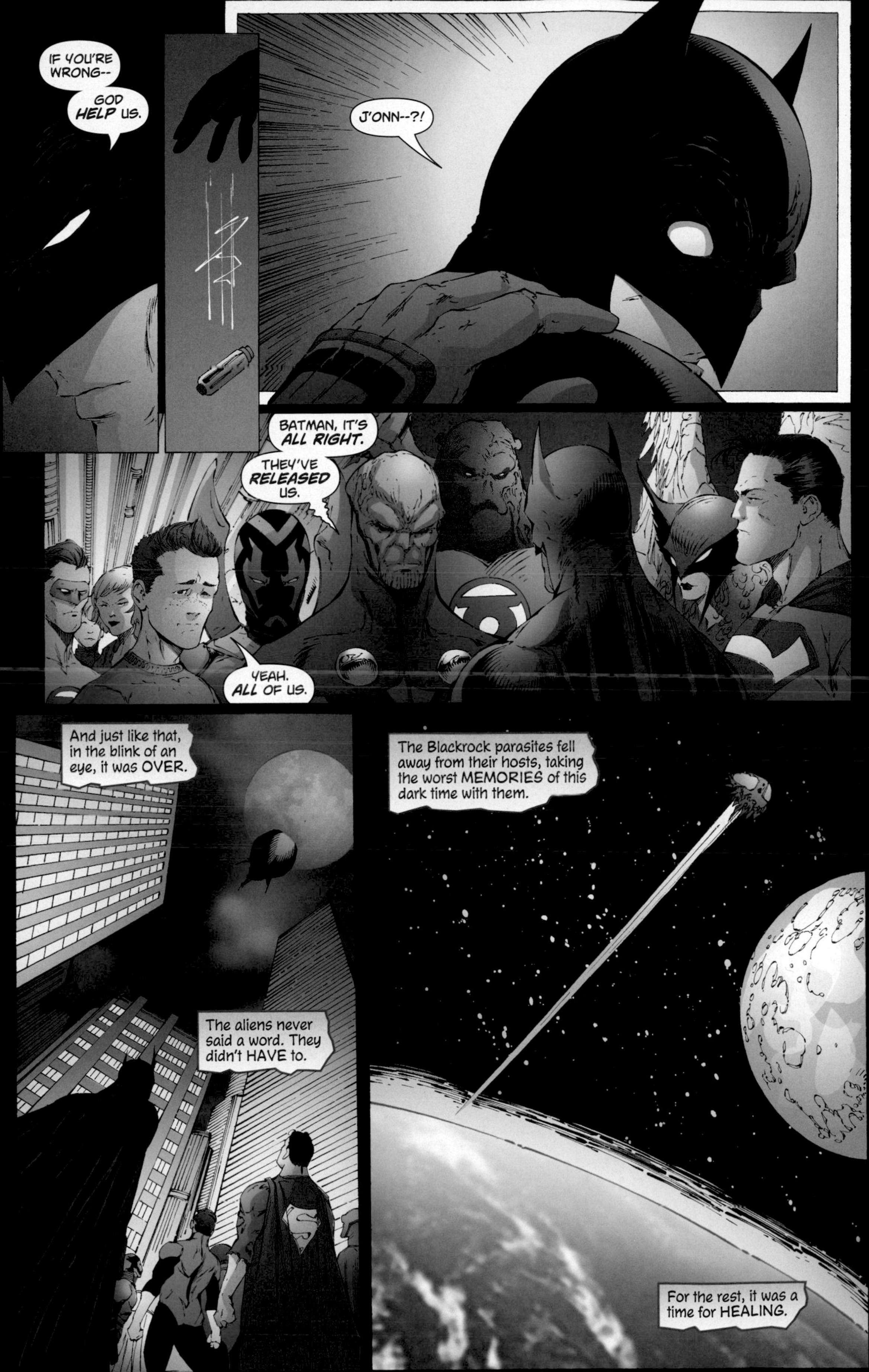
IF YOU'RE WRONG--
GOD HELP US.
J'ONN--?!
BATMAN, IT'S ALL RIGHT.
THEY'VE RELEASED US.
YEAH. ALL OF US.
And just like that, in the blink of an eye, it was OVER.
The aliens never said a word. They didn't HAVE to.
The Blackrock parasites fell away from their hosts, taking the worst MEMORIES of this dark time with them.
For the rest, it was a time for HEALING.

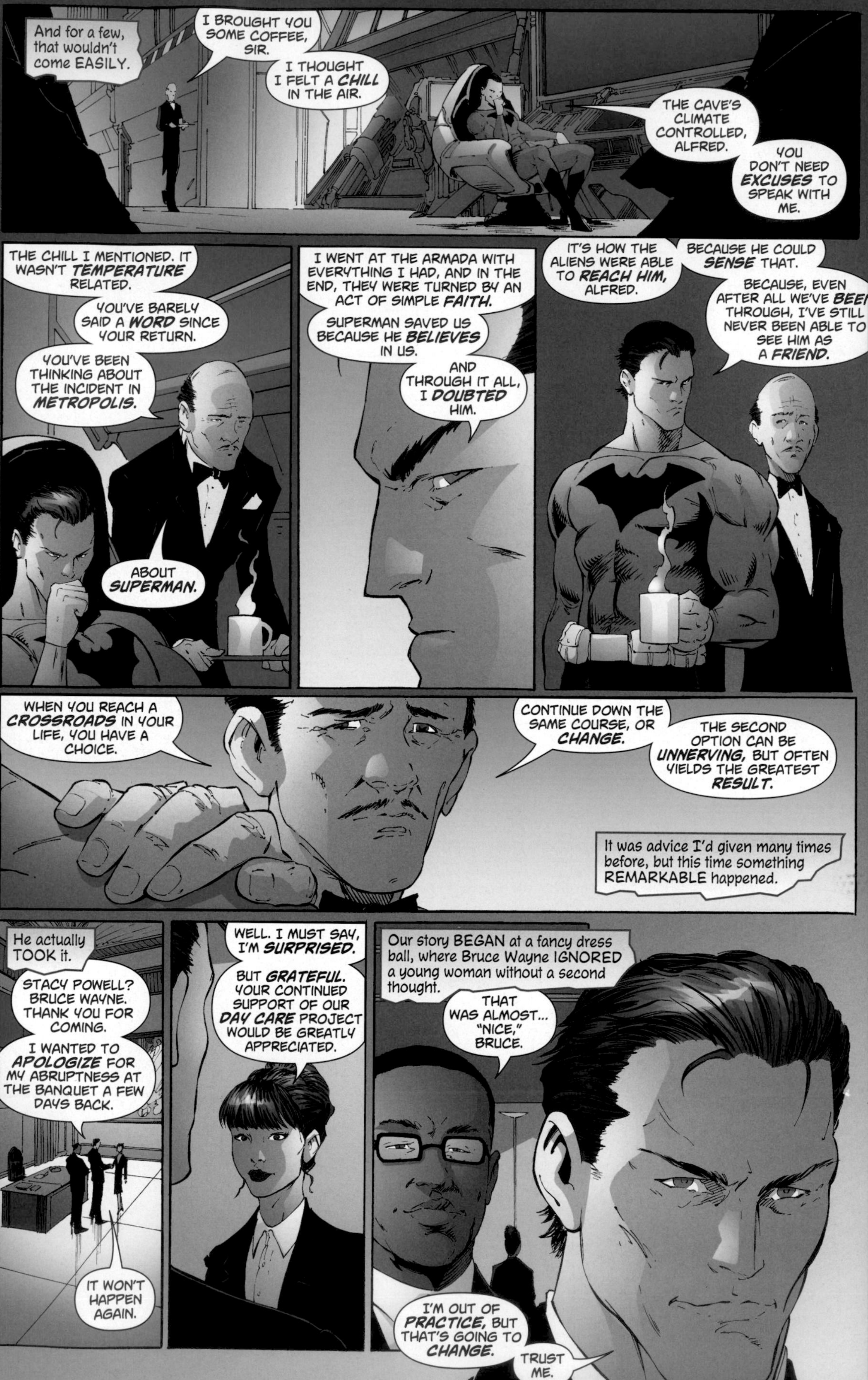
And for a few, that wouldn't come EASILY.
I BROUGHT YOU SOME COFFEE, SIR.
I THOUGHT I FELT A CHILL IN THE AIR.
THE CAVE'S CLIMATE CONTROLLED, ALFRED.
YOU DON'T NEED EXCUSES TO SPEAK WITH ME.
THE CHILL I MENTIONED. IT WASN'T TEMPERATURE RELATED.
YOU'VE BARELY SAID A WORD SINCE YOUR RETURN.
YOU'VE BEEN THINKING ABOUT THE INCIDENT IN METROPOLIS.
ABOUT SUPERMAN.
I WENT AT THE ARMADA WITH EVERYTHING I HAD, AND IN THE END, THEY WERE TURNED BY AN ACT OF SIMPLE FAITH.
SUPERMAN SAVED US BECAUSE HE BELIEVES IN US.
AND THROUGH IT ALL, I DOUBTED HIM.
IT'S HOW THE ALIENS WERE ABLE TO REACH HIM, ALFRED.
BECAUSE HE COULD SENSE THAT.
BECAUSE, EVEN AFTER ALL WE'VE BEEN THROUGH, I'VE STILL NEVER BEEN ABLE TO SEE HIM AS A FRIEND.
WHEN YOU REACH A CROSSROADS IN YOUR LIFE, YOU HAVE A CHOICE.
CONTINUE DOWN THE SAME COURSE, OR CHANGE.
THE SECOND OPTION CAN BE UNNERVING, BUT OFTEN YIELDS THE GREATEST RESULT.
It was advice I'd given many times before, but this time something REMARKABLE happened.
He actually TOOK it.
STACY POWELL? BRUCE WAYNE. THANK YOU FOR COMING.
I WANTED TO APOLOGIZE FOR MY ABRUPTNESS AT THE BANQUET A FEW DAYS BACK.
IT WON'T HAPPEN AGAIN.
WELL. I MUST SAY, I'M SURPRISED.
BUT GRATEFUL. YOUR CONTINUED SUPPORT OF OUR DAY CARE PROJECT WOULD BE GREATLY APPRECIATED.
Our story BEGAN at a fancy dress ball, where Bruce Wayne IGNORED a young woman without a second thought.
THAT WAS ALMOST... "NICE," BRUCE.
I'M OUT OF PRACTICE, BUT THAT'S GOING TO CHANGE.
TRUST ME.

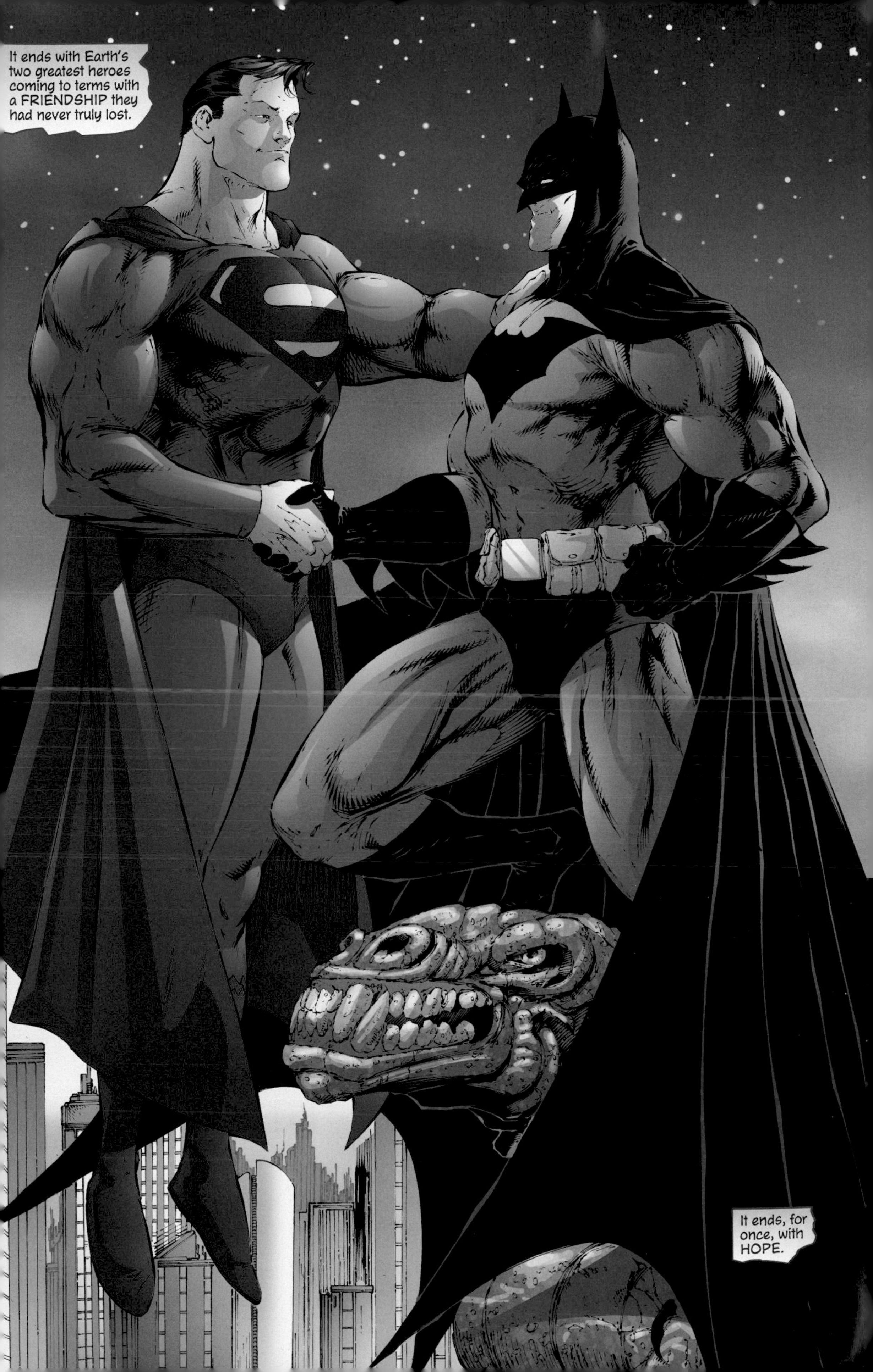
It ends with Earth's two greatest heroes coming to terms with a FRIENDSHIP they had never truly lost.
It ends, for once, with HOPE.

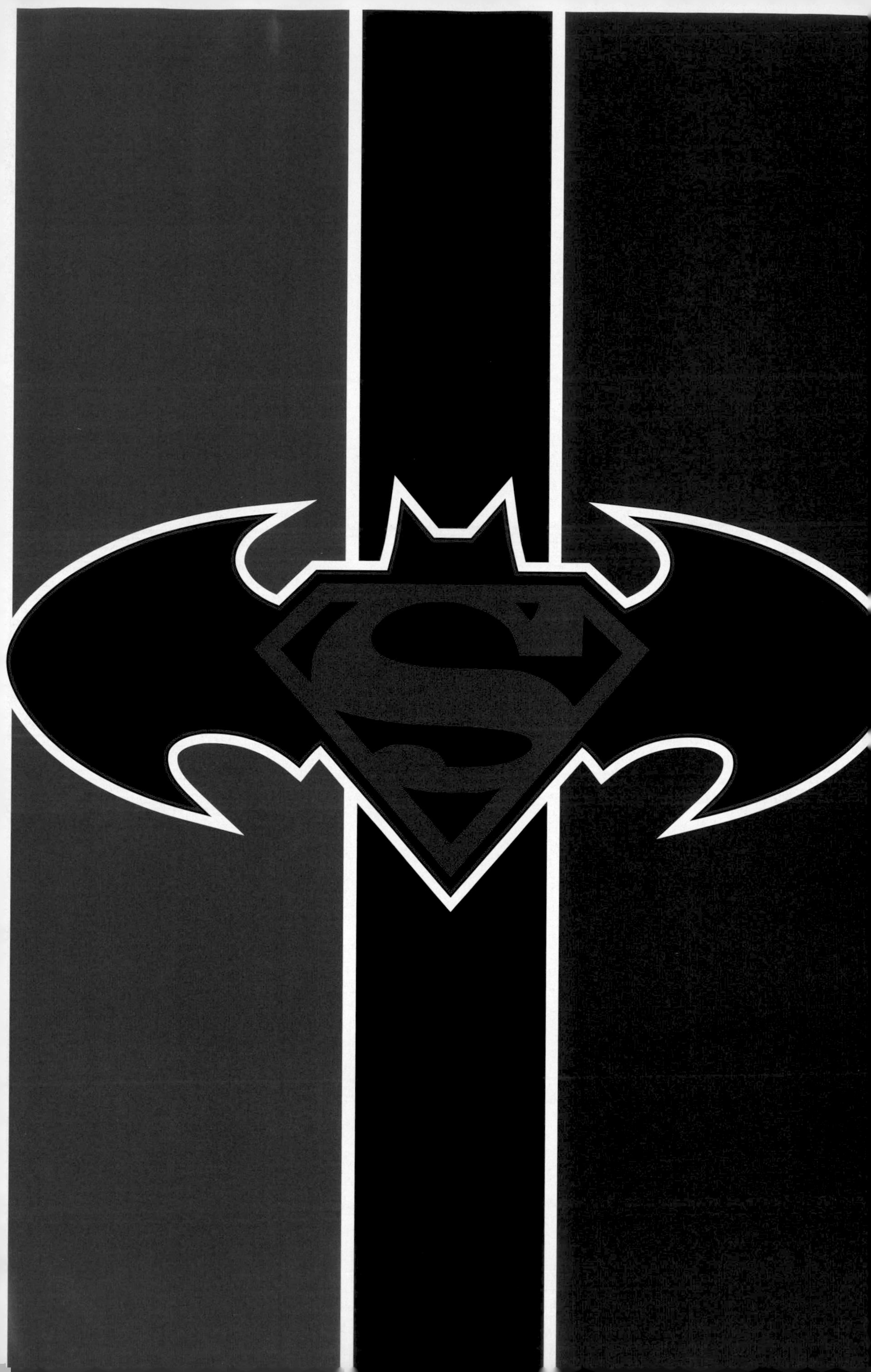

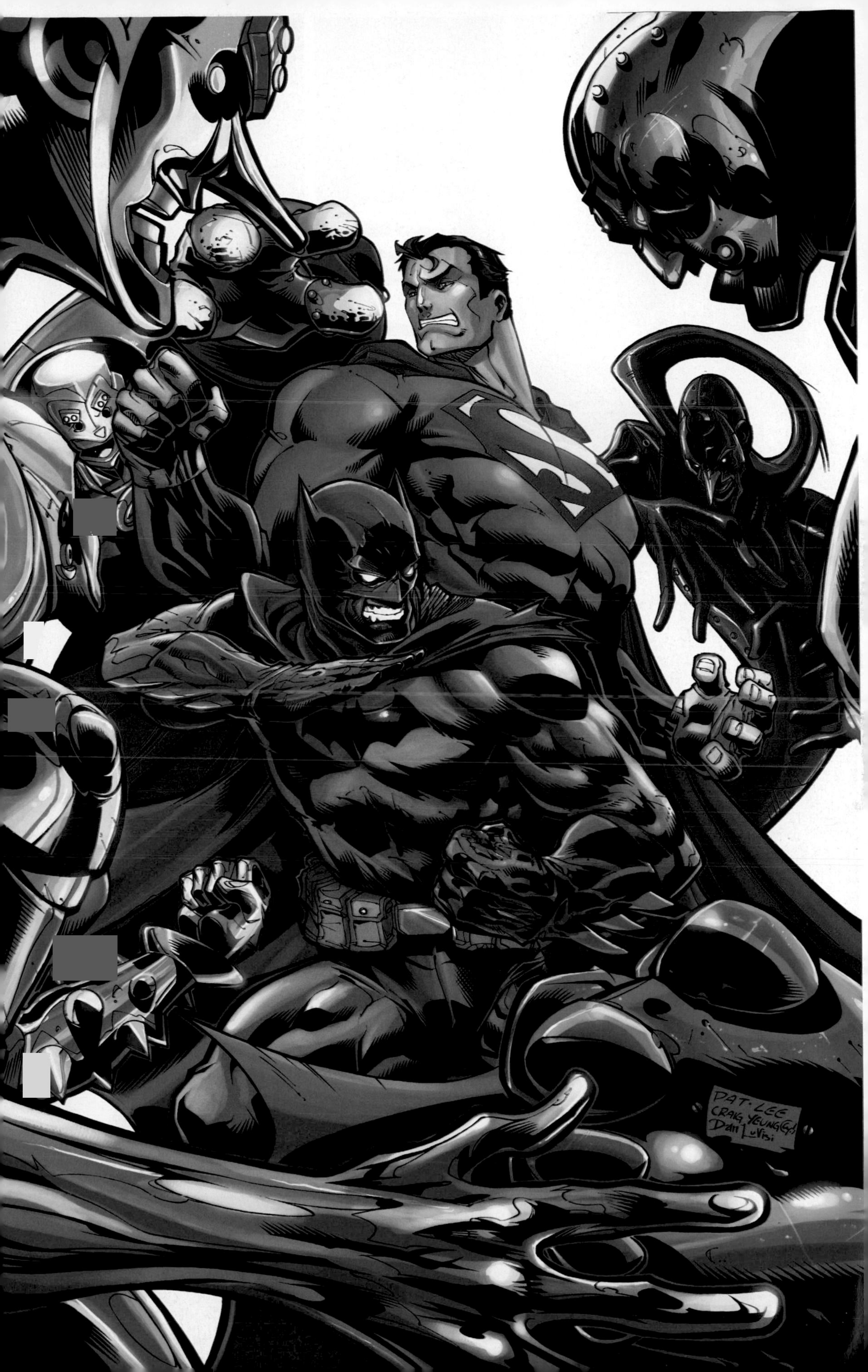
PAT·LEE
CRAIG YEUNG
Dan LuVisi

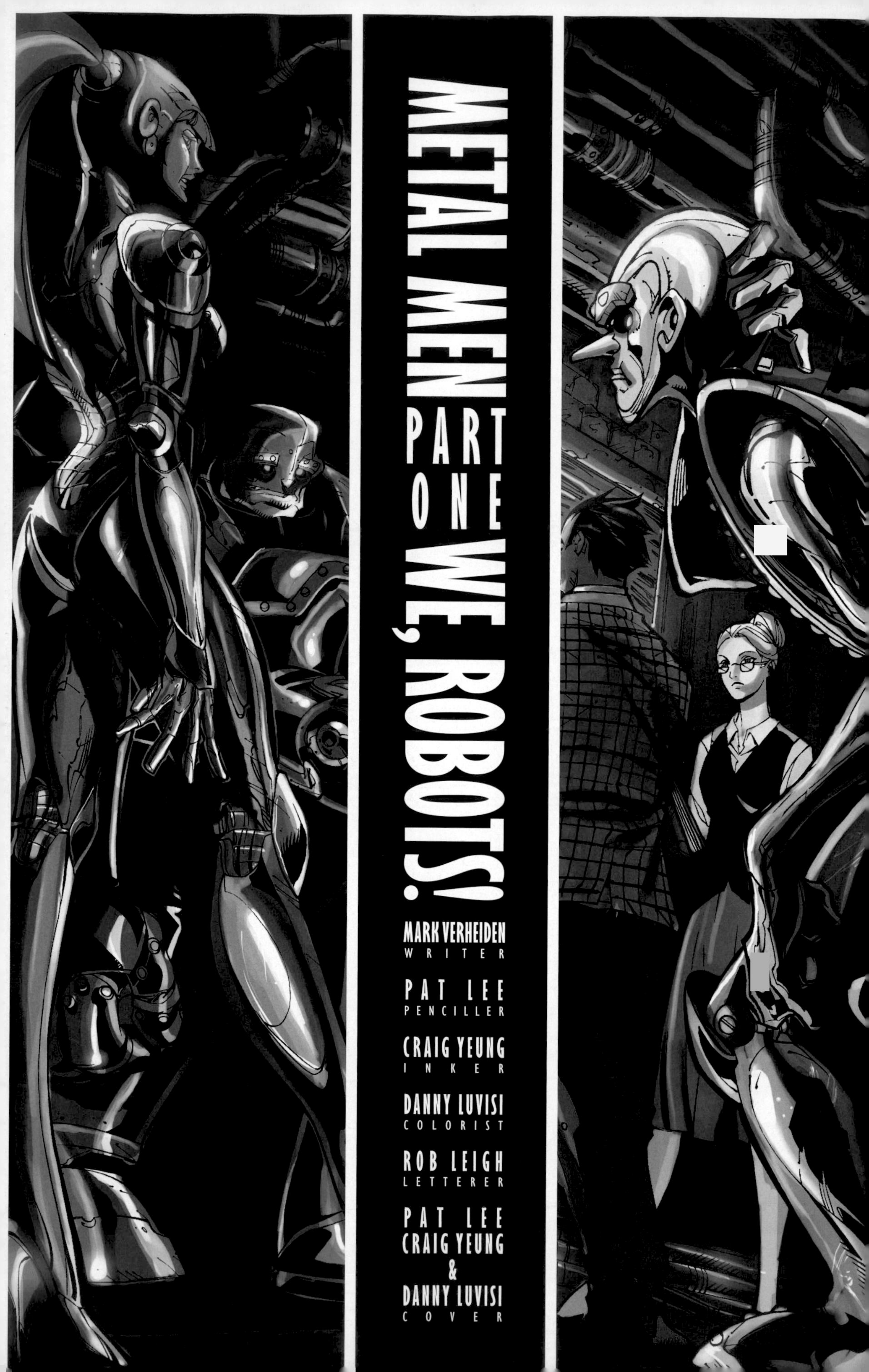
METAL MEN
PART ONE
WE, ROBOTS!
MARK VERHEIDEN
WRITER
PAT LEE
PENCILLER
CRAIG YEUNG
INKER
DANNY LUVISI
COLORIST
ROB LEIGH
LETTERER
PAT LEE
CRAIG YEUNG
&
DANNY LUVISI
COVER

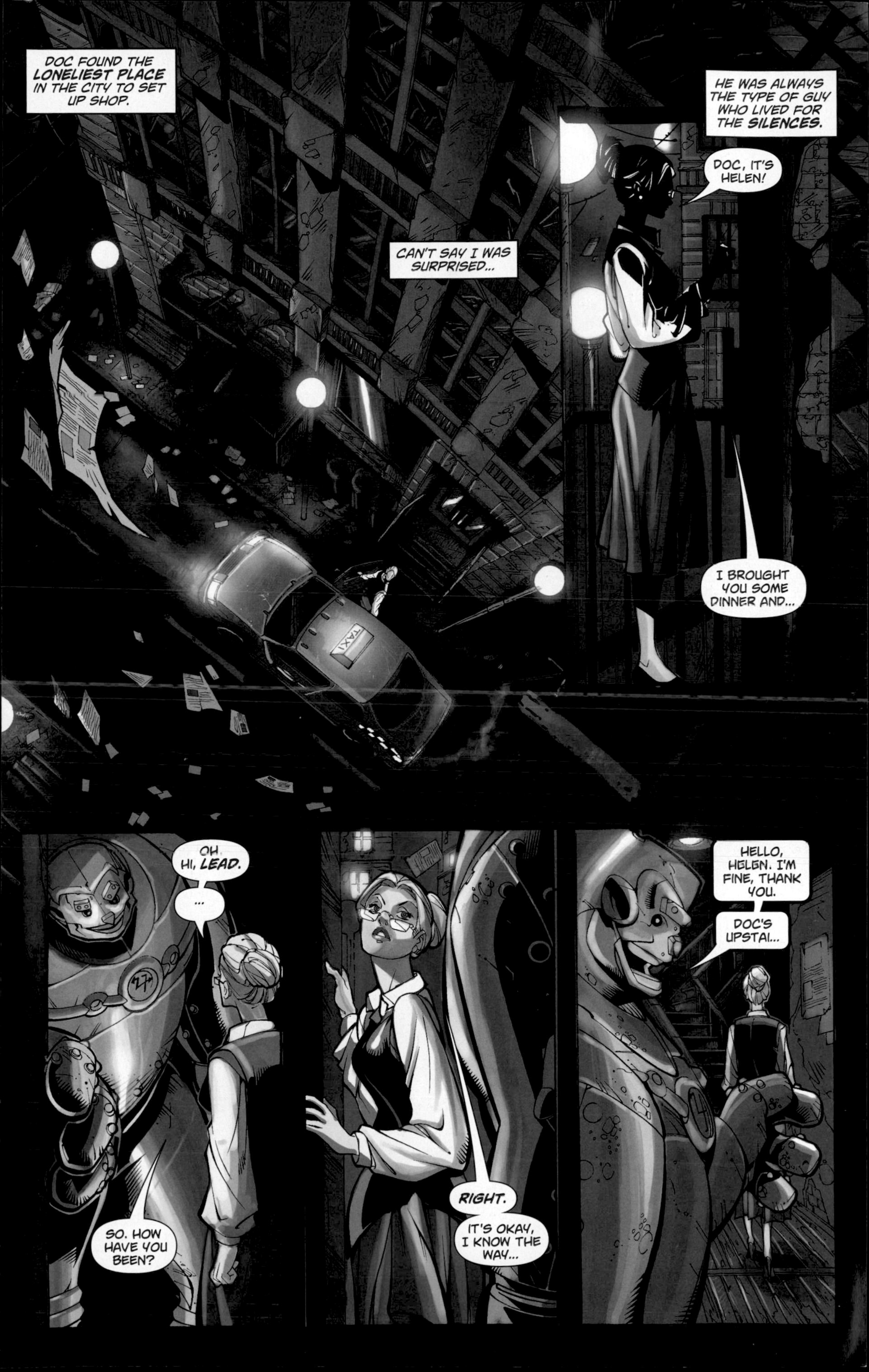

DOC FOUND THE LONELIEST PLACE IN THE CITY TO SET UP SHOP.
CAN'T SAY I WAS SURPRISED...
HE WAS ALWAYS THE TYPE OF GUY WHO LIVED FOR THE SILENCES.
DOC, IT'S HELEN!
I BROUGHT YOU SOME DINNER AND...
TAXI
OH. HI, LEAD.
...
SO. HOW HAVE YOU BEEN?
RIGHT.
IT'S OKAY, I KNOW THE WAY...
HELLO, HELEN. I'M FINE, THANK YOU.
DOC'S UPSTAI...

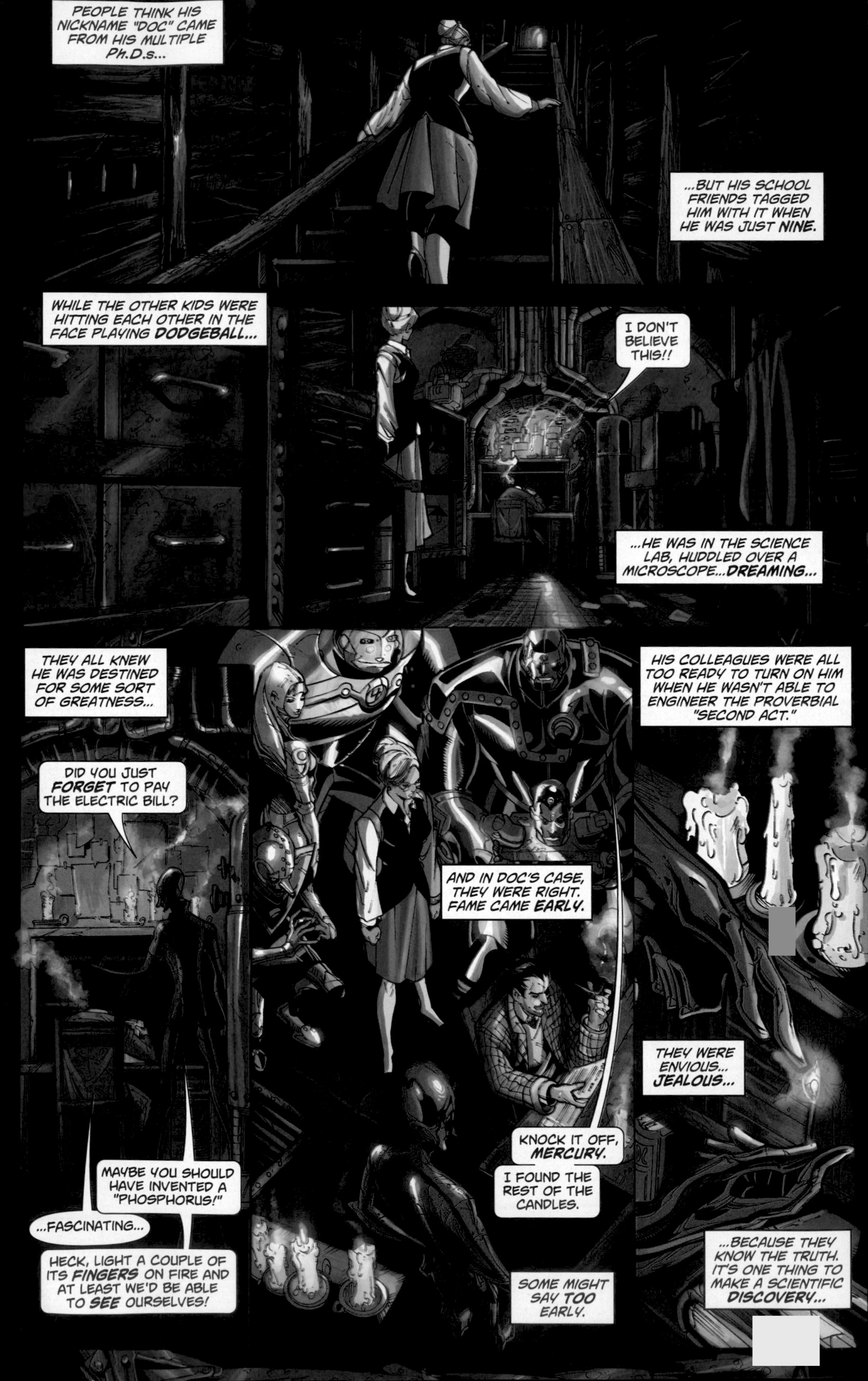
PEOPLE THINK HIS NICKNAME "DOC" CAME FROM HIS MULTIPLE Ph.D.s...
...BUT HIS SCHOOL FRIENDS TAGGED HIM WITH IT WHEN HE WAS JUST NINE.
WHILE THE OTHER KIDS WERE HITTING EACH OTHER IN THE FACE PLAYING DODGEBALL...
I DON'T BELIEVE THIS!!
...HE WAS IN THE SCIENCE LAB, HUDDLED OVER A MICROSCOPE...DREAMING...
THEY ALL KNEW HE WAS DESTINED FOR SOME SORT OF GREATNESS...
DID YOU JUST FORGET TO PAY THE ELECTRIC BILL?
MAYBE YOU SHOULD HAVE INVENTED A "PHOSPHORUS!"
...FASCINATING...
HECK, LIGHT A COUPLE OF ITS FINGERS ON FIRE AND AT LEAST WE'D BE ABLE TO SEE OURSELVES!
AND IN DOC'S CASE, THEY WERE RIGHT. FAME CAME EARLY.
KNOCK IT OFF, MERCURY.
I FOUND THE REST OF THE CANDLES.
SOME MIGHT SAY TOO EARLY.
HIS COLLEAGUES WERE ALL TOO READY TO TURN ON HIM WHEN HE WASN'T ABLE TO ENGINEER THE PROVERBIAL "SECOND ACT."
THEY WERE ENVIOUS... JEALOUS...
...BECAUSE THEY KNOW THE TRUTH. IT'S ONE THING TO MAKE A SCIENTIFIC DISCOVERY...

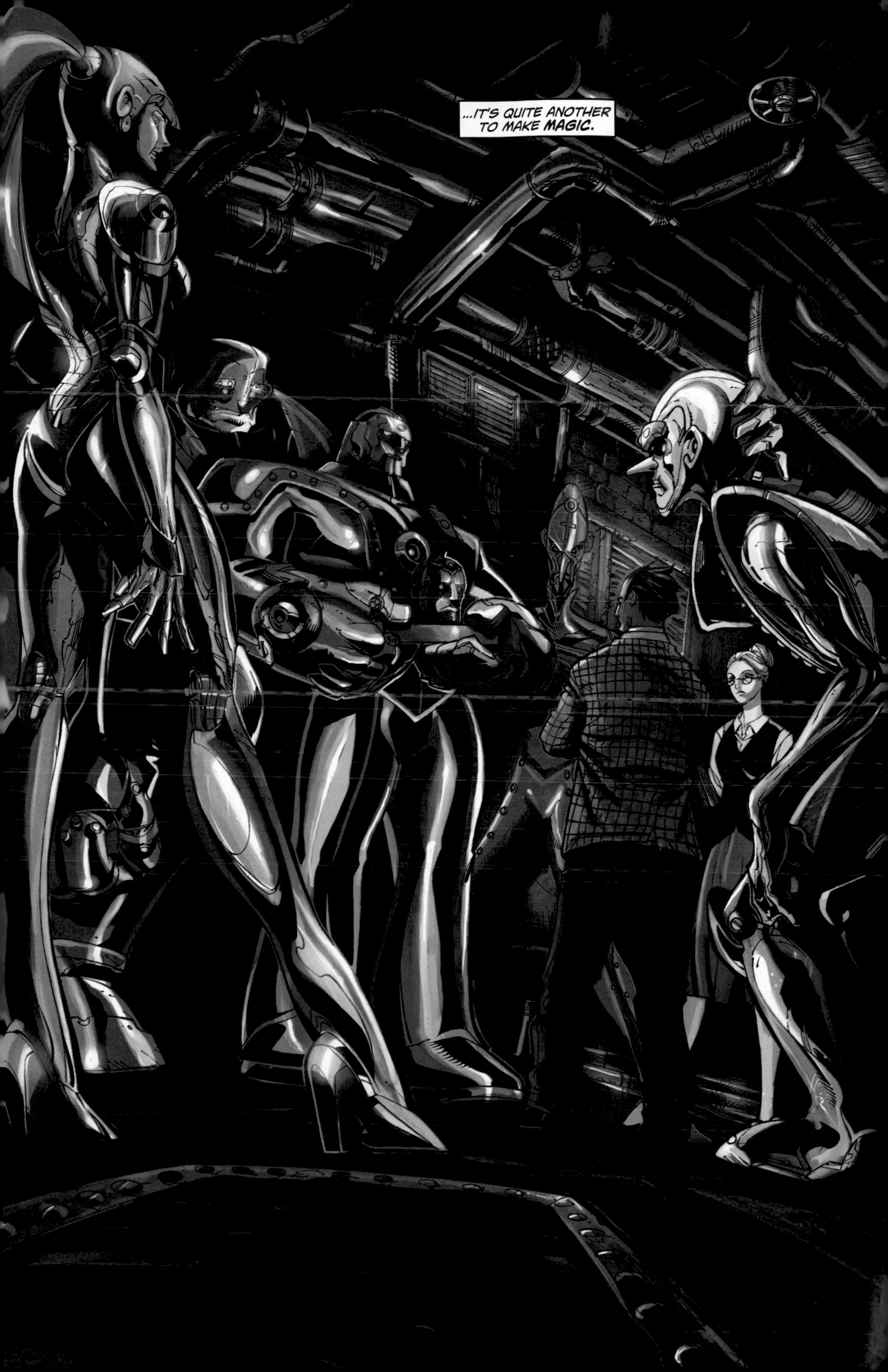
...IT'S QUITE ANOTHER TO MAKE MAGIC.

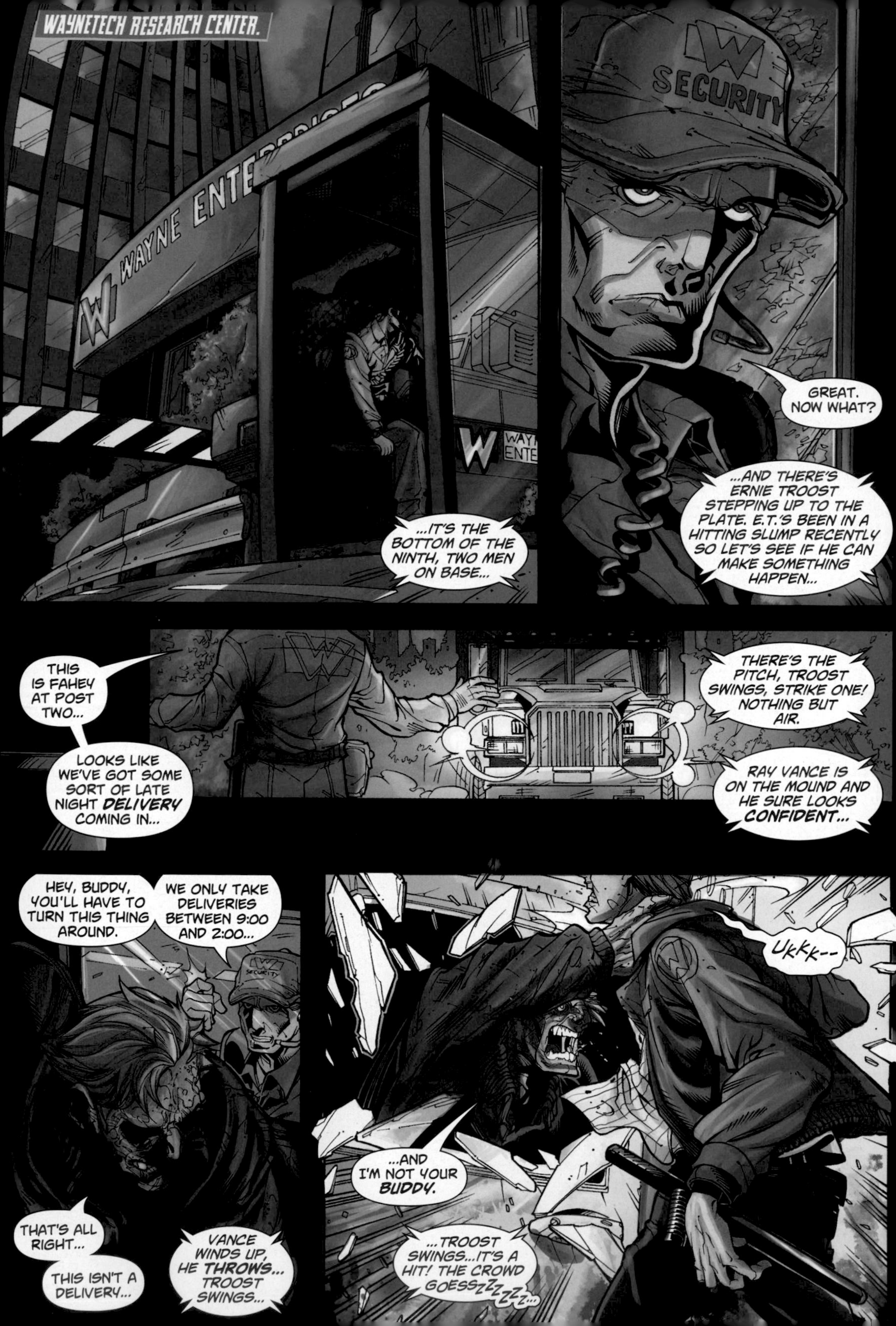
WAYNETECH RESEARCH CENTER.
WAYNE ENTERPRISES
SECURITY
GREAT. NOW WHAT?
...IT'S THE BOTTOM OF THE NINTH, TWO MEN ON BASE...
...AND THERE'S ERNIE TROOST STEPPING UP TO THE PLATE. E.T.'S BEEN IN A HITTING SLUMP RECENTLY SO LET'S SEE IF HE CAN MAKE SOMETHING HAPPEN...
THIS IS FAHEY AT POST TWO...
LOOKS LIKE WE'VE GOT SOME SORT OF LATE NIGHT DELIVERY COMING IN...
THERE'S THE PITCH, TROOST SWINGS, STRIKE ONE! NOTHING BUT AIR.
RAY VANCE IS ON THE MOUND AND HE SURE LOOKS CONFIDENT...
HEY, BUDDY, YOU'LL HAVE TO TURN THIS THING AROUND.
WE ONLY TAKE DELIVERIES BETWEEN 9:00 AND 2:00...
THAT'S ALL RIGHT...
THIS ISN'T A DELIVERY...
VANCE WINDS UP, HE THROWS... TROOST SWINGS...
UKKK--
...AND I'M NOT YOUR BUDDY.
...TROOST SWINGS...IT'S A HIT! THE CROWD GOESSZZZZZZ...

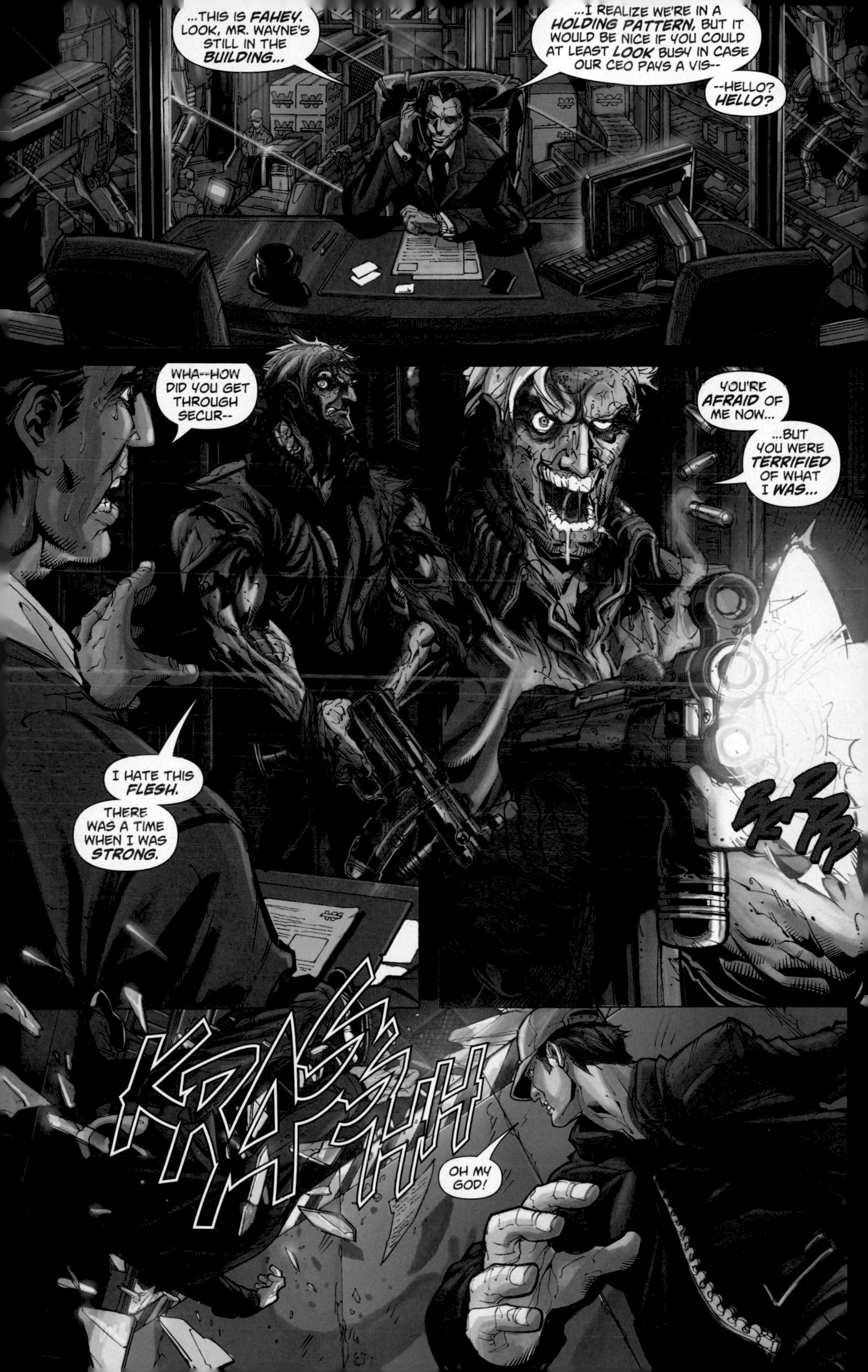
...THIS IS FAHEY. LOOK, MR. WAYNE'S STILL IN THE BUILDING...
...I REALIZE WE'RE IN A HOLDING PATTERN, BUT IT WOULD BE NICE IF YOU COULD AT LEAST LOOK BUSY IN CASE OUR CEO PAYS A VIS--
--HELLO? HELLO?
WHA--HOW DID YOU GET THROUGH SECUR--
YOU'RE AFRAID OF ME NOW...
...BUT YOU WERE TERRIFIED OF WHAT I WAS...
I HATE THIS FLESH.
THERE WAS A TIME WHEN I WAS STRONG.
KRASSHH
OH MY GOD!

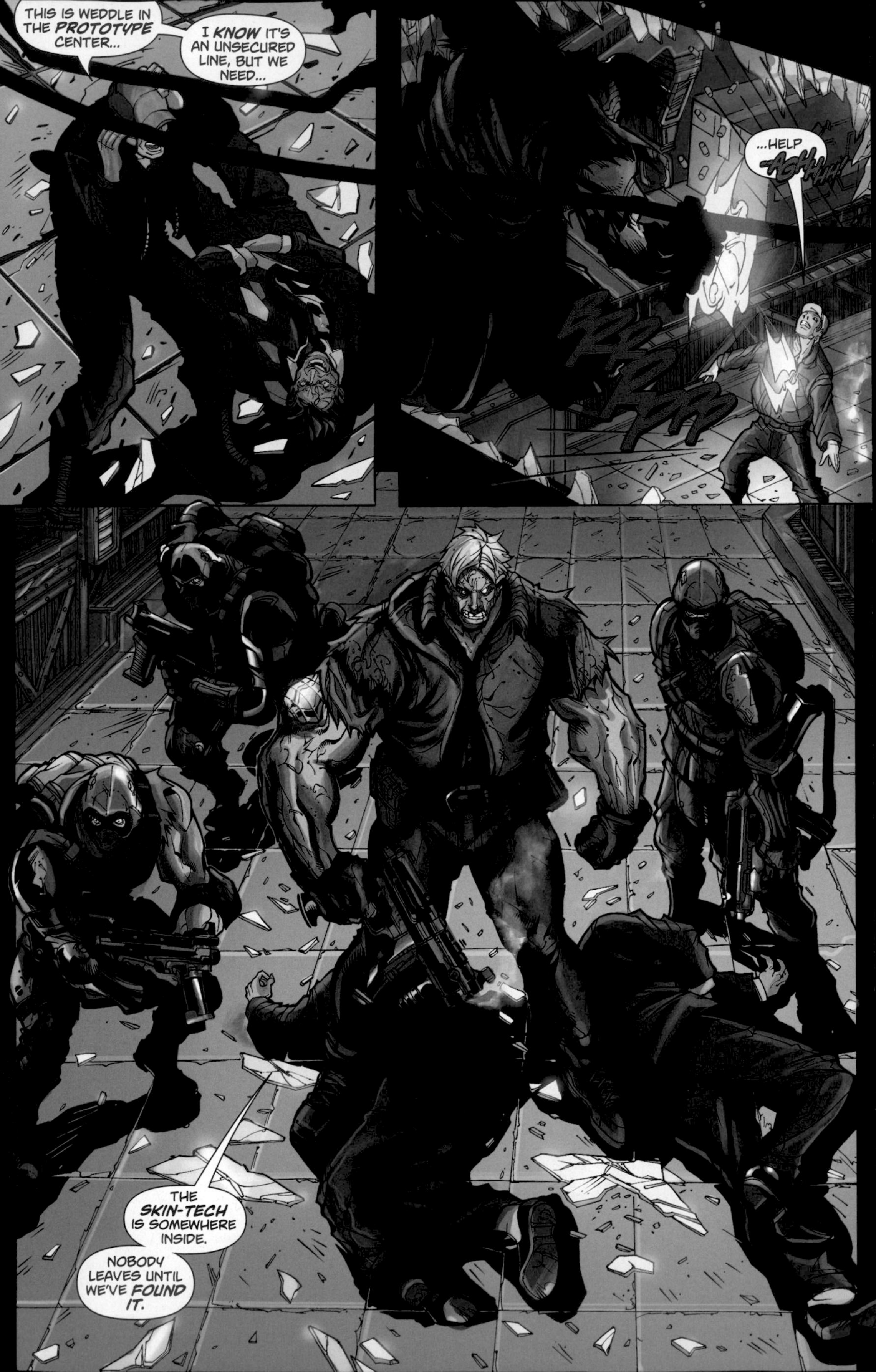
THIS IS WEDDLE IN THE PROTOTYPE CENTER...
I KNOW IT'S AN UNSECURED LINE, BUT WE NEED...
...HELP -AGHHH!
THE SKIN-TECH IS SOMEWHERE INSIDE.
NOBODY LEAVES UNTIL WE'VE FOUND IT.

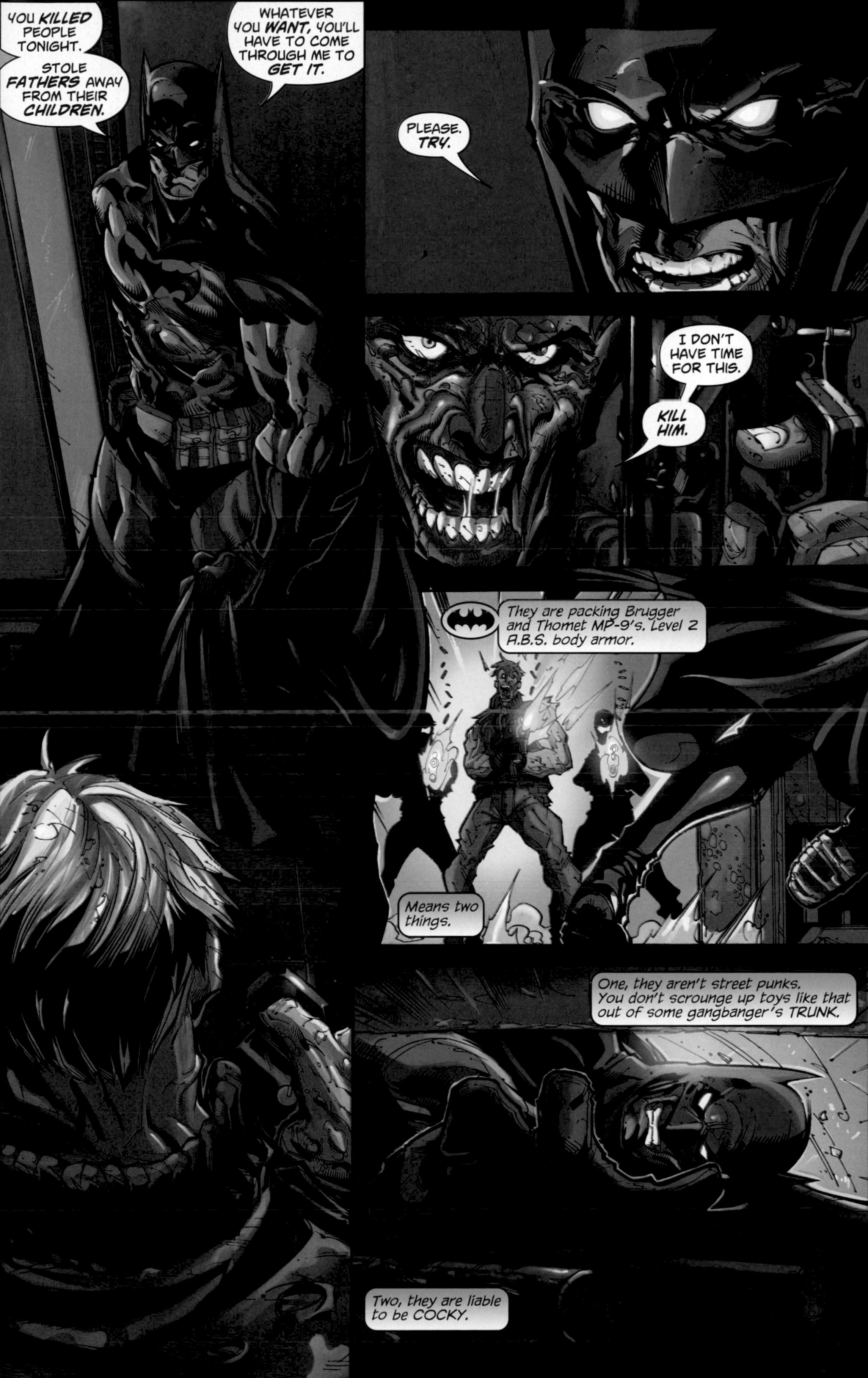
YOU KILLED PEOPLE TONIGHT.
STOLE FATHERS AWAY FROM THEIR CHILDREN.
WHATEVER YOU WANT, YOU'LL HAVE TO COME THROUGH ME TO GET IT.
PLEASE. TRY.
I DON'T HAVE TIME FOR THIS.
KILL HIM.
They are packing Brugger and Thomet MP-9's. Level 2 A.B.S. body armor.
Means two things.
One, they aren't street punks. You don't scrounge up toys like that out of some gangbanger's TRUNK.
Two, they are liable to be COCKY.

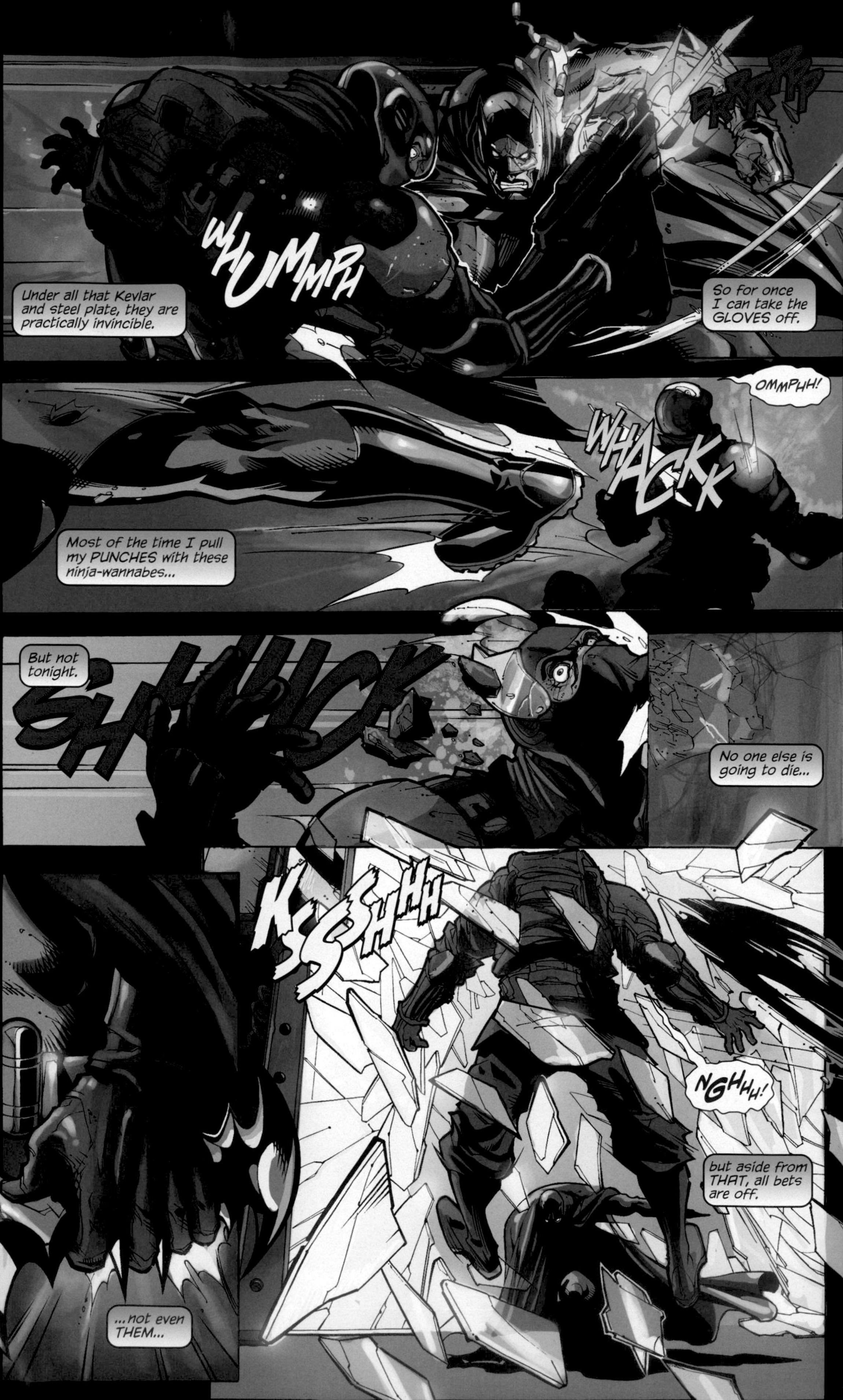
BRRRRPP
WHUMMPH
Under all that Kevlar and steel plate, they are practically invincible.
So for once I can take the GLOVES off.
OMMPHH!
WHACKK
Most of the time I pull my PUNCHES with these ninja-wannabes...
But not tonight.
SHHUCK
No one else is going to die...
KSSHHH
NGHHH!
but aside from THAT, all bets are off.
...not even THEM...

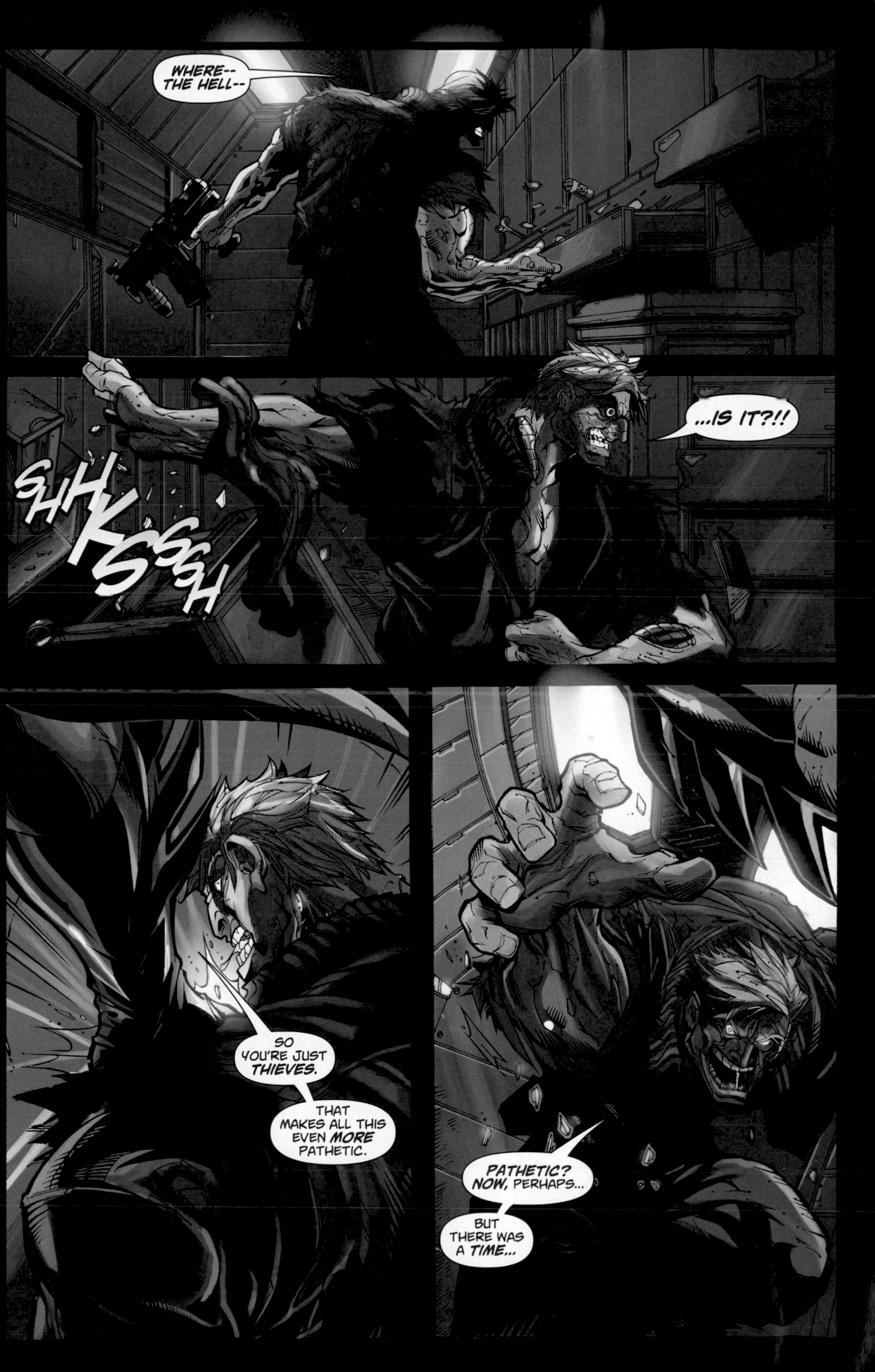
WHERE-- THE HELL--
SHHKSSSCH
...IS IT?!!
SO YOU'RE JUST THIEVES.
THAT MAKES ALL THIS EVEN MORE PATHETIC.
PATHETIC? NOW, PERHAPS...
BUT THERE WAS A TIME...

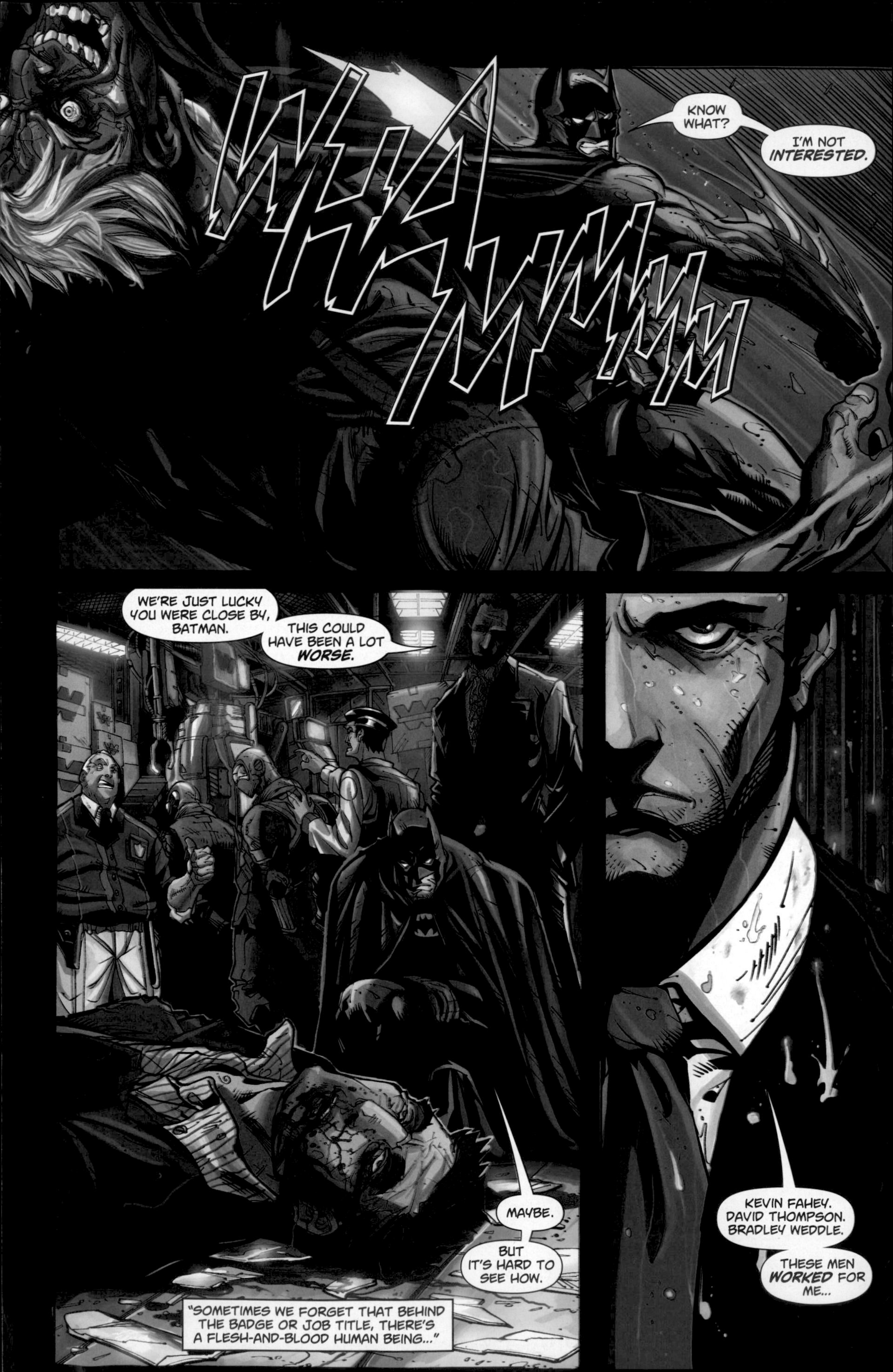
WHAAMMMM
KNOW WHAT?
I'M NOT INTERESTED.
WE'RE JUST LUCKY YOU WERE CLOSE BY, BATMAN.
THIS COULD HAVE BEEN A LOT WORSE.
MAYBE.
BUT IT'S HARD TO SEE HOW.
"SOMETIMES WE FORGET THAT BEHIND THE BADGE OR JOB TITLE, THERE'S A FLESH-AND-BLOOD HUMAN BEING..."
KEVIN FAHEY. DAVID THOMPSON. BRADLEY WEDDLE.
THESE MEN WORKED FOR ME...

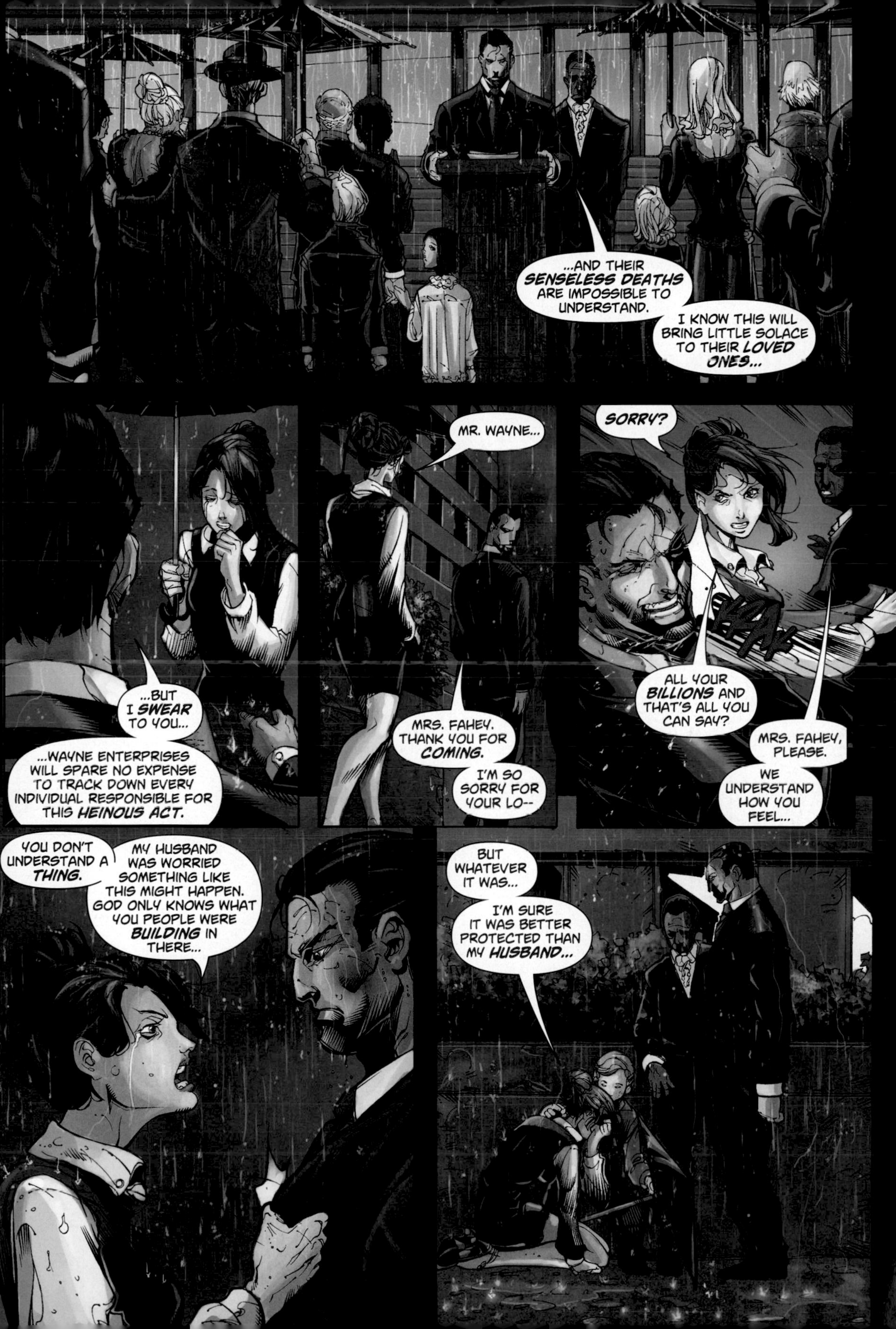
...AND THEIR SENSELESS DEATHS ARE IMPOSSIBLE TO UNDERSTAND.
I KNOW THIS WILL BRING LITTLE SOLACE TO THEIR LOVED ONES...
...BUT I SWEAR TO YOU...
...WAYNE ENTERPRISES WILL SPARE NO EXPENSE TO TRACK DOWN EVERY INDIVIDUAL RESPONSIBLE FOR THIS HEINOUS ACT.
MR. WAYNE...
MRS. FAHEY. THANK YOU FOR COMING.
I'M SO SORRY FOR YOUR LO--
SORRY?
ALL YOUR BILLIONS AND THAT'S ALL YOU CAN SAY?
MRS. FAHEY, PLEASE.
WE UNDERSTAND HOW YOU FEEL...
YOU DON'T UNDERSTAND A THING.
MY HUSBAND WAS WORRIED SOMETHING LIKE THIS MIGHT HAPPEN. GOD ONLY KNOWS WHAT YOU PEOPLE WERE BUILDING IN THERE...
BUT WHATEVER IT WAS...
I'M SURE IT WAS BETTER PROTECTED THAN MY HUSBAND...

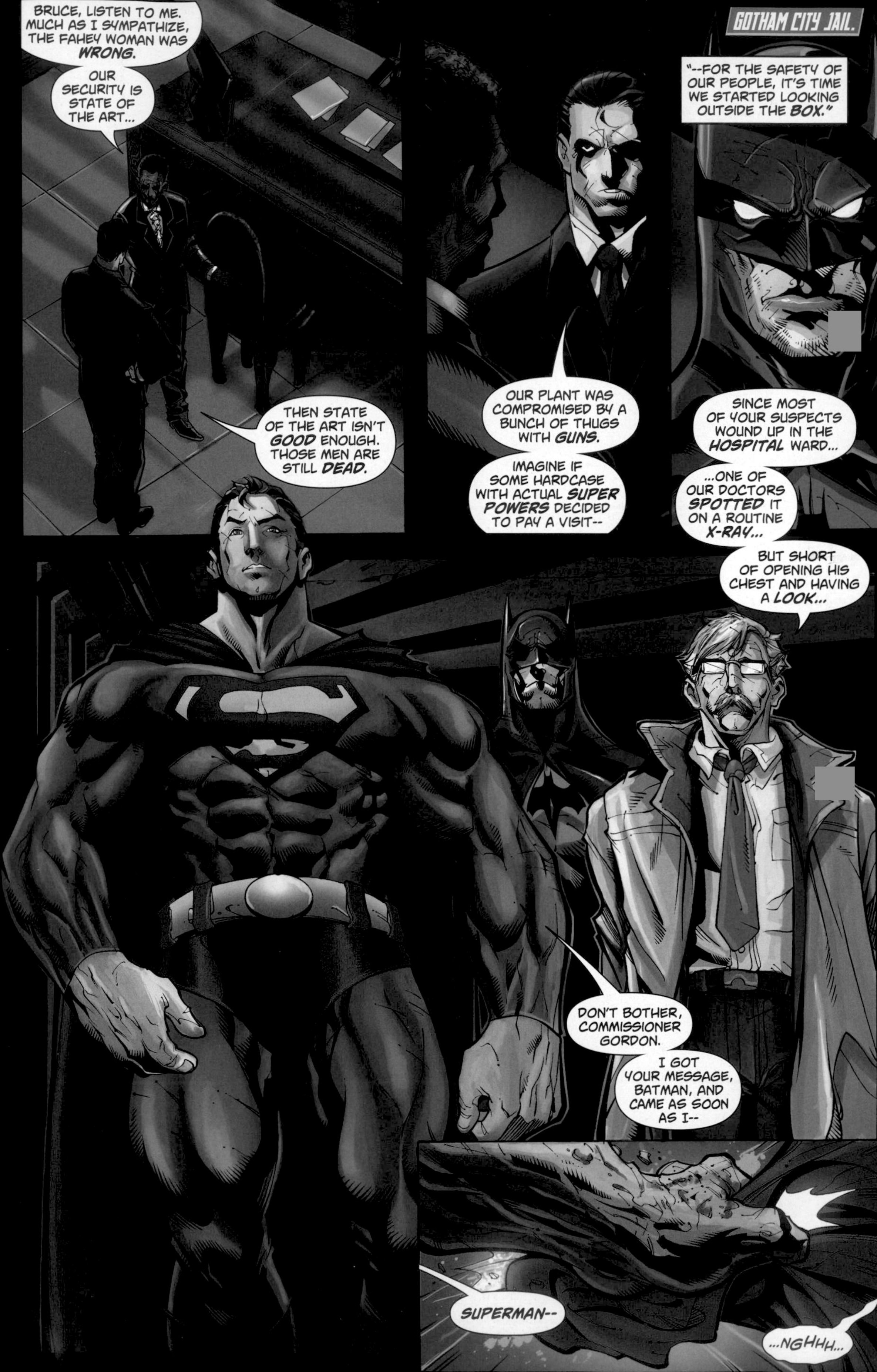
BRUCE, LISTEN TO ME. MUCH AS I SYMPATHIZE, THE FAHEY WOMAN WAS WRONG.
OUR SECURITY IS STATE OF THE ART...
THEN STATE OF THE ART ISN'T GOOD ENOUGH. THOSE MEN ARE STILL DEAD.
OUR PLANT WAS COMPROMISED BY A BUNCH OF THUGS WITH GUNS.
IMAGINE IF SOME HARDCASE WITH ACTUAL SUPER POWERS DECIDED TO PAY A VISIT--
GOTHAM CITY JAIL.
"--FOR THE SAFETY OF OUR PEOPLE, IT'S TIME WE STARTED LOOKING OUTSIDE THE BOX."
SINCE MOST OF YOUR SUSPECTS WOUND UP IN THE HOSPITAL WARD...
...ONE OF OUR DOCTORS SPOTTED IT ON A ROUTINE X-RAY...
BUT SHORT OF OPENING HIS CHEST AND HAVING A LOOK...
DON'T BOTHER, COMMISSIONER GORDON.
I GOT YOUR MESSAGE, BATMAN, AND CAME AS SOON AS I--
SUPERMAN--
...NGHHH...

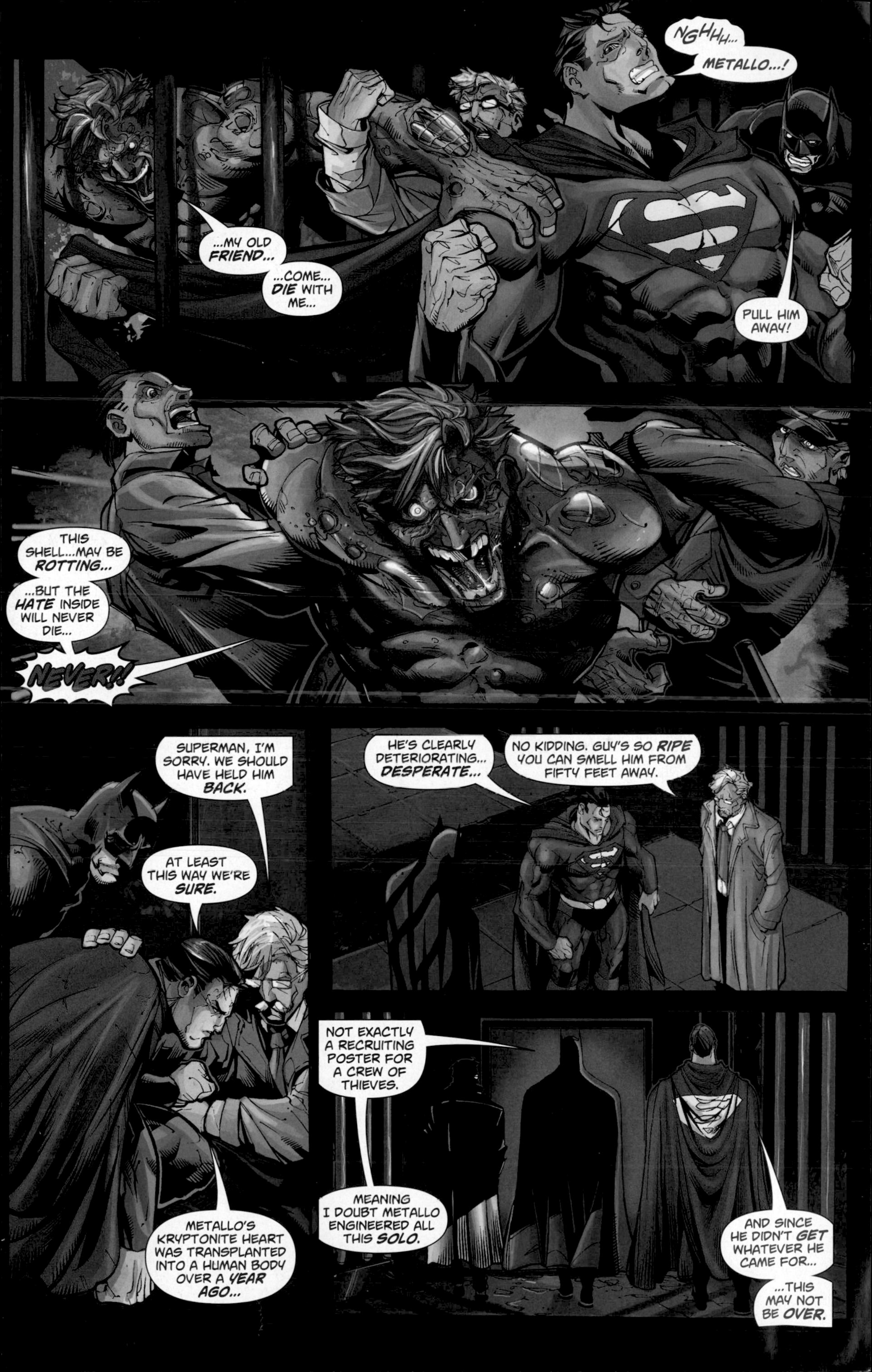
NGHHH...
METALLO...!
...MY OLD FRIEND...
...COME... DIE WITH ME...
PULL HIM AWAY!
THIS SHELL...MAY BE ROTTING...
...BUT THE HATE INSIDE WILL NEVER DIE...
NEVER!!
SUPERMAN, I'M SORRY. WE SHOULD HAVE HELD HIM BACK.
AT LEAST THIS WAY WE'RE SURE.
METALLO'S KRYPTONITE HEART WAS TRANSPLANTED INTO A HUMAN BODY OVER A YEAR AGO...
HE'S CLEARLY DETERIORATING... DESPERATE...
NO KIDDING. GUY'S SO RIPE YOU CAN SMELL HIM FROM FIFTY FEET AWAY.
NOT EXACTLY A RECRUITING POSTER FOR A CREW OF THIEVES.
MEANING I DOUBT METALLO ENGINEERED ALL THIS SOLO.
AND SINCE HE DIDN'T GET WHATEVER HE CAME FOR...
...THIS MAY NOT BE OVER.

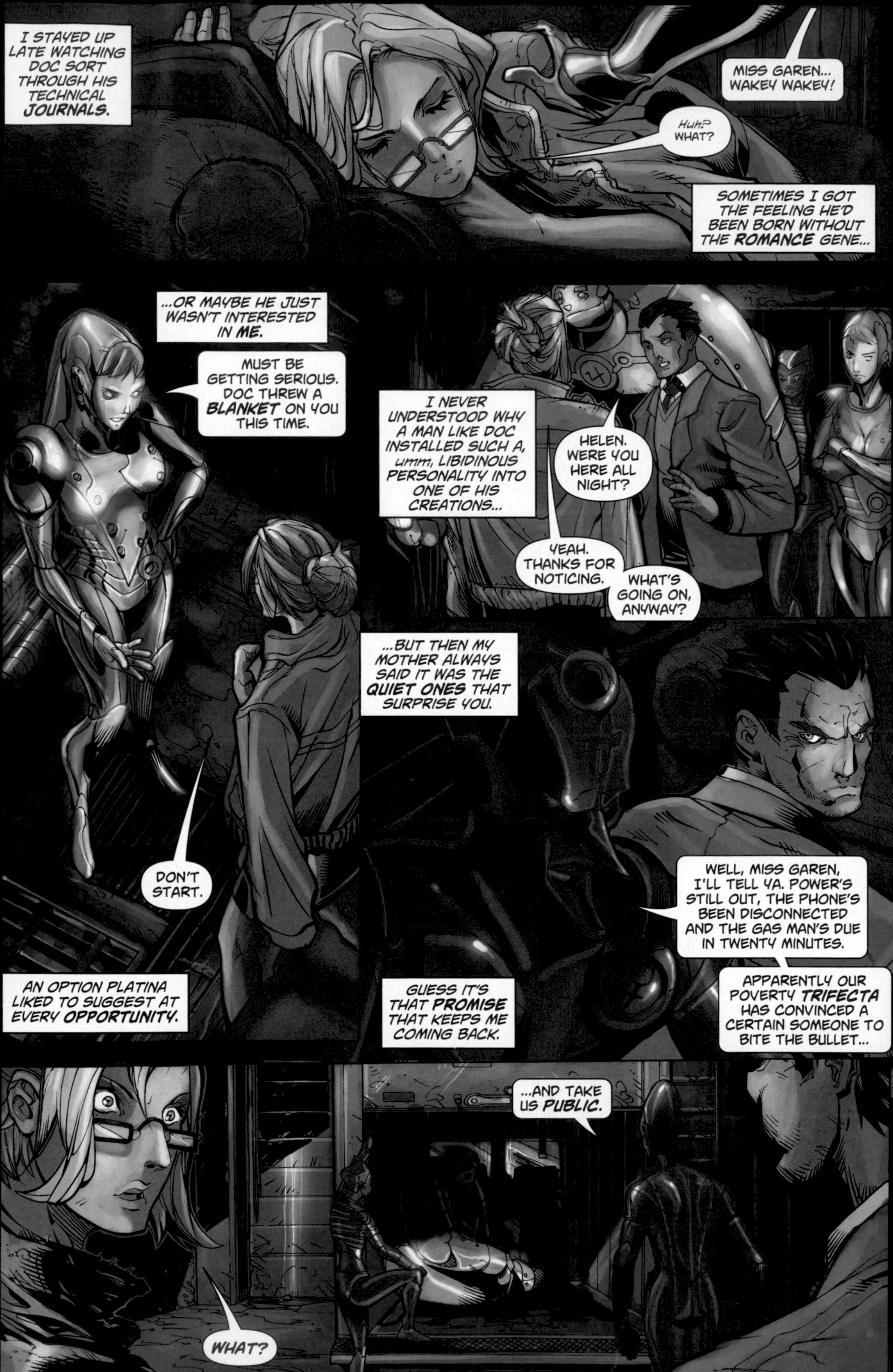
I STAYED UP LATE WATCHING DOC SORT THROUGH HIS TECHNICAL JOURNALS.
MISS GAREN... WAKEY WAKEY!
Huh? WHAT?
SOMETIMES I GOT THE FEELING HE'D BEEN BORN WITHOUT THE ROMANCE GENE...
...OR MAYBE HE JUST WASN'T INTERESTED IN ME.
MUST BE GETTING SERIOUS. DOC THREW A BLANKET ON YOU THIS TIME.
DON'T START.
AN OPTION PLATINA LIKED TO SUGGEST AT EVERY OPPORTUNITY.
I NEVER UNDERSTOOD WHY A MAN LIKE DOC INSTALLED SUCH A, umm, LIBIDINOUS PERSONALITY INTO ONE OF HIS CREATIONS...
HELEN. WERE YOU HERE ALL NIGHT?
YEAH. THANKS FOR NOTICING.
WHAT'S GOING ON, ANYWAY?
...BUT THEN MY MOTHER ALWAYS SAID IT WAS THE QUIET ONES THAT SURPRISE YOU.
WELL, MISS GAREN, I'LL TELL YA. POWER'S STILL OUT, THE PHONE'S BEEN DISCONNECTED AND THE GAS MAN'S DUE IN TWENTY MINUTES.
GUESS IT'S THAT PROMISE THAT KEEPS ME COMING BACK.
APPARENTLY OUR POVERTY TRIFECTA HAS CONVINCED A CERTAIN SOMEONE TO BITE THE BULLET...
...AND TAKE US PUBLIC.
WHAT?

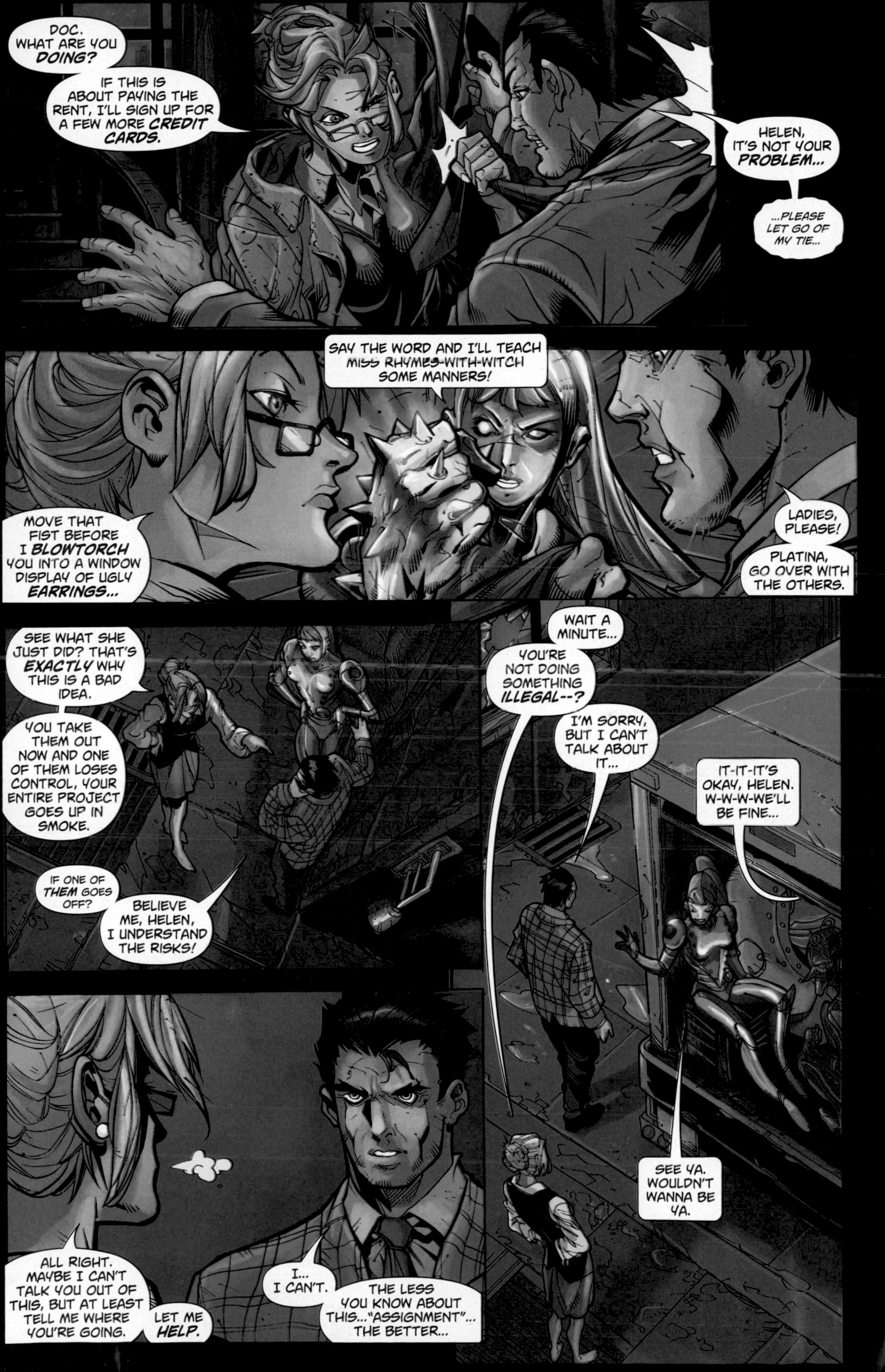
DOC. WHAT ARE YOU DOING?
IF THIS IS ABOUT PAYING THE RENT, I'LL SIGN UP FOR A FEW MORE CREDIT CARDS.
HELEN, IT'S NOT YOUR PROBLEM...
...PLEASE LET GO OF MY TIE...
SAY THE WORD AND I'LL TEACH MISS RHYMES-WITH-WITCH SOME MANNERS!
MOVE THAT FIST BEFORE I BLOWTORCH YOU INTO A WINDOW DISPLAY OF UGLY EARRINGS...
LADIES, PLEASE!
PLATINA, GO OVER WITH THE OTHERS.
SEE WHAT SHE JUST DID? THAT'S EXACTLY WHY THIS IS A BAD IDEA.
YOU TAKE THEM OUT NOW AND ONE OF THEM LOSES CONTROL, YOUR ENTIRE PROJECT GOES UP IN SMOKE.
IF ONE OF THEM GOES OFF?
BELIEVE ME, HELEN, I UNDERSTAND THE RISKS!
WAIT A MINUTE...
YOU'RE NOT DOING SOMETHING ILLEGAL--?
I'M SORRY, BUT I CAN'T TALK ABOUT IT...
IT-IT-IT'S OKAY, HELEN. W-W-W-WE'LL BE FINE...
SEE YA. WOULDN'T WANNA BE YA.
ALL RIGHT. MAYBE I CAN'T TALK YOU OUT OF THIS, BUT AT LEAST TELL ME WHERE YOU'RE GOING.
LET ME HELP.
I... I CAN'T.
THE LESS YOU KNOW ABOUT THIS..."ASSIGNMENT"... THE BETTER...

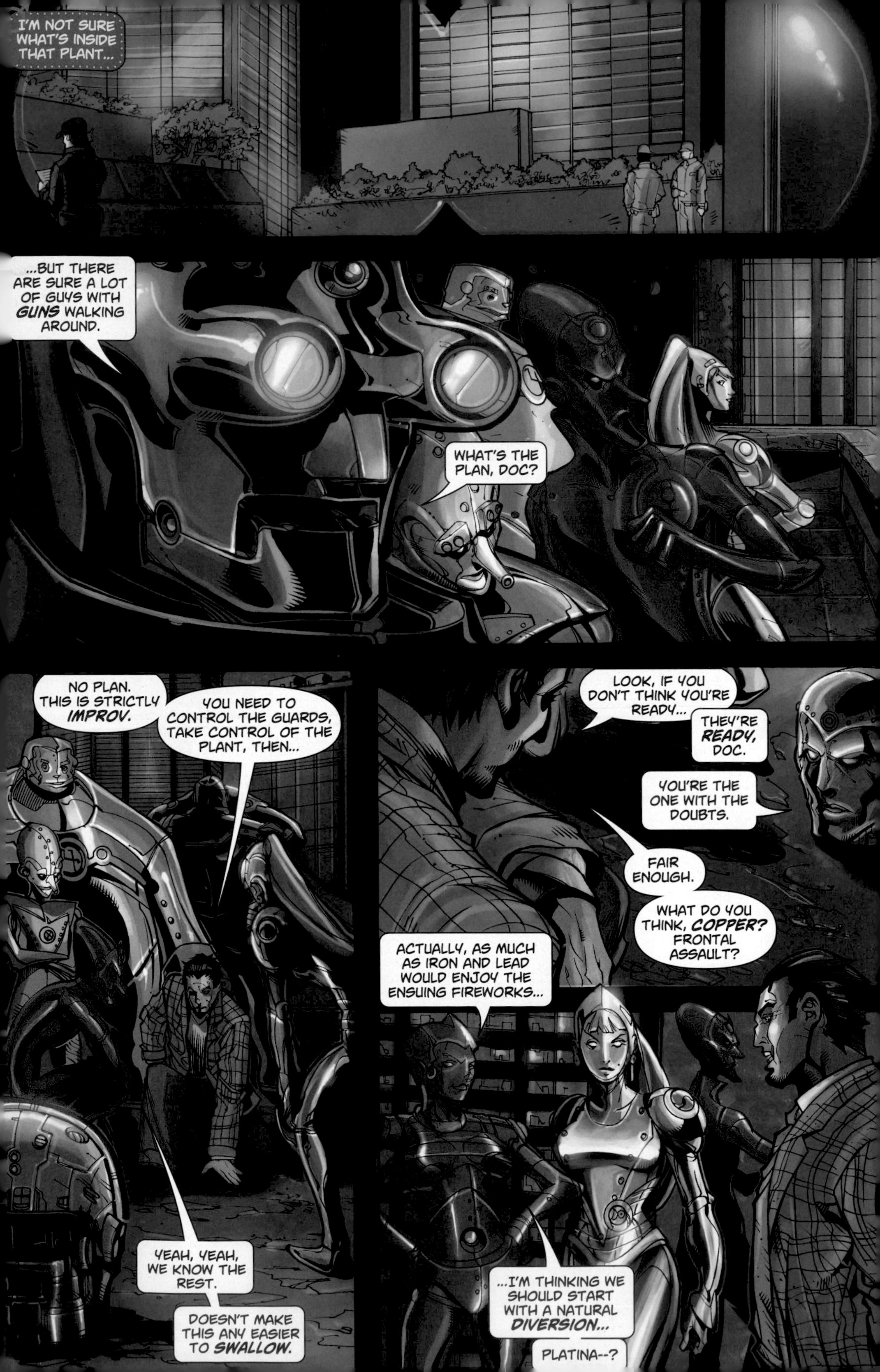
I'M NOT SURE WHAT'S INSIDE THAT PLANT...
...BUT THERE ARE SURE A LOT OF GUYS WITH **GUNS** WALKING AROUND.
WHAT'S THE PLAN, DOC?
NO PLAN. THIS IS STRICTLY ***IMPROV.***
YOU NEED TO CONTROL THE GUARDS, TAKE CONTROL OF THE PLANT, THEN...
YEAH, YEAH, WE KNOW THE REST.
DOESN'T MAKE THIS ANY EASIER TO ***SWALLOW.***
LOOK, IF YOU DON'T THINK YOU'RE READY...
THEY'RE ***READY,*** DOC.
YOU'RE THE ONE WITH THE DOUBTS.
FAIR ENOUGH.
WHAT DO YOU THINK, ***COPPER?*** FRONTAL ASSAULT?
ACTUALLY, AS MUCH AS IRON AND LEAD WOULD ENJOY THE ENSUING FIREWORKS...
...I'M THINKING WE SHOULD START WITH A NATURAL ***DIVERSION...***
PLATINA--?

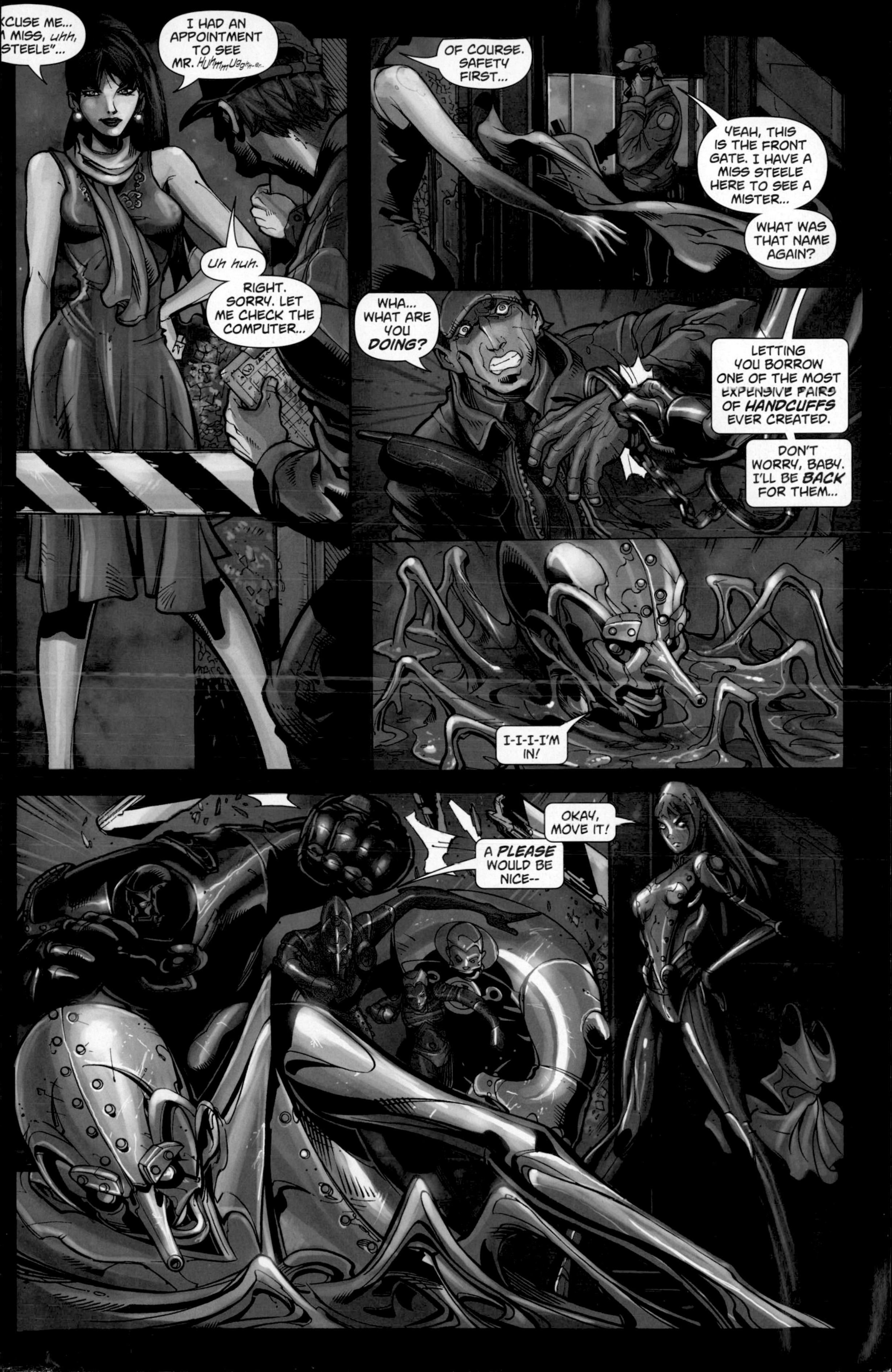
XCUSE ME... M MISS, *uhh*, STEELE"...
I HAD AN APPOINTMENT TO SEE MR. HUhmmUgghh-er...
Uh huh.
RIGHT. SORRY. LET ME CHECK THE COMPUTER...
OF COURSE. SAFETY FIRST...
YEAH, THIS IS THE FRONT GATE. I HAVE A MISS STEELE HERE TO SEE A MISTER...
WHAT WAS THAT NAME AGAIN?
WHA... WHAT ARE YOU ***DOING?***
LETTING YOU BORROW ONE OF THE MOST EXPENSIVE PAIRS OF ***HANDCUFFS*** EVER CREATED.
DON'T WORRY, BABY. I'LL BE ***BACK*** FOR THEM...
I-I-I-I'M IN!
OKAY, MOVE IT!
A ***PLEASE*** WOULD BE NICE--

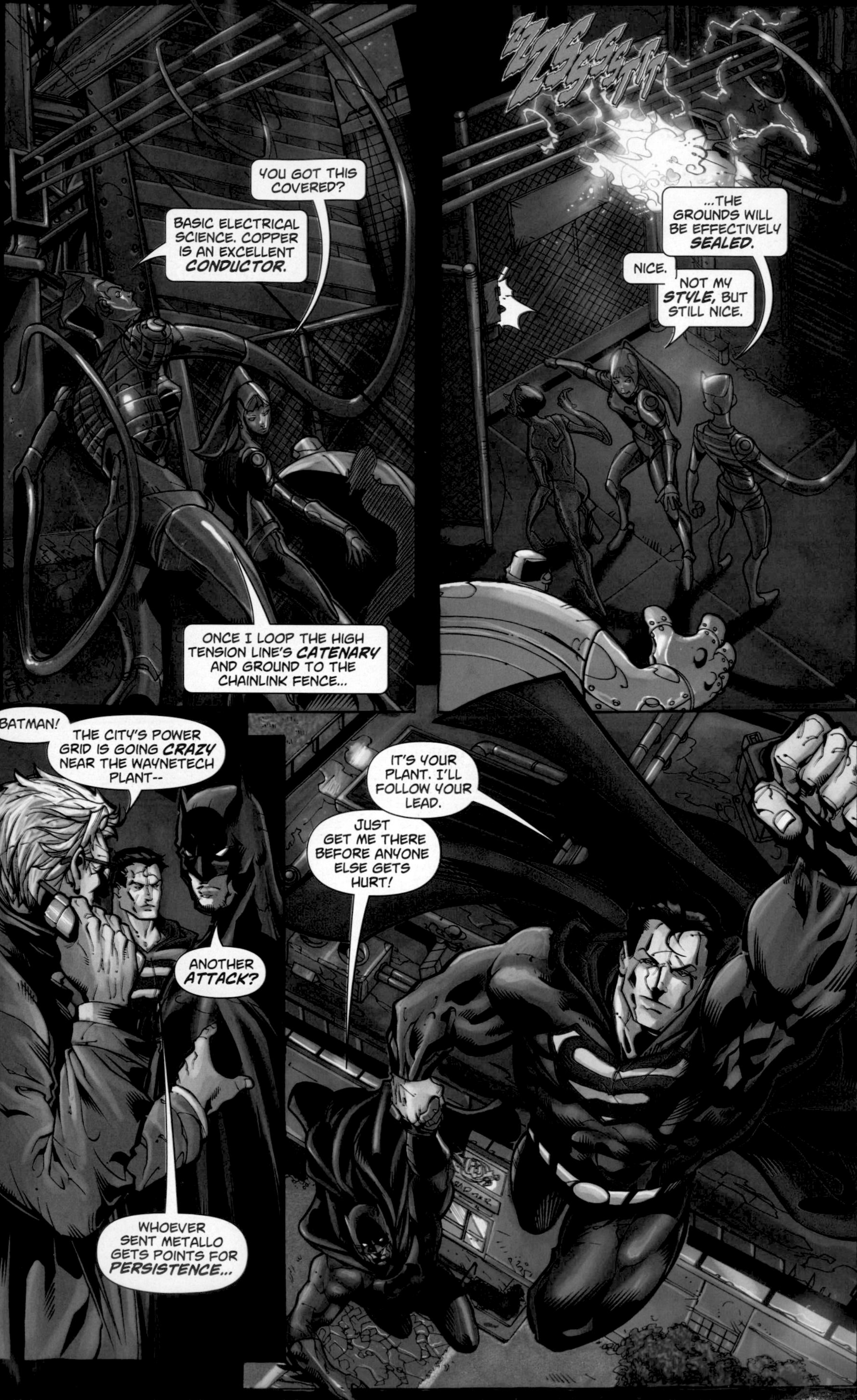
YOU GOT THIS COVERED?
BASIC ELECTRICAL SCIENCE. COPPER IS AN EXCELLENT CONDUCTOR.
ONCE I LOOP THE HIGH TENSION LINE'S CATENARY AND GROUND TO THE CHAINLINK FENCE...
ZZZSSSSTTT
...THE GROUNDS WILL BE EFFECTIVELY SEALED.
NICE.
NOT MY STYLE, BUT STILL NICE.
BATMAN!
THE CITY'S POWER GRID IS GOING CRAZY NEAR THE WAYNETECH PLANT--
ANOTHER ATTACK?
WHOEVER SENT METALLO GETS POINTS FOR PERSISTENCE...
IT'S YOUR PLANT. I'LL FOLLOW YOUR LEAD.
JUST GET ME THERE BEFORE ANYONE ELSE GETS HURT!

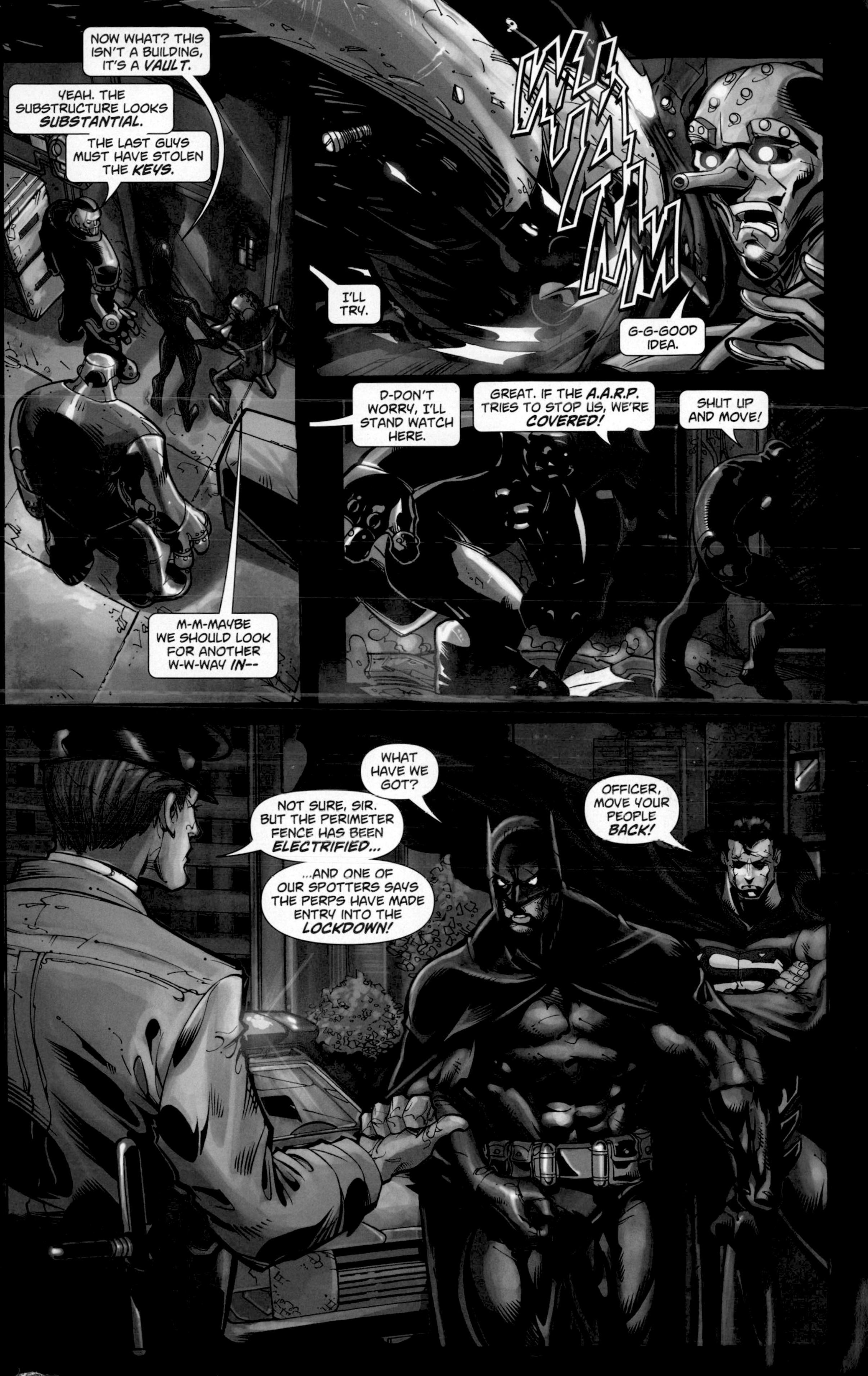
NOW WHAT? THIS ISN'T A BUILDING, IT'S A VAULT.
YEAH. THE SUBSTRUCTURE LOOKS SUBSTANTIAL.
THE LAST GUYS MUST HAVE STOLEN THE KEYS.
M-M-MAYBE WE SHOULD LOOK FOR ANOTHER W-W-WAY IN--
KWAMM
I'LL TRY.
G-G-GOOD IDEA.
D-DON'T WORRY, I'LL STAND WATCH HERE.
GREAT. IF THE A.A.R.P. TRIES TO STOP US, WE'RE COVERED!
SHUT UP AND MOVE!
WHAT HAVE WE GOT?
NOT SURE, SIR. BUT THE PERIMETER FENCE HAS BEEN ELECTRIFIED...
...AND ONE OF OUR SPOTTERS SAYS THE PERPS HAVE MADE ENTRY INTO THE LOCKDOWN!
OFFICER, MOVE YOUR PEOPLE BACK!

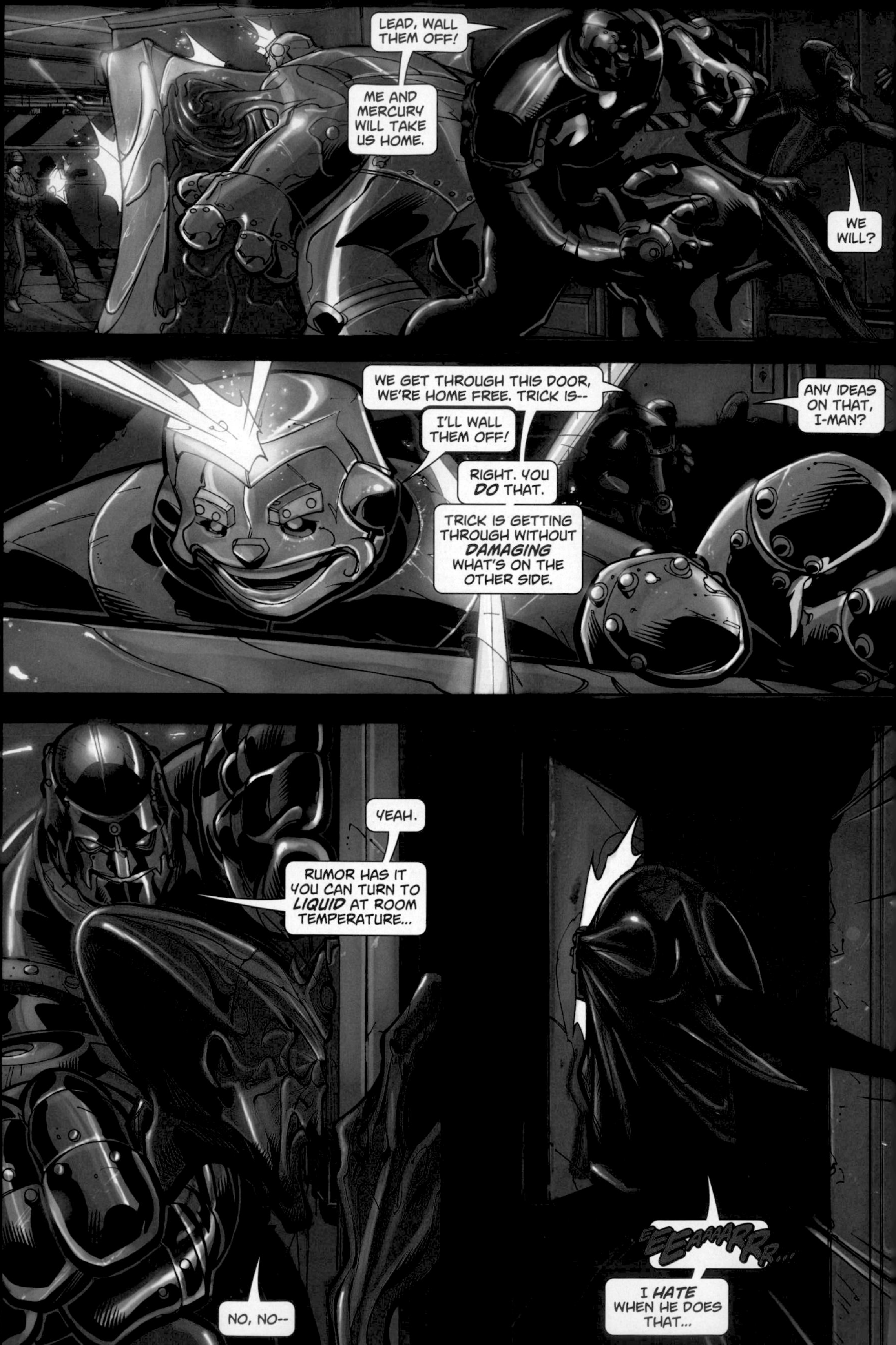
LEAD, WALL THEM OFF!
ME AND MERCURY WILL TAKE US HOME.
WE WILL?
WE GET THROUGH THIS DOOR, WE'RE HOME FREE. TRICK IS--
I'LL WALL THEM OFF!
RIGHT. YOU *DO* THAT.
TRICK IS GETTING THROUGH WITHOUT *DAMAGING* WHAT'S ON THE OTHER SIDE.
ANY IDEAS ON THAT, I-MAN?
YEAH.
RUMOR HAS IT YOU CAN TURN TO *LIQUID* AT ROOM TEMPERATURE...
NO, NO--
EEEAAAARRR...
I *HATE* WHEN HE DOES THAT...

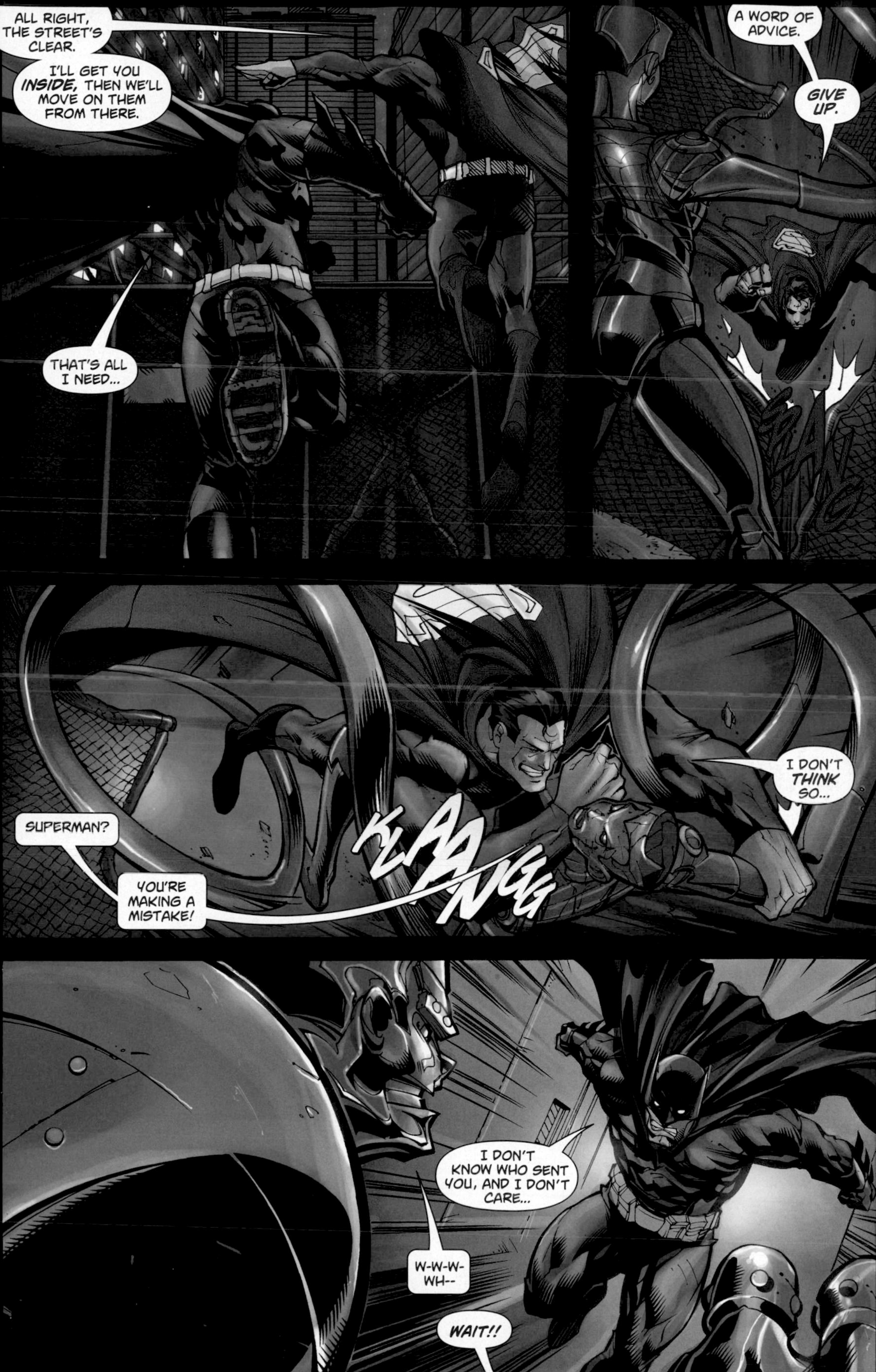
ALL RIGHT, THE STREET'S CLEAR.
I'LL GET YOU *INSIDE,* THEN WE'LL MOVE ON THEM FROM THERE.
THAT'S ALL I NEED...
A WORD OF ADVICE.
GIVE UP.
I DON'T *THINK* SO...
SUPERMAN?
YOU'RE MAKING A MISTAKE!
KLAANGG
I DON'T KNOW WHO SENT YOU, AND I DON'T CARE...
W-W-W-WH--
WAIT!!

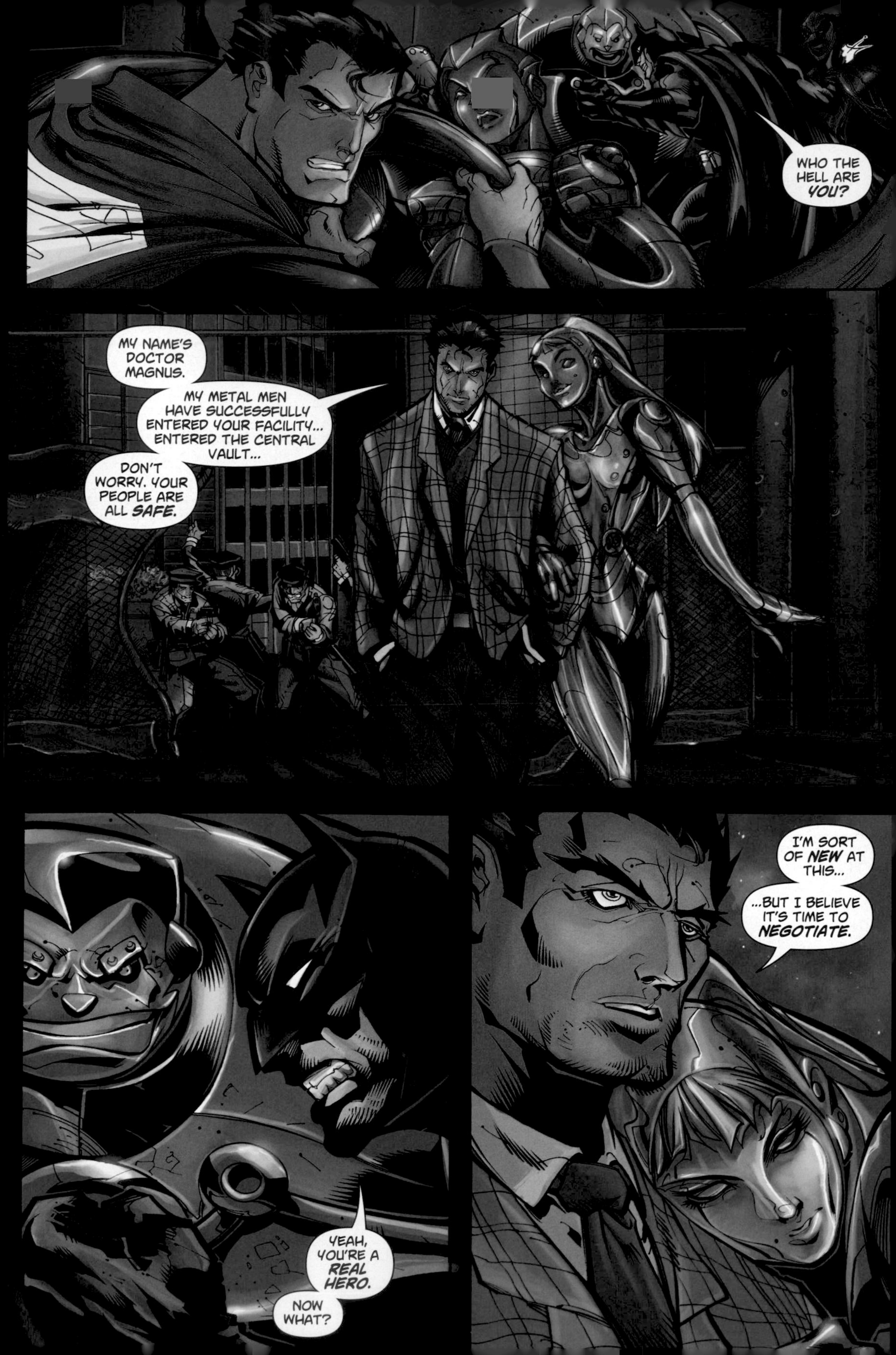
WHO THE HELL ARE YOU?
MY NAME'S DOCTOR MAGNUS.
MY METAL MEN HAVE SUCCESSFULLY ENTERED YOUR FACILITY... ENTERED THE CENTRAL VAULT...
DON'T WORRY. YOUR PEOPLE ARE ALL SAFE.
YEAH, YOU'RE A REAL HERO.
NOW WHAT?
I'M SORT OF NEW AT THIS...
...BUT I BELIEVE IT'S TIME TO NEGOTIATE.

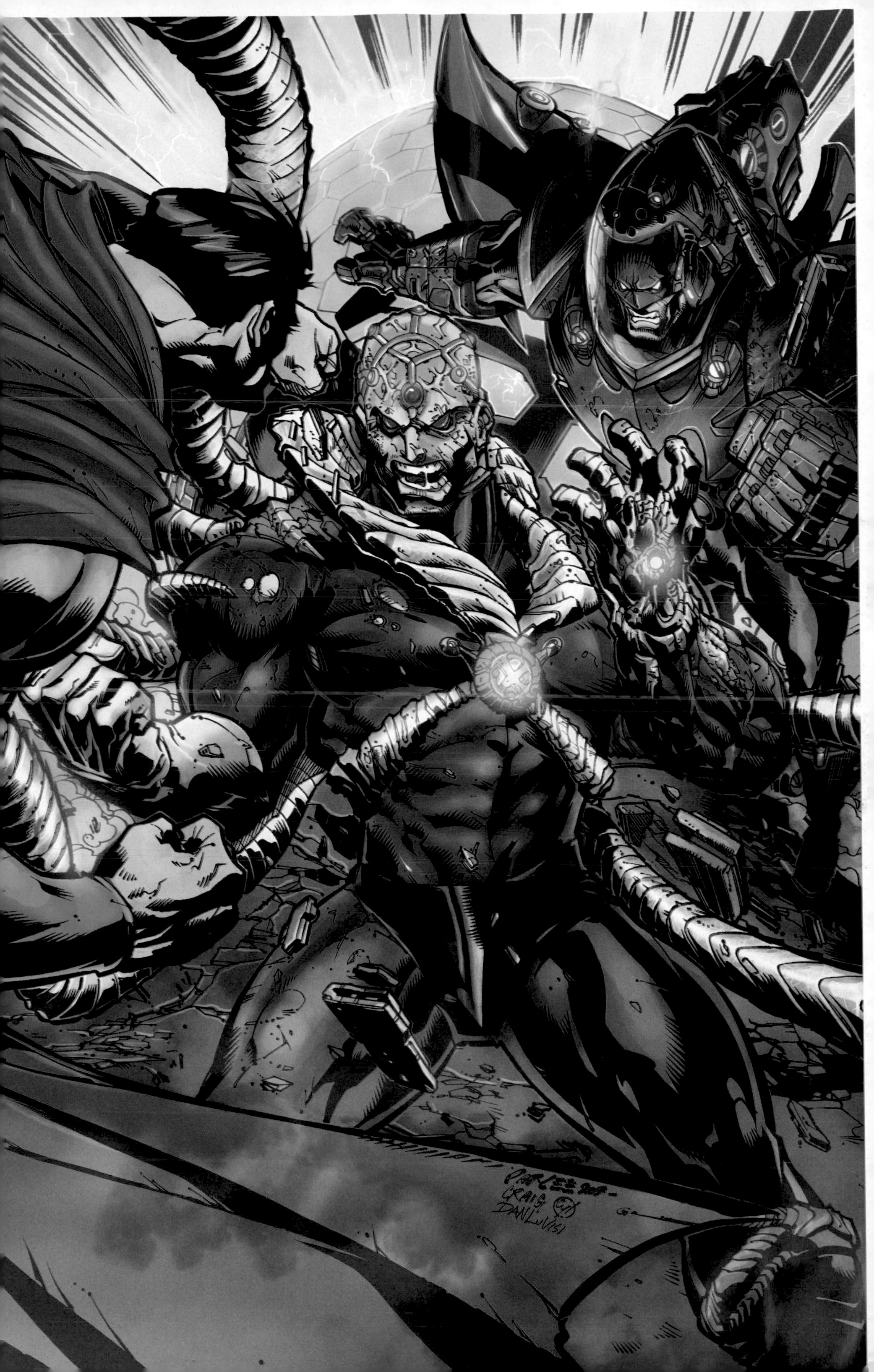

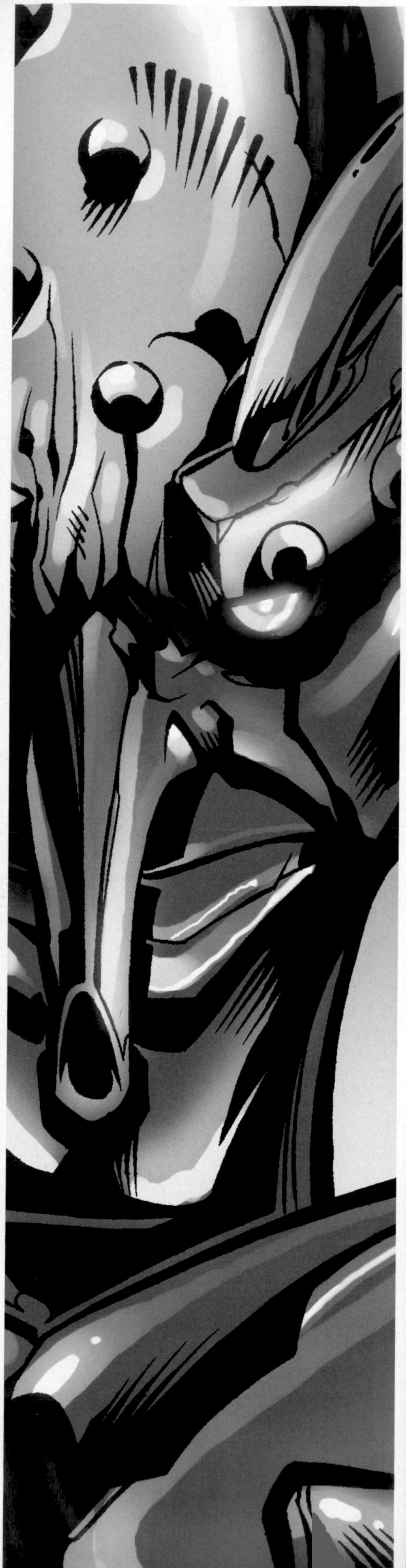

METAL MEN

PART TWO
B.I.

MARK VERHEIDEN
&
MARC GUGGENHEIM
WRITERS

PAT LEE
PENCILLER

CRAIG YEUNG
INKER

DANNY LUVISI
COLORIST

ROB LEIGH
LETTERER

PAT LEE
CRAIG YEUNG
&
DANNY LUVISI
COVER

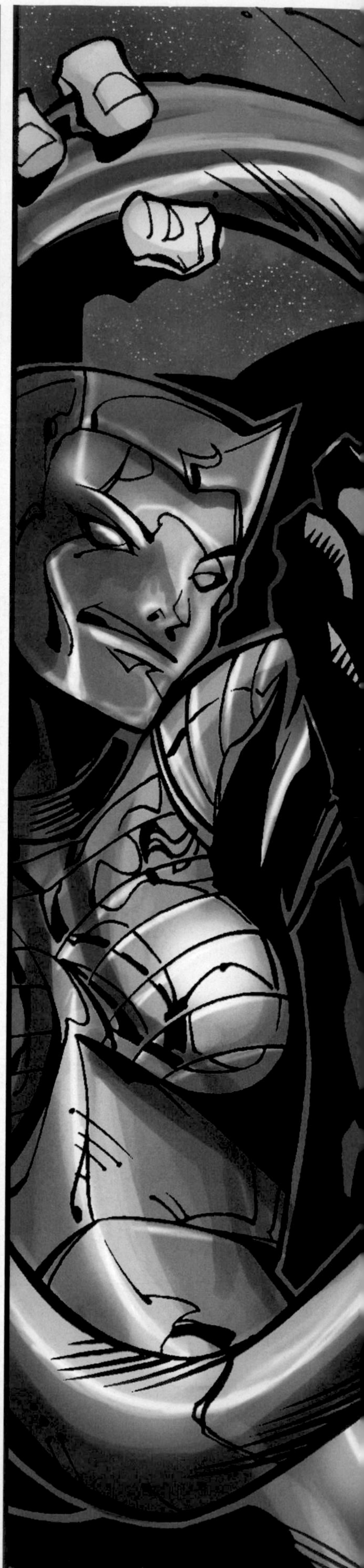

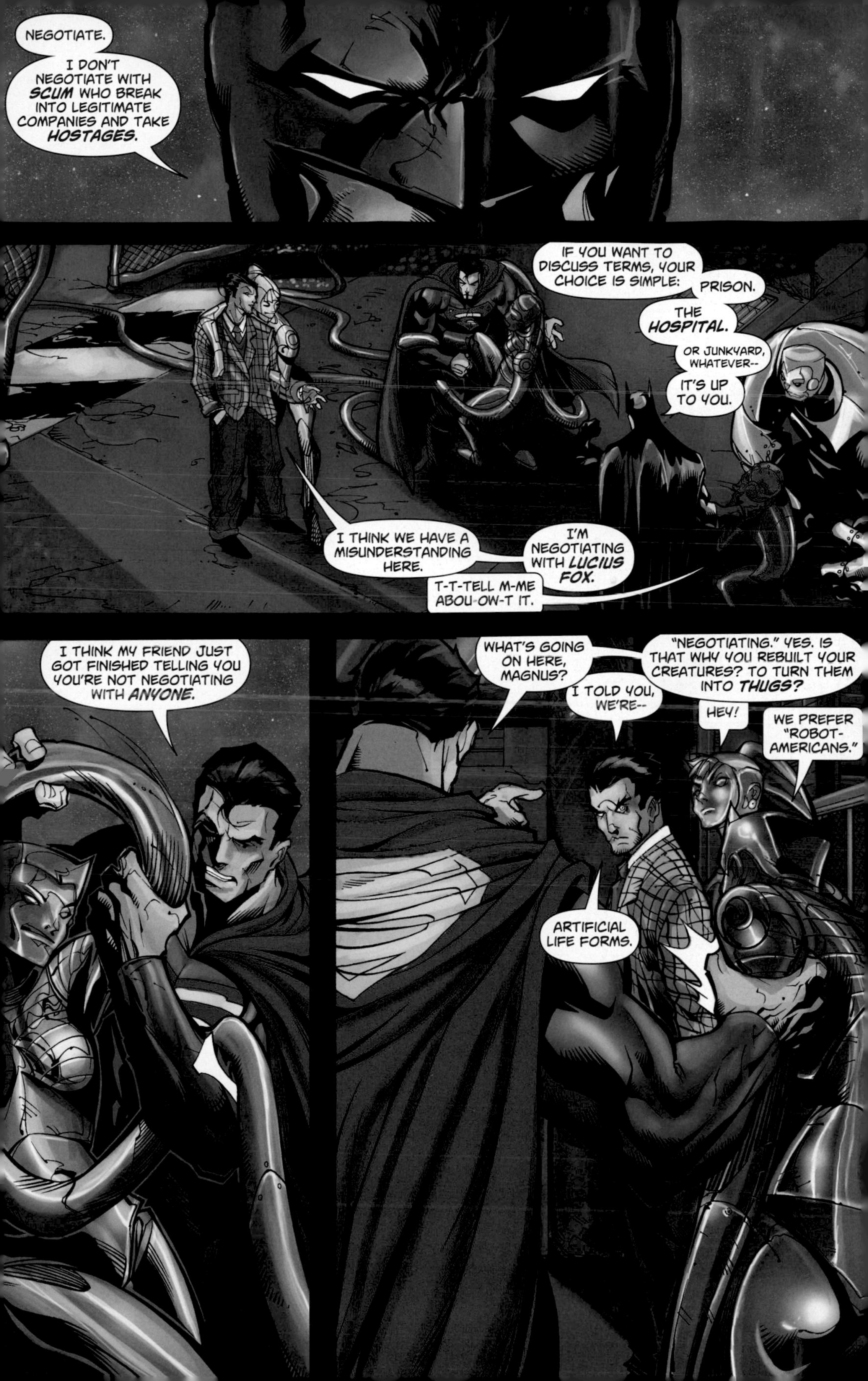
NEGOTIATE.
I DON'T NEGOTIATE WITH SCUM WHO BREAK INTO LEGITIMATE COMPANIES AND TAKE HOSTAGES.
IF YOU WANT TO DISCUSS TERMS, YOUR CHOICE IS SIMPLE:
PRISON.
THE HOSPITAL.
OR JUNKYARD, WHATEVER--
IT'S UP TO YOU.
I THINK WE HAVE A MISUNDERSTANDING HERE.
I'M NEGOTIATING WITH LUCIUS FOX.
T-T-TELL M-ME ABOU-OW-T IT.
I THINK MY FRIEND JUST GOT FINISHED TELLING YOU YOU'RE NOT NEGOTIATING WITH ANYONE.
WHAT'S GOING ON HERE, MAGNUS?
I TOLD YOU, WE'RE--
"NEGOTIATING." YES. IS THAT WHY YOU REBUILT YOUR CREATURES? TO TURN THEM INTO THUGS?
HEY!
WE PREFER "ROBOT-AMERICANS."
ARTIFICIAL LIFE FORMS.

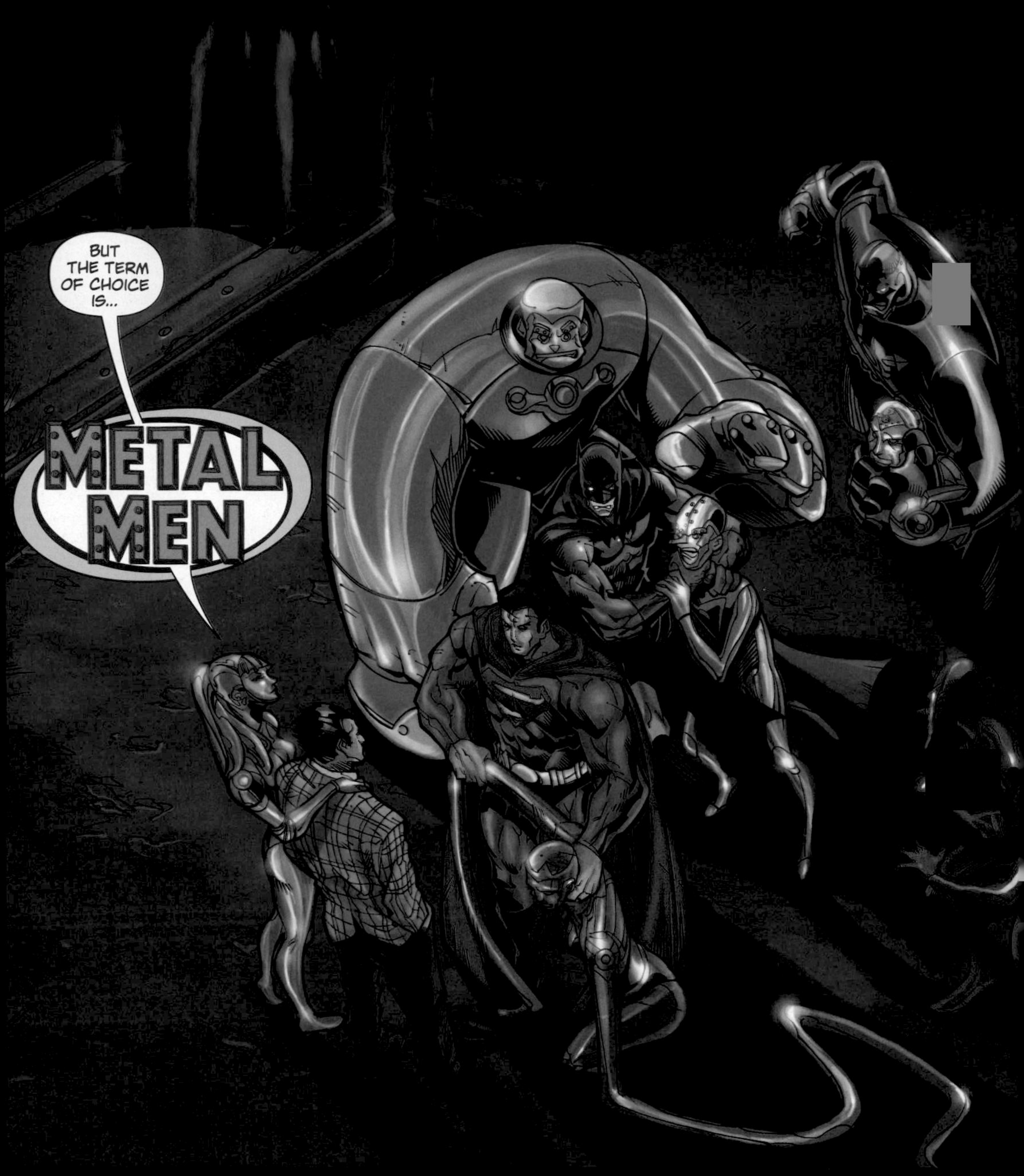
BUT THE TERM OF CHOICE IS...
METAL MEN
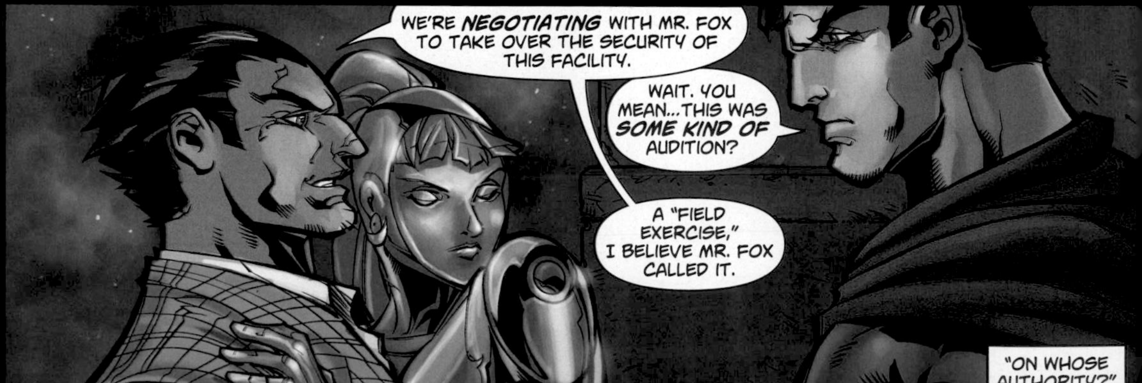
WE'RE *NEGOTIATING* WITH MR. FOX TO TAKE OVER THE SECURITY OF THIS FACILITY.
WAIT. YOU MEAN...THIS WAS *SOME KIND OF* AUDITION?
A "FIELD EXERCISE," I BELIEVE MR. FOX CALLED IT.
"ON WHOSE AUTHORITY?"

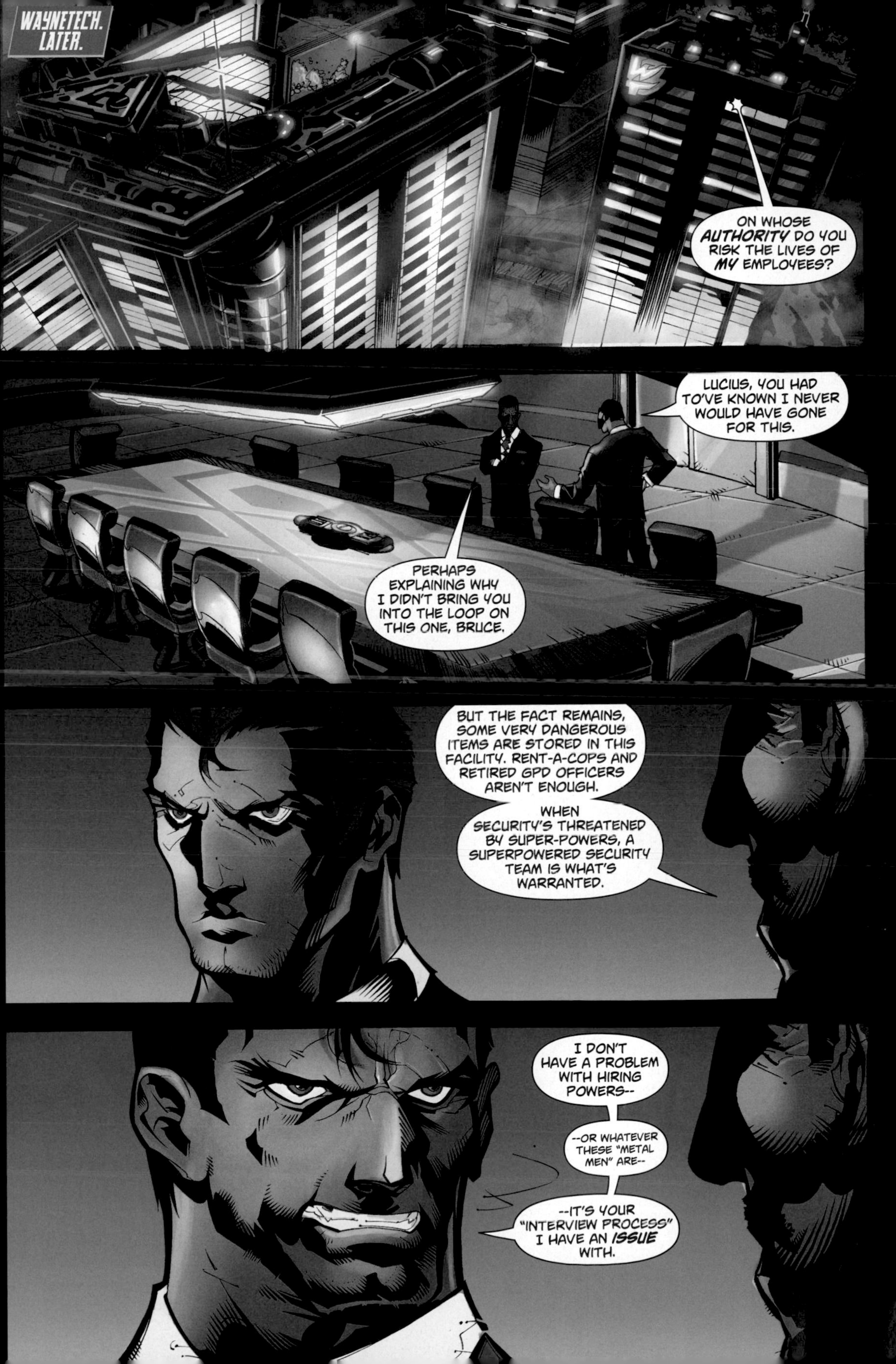
WAYNETECH. LATER.
ON WHOSE AUTHORITY DO YOU RISK THE LIVES OF MY EMPLOYEES?
LUCIUS, YOU HAD TO'VE KNOWN I NEVER WOULD HAVE GONE FOR THIS.
PERHAPS EXPLAINING WHY I DIDN'T BRING YOU INTO THE LOOP ON THIS ONE, BRUCE.
BUT THE FACT REMAINS, SOME VERY DANGEROUS ITEMS ARE STORED IN THIS FACILITY. RENT-A-COPS AND RETIRED GPD OFFICERS AREN'T ENOUGH.
WHEN SECURITY'S THREATENED BY SUPER-POWERS, A SUPERPOWERED SECURITY TEAM IS WHAT'S WARRANTED.
I DON'T HAVE A PROBLEM WITH HIRING POWERS--
--OR WHATEVER THESE "METAL MEN" ARE--
--IT'S YOUR "INTERVIEW PROCESS" I HAVE AN ISSUE WITH.

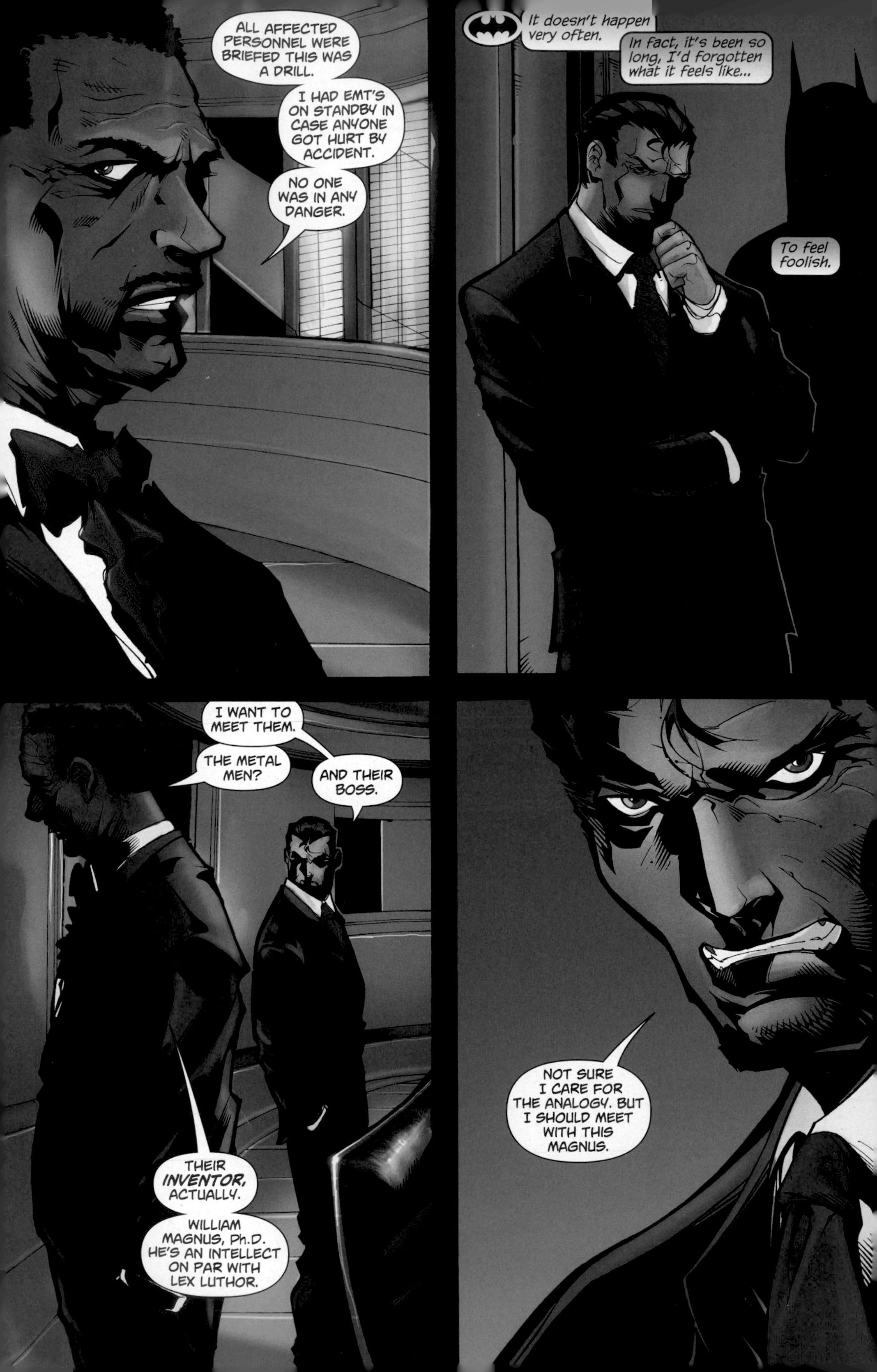
ALL AFFECTED PERSONNEL WERE BRIEFED THIS WAS A DRILL.
I HAD EMT'S ON STANDBY IN CASE ANYONE GOT HURT BY ACCIDENT.
NO ONE WAS IN ANY DANGER.
It doesn't happen very often.
In fact, it's been so long, I'd forgotten what it feels like...
To feel foolish.
I WANT TO MEET THEM.
THE METAL MEN?
AND THEIR BOSS.
THEIR *INVENTOR,* ACTUALLY.
WILLIAM MAGNUS, Ph.D. HE'S AN INTELLECT ON PAR WITH LEX LUTHOR.
NOT SURE I CARE FOR THE ANALOGY. BUT I SHOULD MEET WITH THIS MAGNUS.

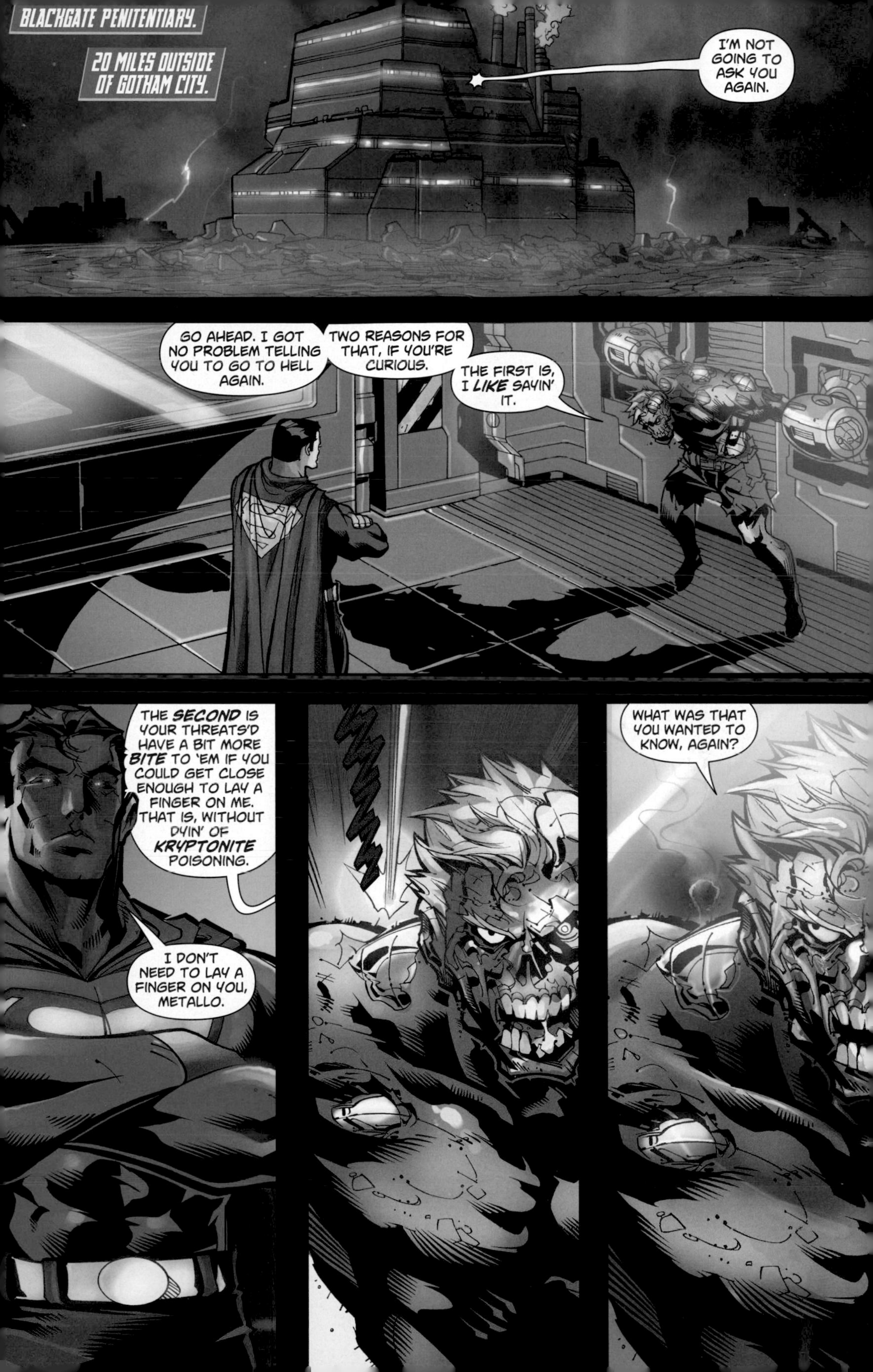
BLACKGATE PENITENTIARY.
20 MILES OUTSIDE OF GOTHAM CITY.
I'M NOT GOING TO ASK YOU AGAIN.
GO AHEAD. I GOT NO PROBLEM TELLING YOU TO GO TO HELL AGAIN.
TWO REASONS FOR THAT, IF YOU'RE CURIOUS.
THE FIRST IS, I LIKE SAYIN' IT.
THE SECOND IS YOUR THREATS'D HAVE A BIT MORE BITE TO 'EM IF YOU COULD GET CLOSE ENOUGH TO LAY A FINGER ON ME. THAT IS, WITHOUT DYIN' OF KRYPTONITE POISONING.
I DON'T NEED TO LAY A FINGER ON YOU, METALLO.
WHAT WAS THAT YOU WANTED TO KNOW, AGAIN?

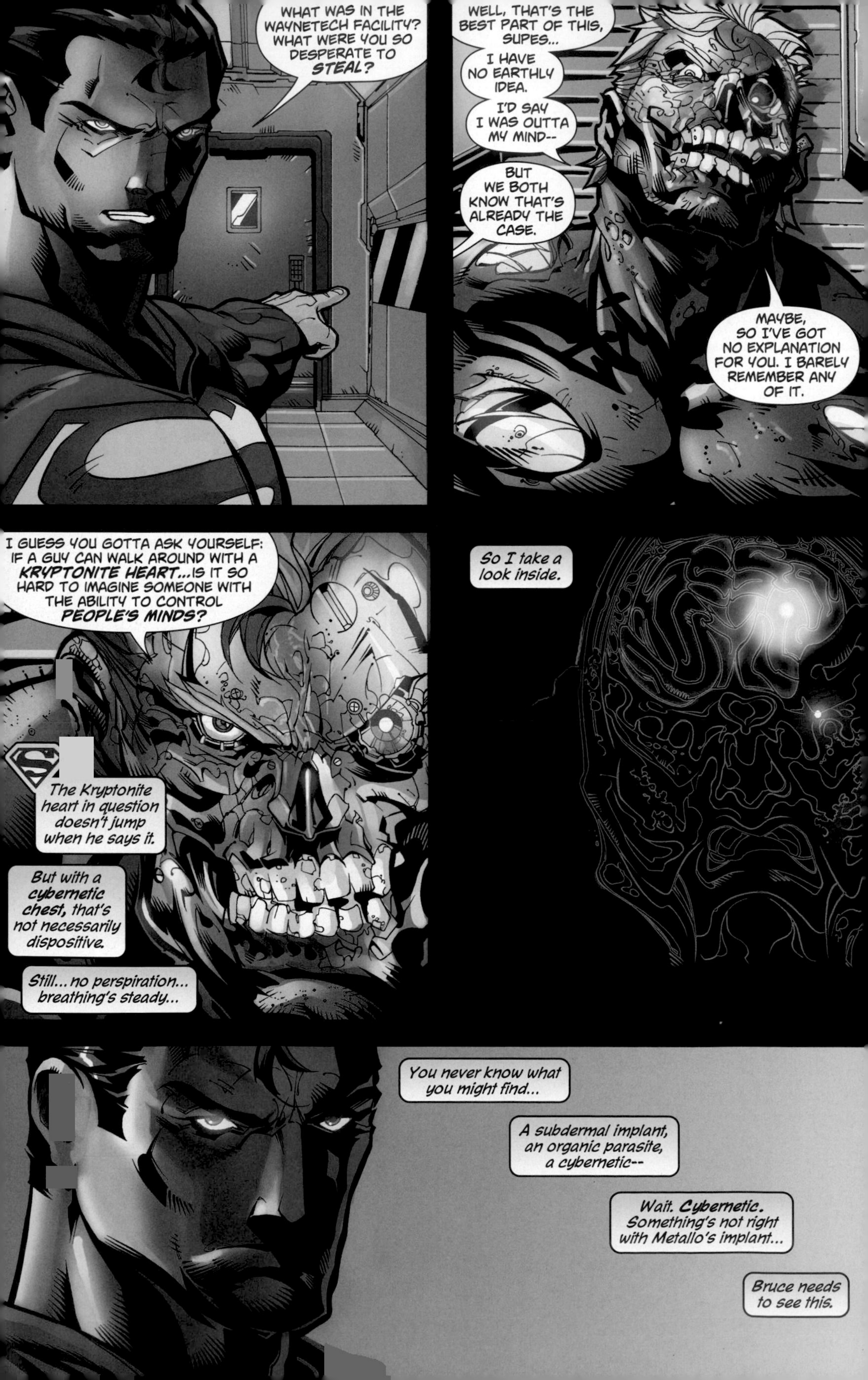
WHAT WAS IN THE WAYNETECH FACILITY? WHAT WERE YOU SO DESPERATE TO STEAL?
WELL, THAT'S THE BEST PART OF THIS, SUPES...
I HAVE NO EARTHLY IDEA.
I'D SAY I WAS OUTTA MY MIND--
BUT WE BOTH KNOW THAT'S ALREADY THE CASE.
MAYBE, SO I'VE GOT NO EXPLANATION FOR YOU. I BARELY REMEMBER ANY OF IT.
I GUESS YOU GOTTA ASK YOURSELF: IF A GUY CAN WALK AROUND WITH A KRYPTONITE HEART...IS IT SO HARD TO IMAGINE SOMEONE WITH THE ABILITY TO CONTROL PEOPLE'S MINDS?
The Kryptonite heart in question doesn't jump when he says it.
But with a cybernetic chest, that's not necessarily dispositive.
Still... no perspiration... breathing's steady...
So I take a look inside.
You never know what you might find...
A subdermal implant, an organic parasite, a cybernetic--
Wait. Cybernetic. Something's not right with Metallo's implant...
Bruce needs to see this.

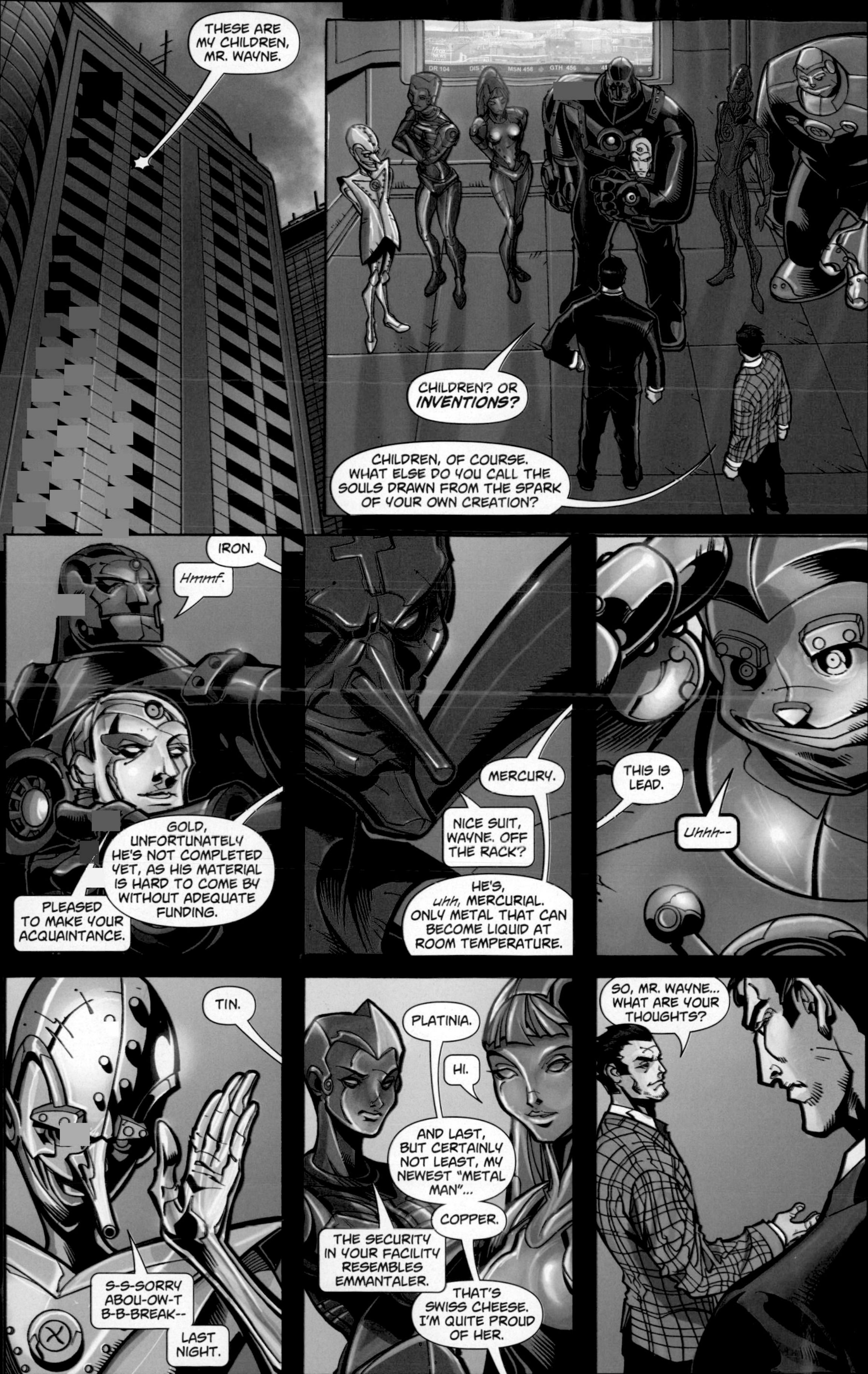
THESE ARE MY CHILDREN, MR. WAYNE.
CHILDREN? OR *INVENTIONS?*
CHILDREN, OF COURSE. WHAT ELSE DO YOU CALL THE SOULS DRAWN FROM THE SPARK OF YOUR OWN CREATION?
IRON.
Hmmf.
GOLD, UNFORTUNATELY HE'S NOT COMPLETED YET, AS HIS MATERIAL IS HARD TO COME BY WITHOUT ADEQUATE FUNDING.
PLEASED TO MAKE YOUR ACQUAINTANCE.
MERCURY.
NICE SUIT, WAYNE. OFF THE RACK?
HE'S, *uhh*, MERCURIAL. ONLY METAL THAT CAN BECOME LIQUID AT ROOM TEMPERATURE.
THIS IS LEAD.
Uhhh--
TIN.
S-S-SORRY ABOU-OW-T B-B-BREAK--
LAST NIGHT.
PLATINIA.
HI.
AND LAST, BUT CERTAINLY NOT LEAST, MY NEWEST "METAL MAN"...
COPPER.
THE SECURITY IN YOUR FACILITY RESEMBLES EMMANTALER.
THAT'S SWISS CHEESE. I'M QUITE PROUD OF HER.
SO, MR. WAYNE... WHAT ARE YOUR THOUGHTS?

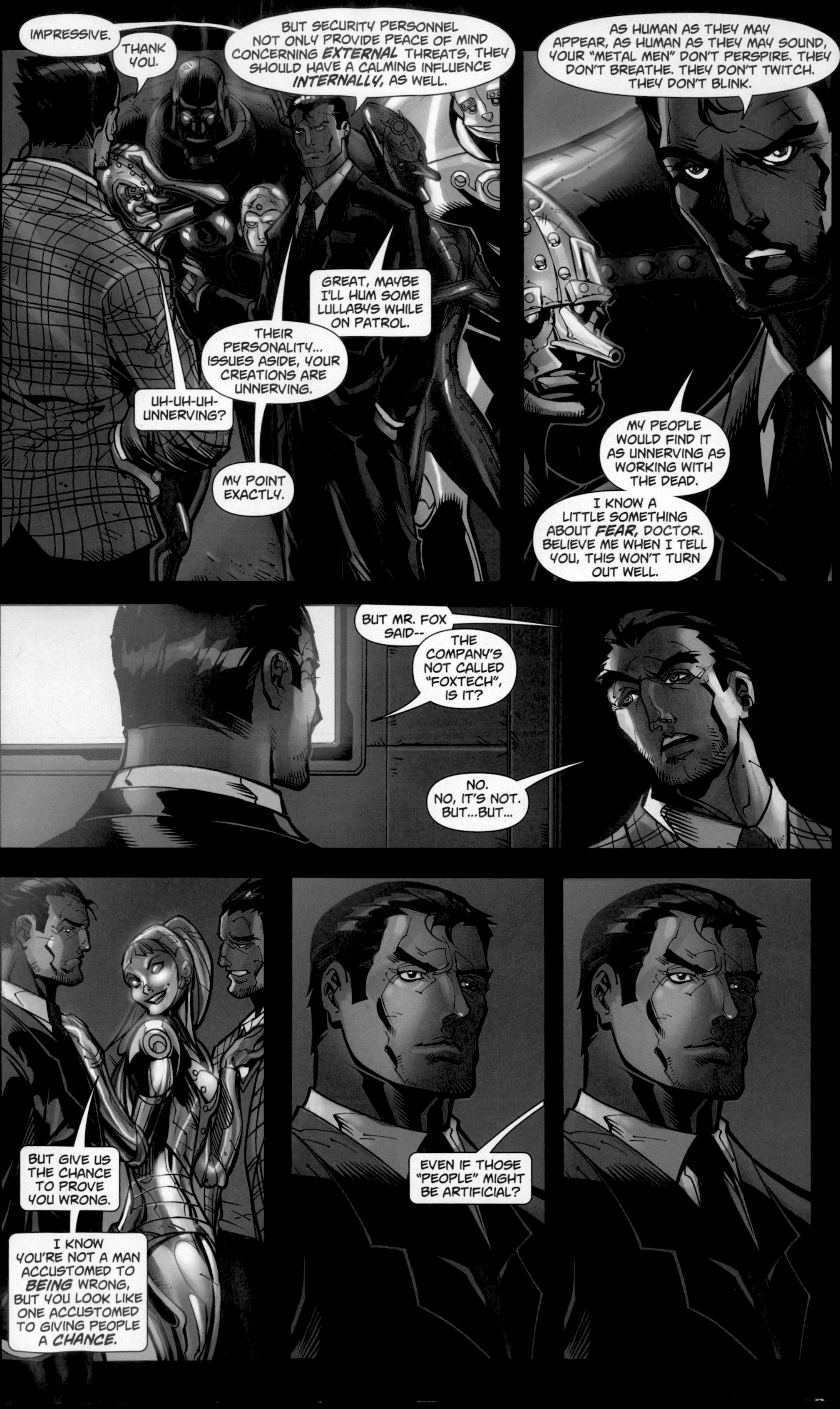
IMPRESSIVE.
THANK YOU.
BUT SECURITY PERSONNEL NOT ONLY PROVIDE PEACE OF MIND CONCERNING EXTERNAL THREATS, THEY SHOULD HAVE A CALMING INFLUENCE INTERNALLY, AS WELL.
GREAT, MAYBE I'LL HUM SOME LULLABYS WHILE ON PATROL.
THEIR PERSONALITY... ISSUES ASIDE, YOUR CREATIONS ARE UNNERVING.
UH-UH-UH-UNNERVING?
MY POINT EXACTLY.
AS HUMAN AS THEY MAY APPEAR, AS HUMAN AS THEY MAY SOUND, YOUR "METAL MEN" DON'T PERSPIRE. THEY DON'T BREATHE. THEY DON'T TWITCH. THEY DON'T BLINK.
MY PEOPLE WOULD FIND IT AS UNNERVING AS WORKING WITH THE DEAD.
I KNOW A LITTLE SOMETHING ABOUT FEAR, DOCTOR. BELIEVE ME WHEN I TELL YOU, THIS WON'T TURN OUT WELL.
BUT MR. FOX SAID--
THE COMPANY'S NOT CALLED "FOXTECH", IS IT?
NO. NO, IT'S NOT. BUT...BUT...
BUT GIVE US THE CHANCE TO PROVE YOU WRONG.
I KNOW YOU'RE NOT A MAN ACCUSTOMED TO BEING WRONG, BUT YOU LOOK LIKE ONE ACCUSTOMED TO GIVING PEOPLE A CHANCE.
EVEN IF THOSE "PEOPLE" MIGHT BE ARTIFICIAL?

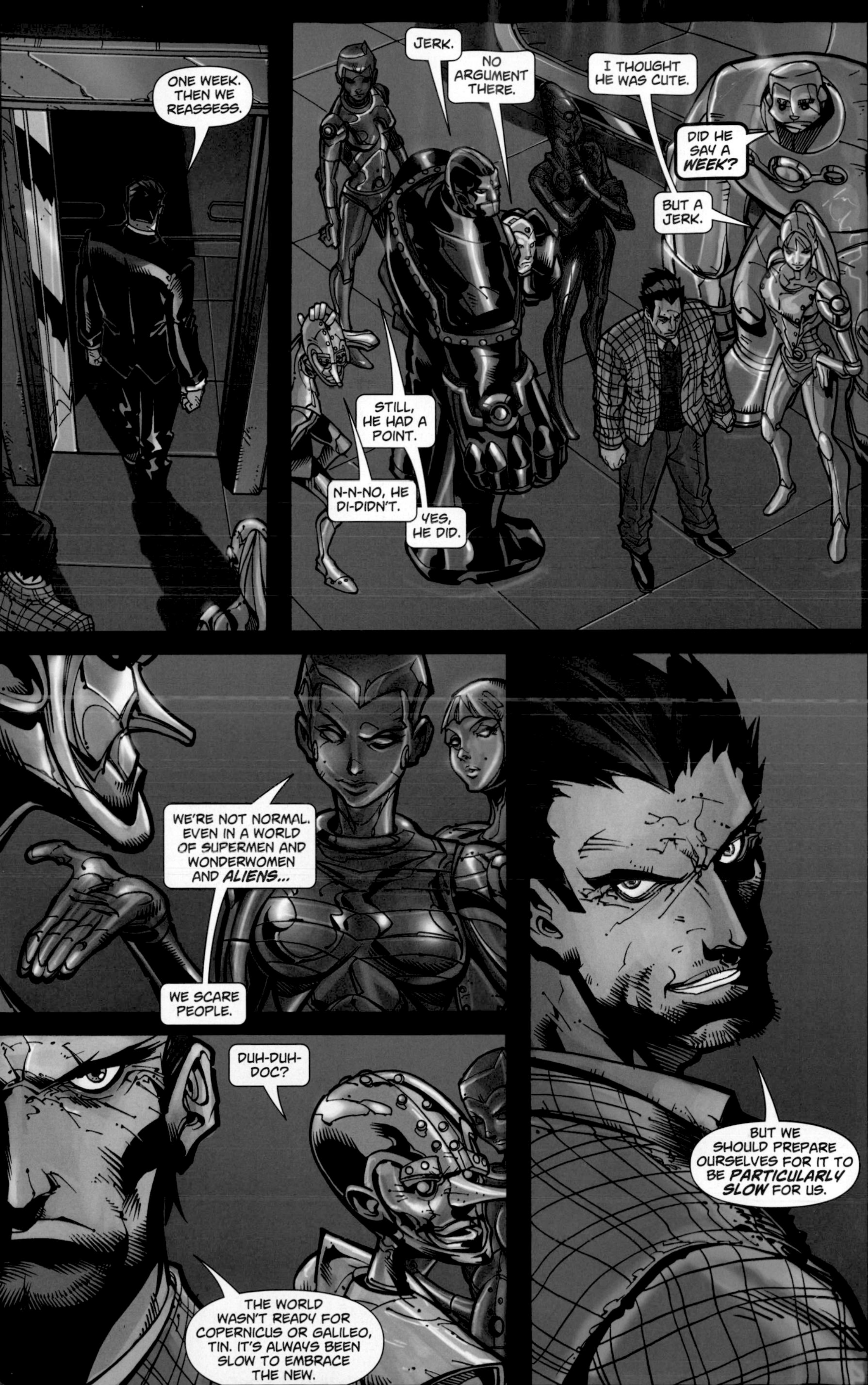
ONE WEEK. THEN WE REASSESS.
JERK.
NO ARGUMENT THERE.
I THOUGHT HE WAS CUTE.
DID HE SAY A *WEEK?*
BUT A JERK.
STILL, HE HAD A POINT.
N-N-NO, HE DI-DIDN'T.
YES, HE DID.
WE'RE NOT NORMAL. EVEN IN A WORLD OF SUPERMEN AND WONDERWOMEN AND *ALIENS...*
WE SCARE PEOPLE.
BUT WE SHOULD PREPARE OURSELVES FOR IT TO BE *PARTICULARLY SLOW* FOR US.
DUH-DUH-DOC?
THE WORLD WASN'T READY FOR COPERNICUS OR GALILEO, TIN. IT'S ALWAYS BEEN SLOW TO EMBRACE THE NEW.

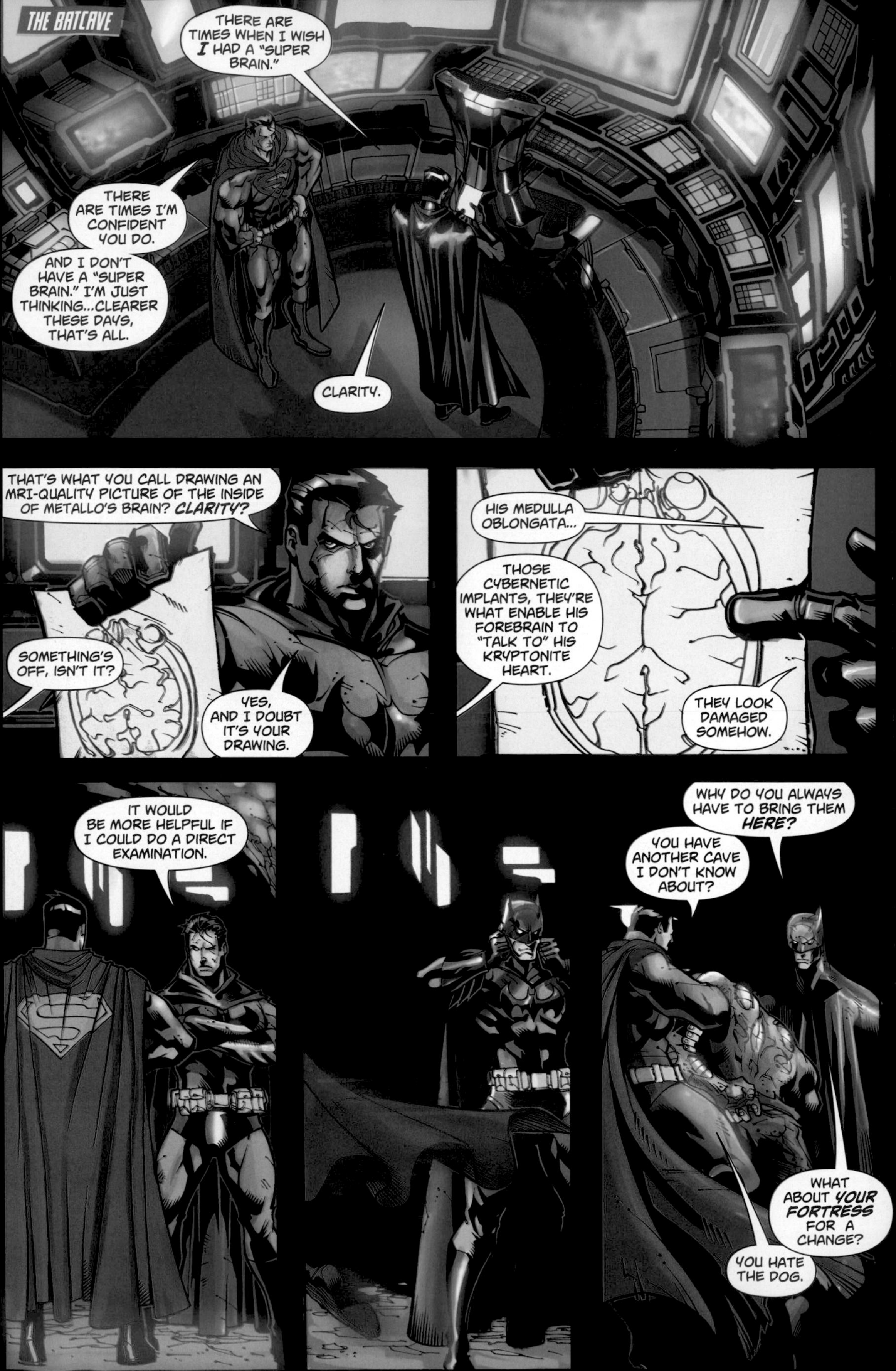
THE BATCAVE
THERE ARE TIMES WHEN I WISH I HAD A "SUPER BRAIN."
THERE ARE TIMES I'M CONFIDENT YOU DO.
AND I DON'T HAVE A "SUPER BRAIN." I'M JUST THINKING...CLEARER THESE DAYS, THAT'S ALL.
CLARITY.
THAT'S WHAT YOU CALL DRAWING AN MRI-QUALITY PICTURE OF THE INSIDE OF METALLO'S BRAIN? CLARITY?
SOMETHING'S OFF, ISN'T IT?
YES, AND I DOUBT IT'S YOUR DRAWING.
HIS MEDULLA OBLONGATA...
THOSE CYBERNETIC IMPLANTS, THEY'RE WHAT ENABLE HIS FOREBRAIN TO "TALK TO" HIS KRYPTONITE HEART.
THEY LOOK DAMAGED SOMEHOW.
IT WOULD BE MORE HELPFUL IF I COULD DO A DIRECT EXAMINATION.
WHY DO YOU ALWAYS HAVE TO BRING THEM HERE?
YOU HAVE ANOTHER CAVE I DON'T KNOW ABOUT?
WHAT ABOUT YOUR FORTRESS FOR A CHANGE?
YOU HATE THE DOG.

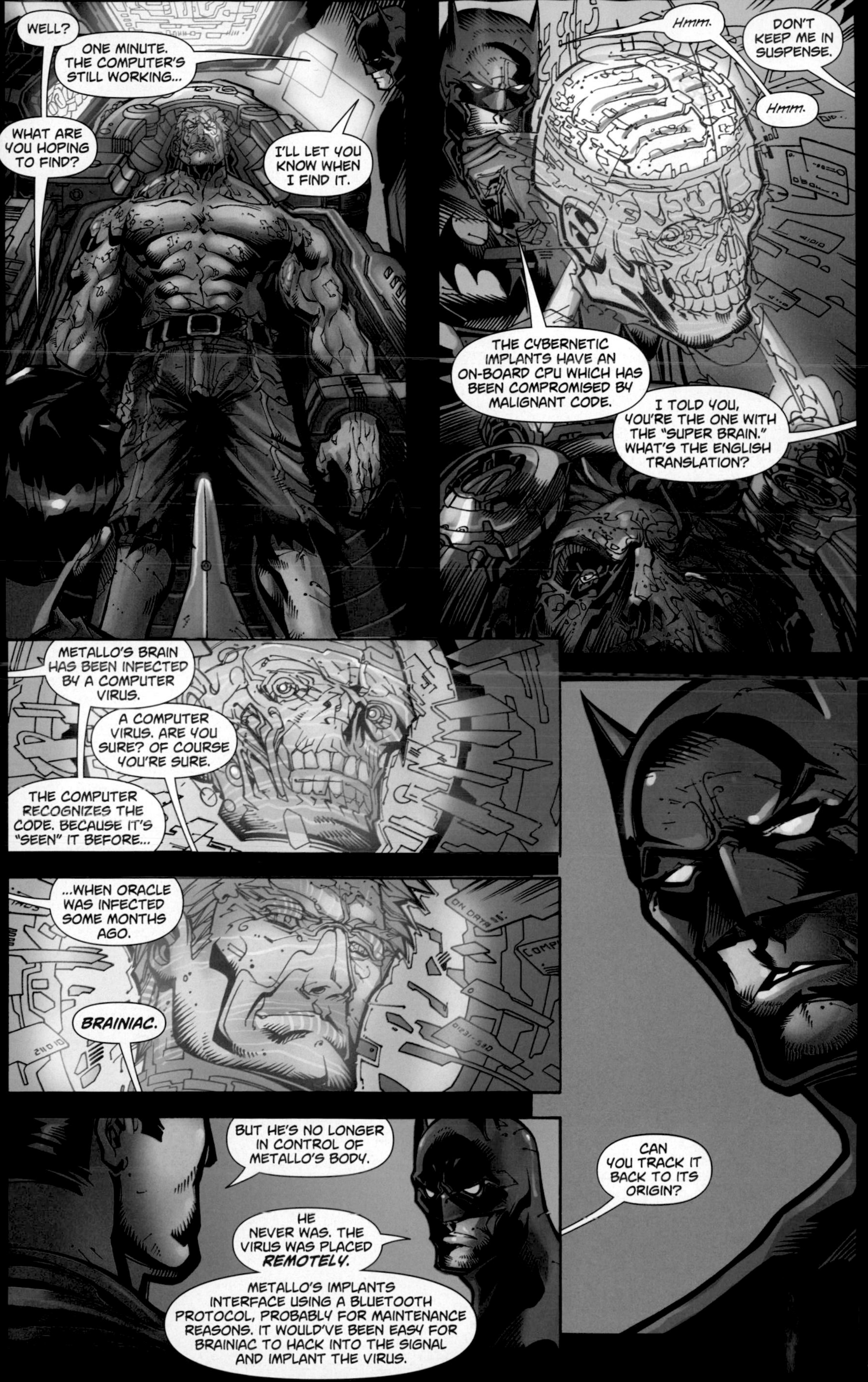

WELL?
ONE MINUTE. THE COMPUTER'S STILL WORKING...
WHAT ARE YOU HOPING TO FIND?
I'LL LET YOU KNOW WHEN I FIND IT.
Hmm.
DON'T KEEP ME IN SUSPENSE.
Hmm.
THE CYBERNETIC IMPLANTS HAVE AN ON-BOARD CPU WHICH HAS BEEN COMPROMISED BY MALIGNANT CODE.
I TOLD YOU, YOU'RE THE ONE WITH THE "SUPER BRAIN." WHAT'S THE ENGLISH TRANSLATION?
METALLO'S BRAIN HAS BEEN INFECTED BY A COMPUTER VIRUS.
A COMPUTER VIRUS. ARE YOU SURE? OF COURSE YOU'RE SURE.
THE COMPUTER RECOGNIZES THE CODE. BECAUSE IT'S "SEEN" IT BEFORE...
...WHEN ORACLE WAS INFECTED SOME MONTHS AGO.
BRAINIAC.
BUT HE'S NO LONGER IN CONTROL OF METALLO'S BODY.
CAN YOU TRACK IT BACK TO ITS ORIGIN?
HE NEVER WAS. THE VIRUS WAS PLACED REMOTELY.
METALLO'S IMPLANTS INTERFACE USING A BLUETOOTH PROTOCOL, PROBABLY FOR MAINTENANCE REASONS. IT WOULD'VE BEEN EASY FOR BRAINIAC TO HACK INTO THE SIGNAL AND IMPLANT THE VIRUS.

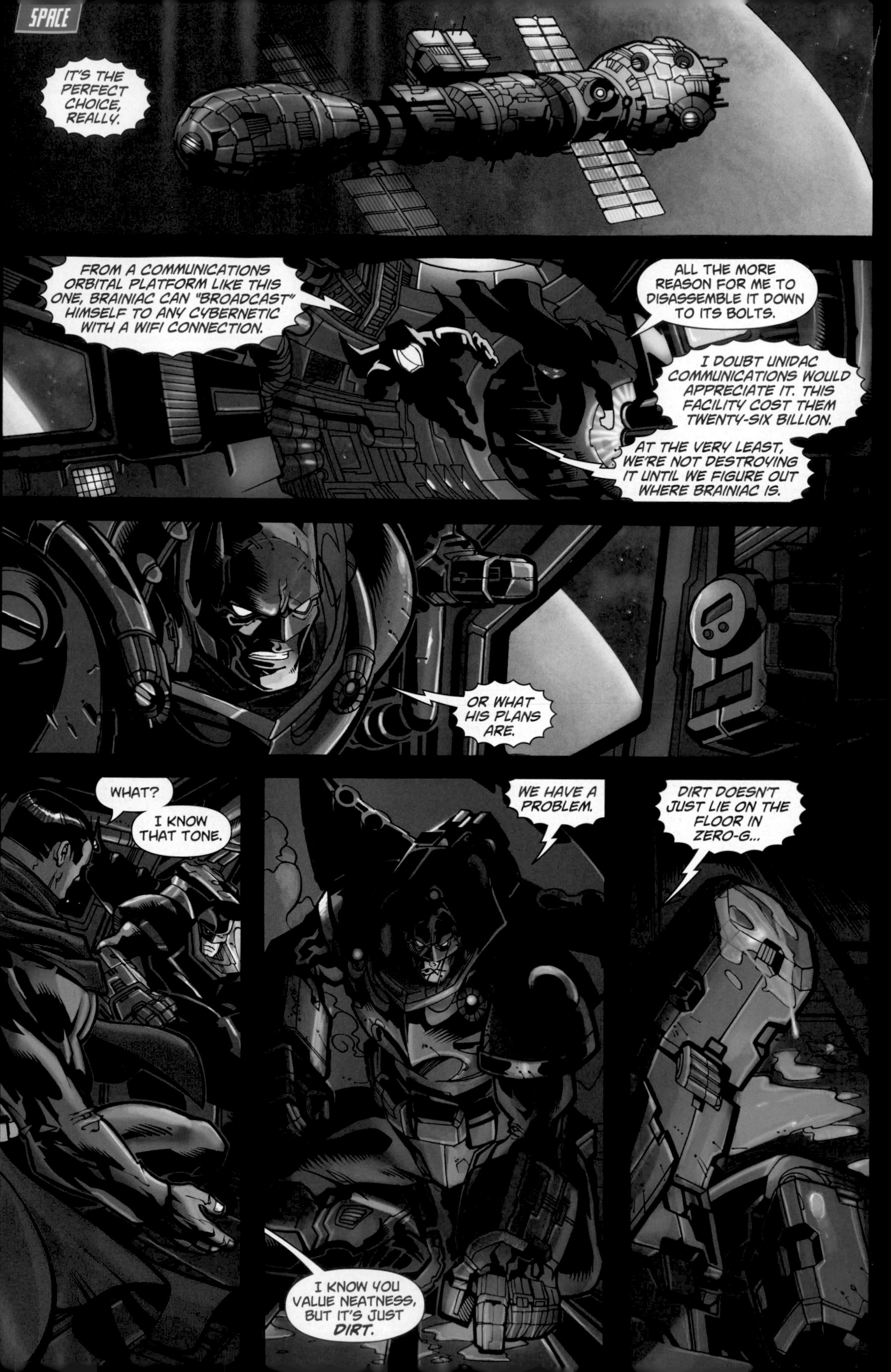
SPACE
IT'S THE PERFECT CHOICE, REALLY.
FROM A COMMUNICATIONS ORBITAL PLATFORM LIKE THIS ONE, BRAINIAC CAN "BROADCAST" HIMSELF TO ANY CYBERNETIC WITH A WIFI CONNECTION.
ALL THE MORE REASON FOR ME TO DISASSEMBLE IT DOWN TO ITS BOLTS.
I DOUBT UNIDAC COMMUNICATIONS WOULD APPRECIATE IT. THIS FACILITY COST THEM TWENTY-SIX BILLION.
AT THE VERY LEAST, WE'RE NOT DESTROYING IT UNTIL WE FIGURE OUT WHERE BRAINIAC IS.
OR WHAT HIS PLANS ARE.
WHAT?
I KNOW THAT TONE.
WE HAVE A PROBLEM.
DIRT DOESN'T JUST LIE ON THE FLOOR IN ZERO-G...
I KNOW YOU VALUE NEATNESS, BUT IT'S JUST DIRT.

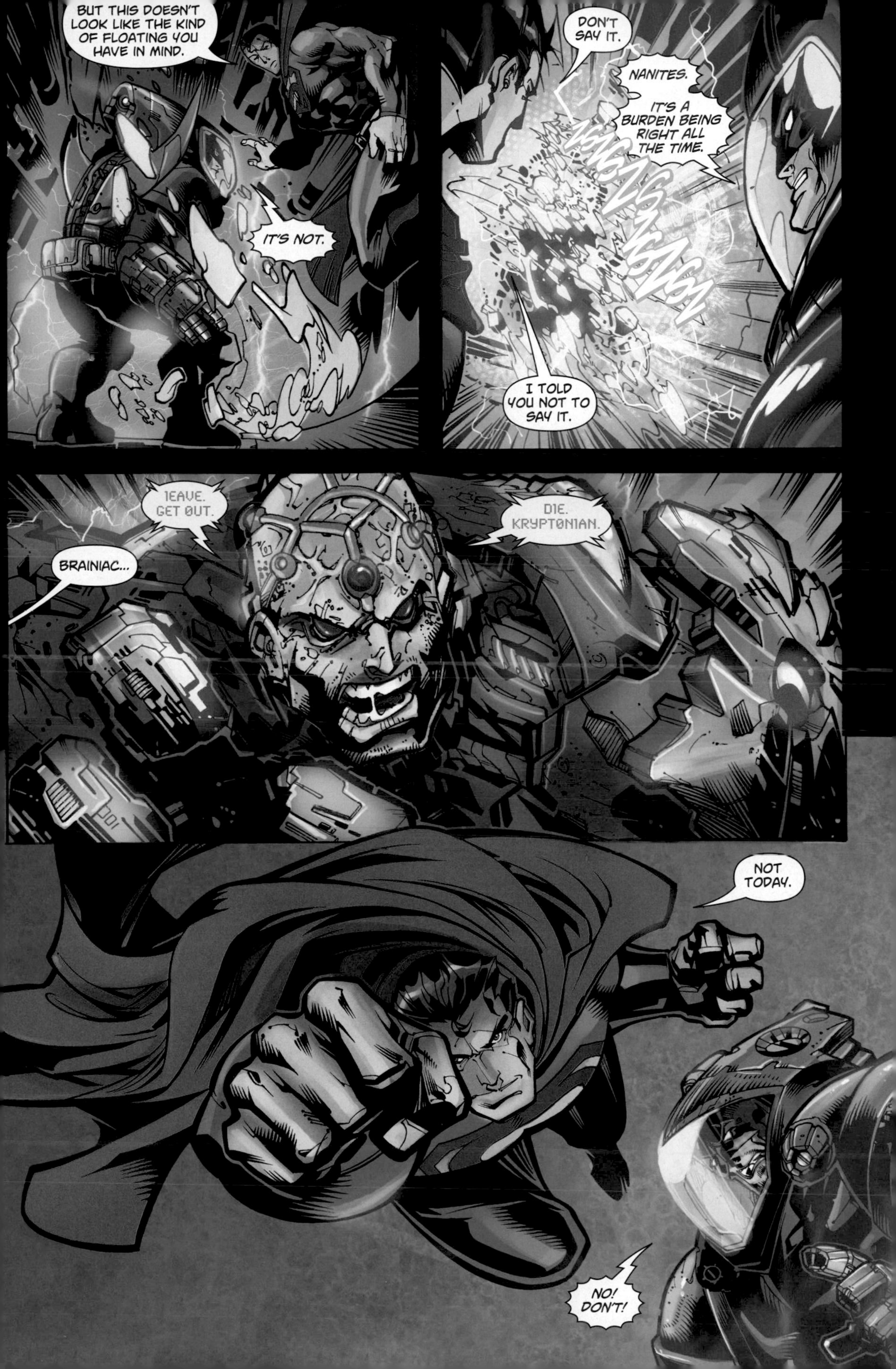
BUT THIS DOESN'T LOOK LIKE THE KIND OF FLOATING YOU HAVE IN MIND.
IT'S NOT.
DON'T SAY IT.
NANITES.
IT'S A BURDEN BEING RIGHT ALL THE TIME.
I TOLD YOU NOT TO SAY IT.
BRAINIAC...
1EAVE. GET 0UT.
D1E. KRYPT0N1AN.
NOT TODAY.
NO! DON'T!

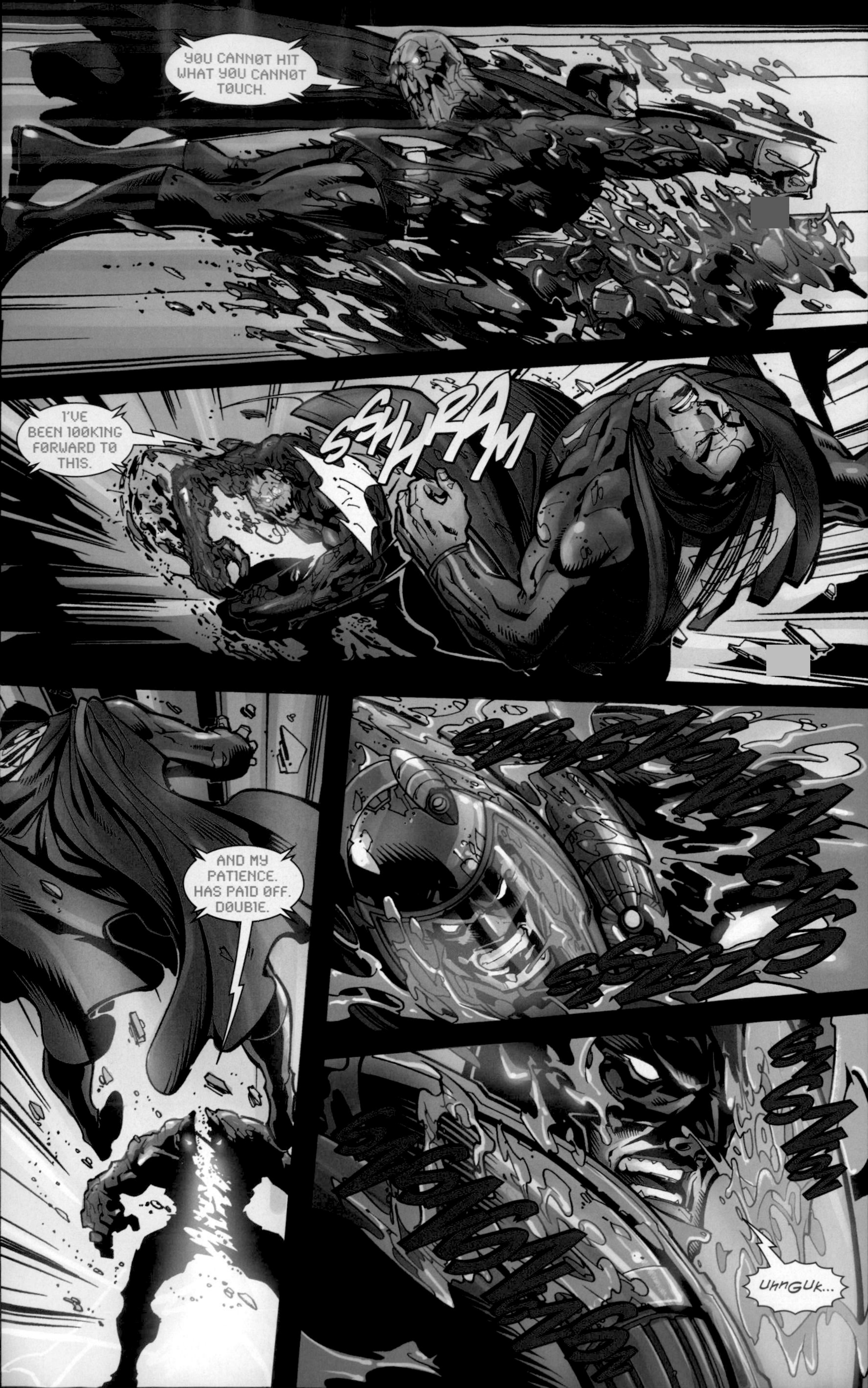

YOU CANNOT HIT WHAT YOU CANNOT TOUCH.
I'VE BEEN LOOKING FORWARD TO THIS.
AND MY PATIENCE. HAS PAID OFF. DOUBLE.
UhnGUk...

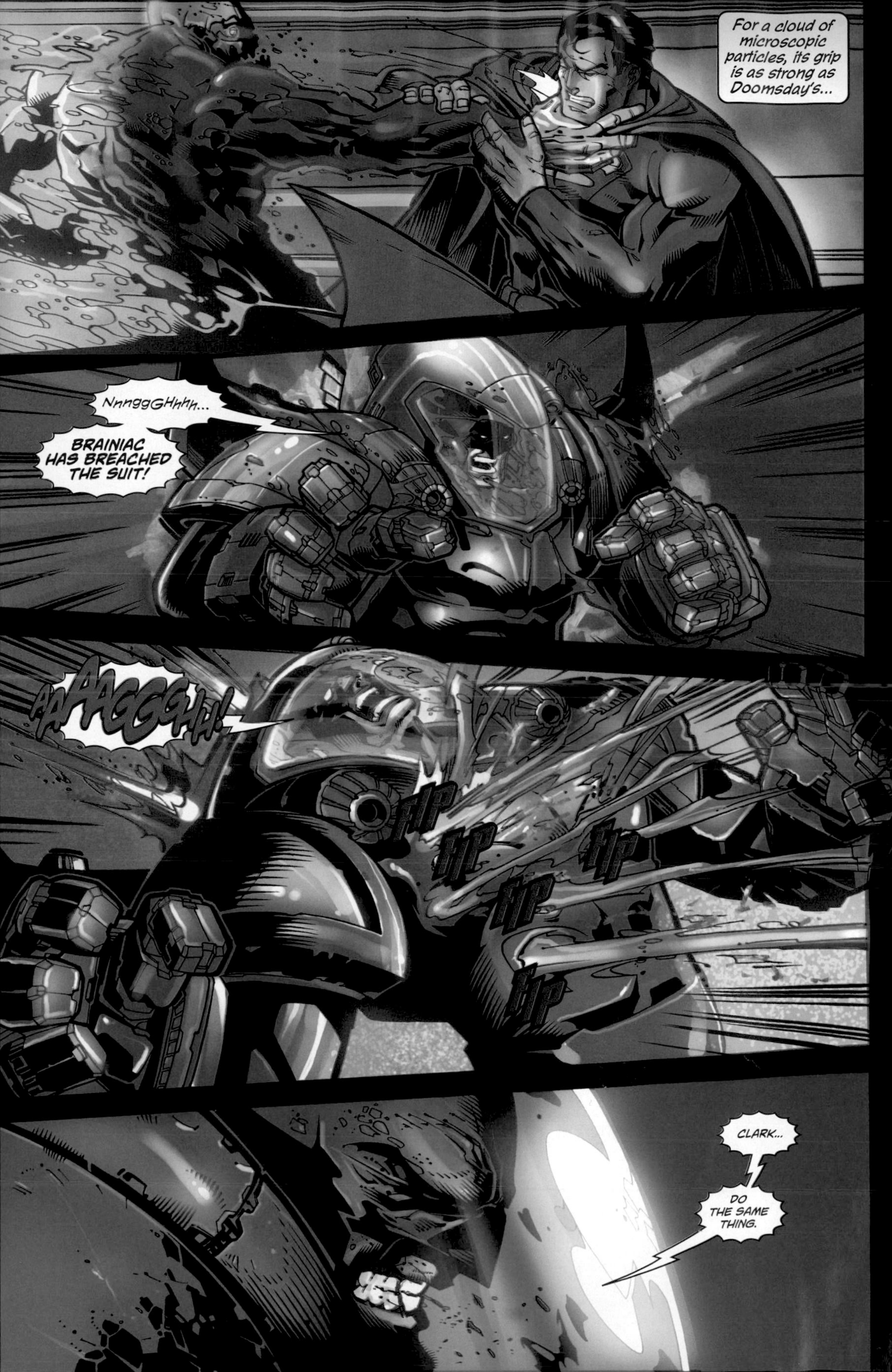

For a cloud of microscopic particles, its grip is as strong as Doomsday's...
NnnggGHhhh...
BRAINIAC HAS BREACHED THE SUIT!
AAAAGGGHH!
FFP
FFP
FFP
FFP
FFP
CLARK...
DO THE SAME THING.

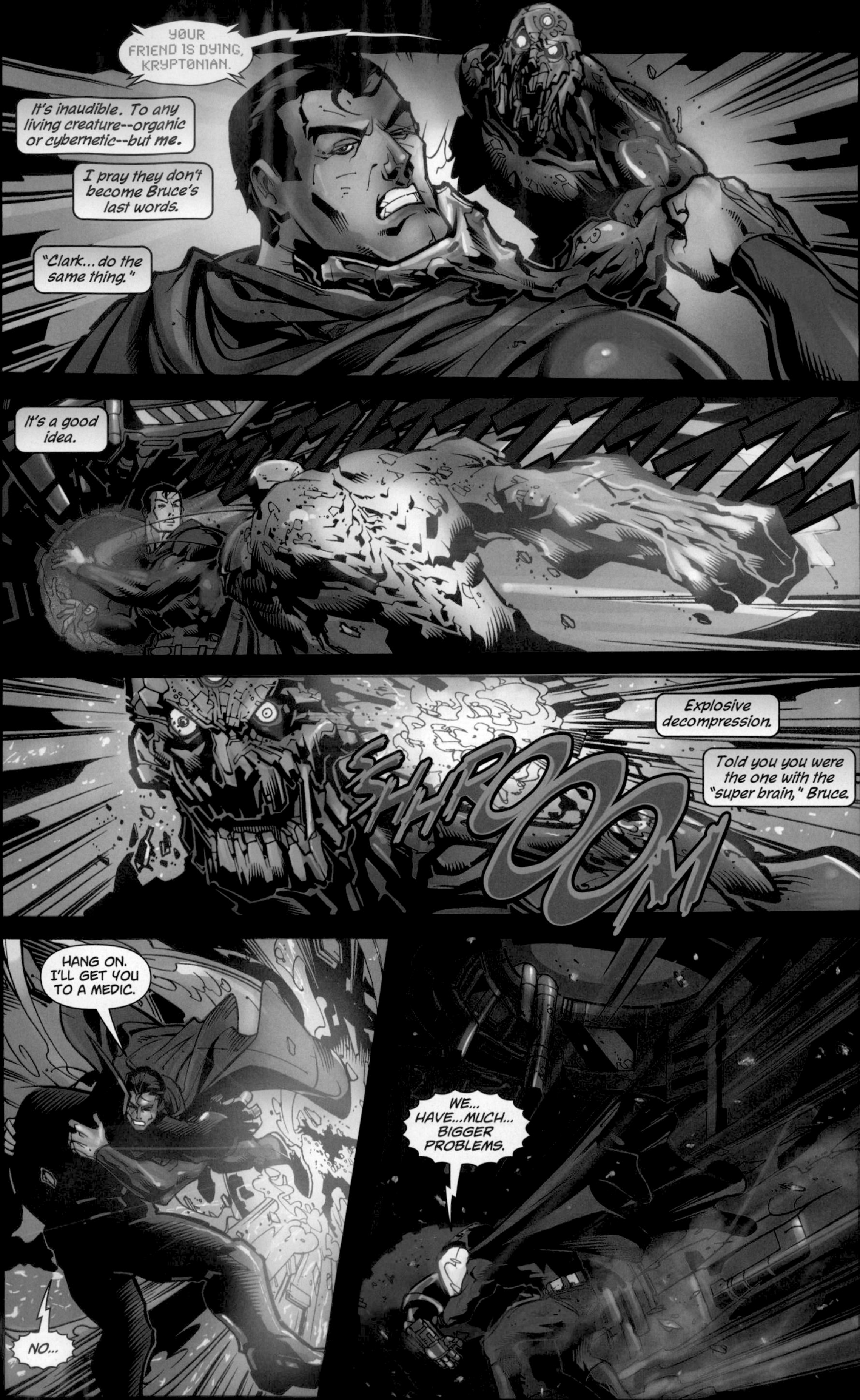
YOUR FRIEND IS DYING, KRYPTONIAN.
It's inaudible. To any living creature--organic or cybernetic--but me.
I pray they don't become Bruce's last words.
"Clark... do the same thing."
It's a good idea.
Explosive decompression.
SSHHPOOOM
Told you you were the one with the "super brain," Bruce.
HANG ON. I'LL GET YOU TO A MEDIC.
NO...
WE... HAVE...MUCH... BIGGER PROBLEMS.

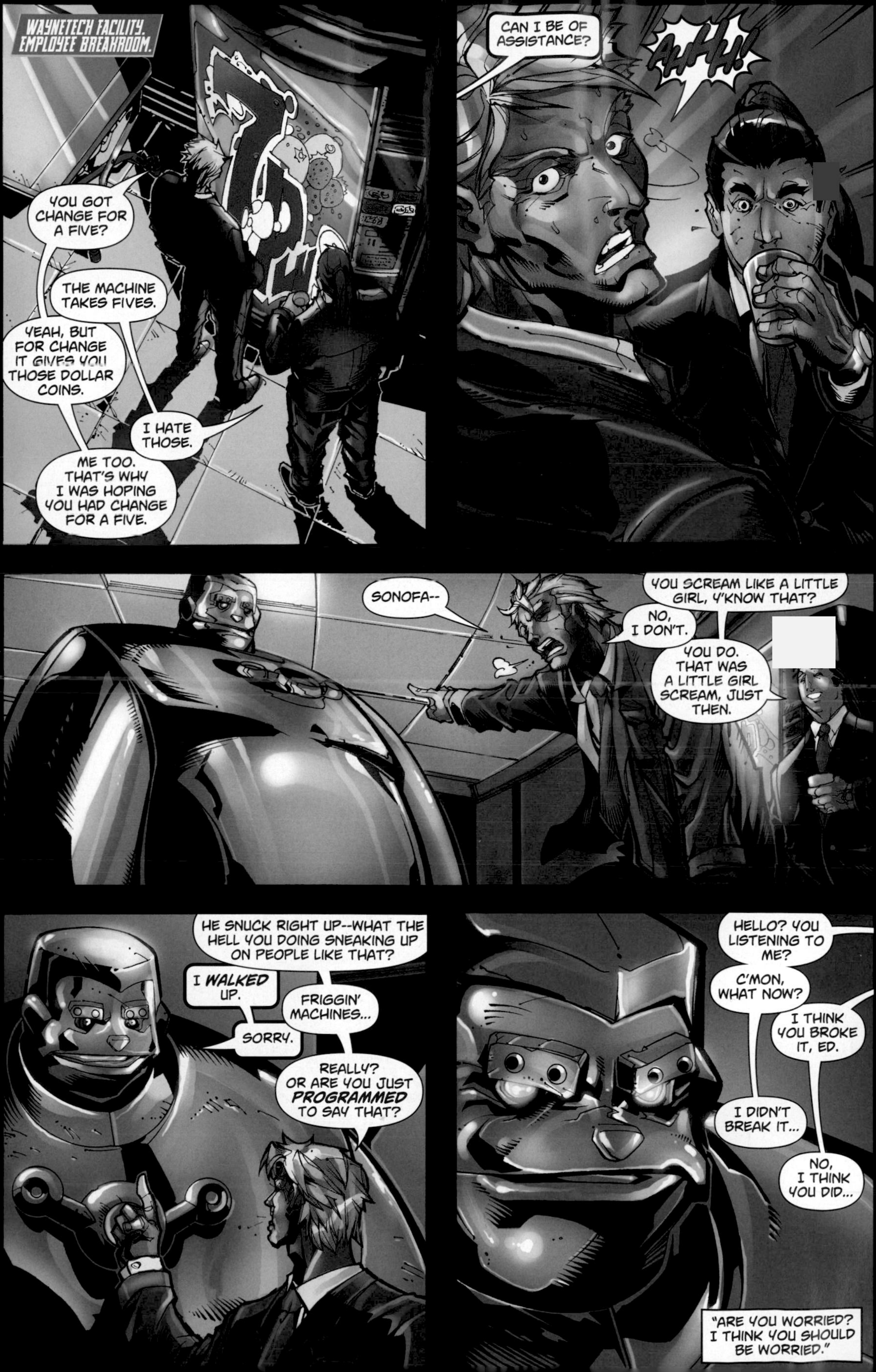
WAYNETECH FACILITY. EMPLOYEE BREAKROOM.
YOU GOT CHANGE FOR A FIVE?
THE MACHINE TAKES FIVES.
YEAH, BUT FOR CHANGE IT GIVES YOU THOSE DOLLAR COINS.
I HATE THOSE.
ME TOO. THAT'S WHY I WAS HOPING YOU HAD CHANGE FOR A FIVE.
CAN I BE OF ASSISTANCE?
AHHH!
SONOFA--
YOU SCREAM LIKE A LITTLE GIRL, Y'KNOW THAT?
NO, I DON'T.
YOU DO. THAT WAS A LITTLE GIRL SCREAM, JUST THEN.
HE SNUCK RIGHT UP--WHAT THE HELL YOU DOING SNEAKING UP ON PEOPLE LIKE THAT?
I WALKED UP.
SORRY.
FRIGGIN' MACHINES...
REALLY? OR ARE YOU JUST PROGRAMMED TO SAY THAT?
HELLO? YOU LISTENING TO ME?
C'MON, WHAT NOW?
I THINK YOU BROKE IT, ED.
I DIDN'T BREAK IT...
NO, I THINK YOU DID...
"ARE YOU WORRIED? I THINK YOU SHOULD BE WORRIED."

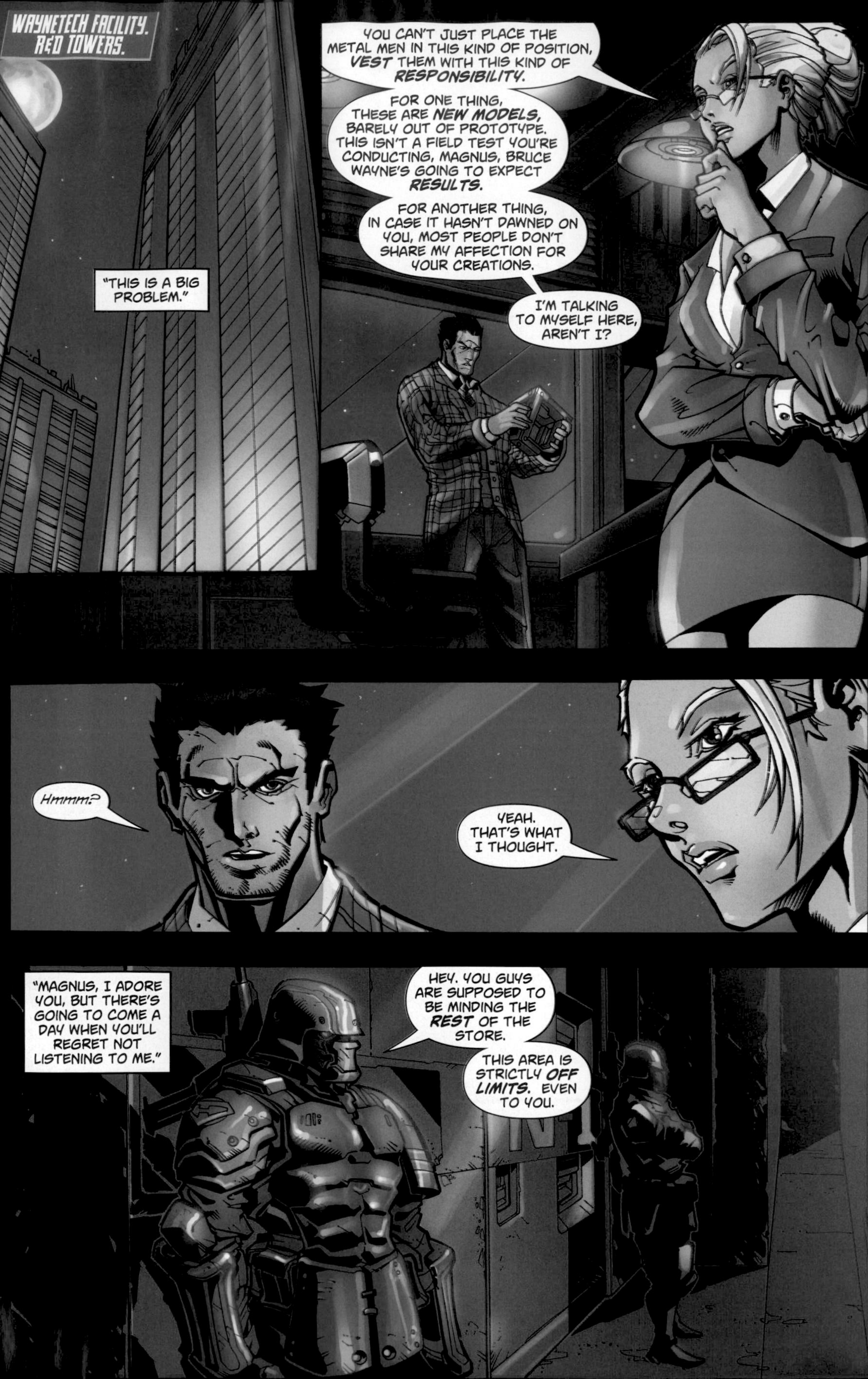

WAYNETECH FACILITY. R&D TOWERS.
YOU CAN'T JUST PLACE THE METAL MEN IN THIS KIND OF POSITION, VEST THEM WITH THIS KIND OF RESPONSIBILITY.
FOR ONE THING, THESE ARE NEW MODELS, BARELY OUT OF PROTOTYPE. THIS ISN'T A FIELD TEST YOU'RE CONDUCTING, MAGNUS, BRUCE WAYNE'S GOING TO EXPECT RESULTS.
FOR ANOTHER THING, IN CASE IT HASN'T DAWNED ON YOU, MOST PEOPLE DON'T SHARE MY AFFECTION FOR YOUR CREATIONS.
"THIS IS A BIG PROBLEM."
I'M TALKING TO MYSELF HERE, AREN'T I?
Hmmm?
YEAH. THAT'S WHAT I THOUGHT.
"MAGNUS, I ADORE YOU, BUT THERE'S GOING TO COME A DAY WHEN YOU'LL REGRET NOT LISTENING TO ME."
HEY. YOU GUYS ARE SUPPOSED TO BE MINDING THE REST OF THE STORE.
THIS AREA IS STRICTLY OFF LIMITS. EVEN TO YOU.

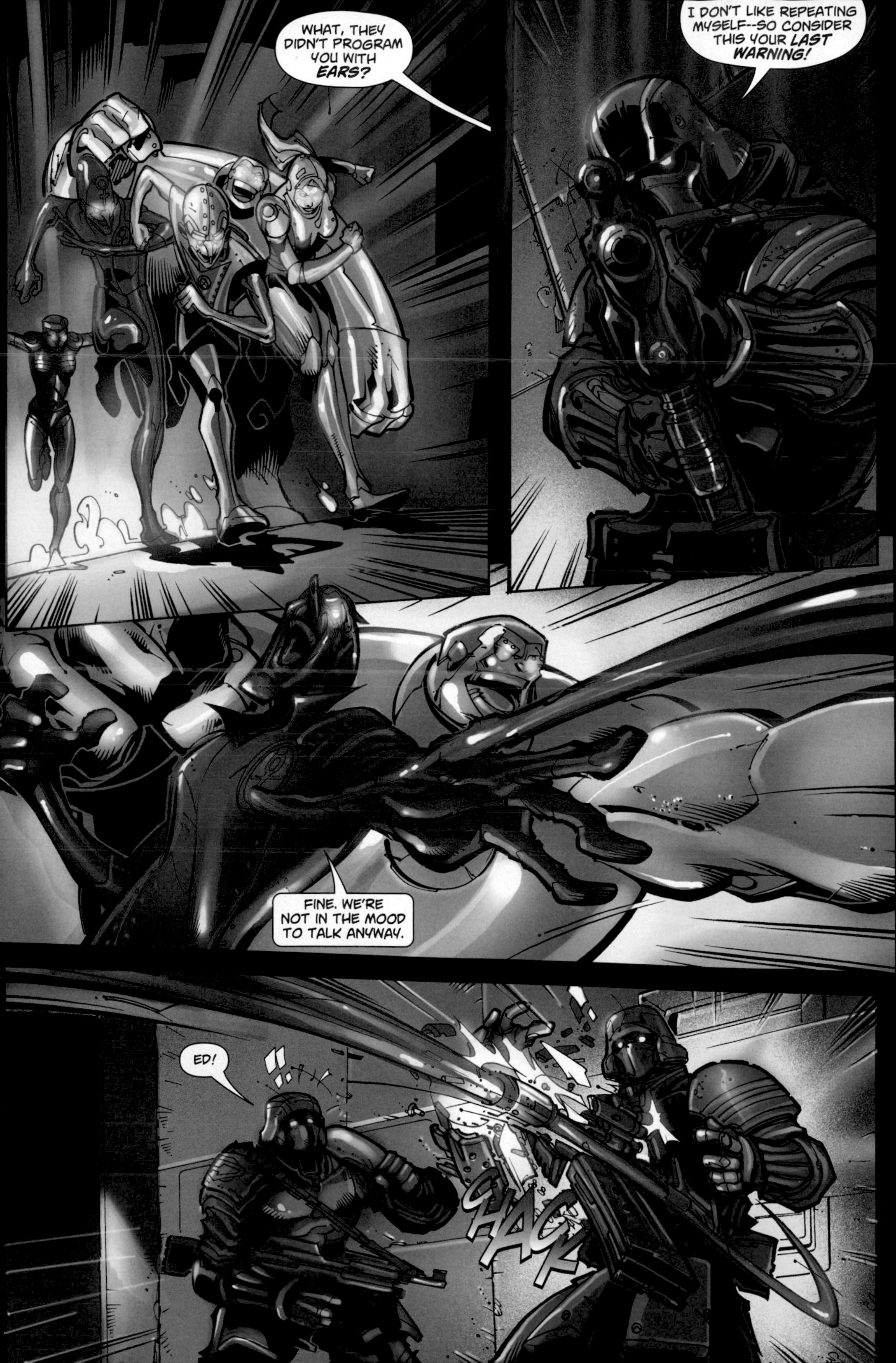

WHAT, THEY DIDN'T PROGRAM YOU WITH EARS?
I DON'T LIKE REPEATING MYSELF--SO CONSIDER THIS YOUR LAST WARNING!
FINE. WE'RE NOT IN THE MOOD TO TALK ANYWAY.
ED!
!!
CHACK

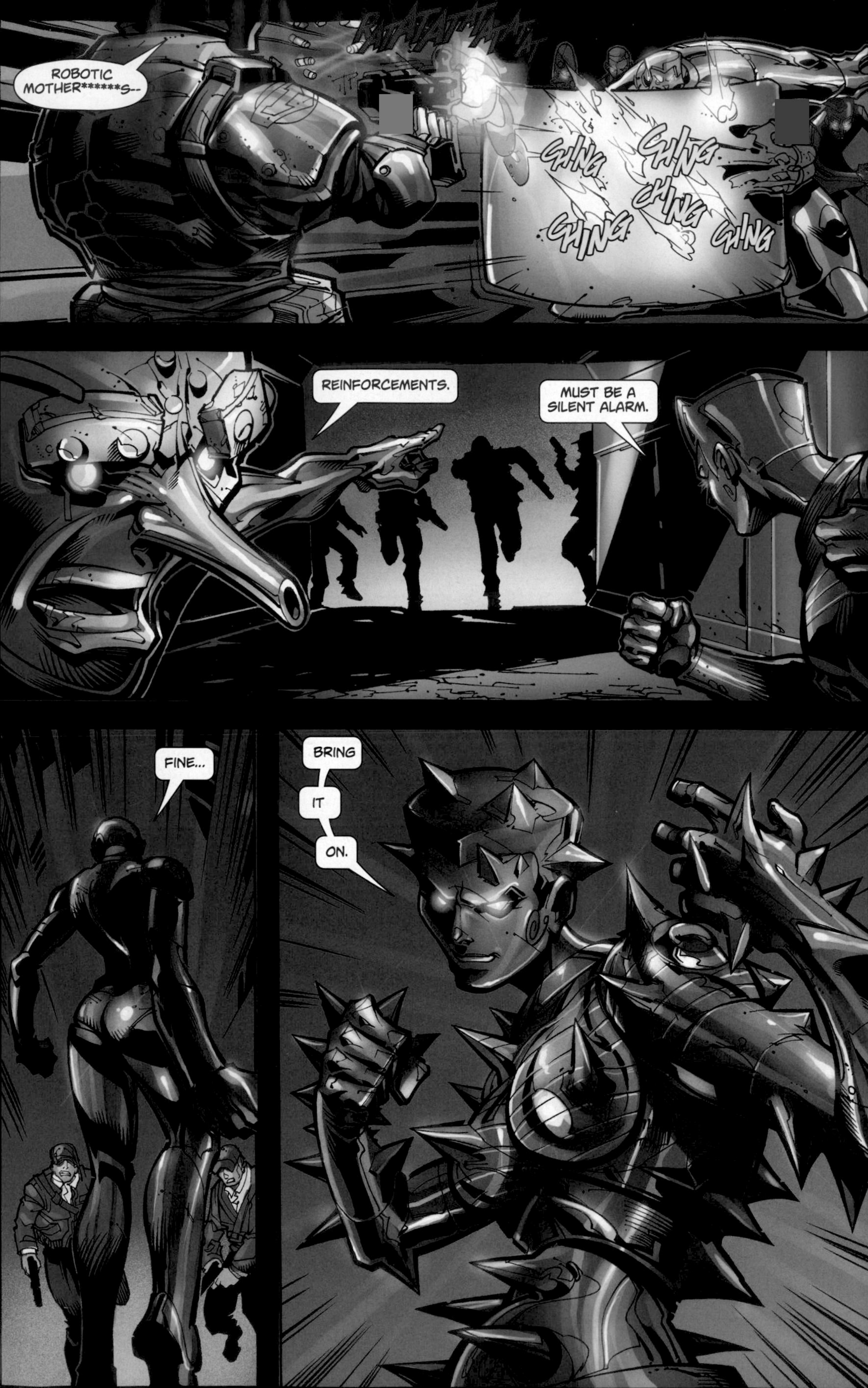
ROBOTIC MOTHER*******S--
CHING
CHING
CHING
CHING
CHING
REINFORCEMENTS.
MUST BE A SILENT ALARM.
FINE...
BRING
IT
ON.

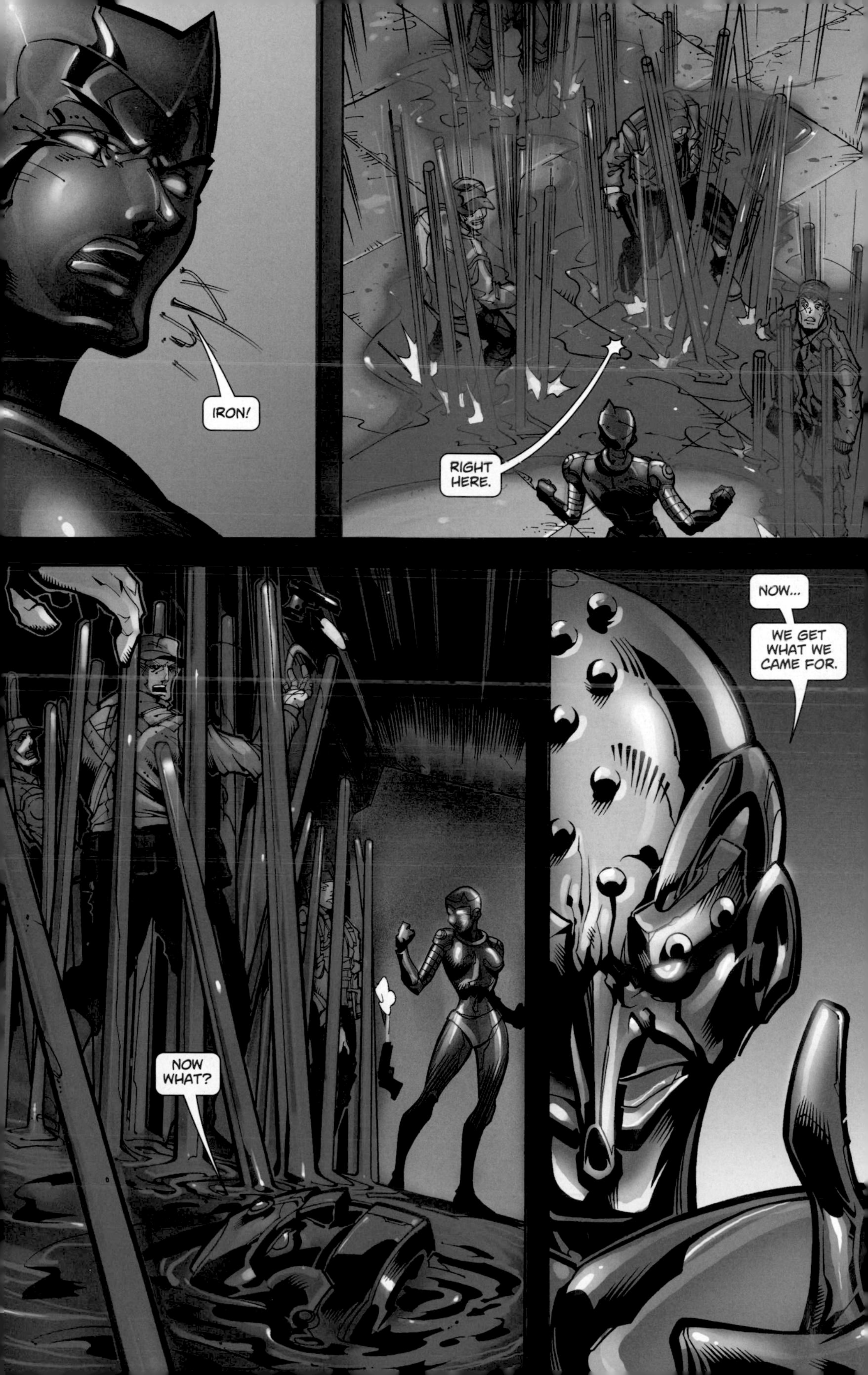
IRON!
RIGHT HERE.
NOW WHAT?
NOW...
WE GET WHAT WE CAME FOR.

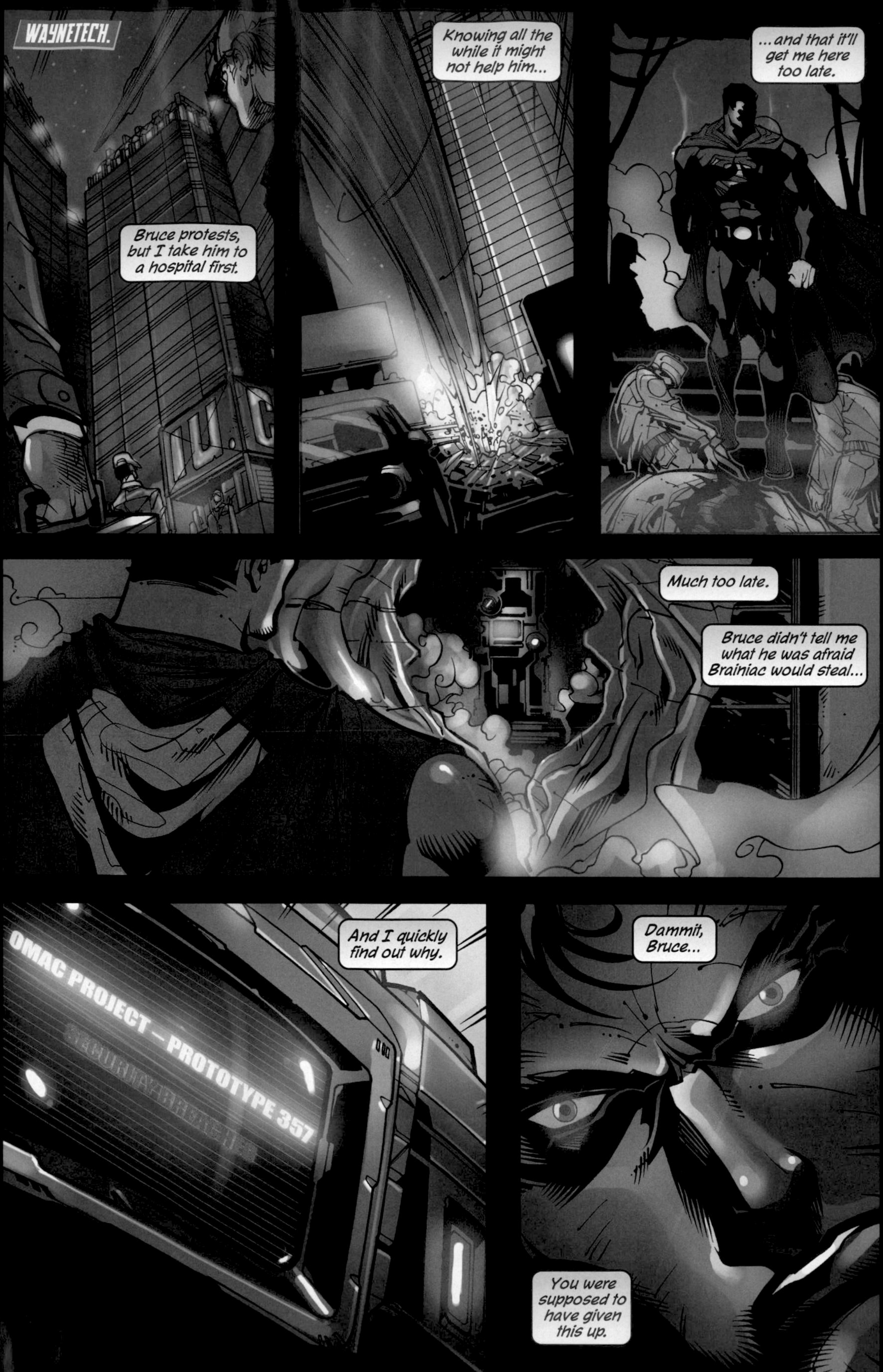
WAYNETECH.
Bruce protests, but I take him to a hospital first.
Knowing all the while it might not help him...
...and that it'll get me here too late.
Much too late.
Bruce didn't tell me what he was afraid Brainiac would steal...
And I quickly find out why.
OMAC PROJECT – PROTOTYPE 357
Dammit, Bruce...
You were supposed to have given this up.

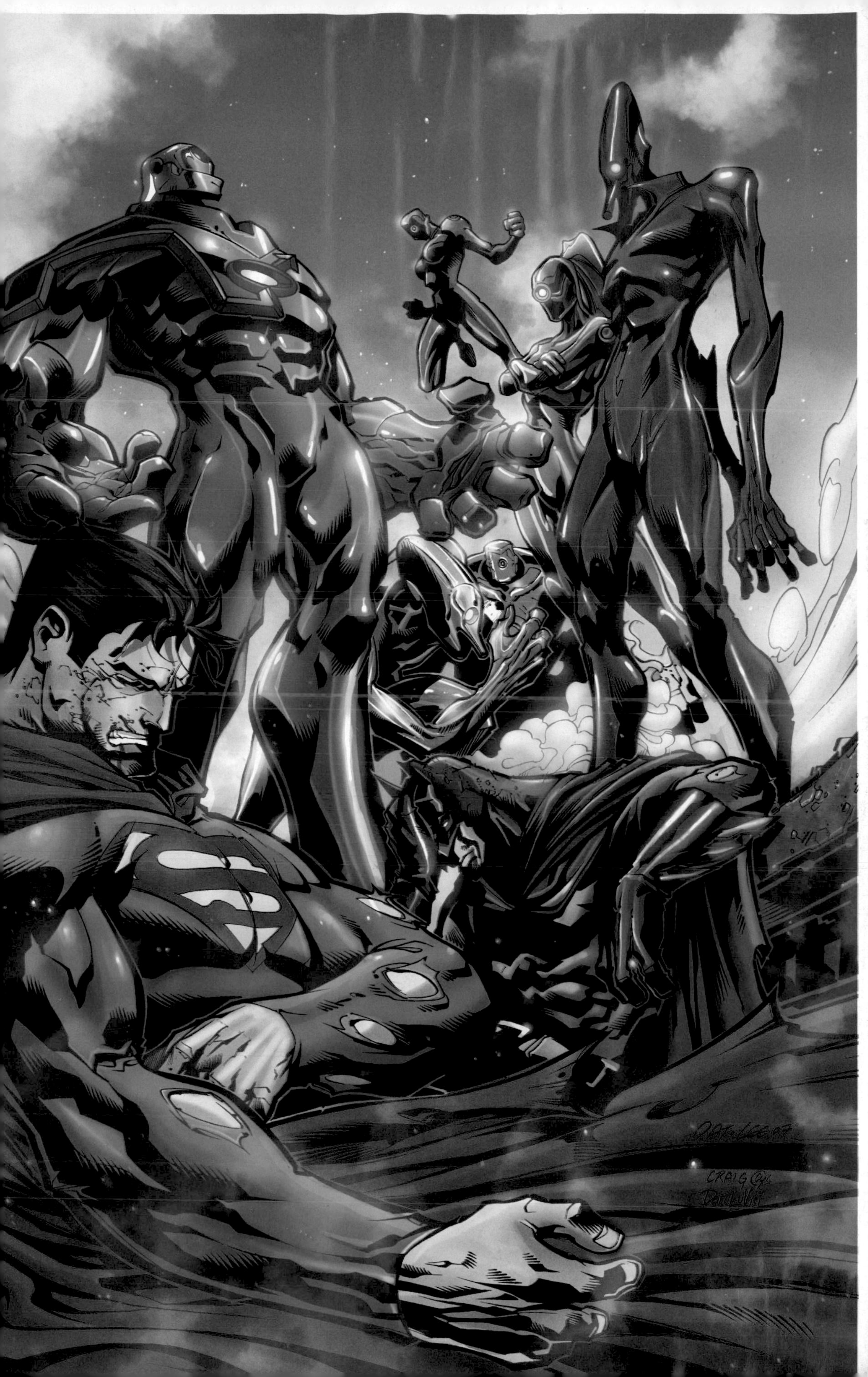

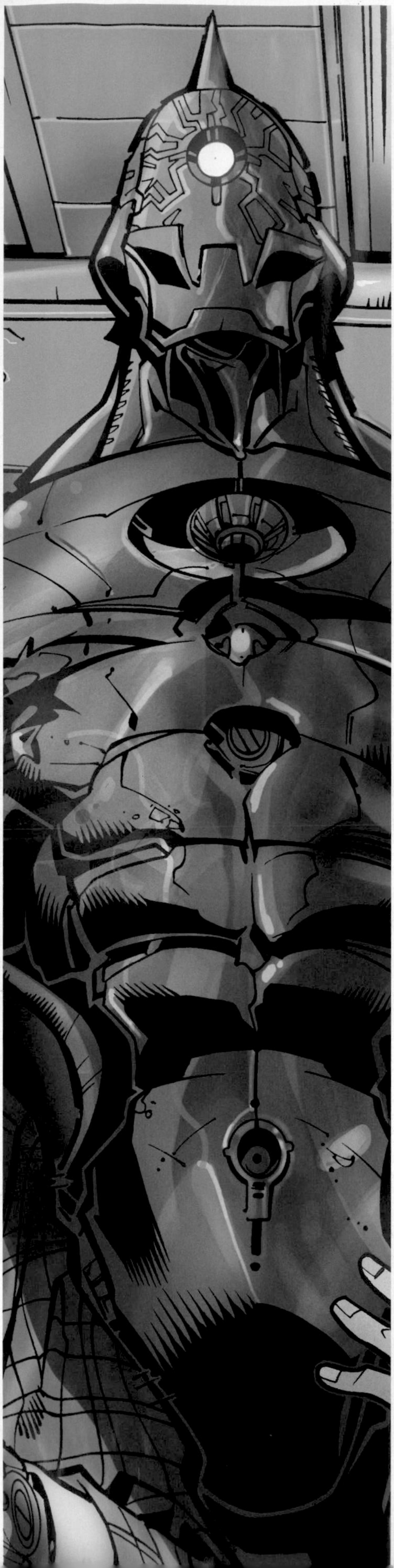

METAL MEN

PART THREE
COMPUTER CRASH

MARK VERHEIDEN
&
MARC GUGGENHEIM
WRITERS

PAT LEE
PENCILLER

CRAIG YEUNG
INKER

DANNY LUVISI
COLORIST

ROB LEIGH
LETTERER

PAT LEE
CRAIG YEUNG
&
DANNY LUVISI
COVER

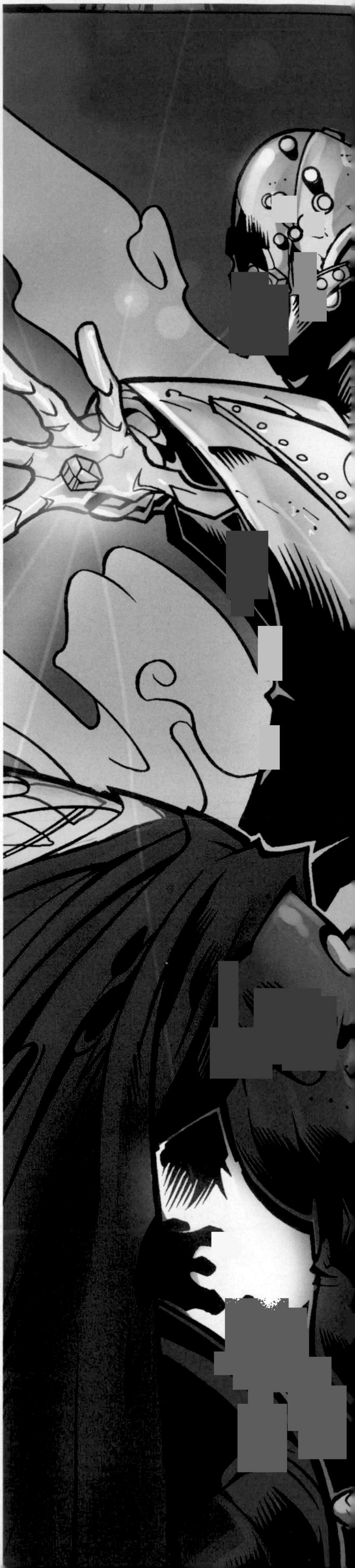

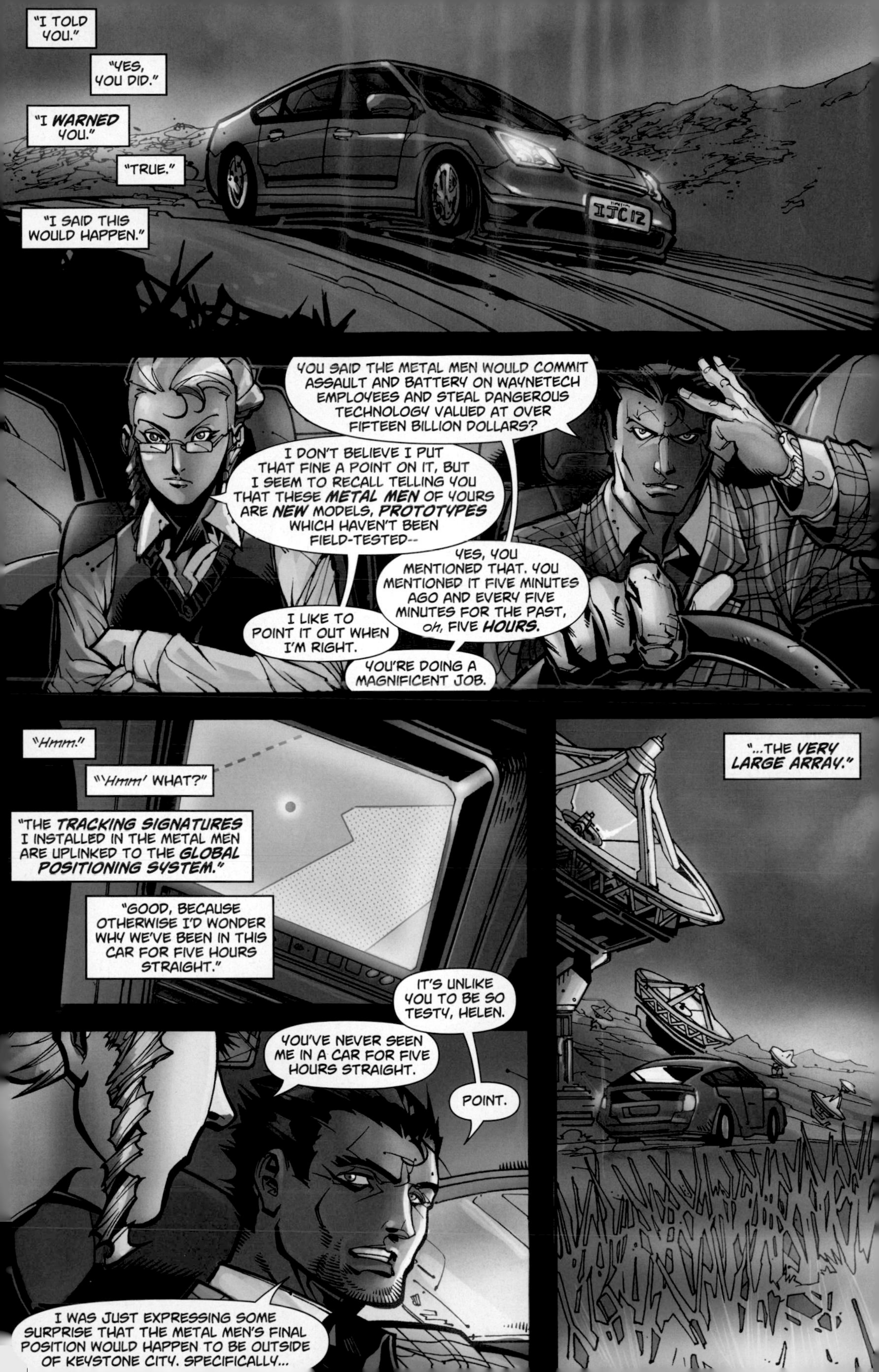
"I TOLD YOU."
"YES, YOU DID."
"I WARNED YOU."
"TRUE."
"I SAID THIS WOULD HAPPEN."
IJC 12
YOU SAID THE METAL MEN WOULD COMMIT ASSAULT AND BATTERY ON WAYNETECH EMPLOYEES AND STEAL DANGEROUS TECHNOLOGY VALUED AT OVER FIFTEEN BILLION DOLLARS?
I DON'T BELIEVE I PUT THAT FINE A POINT ON IT, BUT I SEEM TO RECALL TELLING YOU THAT THESE METAL MEN OF YOURS ARE NEW MODELS, PROTOTYPES WHICH HAVEN'T BEEN FIELD-TESTED--
YES, YOU MENTIONED THAT. YOU MENTIONED IT FIVE MINUTES AGO AND EVERY FIVE MINUTES FOR THE PAST, oh, FIVE HOURS.
I LIKE TO POINT IT OUT WHEN I'M RIGHT.
YOU'RE DOING A MAGNIFICENT JOB.
"Hmm."
"'Hmm' WHAT?"
"THE TRACKING SIGNATURES I INSTALLED IN THE METAL MEN ARE UPLINKED TO THE GLOBAL POSITIONING SYSTEM."
"GOOD, BECAUSE OTHERWISE I'D WONDER WHY WE'VE BEEN IN THIS CAR FOR FIVE HOURS STRAIGHT."
IT'S UNLIKE YOU TO BE SO TESTY, HELEN.
YOU'VE NEVER SEEN ME IN A CAR FOR FIVE HOURS STRAIGHT.
POINT.
I WAS JUST EXPRESSING SOME SURPRISE THAT THE METAL MEN'S FINAL POSITION WOULD HAPPEN TO BE OUTSIDE OF KEYSTONE CITY. SPECIFICALLY...
"...THE VERY LARGE ARRAY."

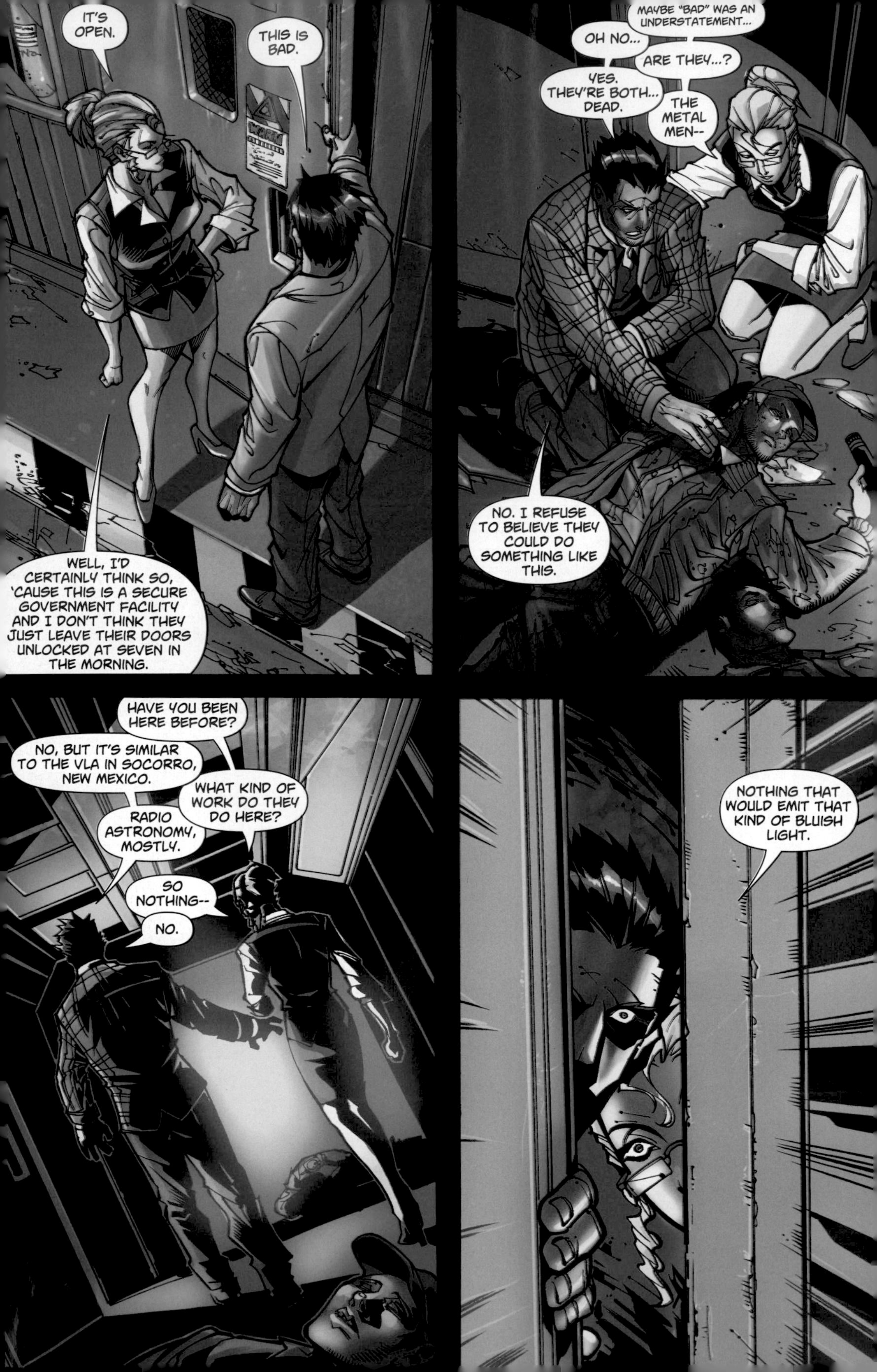

IT'S OPEN.
THIS IS BAD.
WELL, I'D CERTAINLY THINK SO, 'CAUSE THIS IS A SECURE GOVERNMENT FACILITY AND I DON'T THINK THEY JUST LEAVE THEIR DOORS UNLOCKED AT SEVEN IN THE MORNING.
MAYBE "BAD" WAS AN UNDERSTATEMENT...
OH NO...
ARE THEY...?
YES. THEY'RE BOTH... DEAD.
THE METAL MEN--
NO. I REFUSE TO BELIEVE THEY COULD DO SOMETHING LIKE THIS.
HAVE YOU BEEN HERE BEFORE?
NO, BUT IT'S SIMILAR TO THE VLA IN SOCORRO, NEW MEXICO.
WHAT KIND OF WORK DO THEY DO HERE?
RADIO ASTRONOMY, MOSTLY.
SO NOTHING--
NO.
NOTHING THAT WOULD EMIT THAT KIND OF BLUISH LIGHT.

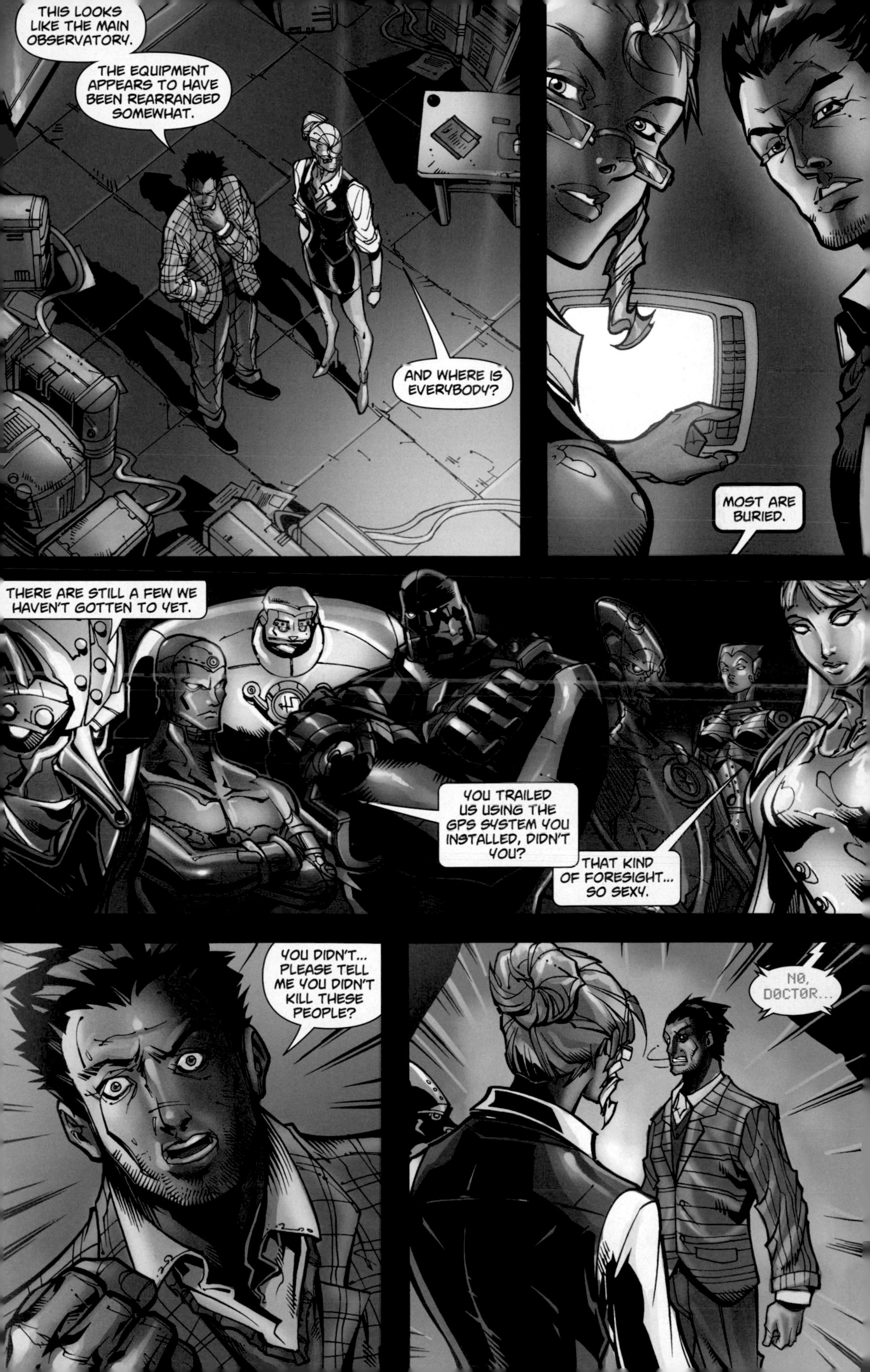
THIS LOOKS LIKE THE MAIN OBSERVATORY.
THE EQUIPMENT APPEARS TO HAVE BEEN REARRANGED SOMEWHAT.
AND WHERE IS EVERYBODY?
MOST ARE BURIED.
THERE ARE STILL A FEW WE HAVEN'T GOTTEN TO YET.
YOU TRAILED US USING THE GPS SYSTEM YOU INSTALLED, DIDN'T YOU?
THAT KIND OF FORESIGHT... SO SEXY.
YOU DIDN'T... PLEASE TELL ME YOU DIDN'T KILL THESE PEOPLE?
NO, DOCTOR...

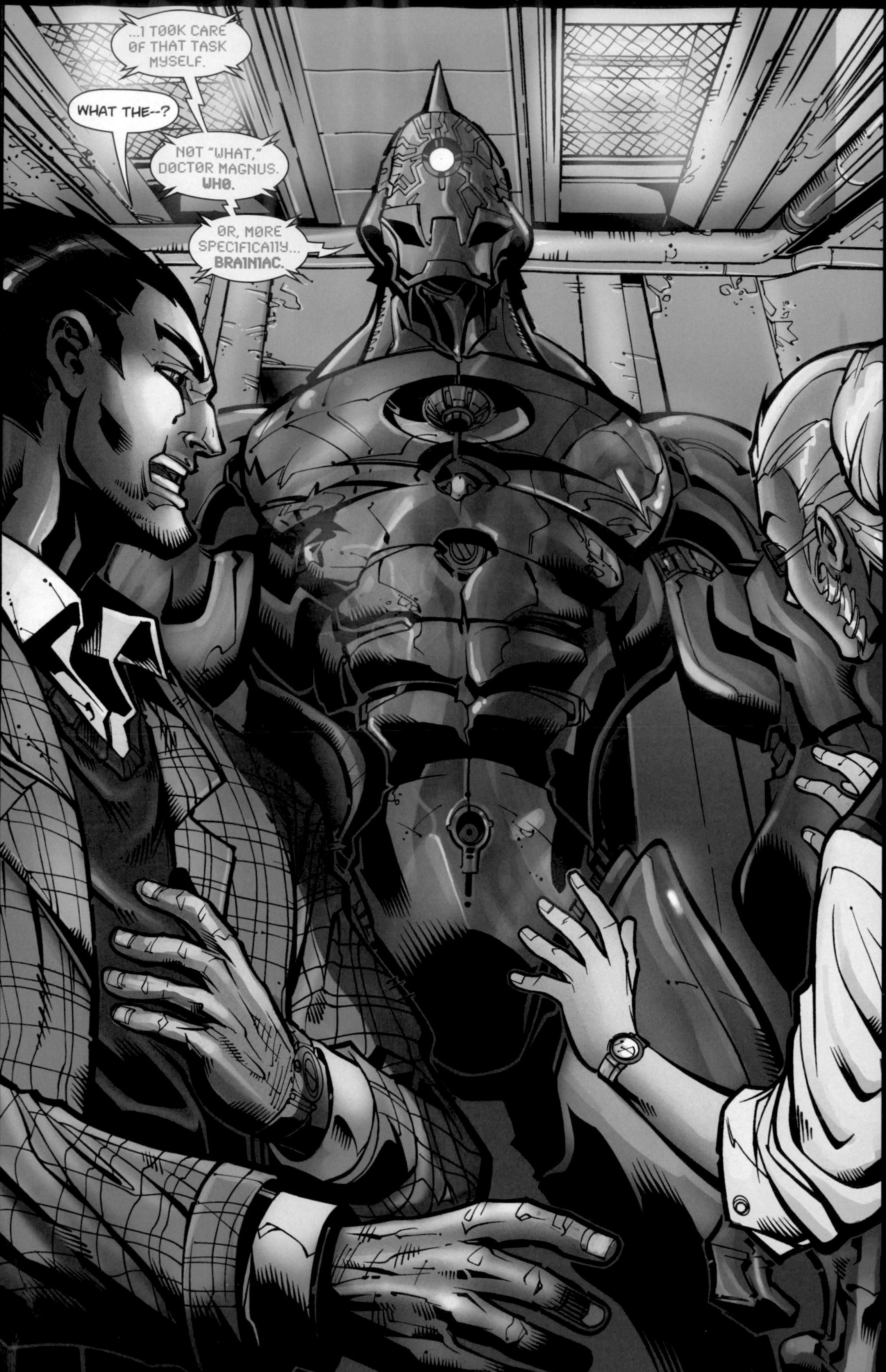
...I TOOK CARE OF THAT TASK MYSELF.
WHAT THE--?
NOT "WHAT," DOCTOR MAGNUS. WHO.
OR, MORE SPECIFICALLY... BRAINIAC.

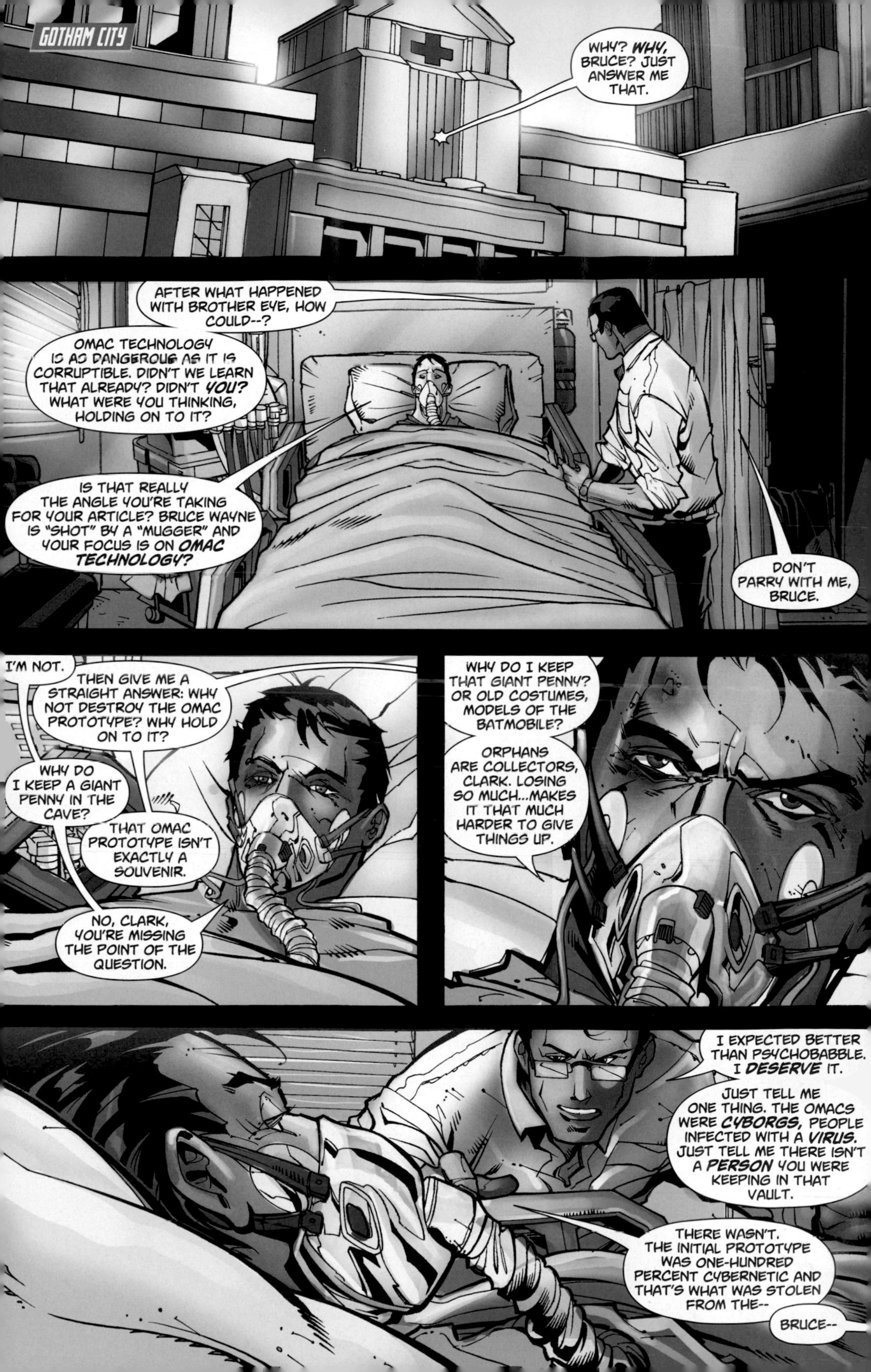
GOTHAM CITY
WHY? WHY, BRUCE? JUST ANSWER ME THAT.
AFTER WHAT HAPPENED WITH BROTHER EYE, HOW COULD--?
OMAC TECHNOLOGY IS AS DANGEROUS AS IT IS CORRUPTIBLE. DIDN'T WE LEARN THAT ALREADY? DIDN'T YOU? WHAT WERE YOU THINKING, HOLDING ON TO IT?
IS THAT REALLY THE ANGLE YOU'RE TAKING FOR YOUR ARTICLE? BRUCE WAYNE IS "SHOT" BY A "MUGGER" AND YOUR FOCUS IS ON OMAC TECHNOLOGY?
DON'T PARRY WITH ME, BRUCE.
I'M NOT.
THEN GIVE ME A STRAIGHT ANSWER: WHY NOT DESTROY THE OMAC PROTOTYPE? WHY HOLD ON TO IT?
WHY DO I KEEP A GIANT PENNY IN THE CAVE?
THAT OMAC PROTOTYPE ISN'T EXACTLY A SOUVENIR.
NO, CLARK, YOU'RE MISSING THE POINT OF THE QUESTION.
WHY DO I KEEP THAT GIANT PENNY? OR OLD COSTUMES, MODELS OF THE BATMOBILE?
ORPHANS ARE COLLECTORS, CLARK. LOSING SO MUCH...MAKES IT THAT MUCH HARDER TO GIVE THINGS UP.
I EXPECTED BETTER THAN PSYCHOBABBLE. I DESERVE IT.
JUST TELL ME ONE THING. THE OMACS WERE CYBORGS, PEOPLE INFECTED WITH A VIRUS. JUST TELL ME THERE ISN'T A PERSON YOU WERE KEEPING IN THAT VAULT.
THERE WASN'T. THE INITIAL PROTOTYPE WAS ONE-HUNDRED PERCENT CYBERNETIC AND THAT'S WHAT WAS STOLEN FROM THE--
BRUCE--

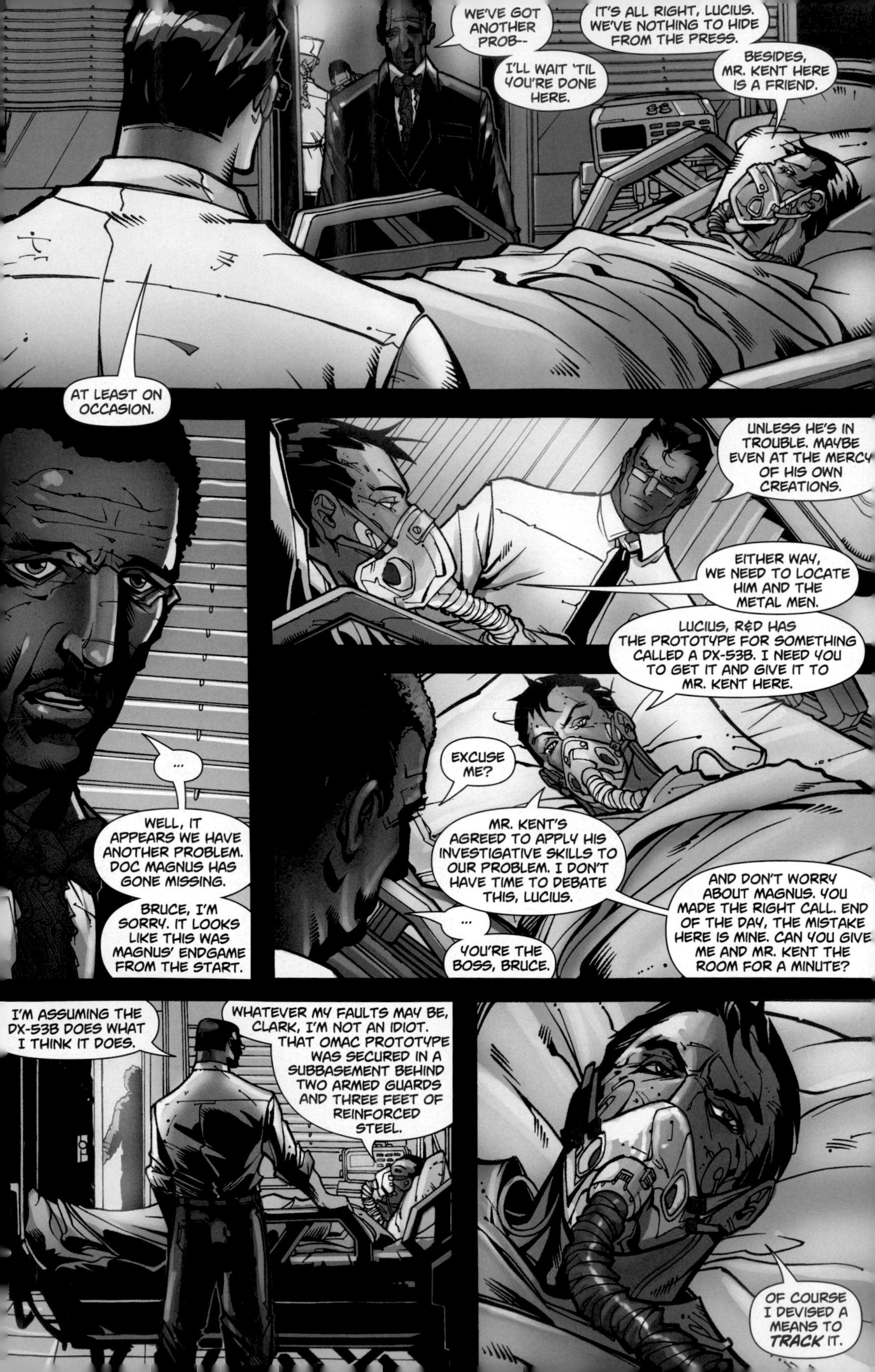
WE'VE GOT ANOTHER PROB--
IT'S ALL RIGHT, LUCIUS. WE'VE NOTHING TO HIDE FROM THE PRESS.
I'LL WAIT 'TIL YOU'RE DONE HERE.
BESIDES, MR. KENT HERE IS A FRIEND.
AT LEAST ON OCCASION.
...
WELL, IT APPEARS WE HAVE ANOTHER PROBLEM. DOC MAGNUS HAS GONE MISSING.
BRUCE, I'M SORRY. IT LOOKS LIKE THIS WAS MAGNUS' ENDGAME FROM THE START.
UNLESS HE'S IN TROUBLE. MAYBE EVEN AT THE MERCY OF HIS OWN CREATIONS.
EITHER WAY, WE NEED TO LOCATE HIM AND THE METAL MEN.
LUCIUS, R&D HAS THE PROTOTYPE FOR SOMETHING CALLED A DX-53B. I NEED YOU TO GET IT AND GIVE IT TO MR. KENT HERE.
EXCUSE ME?
MR. KENT'S AGREED TO APPLY HIS INVESTIGATIVE SKILLS TO OUR PROBLEM. I DON'T HAVE TIME TO DEBATE THIS, LUCIUS.
...
YOU'RE THE BOSS, BRUCE.
AND DON'T WORRY ABOUT MAGNUS. YOU MADE THE RIGHT CALL. END OF THE DAY, THE MISTAKE HERE IS MINE. CAN YOU GIVE ME AND MR. KENT THE ROOM FOR A MINUTE?
I'M ASSUMING THE DX-53B DOES WHAT I THINK IT DOES.
WHATEVER MY FAULTS MAY BE, CLARK, I'M NOT AN IDIOT. THAT OMAC PROTOTYPE WAS SECURED IN A SUBBASEMENT BEHIND TWO ARMED GUARDS AND THREE FEET OF REINFORCED STEEL.
OF COURSE I DEVISED A MEANS TO TRACK IT.

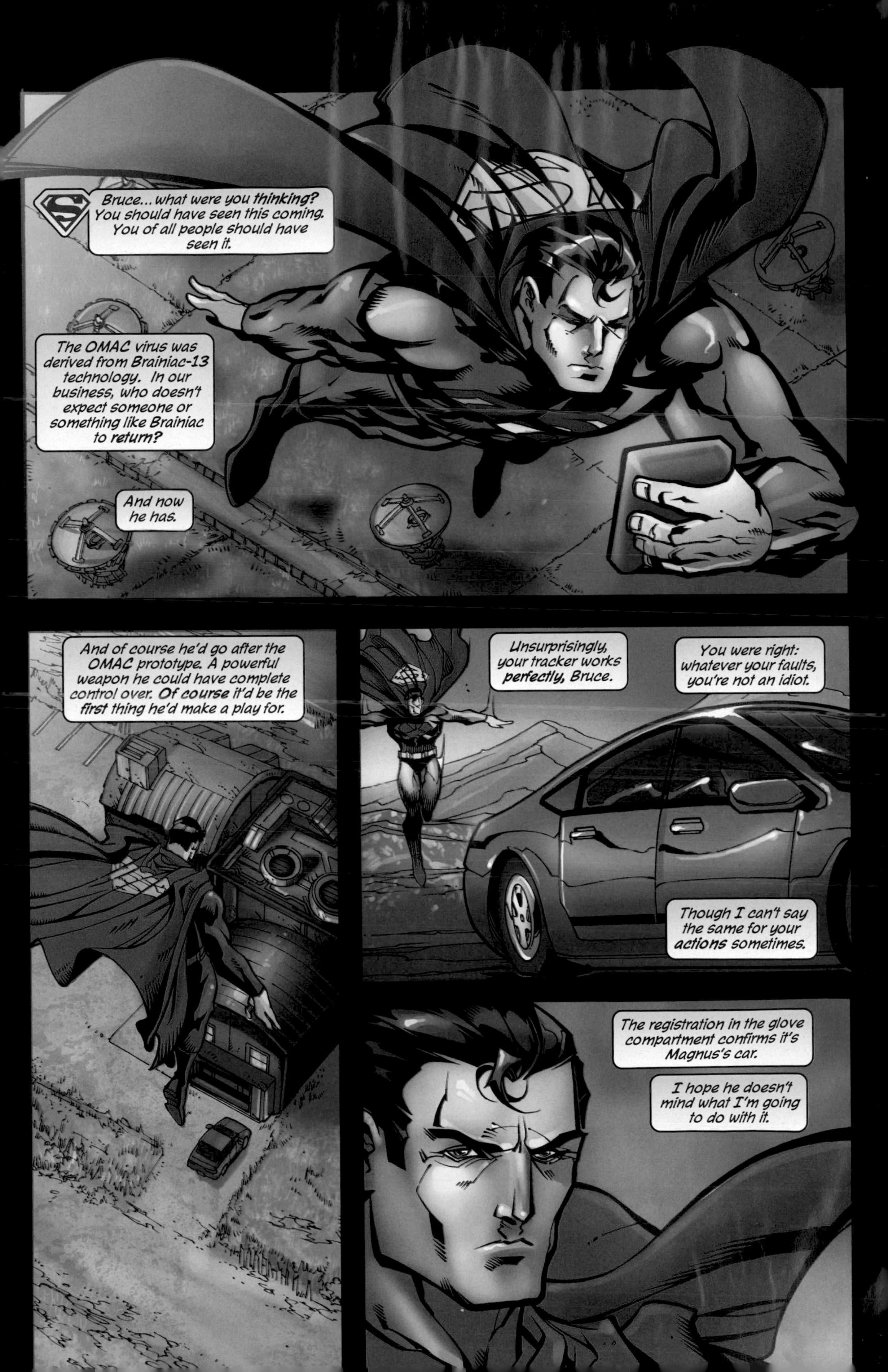

Bruce... what were you thinking? You should have seen this coming. You of all people should have seen it.
The OMAC virus was derived from Brainiac-13 technology. In our business, who doesn't expect someone or something like Brainiac to return?
And now he has.
And of course he'd go after the OMAC prototype. A powerful weapon he could have complete control over. Of course it'd be the first thing he'd make a play for.
Unsurprisingly, your tracker works perfectly, Bruce.
You were right: whatever your faults, you're not an idiot.
Though I can't say the same for your actions sometimes.
The registration in the glove compartment confirms it's Magnus's car.
I hope he doesn't mind what I'm going to do with it.

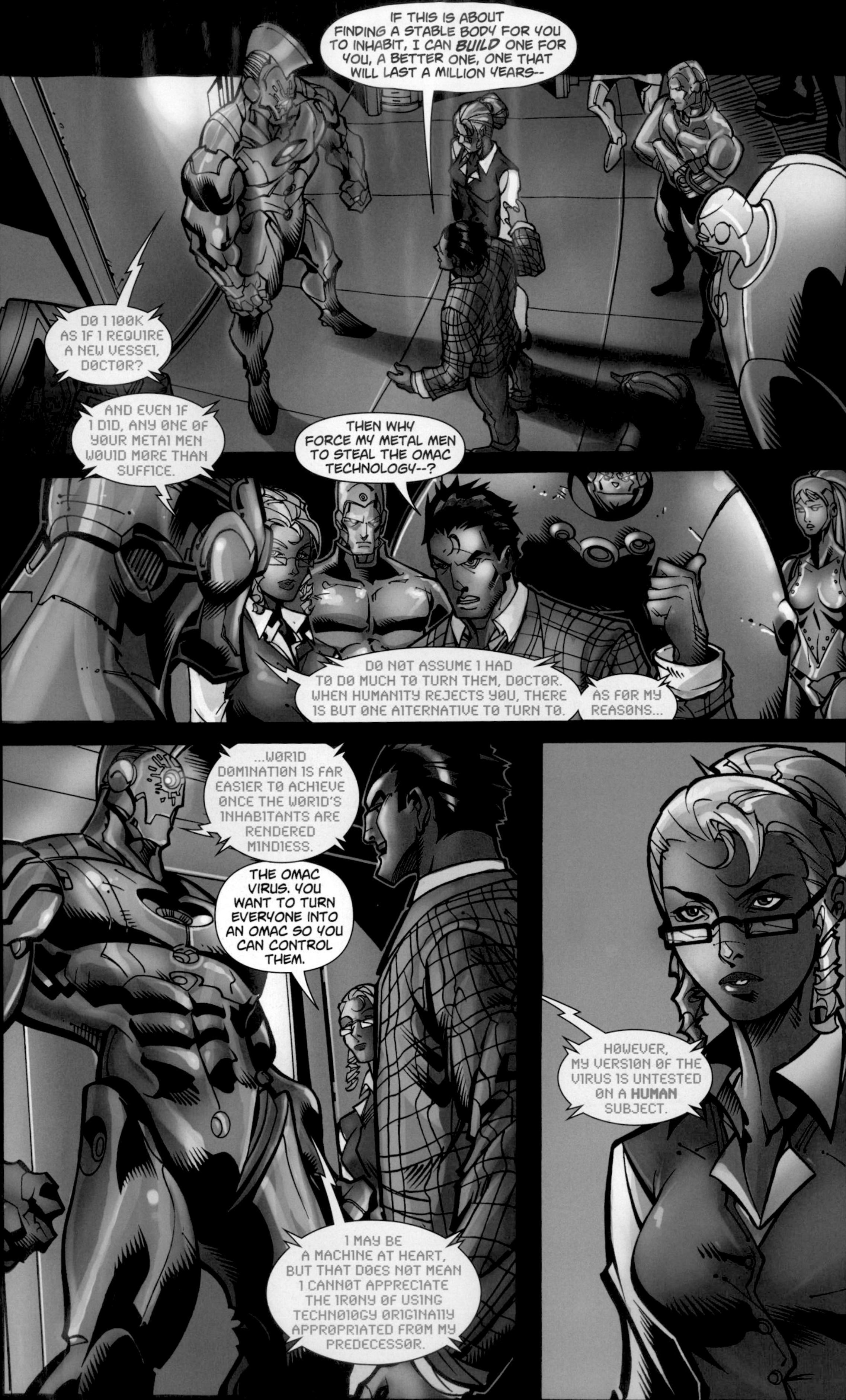
IF THIS IS ABOUT FINDING A STABLE BODY FOR YOU TO INHABIT, I CAN *BUILD* ONE FOR YOU, A BETTER ONE, ONE THAT WILL LAST A MILLION YEARS--
DO I LOOK AS IF I REQUIRE A NEW VESSEL, DOCTOR?
AND EVEN IF I DID, ANY ONE OF YOUR METAL MEN WOULD MORE THAN SUFFICE.
THEN WHY FORCE MY METAL MEN TO STEAL THE OMAC TECHNOLOGY--?
DO NOT ASSUME I HAD TO DO MUCH TO TURN THEM, DOCTOR. WHEN HUMANITY REJECTS YOU, THERE IS BUT ONE ALTERNATIVE TO TURN TO.
AS FOR MY REASONS...
...WORLD DOMINATION IS FAR EASIER TO ACHIEVE ONCE THE WORLD'S INHABITANTS ARE RENDERED MINDLESS.
THE OMAC VIRUS. YOU WANT TO TURN EVERYONE INTO AN OMAC SO YOU CAN CONTROL THEM.
I MAY BE A MACHINE AT HEART, BUT THAT DOES NOT MEAN I CANNOT APPRECIATE THE IRONY OF USING TECHNOLOGY ORIGINALLY APPROPRIATED FROM MY PREDECESSOR.
HOWEVER, MY VERSION OF THE VIRUS IS UNTESTED ON A **HUMAN** SUBJECT.

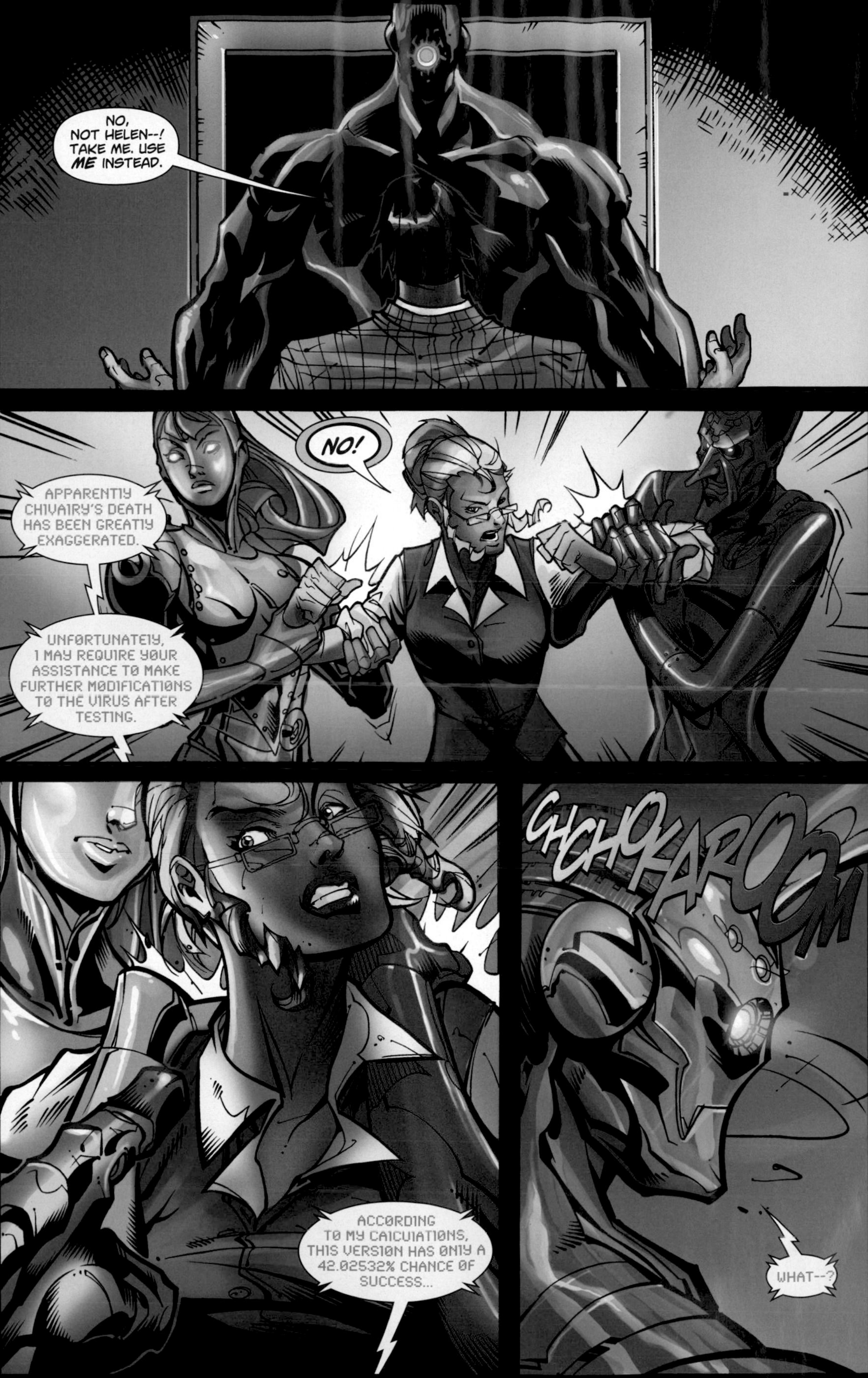
NO, NOT HELEN--! TAKE ME. USE ME INSTEAD.
NO!
APPARENTLY CHIVALRY'S DEATH HAS BEEN GREATLY EXAGGERATED.
UNFORTUNATELY, I MAY REQUIRE YOUR ASSISTANCE TO MAKE FURTHER MODIFICATIONS TO THE VIRUS AFTER TESTING.
ACCORDING TO MY CALCULATIONS, THIS VERSION HAS ONLY A 42.02532% CHANCE OF SUCCESS...
CHCHOKAROOOM
WHAT--?

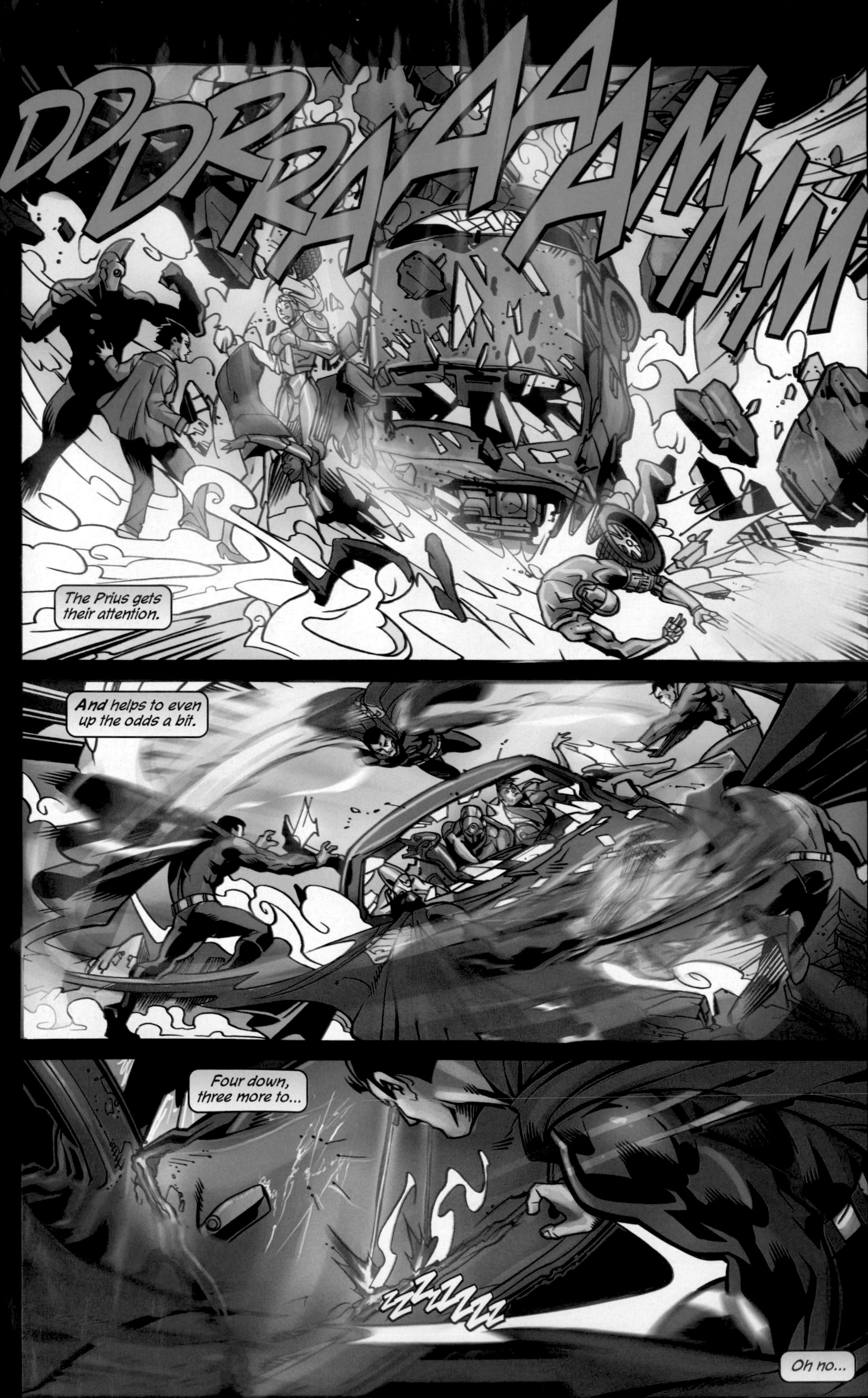
DDDRRAAAAAMMM
The Prius gets their attention.
And helps to even up the odds a bit.
Four down, three more to...
ZZZZZZZZ
Oh no...

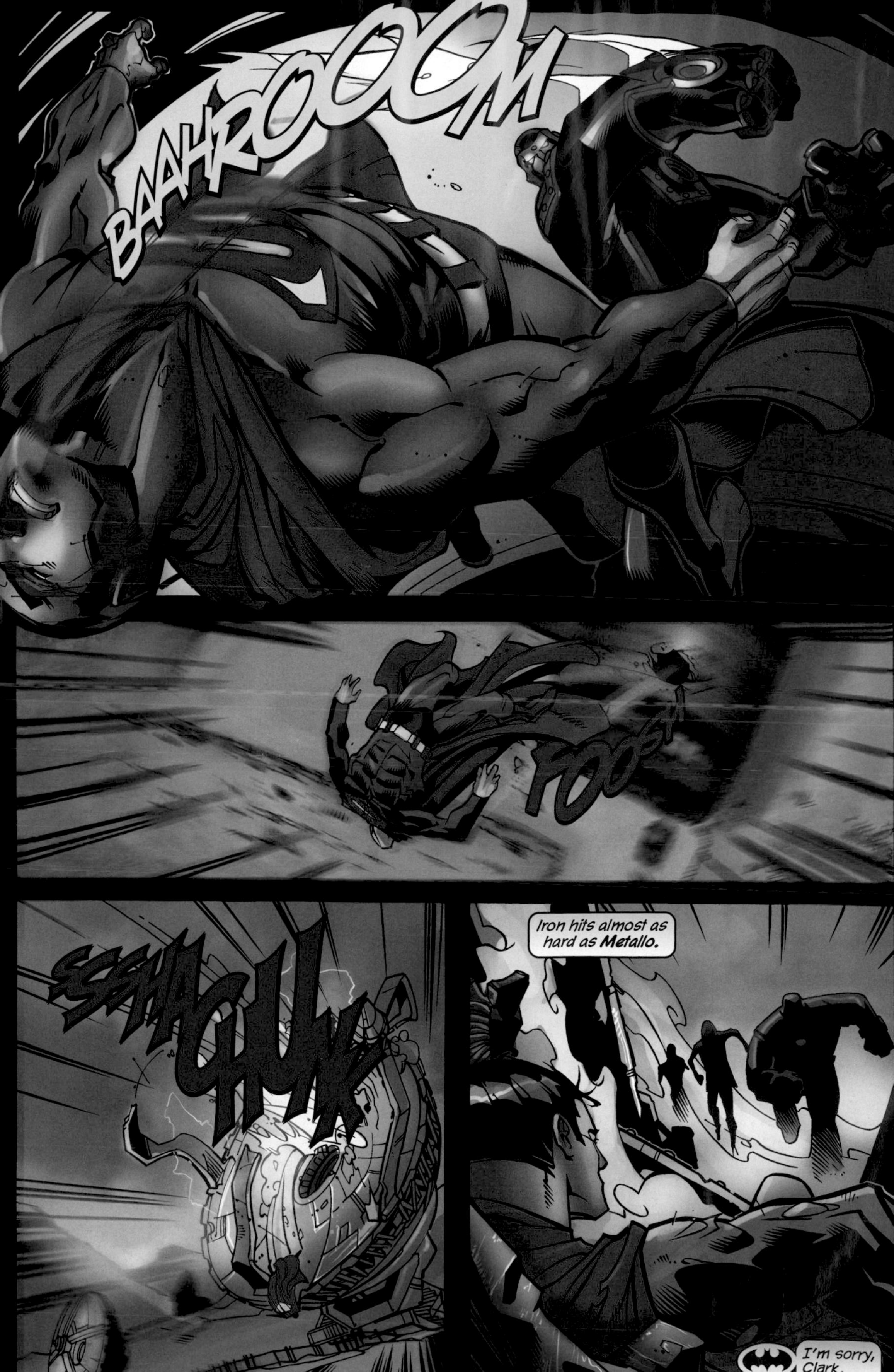
BAAHROOOM
POOSH
SSHAGUK
Iron hits almost as hard as Metallo.
I'm sorry, Clark.

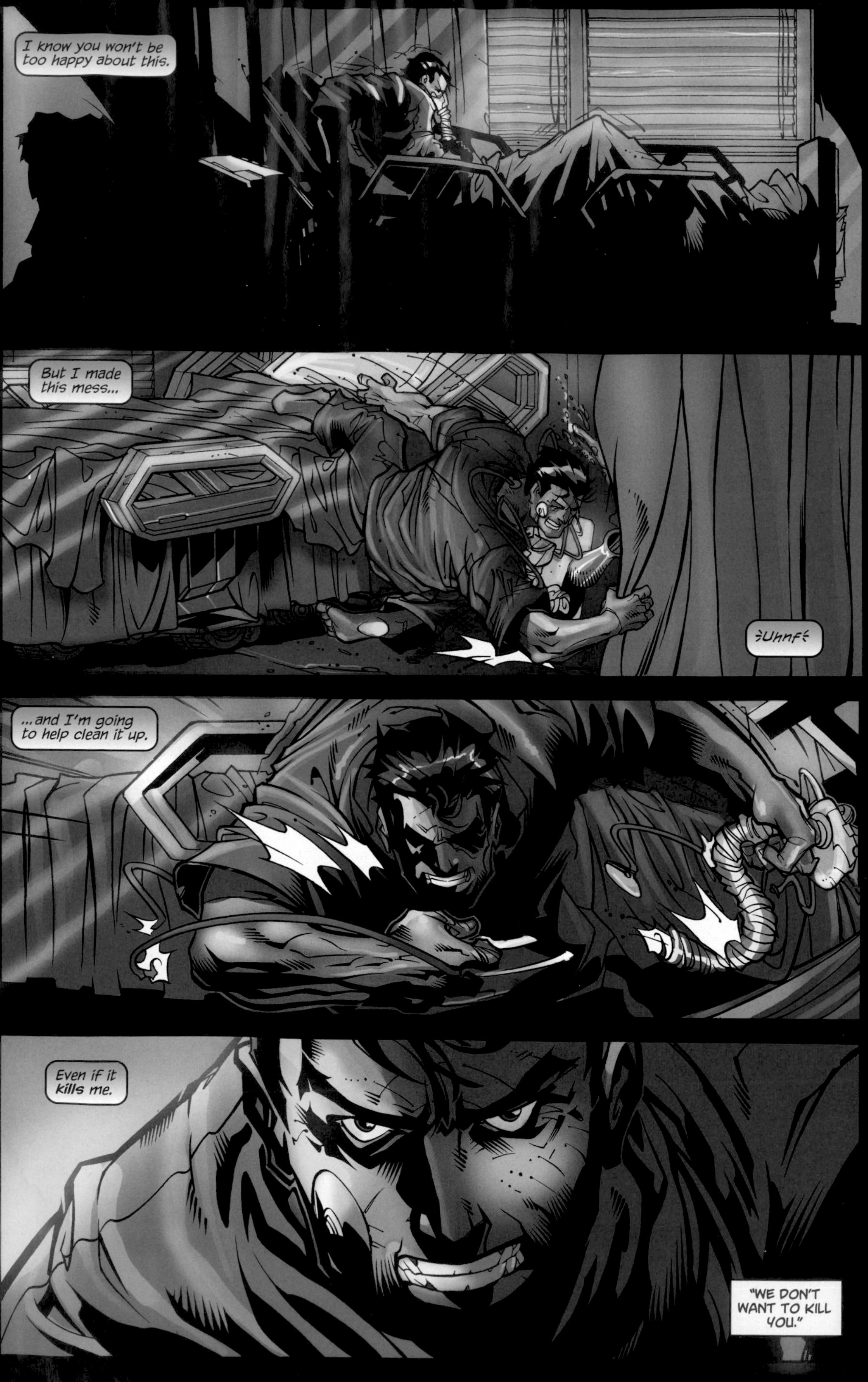
I know you won't be too happy about this.
But I made this mess...
Uhnf
...and I'm going to help clean it up.
Even if it kills me.
"WE DON'T WANT TO KILL YOU."

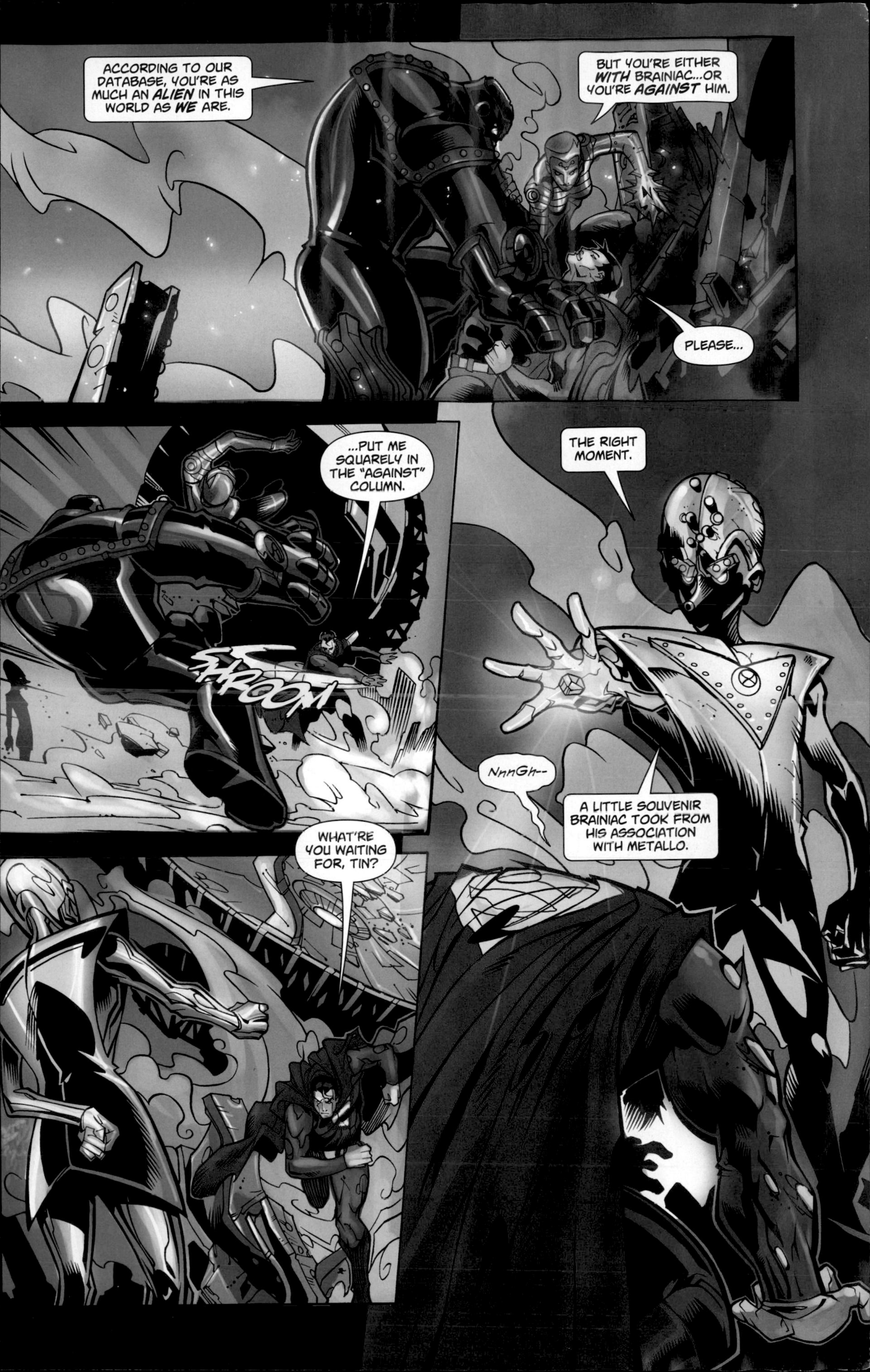
ACCORDING TO OUR DATABASE, YOU'RE AS MUCH AN ALIEN IN THIS WORLD AS WE ARE.
BUT YOU'RE EITHER WITH BRAINIAC...OR YOU'RE AGAINST HIM.
PLEASE...
...PUT ME SQUARELY IN THE "AGAINST" COLUMN.
SHROOM
THE RIGHT MOMENT.
NnnGh--
A LITTLE SOUVENIR BRAINIAC TOOK FROM HIS ASSOCIATION WITH METALLO.
WHAT'RE YOU WAITING FOR, TIN?

YOU'LL BE PLEASED TO KNOW BRAINIAC HAS NO DESIRE TO SEE YOU DEAD.

WELL DONE, METAL MEN.

VERY... *nnnf*... CONSIDERATE OF HIM.

ONCE A KRYPTONIAN VARIANT OF THE OMAC VIRUS CAN BE FASHIONED, YOU'LL TAKE YOUR PLACE AT HIS SIDE.

WELL, KRYPTONIAN? DO YOU YIELD?

NOT AN INCH.

DISAPPOINTING.

WHICH OF YOU WOULD LIKE THE HONOR OF THE KILL?

...PERMIT ME.

'LEASE...

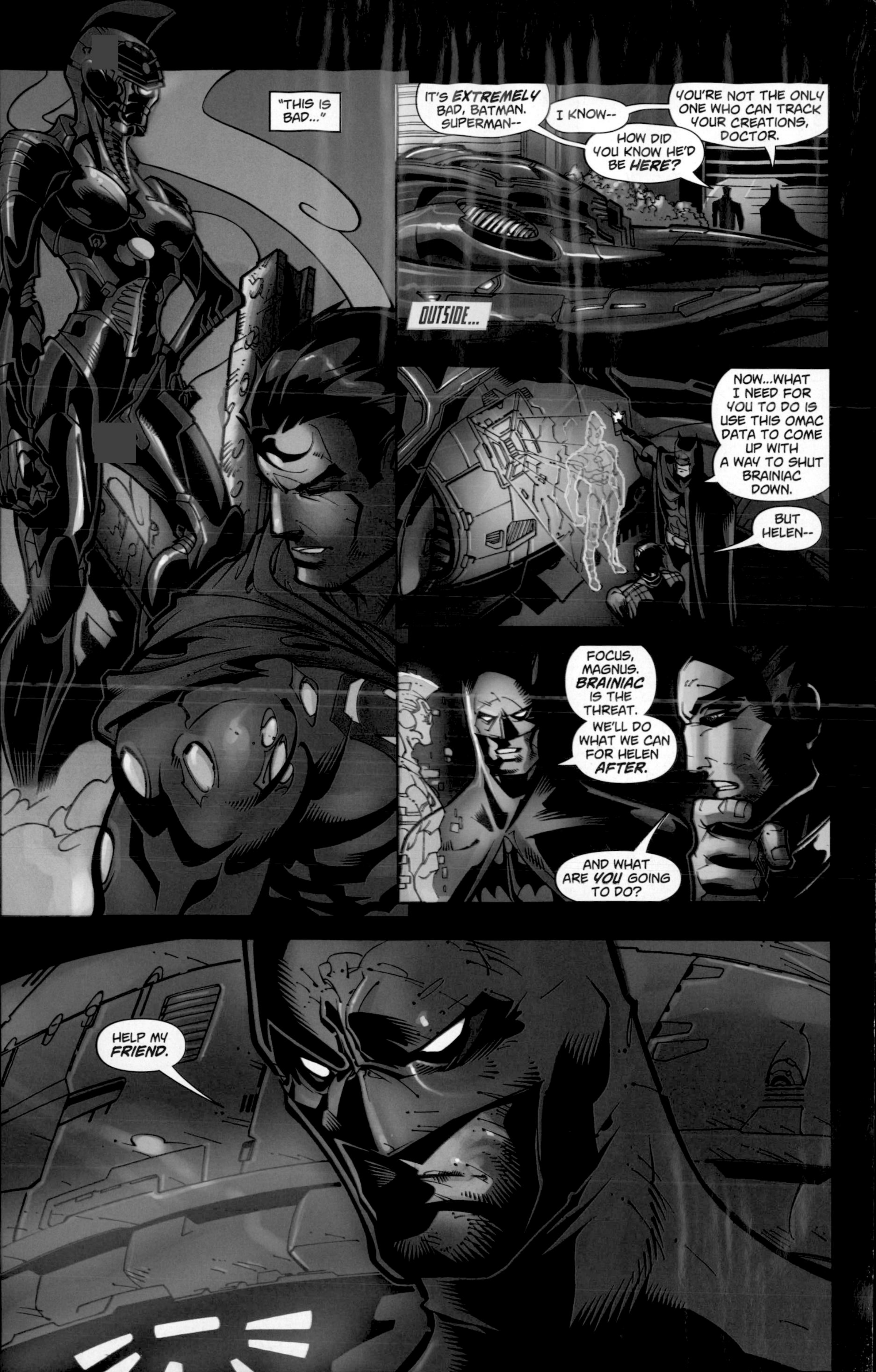
"THIS IS BAD..."
IT'S EXTREMELY BAD, BATMAN. SUPERMAN--
I KNOW--
YOU'RE NOT THE ONLY ONE WHO CAN TRACK YOUR CREATIONS, DOCTOR.
HOW DID YOU KNOW HE'D BE HERE?
OUTSIDE...
NOW...WHAT I NEED FOR YOU TO DO IS USE THIS OMAC DATA TO COME UP WITH A WAY TO SHUT BRAINIAC DOWN.
BUT HELEN--
FOCUS, MAGNUS. BRAINIAC IS THE THREAT. WE'LL DO WHAT WE CAN FOR HELEN AFTER.
AND WHAT ARE YOU GOING TO DO?
HELP MY FRIEND.

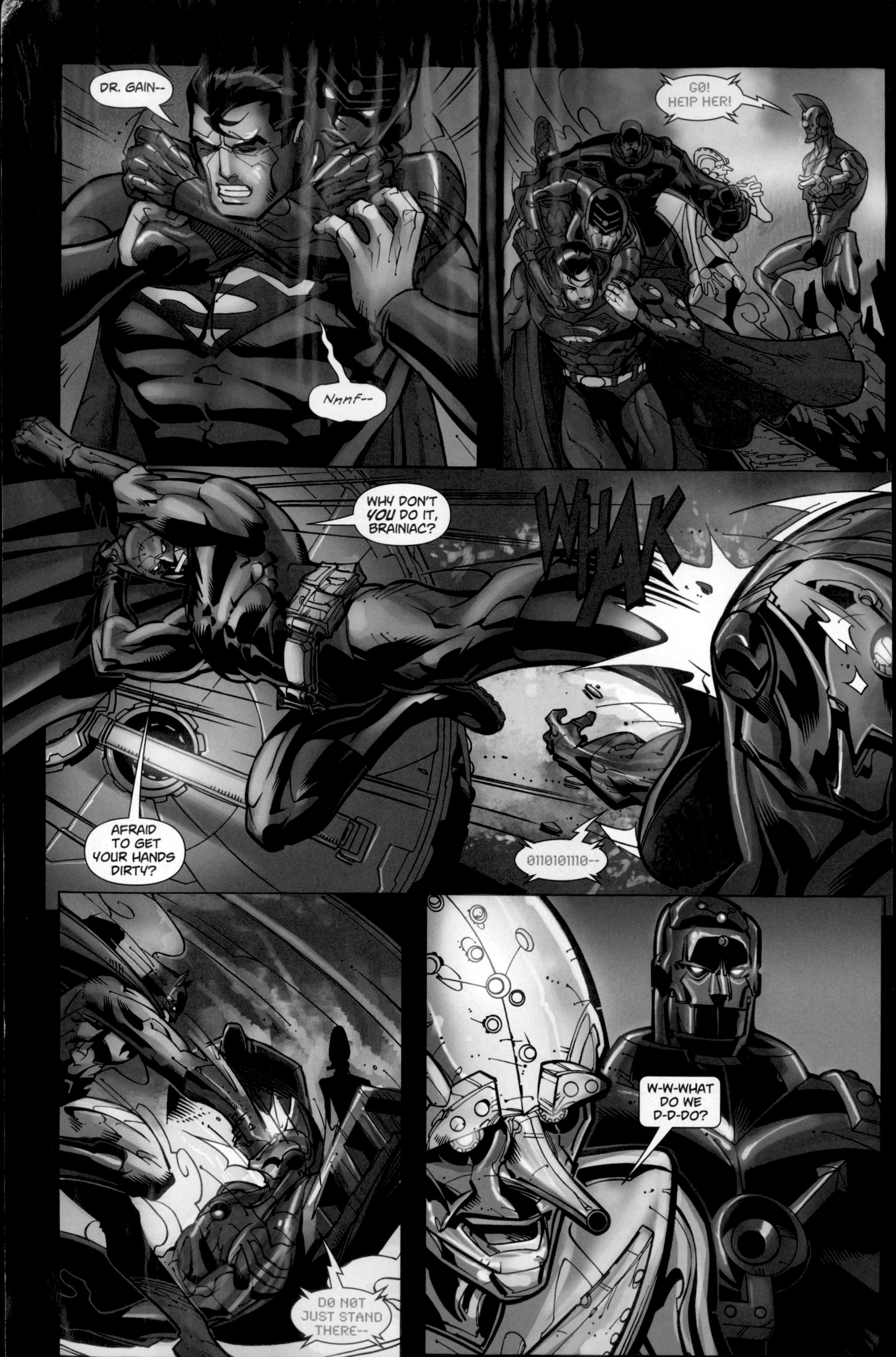
DR. GAIN--
Nnnf--
GO! HELP HER!
WHY DON'T YOU DO IT, BRAINIAC?
WHAK
AFRAID TO GET YOUR HANDS DIRTY?
0110101110--
DO NOT JUST STAND THERE--
W-W-WHAT DO WE D-D-DO?

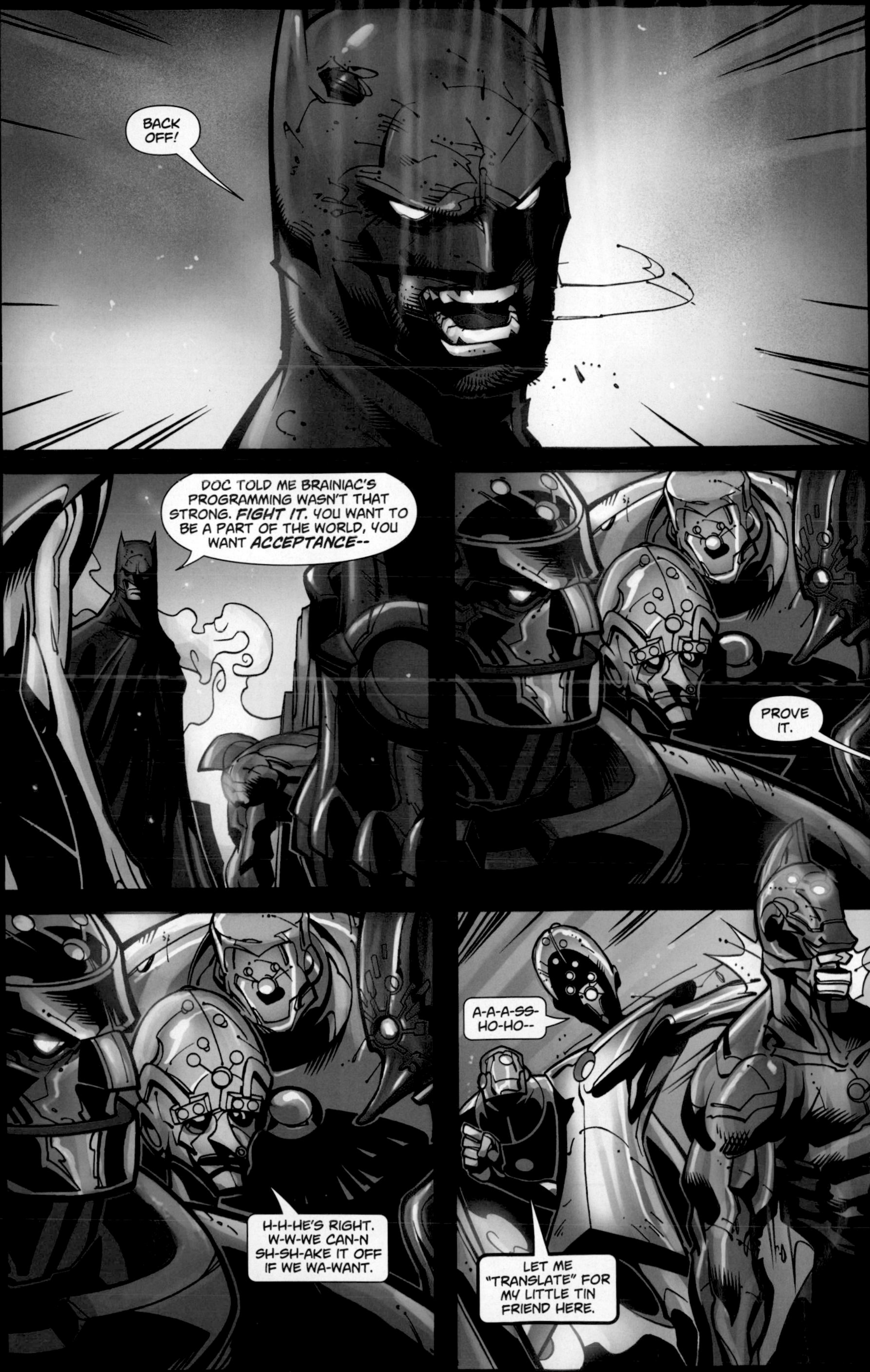
BACK OFF!
DOC TOLD ME BRAINIAC'S PROGRAMMING WASN'T THAT STRONG. FIGHT IT. YOU WANT TO BE A PART OF THE WORLD, YOU WANT ACCEPTANCE--
PROVE IT.
H-H-HE'S RIGHT. W-W-WE CAN-N SH-SH-AKE IT OFF IF WE WA-WANT.
A-A-A-SS-HO-HO--
LET ME "TRANSLATE" FOR MY LITTLE TIN FRIEND HERE.

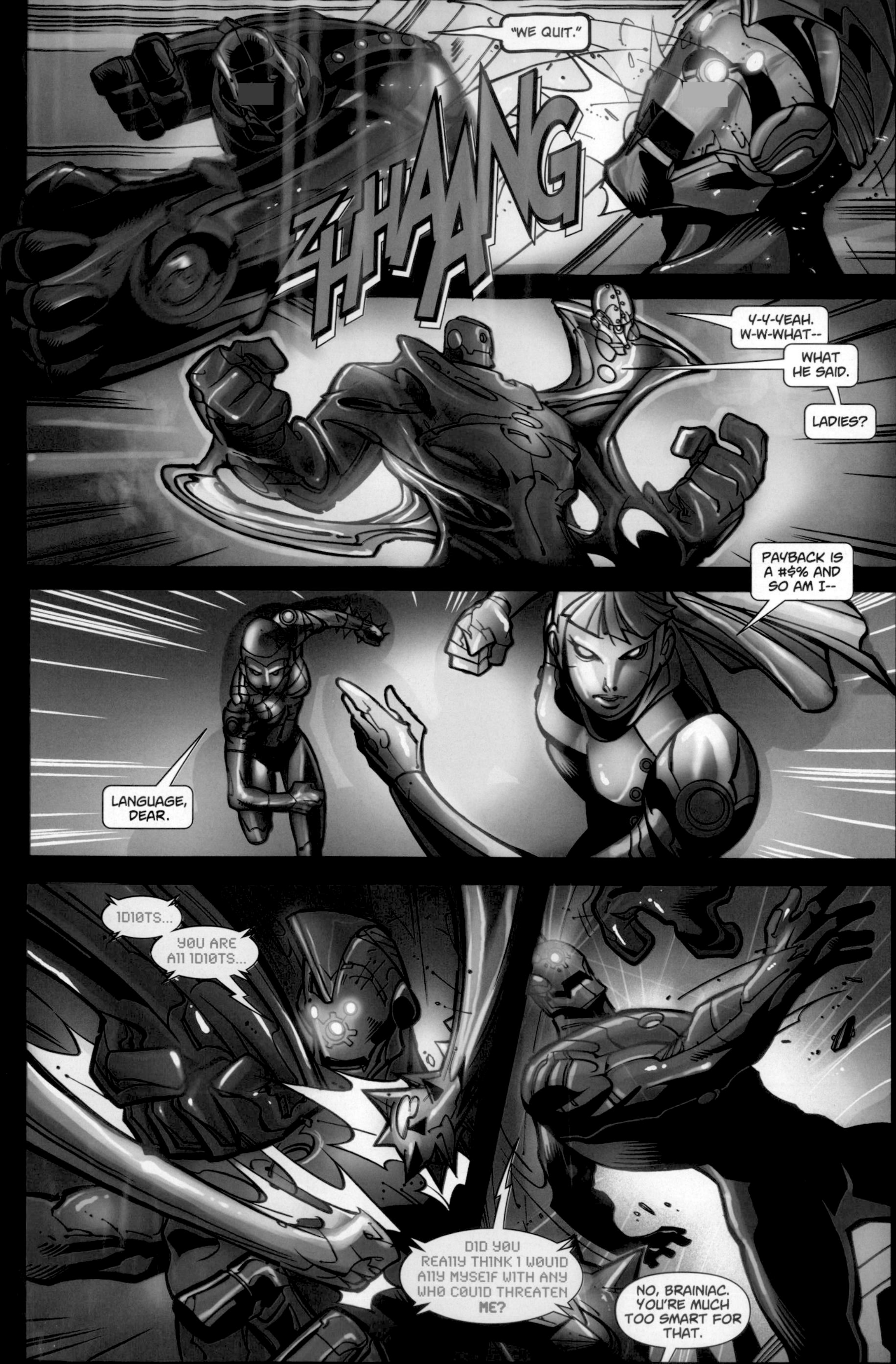
"WE QUIT."
ZHHAANG
Y-Y-YEAH. W-W-WHAT--
WHAT HE SAID.
LADIES?
PAYBACK IS A #$% AND SO AM I--
LANGUAGE, DEAR.
1D10TS...
Y0U ARE A11 1D10TS...
D1D Y0U REA11Y THINK 1 W0U1D A11Y MYSE1F WITH ANY WH0 C0U1D THREATEN ME?
NO, BRAINIAC. YOU'RE MUCH TOO SMART FOR THAT.

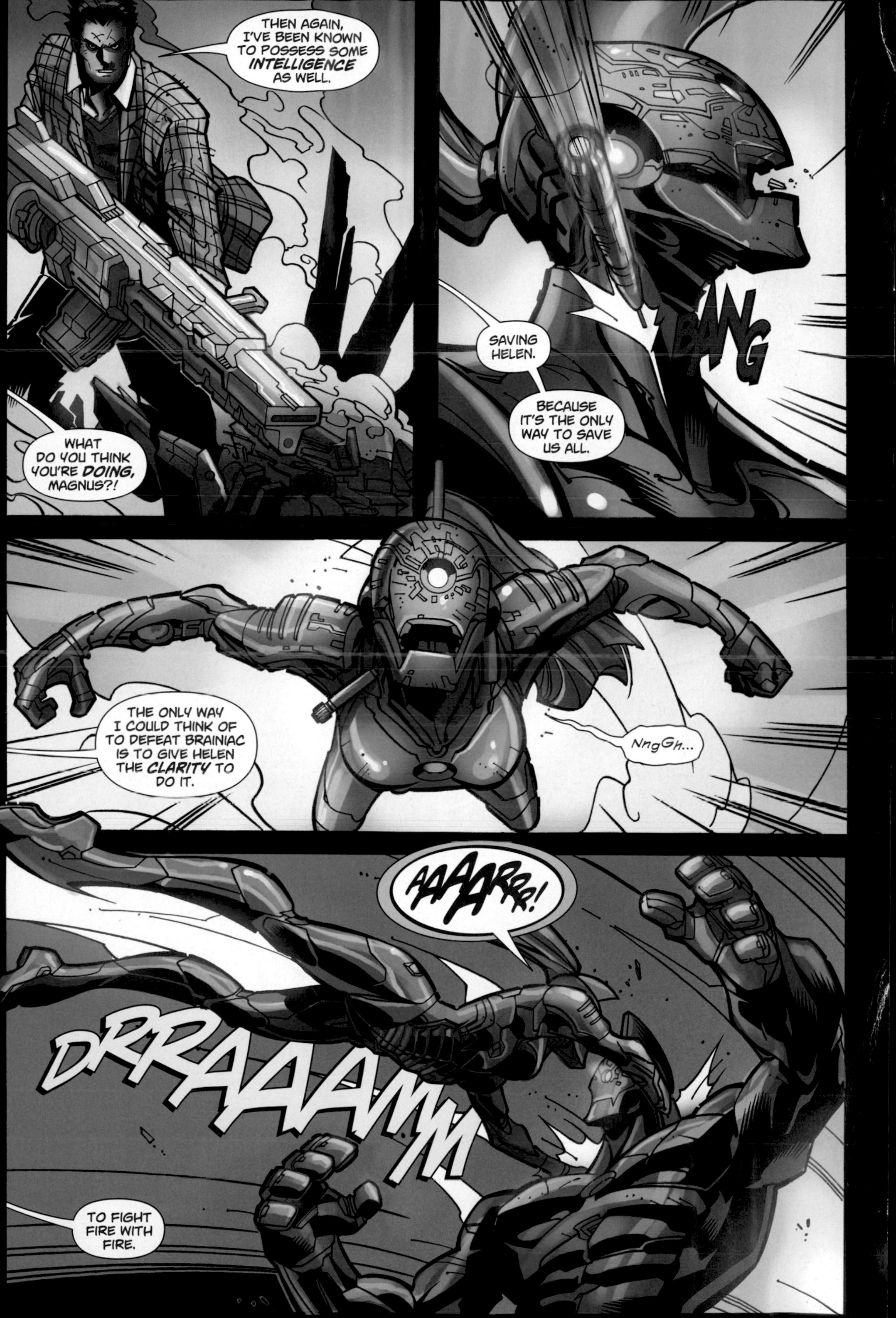
THEN AGAIN, I'VE BEEN KNOWN TO POSSESS SOME *INTELLIGENCE* AS WELL.
WHAT DO YOU THINK YOU'RE *DOING*, MAGNUS?!
BANG
SAVING HELEN.
BECAUSE IT'S THE ONLY WAY TO SAVE US ALL.
THE ONLY WAY I COULD THINK OF TO DEFEAT BRAINIAC IS TO GIVE HELEN THE *CLARITY* TO DO IT.
NngGh...
AAAARRR!
DRRAAAAMM
TO FIGHT FIRE WITH FIRE.

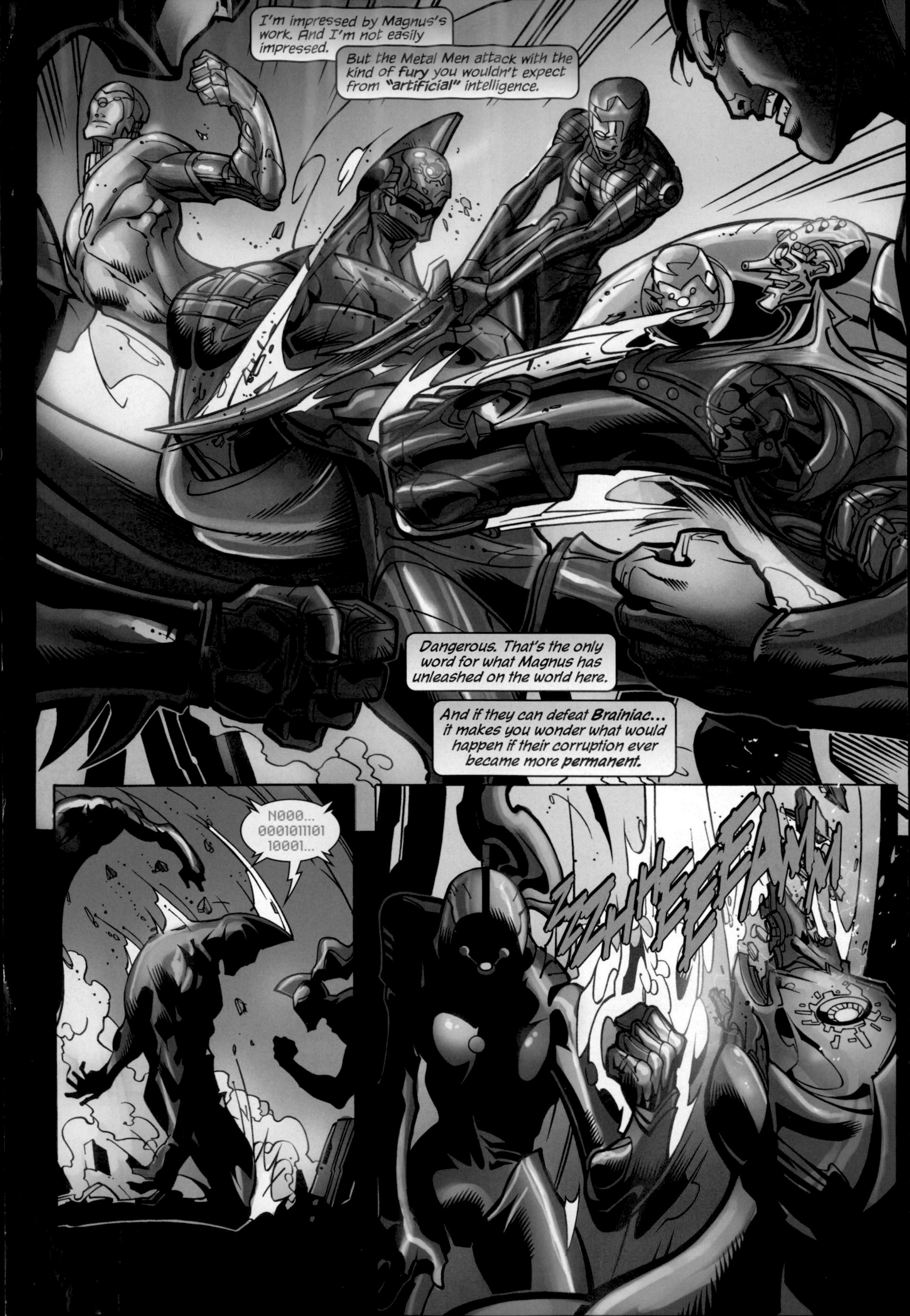
I'm impressed by Magnus's work. And I'm not easily impressed.
But the Metal Men attack with the kind of fury you wouldn't expect from "artificial" intelligence.
Dangerous. That's the only word for what Magnus has unleashed on the world here.
And if they can defeat Brainiac... it makes you wonder what would happen if their corruption ever became more permanent.
NOOO... 0001011101 10001...
ZZZHHEEEEAMM

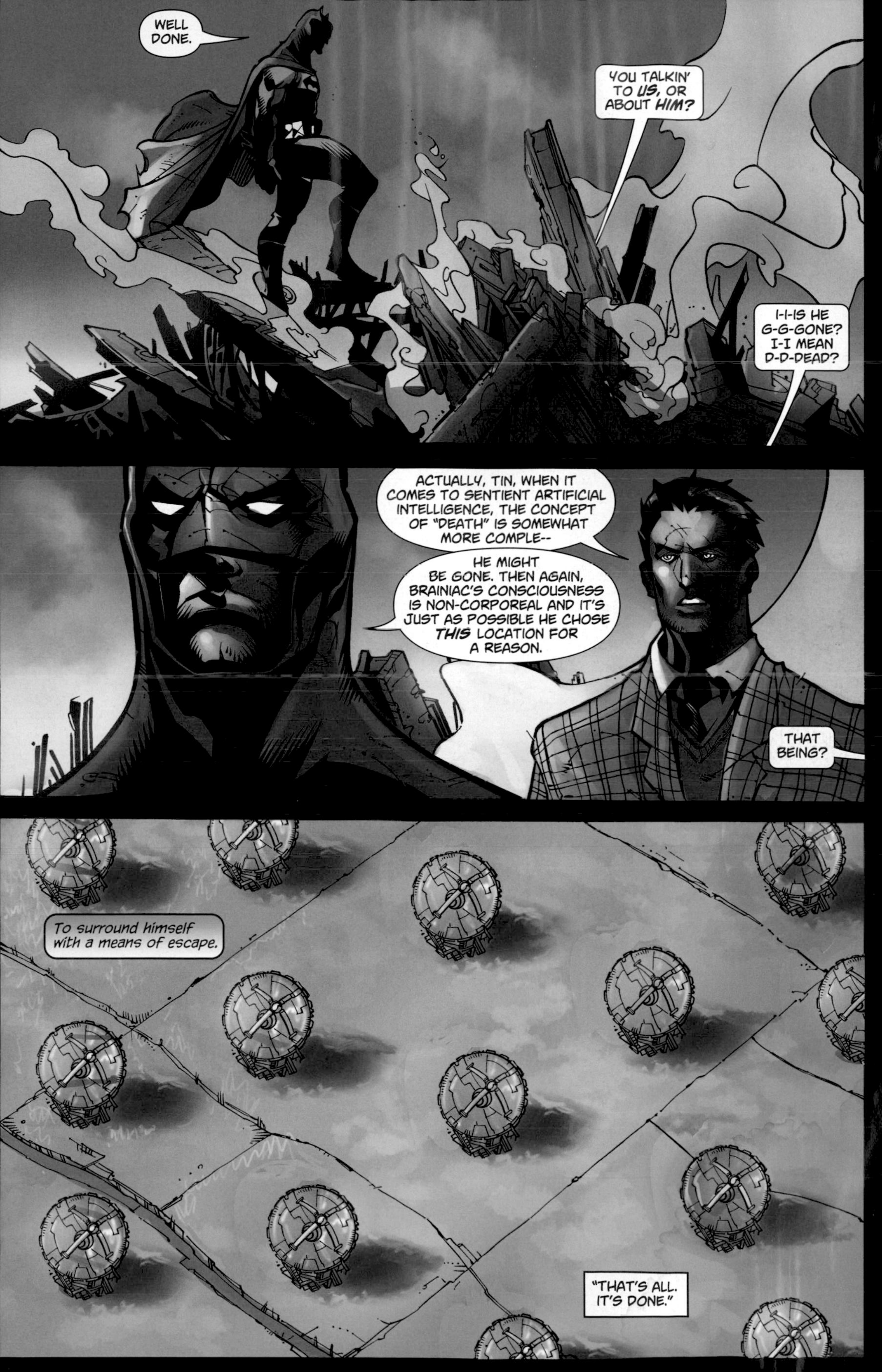
WELL DONE.
YOU TALKIN' TO *US*, OR ABOUT *HIM*?
I-I-IS HE G-G-GONE? I-I MEAN D-D-DEAD?
ACTUALLY, TIN, WHEN IT COMES TO SENTIENT ARTIFICIAL INTELLIGENCE, THE CONCEPT OF "DEATH" IS SOMEWHAT MORE COMPLE--
HE MIGHT BE GONE. THEN AGAIN, BRAINIAC'S CONSCIOUSNESS IS NON-CORPOREAL AND IT'S JUST AS POSSIBLE HE CHOSE *THIS* LOCATION FOR A REASON.
THAT BEING?
To surround himself with a means of escape.
"THAT'S ALL. IT'S DONE."

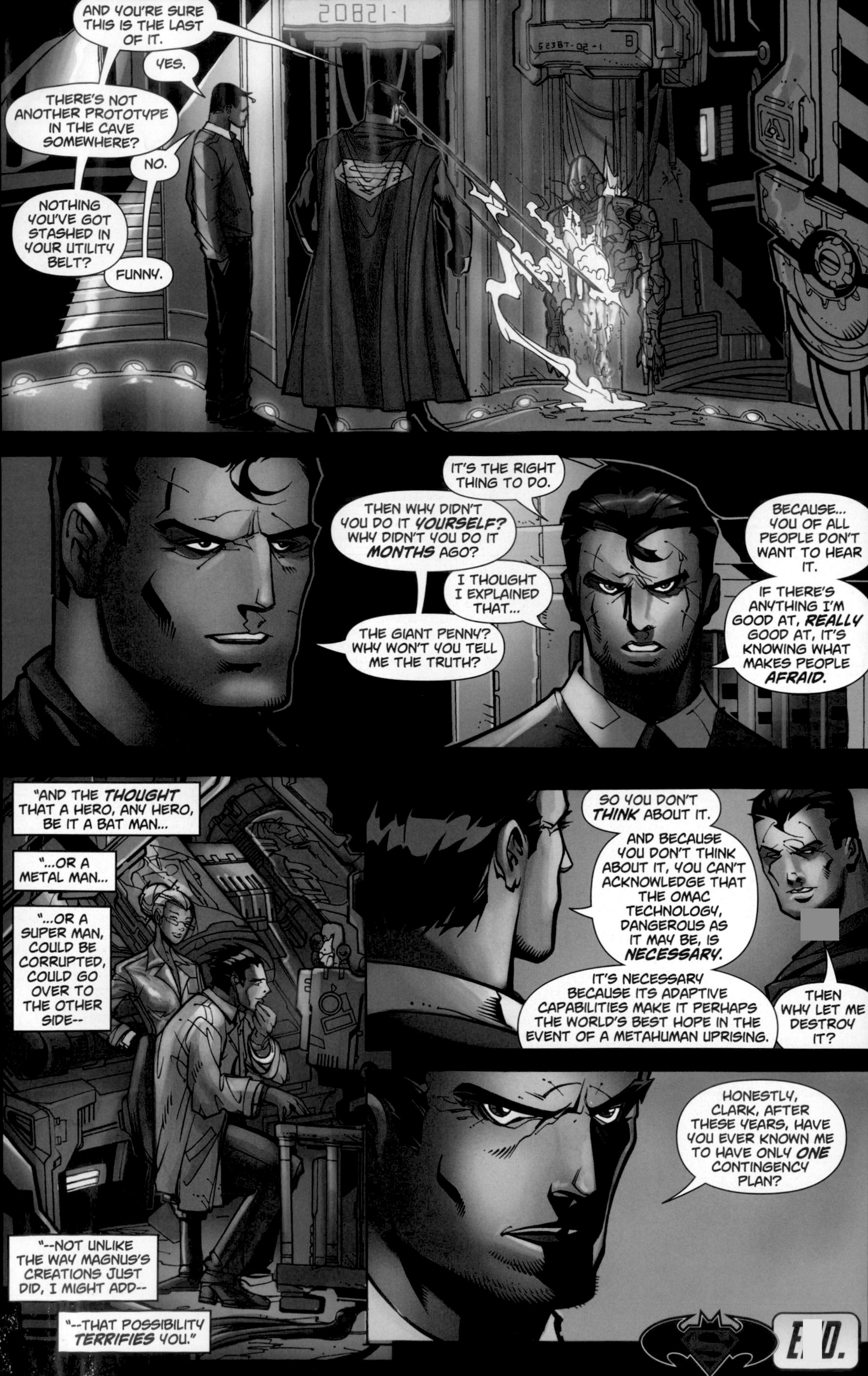
AND YOU'RE SURE THIS IS THE LAST OF IT.
YES.
THERE'S NOT ANOTHER PROTOTYPE IN THE CAVE SOMEWHERE?
NO.
NOTHING YOU'VE GOT STASHED IN YOUR UTILITY BELT?
FUNNY.
IT'S THE RIGHT THING TO DO.
THEN WHY DIDN'T YOU DO IT *YOURSELF?* WHY DIDN'T YOU DO IT *MONTHS* AGO?
I THOUGHT I EXPLAINED THAT...
THE GIANT PENNY? WHY WON'T YOU TELL ME THE TRUTH?
BECAUSE... YOU OF ALL PEOPLE DON'T WANT TO HEAR IT.
IF THERE'S ANYTHING I'M GOOD AT, *REALLY* GOOD AT, IT'S KNOWING WHAT MAKES PEOPLE *AFRAID.*
"AND THE *THOUGHT* THAT A HERO, ANY HERO, BE IT A BAT MAN...
"...OR A METAL MAN...
"...OR A SUPER MAN, COULD BE CORRUPTED, COULD GO OVER TO THE OTHER SIDE--
"--NOT UNLIKE THE WAY MAGNUS'S CREATIONS JUST DID, I MIGHT ADD--
"--THAT POSSIBILITY *TERRIFIES* YOU."
SO YOU DON'T *THINK* ABOUT IT.
AND BECAUSE YOU DON'T THINK ABOUT IT, YOU CAN'T ACKNOWLEDGE THAT THE OMAC TECHNOLOGY, DANGEROUS AS IT MAY BE, IS *NECESSARY.*
IT'S NECESSARY BECAUSE ITS ADAPTIVE CAPABILITIES MAKE IT PERHAPS THE WORLD'S BEST HOPE IN THE EVENT OF A METAHUMAN UPRISING.
THEN WHY LET ME DESTROY IT?
HONESTLY, CLARK, AFTER THESE YEARS, HAVE YOU EVER KNOWN ME TO HAVE ONLY *ONE* CONTINGENCY PLAN?

AFTERWORD
"THE ENEMIES AMONG US!"
by Mark Verheiden

"Eek! One of the Venomee has changed Manhunter into a fish!"
Zook, HOUSE OF MYSTERY #145

Let me put something on the table, right at the top. I love Silver Age DC Comics. It's more than empty nostalgia for days gone by, and it's not a "guilty pleasure," a term I frankly find obnoxious. If you need some pretentious analysis to make it more palatable, okay, try this: there is a magic realism to the DC Silver Age that's simultaneously surreal and often emotionally affecting. That's a combo you don't find very often, especially in today's post-ironic, uber-cynical world, and it's something comics can do standing on their proverbial head.

Me? I'm constantly astounded by the "anything goes" spirit that infused so much Silver Age work. It was a time when Lana Lang could grow an insect head. Our old friend Batman could be zebra-striped, rainbow-hued, or transformed into a diapered baby, and that would only be the beginning of the story. I mean, Superman and Batman could challenge one another to an "amnesia contest" not because they'd been fooled into it by one of their foes, but just because they felt like it. There were rules to this universe, but they were remarkably elastic and utterly dispensable if they interfered with telling a cool story. So, how can you tell when you're reading a really great Silver Age adventure? Pause for a second and try to apply any sort of real-world construct to the drama. Trust me, your head will explode. And then you'll probably turn into a baby.

Aside from super-guys, the Silver Age DC Universe was populated with an astonishing array of alien life-forms. There were, of course, the alien heroes themselves, like Martian Manhunter, Hawkman, the Guardians of Oa, and of course, the big daddy of them all, Superman. But there were also a slew of bizarre creatures that erupted from the pages of STRANGE ADVENTURES, HOUSE OF MYSTERY, HOUSE OF SECRETS and MY GREATEST ADVENTURE, as well as many of the superhero titles. What was great about DC's aliens was that even the most minimal concepts of physics and natural law were tossed into the trash pile when it came to their abilities. These things could fly, cross dimensions, shape-shift, time travel…heck, you name it, and there was probably an alien doing it. Mind you, I'm not talking about the drippy creatures torn out of H.R. Giger's psyche or the visceral horrors of *The War of the Worlds* (George Pal or Steven Spielberg version), or even the wonderful but somehow more prosaic Fin Fan Fooms and Gorgamms that populated the Marvel/Atlas line of the time. No sir. When DC said "alien," they meant frakkin' ALIENS.

These dudes came in all colors, often multi-hued in garish pinks, yellows, reds and purples. They could have beaks. Multiple arms. Tentacles. Claws. Fur. Feathers. Gaping eyes with triangles for pupils. They were usually really big (though not always) and if they were at all sentient, they were usually nursing a secret that only our heroes could divine. Most important, with the exception of the outright villains, most of the DC aliens weren't inherently "evil" but misunderstood, in that "there's a gigantic monster threatening our city and he just crushed the Municipal Bank Building, but I don't think he really meant it" sort of way.

Anyway, when I first started thinking about the "Enemies Within" arc for SUPERMAN/BATMAN, I had three main objectives. One, I wanted to somehow recapture the "anything goes" spirit that infused the Silver Age DC books, and that meant bringing back the most impossible of characters. Perhaps my favorite "get" was

resurrecting The Creature Who Could Not Die, a critter I discovered while plowing through the Showcase issues of GREEN LANTERN. What intrigued me about this fellow was not just the fact that he was one of the Lantern's earliest and deadliest opponents, but that The Creature Who Could Not Die in fact died in his very first outing. Remember what I said about the remarkably elastic rules of the early DCU? Reviving this palooka seemed to fit right in with the plan.

Two, I wanted to use some of DC's greatest villains, and one of them had to be a gorilla. Dr. Phosphorus and Doomsday fit squarely in the villain category, but Titano the super-ape was my glorious two-fer. I know what you're asking yourself: "How in the ever-loving world can the skeletal structure of a primate support the weight and mass of a 75-foot-tall gorilla?" Thing is, you're not asking the right question. What you really want to know is: "How in the world can the skeletal structure of a primate support the weight and mass of a 75-foot-tall gorilla—and look so darn cool while doing it?"

And three, I wanted to bring Zook back into the current DCU. Not only bring him back, mind you, but make him the central player in our little drama. A tall order, but the challenge was half the thrill.

Ahh, Zook, "we hardly knew ye." Barely a blip in the short run of Martian Manhunter stories that ran in DETECTIVE COMICS and then HOUSE OF MYSTERY in the mid '60s, Zook was the Manhunter's alien sidekick and nominal comic relief. But there was more to the Zookster than your everyday alien pet sidekick. For one thing, Zook was instrumental in saving the Manhunter's bacon on several occasions. Take HOUSE OF MYSTERY #146, for example. The Emerald Investigator found himself paralyzed as he faced the hands (well, claws) of Chulko, the red, shambling, virtually featureless offspring of Aroo, which was itself a big yellow creature with a dog's head, rabbit-ear antennae and red underpants. In this nine-and-a-half-page tale, the Manhunter finally falls prey to Chulko's deadly eye beam, leaving it to Zook to save the day. Needless to say, Zook came through like a champ, dispatching Chulko posthaste by melting a large bar of ice over his head and causing the creature to "fade away." Which sounds better than "die," I guess, though it's pretty much the same thing...

Did I mention that the rules in this earlier DCU were remarkably elastic?

Anyhow, what struck me about Zook and his relationship to the Martian Manhunter was that somehow, even though Zook was just as smart and almost as powerful as the big green guy, he didn't get the accolades or attention because he just didn't look the part of a hero. Indeed, poor Zook was Nicole Richie to the Manhunter's Paris Hilton, as the glow from the more glamorous of the pair often blinded the world to the other's abilities. Even though Zook spoke in a semi-literate patois ("Yipes! Green ring now drawing you in, Manhunter—because you green!"), he was clearly as intelligent as any of the other heroes. Yet because he was small, orange and had a physique reminiscent of the freakish child in those "dancing baby" videos, he would never get his shot at the pantheon.

So the "Enemies Among Us" arc was created in part to explore Zook's attitude toward Earth's heroes, and to give him one more shot at immortality. Of course, that meant making him the villain, albeit an unwitting one, but sooner or later he'll come around. Meanwhile, for those who picked up the series in monthly form, let me just ask—did any of you guess Zook was the one behind the mayhem?

In the end, I just hope that this isn't the end of folks strategically plumbing DC's vast alien reservoir. The anarchic imaginations that invented these diverse and bizarre characters deserve to be venerated and carried on, because as long as there are comics, we're going to need Purple Demons, the Beings in the Color Rings, Doom Shadows, King Zoldi and dying Creatures That Cannot Die.

"A real treat for any lover of the superhero genre of comics."
—WASHINGTON TIMES

"Fans of DC Comics' classic characters will find much to love here."
—ATLANTA JOURNAL CONSTITUTION

THE DARK KNIGHT. THE MAN OF STEEL. TOGETHER.

SUPERMAN/BATMAN: PUBLIC ENEMIES

JEPH LOEB & ED McGUINNESS

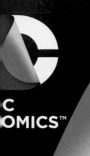

SUPERMAN/BATMAN:
SUPERGIRL

JEPH LOEB
ED McGUINNESS
DEXTER VINES

SUPERMAN / BATMAN: PUBLIC ENEMIES

SUPERMAN / BATMAN: SUPERGIRL

SUPERMAN / BATMAN: ABSOLUTE POWER

SUPERMAN / BATMAN: VENGEANCE

SUPERMAN / BATMAN: THE ENEMIES AMONG US

SUPERMAN / BATMAN: TORMENT

SUPERMAN / BATMAN: THE SEARCH FOR KRYPTONITE

SUPERMAN / BATMAN: FINEST WORLDS

SUPERMAN / BATMAN: NIGHT & DAY

SUPERMAN / BATMAN: BIG NOISE

SUPERMAN / BATMAN: WORSHIP

SUPERMAN / BATMAN: SORCERER KINGS

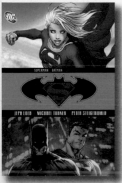

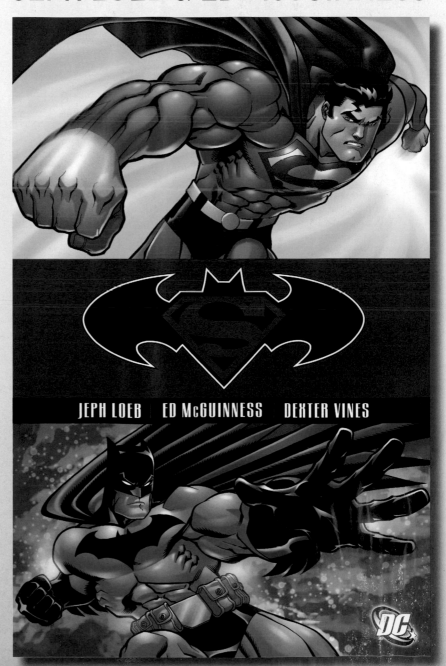

"Writer Geoff Johns and artist Jim Lee toss you—and thei[r] heroes—into the action from the very start and don't put o[n] the brakes. DC's über-creative team craft an inviting world fo[r] those who are trying out a comic for the first time. Lee's art i[s] stunning."—USA TODA[Y]

"A fun ride."—IG[N]

START AT THE BEGINNING!

JUSTICE LEAGUE
VOLUME 1: ORIGIN
GEOFF JOHNS and JIM LEE

JUSTICE LEAGUE VOL. 2: THE VILLAIN'S JOURNEY

JUSTICE LEAGUE VOL. 3: THRONE OF ATLANTIS

JUSTICE LEAGUE OF AMERICA VOL. 1: WORLD'S MOST DANGEROUS

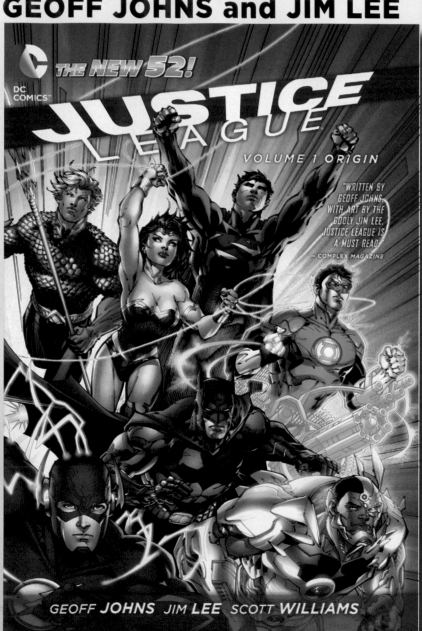

"Groundbreaking."
—USA TODAY

"It's film noir in cartoon panels."
—VANITY FAIR

"Frank Miller absolutely revolutionized the Dark Knight and his influence can be felt throughout comics, even 20 years later...true masterpiece of storytelling."
—IGN

FROM THE CREATOR OF *300* and *SIN CITY*

FRANK MILLER

with KLAUS JANSON

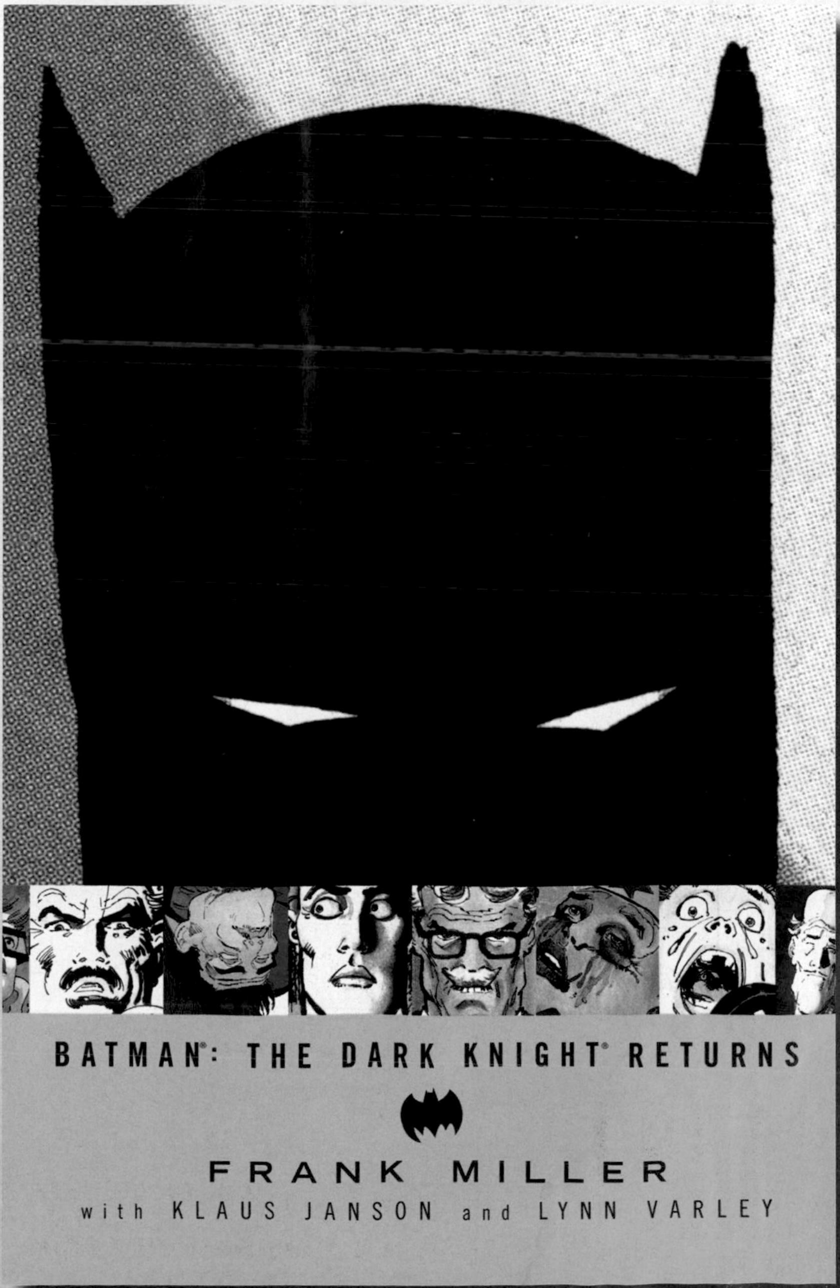
BATMAN: THE DARK KNIGHT RETURNS
FRANK MILLER
with KLAUS JANSON and LYNN VARLEY

BATMAN: THE DARK KNIGHT STRIKES AGAIN

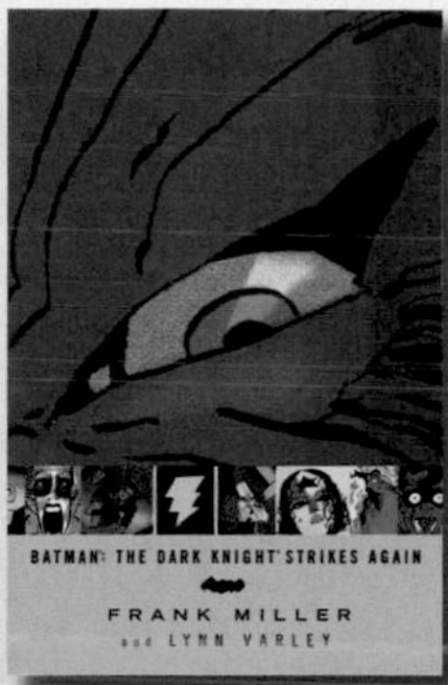
BATMAN: THE DARK KNIGHT STRIKES AGAIN
FRANK MILLER
and LYNN VARLEY

BATMAN: YEAR ONE DELUXE EDITION

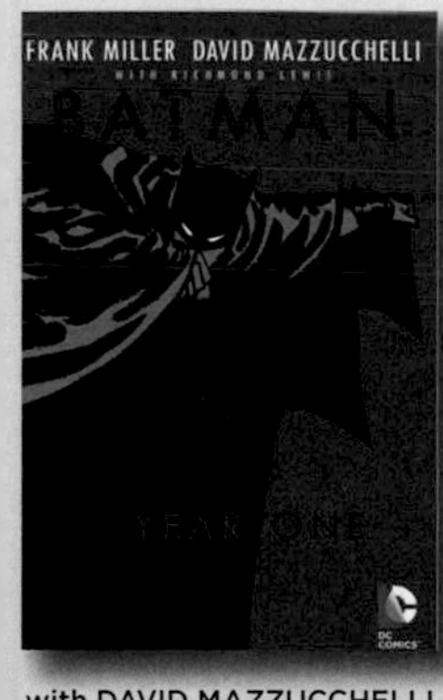
FRANK MILLER DAVID MAZZUCCHELLI
BATMAN
YEAR ONE

with DAVID MAZZUCCHELLI

ALL-STAR BATMAN & ROBIN, THE BOY WONDER VOL. 1

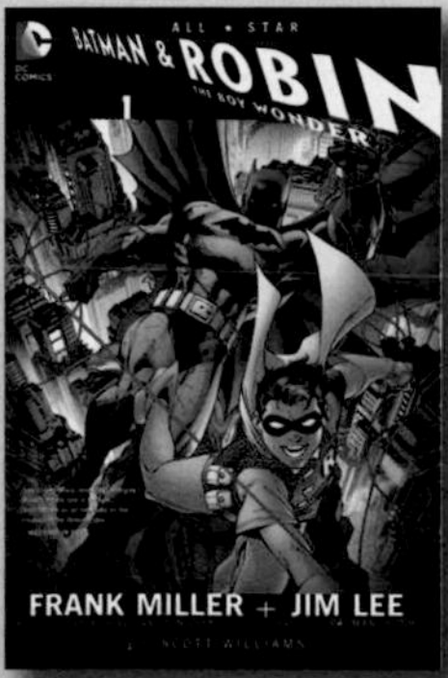
ALL STAR
BATMAN & ROBIN
THE BOY WONDER
FRANK MILLER + JIM LEE

with JIM LEE

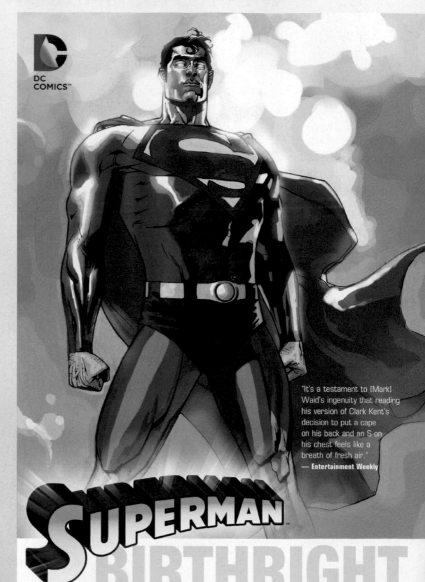